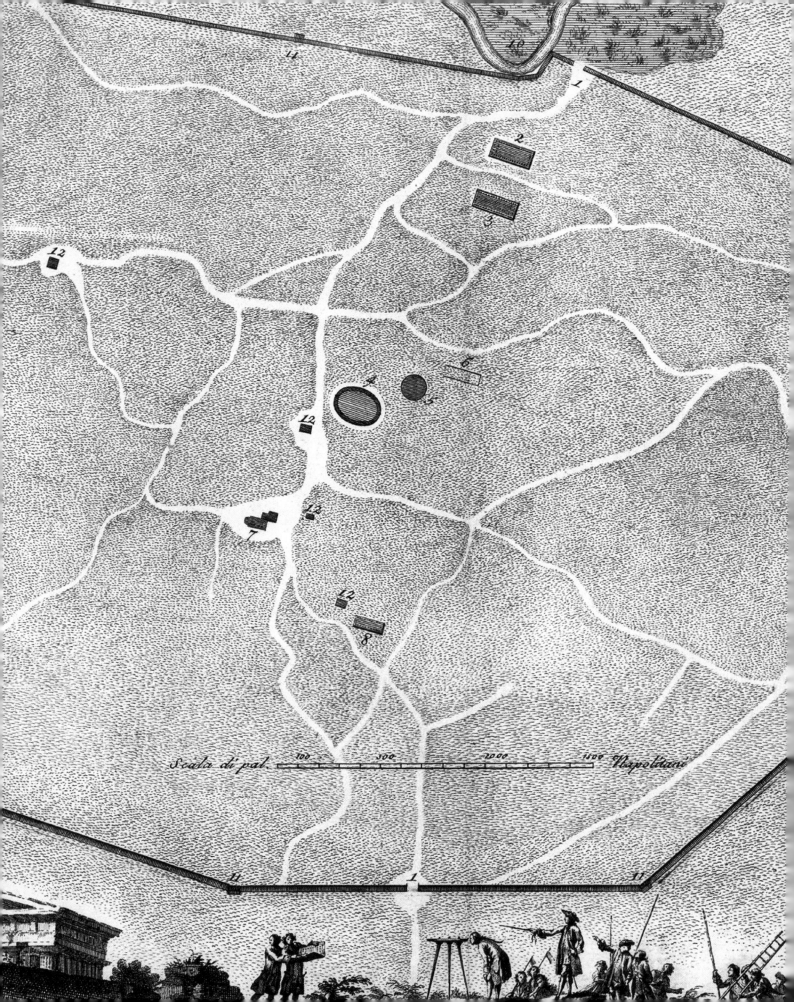

Scala di pal. 100 500 1000 1500 Napolitano

Rediscovering Architecture

PAESTUM IN EIGHTEENTH–CENTURY
ARCHITECTURAL EXPERIENCE AND THEORY

Sigrid de Jong

PUBLISHED FOR
The Paul Mellon Centre for Studies in British Art
BY
Yale University Press
New Haven and London

To Patrick and Philippina

Designed by Elizabeth McWilliams

Printed in China

Library of Congress Control Number 2014953985

ISBN 978-0-300-19575-0

A catalogue record for this book is available from The British Library

Front endpaper   Detail of Fig. 16 (larger than actual size).

Frontispiece   Detail of Fig. 109, with a plan of the city of Paestum (1784) showing the Basilica (2), the Temple of Neptune (3) and the Temple of Ceres (8).

Back endpaper   Detail of Fig. 31 (larger than actual size).

Contents

Acknowledgements

The long journey of researching and writing this book took place in those cities that were major centres of Europe in the eighteenth century: Paris, London, Rome and Naples. The many periods of research I spent in these delightful and inspiring locations could not have been afforded were it not for the support I received from Leiden University, where the book began its life as a doctoral dissertation. I am very grateful to my university for providing intellectual and financial encouragement, both when I was working for my Ph.D. and currently, as a postdoctoral researcher. LUCAS (Leiden University Centre for the Arts in Society, and its predecessors) offered many scholarships for my research in London and Paris and for presenting papers at international conferences. In addition, the Leiden University Fund twice provided a research grant for further archival explorations in London. NWO, the Dutch Organization for Scientific Research, generously funded the final phases towards this book. My sincere gratitude goes to the Paul Mellon Centre for Studies in British Art for funding a travel grant to allow additional research in London. I am grateful also to the Fondation de France and the Institut National d'Histoire de l'Art (INHA) for making a research sojourn in Paris possible, before I settled there.

In France and England I benefited from the help of the staff of many libraries and archives: of the British Library, the British Museum, the Paul Mellon Centre for Studies in British Art, Sir John Soane's Museum, the Royal Institute of British Architects and the Victoria and Albert Museum in London; of the Archives Nationales, the Bibliothèque des Arts Décoratifs, the Bibliothèque Nationale de France, the École Nationale Supérieure des Beaux-Arts, the Fondation Custodia, the Institut de France and the Institut National d'Histoire de l'Art in Paris; of the École Nationale des Ponts et Chaussées in Champs-sur-Marne, of the Bibliothèque Municipale in Besançon and of the Bibliothèque Municipale and the Archives Municipales in Bordeaux. I thank also the staff of the Archivio di Stato in Naples and of the Beinecke Library and the Yale Center for British Art in New Haven. The late Madame Daphné Doublet-Vaudoyer very generously allowed me to consult the archival material in her house in Paris.

Most of all, the ardent, stimulating and thought-provoking discussions I had with my former Ph.D. supervisor and present colleague Caroline van Eck in numerous European cities (including over several dinners) have never ceased to inspire me. Maarten Delbeke shared his time and expertise for supportive and stimulating input, and continues to do so in our NWO-VIDI project, 'The Quest for the Legitimacy of Architecture 1750–1850'. Exchanges of ideas with many other friends and colleagues offered new insights during the writing and rewriting process, and for those I thank especially Barry Bergdoll, Matthew Cohen, Adrian Forty, Mari Hvattum, Lola Kantor Kazovsky, Frank Salmon, Mark Wilson Jones and Richard Wittman. In the Netherlands particularly Nadine Akkerman, Linda Bleijenberg, Stijn Bussels, Petra Brouwer, Joris van Gastel, Lex Hermans, Elsje van Kessel, Eric Moormann, Bram van Oostveldt, Freek Schmidt, Minou Schraven, Esther Starkenburg and Auke van der Woud were generous in critical reading, and shared their inspiring and encouraging thoughts. Marit Eissens energetically arranged all the images for the book, and I thank her for all her work. Students at courses I taught at the Art and Architectural History Department of Leiden University have also helped me to formulate my ideas clearly, and a memorable visit to Paestum with some of them in 2008, when we entered the temples, made us almost live the eighteenth-century experience.

Without the enthusiastic encouragement of Frank Salmon this book would not have been realized in its present form, and the same should be said of the Paul Mellon Centre for Studies in British Art. I owe a tremendous debt of gratitude to its previous Director of Studies, Brian Allen, and to its present one, Mark Hallett, for their confidence in this project. Receiving one of the Centre's publication grants meant that the book could be lavishly illustrated. I would also like to thank David Watkin and John Wilton Ely who both insisted that this work be published and who provided helpful suggestions for improvement. At Yale University Press Gillian Malpass supremely conducted the final phase of turning the manuscript into the present work, and I am grateful for her trust and support. Rosemary Roberts with her wonderfully meticulous editing and pertinent questions made the text so much better and readable, and Elizabeth McWilliams transformed it all into a both elegant and contemporary book, just as the theme of architectural experience required.

My friends and family, and especially my parents and brother, were supportive all along the way, and I am warmly grateful to them. The two people who taught me most about architectural experience are the ones this work is dedicated to: Patrick Leitner, to whom I owe my greatest debt and gratitude for always being there and for shaping my thoughts during all our invigorating and eye-opening conversations and travels, and Pina, our wonderful daughter, who enlightened the final stages towards this book, while dancingly discovering the world.

Introduction

May I suggest to Y[our] M[ajesty] that, in order to save time and expense, it would be possible to take stonework from the ancient city of Paestum situated in Capaccio, an ancient Roman settlement, where there is a great quantity of half-ruined buildings, with more than a hundred huge columns, with their capitals, architraves, friezes and entablatures, built of blocks of stone of such proportions as to give one an idea of the power of the ancient Romans.[1]

The eighteenth-century rediscovery of the ruins of Paestum began in a rather curious way – with a plan to demolish what was left of the temples to use their stones as building material. This plan originated at the royal court of Naples in 1740, and never went beyond the stage of a proposal. In fact, it led instead to a sudden and increasing interest in the ancient architecture of Paestum.

Rediscovery

The building project for which the stones of Paestum were to be used was a royal palace and, ironically, it was intended that the columns of the Greek Doric temples (which were believed to be Roman) should be re-used to represent the power of ancient Rome. The plan was devised by the Neapolitan court architect, Ferdinando Sanfelice (1675–1748), the first architect to mention Paestum in the eighteenth century.[2] In 1740 he suggested to Carlo di Borbone (1716–1788), King of the Two Sicilies, that the columns of Paestum be used as *spolia* in the Palazzo di Capodimonte. Although this proposal was never executed, Sanfelice's letter drew the existence of the temples to the attention of the court in Naples; before long, another Neapolitan architect, Mario Gioffredo (1718–1785), investigated the site more thoroughly and reported his findings to the court commander of the artillery, Count Felice Gazzola (1698–1780). Gazzola would become the agent who diverted many European visitors from Naples to Paestum, which marked the start of an enormous cultural upheaval in eighteenth-century Europe. The rediscovery of Paestum was to cause a great stir in architectural thought and turn existing ideas on classical architecture upside down.

1 (*facing page*) Aerial view of the three temples at Paestum.

Paestum became a source of fascination. Soon after its rediscovery, European travellers began to flock to the site, write about it, draw the temples and publish descriptions and engravings of them in large folios. This fascination was a complex mix: Paestum attracted, captivated, enthralled, tantalised, disturbed, upset, agitated and frightened its visitors simultaneously. The journey to the site, in itself, was an invigorating but often hazardous adventure, through a vast and captivating landscape, and the temples were so different from Roman classical architecture and from everything travellers had seen before, either in publications or at other sites, that the encounter with them raised many questions and became a source of impassioned debates that continued throughout the eighteenth century and well into the nineteenth. Such strongly held opinions are reflected in the numerous published and unpublished accounts that record the reactions of visitors to the site. Compared with other ancient sites in Sicily, Greece and Rome, Paestum is unparalleled for both the number and diversity of the writings it inspired, and for the central role it played among the subjects that dominated eighteenth-century architectural discourse.

Count Gazzola started the dissemination of knowledge about the temples across Europe. It was also at his instigation that the first foreign architect – the Frenchman Jacques-Germain Soufflot (1713–1780) – visited Paestum in 1750.[3] In a lecture given in 1752, Soufflot described how Gazzola, 'a man of great taste', whom he 'had the honour of meeting often in Naples', advised him to examine the 'great Greek temples'.[4] That Soufflot considered the buildings to be Greek is rather striking, because their origin was a source of continuing debate in the eighteenth century. Travellers detected Etruscan, Greek, Roman and even Egyptian elements in the architecture. Soufflot's account is of interest not only because it is the first response of a foreign architect to the site but also because it articulates several aspects that travellers to Paestum would remark upon in the following decades: the impact of the journey, the strong impression the site made, the sense it evoked of establishing contact with the unknown, the state of preservation of the temples, and the strangeness of their proportions and materials. Soufflot also recorded the taking of measurements and the making of drawings, his view that the temples embodied the origins of the Doric order, and his ambition to rewrite architectural history taking these extraordinary monuments into consideration. The first monograph on the site appeared in 1764, based on Soufflot's scale drawings and those made by his travelling companion and the author of the book, the architect Gabriel-Pierre-Martin Dumont (1720–1791). The *Suitte de plans . . . de Poesto* offered no explanatory texts, but only plates. Many publications would follow that included both texts and plates: in the second half of the eighteenth century alone, an impressive total of eight monographs was published.[5]

Towards the end of the century, around 1789, the Italian architect Carlo Vanvitelli (1739–1821) proposed building a replica of one of the Paestum temples in the English gardens at Caserta.[6] While the construction of an artificial ruin as a folly in a landscape garden was by then common practice, it was unprecedented to attempt to copy an entire temple for the visitor to wander around, and thus try to transfer an architectural experience from one place to another. The idea indicates the architect's admiration for the temples, and the importance King Ferdinando di Borbone (1751–1825) attributed to them as part of his kingdom. In the fifty years between 1740, when the temples were under threat of demolition to provide good solid building material for a new palace, and c.1790, when they were so admired that they were to be preserved and their grandeur re-created in the royal gardens, a complete reversal of attitudes had taken place. The development of architectural thinking that occurred between the cautious and exploratory rediscovery of the site and the general strong consensus about the value of the temples are the subject of this book.

Before we turn to the specific questions raised by Paestum and the architectural debates it caused, we shall examine what it was that travellers actually saw and reacted to. What made these buildings so special? A short description of the site and its temples will help us to understand eighteenth-century responses.

The Site

Of the Grecian temples in Magna Graecia,[7] the three in Paestum are the best preserved. They are also the oldest temples on Italian soil. Poseidonia was a colony of Magna Graecia, and is located about 80 kilometres south of Naples and 40 kilometres south of Salerno (Fig. 1). The remains of the city are situated in an extensive plain, with the sea on the west side (the coastline is now 640 metres from the city, but was formerly closer), the River Sele on the north side and the Alburni mountains on the east side. The city walls surrounding the site follow the trapezoidal shape of the calcareous limestone shelf on which the city is built. The walls, which were begun by the Greeks and completed by the Romans, are about 4.8 kilometres long and enclose an area of 96 hectares; they are well preserved and include four gates with towers – the Porta Giustizia on the south side, the Porta Aurea on the north, the Porta Sirena on the east, and the Porta Marina on the west. The city's walls and buildings are made principally of limestone or travertine. The three temples are all east–west orientated and are set in a north–south line – the Temple of Athena at the northern end of the city, and the temples of Hera II and I (in that order) at the southern end (Fig. 2).

The Greek city of Poseidonia was founded *c.*600 BC by the Troizenians, who, with the Achaeans, were the original settlers of the Greek colony of Sybaris in the south of Italy

2 Plan of the city of Paestum showing the three temples: (*north to south*) Athena (Temple of Ceres), Hera II (Temple of Neptune) and Hera I (Basilica).

(now Calabria) *c*.720 BC; after the two groups clashed, the Troizenians were driven out of Sybaris and fled north, where they founded Poseidonia. It was one of the more important colonies in Magna Graecia, and flourished for nearly 200 years. A major staging-post on the trade route from the south, it was situated towards the northern limit of the Greek colony and its inhabitants had contacts with the Etruscan people living nearby, north of the River Sele. The Greeks in the colonies drew on the culture of their homeland but they were also inventive, and while the city prospered they experimented with novel building designs and sculptural styles, and engaged in cultural exchanges with their neighbours. Around 400 BC the Lucanians conquered the city, and they held it until, in 273 BC, a Latin colony grew up there and the name was changed to Paestum. Roman streets were then laid out – the *Cardo maximus* from north to south and *Decumanus* from east to west – and the city was enlarged, with the building of a forum, an amphitheatre, a new temple, shops and houses. The three Greek temples remained standing in the midst of this new Roman city.[8] From the third century AD, the Romans began to leave the city; by the fifth century the Temple of Athena was a Christian basilica, and a medieval village grew up around it.

The three temples, built in different periods and expressing different ideas on building, offer a good overview of the development of early Greek Doric temple architecture (Fig. 3). The oldest temple of the three is the Temple of Hera I, built between 570 and 520 BC (probably *c*.530 BC) (Fig. 4). The ascription to Hera derives from a fragment of pottery bearing her name which was found at the spot. Hera was the city's protectress, and a sanctuary within the walls was dedicated to her. The Temple of Hera I has nine columns from side to side by eighteen columns from end to end. The columns are 1.44 metres in diameter and 6.45 metres tall (a ratio of diameter to height of 1:4.48). The temple is constructed on a stylo-

3 Plans of the three temples at the same scale, in chronological order: (*left to right*) Hera I (Basilica), Athena (Temple of Ceres) and Hera II (Temple of Neptune).

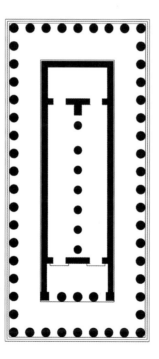
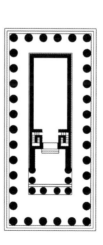
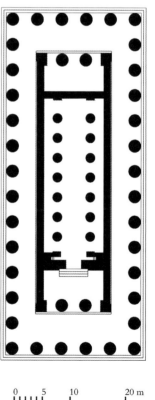

0 5 10 20 m

4a and b The Temple of Hera I (Basilica), *c.*530 BC, interior (*above left*) and exterior (*above right*).

bate of 24.5 by 54.3 metres. The odd number of columns at the front and back is remarkable: it resulted from there being three columns in the porch, which in turn was a consequence of the decision to give the building a central axial colonnade. Another special characteristic is the unusually wide ambulatory. The division of the cella[9] by a single row of columns was possibly designed to provide separate spaces for two cult statues – for example, Hera and Poseidon; but it may also indicate an arrangement favoured in temples from the seventh century BC that later became obsolete.[10] Furthermore, the pronounced entasis and the broad, compressed, convex echinus[11] of the flat capitals are exceptional, and bear out the early construction date. The exterior columns and the cella columns are the same size, which is another notable feature, as cella columns are usually smaller. At the porch, the capitals of the antae have a cylindrical, roll-like projection along the lower edge, a feature found elsewhere only in Sybaris and Argos, and linked to northern Peloponnesian architecture. A further characteristic is the unique flamboyant floral decoration of the neck and echinus of the capitals, including rosettes, lotus and drooping petals (originally painted so that they stood out); according to scholars, the decorative elements provide evidence of the masons competing with one another – the different forms were intended to identify the work of individual craftsmen. In comparison with Greek mainland architecture, the temple is extraordinary in its plan, its structure and its decoration, showing the willingness of the inhabitants of Poseidonia to experiment.

The Temple of Athena was constructed *c.*520 BC (Fig. 5). It measures 14.5 by 33 metres, and has six columns by thirteen, the columns being 1.26 metres in diameter and 6.12 metres tall, a ratio of 1:4.86. It is the smallest of the three temples and is located at the highest point of the city. The external columns are of the Doric order, and the internal ones (smaller in scale) were Ionic, making this the first Greek building to incorporate both Doric and Ionic columns; the cella contained no columns. The interior had a large porch at the east end but no corresponding one at the west end. The porch consisted of eight Ionic columns, of which two functioned as the antae of the porch walls and four presented the façade. Two staircases behind the porch presumably served a platform, from which the statue of the goddess in the cella could be viewed, and the statue and the fabric of the building could be maintained and cleaned. The internal columns were not aligned with the external ones, making the interior an independent space, a common feature in

Magna Graecia. The entasis of the Doric columns is less pronounced than in the Temple of Hera I, the echinus of the capitals is flatter and the shafts are slimmer. The building was constructed from travertine blocks, though some decorations – for example, on the frieze – were of sandstone. Just as at Hera I, this temple featured some unique decorations: it had coffered eaves along the flanks of the building, protected by reliefs with lion heads that functioned as spouts and palmettes. Terracotta figurines of Athena, found at a votive deposit nearby, confirm the dedication to Athena.

The Temple of Hera II, built *c*.460 BC, is the largest of the three temples, having six columns by fourteen on a stylobate of 24.3 metres by 60 (Fig. 6).[12] It is also the best preserved, with all the columns of the peristyle and the interior superstructure still standing. The columns are 2.11 metres in diameter and 8.88 metres tall (a ratio of 1:4.21); their entasis is less pronounced than that of the columns in the Temple of Hera I. The temple has a porch at the east end, with two columns *in antis* (between the antae). A chamber at the west end of the cella – the opisthodomos – has two columns matching those of the porch. The cella is divided into a nave and two aisles by twin colonnades consisting of two storeys of superposed columns, which supported the joists and timber structure of the roof. An internal staircase gave access to a gallery, from which the statue of the goddess could be observed and maintenance of the ceiling could be carried out. As in the other temples, the columns were covered with stucco to imitate marble.

Hera II, constructed as a companion to Hera I, is the most conventional of the three temples (in the arrangement of six by fourteen columns and the porch with two columns *in antis*, for example). Yet in some respects it departs from the norm. The columns have twenty-four flutings, instead of the twenty found in the fully developed Doric order. The echinus of the capitals is still slightly 'baggy', rather than straight-sided, as it is in the columns of the Parthenon at Athens. Towards the corners, the columns are spaced more closely; this so-called 'angle contraction' is common in Greek temples, enabling the triglyphs to be aligned with the columns and the end triglyphs to coincide with the corners, thus avoiding elongated metopes at the corners. Optical correction is used to alleviate the possible perception of distortion: the stylobate is slightly convex and the column shafts curve slightly inwards. The floors were constructed of travertine slabs; the statue was probably of terracotta as no extra supports were found in the floor. These elements indi-

5a and b   The Temple of Athena (Ceres), *c*.520 BC, exterior (*below left*) and interior (*below right*).

6a and b The Temple of
Hera II (Neptune), *c.*460 BC,
exterior (*above left*) and detail
of columns (*above right*).

cate that the architect may well have been trained on the Greek mainland. Several of the temple's features belong to the archaic style rather than the canonical Doric: namely, a plan with fourteen (rather than thirteen) columns on the longer sides, the squat proportions of the columns and entablature, which emphasise the weight and mass of the superstructure, the number of flutings of the columns and the convex profile of the echinus of the capitals. More modern elements are the near absence of decoration and the Doric refinements. There are some similarities to the temple of Zeus in Olympia (470–460 BC), which helps to date the building. Archaeological finds indicate that Hera was the major divinity in the sanctuary, making it probable that the grandest temple was dedicated to her.

In the eighteenth century the temples were called: Basilica (Hera I), Ceres (Athena), and Neptune or Poseidon (Hera II) (Fig. 7). Henceforward, I shall refer to the temples by the names that were most commonly used at the time – Basilica, Ceres and Neptune. The Basilica was so called because eighteenth-century visitors could not believe so idiosyncratic a building to have been a temple: the absence of pediments, the odd number of columns at the front and back, and the colonnade dividing the interior led to the assumption that it was a civic administrative building. The name for the Temple of Neptune derived from the fact that it was the largest of the three buildings, and therefore must be dedicated to Poseidon (the god after whom the city was named). The Ceres temple took its name from some terracotta figures, identified as representing the goddess, found nearby.[13]

Interactions between Architectural Experience and Theory

This book is about Paestum in eighteenth-century architectural thought. It aims to reconstruct Paestum's pre-eminent and crucial role in architectural, aesthetic and artistic debates for more than fifty years after its first rediscovery – *c.*1750 to 1800 – with a brief resurgence of interest around 1830, when the French architect Henri Labrouste (1801–1875) caused a stir with his new ideas about the site.

The eighteenth-century controversies in which Paestum figured so largely took place mainly in France, England and Italy, and more specifically in Paris, London, Rome and Naples. They revolved round the main issues of eighteenth-century architectural, artistic and aesthetic thinking.[14] Aesthetic theory focused on the concepts of the sublime and the picturesque.[15] General ideas on primitivism and the beginnings of civilisation led in architectural thought to a search for the origins of architecture.[16] More specific questions had to do with the cultural meaning of buildings and the impact of a building on the beholder.[17] Many publications – again coming mainly out of France, England and Italy – addressed classical architecture as a model for contemporary buildings, and the writing of the history of architecture.[18]

I shall argue that Paestum made it possible to question many important aspects of eighteenth-century artistic and architectural thinking. Ideas were tested out on Paestum, and Paestum posed questions that fuelled discussion and gave rise to new controversies. Theory was confronted by experience, and the act of visiting and exploring the site led to the development of new theories. Thus Paestum functioned both as the scene where some of these architectural questions were first formulated or tried out, and as an exemplar of new ideas. The site and the temples could be understood, interpreted or accounted for by existing eighteenth-century concepts, but at the same time Paestum explained and exemplified these concepts in a new light. This interaction between architectural thought and the direct observation of the remains at Paestum is at the heart of this study.

The key to reconstructing the processes of eighteenth-century thinking is the concept of architectural experience. This is of vital importance because it will enable us to analyse the reciprocal relationship between theory and reality, and to answer the questions that exercised eighteenth-century architects, historians and theorists – questions about the origins and meaning of architecture, the aesthetics of the sublime and the picturesque, and the continuing validity of classical architecture as a design model. Experiencing the site acted as a pivot between ancient and contemporary ideas, and bred new and experimental thinking. If we study the subject from the point of view of architectural experience we shall uncover how theory and direct exposure to the site interacted, why Paestum came to play such an important role, and exactly what this role was. Penetrating the experience of visitors helps us to understand major changes in architectural and aesthetic thought and gives us privileged access to the shift in ideas about classical architecture that took place in the eighteenth century.

It was only in the actual examination of the temples that their particularity became manifest. I aim to reconstruct these experiences, and to analyse how they were used to inform the architectural debate. The main hypothesis of this book is that the perception of Paestum did not alter as a result of changing architectural ideas, but rather that architectural thought evolved alongside, and on the basis of, the experience of Paestum. The sensations and observations generated by seeing the temples interacted with previously established ideas on classical architecture and led to fundamental changes in architectural thinking in a uniquely varied, intense and concentrated way. In the written accounts of Paestum the crucial importance of being on the spot is constantly emphasised, as is the divergence between expectations based on other descriptions and images and the experience of each visitor *in situ*.

In the eighteenth century the direct experience of architecture acquired a central position in architectural thought and became the basis of many theories. Architects such as Jacques-François Blondel (1705–1774), Julien-David Le Roy (1724–1803) and John Soane (1753–1837) all wrote about their physical acquaintance with buildings in their own countries and abroad, and used these descriptions to support their views about the design of buildings or the importance of particular buildings in the history of architecture. In general, the impact of architecture on the beholder became an essential component of the value that was placed on a building.

The rediscovery of Paestum forced a rethinking of architecture in every sense, from the generally accepted ideas about its history to the relationship of classical Greek to contemporary architecture. This process was initiated and apprehended through the architectural experience. It was the experience of travelling to the site, being there in person, observing the landscape, and exploring the temples – walking around and through them, measuring, drawing and writing on the spot – that produced these new ideas. It was through this immediate and vivid exposure that visitors started to comprehend the site and to appreciate its implications for their assumptions about architecture. Different visitors encountered Paestum in very different ways, and their engagement with it often developed through several stages, marked by the interactions of theory and experience – hence the title of this study: *Rediscovering Architecture: Paestum in Eighteenth-Century Architectural Experience and Theory*.

The structure of the book reflects the diversity of these experiences. It is divided into three parts, each of two chapters. The first part, 'Aesthetic Experiences', examines attempts to understand and interpret the site informed by aesthetic theories. The written and visual records of visitors' impressions of the site are analysed in the light of the two prominent aesthetic concepts of the eighteenth century: the sublime and the picturesque. The second part, 'Experiences of Movement', explores how the temples were observed and represented. In this part we follow the travellers as they enter the temples and experience a sequence of responses that were disseminated in texts, engravings and paintings. The third part, 'Contextualising Experiences', investigates the reflections on the past to which Paestum gave rise, the first attempts to write the history of Doric architecture, and the influence of

7   Antonio Joli, *The Temples of Paestum*, after 1766, oil on canvas. Kulturstiftung Dessau-Wörlitz.

observations and representations of the site on a rethinking of classical architecture as a design model. My purpose is to analyse fifty years of interaction between theory and experience so as to expose the important role of Paestum as it evolved from experience through representation to historiography.

The sources we shall use are both published and unpublished, textual and visual, selected for their focus on Paestum and because they illuminate the different themes of the chapters. They consist of travel diaries, correspondence, sketches and drawings, paintings, models and engravings, and published works such as travelogues, archaeological accounts, treatises and poems. Architects, artists, writers and poets produced them. The analysis of this body of Paestum material operates in three ways. First, I have identified recurrent and prominent themes and pursued their development through the whole corpus. Secondly, I have investigated the role of more general debates and issues in eighteenth-century architectural thought. Thirdly, I have reconstructed the way in which the coverage of Paestum illustrates and contributed to the principal debates. The complexity of the analyses and ideas in this book thus matches the richness of the primary sources.

As we have already seen, the discussions to which Paestum gave rise took place mainly in France, Italy and England, and therefore the sources are mostly from those countries. However, important theorists from elsewhere whose views were influential, such as Johann Wolfgang von Goethe (1749–1832) and Johann Joachim Winckelmann (1717–1768), have also been included. Architects are the main protagonists, complemented by other travellers and theorists, whose writings provide context and background. Because the structure is thematic, several architects, historians, theorists or travellers may appear in more than one part of the book.

Hitherto, scholars have examined accounts of Paestum mainly to offer an insight into the reactions of architects to classical architecture, as demonstrated by its influence on contemporary architectural design. This aspect has been dealt with extensively in studies on neoclassical architecture and the Greek Revival.[19] However, by drawing a straight line from the discovery of the temples to the application of the so-called 'Paestum order' in architecture, these studies overlook the diversity of experiences that architects had at Paestum, and their subsequent impact on architectural issues other than design or form. As architectural history of the eighteenth century remains focused on buildings and architects, the broader themes discussed in this book, including the relation of the sublime, the picturesque and primitivism to architecture, have not been much studied until now.

Nor have historical monographs on the reception of Paestum examined the interaction between experience and theory. The most important publications are the exhibition catalogue *La fortuna di Paestum e la memoria moderna del dorico, 1750–1830* (1986) and the anthology of texts *Paestum: Idea e immagine. Antologia di testi critici e di immagini di Paestum, 1750–1836* (1990), both edited by Joselita Raspi Serra, which provide a very useful starting point. In general, the existing studies give an overview, or focus on the impact of Paestum on design matters.[20] The complexity of the site, the diversity of the experiences that visitors had there and the context of eighteenth-century architectural discourse have largely been ignored. The introduction to *Paestum: Idea e immagine* hints at the historical context and suggests all kinds of impact on eighteenth- and nineteenth-century culture, from Burke to Nietzsche, but goes no further and never substantiates or scrutinises these connections. A recent publication on Italy's Magna Graecia, Giovanna Ceserani's *Italy's Lost Greece: Magna Graecia and the Making of Modern Archaeology* (2012), centres on archaeological concerns and is useful for the intellectual background.[21] But although these works contribute to the picture, there has so far been no comprehensive research into Paestum's central role in eighteenth-century thought.[22]

This book offers, for the first time, an examination of the experience of architecture at a single site, seen from the point of view of its impact on the architectural debate. Existing studies of eighteenth-century visitors to ancient sites – such as Chantal Grell's work on Herculaneum and Pompeii (1982), and MacDonald and Pinto's on Hadrian's Villa (1995) – do not work from so extensive and diverse a range of sources taken from so short a period; nor, crucially, do they treat the subject from the perspective of architectural experience.[23] The many general studies of the Grand Tour and visitors to Italy concentrate on the travels and the travellers themselves and do not go into the impact on contemporary cultural controversies.[24] The first part of Frank Salmon's *Building on Ruins* (2000) comes closest to doing this, but he eventually focuses on architectural design rather than theory. Furthermore, the impact of Italy on architectural theory is usually studied in relation to one country only,[25] whereas here I analyse the wider developments in Western Europe, paying special attention to Italy, France and England.

Studies on architectural experience are rare. Steen Eiler Rasmussen's *Experiencing Architecture* (1957) and Juhani Pallasmaa's *The Eyes of the Skin: Architecture and the Senses* (1996), both concentrate on the role of experience but in relation to contemporary architectural design.[26] Similarly, Heinrich Wölfflin's seminal *Prolegomena zu einer Psychologie der Architektur* (1886) does not survey the history of architectural experience, though it is a very useful analytical tool, as we shall see in Chapter 3. Other scholars have treated the subject in relation to the ideas of one particular architect.[27] Here, however, the subject is approached, for the first time, thematically in a historical context.

Using architectural experience as a focal point leads to several paradoxical results, which not only have significance for an understanding of Paestum's importance but also help us to discern complex trends in eighteenth-century thought as a whole. Only in the light of an analysis of architectural experience can we see, for instance, that the sublime deconstructs classicism, that the picturesque is, in fact, a non-specific viewing method, that primitivism, the search for origins and history are interrelated in a complex way, and that turning Paestum into a design model results, oddly, in its reduction to a type that no longer has anything to do with the real place. Thus, on the basis of this case study of a key site, we shall gain a unique insight into the different topics that came to determine eighteenth-century architectural discourse, seen not from the point of view of technical analysis of built architecture but from that of the human response to it.

8 (*following page*) Detail of Fig. 61.

PART ONE

Aesthetic Experiences

CHAPTER I

Paradoxical Encounters: Paestum and the Sublime

'[The temples] are large long squares, formed by ranges of fluted baseless columns, with capitals that have almost the form of a vase or rather a cup'.[1] Paestum presented itself as strange and fascinating to travellers, so strange that the capitals of the columns in its temples looked to one traveller, the French engraver and draughtsman Abbé Jean-Claude Richard de Saint-Non (1727–1791), like vases or cups rather than Greek classical capitals. To the eyes of eighteenth-century visitors, the temples did not resemble any architecture they were familiar with: Paestum turned accepted ideas of classical architecture upside down. The reactions of travellers to their encounter with this unfamiliar architecture, at a distant, deserted and dangerous site, caused a great stir in architectural thought, and exemplify a broad range of responses to archaeological remains and to classical architecture in general. These accounts are not always easy to interpret, but many of them have one characteristic in common: they describe the experience in terms of the sublime.[2] Here, for example, is the architect Charles Heathcote Tatham, describing his first impressions:

> After alighting & approaching the Temples, my mind became so much expanded from the contemplation of Columns of such grand dimensions that I received an impression I have never forgotten. The Greeks were a wonderful people. They knew too well how simplicity with vastness & continuousness produced sublimity. How calculated are the Fine Arts to elevate the soul when reflected through a pure medium![3]

Great Expectations, Conflicting Experiences

In writing about what they saw at Paestum, many travellers noted a divergence between their experience on the spot and their prior knowledge about the site. The comparison was not always favourable: in the first years after the rediscovery of the temples, before the publication of verbal and pictorial accounts, travellers entertained great expectations of what they would find when they reached Paestum, which were not necessarily borne out by their actual experience. In 1761, for example, the British architect James Adam

9 (*facing page*) Detail of Fig. 36.

10   Charles-Louis Clérisseau, drawing of the interior of the Temple of Neptune from the north-east, after 1761. St Petersburg, State Hermitage Museum ('acquired from the artist by Catherine II on 5 May 1780'), OR-16921.

(1732–1794) undertook a long journey with the French architect Charles-Louis Clérisseau (1722–1820) to study the temples (Fig. 10), but the visit gave him nothing but disappointment. He wrote about:

> the . . . famous antiquitys so much talk'd of of late as wonders but which, curiosity apart, don't merit half the time and trouble they have cost me. They are of an early, an inelegant and unenriched Doric, that afford no detail and scarcely produce two good views. So much for Pesto.[4]

Before he set out, Adam had planned to include the temples in a publication entitled *Antiquities of Sicily and Graecia Major*, but he failed to reach Sicily and abandoned his project.[5] At the time of his visit to Paestum, there were no publications on the temples: the first book on the site appeared in French in 1764, and the first British publication in 1767.[6] Being entirely unprepared and having no knowledge of Paestum or its temples, it was perhaps only to be expected that Adam found it difficult to arrive at a just appreciation of the site. But this sense of disappointment persisted throughout the eighteenth century, even though, as time went on, engravings and publications became available. Indeed, architects who travelled to Paestum at the end of the century could still find themselves perplexed by what they saw.

Although the oddness of Paestum resulted in disillusionment for many, the accounts of visitors testify to their unique experiences *in situ*. Quite often Paestum gave rise to conflicting feelings, as it did in the architect Pierre-Louis Moreau-Desproux (1727–1794), whose travel diary voices his sentiments of both astonishment and pity at the vastness of the site and the spectacle of the magnificent buildings, now partly in ruins.[7] Reactions of this kind demonstrate, more than anything, that a reliance on Vitruvian theory and accepted architectural history did not equip travellers to appreciate what was valuable at Paestum: instead, they tried to express their responses by appealing to their experience of art and nature. How exactly did visitors deal with the strangeness of the site? And how did they make sense of their contradictory sensations? What happened when travellers could not draw on their knowledge of the theory and history of architecture? And what role did the sublime play?

Before being able to answer these questions, we have to define the sublime, and distinguish the various theories that were developed about it and their different purposes. As a rhetorical and aesthetic concept it was formulated in the theories of Longinus (first century AD), the poet and critic Nicolas Boileau-Despréaux (1636–1674) and the philosopher Edmund Burke (1729–1797). 'The sublime' also describes an experience – the powerful reaction of the senses, the emotions and the intellect to nature, art or architecture – and it was this perception of the true Paestum that caused visitors to invoke the sublime to account for what they saw, even when they did not explicitly use the term. In the large number of first-hand accounts of the temples, we can distinguish different varieties of the sublime, which the definitions offered by the three main theorists will help us to identify and explain. Having determined the different theories, we shall then apply them to architecture and see how the sublime informed architectural thought and the responses of visitors to the architecture at Paestum; this, in turn, will enable us to analyse the peculiarity of the site and explain why it shattered common concepts of classical architecture.

Starting from some first impressions of Paestum in written accounts, this chapter examines the different definitions of the sublime in the theories of Longinus, Boileau and Burke, and their influence on rhetorical, artistic and aesthetic thought. We shall then turn to writings on architecture to define how the concept of the sublime was played out in the eighteenth century in theoretical and two-dimensional expressions as well as in the three-dimensional experience of buildings. Having established an understanding of the general theories and the role of the sublime, with its diverse meanings, in architectural thought, in the last sections of this chapter we shall make a further analysis of the sublime experience *in situ* at Paestum, to see how the concept emerged as a kaleidoscope of paradoxical spatial observations.

Paestum at First Sight

If James Adam and other travellers could not appreciate the architecture of the monuments at Paestum, other aspects of the site struck them forcibly and caused wonderment – the enormous size of the temples, for instance. Lascelles Raymond Iremonger (1718–1793), an Englishman who visited Paestum in July 1752 while on the Grand Tour, described the contrast between the startling dimensions of the temples and the unpleasantness of the architecture in a letter:

> all . . . of the Dorick order, these antiquities surprise you by their greatness, but give you no great pleasure by their elegance or taste, the Pillars in my opinion being short, out of proportion, & vastly overcharged in their Capitals, & the Entablature & pediments are very heavy.[8]

Other travellers commented upon the ugliness of the architecture. In autumn 1753 Frederick, Lord North (1732–1792), wrote of the temples: 'The meanness of their materials & ye badness of their Architecture has been one principal cause of their preservation. Nobody has thought it worth his while to destroy them.'[9] The same letter suggests that distaste was

only augmented by an inability to 'place' the temples at Paestum: 'We were . . . struck with
three great buildings, which stood parallel one to ye other, but at unequal distances . . .
Are they Temples? Are they Basilicae? What are they?' – a reaction found in accounts by
other travellers as well. Lord North commented on the strangeness of the architecture in
these terms:

> The Columns are of an ancient Dorick order, [they] seem to have been made at ye
> time, when t[h]at order was coming out of its original rough state & forming itself to
> that beauty, it afterwards attained. They are very short, clumsy & ill-shaped. Their diam-
> eter is much smaller at ye top, than ye bottom; Their Capitals are flat: They are fluted,
> but ye flutings are very coarse.

In describing the form of the capitals, North's tone descends from puzzlement to ridicule:
'I think they resemble in shape pretty much those props, on which our peasants in England
sometimes put their corn, to prevent its being eaten by vermin.' The French art dealer
Pierre-François Hugues, known as Baron d'Hancarville (1719–1805), who went to Paestum
in 1766 with the English diplomat and art collector William Hamilton (1730–1803), envoy-
extraordinary to the Spanish court at Naples from 1764 to 1800, was similarly amazed by
the temples:

> In the midst of [these] ruins stand three Edifices of a sort of Architecture whose
> Members are Dorick, altho' its proportions are not so . . . in a fourth journey we
> [Hamilton and d'Hancarville] made to Pœsti a few months since, we remained there
> several days to examine at leisure those magnificent ruins, which astonish and strike the
> more in proportion as they are examined more particularly and oftner seen.[10]

These observations vividly evoke the impression the temples made on visitors accustomed
to the monuments of Rome and classical architecture as presented in books. The most
conspicuous feature of these accounts is the oddity of the architecture, which comes across
even more strongly when travellers tried to write about what they saw and felt on the
spot. The French architect Pierre-Adrien Pâris (1745–1819), who went to Paestum in 1774,
expressed the mixed feelings the temples aroused in him: 'We see in the ruins of Pestum

or Posidonia three temples, of which one especially is quite well preserved. I do not know of anything so terrible, so impressive, or so distinctive as these temples.'[11]

Accounts were often contradictory and ambivalent. The German writer Johann Wolfgang von Goethe (1749–1832), who visited Paestum on 23 March 1787, was at first uncertain whether he was seeing rocks or ruins, until he detected the remains of monuments (Fig. 11). He described the conflict between a prior knowledge of classical architecture and personal observation at Paestum: 'Our eyes and, through them, our whole sensibility have become so conditioned to a more slender style of architecture that these crowded masses of stumpy conical columns appear offensive and even terrifying.'[12] This passage, one of many that demonstrate the disparity between expectation and experience, offers the first hint of an explanation as to why these monuments were so unattractive to Goethe and to other travellers. His reaction shows that the columns – 'offensive and even terrifying' – shocked, fascinated and impressed visitors all at the same time. It is precisely this mixture of paradoxical emotions that characterises the sublime.

Towards Beauty and Terror:
The Foundations of the Sublime

In the many different statements about Paestum, the term 'sublime' occurs remarkably often; travellers and architects referred to the 'sublime' colonnades, the 'sublime' temples, the 'sublime' architecture, 'sublime' ideas and 'sublime' effects. In doing so were they following Longinus and Boileau, or can we detect the influence of Burke's concept of the sublime?

Longinus, Boileau and Burke were the principal theorists of the sublime until the end of the eighteenth century.[13] We know that architects and travellers had read their theories, having been exposed to them at school or university or because they owned copies of their works.[14] The first treatise on the subject, *Peri hupsous* (*On the Sublime*), was probably written in the first century AD, by an unknown Greek author, now named Pseudo-Longinus or simply Longinus.[15] The earliest known manuscript is incomplete, the missing passages including the final section on the emotions. Until the nineteenth century, Cassius Longinus, a Greek orator, was thought to be the author of the text; the attribution has since been challenged, but there is still no consensus about who wrote it. From the 1550s onwards, different Greek and Latin editions of the text appeared,[16] and versions and translations immediately began to circulate in Western Europe. The work exercised a strong influence on literature, the arts and architecture – an influence that is still not very well charted.[17]

Peri hupsous is a rhetorical theory addressed to students of oratory. Its aim is to provide rhetorical methods to enable the orator to move an audience by the power of speech. The text is a literary theory rather than a theory of art, and therefore concentrates on language, though the visual arts, as we shall see, play a part. Longinus was concerned to differentiate between style and the effects of rhetoric, and, like all rhetorical writers, carefully defined and demonstrated stylistic means of achieving persuasion. He focused on the orators, poets and historians who, in their use of language, showed that 'the effect of genius is not to persuade the audience but to transport them out of themselves',[18] and drew on the works of Demosthenes, Plato and Herodotus to illustrate his points.[19] Listening to a speech or reading literature could transport the hearer or reader, he claimed, and could even change the course of their existence.

The text defines five methods of achieving the sublime, or five sources of the sublime in oratory, speech and literature: great thoughts, strong emotion, figures of thought and speech, noble diction, and the dignified arrangement of words.[20] To Longinus, the sublime is what is truly great and 'gives abundant food for thought: it is irksome, nay, impossible, to resist its effect: the memory of it is stubborn and indelible'.[21] The sublime is what strikes you, what continues to haunt you – often a single strong idea, thought or impression. It 'lies in elevation, amplification rather in amount; and so you often find sublimity in a single idea, whereas amplification always goes with quantity and a certain degree of redundance'.[22] Besides the great and the grand, an important aspect is ambivalence. In embodying terrifying beauty, the sublime goes further than mere amazement.

Sublime sensations created by a confrontation with natural phenomena illustrate the aspect of terror: 'the Nile, the Danube, the Rhine, and far above all, the sea [or the] craters of Etna in eruption, hurling up rocks and whole hills from their depths and sometimes shooting forth rivers of the pure Titanic fire'.[23] The force of nature is to be admired not in small details but in its tremendous and impressive upheavals. To Longinus, nature was much more compelling and moving than art – 'art is only perfect when it looks like nature and nature succeeds only by concealing art about her person'[24] – though he conceded that a colossal sculpture can produce similar emotions.[25] In another passage he said of painting:

Though the high lights and shadows lie side by side in the same plane, yet the high lights spring to the eye and seem not only to stand out but to be actually much nearer. So it is in writing. What is sublime and moving lies nearer to our hearts, and thus, partly from a natural affinity, partly from brilliance of effect, it always strikes the eye long before the figures.[26]

Longinus often made analogies between music and words. For example, *periphrasis* contributed to the sublime: 'Just as in music what we call ornament enhances the beauty of the main theme, so periphrasis often chimes in with the literal expression of our meaning and gives it a far richer note, especially if it is not bombastic or discordant but agreeably in harmony.'[27] Choosing the right words:

has a marvellously moving and seductive effect upon an audience and . . . all orators and historians make this their supreme object. For this of itself gives to the style at once grandeur, beauty, a classical flavour, weight, force, strength, and a sort of glittering charm, like the bloom on the surface of the most beautiful bronzes, and endues the facts as it were with a living voice.[28]

Only once did Longinus write about architecture, using it to illustrate what is not sublime in literature:

What [the greatest rhetorical writers] have done is to make a clean sweep, as it were, of all the main points [of their subject] by order of merit, and to bring them together, allowing nothing affected or undignified or pedantic to intervene. For all such irrelevancies [which distract the reader from the main story] are like the introduction of gaps or open tracery [perforations] in architecture: they utterly spoil the effect of sublime ideas, well ordered and built into one coherent structure.[29]

This might mean that irrelevant ornament is detrimental to the sublime, in the sense that a coherently constructed sentence should not be undermined by unnecessary additions. But in recent studies of the sublime in seventeenth-century English architecture, it has been suggested that the point of the passage is to identify one of the stylistic features of the sublime as the combination of conflicting and contradictory elements in a composition, whether it is a text or a building.[30]

Versions and fragments of Longinus's text circulated until the end of the seventeenth century, when *Peri hupsous* was given new life through a French translation by Nicolas Boileau-Despréaux (1636–1711), published in 1674. Boileau's edition was important because, after being restricted to a circle of humanist scholars for more than a hundred years, *On the Sublime* was now for the first time available to a large public. Some commentators suggest that the dissemination of Longinus's ideas came about only through the success of Boileau's edition, because without it a wide range of readers would never have gained access to the text.[31] As has been shown in recent publications, *Le Traité du sublime* meant a deconstruction of French seventeenth-century classical thought.[32] With Boileau's translation, the rational approach to the arts, which favoured harmonious beauty, was suddenly confronted by an emotional counterpart that sought tension, tolerated ambivalence, and rated amazement or *le merveilleux* on a par with beauty.

In translating Longinus's text, Boileau developed his own ideas about the sublime. Central to his translation is the passage in which the sublime is defined, where he referred to: 'the extraordinary and wondrous thing that strikes you in discourse and that makes a work sweep you away, enrapture you, transport you'.[33] In his *Réflexions critiques*, written twenty years later, Boileau summarised his own ideas:

> The Sublime is a certain forcefulness of speech, fit to elevate and ravish the soul, which originates from the grandeur of the thought and the nobility of the sentiment, or from the magnificence of the words, or from the harmonious, lively and animated turn of the expression; in other words, [it originates] from one of these [characteristics], taken in isolation, or – what makes for the highest manifestation of the Sublime – from all these three together.[34]

What Boileau added to Longinus's theory was the significance of experience. Moreover, he departed from Longinus in stressing the importance of simplicity. Where, for Longinus, the sublime exists only in grand effects, Boileau demonstrated that it could equally be found in a simple phenomenon or event:

> One must know that, by Sublime, Longinus did not mean what orators call the sublime style, but rather the extraordinary and wondrous thing that strikes you in discourse and that makes a work sweep you away, enrapture you, transport you. The sublime style relies merely on lofty words but the Sublime can be found in a single thought, in a single figure, in a single turn of phrase.[35]

Thus Boileau diminished the rhetorical focus on stylistic means of achieving the sublime as part of a strategy of persuasion, and eliminated the opposition between *sublimitas* and *simplicitas*. While for Longinus the sublime created a state of ecstasy, for Boileau it gave lasting pleasure;[36] instead of Longinus's sublime as a superlative of beauty, Boileau called it a state between two extremes. Longinus's 'terrifying beauty' was ambivalent enough, but Boileau's exquisite state of balance was even more so. In Boileau's theory, the sublime was located between 'the low and the precious, the burlesque and the spectacular, the rational and the "je ne sais quoi". . . , the unbelievable and the real'.[37]

By extending the group of those who could appreciate the sublime from connoisseurs to amateurs of art and literature, Boileau made the concept available to less learned minds. This was an important step towards the theories of Edmund Burke, according to which the learned mind could even be a hindrance to apprehending the sublime. The contradiction or paradox inherent in Longinus's understanding of the sublime as combining fear with pleasure would achieve its definitive conceptual value in Burke's theories. In his hands the sublime completed the transition from rhetorical theory, aimed at achieving an impact on an audience, to aesthetic theory, focusing on the experience of the beholder, and in this sense it became also more personal.

In line with the ideas of the Roman poet and philosopher Lucretius (first century BC), Burke conceived a theory in which immensity and terror became something to enjoy, provided you were at a distance.[38] His *Philosophical Enquiry into the Origin of our Ideas of the Sublime and Beautiful* (1757), first published anonymously, set out a seminal theory of aesthetics that had a long-lasting influence on his contemporaries and on the way they perceived nature, art and architecture.[39] For the first time, Burke made a division between the sublime and the beautiful. Beauty engenders pleasant and delightful feelings, but the sublime is associated with fear, terror and astonishment: it intimidates and causes awestruck admiration. Although, in the presence of the sublime, the beholder is aware of his or her own littleness and dependence, the simple fact of knowing that he or she is safe can nonetheless give a feeling of pleasure. In that sense the sublime was to Burke the counterpart of beauty. Precisely this combination of terror and pleasure made the apprehension of the sublime a much stronger sensation than the response to beauty, which is what made it a sought-after experience. The sublime was no longer the equivalent of supreme beauty, but its opposite, caused by different phenomena and producing different feelings. Burke was the first to offer a theory about how the process of pleasure through terror takes place.

In his distinction between beauty and the sublime Burke gave an important place to tactile experience. While smoothness and regularity caused sensations of beauty, roughness might lead to an experience of the sublime. When Burke opposed the sublime to the beautiful, he used words that also appear in descriptions of Paestum. The sublime, to Burke, was of vast dimensions, 'rugged and negligent', 'dark and gloomy', 'solid, and even massive'.[40] The passions caused by experiencing sublime architecture would combine pain and pleasure, whereas beautiful architecture would inspire only pleasure. A significant difference between the theories of Longinus and Boileau and Burke's was the latter's focus on the mind of the spectator. While in Longinus the sublime was a quality of speech, art and natural objects, with Burke it became, above all, an operation of the mind; hence, the relationship between the object and the mind that perceived it gained a new significance.

In what way did Burke connect this concept to architecture? At first sight, his *Philosophical Enquiry* hardly even suggests the possibility that architecture can cause sublime sensations. He seems to focus mainly on nature, literature and, to a lesser degree, painting, and uses experiences of art, nature and literature to define the sublime. Only once did he refer to a built object – hardly a building:

When any work seems to have required immense force and labour to effect it, the idea is grand. Stonehenge, neither for disposition nor ornament, has any thing admirable; but those huge rude masses of stone, set on end, and piled each on other, turn the mind on [the] immense force necessary for such a work. Nay the rudeness of the work increases this cause of grandeur, as it excludes the idea of art, and contrivance; for dexterity produces another sort of effect which is different enough from this.[41]

Burke's description of the 'huge rude masses of stone' of Stonehenge resembles accounts of Paestum, as we shall see later in this chapter. Earlier theories of the sublime, notably those of Longinus and Boileau, have mainly been overlooked as far as architecture is concerned,[42] and so too has the *Enquiry*. But if Stonehenge is the only explicit example of architecture that Burke mentioned, his text nonetheless gives many indications of what sublime architecture is, even if only in a general sense. It is important to note, though, that in Burke's thought the conditions for the sublime in buildings are mainly related to experience. His text sheds some light on how the very lack of prior knowledge on the part of visitors to Paestum could enhance their sensation of the sublime on encountering the temples: that is, how their ignorance could be one of the prerequisites for their sublime experience: 'Knowledge and acquaintance make the most striking causes affect but little.'[43]

In the next section we shall look more closely at what Burke and others wrote about the sublime in architecture. Although recent studies create the impression that only nature or art can produce the sublime, the experiences of eighteenth-century travellers to Paestum and many contemporary expressions in architectural thought belie this. In addressing architecture we need to note an observation that Boileau made in his commentary on Longinus: 'in speaking of the sublime [Longinus] is himself very sublime'.[44]

Theories of the Sublime in Architecture

One eighteenth-century architect who thought that he would himself become sublime by creating sublime architecture was Étienne-Louis Boullée (1728–1799). In explaining his design for a cenotaph for Newton (Fig. 12) he exclaimed:

> Sublime mind! Prodigious and profound genius! Divine being! Newton! Deign to accept the homage of my feeble talents! Ah! If I dare to make it public, it is because I am persuaded that I have surpassed myself in the project which I shall discuss. O Newton! With the range of your intelligence and the sublime nature of your Genius, you have defined the shape of the earth; I have conceived the idea of enveloping you with your discovery. That is as it were to envelop you in your own self . . . By using your divine system, Newton, to create the sepulchral lamp that lights thy tomb, it seems that I have made myself sublime.[45]

In his funerary monument (1784) for Isaac Newton (1642–1727), Boullée paid homage to the scientist, and at the same time tried to demonstrate that architecture could rival science. He explained his intentions in his *Architecture: Essai sur l'art* (*c.*1794, unpublished). In the

12a and b Étienne-Louis Boullée, cenotaph for Newton: night-time view of the exterior (*below left*) and daytime view of the interior (*below right*), *c.*1784. Paris, Bibliothèque Nationale de France, Cabinet des Estampes, HA 56-FT 7, plates 7 and 8.

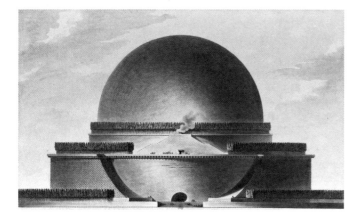

passage just quoted, the parallel with Boileau's comment on Longinus is remarkable. Both reveal how the writer and architect, aiming to transmit or convey the sublime to the public, can through this process become sublime himself. It is as if the sublimity of his work reflects himself: it shows that he is a genius. In Boullée's text the intertwining of artist and art in relation to the sublime is noteworthy and gives an indication of the role that the sublime can play in architecture. It is unfortunate, however, that Boullée has become the epitome of the sublime in architecture, because if we study only Boullée, ignoring other eighteenth-century architects and also the contribution of Burke, a very limited interpretation emerges. Furthermore, the accounts of Paestum take us so much further.

First, we must examine how the sublime was introduced into architectural thought. This demands a two-way analysis, addressing the role of architecture in theories of the sublime and the role of the sublime in the writings of architects. Blondel, Le Camus de Mézières, Chambers, Soane and Reveley will offer us different definitions of the concept, and their ideas will help us to understand what took place at Paestum, and the diversity of sublime reactions to the site itself.

Boileau's French translation of Longinus's text was widely read, but it was not the only, or indeed even the first, means by which the theory of the sublime was disseminated during the seventeenth century: many other publications appeared in which the concept was explained, and related to architecture, and the first manifestations of the sublime in French architecture and urban planning predate Boileau.[46] Similarly, the first English trans-lation of Longinus was published more than twenty years before Boileau's French version.[47] Before the middle of the eighteenth century we can distinguish two rather separate tra-ditions of writing on the sublime, in France and in England; it was only with the publi-cation of Burke's theory that exchanges and interactions between the two took off.

In England, the translations of Longinus that were published by John Hall in 1652, by John Pulteney in 1680 and by William Smith in 1739 were the ones that most influenced English architects. Nicholas Hawksmoor (1661–1736) and John Vanbrugh (1664–1726) drew on these publications in their writings and designs.[48] The English architectural tradition is distinguished by a great awareness of the impact of a building on the beholder. Of his designs for London city churches, for instance, Vanbrugh wrote, in a clear reference to Longinus, that they should have a 'solemn and awfull appearance'.[49] A sublime aesthetic is also suggested by the complex and conflicting composition of Hawksmoor's façades – which cannot be taken in at one glance (see further p. 35 below) – and their tolerance of ambivalence and ambiguity. Rhetorical advice in Longinus's text offered design solutions that combined different styles, emphasising certain elements, favouring variation and rhythm, and working deliberately on the effects of surprise and association that would strike the beholder of a building.

'On the Pleasures of the Imagination', an essay by Joseph Addison (1672–1719) pub-lished in *The Spectator* in 1712, was an important vehicle for the wider dissemination of theories of the sublime.[50] The designs of Vanbrugh have been interpreted as the three-dimensional realisation of his theories.[51] Addison's essay defined his ideas on experience and association, focusing mainly on taste; while he drew on Longinus, giving examples of awe-inspiring natural phenomena and objects, he never used the word 'sublime'. Although he did not address the subject of architecture directly, Addison raised some related issues – for example, offering an aesthetics of the infinite.[52] And in his *Remarks on several parts of Italy*, first published in 1705, he made some comments on architecture, or 'that particular art, which has a more immediate tendency, than any other, to produce those primary pleasures of the imagination', that are of special interest.[53] The 'primary pleasures' to which he referred were caused by greatness, novelty and beauty, of which he explained only greatness because, he said, the other two were easily recognisable in architecture. Pleasures of the imagination, he stressed, are experienced in the mind, but caused by what we perceive or feel. His earlier 'Letter from Italy' (1703) showed how architecture moved him. In his description of the Coliseum we find echoes of the Longinian sublime:

> Immortal Glories in my Mind revive,
> And in my Soul a thousand Passions strive,
> When Rome's exalted Beauties I descry
> Magnificent in Piles of Ruin lye:
> An Amphitheater's amazing Height
> Here fills my Eye with Terror and Delight[54]

In 'On the Pleasures of the Imagination' the size and scale of buildings are said to be a cause of the sublime:

> Let any one reflect on the disposition of mind he finds in himself, at his first entrance into the Pantheon at Rome, and how his imagination is filled with something great and amazing; and, at the same time, consider how little, in proportion, he is affected with the inside of a Gothic cathedral, though it be five times larger than the other; which can arise from nothing else but the greatness of the manner in the one, and the meanness in the other.[55]

Addison claimed, however, that other elements than mere size make for greatness: 'Greatness [in architecture may be an effect of] the manner in which it is built'. He named examples of architecture that impressed merely by their size; these were mainly buildings that had ceased to exist – the wonders of the world, such as the tower of Babel, even the foundations of which 'looked like a spacious mountain', and Babylon with its walls and temple 'that rose a mile high'. The same quality was to be found in the Egyptian pyramids and the Great Wall of China. These were all sublime in their way, but in Italian buildings what he admired more than their dimensions was the way in which they were constructed, in which connection he stressed analogies between nature and architecture. The Pantheon, for example, appealed to the imagination because, just like mountains and the ocean and the wide expanse of the earth, it led man to thoughts of God:

> We are obliged to devotion for the noblest buildings that have adorned the several countries of the world. It is this which has set men at work on temples and public places of worship, not only that they might, by the magnificence of the building, invite the Deity to reside within it, but that such stupendous works might, at the same time, open the mind to vast conceptions, and fit it to converse with the divinity of the place. For every thing that is majestic, imprints an awfulness and reverence on the mind of the beholder, and strikes in [sic] with the natural greatness of the soul.[56]

In his focus on analogies with nature, Addison's approach marks a significant shift in ideas on the sublime at the beginning of the eighteenth century. He showed that feelings of admiration and fear, inspired by magnificent natural phenomena, can be appreciated from a safe distance and put into words, so that (as Lucretius had said) the spectator can see the beauty in terror.[57] This was an important prelude to Burke's theories, and also described a mechanism that would operate in perceptions of Paestum.

While Longinus and Boileau hardly mentioned architecture in relation to the sublime, in composing his aesthetic theory, Burke wrote about it in a clearly defined way. In his *Enquiry* the sublime is often described in terms of the sensations caused by natural objects and phenomena, but Burke also explicitly listed the characteristics of buildings that could result in sublime architecture. These passages, which focus on the experience of a building, its rhetorical and aesthetic effects, read almost like an instruction manual on how to kindle sublime emotions in those who view it. The difference between the sublime and the beautiful is only partly intrinsic in objects, he explained: presenting himself as an empiricist, he claimed that sublime sensations are also – and sometimes purely – an experience that takes place in the mind of the beholder. The sublime is thus not only a quality of the object itself, but is located in the spectator's perception and experience, a direct result of the relation to the object of the human being whose reactions partake of the sublime. As we have already seen, Burke's ideas on architecture remain theoretical: he gave neither positive nor negative examples of buildings, with the sole exception of one mention of Stonehenge.

In the second part of the *Enquiry*, after arguing that astonishment is the highest effect of the sublime, Burke went on to define the cause of sublime emotion as terror: this might be aroused, for example, by a storm at sea, or by obscurity, or by death (in a reference to *Paradise Lost*, Burke remarked that Milton painted a scene of 'Death' in which 'all is dark, uncertain, confused, terrible and sublime').[58] In comparing poetry and painting, Burke maintained that, unlike obscure poetry, painting could never stimulate strong emotions: 'It is our ignorance of things that causes all our admiration, and chiefly excites our passions.' Because we cannot grasp infinity and eternity, the impression that objects or nature make on us is magnificent: 'The mind is hurried out of itself, by a croud [sic] of great and confused images; which affect because they are crouded [sic] and confused.'[59] The claim that paintings can never excite the passions raises the issue of representation. According to Burke (in an echo of Longinus), only direct experience in the unmediated perception of poetry or prose can produce sublime feelings: a transformation of this experience on canvas or wood always fails to succeed in doing the same.

Other important characteristics of sublime objects are vastness and infinity, which reminds us of Addison's theory. In Burke's statement 'Greatness in dimension is a powerful cause of the sublime,' his 'Greatness in dimension' can refer to length, depth or height. Surfaces that are rough and wrecked rather than smooth and polished also have attributes of the sublime.[60] Infinity seems even more powerful: it 'has a tendency to fill the mind with that sort of delightful horror, which is the most genuine effect, and truest test of the sublime'.[61] Even if not infinite in reality, an object that seems infinite to the eye of the beholder can cause the same striking effects. The infinite can be engineered artificially through succession and uniformity. An example of this is the rotunda, which to the eye seems continuous whichever way you turn and thus creates the impression of infinity. Buildings with too many angles, such as churches in the form of a Greek cross, cannot produce grandeur. Furthermore, although 'Greatness in dimension' is essential, if a building were too large it would lose its effect. Burke demonstrated this with an example:

> the perspective will lessen it in height as it gains in length; and will bring it at last to a point; turning the whole figure into a sort of triangle, the poorest in its effect of almost any figure that can be presented to the eye. I have ever observed, that colonnades and avenues of trees of moderate length, were without comparison far grander, than when they were suffered to run to immense distances.[62]

Another significant discussion relates to objects that are not finished – or, we might say, no longer complete. They leave more to the imagination than perfect ones, and are therefore more interesting: young animals, for instance, as opposed to full-grown ones, or unfinished sketches rather than fully executed presentation drawings. Burke argued that imagining something makes it grander, because it is completed in the beholder's mind and therefore occupies the mind more intensely or more lastingly. It is easy to see how this applies to Paestum, which, by its very mysteriousness, left a whole world for its visitors to imagine.

Besides magnificence, two other topics were of importance to Burke's sublime: light and colour. The subject of light in architecture is discussed separately. Dark and gloomy buildings are sources of the sublime. Darkness has a more intense effect on the emotions than light, and contrast is important. On entering a building, one should find the lightness of the open sky opposed by an obscure interior:

> to make the transition thoroughly striking, you ought to pass from the greatest light, to as much darkness as is consistent with the uses of architecture. At night the contrary rule will hold, but for the very same reason; and the more highly a room is then illuminated, the grander will the passion be.[63]

Colours should be dark and gloomy. In architecture the building materials and ornament should not be 'white, nor green, nor yellow, nor blue, nor of a pale red, nor violet, nor spotted, but of sad and fuscous colours, as black, or brown, or deep purple, and the like.' Most decorations, such as mosaics, statues and paintings, do not create sublime responses, but if these are necessary in buildings the sublime should come from other aspects. Above all, the interior of the building must not be too bright, for 'nothing so effectually deadens the whole taste of the sublime'.[64]

Terror, gloom, vastness, infinity, 'difficulty' (that is, of the builder's task), darkness and obscure colours are the elements that Burke defined as conducive to elevated sensations. His ideas were to have a major influence on English architectural thought and had a strong impact in France as well. The first French translation of Burke's *Enquiry* was published in 1765, and received very positive reviews. With a long tradition of the sublime in architecture, based on editions of Longinus and Boileau's translation, the French adopted the Burkean sublime just as eagerly as the English.

Boileau's impact continued in France well into the eighteenth century, notably in the influential and widely read theories of the architect Jacques-François Blondel (1705–1774).[65] Unlike Burke, Blondel did not write on aesthetics; instead he focused on design advice, providing his readership (which consisted of architects) with tools to help them create the sublime in architecture. In chapter IV of his six-volume *Cours d'architecture* (1771–7), Blondel analysed how to distinguish good from mediocre architecture, or a building that possessed 'a sublime, noble, elevated style' from one that had 'a naïve, simple, true character'.[66] According to Blondel, the decorations of a building define its character, a point he made by comparing architecture with poetry, painting and music.[67] In a section of the chapter entitled 'De la sublimité de l'architecture', Blondel advised architects on how to design sublime architecture. The architect should strive for sublimity in himself first.[68] (Boileau's remark on Longinus, subsequently adopted by Boullée, is clearly recognisable here.) After that, he advocated limits to the dimensions of a building, warning of the risks of gigantic dimensions, which lead only to vulgarity in architecture. As Burke had observed before him, too vast is not sublime.[69] So how can an architect achieve sublimity in his buildings? Blondel had the answer:

> One has to reunite . . . knowledge, genius, beauty, regularity, decorum, solidity & convenience; and yet one has to consider that the systematic mind, meditation, composure

can produce a good Architect, & that genius, the soul, enthusiasm, on their own raise the Artist to the sublime: that the mind defines, that the sentiment paints, & that this gives life to all the outputs. In a word, it would be desirable that a building could, by its appearance, entice, move &, so to speak, elevate the soul of the spectator, while it transports him to contemplative admiration, which at first sight he could not himself account for, however well instructed in the profound knowledge of Art.[70]

The kind of architecture that 'could, by its appearance, entice, move & . . . elevate the soul' was necessary for any building that needed to suggest the trace of a divine hand, as was shown in the high-vaulted churches of the Gothic period, with their mysterious light. Blondel criticised contemporary buildings, theatres and palaces where nothing seemed to work: sculpture, painting and architecture, all was mediocre. Sublime buildings elevate the mind, and can be recognised by any real connoisseur, in whom such a building will inspire a feeling that is timeless: the sublime in architecture will thus endure for centuries and will never cease to make that overwhelming impression on the beholder.[71] (In emphasising the importance of connoisseurship, Blondel went against Burke, who had stated that the more ignorant the observer the stronger is his sensation of the sublime.) For Blondel, positive examples of the sublime were the interior of the Val-de-Grâce hospital, the Louvre colonnade and the Porte Saint-Denis, all in Paris, and the orangery at Versailles. These were buildings that had been executed during the reign of Louis XIV and conferred 'a truly immortal glory' on the king and on their architects by the beauty of their mass and the coherence of their details.[72] The sublime could also be found in monuments erected in memory of citizens, great deeds, princes, heroes and captains. The main characteristics of this architecture were that it astonished the beholder and overwhelmed his mind with awe. Real connoisseurs would recognise the harmony between the different parts of the building, achieved through regularity without monotony – a harmony that is infinite and timeless. Like many other eighteenth-century architects, Blondel presented seventeenth-century architecture as the quintessence of the sublime, implying at the same time a veiled criticism of that of his own time, which could not match the distinction of the buildings of Louis XIV's reign.

Blondel aimed to define the aspects of architecture that would excite in the spectator a 'speechless and contemplative admiration'. This admiration could account only for the building as a whole, never for parts or details of buildings.[73] Following the beauty and perfection of the Greeks and Romans, the solidity and lightness of the Arabs and the commodiousness and charm of the French, the defining characteristic of the architecture that he described was originality. In discussing this, he invoked the diverse properties of architecture, among them what he called 'une Architecture terrible'.[74] He used this expression to describe buildings that respond as a whole to the gaze of the observer, seeming to express power and pride through their massive solidity and the use of certain materials; typical examples are military buildings with their large projections and profound recesses, and their high, thick, blank walls, which are pierced only by little openings and cast gigantic shadows.[75]

The French architect Nicolas Le Camus de Mézières (1721–1789) also addressed 'the terrible', but differently from Blondel. In his *Le Génie de l'architecture, ou L'Analogie de cet art avec nos sensations* (1780) he related this concept mainly to nature, but argued that it could also be attained in the arts, and made a connection with terror, beauty and character in architecture.[76] Concentrating on the beholder, he declared that the sublime will be produced when the eye can scarcely penetrate what it sees, or when there is a distant, featureless vista where 'no object meets the eye [and] the soul stands amazed and trembles'.[77] Darkness was an important element to him and designs should seek to exploit the power of light and shadow – for example, by using projecting bays; such contrasts create different characters in a building. Like other theorists, Le Camus de Mézières asserted that merely to build on a colossal scale does not suffice: certain elements are required to provide life and shape to a building, just as the immensity of the ocean needs the defining feature of a shore or an island.[78] He pursued the comparison with nature in describing the different sensations that might overtake someone sitting beside a river, from the drowsiness engendered by the gentle lapping of water to the terror aroused by the noise and motion of a torrent, which, he said, is closely linked to the experience of the sublime.[79] From this example, he argued that the character of a building must have the intended effect on a spectator, and that a building should provide a sequence of different effects on the one who observes it in the course of moving through it. As this account makes clear, Le Camus de Mézières differed from Blondel in thinking about architecture as drama: for him buildings and their interiors could arouse different emotions like the different scenes in a play. We shall revisit this idea in Chapter 4.

The Sublime in the Experience of Buildings

Although some studies have appeared on the sublime and the arts, its relationship to architecture is still a neglected field.[80] Now that we have treated the theory of the sublime, we shall turn to the experience of architecture to demonstrate a different approach. Before focusing on Paestum, this section will first elucidate the sublime in the observation of buildings in the eighteenth century. A built project of this period that can be associated with the sublime is Newgate prison (1768–75) by George Dance the younger (1741–1825). In the vein of Blondel's 'Architecture terrible', Dance designed the prison as a forbidding, rusticated block with small windows.[81] As we saw above, Blondel defined the 'terrible' as an exaggeration of scale and mass, which produced a heaviness that was characteristic of many prison designs in the eighteenth century. This type of architecture aimed deliberately at evoking feelings of fear in passers-by. Dance was an admirer of the aesthetic theories of Burke, and his design reflects the passage: 'Whatever is fitted in any sort to excite the ideas of pain and danger . . . whatever is in any sort terrible . . . is a source of the sublime.'[82] Another oft cited example of architectural sublime achieved through scale and contrasting volumes is the neo-Gothic house Fonthill Abbey in Wiltshire, designed by

13 Friedrich Gilly, perspective view of the rue des Colonnes in Paris, 1798. Universitätsbibliothek, Technische Universität, Berlin (destroyed). From A. Rietdorf, *Gilly: Wiedergeburt der Architektur* (Berlin: Hans von Hugo Verlag, 1940), 108.

James Wyatt. But more striking is the rue des Colonnes (1793–5) in Paris by Nicolas Vestier and Joseph Bénard:[83] a drawing of it, made by Friedrich Gilly (1772–1800) in 1798, represents sublime perception realised through the exaggerated repetition of columns and arches in the seemingly endless colonnades (Fig. 13).[84] It was also depicted by Henry Parke (Fig. 14), whose drawing was to be shown in John Soane's Royal Academy lectures. Parke's depiction presents a more realistic view, showing the end of the street, but still stressing the repetitiveness of the columns. These projects tell us that a sure means of instigating the sublime in architecture is through 'Great dimensions', massive scale and infinity.

The writings of eighteenth-century British architects display a pervasive preoccupation with the sublime. It figures largely in the writings of William Chambers (1722–1796), an admirer and friend of Burke, who, in some notes on Joseph Addison's essay 'On the Pleasures of the Imagination', wrote: 'In architecture sublimity is principally to be aimed at, grace is always to be avoided as much in buildings as in dignified human nature. In both it is equally injudicious and contemptible.'[85] Later he expanded on this idea:

14   Henry Parke, perspective view of the rue des Colonnes in Paris, 1819, for one of John Soane's Royal Academy lectures. London, Sir John Soane's Museum, 22/7/4.

Nothing exalts more nor fills the mind with Sublimer Ideas than the sight of noble actions, valiant exploits or stupendous objects, and next to that nothing fires the imagination so much nor fills [it] with loftier images than bold and spirited descriptions of glorious achievements, prodigious events, extraordinary or wonderful productions of human skill or human power.[86]

This passage shows that Chambers thought about the sublime very much as Burke did about Stonehenge, stressing the human effort necessary to construct such a monument. But, foreshadowing John Soane, Chambers also made a connection with character and its expression through architecture: it is 'an essential quality of beauty and grandeur . . . the gloom and solemnity of a temple or a mausoleum would ill suit a banqueting room or theatre'.[87] In his architecture, as well, Chambers sought sublime effects. For example, according to the architectural historian Barry Bergdoll, Chambers's Somerset House in London (1776–80; Fig. 15) can be seen in terms of the Burkean sublime in its 'infinite extent and a feeling of massive weight and scale'.[88] Chambers and Burke were not only friends but were in close contact about their ideas, as Edward Wendt has recently documented in his study on the sublime as taught at the Royal Academy in London.[89] Wendt's thesis is one of the few studies of the architectural sublime, though owing to its narrow focus on Britain and the figures at the Royal Academy it gives a rather limited view of the topic. It does, however, show how a preoccupation with the sublime at the Royal Academy infiltrated wider artistic and architectural circles in London, as happened also in Paris through the Académie d'Architecture.

The influence of the Royal Academy is embodied in the architect John Soane (1753–1837), who was from 1806 onwards professor of architecture there and gave a celebrated series of Royal Academy lectures starting in 1810. Soane was deeply concerned with the sublime, as the contents of his library demonstrate. He knew Longinus's text from Boileau's translation.[90] In his analyses of Gothic architecture his reactions were thoroughly Longinian, as we can see from his lecture notes, which drew on another book in his library, a collection entitled *Essays on Gothic Architecture* (2nd edn, 1802); from John Milner's contributions to this volume, he borrowed a reference to reactions of 'awe and pleasure' on entering a medieval cathedral, and the observation that 'height and length are among the primary sources of the Sublime'. The infinite also had a place in this: 'the perspective [of a Gothic church] produces an artificial infinite in the mind of the spectator'.[91]

To return to Chambers: he too was to have given some lectures at the Royal Academy in the 1770s, but in the end he never delivered them.[92] However, his lecture notes have been preserved and they offer an interesting insight into his ideas on the sublime, and Burke's influence on them;[93] Chambers published these ideas later in his *Treatise on the decorative part of civil architecture* (1791). In the first lecture, on how to be a good architect, Chambers's notes recommend travel: 'Travelling awakens the Imagination, the Sight of greatness & uncommon Objects, elevates the Mind to sublime Conceptions, and enriches it with numerous & extraordinary Ideas.'[94] The content of the third lecture demonstrates Chambers's concern with achieving the sublime in buildings: 'In Exterior decoration the Grandioso or Sublime is alwais to be aimed at . . . Where the dimensions are Inadequate artifice must be employed to produce the desired Effect.'[95] Further exposition is to be found in notes he made while reading Burke:

> Grandeur which is the first and in Architecture the most Essential quality of the Beau depends in some measure upon the specific dimensions of the Object but Chiefly upon the form & its subdivisions[;] an unskilful hand may render the largest Objects trifling & an Able Artist may Give dignity to trifles . . . Whatever appears difficult whatever bears the mark of distant times or Alludes to Ancient customs & Ceremonies whatever indicates Mystery will raise in the mind these sensations.[96]

Chambers here referred to the idea of mystery as a source of the sublime, but in another passage he drew attention to the element of simplicity, which allows the mind to fix on one aspect and be transported into awe:

> Unity of Colour is likewise productive of the Sublime a Striking Instance of which is the . . . Church of Carignano at Genoa built upon the model of St Peters at Rome which though not one quarter so large as its original hath more Grandeur[.] St Peters at Rome offers ten thousand Colours to the Sight which devide the attention by Confusing the form[;] the Madona del Cargnano is all of one Colour [but] the form is instantaneously Conveyd to the mind And fixes it in a State of Astonishment.[97]

The notes for the second lecture contain some interesting remarks on the origins of architecture, but also some critical passages on Greek temple architecture:

> In the Constructive Part of Architecture the Antients were no great Proficients, I believe many of the Deformities which we observe in the Grecian Buildings must be ascribed to their Ignorance in this Particular such as their Gouty Columns their narrow Intervals their disproportionate Architraves their Ipetral [i.e. hypaethral, wholly or partly unroofed] Temples which they knew not how to cover and their Temples with a Range of Columns running in the Center to support the Roof contrary to every Rule both of Beauty and Conveniency.[98]

In his introduction to the third volume of James Stuart's and Nicolas Revett's *The antiquities of Athens* (1794), the architect Willey Reveley (1760–1799) argued that in this way of reasoning Chambers probably had the temples at Paestum in mind.[99] Reveley was a pupil of Chambers, and (in the words of his obituary) 'had followed the steps of Athenian Stuart, in his travels through Greece and residence at Athens . . . His collection of drawings, universally known to all the lovers of art, and admirers of classic Antiquity, were made during his progress.'[100] Reveley's admiration for Greek architecture was immense, and Paestum fascinated him; in his travel diary he devoted many pages to the site.[101] His master, Chambers, who knew Paestum only through the descriptions and illustrations of others, could not cope with the strange architecture of its temples, which conflicted with

his aesthetic notions of classical architecture.[102] The architect Thomas Hardwick (1752–1829), who had been in Paestum in 1778 and made some captivating drawings of the temples in his sketchbook (Fig. 16),[103] wrote of him:

> Sir William Chambers never trod the classical ground of Attica, nor even visited Sicily or Pæstum, where he might have beheld some of the most antient and imposing works of the Grecian republic. It was evident, therefore, that Mr. Chambers derived from other sources his extensive knowledge in the art, and this he effected, as we have seen . . . by searching into the causes which produced those delightful effects apparent in the remains of Roman grandeur [and] by storing his mind with the excellent precepts laid down by authors who had not only written upon the art, but had likewise practised it.[104]

Chambers's adverse reaction proves that Paestum, in breaking all the proportional and aesthetic rules of classical architecture, could not be judged by established aesthetic criteria. While this recognition led Chambers to reject Paestum as 'deficient', others appreciated different aspects of the site or the temples. Dora Wiebenson, in her study *Sources of Greek Revival Architecture*, reduced the discussion between Chambers and Reveley about Greek architecture to an emotional quarrel about the respective merits of ancient Greek and Roman architecture.[105] She also stated that the sublime made no appearance in archaeological publications until 1794, when Reveley wrote his defence of Greek architecture in the preface to *The antiquities of Athens*.[106] But, as we shall see, the sublime would play a key role in the formulation of a new architectural experience and featured prominently in both archaeological and architectural writings about Paestum from the mid-century onwards.

Reveley's outspoken response to Chambers's views was part of a defence of Greek architecture, in which the sublime found a place, particularly in his admiration of the forceful architecture of the Temple of Neptune:

> The entablature is ponderous, and its decorations few in number, and of a strong character. The awful dignity and grandeur in this kind of temple, arising from the perfect agreement of its various parts, strikes the beholder with a sensation, which he may look for in vain in buildings of any other description.

Paestum's distinctiveness affected Reveley deeply, and in describing his impressions he expressed paradoxical feelings, endowing the building, in its 'awful dignity and grandeur', with almost

16 Thomas Hardwick, the temples at Paestum, 1778, pencil sketch in one of the sketchbooks from his Italian journey. London, Royal Institute of British Architects, Drawings and Archives Collection, SKB105/1.

human characteristics. The sublime character of the temple, in Reveley's estimation, was related to the order and its proportions:

A slight change in the order, or even in the proportions of a building, will always be found to introduce a very different character, even though the general form should be preserved. In the species of temple we are here considering, the causes of the sublime may easily be perceived. The simplicity of the basement, the sweeping lines of the flutings, the different proportions and yet contrasted figure of the outline of the column, and that of the intercolumniation, and the grand straight lines on the entablature crossing in their directions the graceful ones of the flutings, together with the gently-inclined pediment, all contribute to this striking effect.

He went on to describe the specific features of the massive columns and the voids between them: 'The column and intercolumniation approach each other more nearly in apparent superficial quantity, while they contrast more decidedly in form than in any other order.' All these elements contribute to a general impression of endurance and timelessness:

There is a certain appearance of eternal duration in this species of edifice, that gives a solemn and majestic feeling, while every part is perceived to contribute its share to this character of durability . . . These considerations will convince us that no material change can be made in the proportions of the genuine Grecian Doric, without destroying its particular character.[107]

Reveley's travel diary also contains passages about other Italian buildings that evoked feelings of the sublime: the Coliseum in Rome for instance. But these emotions were much less paradoxical and complex:

The Unity of this building is so great, that at any distance, it will produce an effect of Greatness, not to be seen in any other than large Circular or Eliptical buildings & though the particular parts are not to be seen, its general form will be so graceful as to make a strong impression on the mind, an effect only produced by beautiful forms, which must at the same time be so simple that the mind can comprehend them at one view & understand them, without the eye first wandering about in search of reasons why & wherefore; for, wherever the mind is to reason a while before it comprehends any object, the Great Effect & Strong Impression, which in Architecture are the first objects, are sure to be lost; few are the Edifices that will admit of such strict & severe criticisms, but Amphitheatres certainly will.[108]

In discussing the effects buildings can produce, Reveley tried to explain how the mind works in perceiving a sublime object. His discourse is rather similar to Chambers's argument about the unity of colour:

I have always observed that the mind is most satisfyed with objects that entirely occupy it, by leaving no vacancy; & which at the same time are so fully comprehended that time is not spent in reasoning, for the mind like the appetite must be exactly satisfied, by being neither overcharged nor in want. This rule may be deemed general as to the certainty of giving pleasure: but as to the effect of grandeur merely, a prodigious long & high wall only will always produce it & a prodigiously rich ornamented & confused fabrick will also produce the same effect particularly a profusion of Columns tho' ever so ill disposed.[109]

A comparison of Reveley's ideas with Burke's reveals interesting differences in their views of the sublime in architecture. For Reveley, a grand building must be viewed in all its aspects at a single gaze if it is to achieve sublimity, otherwise the mind is confused. The basilica of St Peter in Rome, for example, could evoke sublime feelings, as in the depiction (Fig. 17) by Hubert Robert (1733–1808). According to Reveley's theory, the viewer's first impression must be magnificent, the emotions it inspires overwhelming (Fig. 18):

> The effect of confused grandeur may be seen in the multiplicity of columns in the colonnade of St Peters at Rome in a variety of situations. A spectator walking in the center of one of these colonnades is struck with the magnificence of four ranges of lofty columns, but as he cannot see the end on account of the curving of its course the mind feels a disappointment, & is not satisfied. A man says to himself this is very grand but I see but a small part of it, how much grander would it be if I could see it alltogether! The mind feeling always a desire to know or see all, a part of another greater object for this reason never fully satisfies the mind. This must ever be the effect of objects on the mind as far as I am able to judge.[110]

In this view, Reveley criticised the colonnade of St Peter's for leaving too confusing an impression; its great extent was not visible to the viewer because of its being built in a curve, so it did not produce the overwhelming impression that was the effect of the sublime. He thus contradicted Burke and many other theorists, to whom the possibility of taking in a building at a single gaze was a characteristic of classical beauty, and the need to accumulate an impression of a building from different viewpoints a mark of the sublime.

Given all these French and English ideas on the sublime in architecture, it is remarkable that studies refer mainly to Boullée in this connection. While the enormous volumes and the great spaces of his architectural projects make him an obvious choice, and his

17 Hubert Robert, the cupola of the basilica of St Peter in Rome, c.1760. Besançon, Bibliothèque Municipale, Bibliothèque d'Étude et de Conservation, Collection Pierre-Adrien Pâris, vol. 451, no. 40.

18 Louis-Jean Desprez, interior of the basilica of St Peter in Rome ('La Croix lumineuse de Saint-Pierre, ou L'Illumination de la Croix de carême à Saint-Pierre'), *c.*1783. Palaiseau, École polytechnique.

writings are persuasive, there is a major drawback in attributing the sublime in architecture solely to a Revolutionary architect: Boullée's concept of the sublime is on paper only, and, as we shall see shortly, is worlds away from actual architectural experience. He defined the sublime as suggesting the infinite, marked by a daunting obscurity and an overpowering scale that profoundly affect the spectator.[111] Had the monument to Newton ever been built, this great hollow sphere 150 metres high, resting in a circular base, might have realised in stone Burke's ideas on sublime light:

> Mere light is too common a thing to make a strong impression on the mind, and without a strong impression nothing can be sublime . . . A quick transition from light to darkness, or from darkness to light, has yet a greater effect . . . all edifices calculated to produce an idea of the sublime, ought rather to be dark and gloomy . . . to make an object very striking, we should make it as different as possible from the objects with which you are immediately conversant; when therefore you enter a building, you cannot pass into greater light than you had in open air . . . At night the contrary rule will hold, but for the very same reason; and the more highly a room is then illuminated, the grander will the passion be.[112]

Boullée's design emphasised the natural effects of light shining through holes pierced in the vault. His *Architecture: Essai sur l'art* (*c*.1794), written partly to explain his projects, was never published in his lifetime, but the text was known, and his drawings were engraved and circulated widely (Fig. 19). From the age of 19, Boullée taught at the École Nationale des Ponts et Chaussées, and through his teaching and drawings influenced contemporary architects.[113] But the influence was mutual. The theories of Julien-David Le Roy and Nicolas Le Camus de Mézières are paraphrased in the *Essai*, and similar designs were developed by other architects, including Claude-Nicolas Ledoux, and by students of the École des Beaux-Arts – for example, spherical buildings, such as those by Antoine-Laurent-Thomas Vaudoyer (Fig. 20).[114] Boullée's built architectural work, mostly city and country houses in and around Paris, is rather unimpressive. It was only his drawings of imaginary buildings that influenced his contemporaries and successors. These can be seen as forceful expressions of Burke's ideas but, as they remained on the drawing-board and are more dreamlike than real, they have nothing to do with actual spatial experience.

Boullée's text stressed the advantages of the sphere in architecture:

> it offers the greatest possible surface to the eye and this lends it majesty. It has the simplest possible form, the beauty of which derives from its uninterrupted surface; and, in addition to all these qualities, it has grace for its outline and is as smooth and flowing as it could be.[115]

His theories were influenced by scientific studies – by Copernicus, Buffon and Newton, for example – copies of which were in his library, and his ideas on volumes such as the sphere, cube and pyramid arose from his conviction that natural laws took precedence over antiquity. He explained how his definition of architectural character prompted him to concentrate on the essential – to him, the simplest stereometric forms nature could offer; the sphere, in Boullée's opinion, is the most perfect shape, and expresses immensity, eternity and the infinite.

19a–c Étienne-Louis Boullée, design for the Métropole (a domed cathedral in the shape of a Greek cross), interior on the feast of Corpus Christi, *c*.1781 (*top, left*); design for the Royal Library, interior, 1785 (*top, right*); design for the Métropole, exterior, *c*.1781 (*bottom*). Paris, Bibliothèque Nationale de France, Cabinet des Estampes, HA. 56-FT 7, plate 8-2, 4, 36.

20 Antoine-Laurent-Thomas
Vaudoyer, design for 'Maison
d'un Cosmopolite', *c.*1784.
Paris, private collection.

He appealed to nature again in the importance he attached to the seasons and their influence on the impact of a building. Monumentality, poetry and philosophy were combined in his projects, and informed his ideas of the effect of a building on the spectator: 'Let us consider an object. Our first reaction is, of course, the result of how the object affects us. And what I call character is the effect of the object, which makes some kind of impression on us.'[116]

Significant as his ideas may be, Boullée's buildings are nothing more than utopian projects, aimed at creating sublime effects. The experience of architecture that they purvey is fictional, expressed in two-dimensional drawings. The real experience of being at a site, walking through it, feeling and sensing the architectural space is entirely different – a difference borne out, as we have seen, in Burke's text, and as we shall see in Goethe's, Vaudoyer's and Turner's accounts of Paestum. As Burke stated, paintings – or drawings, for that matter – can never excite the passions. Paestum will make clear the essentiality of this experience for architectural thought.

We shall now turn to eighteenth-century accounts of Paestum and examine them in the light of the theories of the sublime discussed above, following themes from Longinus,

Boileau and Burke. Then we shall trace how the sublime continued to figure in early nineteenth-century reactions to Paestum. These analyses will provide us with a clear picture of architectural experience and the sublime, by means of which we can redefine the sublime in architectural thought. This will shed an important light on the main theme of this book, the changing appreciation of Paestum, and the role of experience in it.

Astonishment and *Je ne sais quoi*: Dupaty and Tatham at Paestum

Astonishment, already associated with the sublime by Longinus and Boileau, was explained by Burke in his *Enquiry* as 'the effect of the sublime in the highest degree'. The 'inferior effects' of the sublime are admiration, reverence and respect: only astonishment 'hurries us on by an irresistible force'.[117] Burke changed 'admiration' into 'awe' when he came to expand on these three subordinate degrees of the sublime, 'which by the very etymology of the words shew from what source they are derived, and how they stand distinguished from positive pleasure'.[118] As we have already seen, Burke believed that some degree of horror is needed for the spectator to feel completely astonished – that is, for the mind of the spectator to be entirely occupied by this passion or emotion.[119] In combining the sublime with feelings of fear and terror, Burke argued: 'do not the french *etonnement*, and the english *astonishment* and *amazement*, point out as clearly the kindred emotions which attend fear and wonder?'[120] In stressing the difference between the beautiful and the sublime, he introduced the important factor of modification. The apprehension of what is great is based on terror, but terror, 'when it is modified causes that emotion in the mind, which I have called astonishment; the beautiful is founded on mere positive pleasure, and excites in the soul that feeling, which is called love.'[121] In the accounts of Paestum we find both the Longinian astonishment of awe, and the Burkean astonishment combined with terror.

A travel account, written in 1785, illustrates these different levels of sublime experience at Paestum. The French magistrate and politician Charles Dupaty (1746–1788) wrote of finding himself in 'a truly horrible desert',[122] and in a passage reminiscent of Burke's description of Stonehenge, questioned how the Greek builders could have constructed such rough and massive buildings: 'How could Sybarites imagine and erect so prodigious a number of columns of such vile materials, of such uncouth workmanship, of so heavy a mass, and such sameness of form?'[123] His remarks emphasise that the very fact of the temples' being ancient and manmade could inspire sublime reflections. Not all Dupaty's reactions were negative: 'It must be admitted . . . that, notwithstanding their rusticity, these temples do possess beauties; they present at least simplicity, unity and a whole, which constitute the first of beauties: the imagination may supply almost all the others, but it never can supply these.'[124] The experience was further enhanced by certain characteristics of the site that have little to do with architecture, but all the more to do with being on the spot. These sensations worked together to create the overall impression that Paestum left in the mind of its beholder, paradoxical but fascinating.

> How much do I regret to be so soon obliged to quit this spot . . . But the heat is excessive; and there is no where any shelter. I could wish, however, thoroughly to collect and carry off in my heart all the sensations I have just experienced. – Why cannot I be still left to treasure up in this solitude, in this desert, amid these ruins, something of that melancholy feeling that enchants me.[125]

The solitude Dupaty felt in the vastness of the plain in which the temples were situated and the magnificence of the deserted ruins caused him to invoke the sublime. The anonymous translator of his work vitiated the intensity of the original French at the end of the passage quoted above: 'melancholy feeling' is his rendering of Dupaty's 'je ne sais quelle horreur', which, moreover, connects the sublime with the concept of 'je ne sais quoi'. The expression 'je ne sais quoi' (literally 'I do not know what') seems first to have been used by the Jesuit essayist and neo-classical critic Dominique Bouhours in *Les entretiens d'Ariste et d'Eugène* (1671): 'Genius . . . is independent of chance and fortune; it is a gift from heaven in which the earth plays no part at all; it is the je ne sais quoi of the divine.'[126] At this early date Bouhours already connected the 'je ne sais quoi' with the sublime style as an expression of the inexpressible. Another seventeenth-century Jesuit, René Rapin, did the same in *Les comparaisons des grands hommes de l'antiquité qui ont le plus excellé dans les belles-lettres* (1684); in comparing Homer and Virgil, he stated that Homer has 'a much vaster plan and a more noble manner than Virgil, that he has a greater breadth of character, that he has a grander air and a more sublime je ne sais quoi, that he describes things much better; that even his images are more accomplished'.[127] Boileau, writing at much the same time as Bouhours and Rapin, emphasised that the sublime was not explicable: it could only be felt. Because the architecture of Paestum was difficult to interpret and did not relate to the classical architecture that travellers were familiar with, they would often refer to the 'inexplicable'.[128]

The idea of perceiving something beyond one's grasp also found expression in the account of the British architect Charles Heathcote Tatham (1772–1842), who went to Paestum in 1795.[129] The only images that survive from his visit are some scale drawings,[130] but Tatham's written record passionately expresses his feelings. For him the sublime provided the perfect framework within which to articulate his sensations. His account draws on Longinus's ideas about the contrast between darkness and light in describing how, on their arrival, he saw the temples struck by a stormy light from above: 'We were overtaken by a storm. It was in the month of January. We weathered it with difficulty the horizon however cleared as if on purpose to salute my eye with the most perfect coup d'oeul [*sic*] of sublime effect.' He vividly described his astonishment at the first sight of Paestum's scenery: 'We found ourselves within a short distance of the Temples, about which buffaloes were feeding, with a fine background of blue sky, the blue sea on the left and the Appenines on the right. I arose from my seat & exclaimed *Dio mio!*' As he alighted from the carriage and moved towards the temples, Tatham reflected on the Greeks' ability to create the sublime by using vastness and infinity to transport the spectator. Then, as he came closer:

> my mind became so much expanded from the contemplation of Columns of such grand dimensions that I received an impression I have never forgotten. The Greeks were a wonderful people. They knew too well how simplicity with vastness & continuousness produced sublimity. How calculated are the Fine Arts to elevate the soul when reflected through a pure medium![131]

The journey that acts as a prelude to such an experience, the immensity that produces the sublime, and the elevation of the mind and the soul in perceiving it recall *Peri hupsous*. Dupaty's and Tatham's writings bear witness to the experience of the most basic sensations of the sublime: astonishment, elevation and a sense of the inexpressible. They also testify to the power of grandeur to transport the viewer. But Paestum also gave rise to more complex, paradoxical, sentiments, as we shall see next.

From Grandeur to the Paradox in the Sublime

Like Longinus and Boileau, Burke often used the word 'grandeur', sometimes as a synonym for 'the sublime', but also as part of its definition. For instance, in the sections on architecture in his *Philosophical Enquiry*, 'grandeur' appears in relation to magnificence, which Burke considered a source of the sublime, and to light and colour as productive of the sublime; it also comes up in his discussion of smell and taste. In a section on the effects of succession on the way the eye perceives architecture, Burke explained that to produce perfect grandeur there must be perfect simplicity, an absolute uniformity in disposition, shape and colouring:

> When we look at a naked wall, from the evenness of the object, the eye runs along its whole space, and arrives quickly at its termination; the eye meets nothing which may interrupt its progress; but then it meets nothing which may detain it a proper time to produce a very great and lasting effect.[132]

The point is that to observe and take in a bare wall may consume only an instant, and the sensation of grandeur is thus less intense because the process of perception does not provide a repetition – or succession – of impressions. Burke explained step by step how a colonnade is perceived:

> let us set before our eyes a colonnade of uniform pillars planted in a right line; let us take our stand, in such a manner, that the eye may shoot along this colonnade, for it has its best effect in this view. In our present situation it is plain, that the rays from the first round pillar will cause in the eye a vibration of that species; an image of the pillar itself. The pillar immediately succeeding increasing it; that which follows renews and enforces the impression; each in its order as it succeeds, repeats impulse after impulse, and stroke after stroke, until the eye long exercised in one particular way cannot lose that object immediately; and being violently roused by this continued agitation, it presents the mind with a grand or sublime conception.[133]

Burke's observations on the effects of a colonnade would be echoed in Julien-David Le Roy's theories, which were developed from the experience of a moving spectator, observing the colonnade of the Louvre in Paris (see Chapter 4).

In the descriptions of Paestum, the word 'grandeur' appears frequently. The travel writer Henry Swinburne (1743–1803), in his account of a tour made in the last quarter of the eighteenth century, applied it to the Temple of Neptune, defining it as an important characteristic of the sublime:

> This is one of the noblest monuments of antiquity we have left; though built in a style few modern architects will adopt, it may perhaps serve to inspire them with sublime ideas, and convince them how necessary to true grandeur in architecture are simplicity of plan, solidity in proportions, and greatness of the component members; they may perhaps discover that a profusion of ornaments rather diminishes the general effect of a large building than adds to its real dignity.[134]

The simplicity of the temples and their lack of ornament allowed the viewer to focus on the principal architectural parts, which, together with their sheer size, contributed to their grandeur. To the British sculptor and illustrator John Flaxman (1755–1826), who visited in 1788 (Fig. 21), the grand simplicity of the temples was a feature of their sublimity:

21   John Flaxman, sketch of
the temples at Paestum, 1788,
in John Romney, *Memoirs of
the Life and Works of George
Romney* (1830).

I have been at Poestum and seen the three fine temples of the ancient Doric order in
that city; they are in better preservation than any ancient temple in Rome, except the
Pantheon. The idea of each of these buildings is so simple, the larger parts so truly great,
the small members done with so much feeling and delicacy that my mind was filled
with the sublime of architecture.[135]

The uniqueness of Paestum to Flaxman becomes manifest in another of his letters. It was,
for him, the only place in Italy where elevated feelings were produced by the effect of
the buildings on the beholder:

> [in] the Ancient Greek City of Poestum, you [find] remains . . . [of] 3 Temples intire all
> but the roofs, a [w]all round the City about 2 miles & a half in circumf[erence] with
> its towers . . . Here are the traces of streets & square tombs still visible with some of
> the foundations of a Music Theatre. The Temples are of the earliest Doric order[,] the
> Columns thick fluted & without bases[.] [The] simple greatness of their effect . . . ele-
> vated & delighted my mind more than all the other Architecture I have seen in Italy,
> which have been raised under the auspices of Roman taste & perfected in the elegance
> of Imperial corruption[. From] the top of Vesuvius . . . I saw the bay of Naples whose
> shore was formerly lined with Greek colonies, all of whose Cities . . . are either
> destroyed by the lava of the Mountain or thrown down by barbarians.[136]

Even if visitors did not always use the term 'sublime', they made use of the concept in
speaking of their astonishment or elevation, or in evoking the grandeur of the buildings.
In 1771 the traveller and author Patrick Brydone (1736–1818) referred to Paestum's 'lofty
temples', echoing William Smith, who in his translation of Longinus used the words 'lofty'
and 'grand' as synonyms for 'sublime'.[137]

While attributing the grandeur of the temples to their solidity and mass, Uvedale Price
(1747–1829), theorist of the picturesque, also used the term 'sublime' in referring to the
site. Price, who never went to Paestum (he went only as far as Rome on his Italian travels
in 1767–8), mentioned it twice in his *Essay on the picturesque* (first published in 1794):

> Among the various remains of antient temples, none, perhaps, have so grand an effect
> as the old Doric temples in Sicily, and at Paestum; though, from their general look of
> massiness, and from the columns being without bases, none are more opposite to what
> are usually considered as light buildings; but may it not be doubted, whether the giving
> of bases to those columns, and consequently a greater degree of lightness and airiness
> to the whole, might not proportionally diminish that solid, massive grandeur, which is
> so striking to every eye?[138]

Although this reference to Paestum occurs in his writings on the picturesque, Price's description of impressive solidity and massive grandeur is more redolent of the sublime than the picturesque.[139] In Thomas Dick Lauder's edition of Price's *Essay*, he suggested a connection between Paestum and Price's theory of the sublime, and referred to the mystery of the buildings on the site: 'what . . . can be more sublime than the Paestan temples, the very origins of which can only be guessed at'.[140] It may seem strange that someone who never visited the site described sublime sensations in relation to the temples, but if we read Price's comments carefully it appears that his reactions are more scholarly than those of travellers to Paestum. They are clearly based on the experiences described in the publications that were widely available to every educated reader around 1800. The solid and massive grandeur of the temples is a recurring feature of these accounts, as is the mystery of the origin of Paestum and its unfamiliar architecture.

As a contrast to Paestum, Price used Athenian architecture, which he labelled generally as 'beautiful', identifying the Monument of Lysicrates and the Tower of the Winds in Athens as 'picturesque'.[141] Price's writings on the picturesque contain many references to the sublime, often opposing the two concepts. In reaction to Burke's definition of sublime architecture as succession and uniformity combined with vastness, Price added other, opposite, elements, stressing the paradoxes that are united in the concept.

> With respect to the sublime in buildings, Mr. Burke, without entering into a minute detail, has pointed out its most efficient causes; two of which are succession, and uniformity. These he explains and exemplifies by the appearance of the ancient heathen temples, which, he observes, were generally oblong forms, with a range of uniform pilasters on every side; and, he adds, that from the same causes, may also be derived the grand effects of the aisles in many of our own Cathedrals. But although succession and uniformity, when united to greatness of dimension, are among the most efficient causes of grandeur in buildings, yet causes of a very opposite nature (though still upon one general principle) often tend to produce the same effects. These are, the accumulation of unequal, and, at least apparently, irregular forms, and the intricacy of their disposition. The forms and the disposition of some of the old castles built on eminences, fully illustrate what I have just advanced: the different outworks and massive gateways; towers rising behind towers; the main body perhaps rising higher than them all, and on one side descending in one immense solid wall quite down to the level below – all impress grand and awful ideas.[142]

Here, Price explained the role of intricacy in the sublime (though, in his theories, this attribute actually belongs to the picturesque). In the following passage, he characterised the sublime by roughness and abruptness:

> When suspense and uncertainty are produced by the abrupt intricacy of objects divested of grandeur, they are merely amusing to the mind, and their effect simply picturesque. But where the objects are such as are capable of inspiring awe or terror, there suspense and uncertainty are powerful causes of the sublime; and intricacy may, by those means, create no less grand effects than uniformity and succession.[143]

These ideas elucidate one particular reference to the sublime in relation to Paestum in the travel account of the French architect Pierre-Louis Moreau-Desproux (Fig. 22). In his account of his expedition to Paestum in 1757,[144] he used the word 'grandeur' four times to describe the site and to comment upon the 'unhappy city' and the great plain on which it stood.[145] He also applied the term specifically to the architecture: 'the Doric order is

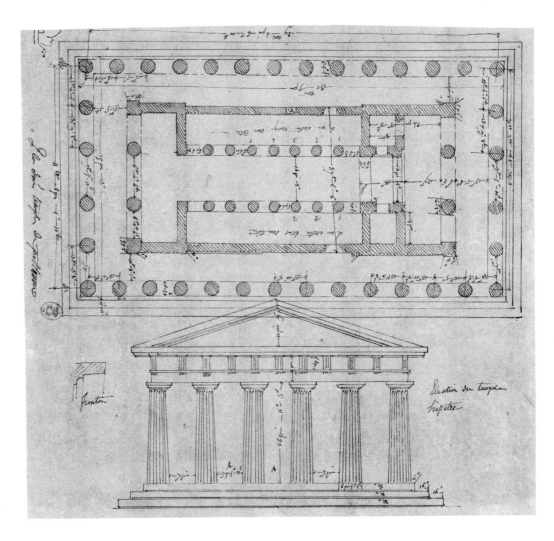

employed in all three [temples] in all the severity and grandeur of style that [the Greeks]
alone have practised'.[146] Moreau's 'journal intime' gives an interesting insight into the different stages of the Paestum experience at a time when no publications about the site
were yet available: the dangers and fatigues of travelling, and his first reflections on the
temples. It also shows that architecture is only one part in a sublime experience: the buildings in Paestum were perceived as sublime, but many other elements also contributed to
this experience. With Jacques-Germain Soufflot, who gave a lecture on Paestum in 1752,
Moreau was one of the first architects to write about the temples, and his visit took place
before Burke's *Philosophical Enquiry* had appeared. Throughout the eighteenth century,
Paestum continued to be associated with mystery, vastness, the curiosity of rediscovery and
the adventure of travelling, and the aesthetic theories of Burke and the various editions
of Longinus gave travellers a means of understanding and expressing specifically the nature
of their experiences.

   On his journey through Italy, before travelling to Naples, Moreau visited Tivoli to the
north of Rome to see the natural spectacle of its waterfalls. He saw Tivoli mainly in terms
of the beautiful and the picturesque, rather than the sublime. But, while viewing the phenomenon from a safe vantage point, he experienced a sense of danger often associated with

the sublime,[147] and this feeling of adventure plainly enhanced his experience. In the same vein, after having visited the temples, Moreau mentioned in his travel diary the dangers of the journey to Paestum. At the site itself, Moreau was assailed by paradoxical sensations. He was astonished by the city and the magnificence of its buildings, but at the same time its condition inspired pity:

> The view of this city strikes us with astonishment and pity when we consider its extent, and the magnificence of the buildings, of which we still see the remains and the entirely ruined state of most of the edifices that once adorned it, the site of which is ploughed up or covered with heaps of stone.[148]

This mixture of two different emotions is typical of a sublime experience. It is precisely these conflicting emotions and the awareness of the contradiction that characterise the sublime. Moreau's description of stark contrasts – astonishment and pity, splendour and sadness, severity and grandeur, a long and difficult journey through wild country rewarded by the sight of a magnificent city on a great plain, the people dressed like savages in animal skins wandering where once all was urban civilisation – perfectly illustrates the paradox in the sublime.[149] His experiences are more intense, profound and overwhelming just because of the combination of dissonant emotions. If we compare his notes on the architectural monuments at Tivoli, where nature and the ruins of great buildings are similarly combined, we find that there Moreau did not experience these opposing sensations: his reactions were clear, straightforward and uncomplicated.[150]

Although Burke's treatise had not appeared when Moreau wrote about his Italian journey, his account presents the same combination of emotions that Burke would describe and for which his *Philosophical Enquiry* would provide a theoretical basis. Moreau's diary demonstrates that experience of architecture and travel preceded theorising about them. It also shows, by comparison with other accounts of ancient sites, that Paestum was extraordinary in offering a specific combination of paradoxical elements and triggering contradictory sensations. The dangers of travelling, the wild surroundings, the strangeness of the architecture, the expansive scale of the landscape and the size of the temples all contributed to the mixed emotional experience. More than any other ancient site, Paestum inspired such ambivalent feelings, and the concept of the sublime lent itself perfectly to the expression of them.

We shall turn now to accounts of Paestum in which the architecture is associated with a certain character. None of the sublime elements we have encountered so far had much to do with classicism, nor did the accounts we have looked at draw on a knowledge of architectural theory or history. Those experiences were, in fact, ahistorical, and only the immediate sensations evoked on the spot counted; such feelings made no use of knowledge but were intense impressions that overwhelmed the viewers, whether they were architects, writers or sculptors. In the next section we shall focus on three architects and a poet to see how they experienced Paestum, with ideas about the character of the architecture in mind.

Character and the Male Aspect: Observations of Vaudoyer and Reveley

The French architect Antoine-Laurent-Thomas Vaudoyer (1756–1846) had a clear image of Paestum in his mind even before he visited the site in 1787.[151] This image was based on five years' education at the Académie d'Architecture in Paris under the guidance of Julien-David Le Roy (1724–1803), a period spent working in the architectural office of Antoine-François Peyre (1739–1823), and reading books and journals, studying drawings and engravings and debating with other architects. Vaudoyer's picture of Paestum was further developed during his time at the Académie de France in Rome as a winner of the Prix de Rome. Not only did he encounter other architects there, who had already visited the temples, but he started to plan his own visit. He bought the latest work on the temples of Paestum, by Padre Paoli, published in Rome in 1784 – the seventh monograph to appear on Paestum in the eighteenth century.[152] He annotated his copy of the book in the margins and under one of his comments he wrote: 'Rome June 1786, Vaudoyer architect'.[153] In these marginalia he suggested that Paoli had never seen Paestum with his own eyes, and though he had not yet seen the temples either, he allowed himself to think that Paoli was wrong. This suggests that Vaudoyer must have discussed the subject with his fellow students at the Académie de France, or with foreign architects and travellers who were passing through Rome and who had seen the architecture of Paestum themselves.[154]

By whatever means Vaudoyer acquired his knowledge of Paestum, in 1785, he applied the Paestum order to a design for a funerary monument (Fig. 23). In a long letter to his brother-in-law Hippolyte Lebas he explained why he chose it: 'This order conveys sadness in its character and its proportions, but at the same time a sense of closure, an allusion to what one experiences during misfortunes.'[155] In this description we can trace the influence of the theories on 'caractère' set out by Jacques-François Blondel in his *Cours d'architecture* (1771–7) and those of Etienne Boullée on both character and 'the architecture of sadness' in his *Architecture: Essai sur l'art* (*c.*1794).[156] As we have seen, Boullée defined character in architecture as 'the effect of the object, which makes some kind of impression on us':[157] 'To give

23 Antoine-Laurent-Thomas Vaudoyer, design for a funerary monument, symbolizing the passage of time, 1785. Montréal, Canadian Centre for Architecture, DR1987:0111.

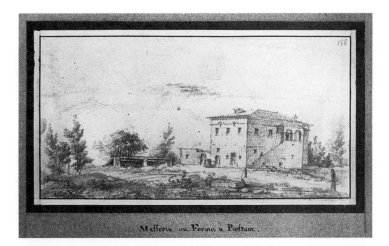

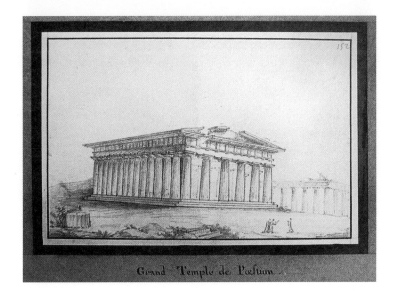

24a and b Antoine-Laurent-Thomas Vaudoyer, *Musseria ou Ferme a Poestum* (top) and *Grand Temple de Poestum* (the Temple of Neptune, with the Basilica in the background) (bottom), 1787. Paris, private collection.

a building character is to make judicial use of every means of producing no other sensations than those related to the subject.'[158]

Thus, by the time Vaudoyer visited Paestum in the summer of 1787 (Fig. 24), an image of the temples had already taken shape in his mind. But his great expectations were not fulfilled. When first confronted with the temples, he found them coarser and rougher than his prior knowledge had led him to expect: 'All this architecture is, in general, of a very heavy and clumsy character; the columns are short, very dense with large capitals, no base; the foot rests on three big steps; the entablature is very weighty and very protruding.'[159] Vaudoyer's reaction to the largest temple suggests a preconditioned comparison: 'this effect, its Male and imposing aspect, has given me great pleasure and I have found there, if one can put it like this, the form, the grace and the subtlety of Hercules'.[160] Other travellers also invoked the idea of the proud and manly character of the Neptune temple; for example, the French architect Hubert Rohault de Fleury (1777–1846) mentioned it in his diary.[161] This may be a direct influence from the writings of Vitruvius, who argued that: 'The temples of Minerva, Mars, and Hercules will be Doric, since it is appropriate for temples to these gods to be built without dainty decoration on account of their virile strength.'[162] Alternatively, the comparison with the Roman hero Hercules may have been suggested by the transportation of the massive marble sculpture known as the Farnese Hercules to the Capodimonte palace in Naples in 1787, where Vaudoyer may have seen it. At all events, like many architects before and after him, Vaudoyer was not certain about the function of the buildings he saw at Paestum; although he recognised that Neptune and Ceres were temples, 'to the right, very close to the Grand Temple, we find a large Colonnade, that rather resembles a portico or covered walk [the Basilica].'[163]

In short, we can say that while Vaudoyer was prepared for what he would find at Paestum, he was not really able to analyse or comprehend the architecture when he saw it for himself. He took the necessary measurements of the temples and made drawings of them, but it is significant that it is impossible to form an understanding of Paestum from the description in his travel journal. Despite this, Vaudoyer did, by actual observation, come closer to the particular characteristics of Paestum than he had been able to when his knowledge was based on publications and experience of other buildings. The Temple of Neptune struck him forcefully as large and virile, but the architecture of the Ceres temple was unimpressive, and that of the 'portico' (the Basilica) even more so.[164] To Vaudoyer, the main impact of Paestum derived from the excitement of undertaking the journey to the site, the whole spectacle of the temples in their setting and their peculiar architecture, all of which are vividly depicted in his text as the result of real experience. But although being there in the flesh and seeing the temples with his own eyes were important conditions for appreciation, experience did not lead to immediate comprehension. Nor did his prior knowledge, so carefully constructed in the preceding years, help him to understand the site: when he finally arrived at the site everything he knew no longer seemed relevant. However, when we look at Vaudoyer's perceptions in the light of the aesthetic concept of the sublime formulated by Burke in his *Philosophical Enquiry*, they become clearer. The sublime, defined by attributes of power, elevation and austerity, was associated in the eighteenth century with masculinity. Considered in these terms, Paestum represented the sublime to Vaudoyer, who discovered that the classical ideals of beauty, which have no place in the sublime, were not to be found there. The architecture of Paestum could not be taken in at a single gaze, as in the classical theories – on the contrary. The vastness and infinity so clearly delineated in the theories of Burke were to be experienced in the extent and spatiality of Paestum. Knowledge from books and engravings was not useful when it came to experience of the reality: Vaudoyer could leave it entirely aside because it had no place in the powerful impressions of the sublime that Paestum imprinted on his mind.

Vaudoyer's contemporary Goethe was similarly confused by his first experience of the temples, which he visited in the spring of 1787 with the painter Christoph Heinrich Kniep (Fig. 25). In his description (quoted in the opening pages of this chapter) Goethe wrote about the 'crowded masses of stumpy conical columns' that to a sensibility 'conditioned to a more slender style of architecture . . . appear offensive and even terrifying'.[165] His reaction to the temples demonstrates not only the discrepancy between a previous knowledge and observation on the spot, but also the ambivalent fascination that the 'offensive and . . . terrifying' columns exercised on his mind, again illustrating the mixed emotions that are peculiar to the apprehension of the sublime. Goethe's account is beautifully constructed, starting with the first strange sensations he experienced as he and his companion approached the site:

Very early next morning, we drove by rough and often muddy roads towards some beautifully shaped mountains. We crossed brooks and flooded places where we looked into the blood-red savage eyes of buffaloes. They looked like hippopotamuses. The country grew more and more flat and desolate, the houses rarer, the cultivation sparser.

25   Christoph Heinrich Kniep, the temples at Paestum, 1787. Düsseldorf, Goethe-Museum, Anton-und-Katharina-Kippenberg-Stiftung, NW 397/1960.

This is all designed to build up to the description of Goethe's first sight of the temples: 'In the distance appeared some huge quadrilateral masses, and when we finally reached them, we were at first uncertain whether we were driving through rocks or ruins.'[166] Goethe's description is a perfect example of the contribution to the sublime experience of the process of travelling towards the site and seeing from a distance the desolate and uncanny scenery around it.

The British architect Willey Reveley, who visited Paestum in 1785 and thoroughly examined the site, equally highlighted the dangers of the journey. His many significant observations are recorded in his travel diary (Figs 26-29). He wrote at some length about the hazards of travelling to Paestum:

26 Willey Reveley, perspective view of the temples at Paestum from the south, 1785, watercolour. New Haven (Conn.), Yale Center for British Art, Paul Mellon Collection, B1977.14.19454.

27 Willey Reveley, the Temple of Neptune from the north-east, 'traced in a camera obscura', 1785, watercolour. New Haven (Conn.), Yale Center for British Art, Paul Mellon Collection, B1977.14.19434.

28 Willey Reveley, the
Temple of Neptune, 1785,
watercolour. London, Victoria
and Albert Museum, Prints
and Drawings Collection,
D.140-1888.

29 Willey Reveley, the
Temple of Ceres, 1785,
watercolour. London, Victoria
and Albert Museum, Prints
and Drawings Collection,
D.446-1887.

As strangers rarely go to Pœsto the people when ever any do come impose upon them as much as possible, & will bully & might murder any person if they chose it, for it is out of the way of all justice or enquiry. Therefore all travellers going should be well armed for their own safety & to secure the civility of people whose unhappy situation reduces them to a level with the beasts of the field.[167]

He claimed that the party had to take weapons to defend themselves from the 'banditti':

It is usual from hence to take guards through Appulia, especially through the wood of Bovino where Banditti frequently harbour; however our company consisting of five priests & an old woman a serjeants wife, besides ourselves, proceeded on our journey without any guards, for as the priests would not contribute to the expence Sir Rd [Richard Worsley] determined to run the risk, we had a sword a hanger 2 brace of pistols & two guns with us, which would however have been of no use, as these banditti make their attack by shooting from behind trees.[168]

In his notes on the temples, Reveley drew attention to the strength, durability, mass and solidity of the Greek monuments – attributes that Burke had exemplified by referring to Stonehenge. Reveley was one of the few architects in this period to travel to Greece as well as Italy, and we find some elements of the Paestum accounts repeated in his reaction to the monuments in Greece. His admiration of the 'masculine character of the great temple' at Paestum and its simple grandeur is matched by his view of the Doric order in the buildings of mainland Greece:

There is a masculine boldness and dignity in the Grecian Doric, the grandeur of whose effect, as Sir William [Chambers] justly observes of the Roman antiquities, can scarcely be understood by those who have never seen it in execution; and which, if understood, would certainly supersede a whole magazine of such objections above. The column has no base, because its great breadth at the bottom of the shaft is sufficient to overcome the idea of its sinking into its supporting bed. The general basement is composed of three steps, not proportioned to the human step; but to the diameter of the columns it supports, and forms one single feature extending through the whole length of the temple, and of strength and consequence sufficient to give stability and breadth to the mass above it. The columns rise with considerable diminution in the most graceful, sweeping lines, and, from the top of the shaft, project a capital of a style at once bold, massive, and simple.[169]

The same idea of the masculinity of the temples appeared in Reveley's introduction to the third volume of James Stuart and Nicolas Revett's *The antiquities of Athens* (1794), where he wrote about his observations of the Greek Doric in general, and Paestum in particular:

The Grecian Doric is by many indiscriminately censured for clumsiness. But those who are so ready to condemn it should first recollect, that it was applied only where the greatest dignity and strength were required. . . . To omit the bases of slender Dorics, as is done in the theatre of Marcellus at Rome, seems to be as erroneous a practice as to add them to the massy ones. Let those who prefer the later Doric indiscriminately, and entirely reject the Grecian, try whether they can, with their slender order, produce the chaste and solid grandeur of the Parthenon, or the still more masculine character of the great temple of Pesto. They will no doubt produce, with their smaller proportions, pleasing affects, but a character lighter and less impressive than in the structure above-mentioned.[170]

While Reveley was impressed by Paestum, it did not terrify him, as it did the French architect Pierre-Adrien Pâris, who visited the site in 1774, and whose reaction demonstrates again the effect of seeing it in person. In his words, too, we find elements of a sublime aesthetics when confronted with the temples: 'We see in the ruins of Pestum or Posidonia three temples, of which one especially is quite well preserved. I do not know of anything so terrible, so impressive, or so distinctive as these temples.'[171] Again the ambivalent combination of feelings proper to the sublime appears, which is achievable only by perceiving the object with one's own eyes. Pâris was certainly familiar with the theories of the sublime, as his extensive library, one of the largest of any Parisian architect, featured a copy of Burke. Pâris was a student of Jacques-François Blondel, and we can also trace some of Blondel's ideas in his account. The use of the word 'terrible', for example, coincides with Blondel's attempt to define 'une Architecture terrible' in his *Cours d'architecture*.[172]

In his *Cours*, Blondel described 'virile' architecture in an article on the 'difference between a male, firm or virile character in architecture'.[173] His example of the male aspect was a strong building, well adapted to its surroundings and purpose, simple and unadorned, but creating large shadows by its mass and projecting structures.[174] He separated the male character in architecture into two different types: the 'firm' and the 'virile'. The first has less heavy forms, though it is still distinctive and imposing enough to excite feelings of amazement in the viewer.[175] The second is of interest in relation to Paestum, because Blondel associated it with the Doric order, claiming that it is a very dominant type because it will not tolerate any detail or decoration that might diminish its virility. Blondel almost personified the 'virile', suggesting that it would refuse to mix with other orders jealously protecting its own character.[176] Virility was often invoked by those who described their experience of Paestum's temples, and played its part in giving rise to the paradoxical feelings that were at work in their responses to the site. Even well into the nineteenth century visitors to Paestum still referred to such contradictory and complex sensations, as we shall see in the accounts of Shelley and Turner.

'The shadow of some half remembered dream': Shelley and Turner

The passionate observations of the English poet Percy Bysshe Shelley (1792–1822) show that there was no diminution in the impact of the sublime experience at Paestum in the nineteenth century. Shelley travelled to Paestum in February 1819.[177] In Chapter 3 we shall examine his journey in more detail, but for now we shall limit our investigation to the way in which the sublime figures in his account. He and his wife, Mary Shelley, visited the site on 24 and 25 February. Mary Shelley's report was remarkably short: 'Go to Pæstum. Stopt at a river five miles from Pæstum, and obliged to walk. A dull day; but a very fine evening until sunset, when it begins to rain again.'[178] Her husband, on the other hand, composed a poetic account of their journey and his encounter with the temples. The opening lines of a letter written on the second day of the visit contain a description of a dark and stormy night, in which the eye could barely see, contrasted with the view by daylight of the mighty plain on which the temples stood, bordered by mountains:

> The night had been tempestuous, & our road lay by the sea sand. It was utterly dark, except when the long line of wave burst with a sound like thunder beneath the starless sky and cast up a kind of mist of cold white lustre. When morning came we found ourselves travelling in a wide desert plain perpetually interrupted by wild irregular glens & bounded on all sides by the Apennines & the sea. Sometimes it was covered with forest, sometimes dotted with underwood, or mere tufts of fern & furze, & the wintry dry tendrils of creeping plants. I have never but in the Alps seen an amphitheatre of mountains so magnificent.[179]

The journey, along muddy roads, was difficult, but the travellers were regaled with the scent of wild flowers. Finally, the monuments that they had glimpsed in the distance came fully into sight:

> After travelling 15 miles we came to a river the bridge of which had been broken, & which was so swollen that the ferry would not take the carriage across. We had therefore to walk seven miles of a muddy road which led to the antient city across the desolate Maremma. The air was scented with the sweet smell of violets of an extraordinary size & beauty. At length we saw the sublime & massy colonnades skirting the horizon of the wilderness.[180]

In an account already characterised by carefully delineated antitheses – darkness and invisible surroundings contrasted with daylight and distant views, the discomforts of travelling with the tantalisation of the senses – Shelley also opposed the architecture of the temples to the colours and lofty contours of the landscape, combining architecture and nature in one sublime view:

> The scene from between the columns of this temple, consists on one side of the sea to which the gentle hill on which it is built slopes, & on the other of the grand amphitheatre of the loftiest Apennines, dark purple mountains crowned with snow & intersected then by long bars of hard & leaden coloured cloud. The effect of the jagged outline of mountains through groupes of enormous columns on the side, & on the other the level horizon of the sea is inexpressibly grand.[181]

At the end of his letter, Shelley again referred to the sublime: 'We only contemplated these sublime monuments for two hours, & of course cd. only bring away so imperfect a conception of them as is the shadow of some half remembered dream.'[182] The impression the journey, the location and the monuments made on Shelley was obviously powerful, and his account offers a rich array of sensations that can be associated with the sublime. It is clear that his perception of stark contrasts and oppositions enhanced the sublime emotions he felt, and his narrative makes us aware that the successive stages of travelling to the site played a significant part. Shelley also underlined how strongly he felt the relationship between nature and architecture at Paestum, and how these interacted to work on his emotions.

The same experience of the sublime is shown in the account of the Countess of Blessington, who went to Paestum in 1823 and described her impressions of the temples in her Neapolitan journals:

> the first view . . . must strike every beholder with admiration. Nor is this sentiment diminished on approaching them; for the beauty of their proportions, and the rich and

warm hues stamped on them by time, as they stand out in bold relief against the blue sky, which forms so charming a background to every Italian landscape, render the spot, even independent of the classical associations with which it is fraught, one of the most sublime and interesting imaginable. The solitude and desolation of the country around, where nought but a wretched hovel, a short distance from the temples, erected for the accommodation of the post-horses of the visitors to Paestum, breaks on a silent grandeur of the scene, adds to the sublime effect of it. The blue sea in the distance, and the chain of mountains as blue, bounding the horizon, complete the picture.[183]

Marguerite, Countess of Blessington (1789–1849), spent two and a half years at Naples and travelled to Paestum with the young architect Charles James Mathews (1803–1878), who measured the temples and later tried to explain their history, and George William Frederick Howard (1802–1864), afterwards a politician and 7th Earl of Carlisle, who recited a poem among the ruins. The countess noted:

> There was something so solemn and imposing in the view of these temples, that the eye and the mind must be accustomed to it, before one could bestow an adequate attention on the ingenious hypotheses connected with them. When I looked on their proud fronts, which had braved the assaults of time during so many centuries, and now stood rearing their heads to the blue and cloudless sky above them, I could not help smiling at the little groups moving round their base, who looked like pigmies near these gigantic monuments.[184]

As is apparent from these passages, the countess was not much interested in the history of the site, but lost herself in sublime feelings of admiration. These feelings seem closest to the definition of the sublime as formulated by Longinus, in which awe was the main element. The more complicated or paradoxical sensations that we found in Shelley's testimony are absent here.

A more interesting account is offered by the representations of Joseph Mallord William Turner (1775–1851). In 1819 Turner stayed in Italy for six months, visiting Turin, Milan, Padua, Venice, Bologna, Rimini, Ancona and Rome; with the architect Thomas Leverton Donaldson (1795–1885), he also travelled to Naples, Sorrento, Amalfi and Paestum.[185] Turner compiled four sketchbooks of southern Italy, entitled *Gandolfo to Naples*; *Pompeii, Amalfi, Sorrento and Herculaneum*; *Naples, Paestum, and Rome*; and *Albono, Nemi, Rome*. A year earlier he had executed watercolours of Italy for *A Picturesque Tour of Italy*, published in 1820 by

30a and b   Joseph Mallord William Turner, interior view of the Temple of Neptune, looking towards the Basilica (*below left*), and interior view of the Temple of Neptune (*below right*), 1819, pencil sketches. London, Tate Britain, D15996, D15995.

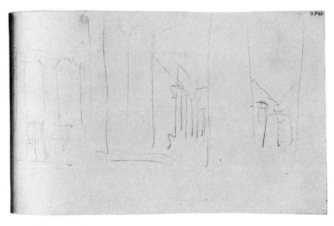

31 Joseph Mallord William Turner, study of the temples at Paestum, c.1826–7, watercolour and pencil. London, Tate Britain, D27609. The finished drawing was used to illustrate Samuel Rogers, *Italy: A Poem* (1830; see Fig. 35).

the architectural draughtsman James Hakewill (1778–1843), but without, at that stage, having been there himself.[186] The contrast with his own travel sketches could not be more compelling. The rather dull, straightforward perspective Turner adopted for Hakewill's book, which drew on existing travelogues of Italy, is worlds apart from the series of rapid, captivating sketches he made to document his experience at Paestum (Fig. 30) and a delicate study drawing of the tantalising temples, standing in the distance on the empty plain beside the sea in the burning Italian sun, with a group of visitors approaching (Fig. 31).

Turner captured his impressions of the temples from as many different viewpoints as possible, and examined them inside and out;[187] the results recall the way the Italian architect and engraver Giovanni Battista Piranesi (1720–1778) wandered among the ruins when he visited Paestum in 1777, as his engravings show (see Chapter 4). In the Neptune temple, for example, Turner sketched the impressive forest of columns that surrounded him. Every different viewpoint offered another composition of columns and lines; every step he took as he walked around the site gave another outlook. The temples are often pictured in a diagonal perspective, which allowed Turner to capture two temples in one sketch, making the grouping of columns even denser; the choice of a corner viewpoint meant that he could include as many objects as possible in his drawings.[188] Of the columns, Turner recorded in his travel notes their number and the fact that they were cigar-shaped (that is, slightly convex) rather than straight-sided. This observation contrasts strongly not only with his depiction of the temples for Hakewill's book, but also with an earlier watercolour drawing of the Neptune temple made c.1810 in connection with a lecture that Turner delivered at the Royal Academy (Fig. 32). There the columns do have straight sides. When he saw the temples in reality he must have been surprised by their true shape.

Turner was elected professor of perspective at the Royal Academy in 1807 and continued to teach there until 1828; he gave his first lecture in 1811. To accompany his lectures, he made drawings and diagrams – between ten and twenty per lecture. The watercolour of the Temple of Neptune was used to illustrate various topics: 'methods of depicting the architectural orders, shadows in oblique sunlight, and the nature of the Doric order'.[189] Turner's lecture drawing shows nothing of the sublime sensations he depicted when, later, he drew the temple from the life. It was probably based on engravings in existing publications, specifically plate XIV in Piranesi's *Différentes vues de . . . Pesto* (1778), which has exactly the same viewpoint (Fig. 33).[190] Turner omitted the figures and cattle, and the vegetation growing on the stonework. More importantly, he changed the columns, straightening out the entasis and making the capitals smaller and less pronounced; he also altered the entablature and left out the pediment. When he went to Paestum himself, however, he perceived something entirely different.

Strangely, when, eight years after his Italian journey, Turner illustrated Samuel Rogers's *Italy: A Poem* (1830), the Neptune temple again took on a different form (Figs 34–5).[191] Now the columns are straight again, and the temple has six by eleven columns, rather than the six by fourteen that he rightly noted in his sketchbook. In her study *Turner in the South*, Cecilia Powell suggested that, under the influence of Piranesi's argument for the superiority of Roman architecture, Turner simply forgot that the temple at Paestum was Greek;[192] but this seems unlikely – not least because, as we shall see in Chapter 4, Piranesi argued something completely different in his *Différentes vues*. The true explanation is probably that Turner was not particularly interested in depicting the temple accurately. His sketches indicate that his interest was in the general impression the temples made, the density of the architecture, their sublimity and mystery. The vignette he drew for Rogers, which depicts the Temple of Neptune in the foreground with the Basilica behind, suggests the same intention. Here the Basilica is no more than a structure of columns, roughly indicated by some lines; the imprecision of the drawing clearly follows Turner's earlier sketches, made on the spot. The stormcloud that darkens the sky above the temples increases the impression of mystery, though the drawing, if other-worldly, is still quite orderly. We have to turn to some other drawings he made of Paestum to experience the full force of what Turner saw in these temples.

32 (*below left*) Joseph Mallord William Turner, interior of the Temple of Neptune from the north-east, watercolour drawing for a Royal Academy lecture, *c.*1810. London, Tate Britain, D17072.

33 (*below right*) Giovanni Battista Piranesi, interior of the Temple of Neptune from the north-east, in *Différentes vues . . . de Pesto* (1778), plate XIV.

34   Joseph Mallord William Turner, the temples at Paestum, *c.*1826–7, for Samuel Rogers, *Italy: A Poem* (1830). London, Tate Britain, D27665.

'Lines Written at Paestum March 4, 1815', from *Human Life: A Poem by Samuel Rogers* (1819)

They stand between the mountains and the sea;
Awful memorials, but of whom we know not!
The seaman, passing, gazes from the deck.
The buffalo-driver, in his shaggy cloak,
Points to the work of magic and moves on.
Time was they stood along the crowded street,
Temples of Gods! and on their ample steps
What various habits, various tongues beset
The brazen gates for prayer and sacrifice!
Time was perhaps the third was sought for
    Justice;
And here the accuser stood, and there the
    accused;
And here the judges sate, and heard, and judged.
All silent now! – as in the ages past,
Trodden under foot and mingled, dust with dust.

How many centuries did the sun go round
From Mount Alburnus to the Tyrrhene sea,
While, by some spell rendered invisible,
Or, if approached, approached by him alone
Who saw as though he saw not, they remained
As in the darkness of a sepulchre,
Waiting the appointed time! All, all within
Proclaims that Nature had resumed her right,
And taken to herself what man renounced;
No cornice, triglyph, or worn abacus,
But with thick ivy hung or branching fern,
Their iron-brown o'erspread with brightest
    verdure!

From my youth upward have I longed to tread
This classic ground – And am I here at last?
Wandering at will through the long porticoes,
And catching, as through some majestic grove,
Now the blue ocean, and now, chaos-like,
Mountains and mountain-gulphs, and, half-way
    up,
Towns like the living rock from which they
    grew?
A cloudy region, black and desolate,
Where once a slave withstood a world in arms.

The air is sweet with violets, running wild
Mid broken sculptures and fallen capitals;
Sweet as when Tully, writing down his thoughts,
Those thoughts so precious and so lately lost,
Turning to thee, divine Philosophy,
Who ever cam'st to calm his troubled soul,
Sailed slowly by, two thousand years ago,
For Athens; when a ship, if north-east winds
Blew from the Pæstan gardens, slacked her
    course.

On as he moved along the level shore,
These temples, in their splendour eminent
Mid arcs and obelisks, and domes and towers,
Reflecting back the radiance of the west,
Well might he dream of Glory! – Now, coiled up,
The serpent sleeps within them; the she-wolf
Suckles her young; and, as alone I stand
In this, the nobler pile, the elements
Of earth and air its only floor and covering,
How solemn is the stillness! Nothing stirs

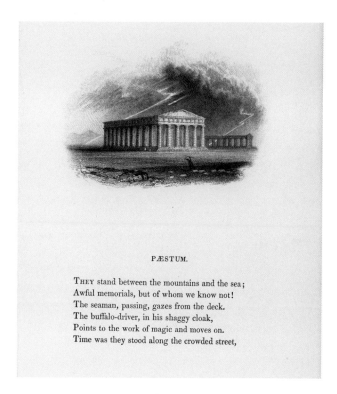

35   Samuel Rogers, 'Pæstum', part of *Italy: A Poem* (1830), 207, illustrated with Turner's drawing, engraved by John Pye, 1830.

PÆSTUM.

THEY stand between the mountains and the sea;
Awful memorials, but of whom we know not!
The seaman, passing, gazes from the deck.
The buffalo-driver, in his shaggy cloak,
Points to the work of magic and moves on.
Time was they stood along the crowded street,

Save the shrill-voiced cigala flitting round
On the rough pediment to sit and sing;
Or the green lizard rustling through the grass,
And up the fluted shaft with short quick
       motion,
To vanish in the chinks that Time has made.

In such an hour as this, the sun's broad disk
Seen at his setting, and a flood of light
Filling the courts of these old sanctuaries,
(Gigantic shadows, broken and confused,
Across the innumerable columns flung)
In such an hour he came, who saw and told,
Led by the mighty Genius of the Place.

Walls of some capital city first appeared,
Half razed, half sunk, or scattered as in scorn;
– And what within them? what but in the midst
These Three in more than their original
       grandeur,
And, round about, no stone upon another?
As if the spoiler had fallen back in fear,
And, turning, left them to the elements.

'Tis said a stranger in the days of old
(Some say a Dorian, some a Sybarite;
But distant things are ever lost in clouds)
'Tis said a stranger came, and, with his plough,
Traced out the side; and Posidonia rose,
Severely great, Neptune the tutelar God;
A Homer's language murmuring in her streets,
And in her haven many a mast from Tyre.
Then came another, an unbidden guest.
He knocked and entered with a train in arms;

And all was changed, her very name and
       language!
The Tyrian merchant, shipping at his door
Ivory and gold, and silk, and frankincense,
Sailed as before, but, sailing cried, "For Pæstum!"
And now a Virgil, now an Ovid sung
Pæstum's twice-blowing roses; while, within,
Parents and children mourned – and, every year,
('Twas on the day of some old festival)
Met to give way to tears, and, once again,
Talk in the antient tongue of things gone by.
At length an Arab climbed the battlements,
Slaying the sleepers in the dead of night;
And from all eyes the glorious vision fled!
Leaving a place lonely and dangerous,
Where whom the robber spares, a deadlier foe
Strikes at unseen – and at a time when joy
Opens the heart, when summer-skies are blue,
And the clear air is soft and delicate;
For then the demon works – then with that air
The thoughtless wretch drinks in a subtle poison
Lulling to sleep; and, when he sleeps, he dies.

But what are These still standing in the midst?
The Earth has rocked beneath; the Thunder-
       stone
Passed thro' and thro', and left its traces there;
Yet still they stand as by some Unknown
       Charter!
Oh, they are Nature's own! and, as allied
To the vast Mountains and the eternal Sea,
They want no written history; theirs a voice
For ever speaking to the heart of man!

A drawing of *c*.1825 shows the Paestum temples in even less detail, focusing on their unadorned sublimity to produce feelings of fascination, fear and awe: here the two temples depicted are no more than dark, mysterious forms, seen under menacing clouds that shed torrents of rain (Fig. 36). Another image, this time of Stonehenge, has the same atmospheric rather than literal purpose (Fig. 37). As we saw earlier in Burke's *Enquiry*, the great age of the enormous monoliths and the insoluble enigma of their purpose rendered Stonehenge sublime.[193] Turner depicted them in a thoroughly Burkean fashion as mysterious masses of stone in a gloomy setting, at the moment of a lightning strike that dramatically illuminates the structure. The images show that he viewed the two sites in a similar way. The history or classical background of Paestum was of no interest to him at all. What fascinated him in these monuments was their obscurity, vastness and strangeness of form. The comparison can be taken even further if we look at the foreground of each image. In the Stonehenge depiction there appear to be dead sheep, at Paestum a dead buffalo (Fig. 38), rendered even more sinister because it is a skeleton. The lost civilisation of the Greeks and the religion of the temples, forever disappeared, are both portrayed symbolically in this drawing. According to John Ruskin, Turner commonly associated lightning with the monuments of dead religions, as we see in both Paestum and Stonehenge.[194]

36   Joseph Mallord William Turner, Paestum in a thunderstorm, *c*.1825. London, Tate Britain, D36070.

Rediscovering Architecture

37 (*left*) Joseph Mallord William Turner, Stonehenge in a thunderstorm, *c.*1827, engraved by Robert Wallis, 1829. London, Tate Britain, T04549.

38 (*below*) Joseph Mallord William Turner, Paestum under a stormy sky, *c.*1825. London, British Museum, Department of Prints and Drawings, 1940,0601.30.

39 Joseph Mallord William Turner, *Rome: The Portico of St Peter's with the entrance to the Via Sagrestia 1819*, pencil and watercolour. London, Tate Britain, D16332.

It was rather extraordinary for Turner to picture architecture in such a gloomy way.[195] The same approach is not found in other depictions of monuments – as we can see, for example, in a drawing of Rome under a rainbow.[196] But although they may not be so dark and forbidding, his architectural drawings do often evoke the sublime. As Wilton suggested, Turner 'sought to imbue the buildings' watercolours with the same awe that he would experience in the building itself'.[197] The architecture he met with on his Italian travels was sometimes portrayed as an immense space, and he often represented the astonishment felt by the viewer by means of distortion of scale, as in his drawings of the Coliseum or (an even more pronounced example) one of the basilica of St Peter, in which a tiny figure is placed beside the soaring, exaggerated structure with its colossal columns (Fig. 39).[198] Turner's watercolours capture the experience of architecture and, like no artist before him, the sublime character of that experience. And they prove that the sublime in architecture cannot exist except through experience.

Mastering a Sublime Experience

As the accounts in this chapter have shown, the sublime architectural experience was encountered for the first time unmistakably and comprehensively at Paestum. Travellers appealed to the sublime in their attempt to do justice to their contradictory feelings, ranging from the unpleasant to the overwhelming, their reaction to the vast scale, great age and rugged qualities of Paestum, and their experience *in situ*. The verbal and pictorial language of the sublime helped them to capture their paradoxical experience of the architecture, and to make sense of its strangeness, the conflicting sensations it aroused, and the contrast between expectation and actual experience – that is, between representations of Doric architecture in images or in the literature and their observations at the site itself.

In their diversity, the reports of visitors have this one element in common: no matter how they are expressed, they make use of the concept of the sublime. As we have seen, the sublime could have different definitions. While Longinus wrote a rhetorical theory, explaining how to move an audience by means of a grand and elevated style, Boileau emphasised the experiential character of the sublime, stressed simplicity and intensified the focus on ambivalence. Furthermore, he argued that the sublime was not something that only connoisseurs could experience: it was accessible to any enthusiast – a view that paved the way for Burke's contention that the sublime was most keenly felt by the ignorant, who approached the experience without preconceptions. With Burke, theories of the sublime moved on from the realm of rhetoric to that of aesthetics. He was the first to define clearly how architecture could be sublime, by identifying the characteristics of buildings that could create a sublime experience, and he stressed that the sublime takes shape in the mind of the spectator.

Although Burke was widely read during the second half of the eighteenth century and had a profound influence on architectural thought, accounts of Paestum show that the theories of Longinus and Boileau still provided an excellent resource for travellers struggling to articulate the contradictory and confusing experience of an architecture unknown to them. In the theories that we have treated, the sublime experience is fuelled by a sense of awe and a feeling of elevation in the presence of art or nature. When they evoke grandeur and immensity, the elevation of the mind and the soul, admiration, surprise and wonder, the descriptions we have discussed echo Longinus and Boileau. The sublime as a strategy of persuasion (Longinus) and the sublime as an experience (Boileau and Burke) are equally present in the accounts.

Paestum baffled the visitors. Looking in vain for connections in architectural theory or history, they had to fall back on their own observations and their personal experience on the spot. The various accounts often refer to the particularity of the site, and the discrepancy between expectation and experience. Some travellers found it impossible to admire the architecture of the temples, but responded to other aspects of the site, such as its overwhelming scale. Others described a disparity between the startling dimensions of the temples and their uncouth design. But while they commented on the ugliness of the architecture, visitors were aware that their perception of the buildings was intensified by unfamiliarity: in its many paradoxical aspects, Paestum was very different from any other monuments they had visited. Thus the concept of the sublime was used to describe not only the architecture and the site themselves but also the visitor's confrontation with them: it provided travellers with both the categories and the vocabulary to define the peculiar characteristics of the natural surroundings, the buildings and the experience of being there, so that they could preserve something of the specificity of a place that had evoked such strong feelings.

Unlike ideas of beauty or the picturesque, the concept of the sublime is able to do full justice to the specifically architectonic experience of Paestum. The emphasis on infinity and huge scale in Longinus and Burke, exemplified in Burke's reaction to Stonehenge and Turner's paintings, caters for Paestum's conspicuous spatiality. The sheer size of the temples standing on the boundless plain was one of the main reasons why Paestum was considered sublime. It is precisely in such vastness that architecture distinguishes itself from the visual arts, because only architecture is capable of such a spatial quality. Consequently the sublime in architecture is something particular, something fundamentally different from the sublime in art or in nature. Architecture differs from art in that it is three-dimensional, and differs from nature in that it is constructed by man. The latter aspect, highlighted by Burke in his discussion of the difficulty of building an immense spatial structure, was a crucial component of the feeling of the sublime: the awareness that the great structures at Paestum were manmade conspired with their antiquity and air of mystery to produce a sensation of awe.

So the sublime functioned perfectly to express the unique character of the Paestum experience. Three-dimensional space and the scale of the real world could not be experienced by looking at a reduced representation of the temples on a flat surface: one had to be there in real life. The sublime can be an unmediated experience, in the sense that both nature and art themselves, in all their manifestations, can create that experience. But the responses to Paestum illustrate powerfully that the experience was generated in and through the very confrontation of the beholder with the temples. Although Burke gave only one concrete example of architecture, his book offers a much wider range of clues to connecting architecture and the sublime than the short discussion of Stonehenge might suggest. What was merely theoretical in Burke's writings was realised in the encounter with Paestum and made manifest in the impressions recorded by travellers.

In existing studies, notably those that focus exclusively on Boullée, architecture and the sublime are connected in a rather limited way. The Paestum accounts clearly show that, on the contrary, the connection is not restricted to size, but is far more complex. Lack of refinement, irregularity and characteristics that shock do not fall within the boundaries of purely aesthetic rules, any more than do the vast and the infinite. The experience that architects had at the site proves this. Different elements of that experience worked together: besides the attributes of the site itself, danger, heat, fatigue, physical discomfort, strangeness, perplexity and disappointed expectations all combined to make the experience complex and hard to define. The sublime proved to be an excellent framework within which to account for the whole gamut of spontaneous feelings and thoughts.

The confrontation with the oldest Greek temples called into question the classical idea of beauty, harmony, unity and purity, and the spatial experience prompted viewers to redefine the sublime in architectural thought. Accepted architectural theory and history could not be used to make sense of the paradox of Paestum, but the sublime could. From this we may conclude that at Paestum the sublime has nothing to do with classicism. It was precisely the spatial quality, and the ahistorical and primitive character of Paestum that made the experience of the site so destructive of classical laws and ideas of beauty. According to classical principles, it must be possible to take in a building at a single glance, but this could not be done at Paestum. We have seen that Burke broke with this idea and introduced the process of viewing endless regularity in a building, which cannot be comprehended at one gaze but demands a sequence of views. The sublime was a strong alternative voice, responding to many more attributes than beauty, harmony and regularity alone. As such, in the later eighteenth century it offered a challenge to classicism. Paestum – gloomy, rough and overwhelmingly huge – excited sublime feelings, and therefore offered incontrovertible, visible proof that, to achieve the sublime, architecture did not need to conform to the rules of classical beauty. Paradoxically, a direct experience of the temples at Paestum, which had themselves been constructed in antiquity, served to undermine the claims of classicism to aesthetic supremacy.

CHAPTER 2

Scenic Associations: Paestum and the Picturesque

As the eighteenth century went on, pictures and descriptions of Paestum by those who had visited the site reached prospective travellers as they made preparations for their own visits. These reports aroused certain expectations of what they would see there, but their accounts often testify to how far the reality departed from their assumptions:

> We make such strange descriptions, and form such monstrous ideas when we read and hear about it, that I expected to find Paestum in a marshy wilderness, the temples lost or hidden by rushes or undergrowth, the foul air giving off the smell of mud; instead of that I found a beautiful situation, a bay, a beautiful plain surrounded by beautiful mountains, a cultivated land with vineyards and wheat.[1]

This first-hand account shows that the reaction of every visitor was personal and might be unique. In this case, the traveller's expectations, produced by the sublime accounts he had read before, were thoroughly unpleasant and were overturned by the reality of a peaceful and beautiful landscape, in which crops rather than bog plants were growing. This passage was written in 1778 by the French diplomat and subsequent founder of the Louvre, Dominique Vivant Denon (1747–1825), in his *Voyage au Royaume de Naples*.[2] Denon's sombre preconceptions must have been based on existing travel accounts of Italy and Paestum. At that time, besides Italian travelogues, there were already six folio publications with engravings of Paestum available (of which at least four had been first published in Paris or were available in French editions), and drawings and engravings were also circulating in Europe.[3]

A few years later, Denon's account was partly published in a four-volume folio, entitled *Voyage pittoresque, ou Description des royaumes de Naples et de Sicile* by the Abbé Jean-Claude Richard de Saint-Non (1727–1791).[4] The 'picturesque journey' of the title was organised and undertaken by the Abbé de Saint-Non together with Denon in 1778. They hired a group of artists and architects, among whom were Claude-Louis Châtelet (1753–1795), Louis-Jean Desprez (1743–1804) and Jean-Augustin Renard (1744–1807), to accompany them for the purpose of drawing and taking measurements of monuments in Italy (Figs 41–3); in

40 *(facing page)* Detail of Fig. 42.

41 (*right*) Claude-Louis Châtelet, the three temples at Paestum from the south-west, engraved by François Desquauvilliers, in Jean-Claude Richard de Saint-Non, *Voyage pittoresque, ou Description des royaumes de Naples et de Sicile*, vol. III (Paris, 1783), plate 83.

42 (*below*) Claude-Louis Châtelet, the three temples at Paestum from the south-west, 1771, watercolour. London, British Museum, Department of Prints and Drawings, 1918,0509.1.

43 Louis-Jean Desprez, the three temples at Paestum from the south-west, engraved by Carl or Heinrich Guttenberg, in Jean-Claude Richard de Saint-Non, *Voyage pittoresque, ou Description des royaumes de Naples et de Sicile*, vol. III (Paris, 1783), plate 82.

44 Hubert Robert, the Temple of Neptune and the Basilica from the north-west, engraved by Louis Germain and Marie-Alexandre Duparc, in Jean-Claude Richard de Saint-Non, *Voyage pittoresque, ou Description des royaumes de Naples et de Sicile*, vol. III (Paris, 1783), plate 11.

45 Hubert Robert, interior of the Temple of Neptune from the east, engraved by Louis Germain and Marie-Alexandre Duparc, in Jean-Claude Richard de Saint-Non, *Voyage pittoresque, ou Description des royaumes de Naples et de Sicile*, vol. III (Paris, 1783), plate 12.

46 Hubert Robert, the Temple of Ceres, engraved by Karl Wilhelm Weisbrod and Jacques Aliamet, in Jean-Claude Richard de Saint-Non, *Voyage pittoresque, ou Description des royaumes de Naples et de Sicile*, vol. III (Paris, 1783), plate 84.

the published account, Saint-Non also used drawings by other artists and architects who had visited southern Italy, such as Pierre-Adrien Pâris, Hubert Robert and Jean-Honoré Fragonard (Figs 44–6).[5] The *Voyage pittoresque* is part of a tradition of eighteenth-century travelogues the titles of which include the word 'pittoresque' or 'picturesque'. In such literary descriptions, which deal not only with Italy but also with sites and landscapes in England, tourism and the picturesque are connected.[6]

Apart from underlining the divergence between prior expectation and experience of the site itself, Denon's remarks illustrate how receptive travellers were to the scenery of Paestum, though in a way that differed from the sublime responses to the vast scale of the landscape, the valley in which the temples stood, and the strangeness of the architecture. This chapter will focus on an aesthetic experience that played an important role in eighteenth-century reactions to Paestum, and that may be regarded as opposed or at least contrasted to the sublime: namely, the picturesque.

First, we shall analyse the origins of the picturesque and its evolution into an aesthetic theory, and then turn to theoretical thinking on architecture in relation to the picturesque. Next, we shall examine accounts of Paestum, focusing specially on a noteworthy example by Richard Payne Knight (1751–1825), one of the major theorists of the picturesque. As a result of these explorations we shall be able to define two aspects of the picturesque as it relates to architecture, one of which is found only in picturesque theories, the other in writings on architecture and the picturesque alike. For now, we can call these 'framing from a distance' and 'movement'. By analysing these two facets we shall gain a clearer view of what the picturesque meant for architectural experience, and in turn what this implied for the understanding of Paestum at the time.

Framing from a Distance: The Origins of the Picturesque

Originally, the term 'picturesque' (from Italian *pittoresco* and French *pittoresque*) meant nothing more than 'in the manner of painters'; but in time it developed new definitions, and the concept developed through different phases.[7] From a painting term, the picturesque evolved, via a theory related to garden design, into a general aesthetic theory. As an independent aesthetic category, it would figure in eighteenth-century cultural debates. The theory of the picturesque, the origins of which lie in the seventeenth century, offered a new definition of man's aesthetic sensibility to art and nature. It gave rise to an important aesthetic cult in the eighteenth century and offered a new conceptual framework within which to describe the sensations aroused by the visual arts, poetry, architecture, gardens, landscape and the art of travel. Characteristic of all varieties of the picturesque is that it considered nature as if it were a landscape painting, and by extension assessed all art for its pictorial value as part of a landscape. Hence, in picturesque travelogues, landscape and the buildings, artworks or other manmade structures in it were appreciated for their pictorial qualities. Traits that had a direct impact on the eye came to be isolated, and were viewed using painting as the point of reference. The principal artists who inspired these associations were the landscape painters Nicolas Poussin (1594–1665), Claude Lorrain (1600–1682) and Salvator Rosa (1615–1673).

Studies of the picturesque have identified four phases. The first phase – 'discovery' (*c.*1690–1730) – is represented in the writings and designs of William Temple (1628–1699), Anthony Ashley Cooper, 3rd Earl of Shaftesbury (1671–1713), Joseph Addison (1672–1719),

Alexander Pope (1688–1744), William Kent (1686–1748) and Batty Langley (1696–1751). The second phase is identified with the designs of Kent and the theories of William Shenstone (1714–1763) of The Leasowes, near Halesowen, and the first writings of William Gilpin (1724–1804).[8] The third phase is defined by the designs of the landscape and garden designer Lancelot 'Capability' Brown (1716–1783) and the writings in the period 1760–1775 of Henry Home, Lord Kames (1696–1782), William Chambers (1722–1796) and Thomas Whately (1726–1772).[9] The fourth phase started in 1794–5, when three publications saw the light: Uvedale Price's *Essays on the Picturesque as Compared with the Sublime and the Beautiful* (1794), Richard Payne Knight's *The Landscape* (1794), and *Sketches and hints on landscape gardening* (n.d. [1795]) by Humphry Repton (1752–1818); and it developed as other publications appeared at the beginning of the nineteenth century.[10] Only then were the significant theories formulated that clearly connected the picturesque with architecture or included architecture within the sphere of the picturesque.

The idea of seeing art and nature through the prism of landscape painting influenced not only connoisseurs and landscape and garden designers but also travellers, in the sense that the focal point of their tours became aesthetic and visual enjoyment, and the search for views in nature that lent themselves to representation in painting. There was even, according to William Gilpin, an ideal picturesque traveller:

> The first source of amusement to the picturesque traveller, is the pursuit of his object – the expectation of new scenes continually opening, and arising to his view. We suppose the country to have been unexplored. Under this circumstance the mind is kept constantly in an agreeable suspense. The love of novelty is the foundation of this pleasure. Every distant horizon promises something new; and with this pleasing expectation we follow nature through all her walks.[11]

Travellers sometimes used a so-called 'Claude glass' (Fig. 47) to frame their chosen views, which made them appear more striking to the eye of the beholder and made gazing at a landscape a personal experience. The Claude glass was a small convex mirror with a dark-tinted surface; it was named after Claude Lorrain because it was the colouring of his paintings that the glass conferred upon the landscape. The user selected and framed his own idea of the finest composition within the scenery spread out around him. Before his eyes the scene, reflected in the mirror, took on the sought-after mixture of tints that was characteristic of Claude's landscapes, and which was often referred to by Richard Payne Knight in his writings on the picturesque. As the landscape historian John Dixon Hunt put it: '[Using the Claude glass] was both an objective, cognitive activity and a private, creative one, as the mirror's user turned his back upon the scene and withdrew into his own reflections.'[12] The glass was mainly used in natural scenery, much less often in the landscaped garden, where the designer had predetermined the appropriate framings. In literature, travelogues and picturesque poetry describing natural scenery and sites of interest formed a sequence of verbal paintings, intended to appeal to the visual imagination of the reader.

Since Christopher Hussey published the first comprehensive study on the subject in 1927, many works on the picturesque have appeared. They present different tendencies. In Hussey's *The Picturesque: Studies in a Point of View*, the picturesque is described as a visual category in arts that relate to the landscape – poetry, painting, architecture, garden architecture and travelogues – in which one focuses on the associations and thoughts that occur to the beholder.[13] Another seminal work, by Walter Hipple, *The Beautiful, the Sublime, & the Picturesque* (1957),[14] analyses the three concepts of the title in relation to one another. Hipple concentrated on

47 Thomas Gainsborough, an artist using a 'Claude glass', c.1750, graphite. London, British Museum, Department of Prints and Drawings, Oo,2.27.

the philosophical context, identifying Burke's *Philosophical Enquiry into the Origin of our Ideas of the Sublime and Beautiful* (1757) and John Locke's and David Hume's empirical theories as the main basis of the picturesque discourse in the second half of the eighteenth century. John Dixon Hunt has used art theory and literary history to analyse the picturesque, which he sees – following Hussey – as the relation between human beings and nature, represented by the individual's observations and associations.[15] While Hussey and Hipple treated the picturesque as an English phenomenon, Hunt and Dora Wiebenson have considered the French context and van Eck the Dutch.[16] Hunt devoted a chapter in *The Picturesque Garden in Europe* (2002) to the Scandinavian, German, Austrian, Eastern European, Russian and Italian variations of the picturesque.[17]

Whereas, traditionally, the picturesque has been viewed in relation to landscape, or to buildings in a landscape that frames them, as in a painting, there is another version of the picturesque based solely on architecture. I am not speaking here of the viewpoint of scholars such as Nicolas Pevsner and Emil Kaufmann, who regarded the picturesque in architecture merely as one element in nineteenth-century stylistic pluralism and as a prelude to modernism.[18] For them, the picturesque was simply the guiding principle in the selection of historical styles on the basis of cultural memory and association. But there is much more to the picturesque in architecture than style or the foreshadowing of nineteenth-century eclecticism, as we shall see in the next section.[19]

Towards Movement:
The Picturesque in Architecture

Although eighteenth- and nineteenth-century theorists of the picturesque mainly discussed the relationship between nature and architecture – that is, buildings situated in the landscape – some of them also wrote extensively on the picturesque in the buildings themselves. For instance, in the second part of *An Analytical Inquiry into the Principles of Taste* (1805), Richard Payne Knight wrote lengthily on architecture, and Uvedale Price composed 'An Essay on Architecture and Buildings as Connected with Scenery', first published in the second edition of *An essay on the picturesque* (vol. II, 1798) and then again in the third, re-edited, annotated and enlarged edition (*Essays on the Picturesque*, 1810).[20] These provide interesting insights into the role of the picturesque in architectural thought, though they seem to have been ignored in studies of architectural history, where the picturesque is mainly seen as a style, or as a step towards modernism. It is only in some of the more general historical studies of the picturesque – for instance, those by Hussey and John Mordaunt Crook, that the picturesque is not treated merely in these terms.[21] To these two scholars, the picturesque in architecture – the practice of building – is not itself a style but a method of using and combining styles.[22] Similarly, in studies by Caroll L. V. Meeks and Reyner Banham, the picturesque in architecture is concerned not with a style or a period but with general values and a design method.[23] According to these commentators, architecture may have picturesque qualities in itself, or it may display certain characteristics that evoke picturesque associations.

However, if we investigate the topic and its sources more deeply, the picturesque can be seen even more broadly. I suggest exploring it not only as a design method but also as a way of observing and experiencing architecture. It is important both to analyse buildings in this respect, and also to take written theories into consideration. The first step is the reading of contemporary sources, in which we find definitions of the characteristics of picturesque architecture.

In 'An Essay on Architecture and Buildings', Uvedale Price defined five qualities that delineate the picturesque in buildings: roughness, irregularity, variety, intricacy, and especially movement.[24] All these qualities (which appear in other eighteenth- and nineteenth-century sources as well) have to do with the visual impression the building makes on the beholder – that is, with the experience of architecture. Elsewhere in the *Essays*, Price argued that, while architecture in cities could be independent and self-sufficient, country houses should be subdued to their surroundings and to the landscape. The architect should be an 'architetto–pittore' and paint the landscape with his designs. The word 'picturesque', he said,

> is applied to every object, and every kind of scenery, which has been, or might be represented with good effect in painting; just as the word beautiful (when we speak of visible nature) is applied to every object, and every kind of scenery, that in any way gives pleasure to the eye.[25]

By defining a category separate from the sublime and the beautiful, he used these two aesthetic concepts to better delineate the picturesque: 'Picturesqueness, therefore, appears to hold a station between beauty and sublimity; and on that account, perhaps, is more frequently and more happily blended with them both than they are with each other.'[26] He claimed that 'a certain degree of stimulus or irritation is necessary to the picturesque, so, on the other hand, a soft and pleasing repose is equally the effect and the characteristic of the beautiful'.[27] To achieve picturesque effects one would need the 'qualities of roughness, and of sudden variation, joined to that of irregularity';[28] and he explained irritation as a positive reaction or emotion. In writing about the effects of light and shadow, Price referred to the 'operation on the mind', showing – as he did throughout the book – how the picturesque depends on the effect of art or landscape on the beholder.[29]

Price used the ruins of Greek temples to support his theory: 'when they are still in perfect condition, we call them beautiful, when they are in decay, they become Picturesque'.[30] In the first edition of the book Price had already commented on this difference: 'A temple or palace of Grecian architecture in its perfect entire state, and its surface and colour smooth and even, either in painting or reality, is beautiful; in ruin it is picturesque.'[31] In his view, the picturesque was not simply something to be deployed by painters, but was the outcome of specific qualities that were already present in nature and that architecture ought to have: roughness, variety and intricacy. When he described how Gothic architecture is more picturesque than Greek, his argument became more explicit:

> The first thing that strikes the eye in approaching any building is the general outline against the sky (or whatever it may be opposed to) and the effect of openings: in Grecian buildings the general lines are straight; and even when varied and adorned by a dome or a pediment, the whole has a character of symmetry and regularity.[32]

That is why Greek buildings are picturesque only when they fall into decay, because only then has the original symmetry become asymmetrical. To continue this thought, the roughness of ruins adheres to its natural surroundings, and architecture and nature can merge and become nearly one. William Gilpin defined ruins in exactly those terms: 'A ruin is a sacred thing. Rooted for ages in the soil; assimilated to it; we consider it rather as a work of nature than of art. Art cannot reach it.'[33]

Let us examine Price's five characteristics a little further. Various theorists wrote on roughness, but it was not only theorists of the picturesque who reflected on this theme. Edmund Burke, in differentiating between the sublime and the beautiful, named the sensation of smoothness as one of the characteristics of beauty, by definition, therefore, attributing roughness to the sublime. As we saw in Chapter 1, in Burke's thesis the rudeness of the ruins of Stonehenge excites sublime sensations. Further, objects that are rough to the touch (and by extension human beings who are harsh) cause pain, whereas soft, smooth objects give a tactile pleasure that creates a sense of beauty. In defining the picturesque, both Richard Payne Knight and Uvedale Price argued the importance of roughness, as opposed to smoothness. But their case is different from Burke's. For them, smoothness is uninteresting because it does not reflect the light in a variety of ways, as a rough surface does. For Knight, the reflections from rough and rugged surfaces create the 'most harmonious and brilliant combinations of tints to the eye'.[34] Again, we see here that the picturesque theorists were concerned with the visual: they concentrated on the eye, on viewing an object from a distance, whereas in defining the sublime Burke dealt with the other senses, including touch. The variations of light are delightful, Knight said, because they stimulate 'irritations upon the optic nerves', and irritation is a positive sensation.[35] He rejected smooth surfaces because their reflection is 'monotonous and feeble', and the reflections of extremely smooth surfaces like glass or polished metal are even disagreeable.[36] Roughness is also, of course, related to ruins, and to the decay of architecture on which time and the natural elements have left their traces. Price favoured ruins, for their picturesque quality, over buildings that were intact.

Price's five qualities of the picturesque were also adopted by other theorists. In his lectures for the Royal Academy (*Discourses* (1797)), Joshua Reynolds (1723–1792) proposed irregularity as the way to create 'something of scenery' in architecture. He claimed that this was sometimes the result of accident, arising from random additions made to a building for reasons of utility or pleasure; such additions led to asymmetry, which is a kind of irregularity.[37] Knight pursued this idea, arguing in favour of a mixture of different styles, in opposition to the monotony of pure classical architecture. The pictorial qualities of intricacy and variety were to be achieved by designing a new and innovative architectural plan – namely, one that was irregular or asymmetrical. Knight's own house at Downton in Herefordshire (1774–8) was a good example; in fact, it was the first, as Nikolaus Pevsner and Andrew Ballantyne showed, to be designed from the start to an asymmetrical ground plan.[38] It is interesting to note, however, that even a symmetrical building could be enjoyed as picturesque: by observing it from certain vantage points, the beholder could engineer various asymmetrical views, suggesting different architectural compositions. If a building was surrounded by curved streets, one could approach it from different directions and angles, thus altering the perspective and achieving asymmetrical and varied effects. The English architect Charles Barry (1795–1860) wrote about this in 1820, when he explained that he preferred St Paul's Cathedral in London to St Peter's in Rome, because it was 'perfectly insulated, and one has many gratifying views of it in perspective – which is not the case with St Peters'.[39]

Although irregularity required the conscious application of 'accidents', it was not an aim in itself. A building had to express its character: that is, the function of the building must be visible from the outside. According to Knight's theories, the impression and the effect a building makes on the spectator are crucial, as is the expression of its character in its exterior. Irregularity in architecture could be achieved in various ways: the ground plan, a mixture of different styles, the outline of the façades against the sky, the placement of windows, the different colours and textures of materials and of plants positioned against or close to the walls. Buildings should be a combination of different masses, inspired by the effect of the architecture in the backgrounds of Italian pictures: in other words, the architecture must harmonise with its setting, as it did in paintings; a building should be well adapted to the contours of the site. For Price, it had also to be conceived according to the views from inside the house, with 'windows turned towards the points where the objects were most happily arranged' so as to 'accommodate [the] building to the scenery'.[40] In that way the building would become an ornament to the landscape, and the blank surfaces of its walls could be 'transformed into beauties' by 'trees and shrubs or . . . climbing plants'.

Eighteenth-century architects started to conceive their buildings with observation from a distance in mind, so that the building in its surroundings constituted an imaginary picture, in which the general effect rather than the detail was important. Because viewing buildings from close to became less important, materials, detailing in decorations, and the structural use of architectural members became subordinate. The importance of examining buildings from a distance thus had its effect on architecture, and irregularity, mystery, romance and texture came to the fore.[41] The landscape could either provide the setting for the architectural design, or be reflected in the building. The main effect of the picturesque on architecture was that it put irregularity in place of symmetry as the essence of design.

As we have seen, Price argued that the picturesque resides in 'qualities of roughness, and of sudden variation, joined to that of irregularity'. The element of variety was partly intrinsic in roughness, movement and irregularity in respect of surface texture, materials, masses and parts of the building. But for Price variety was also synonymous with grandeur and richness.[42] By 'intricacy' he meant that architectural forms were complex and could not be distinguished at a single gaze. The awakening of curiosity and the effort the spectator had to make to interpret the forms were important. Architects should see architecture with a painter's eye. As one of England's principal painters and President of the Royal Academy, the aforementioned Reynolds said: 'Variety and intricacy is a beauty and excellence in every other of the arts which address the imagination: and why not in Architecture?'[43] According to him, architects should make their buildings affect the beholder, either by suggesting associations – as John Vanbrugh did with references in his designs to the architecture of castles – or by creating a 'striking novelty of effect', by which he meant favouring irregularity over symmetry. In arguing that architecture should have 'something of scenery', Reynolds aimed at the picturesque effect, comparing the work of Vanbrugh with that of painters:

> To speak then of Vanbrugh in the language of a Painter, he had originality of invention, he understood light and shadow, and had great skill in composition. To support his principal object, he produced his second and third groups or masses; he perfectly understood in his Art what is the most difficult in ours, the conduct of the back-ground; by which the design and invention is set off to the greatest advantage. What the background is in Painting, in Architecture is the real ground on which the building is erected; and no Architect took greater care than he that his work should not appear crude and hard; that is, it did not abruptly start out of the ground without expectation or preparation.[44]

Price, too, examined the work of Vanbrugh and, in a passage on Blenheim Palace, explained how he achieved his picturesque effect:

> His first point seems to have been massiveness, as the foundation of grandeur. Then, to prevent that mass from being a lump, he has made various bold projections of various heights, which from different points serve as foregrounds to the main building. And, lastly, having probably been struck with the variety of outline against the sky in many Gothic buildings, he has raised on the top . . . a number of decorations of various characters.[45]

As this passage shows, Price insisted on the importance of distant views. Diversity in the skyline of a building was therefore a significant element.

In theories of the picturesque and in eighteenth-century books on architecture, one element is particularly striking: that of movement. A number of recent studies on the subject have given this aspect some attention.[46] Because, in my opinion, this characteristic is essential for understanding the particularity of the picturesque, and because it is, as we shall see, the main theme of the five features essential to the concept, we shall analyse it here in more depth than the other characteristics.

Many eighteenth-century authors saw movement in Vanbrugh's architecture.[47] Theorists of the picturesque applied their ideas not so much to an analysis of Vanbrugh's buildings, which by then were some fifty years old, but to the effects his architecture had on the beholder. John Soane, who called Vanbrugh the Shakespeare of architects, stated:

> His great work is Blenheim. The style of his building is grand and majestically imposing, the whole composition analogous to the war-like genius of the mighty hero for whom it was erected [the Duke of Marlborough]. The great extent of this noble struc-

ture, the picturesque effect of its various parts, the infinite and pleasing variety, the breaks and contrasts in the different heights and masses, produce the most exquisite sensations in the scientific beholder, whether the view be distant, intermediate, or near.[48]

The British architect Robert Adam (1728–1792) had met Piranesi in Rome and admired his etchings for their expression of variety and movement; he stated that they recalled to him the qualities that existed in Vanbrugh's work, of whom the Adam brothers wrote: 'Sir John Vanbrugh's genius was of the first class; and, in point of movement, novelty and ingenuity, his works have not been exceeded by anything in modern times.'[49] Not only did Adam connect architecture to art in its composition, in *Works in Architecture* (1778), written with his brother James Adam, he also established the relationship between a building and its setting. In the same passage they expressed their hope that British architecture would soon improve 'in the form, convenience, arrangement, and relief of apartment': what was needed was 'a greater movement and variety, in the outside composition, and in the decoration of the inside, an almost total change'. In a footnote to the word 'movement' they added:

> Movement is meant to express, the rise and fall, the advance and recess, with other diversity of form, in the different parts of a building, so as to add greatly to the picturesque of the composition. For the rising and falling, advancing and receding, with the convexity and concavity, and other forms of the great parts, have the same effect in architecture, that hill and dale, fore-ground and distance, swelling and sinking have in landscape: That is, they serve to produce an agreeable and diversified contour, that groups and contrasts like a picture, and creates a variety of light and shade, which gives great spirit, beauty and effect to the composition.[50]

Movement in a building is related to its natural surroundings and is therefore best seen from a distance: it requires the viewer to step back so that the masses and elements can be distinguished. Price referred to the 'massiness' of a building, which is 'the accompaniment and, as it were, the attendance of the inferior parts in their different gradations . . . to the principal building'.[51] To perceive movement in architecture, the spectator had to move.

James Adam had already written about movement in architecture, in 1762 during his visit to Rome on the Grand Tour. In this text, the draft of an essay on architectural theory that was never published, he compared architects to landscape painters:

> Nothing contribut[es] half so much to the beauty of buildings viewed from a distance as movement, for at a considerable distance we must of necessity lose all the graces of detail and decoration so that we have nothing remaining but the beauty of a well disposed variety of high and low projections and recesses. For with us, as with landscape painters who chose for their subjects a variety of hill and dale to render their scenes interesting, nor are they less attentive to the disposition of light and shade, upon which likewise much of their success depends; for this reason they who study after nature take the evening or the morning when the sun is low and the shadows are broad.[52]

In another passage the composition of landscape and of architecture were put on a par: 'What is so material an excellence in landscape is not less requisite for composition in architecture, namely the variety of contour, a rise and fall of the different parts and likewise those great projections and recesses which produce a broad light and shade.' As an example of this, Adam again named Blenheim Palace by Vanbrugh.[53]

Such ideas were not unique to Britain, nor were the Adam brothers the first to formulate them. The French architect Jacques-Germain Soufflot's observations on the cathedral of Notre-Dame also addressed the significance of movement:

[The tribunes] of Notre Dame in Paris are of a considerable extent and produce a surprising effect in that they offer to the eye, as it were, a second church; its brightness, contrasting with the sort of dimness that reigns beneath, makes it appear both more indistinct and more elevated, and reveals to the spectators, as if in the distance, a thousand objects that – sometimes fading, sometimes reappearing – offer spectacles that delight them as they move away or approach.[54]

In 1764 Julien-David Le Roy presented to Louis XV (1710–1774) his *Histoire de la disposition et des formes différentes que les Chrétiens ont données à leurs Temples, depuis le règne de Constantin le Grand, jusqu'à nous*, to commemorate the laying of the foundation stone of Soufflot's Sainte-Geneviève (now the Panthéon) in Paris. Le Roy's aim was to explain in an experimental way how movement in architectural space works. He called it the 'metaphysical part of architecture'.[55] To him, architecture should be understood as the unfolding of form through movement.[56] In his 'Essai sur la théorie de l'architecture', the introduction to the second edition of his *Les ruines des plus beaux monuments de la Grèce* (1770), Le Roy suggested that architecture touches the soul, and described how our apprehension of its effects depends on our view of it, in this case while walking through a garden:

If you walk in a garden along and at some distance from a row of trees, regularly planted so that their trunks touch a wall pierced by arched openings, the apparent relation between trees and arches will change almost imperceptibly, and your soul will receive no new sensations, though you keep your eyes fixed on the trees and the openings in the wall and though you cover a considerable distance in a short time. But if the line of trees is set at a distance from the wall, you may walk in just the same way and enjoy a new view at every successive step as the trees mask a different section of the wall.

The Scottish philosopher Henry Home, Lord Kames, also believed this phenomenon:

Avoid a straight avenue directed upon a dwelling house; better for an oblique approach is a waving line . . . In a direct approach, the first appearance is continued to the end . . . In an oblique approach, the interposed objects put the house seemingly in motion; it moves with the passenger . . . seen successively in different directions, [it] takes on at every step a new figure.[57]

The movement of the spectator causes the architecture to move as well, according to Le Roy:

As you move closer or farther away, the top of the wall will appear to rise level with the lowest branches or to intersect the trunks at widely differing heights. And so, though we have assumed the wall to be regularly decorated and the trees equally spaced, the former scheme will seem immobile, while the latter will come to life as the spectator moves, presenting him with a succession of highly varied views created by the infinity of possible combinations of the simple objects that he perceives.[58]

Étienne-Louis Boullée, almost twenty-five years later, addressed in the same vein how the movements of the spectator make architecture come alive:

[the vault] crowns the colonnade in most majestic fashion; in that the columns are not overloaded by the massive vaulting above them and thus preserve their dignity and characteristic grace; finally, in that the architecture would have the most stimulating effect on the onlooker at every step – the stimulating effect that stems from the fact that our glance cannot wander over isolated objects arranged symmetrically in every direction without our forming the impression that the objects move with us and without it appearing that we have imparted life to them.[59]

When Arthur Young (1741–1820), a scientist and farmer, wrote that ruins 'generally appear best at a distance', he was aiming at the general effect: 'if you approach them the effect is weakened, unless the access is somewhat difficult: And as to penetrating every part by means of artificial paths, it is a question whether the more you see by such means does not proportionally lessen the general idea of the whole.'[60] Young was not interested in the style or the details of the ruins, but considered the scene as a whole – 'a mighty picture in three dimensions'. In describing the different shades of old and new buildings, Knight preferred ruins (just as Price did): 'The mouldering ruins of ancient temples, theatres, and aqueducts, enriched by such a variety of tints, all mellowed into each other, as they appear in the landscapes of Claude, are, in the highest degree, picturesque.' Thus, new buildings are less picturesque: 'for new buildings have an unity of tint, and sharpness of angle, which render them unfit for painting, unless when mixed with trees or some other objects, which may break and diversify their colour, and graduate and harmonise the abruptness of lights and shadows'.[61] According to Knight new buildings could better be described as beautiful, for their neatness, freshness, lightness, symmetry, regularity, uniformity and propriety.

The texts analysed above define the picturesque in architecture as consisting in variation, differentiation, the changing effects of light, the use of materials, elements of different architectural styles and periods, the combination of a building and its surroundings, and, principally, movement. Although we can distinguish different types of movement in architecture, the movement of the spectator is essential in all types. For a building to appear to move, the beholder has to move first; thus movement in architecture occurs only with the act of the beholder's being in motion. This kind of movement of architecture – or movement of the spectator – became a crucial element in eighteenth-century architectural thought. The picturesque theorists Knight, Price and Kames all wrote about it, and so did the art and architectural theorists Reynolds, Adam, Soane, Le Roy and Boullée. Now that we have defined two types of the picturesque in relation to architecture, the first using distance and framing, as in a painting, the second focusing on movement, let us turn to the accounts of Paestum to see how these types are represented there.

Pictorial Impressions and Hasty Views: Picturesque Elements at Paestum

The picturesque figures prominently in the accounts of Paestum. Some travellers used the term 'picturesque' itself, while others were concerned with the concept or formulated their observations in a way that can be related to it. For instance, the writer and politician Auguste Creuzé de Lesser (1771–1839), who visited Paestum in 1802, wrote of the striking contrast between the beautiful scenery and the site itself: 'One reaches Paestum via a route where friends of nature will find everything beautiful. Nothing more fresh, more varied, more picturesque than the aspects it presents . . . as also nothing more arid, more sad than Paestum itself.'[62] Several travellers reported that Paestum's location offered interesting scenes for painters: 'painters can find there studies to be made. We encountered

48   Hubert Rohault de Fleury, interior view of the Temple of Neptune at Paestum, c.1805, graphite. Montréal, Collection Canadian Centre for Architecture, DR1974:0002:030:032.

Buffaloes, horrible, mean animals in a very beautiful site[;] they were all submerged in the water, which animated the landscape,' wrote the architect Rohault de Fleury in 1804 (Fig. 48).[63] The Italian architect Giovanni Battista Piranesi observed in 1778 that Paestum lent itself very well to being painted: 'Painters will . . . find there a number of very interesting viewpoints, whether it be the [scenes framed by the] different openings [between the columns], or the variety of rural plants that surround every part; or else the various colours of the many herds that the shepherds lead there.'[64]

Whereas, for many travellers, the picturesque aspects of the scenery or the painterly associations the site conjured up were positive aspects, some authors revealed a hostile attitude to the picturesque in their accounts. In 1798 the French architect Claude-Mathieu Delagardette (1762–1805) wrote: 'even some of these authors [those who admired the site] seem to have gone to Paestum out of nothing more than simple curiosity, or with no other purpose than to enjoy a picturesque picnic there'.[65] Delagardette was aiming to show how different he was from the layman–traveller, who went to Paestum only to enjoy the atmosphere, as the English writer Mariana Starke (1762–1838) did in 1797: 'We took a cold dinner, wine, bread, knives, and forks, in our carriage, and dined in one of the Temples.'[66] Besides dining in the ruins, travellers also used the temples as a stage or a backdrop to their own performances: in 1823 Lady Blessington and her companions listened to a poem spoken by one of their party, whose recitation was presumably enhanced by the setting provided by the ruins.[67] The French architect Henri Labrouste, probably writing out of motives similar to Delagardette's, voiced negative feelings in discussing the reactions of earlier travellers:

These ruins have what is perhaps a dangerous appeal for architects: their picturesque form, the sense of abandonment and even desolation that characterises the land around them, strike the eye too powerfully at first acquaintance; often people fail to resist the desire to draw picturesque views, and these views, executed hastily and imprecisely, exaggerate the strong character of the architecture so that it becomes heavy and defective, thus perpetuating the errors that are unfortunately authorised in the schools.[68]

By criticising the fleeting observation of travellers, for whom the temples were merely a scenic group which they captured in hasty sketches, Labrouste meant to highlight his own, more profound way of examining the temples. He used the picturesque to describe a superficial way of looking at architecture. The reactions of Delagardette and Labrouste show how, according to architects who favoured a more scientific method of observation, the picturesque could be reduced to a mere Romantic concept. These testimonies demonstrate how differently travellers perceived elements of the picturesque, but, more important, they show how the term was used in descriptions of the site: it was applied to the scenery, the pictorial possibilities of the site as a whole, to the temples as a backdrop for activities, to their forms and to the drawings made of them. While the term could be used positively or negatively, it was always related to a particular mode of observation, characterising how travellers viewed the landscape, the ruins, or the combination of the two.

Richard Payne Knight, one of the main champions and theorists of the picturesque, left behind a diary of his journey to Sicily in 1777, in which Paestum and the picturesque play an important part. An English connoisseur, art collector and amateur architect, Knight published eight books, which were widely read and discussed in the eighteenth and nineteenth century: two of them were on the picturesque.[69] It will be instructive to analyse a specific use of the concept of the picturesque in Knight's report of Paestum, and to determine how he formulated a picturesque experience in his writings. Other travellers to the site who engaged with the picturesque did not further theorise their ideas. What is striking in Knight's case is not only that he described his tour as a train of picturesque sensations, but that, having returned to England, he used his ideas and observations to develop a theory of the picturesque.

As we have seen, accounts of Paestum give the term 'picturesque' different meanings: the picturesque as fit for painting, the picturesque as scenery that brings a painting to mind, and the picturesque as superficial observation or as the stage set for a pastime. But all these diverse connotations belong to the traditional aspect of the picturesque as a frame for a view of the landscape – in the case of Paestum the framing of the temples within their setting, as in a painting. It seems as if the other aspect of the picturesque – movement – played no role. So let us turn to Knight's narrative to explore how he utilised the picturesque and to see if can we find movement there.

In Search of the Picturesque: Knight's Paestum Account

Richard Payne Knight was privately educated and a man of letters. Two portraits, made in 1775 and 1794, show him as a cultured person, scholar, collector and critic. His erudition is also evident from all the references he included in his published writings and in his travel diary.[70] As an amateur architect, classical scholar and art collector, he was a prominent figure in British society: a trustee of the British Museum, an MP (1780–1806), a member of the Society of Dilettanti (from 1781), deputy president of the Society of Antiquaries, and a founder of the British Institution.[71] When he embarked on his expedition to Sicily in 1777, the 26-year-old Knight was probably aiming to become a connoisseur and 'gentleman-scholar'. His journey was inspired by the Grand Tour made by the young aristocrats of the Society of Dilettanti.[72]

Knight's Sicilian tour seems to have been carefully prepared: he was to visit Paestum first and then spend two months travelling round the island of Sicily. This 'Expedition into Sicily' was part of Knight's second journey to Italy in 1776–8; the first had taken place in 1772–3,[73]

49 John Robert Cozens,
the Coliseum from the north,
1780, graphite and water-
colour. Edinburgh, Scottish
National Gallery.

and it has been suggested that the trip to Sicily had been planned earlier, even as long
before as that first visit to Italy. Knight left England in 1776, accompanied by the landscape
painter John Robert Cozens (1752–1797), and during the summer of that year they travelled via Switzerland to Italy.[74] Four years earlier, Knight had been to Florence, Rome,
Capua and Naples; this time, the itinerary took the two men to Rome, Naples, Paestum
and Sicily, and then back to Rome. From there they travelled to Paris and in 1778 returned
to England. It was in Rome, where Cozens and Knight arrived in autumn 1776, that Knight
met the German landscape painter Jakob Philipp Hackert (1737–1807) and the English ship-
builder and amateur artist Charles Gore (1729–1807), who was Hackert's pupil.[75] Knight,
Hackert and Gore decided to study the remains of Greek architecture in Italy together.
Cozens stayed in Rome (Fig. 49), perhaps because he was too ill to go with them.[76] The
threesome decided to travel to Sicily in the spring of 1777, when everything was in bloom.
Their route went from Naples to Paestum and thence to Stromboli and Lipari, and on via
Palermo to Segesta, Selinunte, Agrigento, Syracuse, Mount Etna, Taormina and Messina.
They left in April and were back in Rome in July.[77] Knight wrote a 120-page travel diary,
recording his impressions of the landscape, the architecture, local customs and the political
situation. Hackert and Gore captured the sights in vivacious pencil sketches, some of which
they later transferred to impressive watercolours (Fig. 50). The interaction between the connoisseur and the painters must have been stimulating.[78] Knight's plan was probably that

50 Jakob Philipp Hackert,
landscape with ruins at
Selinunte, Sicily, 1777, pen
and grey ink with water-
colour. London, British
Museum, Department of
Prints and Drawings,
Oo,4.17–18.

51 Jakob Philipp Hackert, the temples at Paestum from the north-east, 1777. Private collection.

Cozens would use Hackert's and Gore's sketches to make finished watercolours of the more romantic scenes, and that the text, with Cozens's illustrations, should be published on their return to England, but this project never came to fruition.[79]

The journey, undertaken in a felouk, seems to have been planned to take in places that offered magnificent scenery and would generate a powerful response in the viewer: the volcanoes of Stromboli and Etna, and sites where Greek architecture could be admired – Paestum, Syracuse, Agrigento and Taormina. Knight had read a considerable amount about the subject and knew what to expect. Besides publications about Paestum by Gabriel-Pierre-Martin Dumont, Filippo Morghen, Thomas Major and John Longfield, there were accounts of Sicily published in the 1760s and 1770s by earlier travellers to the island, who included John Dryden (1701), J. P. d'Orville (1727), Patrick Brydone (1770) and Baron von Riedesel (1771).[80] As far as is known, only Brydone and von Riedesel (who was a friend of Johann Joachim Winckelmann) visited Paestum on the way to Sicily, which began to be of interest at a later date in the eighteenth century than Paestum.[81] Except that Sicily had Greek temples on Italian soil – at Agrigento, Segesta and Selinunte – the sites there differed greatly from Paestum, where the state of preservation of the temples, their number and their situation were unique. Knight's travel diary, which was inspired by Brydone's and sometimes followed it closely, shows how different a visitor's reactions to Paestum and Sicily could be.[82]

Early on the morning of 12 April 1777, Knight, Hackert and Gore sailed from Naples for Sicily; their route would take in Paestum and the Lipari Islands on the way.[83] Knight described the view of Naples as the boat drew away from the shore: the sight of the city and the islands, Vesuvius smoking in the distance, and Sorrento, all

> extending round to Cape Miseno in the form of an Amphitheatre, enriched with Palaces, Gardens, Woods and Ruins, are such an assemblage of objects, as are no where else to be seen. We enjoyed it in the utmost perfection, as the weather was extremely fine and the Spring in its bloom.[84]

The weather conditions gave Knight an impressive sight: 'The infinite variety of tints were all harmonised together by that pearly hue, which is peculiar to this delicious climate.' The comment about the mingling of colours is interesting in itself, but Knight added a more significant remark: 'This Tint very particularly marks Claude Lorraine's Coloring.'

He went on to describe how the city gradually disappeared from view as they sailed on: 'As we advanced into the open sea, the colours and forms seemed to sink into the Atmosphere and grow gradually indistinct, till at last the Sun withdrew its rays and left all in darkness.' Knight's description creates a stark contrast between the soft colours of the day and the dark night, in which nothing could be seen and the role of the spectator became null and void. The visual experience of leaving Naples, which is reminiscent of looking through a Claude glass and indeed reminded Knight of Claude's paintings, was enhanced by his observation of colour and light and their gradual fading into darkness and obscurity. This opposition was to become very important in Knight's later theories on the picturesque, and it recalls the strong contrast between night and day that Shelley described in his depiction of the landscape around Paestum. Yet Shelley's account was very different: to him these elements added to the sublime experience, an experience that was related to the specificities of the site.

The travellers spent the night in their boat and disembarked on 13 April at Agropoli, a small village close to Paestum. They continued on horseback in order to reach 'those venerable remains' (Fig. 51); this way of putting it makes clear that Knight was prepared to see something that was already well known and had been admired by earlier travellers. At his first sight of the ruins, Knight's expectations were satisfied or even surpassed: 'The first appearance of them is exceedingly striking.' In his initial description, Knight concentrated on the landscape setting of the temples: 'the three Temples, which are tolerably well preserved, rise one beyond the other in the midst of a rich and beautiful vale, surrounded by romantic Hills, covered with flowering Shrubs and Herbs'. He tried to give some historical depth to his observations by referring to Virgil's *Georgics*, in which the poet mentioned Monte Vostiglione (then named 'Mons Alburnus'), situated near the confluence of the Sele and Tanagro (Silarus and Tanager) rivers, and took this mountain as the starting point for an examination of the landscape around Paestum.[85] Just as in Virgil's times, Knight recorded, the mountain was covered with 'Ilexes'; he also quoted Virgil on the dense forests that covered the banks of the River Silarus, which are infested in summer by a type of 'stinging fly'.[86] In a third reference to Virgil, Knight called the Tanager an insignificant river that had occasionally run dry during the summer – Virgil's 'sicci ripa Tanagri'. Was Knight citing an ancient author to emphasise the history of the site and to show that Paestum was known in Roman times, or merely to show off his erudition? Perhaps he wanted to suggest that, in walking round the site the traveller can somehow relive Roman times, though he believed that such echoes could be set off only by the aspect of Paestum that was unchanged – its natural setting. Quotations from Virgil were a common feature in publications on Paestum, and, far from showing his credentials as a connoisseur, all that Knight proved by repeating them was that he had read the accounts of his predecessors. By studying these beforehand, he had equipped himself with a plentiful stock of historical descriptions and references, which he could call to mind as he viewed the sites where these historical events had taken place.

After taking in his first impression of the temples and their location in the fertile valley, Knight approached to examine them more closely; his diary minutely records his observations. First, he described their architecture:

The Architecture of Paestum is the old Doric – the Columns, short and fluted, and near together, with broad flat Capitals and no bases. They are executed in a kind of porous petrifaction like that of the Lago del Tartaro near Tivoli. The Stones are exquisitely wrought and joined with the nicest exactitude, and like all the fine Works of the Ancients without Cement.

What is interesting about these remarks is not the description of the architecture as such, but the briefness of the comments. In fact, this passage constitutes Knight's only observation about the architecture of the temples in the whole account.

Next, Knight made some interesting remarks about the colours of the stone:

> The colour is a whitish yellow, stained and corroded by the vicissitudes of weather, and overgrown with Moss and herbage; without being blackened by Smoke or intermixed with modern Buildings like the Ruins of Rome: hence the tints are extremely beautiful and picturesque.

The colours were harmonious, attractive and (most important of all) 'beautiful and picturesque'. In this significant passage, not only did Knight apply the word 'picturesque' to the temples of Paestum, he put it on a par with the beautiful. Two aesthetic viewpoints that he would define separately in his later theories were here combined in one phrase.

These comments about the porous stone, and the picturesque colours of the temples were a sort of prelude to Knight's next observation. Of the temples and his own closer examination of them, he wrote:

> 'When one examines the Parts near, they appear rude, massive and heavy; but seen at a proper distance, the general effect is grand, simple and even elegant. The rudeness appears then an artful negligence, and the heaviness a just and noble Stability.'

This comment is crucial for an understanding of Knight's experience of Paestum as a spectator. While the temples from close up appeared rough, massive and heavy, at a distance they made a magnificent overall effect. In studying the temples at close quarters, Knight seems to have been unimpressed: his only positive comment related to the jointing of the stones. It was only from far away that the synthesis of landscape and ruins could be apprehended. Seen from a distance, enormous masses of rough stone, clearly defined, marked by shadows and separated by open spaces, resolved into a soft-coloured texture.

From the descriptions in his Sicilian diary it becomes clear that Knight's view may have been influenced by the painters with whom he travelled, the three of them observing the landscape as if it were a painting. Looking at Paestum with a painter's eye may have been easier than examining the temples in detail: the most interesting image was the one seen from a distance. Knight's record encapsulates all the problems and conflicts that the site could excite in an observer: the conflict between expectation and observation *in situ*, the confrontation with the strangeness of the architecture, and the difficulty of finding ways to appreciate an architecture that was unknown and, to the viewer's own taste, too rough and too heavy. As we saw in Chapter 1, some visitors tried to explain their experiences by means of the sublime, but Knight took a different path, determined by picturesque experiences of ancient Greek ruins. The fact that the ruins did not live up to his expectations or conform with his idea that Greek art was of a higher order than that of Rome exemplifies the dilemma that many eighteenth-century visitors faced who had an *a priori* preference for Greek art, based on their reading and the images they had seen. The reactions of Étienne-Louis Boullée and William Chambers to Greek architecture, discussed in Chapter 1, bear this out. Confronted with the real thing and disappointed by it, travellers somehow had to come to an appreciation of what they saw. Knight's solution was to view the monuments from a distance. In fact, he returned to the position from which he had experienced his first striking sight of the temples; the combination of ruins and landscape dissolved into a blur of colours, like a landscape painting, and as such became aesthetically satisfying.

It is clear that Knight did not appreciate the architecture of the three temples, finding it too rough, massive and heavy. But when he turned to the Roman remains at the site, he was moved to a long reflection on the Corinthian order, commenting upon what little remained of a fourth, Roman, temple. In these observations he unfolded his ideas on history and progress in architecture. Because the remains of the fourth temple were rude, simple and pure, Knight concluded that it had been built before the perfection, or after the decline, of the Corinthian order – probably the first; this led to reflections on the beginnings of the Corinthian order, in which Knight showed that the Greeks were inventors and no imitators, and that the trajectory in the arts is always to evolve:

> Human Genius is always progressive in its operations, and in things of this kind generally slow. Men improve in works of taste more from observing the faults of others, than from any preconceiving Ideas of perfection. The first rudiments of the Corinthian order are to be found among the Ruins of Thebes and Persepolis, and were brought into Europe probably about the time of Alexander the Great: but the Pride of the Greeks would never permit them, to acknowledge themselves Imitators in any thing. They claimed the invention and improvement of all arts, as owing to their own superior Genius, and not the effect of accident[,] observation and experience.[87]

Thus he dismissed the origin of the Corinthian order in the Vitruvian sense. (We shall examine the topic of the origins of architecture in Chapter 5.)

In his long discourse on the Corinthian order, Knight cited another ancient author, in this case Strabo, who was often quoted in eighteenth-century descriptions of Paestum.[88] For example, Thomas Major referred to him in *The ruins of Paestum* (1768), and also cited poets who spoke of the Paestan roses that bloom twice a year (Virgil, Ovid, Propertius, Martial, Ausonius and Claudian).[89] The same quotations appear in Saint-Non's *Voyage pittoresque*. Although the use of texts from antiquity to demonstrate Paestum's ancient history was a common device in eighteenth-century writings, if only to show that Paestum was known to authors in Roman times, it is worth noting that the Roman authors in question mainly referred to the natural surroundings of Paestum and never gave a description of the city. Knight next dealt with the stones used at Paestum, stating that, unlike the Romans, the Greeks had no access to refined materials, which was one reason for the coarseness of their buildings.[90] He further explained the porous appearance of the columns by the vicinity of a salt stream.[91] In this connection, he seems to say that some writers believed architecture to be created by or born out of nature. He ended by describing the soil, and, just like other eighteenth-century authors, the roses, so celebrated by Virgil.[92]

Knight's account of Paestum moves from a general impression, to ancient authors, architecture, stone and colour, via the notion of distance, other monuments and the fourth temple to his reflections on the Corinthian order, the city's decay, the Romans and the Greeks, the air, and the situation and form of the city; it ends with the roses. In fact, there is no clear structure to his description: it is simply a chain of impressions, references and trains of thought. The lack of method proves that Knight was not really interested in the architecture of the temples, but he was fascinated by the landscape, the scenery, the colours, the stone, and the quality of the air. Having received these impressions, he quickly walked away, and started to think about the history of the place. The text, which seems to be random, is in fact structured according to the associations suggested by the experience of being at the site. Having briefly described the temples and viewed them from a distance as part of the landscape, Knight seems to have lost interest in them and quickly turned to the other remains. One wonders whether his preparatory reading had raised his expectations too high and he was disillusioned by the reality. It is important to recognise that in viewing the site as one might view a painting Knight was no different from other travellers who saw the picturesque in Paestum, though his description was exceptionally precise and particular. We should also note that Knight's account of Paestum was not entirely exceptional among the descriptions of ancient sites in his diary: his reaction to others was similar. Yet there were some important differences, as we shall see shortly.

Picturesque versus Sublime:
The Expedition into Sicily and Cozens's View

Paestum was not the only site to which Knight responded as though it were a work of art or the subject of classical references. In some respects he approached Sicily in a similar way, drawing on the picturesque and quoting ancient authors such as Euripides, Homer, Strabo, Theocretius and Virgil. Knight used the word 'picturesque' three times in his descriptions of Sicily. Of Lipari, which the party visited on 24 April, he wrote:

> The Town is situated at the bottom of a small Bay upon a Rock of Lava, projecting into the Sea, beautifully broken and hung with Shrubs. At a small distance it appears very elegant and picturesque, being surrounded by a small plain, cover'd with Houses and Gardens, beyond which rise the Mountains, formely Volcanos, but now turned into rich Vineyards, interspersed with Figtrees, Mulberries etc.[93]

At Agrigento, he related the picturesque to the situation of the temple:

> The present appearance of the Temple of Juno is the most picturesque that can be imagined. It is situated upon a small Hill, cover'd with trees, among which lie the broken Columns etc. that have fallen down, for the material is so coarse that they are not thought worth carrying away.[94]

And at Syracuse he applied the term to its gardens: 'The Latomiae of Acridina are nearer the Sea, and are now the Gardens of a Capuchin Convent. They are in the same stile as the others, but still more beautiful and picturesque.'

Although these examples suggest that he often retreated to a distance in order to appreciate a site and gain a picturesque view, only at Messina did Knight explicitly refer to

52 (*below left*) Jakob Philipp Hackert, the Temple of Hercules at Agrigento, Sicily, 1777, pen and brown ink, with brown wash, over graphite. London, British Museum, Department of Prints and Drawings, Oo,4.27.

53 (*below right*) Jakob Philipp Hackert, the Temple at Segesta, Sicily, 1777, pen and black ink with watercolour. London, British Museum, Department of Prints and Drawings, Oo,4.7.

viewing a city in its surroundings as if it were a painting. In this account he used the words 'beautiful' and 'romantic', and (as at Paestum) combined two different views – one from far away and the other from close by:

> As one enters [the Straits of Messina], the view is very beautiful and romantic, the Coasts being high and rocky, adorn'd with Towns & Villages . . . The entrance into the Harbour is still more striking – a beautiful Lake discloses itself gradually . . . bounded on one side by a vast range of Houses . . . which, tho' of bad Architecture, form a noble & magnificent scene. Behind these rise the Heraean Mountains, cover'd with Woods & Vineyards, interspersed with Churches, Villas & Convents. On the other side a long Arm of land projects into the Sea . . . Upon this are the Lighthouse, Lazzaretto & fortress, which is apparently built, not to defend the Town, but to command it.
>
> Upon approaching nearer this fine Scene loses all it Splendor, and every object assumes an Air of melancholy and dejection. The Houses are many of them uninhabited, & the rest falling into ruin and decay . . . When we disembarked and enter'd the Town, the Prospect still blackened – the Inhabitants were poor and ragged and the Houses, that seemed once to have been the residence of the Great and Affluent, were cover'd with filth and falling into ruin.[95]

Here, too, the view from a distance was delightful but when he approached the town its miserable state became apparent and his reaction was adverse. It also seems that, in Sicily, Knight was more enthusiastic when there was less left of a building, as was the case, for example, at Agrigento (Fig. 52). This recalls the lines by William Gilpin (quoted earlier) on the superior beauty of ruins as compared to buildings that are intact.

Although there are, therefore, similarities between Knight's view of Paestum and his response to the Sicilian sites, there are also differences. His explorations at Segesta inspired observations very dissimilar to those he noted at Paestum. Rather than taking a distant view and ignoring the architecture, at Segesta he immediately started to examine the ruins, counted the columns of the temple, aimed to take measurements and even looked for a ladder so that he could do so more exactly.[96] At Paestum he had not even attempted this, or at least he did not write about it. It was not that he was not impressed by the situation of the temple at Segesta – indeed, he was captivated by it: 'On approaching one is

54 (*below left*) Jakob Philipp Hackert, the ruins of the Temple of Juno Lacinia at Agrigento, Sicily, 1777, pen and brown ink with water-colour. London, British Museum, Department of Prints and Drawings, Oo,4.28.

55 (*below right*) Thomas Hearne, the ruins of the great temple at Selinunte, Sicily, after 1777, pen and grey and brown ink with watercolour, over graphite. London, British Museum, Department of Prints and Drawings, Oo,4.13.

struck with a view of a noble temple, which stands alone upon a small Hill surrounded by high Mountains.'[97] Hackert and Gore both drew the temple in that way, taking a viewpoint from downhill (Fig. 53). The relationship between the text of the diary and their images is often close: the viewing points and descriptions recorded by Knight are repeatedly represented in the artists' watercolours. The drawings also show that the corrosion of stone and damage to a pediment were not at all considered insignificant details, but were important for the picturesque aspect of the building. At Agrigento, too, the group took measurements of the buildings – they can be seen at work in one of Hackert's watercolours (Fig. 54); Knight wrote of one of the temples: 'It has six columns in front and fourteen deep, all entire with their entablatures.' At Selinunte, Knight commented: 'The Capitals are like those of the Great Temple [of Neptune] or Basilica at Paestum & the Columns diminished regularly from bottom to top.'[98] He again busied himself with measuring, and took two days to draw and measure the ruins. Even at Mount Etna, Knight mentioned making measurements. By comparison with this attention to detail, Knight gave an astonishingly general impression of Paestum.

56 Jakob Philipp Hackert, interior of the Ear of Dionysos, a cave at Syracuse, Sicily, 1777, pen and brown ink with brown wash, over graphite. London, British Museum, Department of Prints and Drawings, Oo,4.33.

Rediscovering Architecture

The seriousness with which Knight examined the ruins in Sicily may have had to do with his plan to publish his findings on the island's remains in an illustrated folio, the aim being to further his scholarly ambitions.[99] Knight had proposed that Cozens, who had stayed in Rome, should make finished watercolours of the sketches of Hackert and Gore for publication with his text.[100] Cozens had already made drawings for Knight in Switzerland, on their way to Italy. During the same period, both Cozens and Knight were preoccupied with the element of light.[101] It has been suggested that Cozens was chosen to depict the more poetic scenes of Sicily, while the other painters were to make the more archaeologically accurate views, both on the spot and afterwards.[102]

An important difference between Knight's accounts of Paestum and of Sicily is his use of the sublime. Although it is not mentioned explicitly in his text on Sicily, the concept colours his descriptions from time to time. For example, Knight and his companions explored the ruins at Selinunte (Fig. 55), which Knight called 'stupendous', and at Agrigento he commented upon the 'awful discrepancy between ancient grandeur and modern poverty'. The so-called 'Ear of Dionysos' (Fig. 56), a cave at Syracuse, inspired sublime associations: crimes and misery, gloom, horror and despair. Knight felt the strongest sense of the sublime when he climbed Mount Etna. He wrote: 'I felt myself elevated above humanity, & looked down with Contempt upon the mighty objects of Ambition under me.' The sublime feelings that nature could evoke in a spectator would appear again in his theories in *An Analytical Inquiry into the Principles of Taste* (1805). By contrast with Knight's rather general descriptions of Paestum, these brief quotations demonstrate how much stronger and more impressive a reference point the sublime was when describing a site, because it gave expression to its specific qualities.

Whereas Knight did not characterise Paestum as sublime, John Robert Cozens, when he visited Paestum himself five years later, saw the site in an entirely different way (Figs 57–8). Cozens executed the watercolours for Knight's intended publication without having seen Paestum. After having worked for a patron with a picturesque eye, in November 1782 he made some striking observations of his own at Paestum, captured in impressive images that express nothing but the sublime (Figs 59–62).[103] Cozens thus foreshadows Turner, who drew for James Hakewill before seeing Paestum with his own eyes (see Chapter 1);

57 (*above left*) John Robert Cozens, the three temples at Paestum, 1782. Manchester, Whitworth Art Gallery.

58 (*above right*) John Robert Cozens, the temple of Ceres at Paestum, 1782. Manchester, Whitworth Art Gallery.

59 (*above*)   John Robert
Cozens, *The Two Great Temples
at Paestum*, 1782, watercolour
and graphite. London, Victoria
and Albert Museum, P.2-1973.

60 (*right*)   John Robert
Cozens, *The Small Temple at
Paestum, Italy*, 1782, water-
colour and graphite
Manchester, Whitworth
Art Gallery.

61 (*above*) John Robert
Cozens, the three temples at
Paestum, 1782–3. Oldham,
Gallery Oldham.

62 (*left*) John Robert
Cozens, *Two Great Temples at
Paestum*, 1782–3. Oldham,
Gallery Oldham.

when he was actually present at the site Turner was struck by its sublimity, and represented it magnificently in his drawings. Like Turner, before visiting the site himself, Cozens reworked someone else's drawings of Paestum into finished watercolours. And like Turner, when he saw the temples in reality, his observations were entirely different and evoked the same feelings of the sublime. Cozens's watercolours, painted more than thirty years before Turner's famous drawings, represent a similar dark, gloomy, mysterious aspect, with the temples captured in a few strokes indicating the rude, massive forms of the columns. In capturing his sublime experience of Paestum, Cozens managed to represent, much more effectively than Knight did, the peculiarity of the site. Whereas Knight kept at a distance, viewing some ruins in a landscape, Cozens represented the strangeness and drama of Paestum's architecture.

Interestingly, many years after the tour on which he viewed Paestum and Sicily according to traditional picturesque ideas, Knight developed a largely new theory of the picturesque, which changed the debate from a focus on design to one on aesthetics. The role of the beholder's eye in framing a view from a distance and the role of the body in creating movement in the view were now joined by a third element, the central role of the mind in interpreting the picturesque.

The Educated Mind:
The Theories of Knight and Price

Long after his travels of the 1770s, Knight formulated his aesthetic ideas in two theories of the picturesque, one in the form of a poem, *The Landscape: A didactic poem, in three books* (1794), and the other as an essay, *An Analytical Inquiry into the Principles of Taste* (1805). His aesthetics is distinguished by the interweaving of archaeological interests with the emotions aroused by a landscape as the focal point. In a note to the second edition of *The Landscape* (1795), Knight stated that the picturesque is 'merely that kind of beauty which belongs exclusively to the sense of vision; or to the imagination guided by that sense'.[104]

His ideas become clearer when we see them in the light of the writings of his contemporary Uvedale Price, because some of them were formulated as a direct reaction to Price's views (*The Landscape*'s title indicates that it was 'Addressed to Uvedale Price'). Price lived at Foxley, close to Payne's house at Downton, and published his *Essay on the Picturesque* in 1794, just a few months after Knight's poem. In *The Landscape*, which is illustrated with drawings by Thomas Hearne (Fig. 63), Knight formulated in poetry how art, architecture and landscape influence the sentiments of the spectator, but also how the spectator could influence these sentiments himself. In taking a certain position towards the objects he was looking at, the beholder could guide the outcome of his perception, so that the ensemble – the combination or fusion of architecture and landscape – became a harmonious, blended, picturesque whole.

In his poem, Knight criticised the landscape gardens of Lancelot 'Capability' Brown for being too 'perfectly' irregular. Instead, inspired by the paintings of Claude Lorrain and of Dutch and Flemish artists, he proposed as an ideal of picturesque beauty the rougher natural landscape. (Knight owned a large collection of drawings by Claude.) In other words, he concentrated on the impressions a landscape makes on the beholder, rather than focusing on the design of landscape gardens, which was Price's subject in his *Essay on the picturesque*. As Price's work was first published after *The Landscape*, Knight was compelled to bring out a second edition of his poem in order to counter Price's

ideas, which he did only a year later. Here he rejected Price's endeavour to define the picturesque as an aesthetic category between the beautiful and the sublime, a stance he maintained in his other publication treating the subject, the successful *Analytical Inquiry into the Principles of Taste.*

The most important difference between Knight and Price lay in their views of the basis of the picturesque. For Price the picturesque was an intrinsic characteristic of objects; for Knight it was a sensation produced in the beholder by the experience of viewing. In the idea that the picturesque was created largely in the mind of the observer, Knight may have drawn on David Hume's theory, according to which 'beauty is no quality in things themselves, it exists merely in the mind which contemplates them'.[105] His theory took this principle so far that he claimed no garden designer was necessarily required to design a landscape, because the design was, so to speak, conceived in the observers' minds. We find the same idea in William Gilpin's publications on picturesque tours,[106] where the observer, having the well-stocked mind of a connoisseur, functioned as a painter. To Price, the picturesque was present in all objects that were, for example, old, rough, irregular, shaggy or decaying. For Knight, there was a subjective concept of beauty.

In exploring the debate between Knight and Price, it will pay to turn aside for a moment to look at the influence on Knight of two Scottish thinkers of the next generation to David Hume (1711–1776) – Archibald Alison (1757–1839), clergyman and writer on aesthetics, and Francis, Lord Jeffrey (1773–1850), writer, judge and editor of the *Edinburgh Review*, to which Knight was a contributor. To them, beauty did not reside in the object itself but could arise only from an experience that caused an association of ideas in the mind. Thus the perception of beauty was considered an emotion. In his *Essays on the nature and principles of taste* (1790), Alison stated that aesthetic ideas emerge from the association of sensory impressions with emotions and ideas in the mind of the spectator. A second, enlarged, edition of his book was published in 1810, and by 1825 it had reached the sixth edition – an indication of its popularity. Francis Jeffrey shed an interesting light on the subject in his review of Alison's work in the *Edinburgh Review*, which he entitled 'Essay on Beauty' (1811). Both Alison and Jeffrey made clear that associations take place in the mind of the observer, so that the picturesque is a product of the recollection of various objects that are associated with it.[107] Only when the imagination makes a connection between the object and the

63a and b   Thomas Hearne, picturesque landscape (*above left*) and dressed landscape (*above right*), etched by Benjamin Thomas Pouncy, in Richard Payne Knight, *The Landscape* (1794), plates 1 and 2.

emotions, or the circumstances under which these emotions have previously been felt, can such associations be created.[108] Alison was influenced by Burke in thinking that the imagination's response to objects produced the beautiful or the sublime, but differed from him in believing that these were created through the association of ideas. As the ideas in question were linked to age, education and experience, they were reserved to the educated elite.

Knight applied the concept of the source of beauty propounded by Alison and Jeffrey to his theory that taste is always changing and cannot be fixed. Price's ideas are much closer to Burke's, though he added the third category of the picturesque to Burke's beauty and the sublime. But, as we have seen, while Price located the picturesque in objects, Knight connected it with the actions of the mind. Knight combined a pictorial and an associative picturesque. Visual beauty was not enough for him. Only by association is beauty heightened, and the pleasure of the mind enhanced. According to Knight, the associative picturesque helps in the appreciation of beauty in landscape and art in the sense that, even if the eye perceives something harsh or offensive, the imagination can correct the impression made upon the eye. Beauty is therefore no longer in the objects perceived, or intrinsic as Price argued, but is a mode of perception in the mind of the beholder.

Besides challenging Price, Knight also reacted to Burke, in his *Analytical Inquiry* almost ridiculing Burke and his writings.[109] Knight referred often to Longinus, and how grand and sublime ideas could be caused by nature.[110] But in his opinion the element of the terrible in the sublime, an element introduced in Burke's theories, was disputable.[111] In his critique of Burke's aesthetics, Knight referred to the latter's ambivalence about whether the sublime resides in the object or in the beholder. However, although Knight rightly detected the weak point in Burke's argument, he seems not to have comprehended – or simply to have disagreed with – Burke's point: that you have to be in a safe place to allow for sublime feelings. In Knight's view, fear is the opposite of the sublime.[112] Although *An Analytical Inquiry* is, in a sense, a reaction to Burke's *Philosophical Enquiry*, it principally demonstrates how perception, reaction and appreciation of art or nature take place, and how the pleasure taken in them can be enhanced. Given that he did not consider the picturesque an intrinsic property of objects, Knight focused on the aspect of experience that is the essence of the picturesque, and rejected the idea of fixed characteristics that are in themselves, of their nature, picturesque. To put it another way, because associations in the mind of the spectator create the picturesque, the object itself cannot possess this quality.

In his book, Knight wrote about poetry, literature, theatre, painting, sculpture and also architecture. He argued that 'the connection between [sensations, ideas and objects], howsoever spontaneous and immediate it may seem, is merely habitual, and the result of experience and observation.' In support of this point, he referred to John Locke, George Berkeley, Hume and Thomas Reid. He stated also that 'all sensation is really produced by contact' and 'immediate contact of the exciting cause with the organ'.[113] In order to enjoy the pleasure of a picturesque perception, associations were essential:

> pleasure . . . from painting, sculpture, music, poetry, &c. arises from our associating other ideas with those immediately excited by them . . . Nor are the gratifications, which such persons receive from these arts limited to mere productions, but extended to every object in nature or circumstance in society, that is at all connected with them: for, by such connection, it will be enabled to excite similar or associated trains of ideas, in minds so enriched, and consequently to afford them similar pleasures.[114]

People with a knowledge of the history of painting would, for example, make associations between any of the arts Knight named and landscape paintings by Claude, Poussin or

Giorgione, and this would cause pleasure in their minds because it would remind them of their enjoyment of these paintings. Like the 'je ne sais quoi' discussed in Chapter 1, such associations were restricted to an elite group of connoisseurs, 'persons conversant with the art of painting, and sufficiently skilled in it to distinguish, and be really delighted with its real excellences'.[115] Laymen, with their untrained eyes could not attain this:

> To all others, how acute soever may be their discernment, or how exquisite soever their sensibility, it is utterly imperceptible: consequently there must be some properties in the fine productions of this art, which, by the association of ideas, communicate the power of pleasing to certain objects and circumstances of its imitation, which are therefore called picturesque.[116]

In this discussion, Knight emphasised the act of perceiving an object and the effect this had on the beholder. The associations it set up could differ greatly, depending on one's knowledge of the subject. Perception was connected with memories of familiar images and threw a new light on images that were already known. The beholder, with his well-educated mind, could share his associations with other educated human beings, so that they became inter-subjective. This was another sense in which the picturesque differed from the sublime, which according to Burke could be appreciated by the ignorant no less – perhaps, in fact, even better – than the educated.

Gilpin, Price and Knight all made a connection between the picturesque and the Italian term *pittoresco*, used by the painters Giorgione and Titian to emphasise perception expressed in a harmonious ensemble of light–dark effects and colours.[117] As in *The Landscape*, in *An Analytical Inquiry* Knight demonstrated how the picturesque could be achieved in viewing a fusion of tints, either in ruins or landscapes, that would call to mind the works of Claude or other paintings: 'buildings, that are mouldering into ruin, whose sharp angles are softened by decay, and whose crude and uniform tints are mellowed and diversified by weather-stains and wall plants'.[118] These tints were blended after the manner of painters:

> Tints happily broken and blended, and irregular masses of light and shadow harmoniously melted into each other, are, in themselves, as before observed, more grateful to the eye, than any single tints, upon the same principle that harmonious combinations of tones or flavours are more grateful to the ear or the palate, than any single tones or flavours can be.[119]

In finding a definition for the picturesque as 'after the manner of painters', we can identify another opposition to the sublime: 'this very relation to painting, expressed by the word picturesque, is that, which affords the whole pleasure derived from association; which can, therefore, only be felt by persons, who have correspondent ideas to associate; that is, by persons in a certain degree conversant with that art'.[120] That this is contrary to the sublime can be easily explained by the accounts of Paestum. Chapter 1 showed that the temples baffled visitors. But this could not have happened if the architecture had set off trains of association in their minds, as Knight's theory of the picturesque prescribed. According to picturesque theories, visitors to Paestum would have been able to make associations only with the landscape, or with the combination of scenery and ruined temples, perceiving the scene before their eyes as if it were a painting, or an illustration of the classical texts that mentioned the site, as we have seen in Knight's narrative. They would have been quite unable to make any associations with the architecture itself, because it was so unfamiliar and strange: even a well-stocked mind did not help them there.

Of the contemplation of ruined buildings and scenery, Knight would claim:

Ruined buildings, with fragments of sculptured walls and broken columns, the moul-dering remnants of obsolete taste and fallen magnificence, afford pleasure to every learned beholder, imperceptible to the ignorant, and wholly independent of their real beauty, or the pleasing impressions, which they make on the organs of sight; more espe-cially when discovered in countries of ancient celebrity, renowned in history for learn-ing, arts, or empire. The mind is led by the view of them into the most pleasing trains of ideas; and the whole scenery around receives an accessory character.[121]

It is easy to see how far the evolution of his theory had carried Knight since his first exposure to Paestum: then the ruins were no more than an ornament of the landscape, subsumed in its picturesque qualities when the whole panorama was viewed from a dis-tance. Now, in his fully developed version of the theory, the historical facts relating to the site are a crucial element in its picturesque quality. An awareness in the mind of the observer of the lost ages and empires that the ruined temples represent is more impor-tant than the appearance of the ruins themselves, and gives the surrounding landscape an extra depth. By means of the trains of thought that arise from these associations, the scenery may become, in fact, an ornament of the ruins.

Associating Paestum

In spite of Knight's disenchantment with the temples and his judgement that a direct application of Paestum to architectural projects was impossible, the site did have signifi-cance for him. This was because it was at Paestum that, for the first time, he applied the picturesque to an observation in which landscape and ruins were combined. In his Sicil-ian diary, Knight put into words ideas that can be connected with the traditional meaning of the picturesque – the framing of a view as though it were a picture. Paestum gave him a lifelike and outstanding example of how to 'frame' a landscape containing ruins. Only some thirty years after his journey would Knight himself conceive a more complex theory of the picturesque.

In reading *The Landscape*, we can see that Knight was still making associations with his Sicilian tour: for instance, he referred to the 'pestilential flies' of Virgil's *Georgics*, but he also invoked less trivial elements in his comparison of the English landscape with the Italian:

> Bless'd land! – though no soft tints of pearly hue
> Mellow the radiance of the morning dew,
> And melt the tender distance to the eye,
> In one clear tinge of vary'd harmony[.][122]

In these lines appear the 'pearly hue' and the blending of colours that Knight had observed when leaving Naples in 1777, and which he had connected with Claude's paintings. But more significant than these references are the passages on the observation of nature or archi-tecture from a distance, where Knight emphasised the role of the beholder, and showed the importance of his position in relation to the object he perceived. Elsewhere in the poem he expanded on the idea of fusing tints, touched on in the passage quoted above, suggest-ing that this effect occurs when the observer contemplates the landscape at a distance:

> Where tow'rs and temples, mould'ring to decay,
> In pearly air appear to die away,

And the soft distance, melting from the eye,
Dissolves its forms into the azure sky[.][123]

In another passage Knight described what happens when the spectator retreats to a distance in order to appreciate the landscape:

For pond'rous masses, and deep shadows near,
Will shew the distant scene more bright and clear;
And forms distinctly mark'd, at once supply
A scale of magnitude and harmony;
From which receding gradually away,
The tints grow fainter and the lines decay.[124]

Then the aim of the picturesque is attained:

To lead, with secret guile, the prying sight
To where component parts may best unite,
And form one beauteous, nicely blended whole,
To charm the eye and captivate the soul.[125]

Although some experiences from the Sicilian journey appear in *The Landscape*, it would be too simple to state that the journey influenced the publication. In *An Analytical Inquiry*, Knight developed his theory of the picturesque much further and moved away from the traditional interpretation that was so evident in his Sicilian diary. However, some studies of architectural history in general or of Knight in particular have suggested that his visit to Paestum directly influenced his architecture and led to his use of the so-called Paestum order. While Knight was on his second tour of Italy, his house, Downton Castle in Herefordshire (designed by Thomas Farnolls Pritchard, 1774–8), was under construction, and from abroad he stayed in contact with his uncle and agent Samuel Nash about the progress of the building (Fig. 64). The architectural forms of the house were a translation of his ideas into stone: the exterior Gothic, the interior Greek. According to some scholars, the architect used the baseless Doric order of Paestum.[126] Knight himself never referred to Paestum in talking about his house. Rather, as he would explain later, the house was: 'ornamented with what are called Gothic towers and battlements without, and with Grecian ceilings, columns, and entablatures within'.[127] Another picturesque theorist, Humphry Repton, also approved the combination of Greek and Gothic:

64   James Sherriff, *View of Downton Castle, c.1780.* Herefordshire Record Office.

No critic has ever yet objected to the incongruity of it: for, as the temples, tombs, and palaces of the Greeks and Romans in Italy were fortified with towers and battlements by the Goths and Lombards of the Middle Ages, such combinations have been naturalized in that country, and are therefore perfectly in harmony with the scenery; and so far from interrupting the chain of ideas, they lead it on and extend it.[128]

In my opinion, linking the use of a baseless Greek order at Downton Castle to Paestum is far too direct: Knight could have chosen this order for the simple reason that it was in fashion. Moreover, these columns need not have derived from Paestum: they could just as easily have been inspired by the Sicilian temples Knight had seen. The application of a baseless order was not a direct result of his visit to Paestum, nor did it, as some scholars argue, prove that he had appreciated the temples for their architectural forms – we have seen that this was not the case. In fact, the order Knight used at Downton was probably derived partly from Greek baseless orders that he had seen during his expedition and partly from publications or engravings. It was an amalgamation of elements, a newly invented baseless Doric order, an abstraction, and not a direct copy of what he had observed. (We shall return to this argument in Chapter 6.)

Knight's poem *The Landscape*, written almost twenty years after the construction of his house, reveals his thoughts on the role of Paestum and other classical sites as design models:

> Still happier he (if conscious of his prize)
> Who sees some temple's broken columns rise,
> 'Midst sculptur'd fragments, shiver'd by their fall,
> And tott'ring remnants of its marble wall; –
> Where ev'ry beauty of correct design,
> And vary'd elegance of art, combine
> With nature's softest tints, matur'd by time,
> And the warm influence of a genial clime.
> But let no servile copiest appear,
> To plant his paltry imitations here;
> To shew poor Baalbec dwindled to the eye,
> And Pæstum's fanes with columns six feet high!
> With urns and cenotaphs our vallies fill,
> And bristle o'er with obelisks the hill!
> Such buildings English nature must reject,
> And claim from art th' appearance of neglect:
> No decoration should we introduce,
> That has not first been nat'raliz'd by use.
> And at present, or some distant time,
> Become familiar to the soil and clime[.][129]

Knight's remarks on the impossibility of replicating Mediterranean design in muddy Britain, and the need to make 'imported' classical architecture conform to local characteristics bring to mind John Soane's discourse on character in architecture and the conditions provided by regional characteristics:

If miniature representations of Grecian or Roman temples are placed in our gardens without consulting the genius of the place, and without proper attention to those circumstances and scenery which made the architects of antiquity prefer one style of building to another; if correct representations of the temples of Segesta and Paestum were placed on a fine dressed lawn, surrounded by beautiful shrubberies, from the want of appropriate scenery, they would appear clumsy and misapplied.[130]

Soane may have been inspired by Knight's ideas, propounded in *An Analytical Inquiry*, on the Italian style of gardening, with its imitation of Greek temples in town and country houses and its attempt to conform the surrounding scenery to the architecture:

Since the introduction of another style of ornamental gardening, called at first oriental, and afterwards landscape gardening (probably from its efficacy in destroying all picturesque composition) Grecian temples have been employed as decorations by almost all persons, who could afford to indulge their taste in objects so costly: but, though executed, in many instances, on a scale and in a manner suitable to the design, disappointment has, I believe, been invariably the result . . . In the rich lawns and shrubberies of England . . . they lose all that power to please which they so eminently possess on the barren hills of Agrigentum and Segesta, or the naked plains of Pæstum and Athens. But barren and naked as these hills and plains are, they are still, if I may say so, their native hills and plains – the scenery, in which they sprang; and in which the mind, therefore, contemplates them connected and associated with numberless interesting circumstances, both local and historical – both physical and moral, upon which it delights to dwell.[131]

In light of this general coverage of the status of classical architecture in the English context, other passages in *An Analytical Inquiry* clarify Knight's ideas about his house. He wrote that, after many years, 'the author of this inquiry' was still satisfied with 'the success

65   Thomas Hearne, the alpine bridge on the River Teme at Downton Castle, Herefordshire, 1785–6, ink and sepia, etched by Benjamin Thomas Pouncy, 1794. London, Victoria and Albert Museum, Prints and Drawings Collection, 2933-1876.

66 Thomas Hearne, distant view of Downton Castle. Private collection.

of the experiment . . . having at once, the advantage of a picturesque object, and of an elegant and convenient dwelling; though less perfect in both respects than if he had executed it at a maturer age'.[132] From this it seems clear that Knight believed the building of his own house to have been an expression of his ideas of the picturesque. The landscape at Downton consisted of the sparkling stream of the River Teme, running through a small gorge, in a surrounding ancient forest (Fig. 65); the garden and the house, looking out over the valley, were conceived as a combination of landscape and architecture in the mode of the paintings of Claude Lorrain that were in Knight's own art collection (Fig. 66). 'In the pictures of Claude and Gaspar [van Wittel],' he wrote, 'we perpetually see a mixture of Grecian and Gothic architecture employed with the happiest effect in the same building.'[133] The concept was still that of the early, painterly definition of the picturesque. Ballantyne, in his study of Knight, formulates it as follows: 'The fusion of the landscape at Downton with his body of ideas was Knight's authentically great aesthetic achievement, and having made it, initially in his mind and then in verse and in his purchases of paintings, he was able to draw on it for sustenance later in his retirement.'[134]

The picturesque concept had another advantage, that 'of being capable of receiving alterations and additions in almost any direction, without any injury to its genuine and original character'.[135] The house, with its asymmetrical plan inspired by medieval castles, became an example for architects designing castellated buildings in the period of the picturesque movement,[136] though it was not the first of its kind: it was preceded by two other asymmetrical, castle-like houses – Horace Walpole's Strawberry Hill (1748–77) and Vanbrugh Castle (1718–19) by John Vanbrugh.[137] Downton is often compared with Strawberry Hill and the later Fonthill (1795–1807), designed by James Wyatt for William Beckford; although they also have asymmetrical plans, they were not country houses like Downton but suburban villas.[138] For Knight it was not only the design of the building itself that was important, but its situation in the landscape, and Downton gave Knight a concrete opportunity to realise his early ideas on the picturesque. It is not difficult to draw parallels between what Knight was aiming for in Herefordshire and the picturesque scenic associations that some travellers, including Knight himself, perceived at Paestum.

Can we say, then, that the final stage in the development of the picturesque – that of association – was experienced at Paestum? As we have seen, on the spot Knight made associations with the writings of ancient authors. But those associations were not the spontaneous result of observing the monuments: they were conditioned by his earlier acquaintance with publications about Paestum, which quoted the same passages from those same authors. Apart from some passing references, Knight never again dealt with Paestum in his theoretical writings, and this raises an interesting point. Knight's theorising about how to observe in a picturesque way is very general and could be applied to many sites in Italy, England or indeed anywhere else. As we saw in his travel diary, the picturesque is a method of observing that can be used in any landscape, with or without ruins or buildings. In this sense Knight was never specific: he was explicit only in explaining how to apprehend picturesqueness, focusing on the beholder's mind, but never with reference to particular sites or works of architecture. In other words, he was somewhat imprecise about the picturesque architectural experience. There is an important difference between this approach and the sublime. Whereas the particular characteristics of a site or building cause sublime sensations, the reverse is true of the picturesque: here, the particularity of the site is of no significance – it is the characteristics of a distinct view that arouse the emotions.

Architecture as Painting

The picturesque enabled visitors to Paestum to formulate in words an experience of landscape and architecture: that is, it helped them to define a new awareness of the relationship between architecture and nature. In this sense, the stylistic changes that, according to many studies, the picturesque caused in nineteenth-century architecture can no longer be considered its only outcome. Because, in one of its manifestations, the picturesque framed the landscape and architecture and made it into a picture, it helped travellers to enjoy the sites they visited. Knight's report on Paestum is the perfect example of this process. This chapter has shown that the picturesque could provide other ways of viewing a site than the sublime. We have seen how an appreciation of the picturesque depended on distance, movement and the response of the mind through association, whereas the sublime overwhelmed the observer in the act of perceiving a work of art, a landscape or an object.

No traveller to Paestum who wrote about its scenery was so clear in speaking of the picturesque effect as Knight, who used the word itself in writing about the site at a notably early date, before much had been published on the subject. Although his travelogue predates the full working out of his theory of the picturesque, it is possible to see the seeds of his later thinking in his description of his response to the site: the text is a record of impressions and references, trains of thought and associations; it is clear that his interest was not in the temples themselves, but in their role as a feature in the landscape and the connections they suggested. The essence of the picturesque, the visual experience and the importance of sight, was expressed in the description of the object as it represented itself to the eye. The beholder viewed and described masses, colour and light, the elements of the architecture that were visible from a distance, and not what he thought it was really like. As such, the landscape and the building became a sort of theatre set.

It is possible to argue that Knight's ideas about the picturesque originated at Paestum. All the ingredients are there in his narrative. Paestum was the first stop on his picturesque tour. The landscape reminded him of paintings by Claude. And in retreating to observe the temples from a distance he created a view that resembled a painting of ruins in a landscape. After this quite connected beginning, his record becomes a free-form sequence of observations and thoughts with no clear structure, passing from colours, to the appearance of the stone, back to the landscape, and then to associations with ancient authors. Elements of his Paestum experience clearly informed his theories of the picturesque as they are expressed in *The Landscape* and *An Analytical Inquiry*.

However, another reading is possible. Knight did not go to Paestum unprepared. His account of the visit was composed around a stream of picturesque sensations. It was not accidental that Paestum fitted into this picturesque framework; in fact, it was moulded into it. When at first the site did not accommodate itself to his purpose, Knight consciously took the necessary position to make it fit: that is, he imposed his concept of the picturesque on Paestum. In his fully developed picturesque theory, Knight explained how the mind works and how the picturesque depends on associations. In actively directing his mind towards this outcome, he arrived at a projection of ideas onto Paestum rather than undertaking a creative process in the mind inspired by Paestum. In this sense, picturesque perception was different from sublime sensations, which were a direct reaction to the site. Instead of being baffled or overwhelmed by the object, the spectator, aiming to experience the picturesque, purposively adopted a certain position.

The outcome of this distance from the object of interest was that it no longer mattered whether Knight was at Paestum or at one of the sites in Sicily. The important thing was to observe Greek ruins in a vast landscape, taking a distant viewpoint so that, through the working of associations in the mind, he could come to a picturesque experience. Whereas Chapter 1 showed how the sublime helped to define what went on in the minds of travellers confronted by Paestum, the picturesque shows how Paestum could be adapted to an eighteenth-century learned mind. But, in the process, the site lost its particularity and became just like any other ancient site laid out in a beautiful landscape.

Movement, roughness, irregularity, variety and intricacy were the five characteristics described by Uvedale Price as the necessary constituents of picturesque architecture. While these elements were to be found at Paestum, travellers did not relate them to the picturesque. In the travelogues of Knight and also of Labrouste, Delagardette, Piranesi and Rohault de Fleury only the initial meaning of the picturesque – in the sense of architecture and scenery observed from a distance as if in a painting – is prominent. This kind of observation makes the site almost two-dimensional, and the beholder is important only in that someone must have the visual experience, an experience that does not involve spatial awareness. The three-dimensional site is flattened: architecture and landscape become painting. Even if the beholder moves around and takes different viewpoints, he frames each one so as to obtain the most picturesque view.

Whereas the sublime offers a kaleidoscope of experiences, the picturesque is rather limited. Paestum may have offered a unique experience of the sublime, but it did not do so for the picturesque. Although Richard Payne Knight was indebted to Paestum, the question remains whether he would not have had the same experience if he had first visited a site in Sicily. The sublime tells us more than the picturesque about Paestum. It helped travellers to comprehend and put into words the strangeness of it; it is site-specific. The picturesque is more restricted in this respect, and connects less effectively to the peculiarity of Paestum. Seen from a picturesque point of view, the temples themselves were not of interest: picturesque theorists were concerned with ruins and landscape in general. Viewed from close to, the ruins could not function as a picturesque object: the picturesque had little to say about the architectural details of the temples because it was mainly concerned with their situation as a scenic feature in their setting. In this way the temples became almost like follies in a garden.

Should we, therefore, conclude that the picturesque is useless for Paestum? Rather not, for it can offer insights if we connect it to the experience of architecture. In the traditional pictorial sense, the picturesque tells us nothing specific about the site, but the picturesque concept of movement does. What Knight failed to do, others did. Instead of moving within the architecture, Knight walked away in order to gain his painterly view of Paestum. But many travellers, in the attempt to comprehend the architecture, moved around the site, entered the temples and observed them from different viewpoints, in different weather, and in changing light. As we shall see, movement played a very significant role in the examination of Paestum, and the published descriptions stress this, though without calling the resulting perceptions 'picturesque'.

This chapter has analysed in depth the painterly way of seeing, through the educated eye, in terms of framing a scene from a distance. Knight's theory of the picturesque focusing on association was just as non-specific. The only aspect of the picturesque that says more about the architecture itself is movement. Picturesque experiences that arise from movement are specific because they depend on the changing view of both the inside and the outside of a building, a view that is determined by the features and details of the architecture. Here the spectator plays a much more active role. In the travellers' accounts of Paestum that refer to the picturesque this aspect hardly appears, whereas the framing aspect is common. But in the next two chapters we shall see how, in other approaches to Paestum, movement came into its own.

67 (following page) Detail of Fig. 94b.

PART TWO

Experiences
of Movement

CHAPTER 3

Entering Ruins:
A Physical Experience

> Reproductions give a false impression; architectural designs make [the temples] look
> more elegant and drawings in perspective more ponderous than they really are. It is
> only by walking through them and round them that one can attune one's life to theirs
> and experience the emotional effect which the architect intended. I spent the whole
> day doing this, while Kniep was busy making sketches.[1]

One thing is immediately clear from this passage from Goethe's *Italienische Reise*: the true
nature of observation. As Goethe said, there is an enormous difference between looking
at images of Paestum at home, and observing the temples on the spot: only by being inside
the ruins, wandering around them and examining them from different angles can the spectator start to comprehend what the architecture is really about. In representing himself
walking among the ruins, Goethe showed that he was aware of the importance of his own
presence in the process of observing. In the foregoing chapters, on the sublime and the
picturesque respectively, it became clear that in both varieties of aesthetic experience the
role of the observer is crucial. Now it is time to enter the temples. In this chapter we
shall look further into the role of the observer in architectural experience, focusing on
the awareness not of the experience itself but of being an observer having this experience. The experience is physical, one in which observers take the measure of the architecture in relating their own bodies to it.

Relating the architecture to one's own body took on a very literal meaning in John
Soane's case, when at Agrigento in Sicily he lay down to rest in the fluting of one of the
columns lying broken on the ground:

> Where shall we see buildings in this country [Britain] capable of giving a correct impres-
> sion of the magnificence of the Pantheon, the simple grandeur of the temples at
> Paestum, the sublime and imposing effect of the remains of the Temple of Minerva at
> Athens, the aweful and terrific grandeur of those at Segesta, Selinunte, and Agrigentum,
> particularly the Temple of Jupiter, which in its perfect state must have been the admi-
> ration of every beholder? The columns of this immense building, none of which are

68 (*facing page*) Detail of Fig.
74.

now standing, exceeded forty feet in circumference, and each flute, almost two feet in its concavity, presents a cradle of repose to the traveller wearied with wanderings over the frightful ruins of that stupendous pile![2]

Other architects had a similar idea. Jean Rondelet, for example, remarked that the columns of a Sicilian temple were so gigantic that a man could hide in their fluting.[3] By measuring the size of the Sicilian temple through the dimensions of his own body, Soane gained some awareness of the sublimity of the building: he literally took the measure of the flutings. As a consequence, his imagination of how the columns might originally have been when they were in place was stronger than the sensations he received from viewing temples that remained standing in Sicily. At Paestum, where the temples were still largely upright, the bodily sensations they gave rise to could not be so literal. There, the physical experience had more to do with Goethe's attempt to comprehend the temples by wandering through them – a complex and layered process of observing.

How did observation of the temples actually take place? What happened when travellers examined the ruins close to, and how did they relate these observations to themselves? In what way were they aware of being spectators? Before we can analyse the beholder's awareness of the process of observing the ruins at Paestum, and how the specific attributes of the site influenced perceptions, we must gain a more general idea of the consciousness of being a beholder of ruins. In this chapter we shall explore some eighteenth-century texts that show what thoughts were evoked by being inside ruins, first in the imagination, stimulated by accounts and images, and then in reality at Paestum. Were these different and, if so, in what way? Our analysis will thus oppose mind and body – entering the ruins in the mind's eye versus entering them in reality – and establish what this tells us about Paestum itself and, in a larger sense, about experiencing architecture.

Entering Ruins in the Imagination: Diderot and Robert among Painted Remains

As we saw in Chapter 2, texts by Uvedale Price and William Gilpin showed a preference for a ruin over an unimpaired building. Thomas Whately addressed the same issue in his *Observations on modern gardening* (1770):

> All remains excite an enquiry into the former state of the edifice, and fix the mind in a contemplation of the use it was applied to . . . they suggest ideas which would not arise from the buildings if entire . . . Whatever building we see in decay, we naturally contrast its present to its former state, and delight to ruminate on the comparison . . . At the sight of a ruin, reflections on the change, the decay, and the desolation before us, naturally occur, and they introduce a long succession of others, all tinctured with that melancholy which these have inspired.[4]

This passage is interesting because, although Whately, like Gilpin, compared the effect on the viewer of ruins as opposed to a complete building, his remarks are entirely different. Whereas Gilpin preferred ruined buildings for picturesque reasons, Whately went further, relating them to feelings of decay, producing melancholy. Instead of picturesque aesthetic sensations, drawing on cultural memory, ruins here produced sad sentiments in the viewer's soul.

This topos of ruins connoting decay appears also in the reflections of the traveller and member of the French Assemblée Nationale Constantin-François Chasseboeuf, Comte de Volney (1757–1820) in his *Les ruines, ou Méditations sur les révolutions des empires* (1791). The book, an immediate and enduring success, gives an example – both critical and political – of the melancholy that the decay of ruins can produce in the viewer's mind. The text, which contemplates the revolutions of empires, was written when the horrors of the French Revolution were still rife on the streets of Paris,[5] and it shows a certain ambivalence in idealising the human world while criticising present times.[6] Volney had travelled in Syria and Egypt for four years from 1782. The ruins of Palmyra made him meditate on the decline and fall of empires and on the passing of time: 'Often I met with ancient monuments, wrecks of temples, palaces, and fortresses; columns, aqueducts, and tombs: and this spectacle led me to meditate on times past, and filled my mind with serious and profound contemplations.'[7] Edward Gibbon (1737–1794) reflected on this aspect of decay when contemplating ruins in Rome: 'It was at Rome . . . , as I sat musing amidst the ruins of the Capitol, while the barefooted friars were singing vespers in the Temple of Jupiter, that the idea of writing the decline and fall of the City first started to my mind.'[8]

While Volney's and Gibbon's accounts have political implications in their reflections on the fall of lost empires, Whately's focused on the melancholy feelings that only ruins can produce. These were caused by observing the remains, and acknowledging that their former complete condition had changed. Such trains of association, created by the contemplation of times past as embodied in ruins, are to be found in many eighteenth-century texts. Writers used ruins to reflect on the oldness of the world, and in so doing made a connection between the ruins and their own being. For a more original approach we have to turn to Diderot.

The French writer and philosopher Denis Diderot (1713–1784) also reflected on the age of the world while looking at ruins, but instead of remaining a bystander who observed from afar he pictured himself in the world of the past: 'The ideas that ruins awaken in me are grand. Everything comes to nothing, everything perishes, everything passes. Only the world remains. Only time lasts. How ancient this world is! I walk between two eternities.'[9] Diderot's walking among the ruins is particularly intriguing because he was not recounting an experience *in situ*: he was regarding a painting of ruins, and imagining himself strolling inside them. As an art critic for the *Correspondance Littéraire*, Diderot reviewed paintings exhibited in the nine Salons held by the Académie des Beaux-Arts in Paris between 1759 and 1781.[10] In his commentary on the Salon of 1767 he wrote vigorous and fascinating reviews of the paintings of the French artist Hubert Robert (1733–1808).[11] These magnificent architectural compositions of fictive ruins (Figs 69–72) awakened in the mind of their critic a whole range of emotions and ideas. Diderot transformed the sublime, obscure impact of the ruins into a fictional experience, in which he stepped into the painting to observe the remains from close to:

> The lonely darkness, the majesty of the building, the grandeur of the structure, its size, the stillness, the muffled echo in the space would have made me tremble. I would never have been able to prevent myself from dreaming under that vault, from sitting between those columns, from entering your painting.[12]

This is a strikingly synaesthetic passage. All the senses work together to capture a physical experience. And this expression in a literary text – although clearly a fictional mind game – makes the reader sense the spatial experience.

Unlike Volney, who was among the ruins but contemplated them as a detached witness, Diderot truly aimed to enter, live and breathe the remains of a once great building. His

69 Hubert Robert, draughtsman in the ruins of a Doric temple, *c.*1760. Amiens, Musée de Picardie, M.P.Lav. 1894–188.

70 Hubert Robert, an artist among ancient ruins, 1796. St Petersburg, State Hermitage Museum, OR-46524.

71 Hubert Robert, *The Fountains*, 1787–8, oil on canvas. Chicago, Art Institute of Chicago.

72 Hubert Robert, ruins of a Doric temple, 1783. St Petersburg, State Hermitage Museum, GE-1293.

experience became even more personal when he was drawn into the ruins and started to reflect on how time stands still, how he walked between two eternities, how old the world was and how little he had lived. There, in all solitude, he came closer to himself: 'If the site of a ruin is dangerous, I tremble. If I promise myself privacy and safety there, I am more at liberty, more alone, more myself, closer to myself.'[13] In Diderot's musings, being alone was of paramount importance: only when he was alone could he be himself, forget about society and keeping up appearances, and cease to think about other people witnessing his actions: 'In this deserted refuge, lonely and vast, I hear nothing; I have broken with all of life's troubles. Nobody crowds in on me or listens to me. I can talk to myself very loudly, grieve, shed tears without restraint.'[14] The two modes of public and private in the eighteenth century, so accurately described in Richard Sennett's *The Fall of Public Man* (1974), are expressed here: 'The public was a human creation; the private was the human condition.'[15]

Diderot even advised Robert on how to create ruins and what they should look like, suggesting that he place fewer people in his paintings to enhance their effect:

> The effect of these compositions, good or bad, is to leave you in a sweet melancholy. We rest our gaze on the remains of a triumphal arch, of a portico, of a pyramid, of a temple, of a palace; and we reconsider ourselves; we foresee the ravages of time; and our imagination scatters on the earth the very buildings where we live. Immediately the solitude and the silence reign around us. We alone remain out of a whole nation that has ceased to exist. And that is the first line of the poetics of ruins.[16]

In the sublime experience of ruins, as we saw in Chapter 1, the spectator lost himself in his emotions but tried to regroup in order to overcome and formulate those sensations; but in the reflections we are considering here, the spectator consciously recorded the different stages in his observations, and the writer deliberately presented these to the reader. The beholder walked around and within the ruin itself, and in this process became a creator as well: he himself looked, he himself created what he saw. In expressing the effect of ruins on a solitary observer, Diderot referred not to the 'poetry' of ruins, but to their 'poetics' – that is, the poet's conscious creation of certain effects by bringing together all the different elements of the text. In his experience of wandering into Robert's painting, Diderot was himself creating or designing the ruins he was viewing.

We might put it like this: Robert's ruins caused Diderot not only to reflect on his own being but actively to construct the circumstances and associations that gave rise to these reflections. By means of the ruins, he came closer to himself, but he did this consciously: it was as if he built the ruins and devised the experience he had in wandering through them in his mind. Observation is transformed into a conscious act of imaginative creation. He even went so far as to say: 'We have to ruin a palace in order to make it an object of interest'[17] This is an idea that comes to mind when we look at Robert's *Vue imaginaire de la Grande Galerie du Louvre en ruines*, painted in 1796 (Fig. 73).[18] In actively constructing a ruin by destroying an existing building, Robert wanted to represent a meditation on the immortality of art: the Apollo Belvedere, a portrait bust of Raphael and the sculpture of a slave by Michelangelo have survived; thus, in Robert's view, a specific kind of art would live on but architecture would not.

Hubert Robert gained fame as a painter of ruins when he was a *pensionnaire* at the Académie de France in Rome from 1754. He prolonged his stay in Rome until 1765, and in 1760 visited Paestum with the painter Jean-Honoré Fragonard (1732–1806) and Jean-Claude Richard, Abbé de Saint-Non.[19] He was the first foreign artist to represent the

73 Hubert Robert, *Vue imaginaire de la Grande Galerie du Louvre en ruines*, 1796, oil on canvas. Paris, Musée du Louvre.

temples.[20] Unfortunately no travel diary or letters of Robert's have survived from that visit. Seven of his drawings have been preserved, representing three different views of the temples: a view of the Temple of Ceres (in two versions), a perspective view of the Neptune and Basilica temples (in four versions), and a view of the interior of the Neptune temple.[21] Three engravings after these drawings by Robert were included in the third part of Saint-Non's five-part *Voyage pittoresque, ou Description des royaumes de Naples et de Sicile* (1781–6), so it was more than twenty years after his sojourn that Robert's Paestum drawings were published.[22]

Robert's depictions of Paestum stand out for their original viewpoints. The perspective view of the Neptune and Basilica temples had become a rather common way of depicting them, and they were usually shown with people and some remains in the foreground. But Robert chose an unusual low viewpoint (Fig. 74; see also Fig. 44), and he avoided depicting tourists prominently among the ruins, as Antonio Joli and others would do (see Chapter 4); instead he chose to highlight the local people and animals resting among the fallen masonry, and to relegate to the background visitors examining the temples. Another noteworthy feature in this drawing is the Basilica, which has become a massive repetitive volume of columns in the distance. In a different (mirrored) version of this drawing of both temples, the Basilica is pictured in an equally sketchy way, but here Robert introduced a primitive hut in the foreground as a contrast to the two Greek buildings (Fig. 75). In the drawing of the Ceres temple, the site has an even more homely feel, thanks to the laundry hanging out to dry next to the remains of the building (Fig. 76; see also Fig. 46); this rurality alludes to Piranesi's etchings, in which the local farmers inhabited the temples (see Chapter 4). The columns of the temple are depicted as rather widely

74 Hubert Robert, drawing of the Temple of Neptune, with the Basilica in the background, *c.*1760, red chalk. Rouen, Musée des Beaux-Arts, donation George and Louise Chédanne, 1964, AG.1964.4.10.

75 Hubert Robert, drawing of the Temple of Neptune and the Basilica, 1760, red chalk. New York, The Pierpont Morgan Library, 1982.103.

76 Hubert Robert, *Vue du petit temple de Pestum dans le royaume de Naples* (Temple of Ceres), *c.*1760, red chalk. Besançon, Bibliothèque Municipale, Bibliothèque d'Étude et de Conservation, Collection Pierre-Adrien Pâris, vol. 451, no. 43.

spaced, and the focus is on the surroundings rather than the building, which has more of the air of a ruin than in the other drawings, so that nature and ruins almost become one. In this sketch the eighteenth-century archaeological site is far away; the ruin is timeless in its natural scenery. Robert's drawing of the interior of the Neptune Temple is the most remarkable of his depictions of Paestum (see the engraving of it in Chapter 2, Fig. 45). In choosing a very low viewpoint he seems to suggest that the temple has grown out of the soil. Perhaps this image gives us an inkling of how Robert saw the site – as if the rough, stumpy columns are a product of nature, created over time.

To understand more about how a consciously constructed ruin can be connected with the self-awareness of the observer, we have to turn to someone who used the representation of an existing (intact) building as a ruin to express his ideas.

A Self-Portrait in Ruins:
Soane's *Crude Hints*

The British architect John Soane (1753–1837), who was very much influenced by French eighteenth-century thought, used representations of ruins on several occasions, for diverse purposes. For instance, he had his project for the Bank of England (1788–1833) pictured as a ruin by Joseph Gandy (1771–1843) in 1830 (Fig. 77).[23] The design for this building, part renovation part expansion, was Soane's most important and longest-running project, and the one that he had represented most often: in exhibition and lecture drawings for

77 Joseph Michael Gandy,
the Bank of England
imagined in ruins, 1830.
London, Sir John Soane's
Museum, P267.

the Royal Academy, in his memoirs and in models.[24] His design combined Roman and Greek elements, using a Greek baseless Doric order combined with a Roman dome in the Princess Street vestibule, for example. That the project involved the demolition of parts of the existing early eighteenth-century bank may have enhanced the idea of representing his own building in ruins; and the fact that he was among the ruins of the old bank during the construction of the new may have prompted thoughts on the ephemerality of his own work. He designed, as it were, with ruins in mind, conscious of the future possibility of his building's ruined state.

The aerial drawing or cut-away perspective by Gandy might be interpreted both as a way of showing the ingenious structure of the building, and as a more visionary view of the future of Soane's work.[25] It may also have been an exercise in imagining what might eventually be left of the building and which parts would survive, viewing the project with an architect's mind. According to this concept of the *Ruinenwert* (literally 'ruin value'), a building was designed with the thought in mind that if it were to collapse the ruined structure that remained would please the eye and continue to exist. Gandy's view is impressive in setting the edifice in the London streetscape, and showing the erosion of the ground on which the bank stands. Trees grow inside the ruins. One corner of the building is still complete, but the rest consists of spaces open to the sky, broken vaults, solitary columns and extinguished chimneys. The spatiality of the building is emphasised, and although no people occupy the remains one can easily imagine them wandering among the ruins. Soane's masterpiece was depicted in this fashion towards the end of the building process. In 1833 he would resign, by which time he was nearly blind. With his departure in view, he wrote to the governor of the bank: 'The moment I cease to be the architect to the Bank, that moment will be one of the most trying and painful of my life.'[26] While picturing his design in ruins may well indicate the sombre thoughts of a man at the end of his life, that cannot be the only explanation, for much earlier, in 1798, Soane had the Rotunda and the Four and Five Per Cent Office of the Bank of England painted in ruins, also by Gandy, shortly after they were finished. The painting was exhibited at the Royal Academy in 1832 (Fig. 78).[27]

78 Joseph Michael Gandy,
imaginary view of the
Rotunda and the Four and
Five Per Cent Office of the
Bank of England in ruins,
1798. London, Sir John
Soane's Museum, P127.

Under the title *Architectural Ruins: A Vision*, Soane presented his own design as a Roman ruin, explored and excavated by archaeologists. Sadly, Soane's vision became reality when, in 1925, the Bank of England was demolished; a photograph of the Rotunda in ruins, startlingly similar to Gandy's painting, was published in *The Times*.[28]

Two other projects of Soane's involved the demolition of an existing building to make way for a new design. In 1800 he purchased Pitshanger Manor at Ealing, a house he had worked on at the age of 15 in the late 1760s, when the estate was owned by Thomas Gurnell and Soane was still in training in the office of George Dance the younger. Rebuilt in 1800–02, Pitshanger became his country home, and the pendant of his London House at Lincoln's Inn Fields; in both locations he exhibited antiquities and paintings, and both houses had basements where Soane kept plaster casts to educate young architects. During the rebuilding of Pitshanger Manor, Soane conceived the idea of erecting some artificial ruins in the grounds (Figs 79–80),[29] and in 1802 he claimed to have discovered them; to amuse his guests, he wrote a pastiche of an antiquary's letter, in which he speculated upon the origins of these 'Roman' ruins.[30] The house is interesting for another reason as well: the façade was to represent a self-portrait of the architect. In 1813, three years after he had sold Pitshanger Manor, Soane discussed it with his students at the Royal Academy, showing them an image of the façade (Fig. 81) and asking them to guess the function of the building:

> Describe the front. No man will suppose that the architect or owner had attained civic crowns for saving the lives of his fellow citizens . . . To judge of this species of building we should endeavour to discover the object to be attained: for example, in the building before you, if we suppose the person about to build possessed of a number of detached pieces of ornament . . . and . . . a desire to preserve them from ruin, or to form a building to give a faint idea of an Italian villa . . . this building may thus be considered as a picture, a sort of portrait.[31]

In this text the importance of the expressive character of architecture is underscored. While the owner of the house had won no civic awards for saving lives, it was clearly his mission

79 C. J. Richardson, bird's-eye view of Pitshanger Manor, Ealing, with the mock Roman ruins to the right of the house, 1835. London, Sir John Soane's Museum, Vol. 90/7.

to save art. He was a collector of fragments, who constructed the building through exploration. Thus Soane represented himself first and foremost as a collector of antiquities, wanting the façade to express what the house contained within. We might connect this idea to the *Hypnerotomachia Poliphili* (1499), attributed to the Venetian friar Francesco

80 George Basevi, sketch of the 'ruins' at Pitshanger Manor, Ealing, 1810. London, Sir John Soane's Museum, Vol. 87/11.

Colonna (1433–1527), which may have been Soane's model. This architectural book presents, in words and images, a hallucinatory world of classical ruins and gardens, and stresses the use of meaningful ornament, or ornament 'suitable to the use and character of the edifice', as Soane called it in his fifth lecture for the Royal Academy. Although the *Hypnerotomachia* was not well known in England at the time, Soane obtained several copies of it, studied it extensively and made translations of certain passages that he found significant.[32]

Whereas the ruins at Pitshanger were no more than a rather innocent and playful construction of artificial remains, a later project, a project of the mind, came much closer to conjuring up a hallucinatory world. In a manuscript entitled 'Crude Hints towards a History of my House', Soane reflected on his London house in ruins. Now, against the backdrop of representations of ruined buildings, speculations on artificial ruins and architecture as self-portraiture, we can examine how Soane staged his own imagined entry, as a spectator, into the ruins of his house. If Soane's light-hearted manuscript about the 'ruins' at Pitshanger Manor was supposed to entertain his friends, the 'Crude Hints', written in 1812, evolved into a gloomy personal account.[33] Soane drafted the work while he was engaged in remodelling his home at Lincoln's Inn Fields in London. On the 'ruins' of no. 13, which he demolished, he erected a new house, linked to the 'museum', which he had built earlier at the rear of no. 13, and to his existing house at no. 12. Thus, at the time 'Crude Hints' was written, Soane's home was a demolition site, though one that was developing into a complete building rather than decomposing into a ruin, as described in his manuscript.

In 'Crude Hints', Soane took on the persona of an antiquary of the future, presenting his house as a ruin, with visitors exploring the remains and speculating on its origins and function: a Roman temple, a burial site, a monastery or a magician's home. The house itself was envisaged as a chapel or a mausoleum, the staircase as a prison (comparable to Piranesi's etchings of imaginary prisons in the *Carceri d'invenzione* (*c*.1761), Fig. 82), where Soane imagined that victims were 'left to starve to death in all the horrors of endless darkness

81 John Soane, design for the front façade of Pitshanger Manor, Ealing, 1800. London, Sir John Soane's Museum, 14/2/3.

there to pay the forfeit of a little human frailty'; as he put it, 'here is food for meditation even to madness'.[34] The account mingles his ideas for the design of his own house, an evocation of the construction site, a survey of his collections of antiquities and casts, and a vision of the future. The antiquary proposes to 'look at [the ruin] merely as a dwelling, & that of an Artist, either an Architect or painter'.[35] Thus Soane constructed an externalised self-portrait. In presenting the creator of the ruins, he showed a man with failed ambitions, pursued by people who plotted against him:

> then persecutions and other misfortunes of a more direct & domestic nature preyed on his mind – he saw the views of early youth blighted – his fairest prospects utterly destroyed – his lively character became sombre – melancholy, brooding constantly over an accumulation of evils brought him into a state little short of mental derangement, his enemies perceived this – they seized the moment – they smote his rock & he fell as many had done before him and died as was generally believed of a broken heart.[36]

In the ruins of the house the antiquary finds a fragmentary inscription that reads 'et filii filiorum' ('and the sons of his sons'), of which Soane wrote:

> the man who founded this place piously imagined that from the fruits of his honest industry & the rewards of his persistence [and] application he laid the foundation of a family of Artists and that the filii filiorum of his loins might, smitten with the love of Art and anxious to shew their gratitude for the benefits & care & comfort they derived from it, dwell in this place from generation to generation.[37]

But Soane's two sons, John and George, did not live up to their father's ambitions, and neither of them became an architect.

The imagined ruins of his home in Lincoln's Inn Fields became for Soane an externalisation of his inner moods and character, a place where he constructed a melancholy and personal world. In writing an account of an antiquary exploring the ruins, the acts

Rediscovering Architecture

of constructing and externalising came together. Instead of a generation of artists who would occupy the house after him, Soane imagined it haunted by ghosts. The manuscript ends: 'Oh could the dead but for a moment leave their quiet mansions – could they but even look out of their Graves and see how posterity treated them and their Works what Hell could equal their Torments.'[38] An alternative version of the ending reads: 'Oh what a falling off do these ruins present – the subject becomes too gloomy to be pursued – the pen drops from my almost palsied hand . . .'[39] Suddenly here the voice changes from the third to the first person. Now, the ruins represent Soane's own decay. The price of architectural externalisation – of identifying too closely with one's own buildings – is, it seems, that like them one becomes subject to decay.

These writings on ruins by Whately, Volney, Diderot and Soane introduce some ideas that had become eighteenth-century topoi. General themes of decline, decay, the ephemeral life of human beings set beside the passing of endless time, and the smallness of human concerns in the context of unfolding history would occur more and more often in cultural and philosophical writings towards the end of the century. But at the same time, the reflections on ruins that we have examined show a slow shift from the general towards the more personal, until with Soane we find the observer creating a fictive ruin as an image of his life and character.

The descriptions and depictions of ruins by Diderot and Soane, discussed above, are all fictionalised, consciously created accounts. These writers entered ruins only in their minds, and found there the spur to reflect on themselves and their own being. But what happened when ruins in the mind were exchanged for ruins in reality? We shall see that the self still plays a role, but in a different way. Instead of the conventional themes of ruin and decay, the Paestum accounts of the experience of being inside and around the ancient temples are both more individual and more original. They tell us about the process of looking at ruins, and about the awareness of the physical self in space, as opposed to the self of the imagination. From imagined ruins let us therefore turn to actual ruins.

Mass and Space:
Goethe and Forsyth in the Temples

Travellers to Paestum who wrote about their visits all stressed the importance of seeing the monuments with their own eyes, and remarked on the significant difference between looking at images of the site and seeing it in person. It is clear that an awareness of their own presence among the ruins – in actuality as opposed to in imagination – was crucial. The accounts often unfold the process of experiencing and observing the temples, in which physicality played an important part.

The architect Eugène-Emmanuel Viollet-le-Duc (1814–1879), who travelled to Italy at the age of 22, wrote in his diary:

> This morning at 5 we leave for Paestum; sad region, wilderness, marsh, heavy air; at 10 we arrive at Paestum. The three temples, of Ceres, Neptune, and the Basilica; pleasing proportions of the temple of Ceres; the Neptune [temple] is a bit heavy; columns too strained in the Basilica; I draw the temple of Neptune; heavy air, sun, I am not at ease.[40]

Viollet-le-Duc's entire account breathes discomfort. The landscape was miserable, deserted, the atmosphere humid and the sun burned. His first, scribbled impressions of the temples were far from enthusiastic. He found the Temple of Neptune too massive, and the form of the Basilica's columns strange. All in all, Paestum unsettled him and he had difficulty in coming to terms with its architecture. Worse still, he could find nowhere to eat, having refused a meal of rotten figs and suspect meat in a filthy *cantina*, and on the return journey had to share the carriage with a man suffering from the plague. But when he arrived at Salerno, he noted his final thoughts about the site, which were very different from those he had expressed earlier: 'The temple of Neptune is of rare construction, all three [temples] are made of a very hard stone pitted with holes; some stuccoed parts survive.'[41] Now the Neptune temple (Fig. 83), which before had been too massive, with proportions less satisfying than those of the Temple of Ceres, was superior in its construction to the other two. The strong contradiction between his perceptions recorded *in situ* and the entirely different opinions expressed after he had come away is striking.

Many travellers made the same remark about the pre-eminence of the Neptune temple, so we could say that Viollet-le-Duc turned from his first personal impressions to a conventional view. But these fragments show that Viollet-le-Duc focused on the tectonic elements. Although the architecture of the Neptune temple was 'heavy', he admired the way it was constructed, and noted the hard, porous stone and the presence of stucco. So, despite physical distress and his initial qualms about the form of the buildings, what the architect focused on and appreciated at Paestum were the construction of the temples and their materials. Furthermore, although Viollet-le-Duc did not refer to wandering among the ruins, he made clear that being at the site was an intensely physical experience. His feelings of unease in surroundings he found horrible, his difficulty in coming to terms with the architecture of the temples, the unpleasant weather and the lack of facilities for visitors all contributed to a sensation of extreme physical discomfort.

Charles Dupaty, in his travel diary of 1785, remarked upon the vile materials of which the massive columns were made, and stressed how acutely aware he was, in observing them, of their weight, by comparison with Greek columns in general: 'It is not the character of Grecian columns to crush the earth; they lightly mounted into the air; these, on the contrary, weigh ponderously on the earth; they fall.' In evoking human sensations of weight and gravity, Dupaty aptly put into words the singularity of the temples, which was hard to capture visually: 'The Grecian columns had an elegant, slender shape, around which the eye continually glided; these have a wide and clumsy form, around which it is impossible for the eye to turn: our pencils and our graving tools, which flatter every monument, have endeavoured in vain to beautify them.'[42] Dupaty was perhaps alluding here to the experience of wandering about among the ruins. When Goethe visited Paestum in 1787, he asserted that it was only by walking through and around the temples, observing them from every side and angle, that he could understand what it was impossible to see when looking at reproductions (see the quotation with which this chapter begins).[43] Goethe explained how the movement of his body through the temples, the conscious process of relating it to the open spaces and the masses of the architecture, allowed him to come to an understanding of them. In a way, he adjusted himself to the temples, and by doing so tried to experience the sensations this engendered. He believed that this gave him an insight into what the ancient architect had been aiming at in these buildings. By clinging to the tectonic elements of the temples he sought to comprehend their architecture. But he also took account of the spaces between the columns, and described how in the act of walking between them he found that the columns became familiar to him. In a sense, these movements were necessary to him, because the awkward forms of the architecture almost frightened him (as we saw in Chapter 1): 'Our eyes and, through them, our whole sensibility have become so conditioned to a more slender style of architecture

83 Eugène-Emmanuel Viollet-le-Duc, interior of the Temple of Neptune, 1836, brown wash. Paris, Musée d'Orsay, RF 3906.

that these crowded masses of stumpy conical columns appear offensive and even terrify-ing.'[44] In remarking that only through movement could one impart real life to the temples, Goethe suggested feelings of empathy, which would not be theorised as such until Robert Vischer described what he called *Einfühlung* in 1873.[45] We shall see, later in this chapter, how important this concept is for an understanding of bodily observation.

As well as using the experience of bodily movement in space, Goethe employed another means of coming to an understanding of Paestum:

I pulled myself together, remembered the history of art, thought of the age with which this architecture was in harmony, called up images in my mind of the austere style of sculpture – and in less than an hour I found myself reconciled to them and even thank-ing my guardian angel for having allowed me to see these well-preserved remains with my own eyes.[46]

By calling upon his art-historical memory, Goethe transformed his initial bewilderment and confused impressions into comprehension of, and even familiarity with, the architec-ture. One way of coming to terms with the strangeness of Paestum's architecture was to explain it as very ancient, and thus to see the temples as representing the beginnings of architectural history and development – in fact, the origins of architecture. As such, it pre-dated classical architecture and the sophisticated elegance that many eighteenth-century travellers thought was characteristic of buildings in ancient Greece. We shall explore this idea further in Chapter 5. While Goethe described the bodily impact of observing the temples, we must turn to other accounts to find more details of how this physical obser-vation took place.

Joseph Forsyth (1763–1815), a Scottish schoolmaster and traveller, offered an interesting insight into the different roles of the observer in his *Remarks on Antiquities, Arts, and Letters, during an Excursion in Italy in the Years 1802 and 1803* (1813). Forsyth had been arrested 'as a British subject' in Turin in 1803, and remained in prison until 1814; his book was written partly to persuade Napoleon to release him. In the section on Paestum Forsyth recounted his journey to the site, his initial reactions and his examination of the three temples, in all of which he was constantly aware of his own presence in his observations. The perils of the journey[47] were rewarded by a compelling first impression: 'On entering the walls of Pæstum I felt all the religion of the place. I trod as on sacred ground. I stood amazed at the long obscurity of its mighty ruins.'[48] That Forsyth included a religious element in his account is very distinctive. Other travellers to Paestum hardly referred to the sacred associations of the site, or at least mentioned them far less prominently. Perhaps Forsyth was reacting to the aura of the temples, with their connotations of sacrifice, worship and ritual, or simply to the ancientness of the buildings. We might also relate his associations to the sublime: for instance, Longinus connected lofty feelings with divine forces.[49]

The first impact of the temples was confirmed by Forsyth's further observations. He wrote of the antiquity of the temples, their wholeness and simplicity, and the variations of mass and space that they presented:

> These wonderful objects, though surveyed in the midst of rain, amply compensated our little misadventures. Taking into view their immemorial antiquity, their astonishing preservation, their grandeur or rather grandiosity, their bold columnar elevation, at once massive and open, their severe simplicity of design, that simplicity in which art generally begins, and to which, after a thousand revolutions of ornament, it again returns; taking, I say, all into one view, I do not hesitate to call these the most impressive monuments that I ever beheld on earth.[50]

Forsyth related the simplicity of the architecture and lack of ornament to the age of the temples, reasoning that purity of form proved they had been constructed in very early times. But, more significantly, it is clear from his remarks about the massive columns and the open spaces between them, that he came to terms with the architecture by means of the movement of his body. Architecture became dynamic as the beholder perceived the alternation between mass and space, openness and closedness, through physical experience – the responses of the embodied mind.

In this passage, Forsyth tried to express something that was not easy to capture in words: a feeling of awe, but also a sensation that he could not immediately define. The city walls seemed to provide a defence against the dangerous world he had traversed on his way to the site, to the three temples standing on a silent plain. Together with Forsyth, the reader can pause for a moment to breathe in and capture the scene before entering the temples and exploring them thoroughly. After the dangers faced by the travel party and the chaotic circumstances of their arrival, Forsyth was suddenly alone and overwhelmed in his contemplation, in 'one view', of the awe-inspiring temples standing on their almost 'sacred ground'.

Forsyth then turned to the architecture. He did not attempt to date the 'sage, austere and energetic' ruins, but tried to describe their origins by situating their proportions in relation to the Parthenon. Despite the difference between them, he did not believe the temples of Paestum to be older than that in Athens, because the proportions of an order 'are but a matter of convention'. In fact, Forsyth expressed his dislike of, and unfamiliarity with, this specific order, the 'Pæstan Doric', arguing that architects who worked in the metropolis would be bound to construct more elegant buildings than those 'who were confined to the ruder materials and tastes of a remote colony'. He stated that as one approached the temples and studied them in detail, their first impact from a distance was transformed.

Throughout his account Forsyth defined the temples as 'structures', and portrayed them by describing all their tectonic elements: columns, intercolumniations, capitals, architraves, friezes and cornices. His awareness of aspects of load and support led to some interesting observations: 'the members which support are here larger than those supported' (unlike 'Latin Doric'), the architrave larger than the frieze, and the frieze than the cornice; 'these very peculiarities create an exaggeration of mass which awes every eye, and a stability which, from time unknown, has sustained in the air these ponderous entablatures. The walls are fallen, and the columns stand; the solid has failed, and the open resists.'[51] This could almost be a description of Soane's representation of the Bank of England as a ruin, with its emphasis on the vaults and open spaces. But above all, Forsyth here associated architecture with bodily reactions and physical processes such as gravity. These bodily experiences he analysed in terms of the physical laws at work in architecture, noting how at Paestum these laws seemed to have been ignored. Instead of an abstract, intellectual analysis of proportions, Forsyth relied on a dynamic navigation through architectural space, and tried to explain the effects of this on the mind and the imagination: with every step, he experienced another vista. Technical knowledge is not constitutive of these observations: close looking and the appeal to one's own physical experience are.

To Forsyth, the orders in general were a natural necessity in a hot climate:

> In such climates a place of assembly required nothing but shade and ventilation; in other words, nothing but a roof and just as much vertical buildings as could support it – hence the groves of pillars which we find in Egypt; but the angles of pillars were found to obstruct the circulation of a crowd – hence columns; and, as plinths and tores would impede the passage of feet – hence baseless columns, like these of Pæstum.[52]

What is notable here is that Forsyth approached the particular architecture of Paestum from the viewpoint of the user of the architectural space. By analysing his own physical movement and circulation within an architectural structure, he accounted for the choices made in architectural design.

Forsyth also made some interesting remarks on scale and architecture, asserting that, according to Vitruvius,

> intercolumniations should be in direct proportion to the relative thickness of the columns. Now these [the columns at Paestum], in proportion to their height, are the thickest columns that I have seen, and yet their relative distance is the least. This closeness makes the columns crowd advantageously on the eye, it enlarges our idea of the space, and gives a grand, an heroic air to monuments of very moderate dimension.[53]

The contrast between massive limestone and open space, between simplicity and ornament in Forsyth's account is telling. He referred to Vitruvius, but his experience contradicted what Vitruvius wrote, and can much better be understood in terms of nineteenth-century theories of empathy. Thus, Forsyth did not invoke the historical use or function of the buildings, but focused, in an original, very articulate and thoroughly observed way, on the straightforward representation of structure and tectonic processes and on the impression the temples made on him in the present moment. Forsyth's account of Paestum provides us with some clues as to how visitors might examine the temples. Certainly, the way in which he explored the ruins makes one thing clear: to understand the nature of the temples it was necessary not only to visit them in person but, in the course of viewing them, consciously to cultivate an awareness of one's body in the architectural space.

Sensing Ruins: Eustace and Shelley

This same awareness is noticeable in the account of Paestum written by the poet Percy Bysshe Shelley (1792–1822). As we saw in Chapter 1, Paestum was on the itinerary of a tour he made of Italy with Mary Shelley and Claire Clairmont, during which, between April 1818 and April 1819, he wrote extensive letters to Thomas Love Peacock (1785–1866), in the form of a journal.[54] Shelley was familiar with the writings of Forsyth and with another much read narrative of travels in Italy, *A Tour through Italy* (1813) by John Chetwode Eustace (1762–1815), who made his Italian journey in 1802–3.[55] Eustace was an Irish Roman Catholic priest, a Hellenist at Cambridge and an intimate of Burke.

When Eustace visited Paestum he recorded, just as Forsyth had, the dangers of the site. He wrote about the presence in the area of *banditti*, one of whom had shot his own wife and had become 'a wanderer in the forests, and amid the ruins of the plain of Pœstum . . . He was armed with a gun and pistols; and was on the whole an object very unwelcome to the eye in such a solitude.'[56] Besides the hazards of the journey, Eustace's account contains all the elements that are recurrently referred to by travellers to the site. The temples struck Eustace particularly, though he viewed them as strange heaps of stones rather than as buildings: 'The unusual forms of three temples rising insulated and unfrequented, in the middle of such a wilderness, immediately engrossed our attention. We alighted, and hastened to the majestic piles; then wandered about them till the fall of night obliged us to repair to our mansion.'[57] He portrayed the experience as an intense assault on all the senses, working together to take in an impression of Paestum:

> The night was bright, the weather warm but airy, a gale sweet and refreshing blew from the neighboring hills of *Acropoli* and *Callimara*; no sound was heard but the regular murmurs of the neighboring sea. The temples silvered over by the light of the moon, rose full before me, and fixed my eyes till sleep closed them. In the morning the first object that presented itself was still the temples, now blazing in the full beams of the sun; beyond them the sea glittering as far as sight could reach, and the hills and mountains round, all lighted up with brightness. We passed some hours in revisiting the ruins, and contemplating the surrounding scenery.[58]

The contrast between the situation and the ancient remains impressed him: 'Amid . . . scenes rural and ordinary, rise the three temples like the mausoleums of the ruined city, dark, silent, and majestic.'[59] Even the history of the site was a mystery: 'Obscurity hangs over, not the origin only but the general history of this city, though it has left such magnificent monuments of its existence.'[60] True to form, Eustace made reference to Virgil's writings on Paestum, in a passage that recalls Richard Payne Knight's educated response to Paestum:

> Mount *Alburnus* inseparably united with the *Silaris*, in Virgil's beautiful lines, and consequently in the mind of every classical traveller, rises in distant perspective, and adds to the fame and consequence of the stream by the magnitude of his form and the ruggedness of his towering brow. Ilex forests wave on the sides of the mountain, and fringe the margin of the river, while herds innumerable wander through their recesses, and enliven the silence of the scene by perpetual lowings. As the country still continues flat and covered with thickets, the traveller scarce discovers *Pœstum* till he enters its walls.[61]

When Eustace contemplated the antiquity of the temples, he introduced – as other travellers had also done – an important idea that determined the eighteenth-century discourse on Paestum – namely, primitivism (which we shall explore further in Chapter 5):

to judge from their form we must conclude that they are the oldest specimens of Grecian architecture now in existence. In beholding them and contemplating their solidity bordering upon heaviness, we are tempted to consider them as an intermediate link between the Egyptian and Grecian manner, and the first attempt to pass from the immense masses of the former to the graceful proportions of the latter. In fact, the temples of *Pæstum*, *Agrigentum*, and *Athens*, seem instances of the commencement, the improvement and the perfection of the Doric order.[62]

Taken as a whole, Eustace's account presents a very complete picture of the elements that characterised the eighteenth-century debates about Paestum, and summarises the topics that preoccupied their participants. His descriptions of the three temples are not of great interest, except for his remarks on the stylobate, where he alludes to his physical examination of the architecture: 'In common to all it may be observed, that [the temples] are raised upon substructions forming three gradations (for they cannot be termed steps, as they are much too high for the purpose) intended solely to give due elevation and relievo to the superstructure.' In a note he added: 'Ordinary steps seem to sink under the weight, and are quite lost in the cumbrous majesty of the Doric column.'[63] From this it is clear that he investigated the temples by walking around and through them. In considering their substructures he made a comparison between steps that can be climbed and 'gradations' that were far too high to be negotiated in that way; and he explained this feature by observing, in terms suggesting an almost physical sense of the crushing weight of the stone, that the columns demanded a more massive underpinning than simple steps could provide.

Shelley was strongly influenced by Eustace's book. In observing the Coliseum, he took a viewpoint within the structure, just as Eustace had done, and thereby showed the spectator's disorientation and sense of lack of control over the object: 'the effect of the perfection of its [exterior] architecture adorned with ranges of Corinthian pilasters supporting a bold cornice, is such as to diminish the effect of its greatness.'[64] Shelley imagined how the building might have appeared in its original state but could hardly believe that it would have been as sublime and impressive as the ruin. He paid no attention to its historical context or iconography, but simply expressed his awareness of being the building's observer. Because he focused on its material presence, and not on its construction, function or appropriation, the architecture became, for Shelley, almost ahistorical. After visiting the building several times, he wrote a romance entitled *The Coliseum* (1818) in which the same features recur.[65]

Shelley was clearly very susceptible to architecture, and he often expressed the effect it had on the spectator. In comparing St Peter's in Rome with the Pantheon, he stated that the Pantheon is:

> totally the reverse of . . . St. Peter's. Though not a fourth part of the size, it is as it were the visible image of the universe; in the perfection of its proportions, as when you regard the unmeasured dome of Heaven, the idea of magnitude is swallowed up & lost. It is open to the sky, & its wide dome is lighted by the ever changing illumination of the air. The clouds of noon fly over it and at night the keen stars are seen thro the azure darkness hanging immoveably, or driving after the driving moon among the clouds.[66]

His letters contain many reflections on Italian ruins in which the remains of ancient buildings are almost amalgamated with nature. For instance, in his account of the Baths of Caracalla, references to natural and architectural elements are integrated: nature softens the decaying buildings, which seem to borrow some of nature's timelessness – 'their vast desolation softened down by the undecaying investiture of nature'.[67] Shelley associated the Greeks with nature, and often reflected on the harmony between nature and architecture in their culture. In contemplating the Temple of Jupiter in Pompeii, he imagined the Greeks living close to nature, and suggested that it was this that accounted for the quality and perfection of their art:

> They lived in a perpetual commerce with external nature and nourished themselves upon the spirit of its forms. Their theatres were all open to the mountains & the sky. Their columns that ideal type of a sacred forest with its roof of interwoven tracery admitted the light & wind, the odour & the freshness of the country penetrated the cities. The temples were mostly upaithric [open-roofed]; & the flying clouds the stars or the deep sky were seen above.[68]

He connected Pompeii to Greece, asking himself: 'If such is Pompeii, what was Athens?'[69]

Shelley's view of Greece is very particular, underlining the connection of art to nature, and imagining the living conditions of the Greeks. Before his tour Shelley had gained a thorough knowledge of Italy and its ancient sites and of Greek art. He had read Volney's *Les ruines* (1791), and in the summer of 1818, while he was translating Plato's *Symposium* and writing *A Discourse on the Manners of the Ancient Greeks Relative to the Subject of Love*,[70] he read Jean-Jacques Barthélemy's *Voyage du jeune Anacharsis en Grèce* (1788). Barthélemy (1716–1795), a French archaeologist and numismatist, cast his book as a travelogue in which the young Scythian philosopher Anacharsis visited the sites of classical Greece and analysed Greek civilisation. The book became highly esteemed and was an immense success in France and the rest of Europe, contributing to the Greek revival. Then, in December 1818, Shelley began to read Johann Joachim Winckelmann's *Geschichte der Kunst des Altherthums* (1764) and continued to do so almost daily until 3 January 1819.[71] Thanks to this process of self-education, and not least to the influence of Eustace's writings, Shelley developed a fervent admiration for Greek art and architecture, asserting constantly its superiority over that of the Romans, and its simplicity, beauty and grandeur.

Shelley's Italian tour was deliberately planned around sites where he could see Greek art and architecture, about which, even before leaving England, he had very well-defined aesthetic ideas. Unhappily, his plans to visit Greece itself in 1821–2 failed because the political situation in the country was too dangerous. In the preface to his poem *Hellas* (1821), Shelley wrote: 'we are all Greeks . . .', and claimed that he was reading 'scarcely anything but Greek'.[72] We may assume, therefore, that he went to Paestum in February 1819 with his mind full of ideas about the Greeks and their culture. But when he reached the site all this knowledge seems to have been put aside. His account of his observations at Paestum makes nothing of his prior knowledge or his ideas about history. Instead he concentrated on the experience of space.

In light of his extensive reading and thinking about Greek culture, we might expect that, in describing Paestum, Shelley would write about the superiority of Greek temple architecture, or reflect on the lost empire of the Greeks, as Volney had done. His letter to Peacock about his visit can certainly be interpreted as voicing a desire to see the remains of Greek culture. But at Paestum something happened to the poet that needs to be related to his other accounts of architecture in Italy – Pompeii, the Baths of Caracalla, the Coliseum and the Pantheon. Shelley dissociated his Paestum experiences from his Greek erudition. In his record of the visit he pondered on the ideal tourist, who is attracted to what reflects his or her own values and desires: 'neither the eye nor the mind can see itself, unless reflected upon that which it resembles'; this suggests that observation is always a form of self-identification.[73] A projection of bodily recognition was the starting point for real perception, a sequence that took on a clear form in his journal of Paestum.

Shelley started his account by saying that in this Greek city 'there still subsist three temples of Etruscan architecture'. Apart from the fact that this remark is untrue – the temples are Greek, not Etruscan – it is also the only reference Shelley made to any historical context for the site. Just as in his other descriptions of Italian architecture, he was not interested in the history of the ruins, but focused on the relation between nature and architecture and the impression they made on the traveller. The description is constructed around an experience received through the different senses, just as in Eustace's case: Shelley and his companions were regaled by sights, smells, sounds and sensations as they approached the deserted site along muddy roads in stormy weather, through orange and lemon groves carpeted with wild violets. Depicting the relation between the temples and their surroundings, Shelley represented the scenery as if it were a form of architecture, a magnificent 'amphitheatre of mountains', and characterised the temples as 'sublime & massy colonnades skirting the horizon of the wilderness'.[74]

In describing the temples one by one he focused on their proportions, on their great mass and on the simple and unornamented architecture. Of the Ceres temple, he made some puzzling remarks: 'These columns do not seem more than forty feet high, but their perfect proportions diminish the apprehension of their magnitude, it seems as if inequality & irregularity of form were requisite to force on us the relative idea of greatness.'[75] Shelley seems to state that, although the proportions of the whole temple were exceedingly heavy, the 'perfect proportions' of the columns had the effect of reducing the uneasiness (or maybe even fear) that their dimensions produced in the spectator; an idea of comparative size – that is, the ability to see architecture in relation to the human body and scale – depends on differences in form. By this Shelley probably meant that, although the general impression of the temples is vast and massive, the fact that the columns have fine proportions counterbalances this feeling. This effect can be sensed only when the spectator relates his or her body to the architectural space.

Shelley's intentions can be read more clearly in his account of the Neptune temple:

The co[lumns] in all are fluted and built of a porous volcanic stone which time has dyed with a rich & yellow colour. The columns are one third larger & like that of the 1st [temple] diminish from the base to the capital, so that but for the chastening effect of their admirable proportions their magnitude would from the delusion of perspective seem greater not less than it is; though perhaps we ought to say not that this symmetry diminishes your apprehension of their magnitude, but that it overpowers the idea of relative greatness, by establishing within itself a system of relations, destructive of your idea of its relation with other objects, on which our ideas of size depend.[76]

In Shelley's experience, therefore, the fine proportions of the columns moderated the effects that perspective would otherwise create and exercised a restraining influence on the appearance of the building as a whole. The same was true of the Basilica. We might interpret this statement as meaning that one well-proportioned element controls the apparent size of the whole. But the most significant point is that Shelley experienced the disorientation of his earlier learned notions of scale: the Temple of Neptune overturned common ideas of size and scale, which depend on comparison with external objects.

Thus, Shelley argued, the Neptune temple overpowers the spectator because it has its own system of relations (of scale and proportion): common notions of relative size do not apply here, because the building sets its own standards. By walking about inside the temple, Shelley tried to comprehend its perspective, proportions and scale, and the effect they produced on him. In this account, where experience stands above knowledge, he demonstrated how the disruption of common ideas of scale in a monument can lead to an acute awareness of a physical experience: as he allowed himself to depend on physical perception, the architecture became overwhelming.

The Body in Architectural Space

The intense physicality of actual experience at Paestum is compelling. It is entirely different from the eighteenth-century theoretical discourse on ruins, in which the remains of architecture caused the spectator – Diderot or Soane, for example – to reflect on himself, his life and character. While Paestum sometimes inspired reflections on the self, these reflections were not so much thoughts about one's own existence, but rather observations about one's physical relation to the architecture, about the body in space. The temples were puzzling to visitors: because they offered little more than tectonic elements, space, material, scale and situation, it was not easy to comprehend them immediately. But since a building is three-dimensional, one can walk around and through it in order to try to grasp its essence. This is what travellers did: they took the measure of, or positioned themselves in relation to, the temples, by setting the architecture against the human body. This way of observing architecture broke with Vitruvius's ideas in *De architectura*; while Vitruvius described proportions, ground plans and orders, he did not stress the sense of a building as a three-dimensional whole. It was exactly this three-dimensionality that was explored at Paestum, and explained in the accounts – how movement, looking, touching and sensing the architecture enabled the viewer to understand and come to terms with a building.

The temples invited the visitor to move around, to take different viewpoints. This is true of architecture in general simply because it is three-dimensional, but at Paestum a spatial exploration of the architecture was forced on the visitor, for there was really nothing else to see. Because Paestum presented the viewer mostly with columns and architraves, which created and opened up space, the only way to understand these buildings, given the complete absence of iconographical or even functional information, was by experiencing them physically, by looking at them and walking round and through them. The temples made their impact through both sight and sensation.

Although in writings on Paestum we do not find the general topoi of decay and the ephemerality of ruins, many of the texts are no less personal than other descriptions of ruins and the reflections they inspired about the self. As we saw in Chapter 1, the peculiarity of Paestum confronted visitors with paradoxes and defeated their expectations, and this led to an increased awareness of the self as observer. In that sense, the physical measuring of the body against the scale of the architecture may be seen as a continuation or a result of the sublime. Goethe's account makes clear that he succeeded in combining a bodily experience with art-historical memory to give meaning or a sense of identification to what he first perceived as the strangeness of the architecture. If Goethe focused on the art-historical canon, on norms and deviations from norms, Viollet-le-Duc concentrated on structure, Forsyth on tectonic aspects and the design of architectural space, Dupaty and Eustace on gravity, and Shelley on scale and the disruption of our common sense of relative size, which can lead to a sublime experience. We have seen in Shelley's case that a knowledge of Greek culture, history and the distant past was not useful on the spot, as such knowledge was not grounded in experience. What was important for visitors to Paestum was architectural space and the complex, multi-layered physical experience of that space.

Existing architectural studies provide few clues as to how to analyse writings that are rooted in the physical. An exception is the study by Cammy Brothers of a related experience of perception and the body in Michelangelo's Biblioteca Laurenziana in Florence.[77] The interior of the library is described in intensely physical terms, recounting the process of movement through space and its visceral effect on the body. Michelangelo employed the vocabulary of exterior architecture but turned it inwards and applied it to the interior of the library; as a result the visitor does not know where to look or how to move. At Paestum, exterior and interior are almost indistinguishable, but the temples cause similar difficulties. Visitors therefore lighted on the orders, the space, the scale or the age of the buildings to reduce their sense of disorientation. As at the Biblioteca Laurenziana, at Paestum the physical presence of the visitor 'is almost squeezed out of existence by the massiveness of the architectural elements and their imposing physicality, which heightens the visitor's sense of his or her own body'.[78]

Heinrich Wölfflin, one of the few art historians to write on the bodily experience of architecture, can provide a frame to define what happened. In his *Prolegomena zu einer Psychologie der Architektur* (1886), he showed how our experience of and reaction to architecture are rooted in our physical being. We react physically to architecture because only in and through our bodies can we experience the laws of nature:

> Physical forms possess a character only because we ourselves possess a body . . . But as human beings with a body that teaches us the nature of gravity, contraction, strength, and so on, we gather the experience that enables us to identify with the conditions of other forms . . . We have carried loads and experienced pressure and counterpressure . . . and that is why we can appreciate the noble serenity of a column and understand the tendency of all matter to spread out formlessly on the ground.[79]

Columns confront us with our physicality. The anthropomorphic aspect of columns is a subject that has been much studied and features in Wölfflin's text, though writings on Paestum do not mention this phenomenon.[80] They do, however, as we have seen, discuss the physical experience of columns. This can be related to Wölfflin's argument that it is the viewer who animates each object, and defines its expressive capability accordingly: architectural forms 'can communicate to us only what we ourselves use their qualities to express'.[81] Quoting the psychologist Johannes Volkelt's *Symbol-Begriff in der neuesten Ästhetik* (1876), Wölfflin stated that to interpret a spatial form in an aesthetic way we have to move in and around it, and respond to this movement through our senses, 'share in it with our bodily organization . . . The extension and movement of our body is associated with a feeling of pleasure or displeasure, which we interpret as the experience characteristic of the form itself.'[82]

Wölfflin also offered a clue as to how columns can give us a sense of energy. When we experience the openness and closedness of architectural space – for instance in the difference between column and intercolumnium – such alternations harmonise with our respiration. He claimed that we judge the vital feeling of architectural forms according to the physical state they induce in us. Here he quoted Goethe, who, in remarking that we ought to sense the effect of a beautiful room, even if we were led into it blindfold, argued that architectural impression is not a 'reckoning by the eye' but principally based on a direct bodily feeling.[83] This is exactly what we have seen in the accounts of Paestum, where it is clear that not only the eye but also the whole body played a role in the experiences of visitors. The spectator figured not merely as the eye of the beholder, but as an observer using all the senses to explore the site. We can relate this to the aesthetics of *Einfühlung*, which, as we saw earlier, were suggested in Goethe's texts but were defined in those terms only later, by Robert Vischer. The concept of *Einfühlung*, often translated as 'empathy', was explained in Vischer's *Über das optische Formgefühl: Ein Beitrag zur Aesthetik* (1873). Drawing on the associational theory of the picturesque, Vischer proposed the idea that 'we invest in a building . . . with certain emotions'.[84] Wölfflin showed how spectators forget themselves when they are engrossed in the object in an aesthetic experience. This loss of self-awareness happened to visitors who had a sublime experience at Paestum. It was a different – less active and rational – experience than the one we have discussed in this chapter, which involved an enhanced awareness of the body in architectural space. In this case, visitors referred to the basic elements of architecture – form, dimensions, material, space, interior and exterior – which they defined by their own human and physical experience of height, width, force, load, gravity, mass, proportion, scale and perspective.

With Wölfflin in mind, we can identify some general and common aspects in the reactions to Paestum: how observation is related to the way we experience certain physical processes in our bodies and express those experiences through our bodies. Forsyth noted that the solid failed and the open resisted, and Shelley that the experience of Paestum shattered common notions of scale. At Paestum the boundaries between exterior and interior were hardly evident: there were no walls but only columns; the spectator could not walk in and out of the temples but could only make loops and wander through the forest of columns. There was no directional hierarchy, no clear indication of entrance or exit and no differentiation of inside and outside, so visitors lost their sense of orientation.

Travellers to Paestum recorded the manner in which they observed the site, and the aspects of the ruins that were the subject of these observations. Because Paestum was not at all about ornament, decoration or detail, the viewer had only the larger picture to focus on: columns articulating space, their size and scale, their material presence, tectonic elements, load and support. Recognising this illuminates the elevated self-experience that resulted from the perception of the sublime, discussed in Chapter 1: it was a specific architectural experience of space and scale, enclosure and openness, mass and gravity – an experience made possible because Paestum confounded all preconceived ideas. Eighteenth-century travellers invoked art history or the rhetoric of the living building, as Goethe did, or any of several sublime topoi. While texts on other ruins, such as those by Diderot and Soane, chronicled self-discovery through the contemplation of ruins, at Paestum the process was inverted: there, a coming to terms with the ruins relied on an understanding of architecture through bodily awareness.

The sublime experience led to an awareness of the self, reinforced by the confrontation with danger, the incomprehensible and the lofty. The encounter with ruins gave rise to different reflections in the eighteenth-century observer. In Diderot it generated thoughts on his own life, in Soane meditations on his own character. The contrast between expectations conditioned by writings and images and the actual experience on the spot is strong. When seen in actuality, the buildings at Paestum turned out to be no more than columns and entablatures, or forms of façade, and this realisation turned patterns of expectation upside down. The columns had an intense presence: they reminded visitors of the massive architectural load they had been built to carry, and bore down on the consciousness with the sensation of their enormous weight. Observers noted the absence of a base, and foresaw that what Wölfflin called the 'noble serenity of a column' would subsequently crumble, thanks to 'the tendency of all matter to spread out formlessly on the ground'.[85] Wölfflin's ideas on the physicality of architectural experience help to articulate what went on in the mind of the observing subject at Paestum. Visitors were disturbed or moved by the way in which the temples changed their accustomed sense of the relation of architecture to the body. It was exactly this break with conventional interpretations, arising from Paestum's lack of functional or iconological context, that launched an awareness of the process of observation.

Entering actual ruins in person is completely different from entering imagined ruins as a sort of mental game played while one is seated comfortably in one's armchair. The creations of the imagination are conceptualised and culturally influenced; they lead to reflections on the self and on the decay of humankind. At the site of real ruins, one must relate oneself to the building physically, as Wölfflin explained, sensing and understanding its tectonic elements through one's own body. Our investigation of how visitors observed at Paestum makes clear that the bodily experience was a key to the analysis of Greek architecture: the act of relating a building to the body in scale, but also in terms of physical laws such as gravity, enabled travellers to understand the general constructional aspects of architecture. The simplicity of architectural forms, how they supported and carried loads, and how they articulated space could be comprehended only by being there.

The fundamental opposition explored in this chapter between entering ruins in the mind and entering ruins in the flesh has established several crucial ideas. First, entering a real ruin, studying it from close at hand, shows that the physical experience is very different from the mental experience. Secondly, that on-the-spot experience tells us much about the spatial and tectonic characteristics that were clearly felt at Paestum, and that make the temples exceptional. Thirdly, the fact that the temples are ruins made them different in important ways from other architectural sites (for instance, St Peter's in Rome). At Paestum interior and exterior were almost one: the process of wandering and the experience of spatiality were particular. Furthermore, visitors found structure and tectonic elements exposed to view in a way that they are not in buildings that are complete: these elements, how they function and how they relate to one another could be observed and interrogated, and thus they received attention in the written accounts of the site. Lastly, although they are ruins, the temples are still relatively intact, unlike other Greek temples – in Sicily, for example; for the eighteenth-century traveller they were not the kind of remains that had to be reconstructed in the mind. One could actually feel the spatiality in the monument *an sich*, apart from what it had been or might have been: one could imagine what the entire building had looked like, but one could also view it just as it was – as a ruin, or as the structure it was at the very moment of observation. In fact, it seems that this was how visitors saw it.

This chapter has identified the aspects of experience that were important in entering ruined spaces as opposed to contemplating ruins in the imagination. It has demonstrated that, in order to 'feel' space, an awareness of the body in relation to architecture is essential. Some fundamental architectural characteristics can be analysed only in person. Because their form and structure could still be seen, the temples at Paestum were the very example to give a sense of what architecture is about.

CHAPTER 4

Staging Ruins:
Theatrical Sequences

Now that we have followed the eighteenth- and nineteenth-century visitors inside the temples of Paestum, the next step is to see how their experiences were represented in publications that were disseminated across Europe. While the first three chapters of this book have focused on private accounts in letters and travel diaries, the next three will concentrate on representations of Paestum in texts and images for publication. In these published representations, movement plays a major role. We have already considered movement as an aspect of the picturesque in architecture (Chapter 2), but now we shall examine it in relation to Paestum. How did visitors move towards and around the site? How were their movements rendered in published accounts? And how did these representations of movement influence subsequent explorations of the site?

Architecture as Theatre

As we shall see, movement in this context is to be connected not with the picturesque, but with the theatre. The relationship between architecture and the theatre is a compelling one. We find it, for instance, in the ideas of the architect John Soane, who, in the notes for one of his Royal Academy lectures, compared the experience of seeing and walking through a building with that of watching a theatre performance:

> The front of a building is like the prologue of a play, it prepares us for what we are to expect. If the outside promises more than we find in the inside, we are disappointed. The plot opens itself in the first act and is carried on through the remainder, through all the mazes of character, convenience of arrangement, elegance and propriety of ornaments, and lastly produces a complete whole in distribution, decoration and construction.[1]

According to Soane, if a building is to 'perform', or express its character, it needs certain specific elements. In his lecture notes, quoted here, the impression a building makes is inextricably linked to the presence and movements of the observer, the 'stage settings' of

84 (*facing page*) Detail of Fig. 88.

the architecture, and the 'plot' through which the spectator experiences it. Soane made explicit that three elements are of the utmost importance in defining the theatre performance in architecture: the spectator, the script and the stage. And in linking theatre to architecture, he singled out the temporal experience of those two arts, and compared the impact that architecture and the theatre could have on the beholder.

Although a strong connection between architecture and the theatre is well recognised, studies of the subject mainly ignore theoretical parallels, and few provide a concrete and precise definition of this relationship.[2] The eighteenth- and nineteenth-century accounts of Paestum make a clear connection between building and theatricality,[3] so our study of them will make the relationship between architecture and the theatre more explicit. The temples constitute an exceptional case because they bring together the architectural equivalent of audience, script and stage, and these three elements are exceptionally well documented in numerous publications, drawings and manuscripts.

Some travellers to Paestum had a direct involvement with theatre design and used their experiences as the inspiration for stage sets – a literal connection between architecture and the theatre that deserves a brief discussion, though it is not, in my view, the essence of Paestum as theatre. Gabriel-Pierre-Martin Dumont imagined Paestum's temples as the backdrop for *Philoctetes* by Sophocles (see Figs 99e and 104d),[4] and Pierre-Adrien Pâris's

85a–d Pierre-Adrien Pâris, designs for theatre sets, undated, ink and wash. Besançon, Bibliothèque Municipale, Bibliothèque d'Étude et de Conservation, Collection Pierre-Adrien Pâris, vol. 483, nos 68, 69, 170, 196.

Rediscovering Architecture

86a–c Pierre-Adrien Pâris, designs for theatre sets with columns in the form of rocks, undated. Besançon, Bibliothèque Municipale, Bibliothèque d'Étude et de Conservation, Collection Pierre-Adrien Pâris, vol. 483, nos 233, 90, 366.

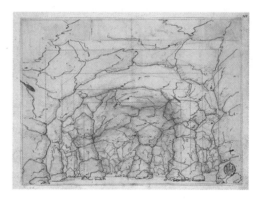

stage designs compellingly demonstrate that the baseless column generated associations of the primitive and the sublime appropriate to the theme of certain plays and operas. As 'Architecte des Menus-Plaisirs' from 1778 to 1792, Pâris was in charge of festivities at the court of Louis XVI,[5] and conceived and designed all the ephemeral *décors des fêtes* and stage sets for operas and plays at the châteaux of Marly, Saint-Cloud, Fontainebleau and Versailles. He was responsible for the design of almost eighty operas, theatre pieces and ballets,[6] and for some of the operas he used a baseless Doric order for his sets (Fig. 85), as in his design for a Greek temple in *Adrien en Syrie*, and an underground chamber in the Temple of Diana in Niccolò Piccinni's *Iphigénie en Tauride* (premiere 1781); the columns for the set of *Iphigénie* are reminiscent of the smooth columns of the temple at Segesta in Sicily. For *Les Danaïdes* by Antonio Salieri (premiere 1784) he drew a crypt-like setting, using fluted columns supporting vaults.

We cannot, however, claim that Pâris was directly influenced by Paestum in his use of a baseless order in these designs.[7] It is too easy to connect the use of baseless Doric columns, in general, specifically to Paestum. The columns in Pâris's stage designs are clearly abstract combinations of those he had seen on his travels in Italy and in publications and engravings. Besides, the origins of the baseless Doric order in his designs are less interesting than what he wanted to express with it. In that sense the underground chambers with their Doric columns are relevant because, in conveying a sense of danger and fear, they reinforce the idea he expressed after his visit in 1774 that there was something terrible about Paestum (see pp. 19, 53). In my view, these designs combine the idea that a building must express a character (as Soane said in his lecture) and Blondel's concept of 'une Architecture terrible' as characterising buildings that purvey power and pride through their massive solidity and the use of certain materials (see Chapter 1). It seems quite understandable that, in pursuit of an effect of the terrible in an opera set, Pâris chose a baseless Doric order rather than the Ionic: in some of his theatre sets his columns were so rustic that they looked like rocks – nature preceding architecture, as it were: a clear primitivist expression (Fig. 86).[8]

So, although these representations of a certain character are interesting, in that they show how architectural theory can find an expression in theatre, the mere application of an order does not tell us much. In short, it is not the use of a particular order that demonstrates how theatre and architecture are connected. At Paestum theatricality had another and more crucial role.

There is an important reason why it is rewarding to study Paestum in this context: it posed problems to architects, as we have already seen. Reading the testimonies of travellers, it is evident that they found the temples, with their rough forms and porous stone, puzzling. The architecture of the temples was completely uncanonical, and the site, partly overgrown and inhabited by peasants and grazing cattle, was quite different from other classical remains, familiar through publications and visits. When they finally reached the temples, after a journey of several stages and fraught with difficulty, travellers found they could not take in these monuments simply by standing still and looking at them: they had to confront the conundrum by walking around and through them.

Because of the peculiarity of Paestum, architects and artists struggled, in writing about it, to define what they had seen and to represent their experiences in drawings and texts. One solution was to take refuge in a positive portrayal of the site, and, despite their negative reactions to the architecture, many travellers hastened to praise the setting of the temples. In fact, it was precisely the landscape and the temples standing in the plain between the mountains and the sea that made so intense an impression on them; like Richard Payne Knight, some preferred to keep their distance and appreciate the temples from afar instead of approaching them. Yet there was also another solution. I believe that by using strategies of representation that had been developed in the theatre or can be associated with it, architects and other visitors found a way to present Paestum that was acceptable to the eighteenth-century public. By appealing to experience of the theatre, they rendered it less curious, bizarre and threatening.

Movement played an important role in this strategy. By adopting different viewpoints to observe and experience a building, observers came to understand it, and, as in the theatre, these different stances affected the representation of the experience. As Roland Barthes expressed it: 'The theatre is precisely that practice which calculates the place of things as they are observed.'[9]

The Sequence of Experience: Acting and Directing

The accounts of eighteenth-century visitors to Paestum often read like a theatrical scenario, with different stage settings for every episode of the experience. The sequence followed in these descriptions is often very similar: the narratives are chronologies, shaped by eighteenth-century culture and drawing on eighteenth-century theatre – a storehouse of representational strategies. But they were also influenced by the information that was available in advance about the site. Having prepared for their journey beforehand, travellers already had an image of Paestum in their minds, engendered by the publications, engravings and paintings that they had consulted or seen. It was in these publications and images that the story of the Paestum experience was created.

The Italian court painter Antonio Joli (1700–1777) played a key role in this dissemination of the image of Paestum among eighteenth-century audiences.[10] Joli produced eleven paintings of Paestum that not only were widely seen in Europe but also formed the basis for the majority of the publications on the site that appeared in this period. Joli was trained as a painter of *vedute*.[11] He also worked in the studios of Giovanni Paolo Panini (1691–1765) and Giuseppe Galli da Bibiena (1696–1757), and designed stage sets for the theatre. At the time he depicted Paestum he was court painter to Charles and Ferdinand de Bourbon in Naples. His paintings show the *veduta* influence but, more than anything, his theatrical background. As a stage designer to the Bourbons, Joli created the sets for sixty operas for the Teatro San Carlo in Naples between 1762 and 1777; these were mostly Italian operas, but in 1774, for instance, he drew for Christoph Willibald Gluck's opera *Orfeo ed Euridice*. From some time in the Naples period there survives an interesting painting, which might have been for Gluck's opera.[12] It shows decayed columns and architraves, clearly delineated in the foreground and fading into the distance (Fig. 87). Although it is possibly no more than a capriccio,[13] it does have scenographic qualities in the pronounced perspectives leading from the three arches into an infinite space. The columns are very similar to those that Joli painted in his canvases of Paestum, rather slim Doric ones, made up of regular blocks of stone. In the background the columns are superposed,

87 Antonio Joli, capriccio of ruins, *c.*1760, oil on canvas. Caserta, Palazzo Reale.

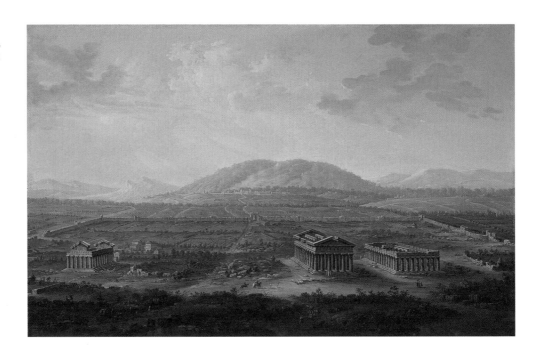

like those he had seen in the Temple of Neptune. The building is clearly in ruins, and
offers an interesting interpretation of the Paestum temples – the Temple of Neptune, in
this case, where arches have been added to the seamless ranks of receding columns to
create the effect of a limitless edifice. Joli placed just one staffage figure in the picture to
give the scale, as in the Paestum painting of the oblique view along the façades (see Fig.
90). The suggestion of infinite space is typical of Galli da Bibiena,[14] and the influence of
his theatre designs is also felt in the painting's strong perspective, pronounced foreground
and misty background. The work is rather extraordinary. Joli drew many other similar
capricci of columns and arches in deep perspective, but these always show Corinthian
columns, and the buildings are more intact, with only minor evidence of vegetation and
the loss of only a few architectural details. In this view the portrayal of ruin is emphasised by the presence of large fragments of fallen masonry in the foreground. This makes
the painting more rustic, which might also be a reference to Paestum, whereas the other
paintings are clearly views of Roman city life, featuring many figures engaged in discussion or debate.

Joli's series of eleven paintings of Paestum, dated 1759, shows an interesting sequence
of different scenes: the distant view of the temples from the west (Figs 88, 91a–b); a
view through the east gate onto the three temples, in which the third temple is nicely
placed in the hole in the gate wall (Figs 89, 92a–b); a slightly nearer view, seen from
the south-east, of the three temples with the mountains in the background (Figs 93a–
c); a still nearer view from the south along the façades of the three temples (Figs 90,
94a); and finally two interior views of the Temple of Neptune (Figs 98a, 100a). These
paintings, and the engravings that were based on them, took eighteenth-century readers
by the hand and led them through the several stages of observation, to give the best
experience of Paestum.[15]

Eight monographs on the temples were published between 1764 and 1799, and in five
of them Joli's paintings were used to make the engravings. In the other three, the

engravers often used the same viewpoints as Joli.[16] The engravings made after his paintings were also sold separately, and played an even greater part in shaping the image of Paestum.[17] *The ruins of Paestum* (1768) by Thomas Major (1714–1799), for instance, used three of Joli's perspective views to introduce his work (Figs 91e, 92c, 94d), together with other views and measured drawings of plans, elevations, cross-sections and details. Sir James Gray (c.1708–1773), envoy-extraordinary and plenipotentiary at Naples from 1753 until 1764, commissioned two views of Paestum by Joli (Figs 89–90), and served as a cultural agent in the dissemination of Joli's images of Paestum through his contacts in Italy, France and England.[18] He was a member of the party when Joli visited Paestum and was present when the artist drew his views of the site, as Major, who obtained the Paestum paintings through Gray, wrote in the footnotes to his plates.[19] Gray was also instrumental in the drawings for a proposed publication on Paestum by the Scottish travel writer James Bruce (1730–1794). Bruce visited the temples in 1763, and, being dissatisfied with the drawings provided by Count Felice Gazzola, with Gray's help he hired the Italian artist Gaetano Magri to draw for him on the spot. While Bruce never published his account of the site, drawings by Magri ended up in Major's publication.[20] Institutions in Italy, such as the Académie de France in Rome, where foreign artists and architects met and debated, also provided a useful outlet for the distribution of such drawings, publications and plates.[21]

Joli's different perspective views followed the path that was taken by the travellers when they approached the temples: first they were offered an overview of the three buildings, then they examined them further from the outside, and finally they entered the temples. After the long adventure of the journey, travellers naturally stopped to observe the site when they arrived. The scenes in Joli's paintings represent the precise points where they paused to take in what they saw, and to savour and analyse what they experienced. Thus the visual representations of these scenes are simultaneously illustrations of the visitor's experience, and a guide to observing the site.

89 (*above left*) Antonio Joli, the three temples, seen through the eastern gate, 1759. Private collection.

90 (*above right*) Antonio Joli, the three temples from the south, 1759. Private collection.

a

b

c

d

e

f

91   The three temples from the west:
(a), (b) Antonio Joli, 1759, Pasadena,
California, Norton Simon Art Foundation,
and private collection; (c) Filippo Morghen,
Sei vedute delle rovine di Pesto ([1765]), plate
2; (d) [John Longfield], *The ruins of Poestum*
(1767), plate 1; (e) Thomas Major, *The ruins
of Paestum* (1768), plate 1; (f) Jérôme de La
Lande, *Voyage d'un françois en Italie* (1769),
vol. VII, plate 1; (g) Gabriel-Pierre-Martin
Dumont, *Les ruines de Paestum* (1769), plate
1; (h) Jean Barbault, *Recueil de divers
monumens anciens* (1770), plate 6; (i) Claude-
Matthieu Delagardette, *Les Ruines de Paestum*
([1799]), plate II; (j) Domenico Romanelli,
Viaggio a Pompei, a Pesto . . . (1811).

g

h

i

j

a

b

c

92 The three temples, seen through the
eastern gate: (a), (b), Joli, 1759, private
collection; (c) Major (1768), plate III.

a

b

c

93 The three temples from the south-east:
(a)–(c) Joli, 1759, Bowhill, Selkirk, Scotland,
collection of the Duke of Buccleuch and
Queensberry, and private collection;
(d) Paolo Antonio Paoli, *Paesti . . . rudera:
Rovine della città di Pesto* (1784), plate IX;
(e) Claude-Matthieu Delagardette, *Les
Ruines de Paestum* ([1799]), plate II.

d

e

a

b

c

d

e

f

g

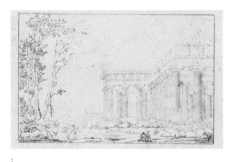

h

i

94 The three temples from the south:
(a) Joli, 1759, private collection; (b) Morghen
(1765), plate 3; (c) [Longfield] (1767), plate
2; (d) Major (1768), plate II; (e) Barbault
(1770), plate 7; (f) Abraham-Louis-Rodolphe
Ducros, c.1785–90, Lausanne, Musée cantonal
des Beaux-Arts; (g) Giovanni Battista Lusieri,
c.1790, private collection; (h) Delagardette
([1799]), plate II; (i) Hubert Rohault de
Fleury, c.1805, Montréal, Collection Canadian
Centre for Architecture, DR1974:0002:030:031;
(j) Joseph Gandy, 1819, private collection;
(k) James Elmes, undated, RIBA Library
Drawings Collection.

j

k

a

b

c

95 The Temple of Neptune: (a) Gaetano
Magri, undated, London, Sir John Soane's
Museum, Vol. 27/8; (b) Major (1768),
plate VII; (c) Gottfried von Neureuther,
1831, Munich, Architekturmuseum TU,
neur_g-68-1.

a

b

c

96 The Temple of Neptune: (a) Paoli
(1784), plate XIV; (b) Lusieri, c.1790, private
collection; (c) Franz Kaisermann, undated,
private collection.

a

b

c

97   The Temple of Neptune: (a) Magri, undated, London, Sir John Soane's Museum, Vol. 27/9; (b) James Bruce, 1763, New Haven (Conn.), Yale Center for British Art, Paul Mellon Collection, B1977.14.8498; (c) Major (1768), plate VIII; (d) Morghen (1765), plate 9; (e) Friedrich von Gärtner, c.1816, Munich, Architekturmuseum TU, gaer_f-127-1.

d

e

a

b

c

98   Interior of the Temple of Neptune from the south-west: (a) Joli, 1759, Caserta, Palazzo Reale; (b) Morghen (1765), plate 4; (c) Pietro Fabris, late 1770s, Warwickshire, Compton Verney.

a

b

c

d

Scene V.du II.e Acte de la Tragédie de Philoctete

e

Internal View of the Hexastyle Spetral Temple, taken from the South.
Vue du dedans du Temple Hexastyle, Spetro, prise du coté du Sud.

f

g

Vue Perspective d'un Temple Hexastyle des ruines de Pæstum.

h

i

j

99 (*previous page*) Interior of the Temple of Neptune from the west: (a) Gabriel-Pierre-Martin Dumont, 1750, Champs-sur-Marne, École Nationale des Ponts et Chaussées, Fonds ancien, MS, fol. 208; (b) Magri, undated, London, Sir John Soane's Museum, Vol. 27/10; (c) Bruce, 1763, New Haven (Conn.), Yale Center for British Art, Paul Mellon Collection, B1977.14.8496; (d) Gabriel-Pierre-Martin Dumont, *Suite de plans . . . de Pesto* (1764), plate 1; (e) Gabriel-Pierre-Martin Dumont, *Parallèle de plans des plus belles salles* ([*c*.1765]); (f) Major (1768), plate IX; (g) Paoli (1784), plate XV; (h) Dumont (1769), plate 4; (i) Ducros, *c*.1785–90, Lausanne, Musée cantonal des Beaux-Arts; (j) Jean-Louis Lefebvre, painted snuffbox, 1809–19, London, Victoria and Albert Museum, Loan: Gilbert.484:1, 2-2008.

a

b

c

d

100 (*right and above right*) Interior of the Temple of Neptune from the east: (a) Joli, 1759, private collection; (b) Morghen (1765), plate 5; (c) [Longfield] (1767), plate 3: (d) Barbault (1770), plate 9.

a

b

c

101 The Basilica: (a) Magri, undated, London, Sir John Soane's Museum, Vol. 27/25; (b) Major (1768), plate XIX; (c) Paoli (1784), plate XXXIV.

a

b

c

102 The Basilica: (a) Magri, undated, London, Sir John Soane's Museum, Vol. 27/26; (b) Bruce, 1763, New Haven (Conn.), Yale Center for British Art, Paul Mellon Collection, B1977.14.8495; (c) Major (1768), plate XIXB.

103 Interior of the Basilica from the east: (a) Major (1768), plate XXI; (b) Paoli (1784), plate XXXVII.

a

b

a

Internal View of the Dieudécépteral Temple or Basilica, taken from the South

b

The Interior part of the 3.ª Temple looking from the West front

c

*Vestiges de l'interieur d'un Temple ou Basilique de l'ancienne ville
de Pæstum tels qu'ils existoient en 1750.
Pirrhus seul dans la Scene premiere de l'Acte V. de la Tragédie de Philoctete*

d

*Vestiges de l'interieur d'un Temple ou Basilique de l'ancienne ville
de Pæstum tels qu'ils existoient en 1750.
(à vue en joint en 1769 par le S.ᵗ Dumont.)*

e

104 Interior of the Basilica from the west:
(a) Dumont, 1750, Champs-sur-Marne, École
Nationale des Ponts et Chaussées, Fonds
ancien, MS, fol. 208; (b) Magri, undated,
London, Sir John Soane's Museum, Vol.
27/27; (c) Bruce, 1763, New Haven (Conn.),
Yale Center for British Art, Paul Mellon
Collection, B1977.14.8499; (d) Dumont
([c.1765]); (e) Dumont (1769), plate 6;
(f) Major (1768), plate XX; (g) Giovanni
Volpato, c.1780, Düsseldorf, Goethe-Museum,
Anton-und-Katharina-Kippenberg-Stiftung,
NW 12/1955; (h) Paoli (1784), plate XXXV.

Internal View of the Pseudodipteral Temple or Basilica, taken from the South.
Vue de dedans du Temple Pseudodiptere ou de la Basilique prise du coté du Sud.

f

g

h

a

b

c

105　The Temple of Ceres from the east:
(a) Magri, undated, London, Sir John
Soane's Museum, Vol. 27/18; (b) Bruce,
1763, New Haven (Conn.), Yale Center
for British Art, Paul Mellon Collection,
B1977.14.8494; (c) Major (1768), plate XIV.

a

b

c

106　The Temple of Ceres from the west:
(a) Joli, 1759, private collection; (b) Morghen
(1765), plate 6; (c) Barbault (1770), plate 8.

107 The Temple of Ceres from the north-east: (a) Magri, undated, London, Sir John Soane's Museum, Vol. 27/19; (b) Major (1768), plate XIV.

a

b

108 The Temple of Ceres: (a) Dumont (1769), plate 8; (b) Paoli (1784), plate XXXVII.

a

b

In one of his Royal Academy lectures, John Soane spoke of the importance of pausing when attempting to look properly at architecture. He compared Blenheim Palace to Paestum:

> there is a constant variety of outline [at Blenheim] that pleases from whatever point it is viewed (as are viewed ancient temples), whether at a distance wherein the great masses only are made out, or at a nearer approach when the prominent features are distinguished, or still nearer where the general details are distinguished. Here the eye reposes to enjoy the whole picture . . . In this respect the interest is kept up as in the ancient temples, but this would not be the case if variety of outline and continuity of character were confined to one front only. To keep up the first impression there must be the same character observed in every part externally and internally. This is seen in the great temple [of Neptune] at Paestum. Its interior is of the same character as the exterior.[22]

The advantage of Paestum as opposed to other ancient sites – those in Rome, for instance – was that it provided the opportunity for the traveller's eye to contemplate the scene and then to come to rest again at another point; by constantly taking a new viewpoint, the beholder could sustain interest in the observation process. Every different view, from far

109 Paolo Antonio Paoli, plan of Paestum, in *Paesti . . . rudera: Rovine della città di Pesto* (1784), plate X.

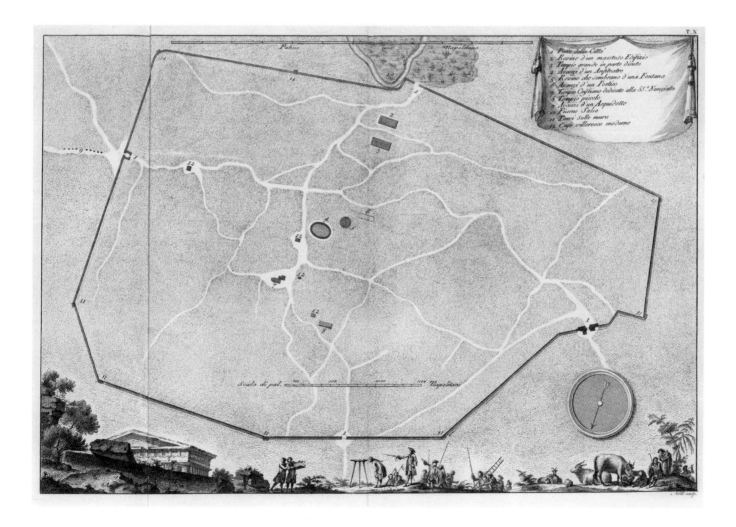

off to nearby, offered a singular scene and generated diverse feelings and associations in the viewer's mind.

We find a similar sequence of perspective views, representing such moments of repose, in Robert Wood's *The ruins of Palmyra* (1753), which, according to Nicholas Savage, 're-enacts the drama of first setting eyes on, and then exploring in detail, the huge expanse of the marble ruins of the deserted city'.[23] In the middle of the eighteenth century, topographical views of ancient sites, depicting the monuments in their setting, were an indispensable feature of volumes on archaeological travels, and the readers of such volumes were not unfamiliar with the way Paestum was represented. James Stuart and Nicholas Revett, Wood, Julien-David Le Roy and Robert Adam all tried to do the same thing in their books: to enable the reader to re-enact their experience.[24] But in the case of Paestum it was far more likely that readers would eventually go there themselves and undergo the same experiences than it was in the case of many other monuments. It was more difficult and dangerous to travel to Palmyra after studying Wood's *Ruins*, or to Athens after reading Stuart's *Antiquities* than it was to make the journey to Paestum after perusing Major's *Ruins* and any of the other monographs. Once the travellers arrived, they could put theory into practice, performing and experiencing for themselves what they had read about before. The number of people who travelled to Paestum is beyond comparison with any other ancient Greek site; and the number of publications – that is, testimonies tracing in detail the reactions of visitors – is greater than that devoted to any other site. Architects and others went to the temples with the publications in their hands, comparing the monuments with what they had read and seen, as Paoli pictured them doing in his *Paesti . . . rudera: Rovine della città di Pesto* (1784; Fig. 109).

It was like reading the script and seeing the stage sets before becoming the protagonist in a play. In their different representations of Paestum, the visitors were simultaneously the directors of the play, staging the ruins in a series of scenes, the audience at the performance in viewing the site itself and the different perspectives that the course of their visit opened up, and the actors in the drama, experiencing their own journey and exploration.

Architecture as Scenographic Experience

The experience of architecture, and the different feelings it arouses when one approaches a building, walks around it and enters it, are a new, and very conspicuous theme in eighteenth-century publications by architects. In the second edition of his work on ancient Greek architecture, *Les ruines des plus beaux monuments de la Grèce* (1770), the French architect Julien-David Le Roy took more than three pages to describe the experience of observing colonnades, taking as an example Claude Perrault's colonnade on the east front of the Louvre (1672). He recounted the various stages of his approach to the colonnade, 'first from afar, then on approaching, then walking alongside or under it, whether in bright sunlight or on a clouded day'.[25] In this way each scene offered new emotions to the spectator.

In Le Roy's text the role of the spectator as director and actor becomes clear: he himself created the spectacle he was to view, phasing his viewing experience as a playwright might build his plot. Le Roy advised his readers how to observe the colonnade:

> Run your eye along the full extent of the colonnade . . . while walking the length of
> the row of houses opposite; stand back to take in the whole; then come close enough

to discern the richness of its soffit, its niches, its medallions; catch the moment when the Sun's rays add the most striking effects by picking out certain parts while plunging others in shadow: how many enchanting views are supplied by the magnificence of the back wall of this colonnade combined in a thousand different ways with the pleasing outline of the columns in front of it and with the fall of the light![26]

Le Roy's instructions on how to observe a building recall Aristotle's ideas on plot, vividness and fictionalisation in the *Poetics*. The essence of the plot, according to Aristotle, is its selectiveness.[27] Similarly, Le Roy allowed the sun to select the architectural elements that would have the most vivid effect on the beholder. This brings to mind another theme in Aristotle's *Poetics*, the important role of *enargeia* in making an impression on the viewer.[28] The Greek *enargeia* derives from *argès*, 'shining light', and originally meant 'clarity', 'distinctness' or 'vividness', as when putting something in the spotlight. Vivid representation, whether by the use of metaphor in speech, or by the use of colour and light in the visual arts, was one of the main instruments to impress and thereby move the public.[29] Taken together, this combination of selectiveness and highlighting allows us to make explicit the sense in which Le Roy's account was a fictionalisation of the experience of looking at the Louvre colonnade. The experience became a narrative, unfolding in time, in which Le Roy suggested that the reader walk along the colonnade in a sequence of scenes. He directed and positioned the gaze of the beholder, selected what was to be seen, and let the sun function as a spotlight to single out conspicuous details.

As we come closer, our view alters. The mass of the building as a whole escapes us, but we are compensated by our closeness to the columns; as we change position, we create changes of view that are more striking, more rapid, and more varied. But if we enter beneath the colonnade itself, an entirely new spectacle offers itself to our eyes: every step adds change and variety to the relation between the positions of the columns and the scene outside the colonnade, whether this be a landscape, or the picturesque disposition of the houses of a city, or the magnificence of an interior.[30]

Le Roy's description of his observations anticipates the treatise *Le Génie de l'architecture, ou L'Analogie de cet art avec nos sensations* (1780) by the French architect Nicolas Le Camus de Mézières (1721–1789), who offered a theory to account for the ways in which experiencing architecture can arouse different emotions. In this study, Le Camus de Mézières used theatre as an analogy for architecture. He postulated that the architecture of a building is akin to the dramatic structure of a play: walking through a sequence of spaces in a house is an experience similar to that of viewing a succession of stage sets during a theatrical performance. 'Each room must have its own particular character. The analogy, the relation of proportions, decides our sensations; each room makes us want the next; and this engages our minds and holds them in suspense. It is a satisfaction in itself.'[31] In his introduction, Le Camus de Mézières discussed the relationship between architecture and stage decor, which he called the 'threefold magic' of painting, sculpture and architecture, claiming that it 'addresses almost all the affections and sensations known to us'. Then, in the part entitled 'Le Génie de l'architecture', he made a connection between the characteristic qualities of well-designed architecture and the effects of the theatre:

The grand ensemble alone can draw and hold the attention; it alone can engage both the soul and the eye. The first glimpse must hold us spellbound; the details, the masses of the decoration, the profiles, the play of light, all conduce to this same end. Large divisions, purity of profiles, a play of light that is neither too bright nor too sombre, grand openings, and great harmony will proclaim the grandeur and magnificence to come.[32]

In making this comparison between the expressiveness of architecture and the evocation of emotion by changes of scenery in the theatre, Le Camus de Mézières underlined the importance of the beholder and the different stages of his experience.

The Landscape as Stage Set

In Le Camus de Mézières's emphasis on first impressions when seeing a play or viewing a building, we find the same elements that travellers to Paestum related. For instance, when Richard Payne Knight described his first encounter with the temples in his travel diary, he recalled in romantic terms the striking effect of his first sight of them, their arrangement in relation to one another on the plain, and the verdant hills that surrounded them (see Chapter 2, p. 85).[33] The impact of the scene and the impression made by coming upon the ruins set in the southern Italian landscape was re-enacted in the reports of many visitors to the site. The French architect Antoine-Laurent-Thomas Vaudoyer went to Paestum with the book by Paoli in his hand. He too appreciated the visual effect from a distance and deliberately chose a far-off viewpoint from which to observe the scene:

> The town is situated half a mile from the coastline, and at the foot of a chain of beautiful mountains. To get far enough away to enjoy this beautiful view of the three monuments, there is nothing like climbing to the top of the tower by the sea, in line with the great temple.[34]

This view from a distance, which is so well captured in Joli's paintings, kept reappearing in publications on the site. One of the printmakers who made engravings after Joli's paintings was Filippo Morghen (1730–1807). He published this initial view from the west in his untitled and undated publication now referred to as *Sei vedute delle rovine di Pesto* ([1765]; Fig. 91c), and made three other engravings from Joli's images in the same work. Employed at the Neapolitan court of Charles of Bourbon, Morghen was responsible for many publications on archaeological sites in the Kingdom of the Two Sicilies, the purpose of which was to disseminate images of the kingdom. Three years later Thomas Major also published an engraved version of Joli's opening scene (Fig. 91e); although he never went to Paestum himself, he bought numerous drawings from architects such as Jacques-Germain Soufflot and from Italian artists, and used them for his engravings.[35] The French architect Gabriel-Pierre-Martin Dumont, who in 1750, with Soufflot, was the first foreign architect to visit the site after its rediscovery, published the same view in 1769 (Fig. 91g). Jérôme de La Lande (1732–1807) also published the same image (Fig. 91f), stating that he had seen Joli's paintings in Naples and had used them for his engravings.[36] La Lande recounted that Count Felice Gazzola had ordered the drawing of plans and elevations of the temples, and that Joli had shown him several paintings, which Morghen later engraved and published.[37] He described Morghen's plates as a sequence, tracing a walk or tour around the site.[38] Although he was writing at an early stage of Paestum's rediscovery, La Lande already had some interesting observations to make. He noted that the temples were composed of 'Doric fluted columns, without a base, as was practised in the remotest past', and that they could 'serve as a model for artists who know and appreciate the beauties of Greek architecture'.[39] He regarded them as being of the same genre as the temples Le Roy had published in his *Les ruines*, and stated that he knew they had appeared in print in London in 1767, though he had not yet seen the book.[40] The fact that authors referred in this way to one another's work illustrates how extensively their publications circulated.

La Lande's *Voyage d'un français en Italie* (1769) had been published in eight volumes in a small format and was widely read. The British architect Richard Norris, who arrived in Rome in 1769 and visited Paestum in 1771, bought the book when his travel party stopped at a bookseller's on his way to the Capodimonte palace in Naples.[41] At Paestum a few days later, he used Thomas Major's *The ruins of Paestum* (1768) as a guide to the site:

> Sett off at 2 past 4 oClock when we got into the Boat which was a small Open One had 4 Watermen to row and a Charcoal Fire in the Middle of the Boat to warm us for it was intensely cold: was extremely Sick all the Voyage which lasted near 6 Hours. arrived at Pestum at 1/4 past ten which appeard like a desolate Place at your first Arrival – and for half an hour before you can see any house or Building excepting the three Temples & meeting some Buffaloes which look quite dreadfull, and a few Oxen you pass before you arrive at the Temples. a . . . Tower and . . . [a] watch House. by which that part of the Coast is guarded from the Enemy – the Temples are situated about a Mile from the Shore (or not quite so much) Dined before the Middle Temple on Provender brought from Salerno. with Wine we bought at a little Distance examin.d the Temples & Gateway with the Book published by Major an Engraver. the remarks of which are in my Sketch Book.[42]

Norris's travel diary concentrates chiefly on the journey to Paestum and the general view of the three temples.[43] The second scene that visitors saw was described by Dominique Vivant Denon, in his account of a visit in 1778: 'We entered through [the gate], and caught sight of the three large temples arranged side by side, which divide the whole width of the city on a slight diagonal.'[44] This perspective, which showed the temples in line with one another, was popular; first depicted by Joli, it was copied by Morghen, Major and Jean Barbault (1718–1762), among others (Figs 94b, d, e).[45]

It is noteworthy that the same sequence that the images follow in the works we have been discussing appears in the written records of visits to Paestum. For instance Charles Dupaty, the French lawyer who published *Lettres sur l'Italie* in 1788, described how a dramatic succession of scenes unfolded before his eyes:

> I proceed across desert field, along a frightful road, far from all human traces, at the foot of rugged mountains, on shores where there is nothing but the sea; and suddenly I behold a temple, then a second, then a third; I make my way through grass and weeds, I mount on the socle of a column, or on the ruins of a pediment.[46]

Dupaty then paused to take in the almost pastoral scene:

> a cloud of ravens take their flight; cows low in the bottom of a sanctuary; the adder, basking between the column and the weeds, hisses and makes his escape; a young shepherd, however, carelessly leaning on an ancient cornice, stands serenading with his reedy pipe the vast silence of this desert.[47]

Dupaty's poetic account of the different scenes, especially the one he observed from a pediment of animals grazing and the shepherd playing his pipe among the ruins, marks him out as a spectator. But he was also a participant in an experience that he quite consciously directed. By walking through the deserted landscape, with the mountains on one side and the sea on the other, allowing himself to encounter the three temples one after

VUES GÉNÉRALES DE LA VILLE DE PÆSTUM.

Vue prise près la Porte de l'Est.

Planche II.

Vue prise près la Porte du Sud.

Vue prise près la Porte de la Mer.

another, and deliberately observing the details of the ruins, he effectively constructed his own sequence of experiences.

The French architect Claude-Mathieu Delagardette likewise interpreted the location of the temples as if it were a stage set, writing in the introduction to his monograph *Les Ruines de Paestum* ([1799]):

And in truth what an impressive scene it is for an artist observer to see on the sea shore, an immense and arid space, enclosed by walls, covered with columns and majestic

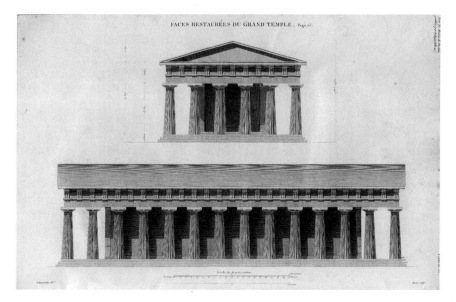

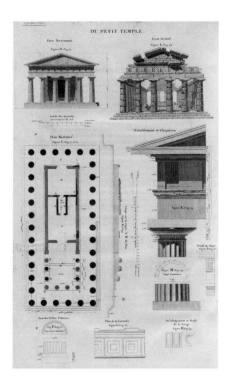

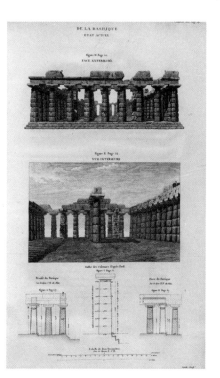

111 (*top*) Claude-Mathieu Delagardette, 'Faces restaurées du grand temple', in *Les Ruines de Paestum* ([1799]), plate IV.

112 (*bottom, far left*) Claude-Mathieu Delagardette, elevations, plan and details of the Temple of Ceres, current and restored states, in *Les Ruines de Paestum* ([1799]), plate X.

113 (*bottom, left*) Claude-Mathieu Delagardette, elevations and details of the columns of the Basilica, current state, in *Les Ruines de Paestum* ([1799]), plate XII.

monuments, where, under a beautiful sky that no cloud darkens, reigns the most absolute silence; having around him no other inhabitants except his travel companions and some peasants busy grazing their buffaloes, nothing but stones and snakes.[48]

Of the next scene, he wrote:

Deeply moved, I was in a sort of delirium, at the sight of the extraordinary scene that stretched out in front of me. But casting my eyes over each of the monuments in turn,

I believed I perceived the sublime genius that had presided over the creation of these masterpieces, and the profound knowledge that directed their execution.[49]

Thus Delagardette recounted pausing twice to observe the scene before his eyes: the setting of the temples in the Italian landscape, and the temples themselves. However, the lyrical style of the introduction is not continued in the rest of the work, which is merely an analysis of the architecture, aiming to prove that he was the first to examine and measure the temples thoroughly. His second plate shows the temples from a distance, a reminder of the way Joli pictured them. But there is an important difference: while other images show almost narrative views of the temples, inhabited by peasants and cattle, Delagardette depicted the ruins as isolated structures in the landscape (Fig. 110), or made clinical draw-

114 Vincenzo Brenna, cross-section and elevations of the Temple of Neptune, *c.*1768. London, Victoria and Albert Museum, Prints and Drawings Collection, VI 8478.12.

115a and b Vincenzo Brenna, details of the order of the Temple of Neptune (*right*) and plan of the temple (*far right*), *c.*1768. London, Victoria and Albert Museum, Prints and Drawings Collection, VI 8478 14, VI 8478 13.

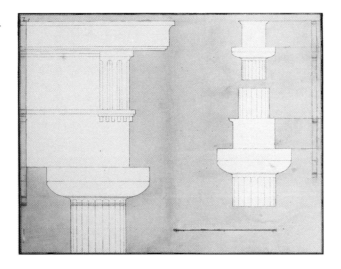

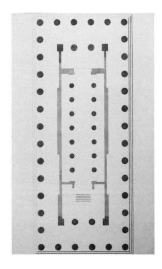

ings of façade, cross-section, plan and details as part of an architectural analysis (Figs 111–13). These images mark the moment when Paestum was canonised and became part of the norm of classical architecture. In all his engravings the lively experience of Paestum is suppressed, an effect that is reinforced even more emphatically in the details, where the specificity of the place is reduced to Paestum's baseless Doric order.

In Delagardette's perspective drawings we see nothing of his being 'deeply moved', as he claimed in his introduction. Rather they express the forceful impression made on him by the immense buildings standing silent on the plain: the temples are not personal to him – they have become objectivised, akin to other ancient monuments. The theatricality that others used to present them to the novice eighteenth-century reader was no longer necessary: for Delagardette they were simply the source of a baseless Doric order, which

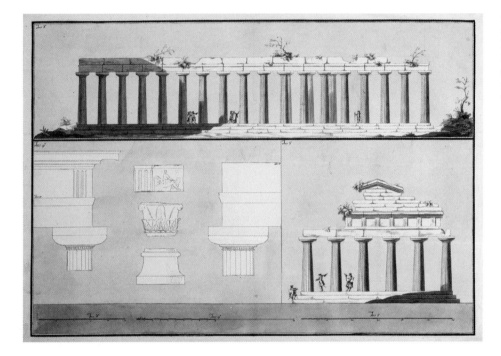

116 Vincenzo Brenna, elevations and details of the Basilica and the Temple of Ceres, c.1768. London, Victoria and Albert Museum, Prints and Drawings Collection, VI 8478 15.

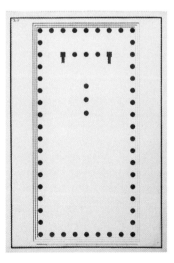 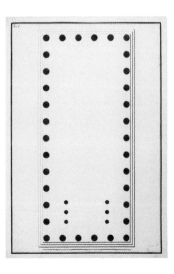

117a and b Vincenzo Brenna, plans of the Basilica (*far left*), and the Temple of Ceres (*left*), c.1768. London, Victoria and Albert Museum, Prints and Drawings Collection, VI 8478 16; VI 8478 17.

118 (*below and facing page*) Giovanni Battista Piranesi, seventeen study drawings for *Différentes vues de . . . Pesto* (1778). London, Sir John Soane's Museum, except *first image*: Paris, Bibliothèque Nationale de France, Département des Estampes et de la Photographie; and *last image*: Amsterdam, Rijksmuseum, Rijksprentenkabinet (for full details see Bibliography).

had become part of a vocabulary, familiar to everyone. But the abstraction required for this canonisation of Paestum involved a departure from the experience that Dupaty and Goethe described and from Piranesi's etchings, as we shall shortly see.

The Temples as a Stage

The next scene in the sequence, after the perspective view from a distance and a view of the ruins from closer at hand, is the aspect of the temples individually, as the visitor approached to enter them. This is the view Paolo Paoli (1720–1790) presented in his monograph on Paestum (see Fig. 109); on the same page as a plan of the site, he depicted visitors hurrying with ladders to measure the monuments, and others, book in hand, comparing the temples with one another and with the plates published by earlier visitors. Paoli's attempt to stage-manage the observations of the architectural connoisseur by picturing these activities is reinforced in the accompanying text, where he claimed that careful

examination would prove the temples to be Etruscan, and thus Italian and not Greek in origin. But Paoli may have had another purpose in showing travellers engaged in their visit: because Paestum was strange and unfamiliar, it helped to place figures among the ruins so that eighteenth-century readers could identify with people who looked and dressed just like them, busy measuring and studying the temples; readers could thus assume the role of the tourist and connoisseur in their imagination, and the temples became a subject fit for cultural discourse.

Vincenzo Brenna (1747–1820), an Italian architect who was hired to draw the temples in 1768 by Charles Townley (1737–1805), the English connoisseur and one of the founders of the British Museum, also portrayed this scene, showing the temples as if they were a stage set.[50] His drawings are an interesting combination of the familiar perspective view, peopled by the grand-tourists as actors, and architectural studies (Figs 114, 116). He also drew plans of the temples, and details of the columns (Figs 115–17). The gesturing figures in the elevations are reminiscent of the typical characters in Piranesi's engravings, but Piranesi pictured Paestum in a radically different way.

There are some strikingly impressive drawings of Paestum by Piranesi, fifteen of which were bought by Soane (Fig. 118);[51] in twenty *vedute*, he presented his own unique vision of the site. While most publications – such as those by Dumont, Morghen, Longfield and Major – tried to bring the monuments to the reader by depicting them like Roman architecture, without the very pronounced entasis that characterises the columns, Piranesi was the only artist to picture them realistically in their ruined state, with an accurate representation of their entasis, and their porous limestone overgrown with vegetation. And while in all existing publications the figures among the ruins were either fictional historical characters or contemporary travellers busy measuring, analysing and discussing the temples, only Piranesi ignored the visitors and depicted simply the local farmers and cattle about their business among the ruins. He represented the actual situation as he saw it – the ruins in decline – without any historical references. In focusing on current reality rather than conjuring up the classical past, he may, like Paoli, have wanted to emphasise that the origin of the temples, a source of debate in the second half of the eighteenth century, was Italian and not Greek. In short his approach eliminated eighteenth-century conventions, and robbed them of their usefulness for contemporary architectural design, because it failed to offer the information the architect needed.

All the monographs on Paestum discussed above have an identical structure: the opening scene is a bird's-eye view or a perspective of the three temples in the landscape, with mountains in the background; in the next scene, identifying easily with the travellers depicted, readers approached the temples, walked around them and entered to take a closer look. The case is quite different in the etchings by Piranesi, who drew local people living and working among the ruins. In some drawings he seems almost to give more attention to the cattle than to the buildings: the temples appear to have become a mere backdrop to the humble life of farmers, who happened to be living around some structures in stone. It is here that we start to comprehend how the ruins functioned for many centuries. They were simply part of familiar surroundings and nobody paid any special attention to them. Only when architects became interested in rediscovering classical architecture and its ancient origins, did the temples begin to be explored. Piranesi's etchings eventually made explicit what eighteenth-century visitors actually knew but had not expressed before: real Greek buildings had very little to do with the Renaissance version of classical architecture.[52]

Theatricality as a Means of Plotting an Architectural Experience

Travellers to Paestum, trying to cope with the strangeness of its architecture, represented their often contradictory experiences in images and texts that used theatrical equivalents. Sequences of experiences, established by earlier representations of the temples, guided them. The landscape surrounding the temples functioned as scenery. The ruins themselves provided a stage.

On this 'stage' an experience in three steps unfolded, which clearly connect the architecture to theatre. First, by the conscious use of certain elements, the beholder employed the temple itself to 'stage' his view, as Soane stated in his Royal Academy lecture, because these elements imbued the building with character. So, by organising the observer's perception of the building, the architectural elements turned it into a stage. Second, the expe-

rience of such a building could follow the intentions of the architect, but through selection the viewer could recreate the building for himself as a sequence of emotions or scenes; Le Roy's account of seeing the Louvre colonnade, and Knight's and Vaudoyer's descriptions of Paestum illustrated this. Third, the representation of this experience could take any of three different forms: it could follow a sequence (as in the images of Paestum by Joli, Major, Morghen and Dupaty) by selecting views that unfold a narrative; it could express the wandering eye (as in Goethe's written and Piranesi's visual accounts) and in that way create a more singular and personal record; or the representation could ignore

119   Giovanni Battista Piranesi, *Différentes vues de . . . Pesto* (1778), plates I–XX.

the experience altogether, by transforming it into an abstraction, conceived by the measuring architect in search of an order, and considered by him in relation to its applicability to contemporary architecture (as Delagardette showed).

In all three steps the spectator's role was crucial – indeed, may even be said to have defined the outcome. In Delagardette's *Ruines de Paestum* the spectator was a measuring architect, in Joli's paintings he was an erudite connoisseur, while in Piranesi's etchings the spectator was endowed with a mood and needed no knowledge of architecture. These different approaches, and the different stages, from the creation of the architecture to the architectural experience to the representation of the experience, show that the role of the spectator was active, not passive, and this, too, tells us something about the analogy between architecture and theatre. In viewing architecture, the observer was not merely a spectator or a witness: architecture is unlike the other arts in that one can step into it and become an actor as well. When an eighteenth-century architect saw the paintings and engravings of Paestum and read the publications about the site, that was not the end of the experience: viewing a representation of architecture could be converted into reality by the experience of actually approaching and entering the building. Architects could travel to Italy, and when they did so in a way they entered the engraving or painting or realised the written description: they could compare their own experience *in situ* to earlier experiences that they had seen depicted or described by those who had gone before them.

One can imagine that looking at the engravings of Paestum and identifying with one of the characters illustrated generated a strong urge to live the exploration of the site oneself. As Denis Diderot put it: 'The performance had been so true to life that on many occasions, forgetting I was a spectator, and an unknown spectator at that, I had been on the verge of getting out of my seat and adding a real character to the scene.'[53] In commenting upon one of Hubert Robert's paintings of ruins in the Salon of 1767, he wrote: 'I would never have been able to prevent myself from dreaming under that vault, from sitting between those columns, from entering your painting.'[54] Elsewhere, Diderot described what he called the invisible fourth wall, which marked the boundary between fiction and reality; when eighteenth-century viewers sat in their armchairs looking at engravings of Paestum, the invisible fourth wall was impenetrable, but it was smashed to pieces when they entered the site themselves and became actors in their own play of architectural experience, instead of mere spectators.

And here another crucial analogy between architecture and theatre comes to the fore: that of temporality. Just as in a play, the narrative structure of a visit to the ruins was created by a temporal experience of successive scenes. Although Joli and Piranesi did not present the same sequence of scenes, both offered a narrative framework to bring Paestum to the eighteenth-century reader, and showed the experience of visiting the site through time. In fact, Piranesi revealed something else as well – in a very graphic form, the experience of wandering around, into and through the temples (Fig. 119). His etchings represented movement so realistically that the reader himself wandered through a forest of columns, continually encountering yet another perspective, illuminated by the changing rays of the sun. As the French architect Rohault de Fleury wrote in his travel diary in 1805: 'the more often I was at Paestum, the more beautiful I found the [Neptune] temple, I have examined it from all sides, [and it] always [presents] a new spectacle, at sunset, in the morning before and after sunrise. It is the character of simplicity not to be so seductive at first sight, but to become more so the longer one looks.'[55]

But Piranesi had something more to say about Paestum. By depicting it in its ruined state he expressed its vulnerability and decay, and presented a powerful message about the porality of the buildings and the visitor's experience of them, and reduced the temples to an abstraction. In his account, the role of the spectator is diminished, whereas in Piranesi's the spectator is essential. The spectator is drawn into Piranesi's vision, which demonstrates, above all, that in the quest for understanding the temples architectural knowledge is of no use, while the experience of the site is vital: like actors on a stage, directed by a pre-conceived script and shadowed by the members of the audience as active participants, eighteenth-century visitors experienced Paestum most keenly through movement.

120 *(following page)* Detail of Fig. 150a.

PART THREE

Contextualising Experiences

CHAPTER 5

In Pursuit of the Primitive:
History in the Making

[J]udging from the heaviness and solidness of their proportions, it is indubitable that these monuments have been constructed by the Greeks in the origin of Architecture, and that they are of a primary antiquity, being very certain that all that remains in Italy of Temples and Monuments constructed by the Romans is of a much lighter architecture, and of a very different proportion and form.[1]

The primitive forms of the temples of Paestum led several travellers to assume that, as these were the oldest temples on Italian soil, they represented the origins of architecture. The Marquis de Sade (1740–1814) wrote: 'it is clear that their construction date goes back to the origin of architecture.'[2] This was a crucial concern at the time that Paestum was rediscovered and explored, when debates on primitivism and on the origins of architecture were at the forefront of architectural discourse. This chapter examines the important role that Paestum and accounts of Paestum played in ideas about primitivism and the origins of architecture.

Primitivism in the Eighteenth Century

In eighteenth-century discussions of the origins of architecture, generally speaking, three tendencies can be discerned: the origins are considered the norm – an example to be followed; the origins are seen historically, as the beginning of a development in architecture; or the origins are seen as a conscious artistic choice. Hence we can distinguish between primitivism as a cultural theory, in which the earliest manifestations were regarded as the best; primitivism as an aetiology, in which a present-day phenomenon was explained by reference to its origins; and primitivism as an aesthetics, in which primitive forms were appreciated and consciously applied. In the first variety, a normative culture and art theory, origins and norms are connected. Norms derive their authority from the mere fact that they represent the origins, because the first beginnings are the most highly valued. The

121 *(facing page)* Detail of Fig. 139.

122 Excavations at Paestum: *Veduta di Pesto, preso fuori della mura presso la porta Settentrionale*, engraving after a painting by Jean-Pierre Péquignot, 1812. Naples, Istituto Suor Orsola Benincasa.

three types of primitivism can be found together, but they also occur separately, as we shall see in this chapter.

Alongside these three tendencies in primitivistic theories, we find another development in the eighteenth century that interacts with them: the archaeological search for historical beginnings by means of excavation or examination of a historical site (Fig. 122). We can differentiate between the primitivists, arguing for origins as norms, and the archaeologists; or, to put it another way, between primitivistic visions and archaeological expeditions. Although the two can work together, archaeological expeditions may, of course, be motivated by other purposes than to prove origins, just as primitivistic theories are not necessarily archaeologically founded. The theoretical quest by the primitivists and the practical quest, through fact-finding, by the archaeologists did not always have the same outcome. On the contrary, more often than not there was a gulf between primitivistic ideas evolved at the desk and the findings about the origins of architecture at an ancient site. This issue became acutely troubling at Paestum.

Primitivists advocated returning to the beginnings of civilisation in the search for origins. The idea that the earliest phase of humankind's existence was superior to contemporary civilisation, and that the 'noble savage' was closer to the arts than any later practitioner because he had been present at their birth originated in antiquity. In their seminal work, Arthur O. Lovejoy and George Boas analysed these ideas in Greek and Roman writings.[3] Primitivism continued during the Middle Ages in the Christian tradition, and on into the eighteenth century, when primitivists such as Jean-Jacques Rousseau drew on classical writings – for example, Seneca's. In modern primitivism, from the Renaissance onwards, exploration and the publication of accounts of newly discovered countries augmented knowledge and provided living examples of primitive cultures. This led to the development of a more critical view of the primitive, as in Montaigne's essay on the barbaric practices of Native Americans.[4] Closer contact with real examples of primitive peoples led to doubts about the theory of primitivism.[5]

In the eighteenth century, ideas about the natural goodness of humankind prompted theorists such as Rousseau and Anthony Ashley Cooper, 3rd Earl of Shaftesbury, to accord primitivism a new importance. They stated that humankind in the primitive state, untouched by later influences, must be good.[6] Shaftesbury argued in favour of nature and simplicity over wealth:

> I shall no longer resist the passion growing in me for things of the natural kind; where neither art, nor the conceit or caprice of man has spoil'd their genuine order, by breaking in upon that primitive state. Even the rude rocks, the mossy caverns, the irregular unwrought grottos, and broken falls of waters, with all the horrid graces of the wilderness itself, as representing Nature more, will be the more engaging, and appear with a magnificence beyond the formal mockery of princely gardens.[7]

In a human being as far removed as possible from society, reason would assert itself, drawing that person close to nature and to God. In *Discours sur les sciences et les arts* (1749) Rousseau argued that intellectual progress had diminished the happiness of humankind, and in *Discours sur l'inégalité* (1755) that luxury leads to vice. In the opening phrase of *Émile, ou De l'éducation* (1762) he urged the living of a virtuous life, far from society: 'Everything is good as it leaves the hand of the Author of things, everything degenerates in the hands of man.'[8] The closer primitive people lived to nature, the freer they were from culture, an idea that appealed in the eighteenth century as a refuge from the decadence and artificiality of the Rococo period.

The term 'noble savage' seems to have appeared for the first time in John Dryden's *The Conquest of Granada* (1669):

> I am as free as Nature first made man,
> Ere the base laws of servitude began,
> When wild woods the noble savage ran.[9]

This savage, not yet touched by sin, appeared often in eighteenth-century literature, as in Daniel Defoe's *The life and strange surprizing adventures of Robinson Crusoe, of York, mariner* (1719). The voyages of Captain Cook in the later eighteenth century uncovered further evidence of uncivilised tribes and regions. At the behest of Louis XV, a similar voyage of circumnavigation was undertaken in the French interest by Louis-Antoine de Bougainville, who memorialised his journey in *Voyage autour du monde* (1771); in his review of Bougainville's book, Diderot stated that this was the only account that had ever made him feel like leaving his own country: 'The wild life is so simple, and our societies are such complicated machines! The Tahitian is in touch with the origin of the world, and the European with its ancientness.'[10]

The first comprehensive definition of primitivism is that given by Giambattista Vico in his *Principi di una scienza nuova* (1725; rev. and enlarged 1744). For Vico language was the means of identifying different levels of civilisation: the moment when language became a written form was the moment culture started. By his account, primitive people were unable to reflect, and so had to rely on their imagination and passions.[11] Burke's conviction that 'savage' people were more susceptible to the sublime (see Chapter 1), follows the same line of thought. The idea that primitive people were subject to deep feelings and strong passions had a powerful appeal. Vico traced the development from the impulsive

towards the rational, reflective mind in the following terms: 'Men at first feel without perceiving, then they perceive with a troubled and agitated spirit, finally they reflect with a
clear mind.' Poetry derived from these wild passions: 'the founders of gentile nations, having
wandered about in the wild state of dumb beasts and being therefore sluggish, were inex-
pressive save under the impulse of violent passions, and formed their first languages by
singing'.[12] Vico was convinced that the arts had originated with primitive people, that
poetry had attained its highest form with them, and that learning, reason and the critical
faculty hindered its production.[13] Primitive people lived only in the immediate present,
and were unconscious of any past or future.

The quest for the origins of architecture made primitivism a focal point of eighteenth-
century architectural theory. Its persistence as a model of thought must be seen in the
light of seventeenth-century developments. In 1673 the architect Claude Perrault published *Dix livres d'architecture de Vitruve corrigés et traduits nouvellement en français*, which
attacked the absolute beauty of the architectural orders as presented by Vitruvius; a decade
or so later, in the Querelle des Anciens et Modernes, the adherents of the two parties dis-
puted whether to take Greek and Roman architecture as a source, or whether to create
new forms.[14] The contradictions that came to light between the principles articulated in
Vitruvius's text and the evidence of Roman monuments stimulated architects to search
for the origins of the orders. Critics of contemporary architecture urged architects to
pursue a model of building that was as close as possible to nature: the so-called primitive
hut. Just as, in general primitivist theories, the myth of origins postulated a return to the
living conditions of primitive societies, in architectural theory it presented the primitive
hut as a design example. Primitivism thus became a new foundation of design theory for
eighteenth-century architecture. In architectural thought the primitivist debate centred on
the origins of architecture as a design solution for contemporary architecture, and sought
these origins in the writing of a history of architecture.

Despite its importance for architectural theory, existing studies of primitivism as a cultural construct pay scant attention to architecture.[15] In the collection of essays *Primitivisme
et mythes des origines dans la France des Lumières, 1680–1820* (1989), for example, architecture
is mentioned only in the introduction and in Christian Michel's article.[16] On primitivism
in the arts generally, a much wider range of scholarship is available, though the focus is
mostly on the twentieth century and the connection with modernism;[17] an exception is
The Sleep of Reason by Frances S. Connelly (1995), which is relevant for eighteenth- and
nineteenth-century primitivism.[18] From the reverse perspective, some monographs on architecture raise the question of origins, but they fail to define the concept in a larger sense.[19]
Joseph Rykwert's *On Adam's House in Paradise* (1972; 2nd edn 1981) is the first important
study of the subject, and is still regarded as authoritative, though it has been challenged.
Ernst Gombrich maintained that Rykwert had no clear argument at all, only an underly-
ing theme – 'man's nostalgia for the past and his desire for renewal' – and dubbed his
methods those of a psychoanalyst rather than an architectural historian.[20] He emphasised
the associative, almost superficial way in which Rykwert connected the several theorists of
the primitive hut and the writings of architects from the sixteenth century to Le Corbusier
and Loos, and accused him of an incoherent approach. In a more recent collection of essays,
Primitive: Original Matters in Architecture (2006), the authors try to define the word 'primitive' in the context of architecture, but they focus mainly on modernism and contemporary architecture.[21]

In this chapter we shall use eighteenth-century sources to analyse how Paestum figured
in the primitivist debates. Bearing in mind the questions about the origins of culture and

architecture that were in the air at that time, what role did Paestum play in eighteenth-century theories on the origins of architecture, and what do we learn about primitivism when the theoretical concept is confronted with Paestum as an exemplar of those origins? To answer these questions, we shall first clarify the distinction between primitivism as a cultural normative theory and as an aetiology by analysing the ideas of two protagonists of these types, Marc-Antoine Laugier and William Chambers. They represent, respectively, the advocacy of the primitive as a design model and the attempt to trace the historical development of architecture from its first 'causes'. We shall trace these trends in demonstrating a slow shift in the interpretation of Paestum from a focus on design towards a focus on history. The following sections will treat the three versions of primitivist theory, by examining the role of Paestum in archaeological and primitivist discussions of the origins of architecture. The difference between origin as norm and origin as aetiology will also feature in our analysis of the primitive as a design solution in Delagardette's and Soane's ideas. Then we shall turn to Piranesi, who straddles the debate because his ideas are relevant to both the design and the historical themes: his ideas on invention will be contrasted with those of Johann Joachim Winckelmann (one of the first to consider the origins of the temples) on imitation. To explore primitivism as an aesthetics, we shall turn to Paolo Paoli, author of a monograph on Paestum and a critic of Winckelmann. Another figure, Quatremère de Quincy, reacted to the ideas of both Paoli and Laugier, and also represents a connection between eighteenth-century thought and nineteenth-century concepts of history. This brings us to the last protagonist, Henri Labrouste. His account forms a kind of ending to the long line of reactions to Paestum, and brings together much of the thinking on the subject, though at the same time it overturns received wisdom on the origins of architecture and the primitive.

Primitive Perfection in Laugier's Mind

To throw a clearer light on eighteenth-century primitivism and its relation to the quest for the origins of architecture we shall examine two versions of the theory of the 'primitive hut', which arise from entirely different reasoning and purposes. In order to make sense of this idea, we first need to review accounts of the origins of architecture in works of classical antiquity. In *De architectura libri decem* Vitruvius situated the origins of architecture in a primitive society, and connected them with the emergence of civilisation. The connection between the development of architecture and that of civilisation gives architecture its *raison d'être* and its importance – an idea that is central in Vitruvius's thought. He described the first beginnings of building as follows:

> Humans, by their most ancient custom, were born like beasts in the woods, and caves, and groves, and eked out their lives by feeding on rough fodder. During that time, in a certain place, dense, close-growing trees, stirred by stormy winds and rubbing their branches against one another, took fire. Terrified by the flames, those who were in the vicinity fled. Later, however, approaching more closely, when they discovered that the heat of the fire was a great advantage to the body, they threw logs into it and preserving it by this means they summoned others, showing what benefits they had from this thing by means of gestures. In this gathering of people, as they poured forth their breath in varying voices, they established words by happening upon them in their daily routines . . . Some in the group began to make coverings of leaves, others to dig caves under the mountains. Many imitated the nest building of swallows and created places of

mud and twigs where they might take cover. Then, observing each other's homes and adding new ideas to their own, they created better types of houses as the days went by.[22]

So, for Vitruvius, the hut, built in imitation of the shelters made by animals, was the first manmade structure.

Other ancient authors also made a connection between nature and architecture. Cicero, a contemporary of Vitruvius, presented nature as a model for functional design:

> Now carry your mind to the form and figure of human beings or even of the other living creatures: you will discover that the body has no part added to its structure that is superfluous, and that its whole shape has the perfection of a work of art and not of accident. Take trees: in these the trunk, the branches and lastly the leaves are all without exception designed so as to keep and to preserve their own nature, yet nowhere is there any part that is not beautiful. Let us leave nature and contemplate the arts: in a ship, what is so indispensable as the sides, the hold, the bow, the stern, the yards, the sails and the masts? Yet they all have such a graceful appearance that they appear to have been invented not only for the purpose of safety but also for the sake of giving pleasure. In temples and colonnades the pillars are to support the structure, yet they are as dignified in appearance as they are useful. Yonder pediment of the Capitol and those of the other temples are the product not of beauty but of actual necessity; for it was in calculating how to make the rain-water fall off the two sides of the roof that the dignified design of the gables resulted as a by-product of the needs of the structure – with the consequence that even if one were erecting a citadel in heaven, where no rain could fall, it would be thought certain to be entirely lacking in dignity without a pediment.[23]

We shall see these ideas return in the writings of the Enlightenment authors who are our chief concern here.

The key eighteenth-century text on the origins of architecture as a design model is the *Essai sur l'architecture* by Abbé Marc-Antoine Laugier (1713–1769), published anonymously in 1753.[24] A second edition, now attributed to Laugier, appeared in 1755;[25] this had a new frontispiece, drawn by Charles Eisen (1720–1778), which would become legendary (Fig. 123). The preface, introduction and first chapter of Laugier's text deal with the origins of architecture.[26] The work was aimed at architects and its main objective was to shape their taste.[27] In an ahistorical, rationalistic thought experiment, the classically educated Laugier proposed that the reader join him in thinking through ideas about the first origins of man:

> It is with Architecture as with all other arts; its principles are founded upon simple nature, and in the proceedings of the latter are clearly shewn the rules of the former. Let us consider man in his original state, without any other help, without other guide, than the natural instinct of his needs.[28]

First nature presents itself in a positive light:

> He wants a place to rest. Beside a gentle stream he notices a grassy place; its fresh verdure pleases his eye, its tender growth is inviting; he approaches and, stretching out lazily upon this spangled carpet, he thinks of nothing but enjoying the gifts of nature in peace: he lacks nothing, he desires nothing.

But soon nature shows a harsher side:

> but presently the Sun's heat, which scorches him, forces him to seek shelter. He perceives a neighbouring wood, which offers him the coolness of its shade; he runs to hide

in its thickets and behold him there content. In the mean time a thousand vapours arise by chance, meet, and gather together, thick clouds obscure the sky, a terrible rain pours down in a torrent upon this delightful forest. The man poorly protected by the canopy of leaves, knows not how to defend himself from the wet, which penetrates everywhere.

Then nature offers him a ready-made dwelling: 'A cave presents itself, he slips into it, and, finding himself in the dry, congratulates himself on his discovery.' However, soon the disadvantages of this refuge emerge:

new sources of annoyance make him discontented with his abode. He finds himself in darkness, he breathes unhealthy air; so he leaves [the cave], resolved to make up for the carelessness and neglect of nature by his own industry. The man wants to make a lodging for himself, which shelters without burying him.

After having analysed the possibilities nature can offer, and their negative outcomes, Laugier proposed the obvious solution: he pictured the moment when man decided to build his primitive hut. Nature presented the materials, but man had to construct his dwelling by himself:

Some fallen branches in the forest are suitable materials for his design. He chooses four of the strongest, which he raises perpendicularly and disposes in a square. On top of these he places four others crosswise, and upon these he raises some that incline from both sides and meet in a point. This kind of roof is covered with leaves packed closely together so that neither the sun nor the rain can penetrate; and so the man is housed.[29]

Laugier argued that the wooden hut was humankind's first built habitation, and that primitive man devised it unaided simply by using his natural common sense. To Laugier, man was at his most intelligent in his primitive state. His 'petite cabane rustique' consisted of four poles, four beams and a roof: tree trunks planted upright in the ground supported the horizontal beams, and the roof was set at an angle to shed rainwater.

How did Laugier arrive at this thought experiment? Which parts of his essay are invented and which are based on real experience or research? The *Essai* was written in opposition to Vitruvius's *De architectura libri decem* and inspired by the writings of the architectural historian Abbé Jean-Louis de Cordemoy (1655–1714). In the preface, Laugier lost no time in positioning himself against Vitruvius, and declaring his admiration for Cordemoy's *Nouveau traité de toute l'architecture* (1706).[30] To Laugier there was only one way to create good architecture, and to explain his ideas he appealed to both erudite knowledge and architectural experience. He started by describing an experience of buildings in terms of a Longinian sublime and different levels of pleasure and distaste:

> In considering with attention our great and fine edifices, my soul hath experienced various impressions. Sometimes the charm was so strong that it produced in me a pleasure mixed with transport and enthusiasm: at other times without being so lively drawn away, I found my self employed in an agreeable manner; it was indeed a less pleasure, but nevertheless a true pleasure. Often I remained altogether insensible: often also I was surfeited, shocked, and mutinied. I reflected a long time upon all these different effects.[31]

Laugier applied experience empirically, explaining how he repeated the same observations to assure himself that the same buildings always produced the same effects. These experiments and his enquiries into the opinions of other people led him to three conclusions: that architecture has essential beauty, that architecture is capable of having an impact, and that the architect has to have genius.[32] And then one day he was struck by a self-evident truth.[33] What followed, necessarily, from early man's search for shelter and its resolution in the invention of the first house, was, of course, that the primitive hut was a model for contemporary architecture to build on. This was the ultimate goal of Laugier's thinking and is entirely in line with the primitivist ideas expressed in the introduction to this chapter.

> Such is the step of simple nature: It is to the imitation of her proceedings, to which art owes its birth. The little rustic cabin that I have just described, is the model upon which all the magnificences of architecture have been imagined, it is in coming near in the execution of the simplicity of this first model, that we avoid all essential defects, that we lay hold on true perfection.[34]

In primitivistic theories, the first beginnings, because of their character of origin, are held to be true and valid for contemporary society. So, for Laugier, because his hypothesis of the origin of architecture represented the simple perfection of building for the sole purpose of giving shelter, it was the perfect model. Laugier did no archaeological research, he did not travel in search of the primitive dwelling, nor did he find it in reality. By thinking about the first dwelling at his writing-table, he created an image of what it may have looked like. But this dwelling is completely ahistorical: it belongs to no specific time frame or chronology; it has no successors; it is not the work of a particular tribe, a certain culture or specific surroundings. It is a product of the mind. From this concept of a dwelling, the closest possible to nature, Laugier moved on to the transformation of the hut into a building of stone – to him the simplest and most rational next step:

> Pieces of wood raised perpendicularly, give us the idea of columns. The horizontal pieces that are laid upon them, afford us the idea of entablatures. In fine the inclining pieces which form the roof give us the idea of the pediment. See then what all the masters of art have confessed.[35]

In switching from the third person – he (primitive man) – to the first person plural – us (the civilised people) – Laugier represented the architectural transformation: civilised man turned the wood of the primitive hut into stone: tree trunks became columns; the wooden beams became the entablature; the roof made the shape of the pediment. In Laugier's theory the hut is the model for architects; it embodies the constructional fundamentals of architecture, which are quite independent of different styles and different periods. He aimed to trace the true and immutable principles of architecture, and like many other primitivists found them in the oldest sources, which, because of their character of origin, have permanent and unchanging value. Laugier was an exponent of primitivism as a normative cultural theory. To him, all architecture should imitate the primitive hut, and the more closely a building resembled it the more nearly it approached good design. In Laugier's view, humankind's first dwelling should supply design principles for all building. But Laugier did not quite maintain the purity of his theory: paradoxically, at the end of his *Essai*, he stated that what is necessary for a temple – namely, the use of columns – is not obligatory for a house; so, while the hut was the model for good architecture, it applied mainly to public buildings.

From establishing the primacy of the primitive hut as the perfect design model, the model for all architecture, Laugier went on to explore the three 'default' elements of architecture: column, entablature and pediment:

> Do not let us lose sight of our little rustic cabin. I can see nothing therein but columns, a floor or entablature; a pointed roof whose two extremities each of them forms what we call a pediment. As yet there is no arch, still less of an arcade, no pedestal, no attique, no door, even nor window. I conclude then with saying, in all the order of architecture, there is only the column, the entablature, and the pediment that can essentially enter into this composition. If each of these three parts are found placed in the situation and with the form which is necessary for it, there will be nothing to add; for the work is perfectly done.[36]

In pursuing his comments on columns, Laugier first argued that the pilaster should be abolished, a statement that was to lead to much criticism.[37] In his foreword to the second edition of the *Essai* he addressed the objections of a critic to this proposal, repeating his argument that 'nature produces nothing square'.[38] The elements of a building were there to support the architecture, he said, and every part should be essential: it should not be possible to remove anything without ruining the building.[39] Here Laugier was obviously drawing on the work of the Renaissance architect Leon Battista Alberti, though his point did not relate to composition but purely to the need for certain structural elements.[40]

Laugier's view of another characteristic of columns is significant in the light of Paestum: the use of an entasis or *renflement*. Laugier stressed that nature has never produced anything that could authorise an entasis,[41] which might suggest that he would not have regarded Paestum as an example of good architecture. Laugier never visited Paestum, and may not have seen the unpublished drawings by Soufflot and Dumont that circulated in Paris from the 1750s onwards.[42] At the time he was writing, nothing had been published on the temples. But the disjunction between Laugier's version of primitivism and the reality of Paestum gives the first indication of a problem: the two were incompatible, for although Paestum was very ancient, it did not conform to the rules Laugier laid down in his theory.

Paestum further undermines Laugier's concept in that the example he gave of perfect architecture was a Roman rather than a Greek building. This was not because he preferred Roman architecture but because the building in question, the Maison Carrée in Nîmes, consisted, in his view, of the simplest forms: columns, entablature and a roof.[43] It represented the perfect example of an architecture constructed on rational principles (Fig. 124). Everyone admired it, he said, connoisseur or not, because: 'all therein is agreeable to the true principles of architecture. A long square, wherein thirty columns support an entablature, and a roof terminated at the two extremities by a pediment, this is all it contained; this collection hath such a simplicity and grandeur that strikes every eye.'[44] In fact, the Maison Carrée has walls, and thus consists of more than just columns, an entablature and a pediment, but for the sake of his argument Laugier ignored this. After discussing the column, Laugier went on to the entablature – good examples were the Louvre colonnade and the chapel of Versailles[45] – and the pediment.[46] While he conceded that his theory reduced architecture 'to almost nothing',[47] Laugier argued that it was up to the genius of the architect to create good architecture.

At first sight, Laugier's theory of the primitive hut may seem to resemble Vitruvius's story of the building of the first dwelling. But there is an enormous difference: that between primitivism as a cultural theory and as an aetiology. Laugier's 'cabane' may well

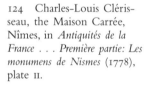

124 Charles-Louis Clérisseau, the Maison Carrée, Nîmes, in *Antiquités de la France . . . Première partie: Les monumens de Nismes* (1778), plate II.

125 Samuel Wale, frontispiece to the first English edition of Marc-Antoine Laugier, *Essai sur l'architecture* (*An essay on architecture* (1755)).

have been influenced by Vitruvius's hut and its successors, but it took a different form and assumed a different meaning. In *De architectura libri decem* Vitruvius argued that architecture originated in the imitation of animal shelters, and that it could develop only with the evolution of civilisation. Many authors after him adopted this point of view and stated that architecture was related to the primitive hut historically: the hut was the origin of architecture and all subsequent buildings were descendants of it. In this interpretation historical progress is an important element.[48] Laugier broke with this notion: in his *Essai* the hut is not a historical reference point but a design principle, and in that sense ahistorical; its form is already perfect and architecture should return to it, not seek to improve on it. Its essence is the constructive principle. We might note that Laugier's thought experiments are very similar to those of Jean-Jacques Rousseau.[49]

An English edition of the *Essai* was published in London in 1755; it was reissued (unchanged except for the title page) in 1756 (Fig. 125).[50] The frontispiece to the English edition was drawn by Samuel Wale, who depicted the primitive hut under construction, following images in the Vitruvius editions by Cesare Cesariano (1521) and Walther Rivius (1548); his depiction is entirely consistent with Vitruvius's ideas. By contrast, the famous frontispiece to the second French edition, by Charles Eisen, showed a hut created by nature, in line with Laugier's primitivist vision of the first phase as representative of the fundamentals of architecture.[51]

Chambers's Concept of the Hut
in Architectural History

The years after the publication of Laugier's *Essai* saw an increase in the number of publications in which the primitive dwelling was discussed.[52] One of them was written by the architect Sir William Chambers (1722–1796). An analysis of his writings can help to explain the important difference between primitivism as a cultural theory and as an aetiology. The latter version is based on the search for origins through architectural history. It makes use of the primitive hut, just as Laugier did, but in a very different way. We have seen the difficulties posed by adopting the primitive hut as a design model; now we shall contrast that idea with theories in which the primitive hut accounts for the birth of architecture and its historical development, taking Chambers as the representative of this approach.

In 1759, shortly after Laugier's *Essai* appeared, Chambers published his *Treatise on civil architecture*.[53] Chambers had studied in Paris at the École des Beaux-Arts in 1749 as a student of Blondel, then from 1750 to 1754 in Rome. He never went to Paestum; in fact, he never went further south than Rome. During his years there he kept company with the French *pensionnaires* at the Académie de France, and frequented Piranesi's circle.[54] The French influence is clearest in his early architectural work, but also emerges in his writings. In his *Treatise*, Chambers developed the form of the primitive hut, starting from a conical structure, which he regarded as the most logical original shape, because it was 'the simplest of solid forms and most easily constructed'. According to Chambers, primitive men evolved this form in imitation of nature:

> At first they most likely retired to caverns, formed by nature in rocks; to hollow trunks of trees; or to holes dug by themselves in the earth; but soon, disgusted with the damp and darkness of these habitations, they began to search after more wholesome and comfortable dwellings. The animal creation pointed out both materials, and manners of construction; swallows, rooks, bees, storks; were the first builders: man observed their instinctive operations, he admired; he imitated; and being endued with reasoning faculties, and of a structure suited to mechanical purposes, he soon outdid his masters in the builder's art. Rude and unseemly, no doubt, were the first attempts; without experience or tools, the builder collected a few boughs of trees, spread them in a conick shape, and covering them with rushes, or leaves and clay; formed his hut: sufficient to shelter its hardy inhabitants at night or in seasons of bad weather. But in the course of time, men naturally grew more expert; they invented tools to shorten and improve labour; fell upon neater, more durable modes of construction, and forms, better adapted than the cone, to the purposes for which their huts were intended.[55]

According to Chambers, man began to be dissatisfied with the initial conical hut, and conceived the cubic hut in its place: 'wherever wood was found, they probably built in the manner above described; but, soon as the inhabitants discovered the inconvenience of the inclined sides, and the want of upright space in the cone; they changed it for a cube'.[56] The next step was the pedimented hut; it was this form that was imitated in stone and was the ancestor of columns and beams, and also of the decorative aspect of architecture, a pediment often being used as an ornament (Fig. 126). Thus Chambers proposed an evolutionary development,[57] and gave the hut a different meaning from Laugier. He was not the profound theorist that Laugier was: an image he drew in about 1759 of a primitive hut might appear to represent a version of Laugier's theory in the *Essai*, but in fact it was probably meant to be a gardener's shed (Fig. 127).

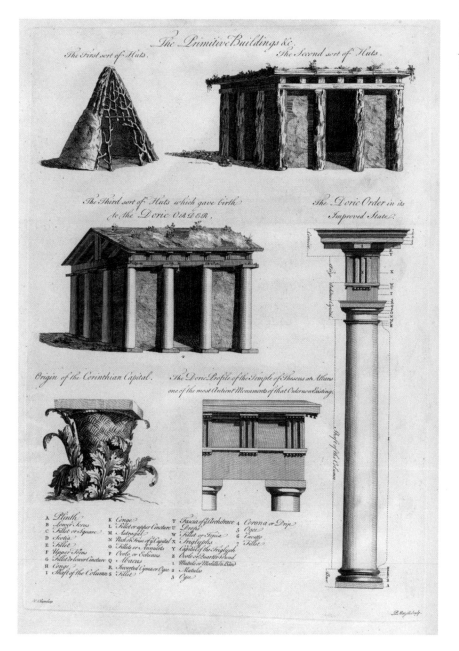

Another important difference between Chambers and Laugier had to do with his ideas on progress. To Chambers, although the Greeks were the first to transform the elements of the primitive dwelling into architecture, it was the Romans who brought them to perfection. The hut itself was not perfect, but it could be perfected through historical development. His explanation of the origins of architecture was no more than a brief introduction to his main argument: the primitive hut supplied the primary elements of architecture – column and architrave – but the secondary elements, the mouldings, were essential to make architecture attractive, indeed to transform a building into architecture. Chambers quickly moved on to the orders, which he regarded as a combination of these primary and secondary elements, and focused on their proportions, following the sequence of Tuscan, Doric, Ionic, Composite and Corinthian identified by the Venetian architect

Vincenzo Scamozzi (1548–1616). To Chambers, therefore, and to many other contemporary critics of Laugier, the primitive hut was not a standard of perfection: it was nothing more than a crude first phase in the evolution of architecture; far from being perfect in itself it was perfected only in the developments that followed. Civilisation was important, because only through civilisation could man improve on these savage forms. As far as Chambers was concerned, origins and reason did not play a major role in architecture; instead he argued from visual appearances. He was not a primitivist, he merely searched for the origins of building to explain the historical development of architecture.

In comparing Chambers and Laugier it becomes clear that the primitive hut could be interpreted in different ways, and functioned differently in architectural theory depending on the perspective and agenda of the author. Laugier can be situated in the intellectual milieu of Rousseau, while Chambers followed in the line of Vitruvius. In one case the primitive hut was a design model for eighteenth-century architects, but in the other it had no useful place in contemporary architecture. Despite the fact that Laugier's theory was much more highly developed than that of Chambers, when the origins of architecture

Rediscovering Architecture

became the subject of archaeological investigation his thought experiment broke down in the teeth of the evidence. Paestum exemplifies what happened when primitivistic theories were confronted with the real beginnings of architecture.

Delagardette and Soane Employ Paestum's Primitive Purity

The three temples at Paestum were the oldest to be found on Italian soil. Many travellers mentioned this in a general way, speculating on their possible origins. In the accounts a connection was often made between two aspects of the temples: their primitive forms and their great age. Paestum was very different from the monuments of Rome, whose building history and functions were well documented through excavation and publication. At Paestum, the so-called Basilica was the most problematic case: its primitive form, lacking a pediment, and the uncertainty about its purpose, history and date of construction led to diverse speculations that went on well into the nineteenth century. In fact, eighteenth-century travellers paid less attention to the question of whether the temples were Greek or Roman than to the fact that they were ancient – Winckelmann referred to them as 'the oldest surviving architecture in the world outside Egypt'.[58] Being so different from the familiar examples of classical architecture, the temples evoked ideas about archaism and the primitive, ideas that were reinforced by their strange architectural forms and the porous stone of which they were built.

Towards the end of the eighteenth century the primitive character of the temples came to be viewed in a more and more positive light. The French architect Claude-Mathieu Delagardette, for example, found the Neptune temple a perfect representative of Greek architecture. He particularly relished its purity and lack of ornament, and the rudeness of the materials:

> It is in these ruins that we find the Doric Order executed in all its primitive purity; it is in these ruins that Architecture bears that character both simple and sublime that the Dorians imparted to all their works, which distinguishes them from other people of Greece.[59]

This passage is significant because Delagardette asserted that primitive means pure, and that the superior character of the ruins at Paestum arises from their simplicity. He also assigned them to a special category, distinct from that of other Greek architecture. We find similar reactions in many other writings, in which visitors stated that its rude and simple forms set the architecture apart, echoing Delagardette's equation of primitive and pure. Delagardette did not underline the antiquity of the temple, but associated its form with the primitive, and represented it as unaltered, unspoiled and unaffected. These statements are reminiscent of Laugier's view that all evolution from the first model is a deterioration, though Delagardette associated the primitive not with humankind's first shelter but with the Doric order, and Paestum's pure version of it. Indeed, Delagardette's approach is quite different from Laugier's. Although he was looking for a model in the primitive architecture of Paestum, he located it in the order, not in the rationality or simplicity of the structure. And he made no direct connection with the primitive hut.

Delagardette first wrote about Paestum seven years before he visited the site and thirteen years before the publication of his monograph about it. His *Règles des cinq ordres d'architecture de Vignole* (1786)[60] was an edition of Vignola's *Regola delli cinque ordini d'architettura* (1562), with an introductory essay in which Delagardette announced the baseless Doric of Paestum as a new order. Later (Chapter 6) we shall see how he tried to present Paestum to young architects as a model for contemporary architecture, but *Règles des cinq ordres* is equally interesting for another reason – namely, his representation of the primitive hut. Plate 4, captioned 'Origine de l'architecture', shows an image of the primitive hut that is far removed from Laugier's: built of wood, it has four columns, with capitals and rings at the bottom to indicate a sort of base, an entablature and a pediment (Fig. 128). It is a building rather than a simple primitive dwelling. In the background are depicted the forest and two other forms of primitive dwelling: a tent and a hut in cone form. In the foreground some people are working large timber beams while others sit watching. Next to the building three people are evidently discussing the structure. In the accompanying text, Delagardette followed the Vitruvian model, but took it somewhat further.[61] Conical huts and other types, he claimed, were the predecessors of the 'cabane', which was a perfected version of the hut; so, like Vitruvius, he attributed the development of architecture to the evolution of civilisation.

128   Claude-Mathieu Delagardette, 'Origine de l'architecture', in *Règles des cinq ordres d'architecture de Vignole* (1786), plate 4.

Pl. 4.   Page 16

P.M. Inv.   Le Pagelet Sculpsit.

ORIGINE DE L'ARCHITECTURE.

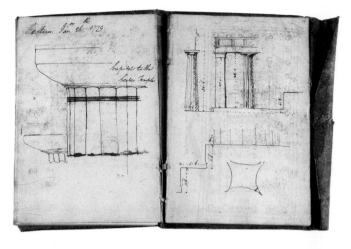
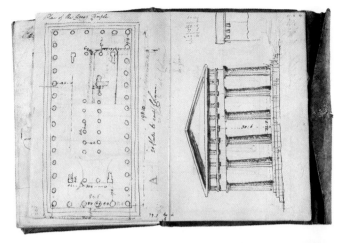
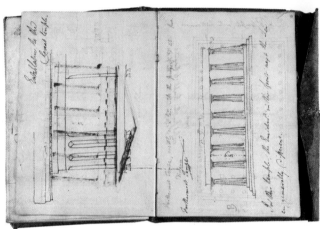
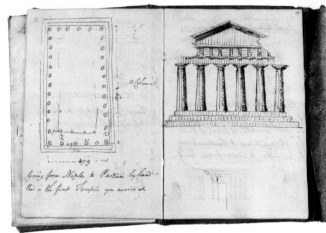

In the prospectus for his Paestum monograph, Delagardette referred back to his Vignola edition and to earlier publications about the site that had informed his ideas about its architecture:

> Stimulated, myself, by the desire to fix the attention of our young students on the primitive purity of the Architecture of these people, I inserted on trust in the first edition of my treatise of the five Orders . . . the details of a Doric order of Pæstum, that were given to me by the Author of one of these publications. But I had not seen the original then.[62]

Evidently Delagardette went to the site (in 1793) on purpose to see for himself the 'primitive purity' of the architecture of the temples: pure primitive forms were aesthetically satisfying and fit to serve as a model for young architects, though not in the sense that Laugier intended. Delagardette concentrated on the simplicity of the order, an aesthetic appreciation of its qualities that made him want to import the order to France. We see here how during the eighteenth century the preference shifted from the elegant Roman orders to the more massive, simple Greek Doric. However, taking Paestum as a model was not straightforward. The quest for the origins of architecture had given eighteenth-century architects an interest in the temples, but although they found ancient architecture at Paestum, they did not find a design model. On the contrary, as John Soane discovered,

129a–d   John Soane, sketches of the temples at Paestum, 1779: (*top, left*) details of the Temple of Neptune; (*top, right*) plan and elevation of the Temple of Neptune; (*bottom, left*) detail of the Temple of Neptune and elevation of the Basilica; (*bottom, right*) plan and elevation of the Temple of Ceres. 'Italian Sketches / J: Soane / 1779', London, Sir John Soane's Museum, Vol. 39/14–19.

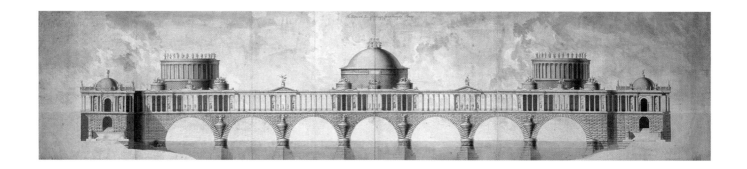

130 John Soane, design for
a triumphal bridge, submitted
to the Royal Academy
competition in 1776, drawing
dated 1777. London, Sir John
Soane's Museum, 12/5/4.

a confrontation with the temples themselves simply led to the deconstruction of the accepted image of antiquity.

Soane visited Paestum in 1779 (Fig. 129) and noted in his diary:

> The Architecture of the Three Temples, is Doric, but exceedingly rude, the Temples at the extremities in particular, they have all the particul[arities] of the Grecian Doric, but not the elega[nt] taste; they seem all form'd with the same Materials, of Stone formd by Petrification which continues to this Day.[63]

Like Delagardette, he observed the Doric character of the temples, but found it 'rude' and inelegant, largely because of the rough building material. Twenty years after his visit to Paestum, Soane designed a barn for Henry Greswold Lewis, a friend from his Grand Tour days, at Malvern Hall in Warwickshire. Soane's 'Barn à la Paestum' featured baseless paired Doric columns in brick, supporting a wooden entablature. But, although the columns are baseless Doric and undecorated, they have neither the proportions of the Paestum temples nor their specific characteristics – the entasis and the wide capitals. So why did Soane refer to Paestum in naming his design? Which elements did he think were characteristic of Paestum? The following year (1799) he applied the baseless Doric order again, in a revision of the design for a triumphal bridge, originally featuring Corinthian columns, with which he had won the Royal Academy's gold medal in 1776 (Fig. 130). (It was with the Academy's travelling scholarship, awarded in 1777, that he had travelled to Italy.) In my view, the baseless Doric order, used in the triumphal bridge, the barn and other designs by Soane – a dog kennel (1779; Fig. 131) and the later church for the Duke of York (1827; Fig. 132) – was not the essence of Paestum's appeal for Soane.[64] Although Soane used the term 'à la Paestum', there was no literal application of a Paestum order in his architectural designs: there is a more noteworthy trace of Soane's experience at Paestum, which can be related to his views on the origins of architecture.

Soane was to translate his ideas on primitive architecture more clearly in a design he made, at the request of Philip Yorke (1757–1834), for a dairy at Hamels in Hertfordshire (1781–3). Yorke had been his companion on his visit to Paestum in 1779 and was one of many patrons Soane came to know in Italy.[65] Soane called his design 'a Dairy in the primitive manner of building' (Fig. 133),[66] and in his description of his design one can detect the traces of Laugier's *Essai*: 'The pillars are proposed to be the Trunks of Elm trees with the bark on and Honey suckles & Woodbines planted at their feet, forming festoons &c. The Roof to be thatched & the ends of the Rafters to appear.'[67] Laugier's influence is hardly surprising, since Soane owned an impressive collection of ten copies of the *Essai*. He also owned many books on primitivism, including Rousseau's *Essai sur l'origine des langues* (1781), Joseph-François Lafiteau's *Moeurs des sauvages ameriquains, comparées aux moeurs*

des premiers temps (1724), and Lord Kames's *Sketches of the History of Man* (1774). Christopher Woodward suggested that the design expressed a conversation between Soane and Yorke on the origins of the Doric order, started at Paestum and resumed at Hamels.[68] In Soane's drawing, the timber columns are similar to the tree trunks supporting the roof of the hut in the frontispiece to the second edition of the *Essai* (1755; see Fig. 123). But while Soane subscribed to Laugier's ideas, the building is above all an interesting combination of the primitive wooden hut, with its thatched roof, and more sophisticated features indicative of the progress of civilisation, such as the vernacular peddle-dash used for the walls and the entablature.

In the first of his Royal Academy lectures, which he read on 27 March 1809, Soane showed a sequence of images to illustrate the evolution of the primitive hut made of wood into the Grecian Doric temple built of stone.[69] The large drawings Soane used during his lectures were specially prepared by his pupils and assistants; one such drawing of a primitive hut (Fig. 134) showed (like Laugier's frontispiece) aboriginal people wearing animal hides;[70] a man, a woman and two children are pictured in the middle of the dwelling, while in the background two men are carrying timber to construct another hut. (These figures were inserted by Antonio van Assen (1767–1817), a topographical artist, who usually drew the stylish Regency figures in Soane's lecture drawings of building

131 (*above left*) John Soane, design for a canine residence, 1779. London, Sir John Soane's Museum, 14/4/2.

132 (*above right*) John Soane, design for a sepulchral church, 1796. London, Sir John Soane's Museum, 13/5/6.

133 John Soane, perspective view of the dairy at Hamels Park, 1781–3. London, Sir John Soane's Museum, 13/7/1.

134 (*above left*) John Soane,
drawing of a primitive hut,
undated, for Royal Academy
lecture I. London, Sir John
Soane's Museum, 27/2/4.

135 (*above right*) Thomas
Major, interior of the Temple
of Neptune, in *The ruins of
Paestum* (1768), plate IX.

perspectives.) The impressive construction, with its four rows of columns, in two tiers in the central rows, perfectly exemplifies Laugier's principles of support and weight. More importantly, Soane's drawing adopts not only the double ranks of columns, as in the Temple of Neptune, but also exactly the same perspective that many artists chose when representing the interior of the Paestum temple (Fig. 135). As we saw in Chapter 4, Dumont, Magri, Major and Paoli all used this same viewpoint. Although the scale of Soane's building is different, and the plan is not precisely the same as that of the temple, the similarities are striking. Furthermore, people appear in the middle of the drawing, as in the Paestum depictions, and the wooden beams lying in the foreground resemble the architectural remains represented in many images of Paestum. And in both Soane's drawing and the views of the Temple of Neptune, the spectator is drawn into the middle of the building by the perspective.

What does this tell us? First that the visual tradition of depicting temples had an influence on the manner in which the construction of the first dwelling was illustrated. Second that a public whose minds were well stocked with architectural examples, found versions of the primitive hut depicted in a similar way acceptable, and were thus convinced by this account of the beginnings of architecture. The more it resembled an abstract version of an antique temple, the more plausible the primitive hut was as the original model for Greek architecture. In Soane's lecture the well-known view of Paestum's temple was mimicked to compose the image of the primitive hut, which was then used – in a sort of reversal – to illustrate the forerunner of Paestum's structure. Thus, in these depictions, history was reversed: Paestum served as a model for the building that was supposed to have been its model.

It must be remembered that the lecture drawing shows a dwelling, not a temple. The origin of architecture was a hut, but at Paestum the oldest architecture was a temple. Laugier had already noted in his *Essai* that the design demands for temples differed from those for houses. For that reason, also, the temples of Paestum as exemplars of the first architecture were problematic. Retrospectively, this offers another insight. If a Greek temple and its wooden predecessor were represented in this way, the construction was evidently of key importance to travellers; the emphasis they put on gravity, weight and support in their descriptions of the temples also found expression in their drawings. In the absence of ornament and decoration to catch the visitor's eye, drawings, engravings and paintings highlighted the two tiers of columns in the Neptune temple, the upper ones smaller than the lower ones, and the way the columns carried the entablature and roof. Thus, the depictions of the primitive hut, in the tradition of the Paestum images, suggest that what mattered to travellers was not the function of the temples or their place in history, but how people used to construct buildings, in the purest and simplest way possible. In a sense, Soane's lecture drawings went back in time to origins: a temple at Paestum, dedicated to the gods, became a primitive dwelling, built by people dressed in animal skins. But the projection of Paestum onto an entirely imaginary construction of the primitive hut was not at all simple, as Delagardette's and Soane's interpretations show. Delagardette concentrated on the order, admiring the primitive forms of the columns of the Neptune temple because they represented ancient and therefore pure architecture. Soane focused on the construction, of which the simple hut offers an account. One made an aesthetic judgement, the other gave an explanation of structure, but both demonstrated how problematic it was to transform Laugier's primitive hut as a theoretical ideal into a workable design model.

In his first Royal Academy lecture Soane began by showing drawings in the following sequence: temples in Egypt, Palmyra and Baalbek; two cave temples near Bombay; tombs in Persepolis, Telmessus and Corneto; a grotto; temples at Luxor, Pozzuoli, Pompeii and Palmyra; and other examples of Egyptian architecture.[71] Then he turned to four images of different types of primitive dwelling (somewhat along the lines of Chambers's engravings of three types of hut in his *Treatise* (see Fig. 126): a 'primitive hut of conical form', which Soane attributed to 'primitive Greece', a 'primitive hut with flat roof', then a 'primitive hut with pedimented roof', and finally a 'primitive hut with a central row of posts' (Fig. 136).[72] Immediately afterwards, Soane showed his students depictions of the Basilica temple at Paestum in perspective and plan. This – the oldest of the Paestum temples – appeared before another image of an Egyptian temple, followed by two drawings of timber buildings with two rows of posts and a hut with supports under the principal rafters (see Fig. 134). The lecture ended with two buildings in Athens: the Parthenon and the Temple of Theseus.

When we examine the text of the lecture, one element emerges unmistakably: Soane made a direct connection between the origins of architecture and Paestum. He argued that when families became larger, dwellings had to be enlarged as well:

> The horizontal beams, in particular, being of course considerably lengthened, curved downwards and threatened ruin. A row of posts or supports however, placed from front to rear, dividing the entire space into two equal parts, removed the defect and gave security to the inhabitants. This mode of construction probably suggested the idea of that particular manner of using columns to be seen in one of the temples at Paestum.[73]

By connecting a private dwelling to a divine temple, Soane showed that, in this context, the function of the building took second place to the construction method: in time, tectonic aspects would become increasingly important, displacing the significance of columns and their role in architectural design. He elaborated on this idea in the lecture, explaining how a larger dwelling called for new design solutions. When the dwelling became much higher, the rafters needed to be longer and therefore required more support:

136a–d John Soane, drawings of primitive huts for Royal Academy lecture I: (*right*) 'primitive hut of conical form', undated; (*far right, top*) 'primitive hut with flat roof', 20 May 1807; (*far right, bottom*) 'primitive hut with pedimented roof', 1807; (*facing page*) 'primitive hut with a central row of posts', undated. London, Sir John Soane's Museum, 27/2/1, 2, 5, 3.

These supports were placed immediately over the others, under the beams, and probably gave the first indication of pillars placed upon pillars; and in this early work we perceive the reason why the Greeks, faithful to their primitive model, made the upper pillars in the hypaethral temples so very short in proportion to those immediately under them.[74]

Soane illustrated this passage, in which he explicitly referred to the primitive hut as a model for the Greeks, with the drawing we have already discussed (see Fig. 134), in which the Paestum perspective is used to show the construction of a primitive dwelling. Soane's primitivism is aetiological: he explained the form of the temples through the form of their primitive predecessor.

Soane began his second Royal Academy lecture with the Temple of Solomon in Jerusalem and went on to treat the Greek Doric order, showing an image of the order of the Temple of Neptune at Paestum.[75] He again referred to the primitive hut, explaining how some theorists stated that columns originated from the trunks of large trees. Other writers, he said, thought that they derived from bunches of reeds or saplings, but that these could only ever have been decorative and could never have provided structural support: 'In Grecian works the column owed its origin to the rudely shaped timbers which were placed as supports to the roofs of the early habitations, and we shall likewise find bases and capitals owe their origin to early constructions in timber.'[76] In the same lecture, Soane claimed, much in the same vein as Laugier, that the primitive hut had provided a model for the ancients, or rather their 'great artists', but that the rich Roman buildings marked a decline of this former greatness; Roman architecture had sacrificed simplicity and no longer demonstrated the 'important truth' that the 'essentials of the Grecian orders, more especially those of the Doric, might and must be explained by the imitative system of construction in timber'.[77]

Rediscovering Architecture

Both Delagardette and Soane had observed the primitive temples with an architect's eye, and in the same spirit as Laugier. But each of them answered Laugier's plea for an architectural model in his own way, which made the relationship between the primitive hut and real ancient architecture problematic. Delagardette tried to make Paestum's purity of form the model, thus focusing on the aesthetic aspects alone; he made no link with the primitive hut. Soane made such a link, in order to show an evolution in architecture – that is, to provide an aetiology; in so doing he may be said to have been more an architectural historian than an architect. He aligned the primitive hut with Paestum, but did not set up either as a design model. We turn now to a theorist who, like Delagardette, observed the temples as an architect and designer, but who was strongly opposed to Laugier's ideas. Piranesi's theories raise more questions about the concept of primitivism – now as an aspect of invention.

Piranesi's Theories on Invention in Architecture

Piranesi presented his ideas in his *Osservazioni sopra la lettre de M. Mariette* (1765), published with the *Parere su l'architettura* and *Della introduzione e del progresso delle belle arti in Europa ne' tempi antichi*.[78] These texts are of great importance because in them Piranesi positioned himself in opposition to Winckelmann and Julien-David Le Roy, in what scholars often refer to as the Graeco-Roman debate. Piranesi presented Roman, rather than Greek, art as the summit of Western art, and, more importantly, pointed to the Etruscans, not the Greeks, as the artistic predecessors of the Romans. By making these claims, he could also prove that the Romans had never been inferior to the Greeks.

The *Osservazioni* was Piranesi's response to a letter by the art collector and connoisseur Pierre-Jean Mariette (1694–1774), a defender of Greek superiority. Mariette published his critique of Piranesi's *Della magnificenza ed architettura de' Romani* (1761) in the *Gazette Littéraire de l'Europe* in 1764. In other articles in the *Gazette*, French readers were exposed to the views of John Locke, David Hume, Lord Kames, Winckelmann and Arthur Young, implicitly illustrating the changing position of Italian culture in modern Europe. Italy was no longer regarded as the source of powerful cultural influence or intellectual leadership; instead, the *Gazette* portrayed it as offering curious treatises on antiquity and pleasing poetry. In the pages of the *Gazette*, Piranesi was the Italian author most often and most minutely criticised: his traditionalist Italian humanist view of Roman splendour, his quotations from famous but dubious sources, and his attempt to shore up Livy's version of Roman history by appealing to the evidence of Roman monuments all came in for adverse comment.

Mariette claimed that the Etruscans were Greek colonists and that Roman art thus had its origins in Greek art, echoing Winckelmann in his belief that the Romans had lost the 'beautiful and noble simplicity' of the Greeks. He argued that the presence of very ancient and impressive architectural structures in Italy, built before contact with the Greeks had been established, did not prove the artistic abilities of the Romans, since these structures had been built by the Etruscans, who were Greek in origin. Piranesi refuted Mariette's philhellenic arguments point by point in his *Osservazioni*. His *Parere su l'architettura*, set out this same polemic on the superiority of the Romans, and is composed as a dialogue between two rival architects: an opponent (Protopiro) and a defender (Didascalo) of Piranesi's own ideas. Protopiro is the rigorist, who defends an architecture based on rules, rationality and imitation, while Didascalo aims at an architecture full of invention, arguing that without it architecture would become a 'vile occupation, in which one could only make copies'.[79] They argue about the power of *sfrenata licenza* ('unrestrained invention') versus the tyranny of aesthetic theories: it was this *licenza*, Piranesi stressed, that rescued architecture from mere copying. He illustrated his ideas with his own designs, and planned in 1767 the addition of a series of full-scale plates to the *Parere* (a project that remained unfulfilled), which showed Greek, Etruscan–Roman and Egyptian motifs in juxtaposition (Fig. 137). These inventive compositions, which show how the architect can be creative, are more than mere stylistic examples: they offer models for how to treat history.

The *Osservazioni* and *Parere* are not only a plea for invention, they also represent a rejection of the authority of Vitruvius. But Piranesi did not restrict his attack to Vitruvius, he also turned his fire on Laugier: Didascalo (Piranesi's alter ego) rejects the rigorist Protopiro's arguments for smooth columns without bases or capitals, architraves without fasciae and friezes without triglyphs. In a passage on the walls of a building, Didascalo demonstrates the absurd outcomes of Laugier's position:

> Let us observe the walls of a building from inside and outside. These walls terminate in architraves and all that goes with them above; below these architraves, most often we find engaged columns or pilasters. I ask you, what holds up the roof of the building? If the wall, then it needs no architraves; if the columns of the pilasters, what is the wall there for? Choose, Signor Protopiro. Which will you demolish? The walls or the pilasters? No answer? Then I will demolish the whole lot. Take note: buildings with no walls, no columns, no pilasters, no friezes, no cornices, no vaults, nor roofs. A clean sweep.[80]

In this *reductio ad absurdum* of Laugier's ideas, Piranesi allowed Didascalo, his mouthpiece, to claim that the architecture of antiquity was no longer relevant as a model for design. The dependence on rules and systems by the so-called rigorist architects were condemned:

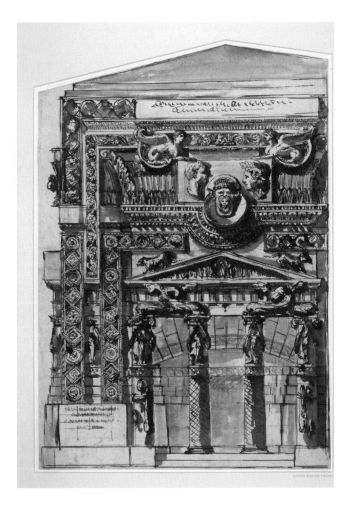

137 Giovanni Battista
Piranesi, design for a
fantastical façade, 1767, pen
and brown ink with brown
wash, over red and black
chalk. London, British
Museum, Department of
Prints and Drawings,
1908,0616.44.

'Didn't I tell you that if you were to build according to the principles you have got into
your heads – that is, to make everything in conformity with reason and truth – you would
have us all go back to living in huts?'[81]

This wink at Laugier's *Essai* and his ideal of the hut is an implicit critique of the primitive dwelling as a model and the rejection of ornament. Piranesi showed that a view of
architecture based on rationalist thought experiments reduced the art of architecture to a
mere hut – indeed, to a state in which architecture is no longer architecture. Conversely,
when ornamentation is beautiful, architecture will be beautiful as well, since ornament
relieves monotony in architecture. He dismissed all architects who followed antiquity, who,
'from the moment when this kind of architecture was invented until it was buried beneath
the ruins always worked in this way'.[82] All the travellers who went to Asia, Egypt and
Greece, searching for inspiration for their own practice in the origins of architecture, did
the same: 'Someone goes off to inspect the antiquities and brings back the dimensions of
a column, a frieze, or a cornice with the intention of enriching architecture with proportions different from those which we have become accustomed to seeing.'[83] To Piranesi,
it was false to think that it is possible to copy the architecture of antiquity, for not one
building from this period has the same proportions as another, nor do the individual parts
of different buildings, such as columns, have the same dimensions. He suggested, for
example, that an examination of all the Doric temples of Greece, Asia and Italy, would

reveal so much variety in their proportions that one could define as many orders as there were temples; this (he claimed) was proven by the publications of Le Roy and Stuart and Revett.

With these ideas in mind, one might assume that Piranesi would reject Paestum for its simplicity and purity. But his description of the architectural forms in *Différentes vues . . . de Pesto* (1778) makes clear that, while he viewed the temples as primitive, he also found in them what we may call ahistorical design solutions. He was certainly in search of the origins of architecture, but without the primitivistic motives of Laugier and others. The distinction we made in the introduction to this chapter between primitivism as a cultural theory and the search for origins in the historical development of architecture is clearly illustrated here.

In Chapter 4 we focused on the engravings Piranesi made after visiting Paestum in 1777, but the text of *Différentes vues* is at least as interesting as the images, though it has received far less attention. In existing studies, this work is often represented as marking Piranesi's conversion to Greek architecture,[84] but because scholars situate his book only in the context of the Graeco-Roman debate, they tend to overlook the many novel aspects of his text. To begin with, the identification of Roman and Greek architecture was not at all clear in the eighteenth century, and in the case of Paestum this was certainly still the subject of debate; there was no consensus about the Greek origin of the temples, and even well into the nineteenth century some architects thought they were Roman or Etruscan. More importantly, this was not what fascinated visitors to Paestum. As Piranesi did not know that the temples were Greek, the *Différentes vues* cannot mark his conversion to the Greek camp in the Graeco-Roman debate and should not be read in that light.

A careful reading of the text leads to other conclusions. In describing the largest temple of the three, the Temple of Neptune (Fig. 138), Piranesi revealed his hand: 'This Work

138 Giovanni Battista Piranesi, interior of the Temple of Neptune, in *Différentes vues de . . . Pesto* (1778), plate XII.

clearly shows that the Architect was master of his art, that he was not held back by Systems dreamed up on a whim, nor even dependent on imitating works in wood.'[85] This passage is, of course, a direct reference to Laugier's proposal of the primitive hut as a model, and is a statement of direct opposition to the idea of architecture as imitation. Piranesi exposed three important ideas here: the architect is an artist; he does not design according to certain rules and systems, and he does not copy. Interesting though his remark on the imitation of works in wood may be as a side-swipe at Laugier and Vitruvius, Piranesi's argument about the architect as inventor is more significant. As he had already presented related ideas in his earlier publications, we should read his work in relation to his earlier published theories.

In the text accompanying plate VI, the interior of the Basilica temple (Fig. 139), Piranesi discussed how the capitals of the columns of the pronaos (the vestibule between the portico and the cella) have an entasis, like the columns of the main body of the temple. To Piranesi, the architect of the temple had done something interesting here: the little volute, he said, gave the columns a sense of lightness, which they would have lacked had the architect copied the Ionic order literally. In condemning imitation and promoting invention, Piranesi stated: 'One sees here . . . features of an invention that one does not expect, and which, despite their boldness, oblige one to admit that one could not have done better in a similar case.'[86] Piranesi's references to the choices an architect has to make in creating a building, suggest a continuation of his earlier thinking, in the *Parere* and the *Della magnificenza*, rather than a break with it; here, as in those publications, Piranesi commented upon an architect's design decisions and the need for invention and genius in the design process, but now he was talking about primitive rather than contemporary architecture. Interestingly, in observing and analysing the temples, Piranesi imagined himself as their architect in antiquity. He evaluated the design choices this architect had made, and

139 Giovanni Battista Piranesi, interior of the Basilica, in *Différentes vues de . . . Pesto* (1778), plate VI.

140 Ribart de Chamoust,
the prototype and development of the 'ordre françois
trouvé dans la nature', 1776,
in *L'Ordre françois trouvé dans
la nature . . . Orné de planches
gravées d'après les dessins de
l'auteur* (1783), plate II.

why he had made them, connecting the architect's invention and genius with his own
theories and experience of decision making. So he regarded Paestum not as a historical
design model (Delagardette) or as a derivation of the primitive hut (Soane), but as inspiration for designing with an inventive mind. The Architect (always written with a capital
initial in his texts) figures here as Artist.[87] These ideas, first formulated in his *Parere*, evidently resonated with his observations of the architectural forms at Paestum.

Because Paestum represented the origins of architecture, Piranesi felt justified in arguing
for a lack of decoration: the absence of bizarre ornamentation made the temples even
more convincing in their grandeur.[88] He again attributed this to the conscious choice of
the architect, made in order to enhance the building's solemnity:[89]

> Regarding this temple, whether it was the custom of the nation to favour the heavy
> and simple, or whether it was the wisdom of the Architect, it is clear that this enter-
> prise was conducted and completed with dignity by omitting the majority of the
> embellishments to make it solid and sober.[90]

The character of the building was explained from a point of view that we can connect
with primitivism. The building is simple and unadorned, because that makes it closer to
nature and to the materials from which is it built: 'for these sorts of monuments, being
constructed in a hard material, it was true to the principles of the art not to change the
nature of it too much[;] . . . a building made entirely of stone should maintain a great air

of strength and solidity'.[91] Thus Piranesi saw the temples almost as an outgrowth of nature, and as dependent on the local conditions at the site.

Ribart de Chamoust, in his *L'Ordre françois trouvé dans la nature* (1783), proposed something similar. Arguing for a French order in architecture (Fig. 140), de Chamoust advised against imitating the Greeks, suggesting a 'return to primitive theory, that is to say, to Nature herself'.[92] De Chamoust's close association of primitive architecture with nature, and its connection with the development of a new architecture are interesting. An order must grow naturally out of French soil, as the Greek orders had grown out of their native soil. In this linking of architecture to nature, de Chamoust approached both Piranesi and Laugier, who in their different ways both proposed that original architecture – whether in stone or wood – had exploited the knowledge acquired by primitive man from nature and natural materials, which he hardly needed to adapt.

What Piranesi saw at Paestum confirmed his long-standing ideas about architecture. He made no attempt to date the temples or to determine their chronological order, so it seems that their history did not much interest him. What he focused on were the different architectural elements and the choices made about them by the architect as artist. For instance, in the Neptune temple, the artist had given the entrance a heavy, majestic effect by means of a cornice. In respect of the Basilica, he again questioned Vitruvius's authority. Along with many other eighteenth-century travellers, Piranesi was puzzled about the function of this temple in antiquity: the building had no architrave and, unusually, had an uneven number of columns; furthermore, there were no independent indications of its use. Piranesi claimed, in *Différentes vues*, that he had searched Vitruvius in vain for any mention of an uneven number of columns in basilicas, curias and temples, and because he knew nothing about the rites and uses of the building, declared that he was unable to explain this unusual feature. The Basilica, therefore, was not only an architectural and functional enigma, but was also deprived of historical context.

Piranesi's preoccupation with the origins of architecture expressed itself in his architectural designs. These display an interesting mixture of forms, derived from the different periods that epitomised to him the first beginnings: Etruscan, Egyptian and Greek. The theme returns in his discourse on Roman architecture. His admiration for the invention and technical skills of the Romans is displayed in his statement that they were the first to build buildings of such magnificent construction. In his observations on Paestum, too, he highlighted progression and invention rather than imitation: the temples were not, in his view, copies of pre-existing models, but were inspired by, and close to nature, and in that sense he foreshadowed Labrouste, as we shall see later.

History as a System in Winckelmann's Thinking

If Piranesi's stand against imitation and in favour of invention constituted a critique of Vitruvius and Laugier, it was also aimed at Johann Joachim Winckelmann. As is well known, Greek art was Winckelmann's ideal, and he argued for *imitatio*, not in the sense of mere copying but as a source of inspiration. He distinguished between *das Nachmachen* as 'copy' and *die Nachahmung* as 'imitation'. If done with intelligence, an imitation (in Winckelmann's sense) could be transformed into something new and autonomous. The praise of pure and perfect beginnings in the history of art implied an appreciation of originality.[93] Conversely, in order to find originality the artist had to go back to the origins of art: 'The only means by which we can become truly inimitable, if it is possible at all, is the imitation of the ancients.'[94] In his quest for the origins of art, Winckelmann longed to visit Greece. But Paestum was the closest he came. In fact, the more he reflected on and wrote about the perfection of Greek art, the less eager he was to travel to Greece. It seems as if he was afraid that his expectations would be disappointed: Greece became a utopian image so perfect that reality could only destroy it.[95] So, instead of travelling to Greece, Winckelmann pursued his quest for the origins of art and architecture through research, seeking to trace their historical development by making comparisons and relating works to one another chronologically. He searched obsessively for origins, in written sources and in the works themselves,[96] strongly motivated by his belief in chronology as a discipline and method;[97] in his view, chronology was to be written through the construction of series and the detection of similarities. Given this approach, Paestum – a unique site – was likely to pose problems for him. And so it did.

The difficulty Winckelmann had in accommodating Paestum in his theories is discernible from his many letters. These evoke the temples from time to time, focusing on the antiquity of the buildings and on his sensation of being one of the first foreigners to visit them, presenting him more as an archaeologist than as an art historian. Winckelmann first mentioned Paestum in 1756, at which time he had been in Rome for almost a year. He did not visit the site until two years later. As he never travelled to Greece or Sicily, Paestum provided him with the only example of ancient Greek architecture he saw for himself: his knowledge of the architecture of temples in Sicily and Athens came from books – for example, those by Stuart and Revett, and Giuseppe Maria Pancrazi – and from information supplied to him by the architect and engineer Robert Mylne.[98] Winckelmann's happy anticipation (*Vorfreude*) of his visit to Paestum is expressed in an enthusiastic letter to Giovanni Lodovico Bianconi, a doctor from Bologna, sent from Rome on 29 August 1756:

> [How] Happy [I should be]! if I could travel all over Magna Graecia. The three temples at Paestum, 50 miles from Naples, [are] of an Architecture perhaps more ancient than that of the period of Pericles; they have been talked of for only two years, although they are almost entire, and have been waiting all this time to be discovered[.] [T]his oversight leads me to believe that there could be an infinity of beautiful things, scattered and neglected, above all in Taranto and its vicinity. I would be determined to go there even if I had to go on foot.[99]

Two years later, when Winckelmann eventually visited the site, the same preoccupations – the situation of Paestum in relation to Naples, the antiquity of the architecture and the fact that the temples had only recently been discovered – continued to dominate his letters. Writing to his friend Heinrich von Bünau on 26 April 1758, he noted: I have made several journeys far into the country, to see everything: among other things I have visited Paestum . . . to see three old Doric temples or Portici, that are in an almost complete state of preservation; this is the oldest surviving architecture in the world outside Egypt.' He stressed his urge to publish about the monuments and his astonishment that the buildings, though always visible, had never been mentioned until only a few years before. He went on to say that now people were making engravings of them, and also that the landscape towards Salerno was more beautiful than anyone could imagine.[100] Winckelmann was plainly very much interested in recently discovered sites, and his reactions to Paestum differ greatly from those of the travellers we have discussed hitherto. He did not describe the site or the temples in any detail, did not relay his feelings or his perceptions to his reader, and said nothing about an architectural experience. Instead, his account voices archaeological interest in an almost unknown site, and declares his eagerness to publish his 'discoveries'. He seems to have been more interested in the simple existence of three ancient temples at an inaccessible site than he was in examining them closely.[101] And this is revolutionary in itself: Winckelmann was the first to think about Paestum as a historical phenomenon, in the sense of its standing at the beginning of a historical development. His feeling of history also manifests itself in a self-conscious reference to his own presence on the spot: 'Maybe I am the first German who has been there.'[102]

After this initial expedition, Winckelmann went back to Paestum in 1762 and 1764, though he seems not to have found these return visits to what we might call 'Greece on Italian soil' particularly rewarding. By constantly repeating how ancient the temples were and referring to his status as the first German to visit them, Winckelmann betrayed his inability to grasp the character and significance of the site. His letters to the painter Adam Friedrich Oeser, Bianconi again, the writer Johann Caspar Füssli, the collector Philipp von Stosch, and the Swiss writer Salomon Gessner, which reiterate the same observations, all suggest that Winckelmann simply could not get his bearings at Paestum.[103] This unease represents the conflict between theory and reality that beset Winckelmann all his life. Apart from the evident connection between Paestum and the origins of architecture, he had little of interest to say about the temples, so the descriptions of Paestum in his letters are usually variations on the same theme.[104] Mostly he wrote about his plans for a publication about the site, or mentioned Paestum only briefly – for example, telling his correspondent to go there.[105] It was only in one letter to Giovanni Lodovico Bianconi that Winckelmann made an interesting comparison between architecture and sculpture, explaining the conical form of the columns, and in that way being one of the first to remark on the entasis in Paestum's temples.[106]

In spite of the cursory treatment it received in his letters, Paestum played some role in Winckelmann's publications on the origins of architecture: *Anmerkungen über die Baukunst der Alten* (1762) and *Geschichte der Kunst des Alterthums* (1764). The letters trace how these ideas came about. It was Winckelmann's aim to write a cyclical history of art, showing how the general processes that determine art returned as art evolved.[107] In the *Geschichte*, Paestum is evoked only once, but at a significant point: the engraving that opens the first chapter shows a column from one of the temples (Fig. 141). The chapter, entitled 'On the Origins of Art and the Reasons for its Diversity among Peoples', begins Part 1 'Investigation of Art with Regard to its Essence'. In a descriptive list of the illustrations, Winckelmann explained that for this chapter he chose a collage of different objects of the most ancient works of sculpture and architecture:

> The section of a column is drawn after a column at a temple at Pesto, on whose buildings I provided the first report in the preface to my *Anmerkungen über die Baukunst der Alten*. These temples were probably built not long after the 72nd Olympiad, and to all appearances they are older than any building that has survived in Greece itself. The column should be more tapered, a fact that the draftsman did not observe.[108]

In the same image, along with the Paestum column, Winckelmann depicted a statue in ancient Egyptian style, a terracotta relief of a sphinx and an Etruscan vessel, demonstrating that the origins of art began with the Greeks, the Egyptians and the Etruscans. In his publications, Winckelmann never failed to emphasise that Paestum was the most ancient example of Greek architecture on Italian soil.

The observations on the temples in the *Geschichte der Kunst* are very general, but the remarks Winckelmann made in the *Anmerkungen* are more relevant. Here he wrote at

141 Title page to Part I,
Chapter 1, of Johann Joachim
Winckelmann, *Geschichte der
Kunst des Alterthums* (1764);
the engraving (by Michael
Keyl) shows a column from
one of the temples at
Paestum.

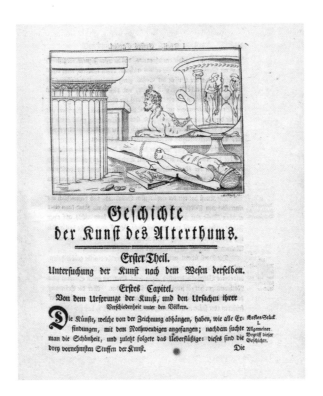

length on Paestum, though his text is descriptive rather than analytical. Winckelmann was aware that he was the first writer to offer a thorough description of the temples, and the first foreigner to publish about them in any detail; he was also the first to found his judgements on a comparison with other ancient architecture: 'These are, without doubt, the oldest Greek buildings, and, apart from the temple of Agrigento in Sicily and the Pantheon in Rome, there is no other work of [ancient] architecture that is so perfectly well preserved.'[109] He remarked that the temples were not designed according to the precepts of Vitruvius's *De architectura*, and that the entasis was proof of their antiquity. In comparison with the temples in Sicily (which he had never seen but which he knew from Robert Mylne's drawings, made on the spot), he thought the Paestum temples extraordinary, chiefly for their capitals, though he also observed that the columns at Agrigento were not as stumpy as those at Paestum. Thus Winckelmann's comments in the *Anmerkungen* consist of comparisons of particular features of the temples at Paestum with those of the Agrigento temple, and his main point relates to their great age.[110]

Winckelmann encountered insurmountable problems in his attempt to integrate Paestum into his chronological approach to art history. He construed the temples as representing the beginnings of architecture, but at the same time as part of a whole group of early buildings, and this caused him to ignore their distinctiveness. His approach contradicted that of Soane, Piranesi and, as we shall see, Labrouste, who all drew attention to the uniqueness of the site, understood the significance of this and aimed to interpret it. Winckelmann's idea of history was one of progression, and the difficulty of engaging Paestum in this history explains the very general nature of his remarks about it. However, Winckelmann's concern with the history of art will shed some light on further developments in the eighteenth and nineteenth centuries, notably the writings of an author whom we met briefly in Chapter 4: Paolo Paoli.

Rediscovering Architecture

Paoli Turns History Around

While Winckelmann presented a careful chronological system that accounted for the origins, decadence and decay of the arts, his critic Paolo Paoli, one of the more controversial authors on Paestum, addressed the topic of origins in terms of a third type of primitivism: the primitive as an aesthetics. In the same year that Paoli's contentious monograph on Paestum appeared, the papal antiquarian Carlo Fea (1753–1836) published a new Italian edition of Winckelmann's *Geschichte*, under the title *Storia delle arti del disegno presso gli antichi, di Giovanni Winkelmann, tradotta dal tedesco e corretta e aumentata dall'abate Carlo Fea* (1783–4). Volume 3 of the translation (1784) included a remarkable text by Paoli in the form of a letter to Fea, entitled 'Lettera sull'origine ed antichità dell'architettura al signor abate Fea'. Twenty years later a French translation of the same letter was published in a French edition of the *Geschichte*.[111] The exclusive focus of scholars on Paoli's false assumption that the temples at Paestum were Etruscan has led to the neglect not only of his monograph, but also of his more significant remarks in the letter, which shed interesting light both on Paestum and on the eighteenth-century pursuit of origins.

Winckelmann's *Geschichte* had first been published in Italian in 1779.[112] Carlo Fea found this first edition badly translated and annotated, and so turned back to the German original, in which he uncovered many errors of facts. In preparing his new edition, he corrected Winckelmann's sources and added his own descriptions of monuments and recent discoveries.[113] Fea's radical treatment of Winckelmann's work and his blunt attack on the reputation of a widely acclaimed intellectual began to receive highly critical reviews almost as soon as it was published.[114]

Paoli's letter, framed as a critique of Winckelmann, began by stating that the *Geschichte* was a seminal work but needed a few corrections.[115] He complimented Fea, as editor of the translation, on presenting the text well and annotating it thoroughly, applauding the addition of further information on the monuments that Winckelmann had written about, and the introduction of new ones. Paoli stated that Fea had, while compiling the translation, asked him to comment upon it, and especially on Paestum; he thanked Fea for having communicated his 'wise observations' and for obliging him to express 'his feelings about Winckelmann's remarks on the architecture of the ancients, and in particular on the ruins of Paestum'.[116] Fea himself had never visited the temples, so he had used Paoli's measurements to correct those given by Winckelmann; Paoli boasted that the dimensions given in his monograph were the most accurate so far published and that they corresponded exactly to the temples themselves.[117] He also referred to an Italian edition of the *Anmerkungen*,[118] in which, he claimed, Winckelmann adopted the false idea, originally proposed by Le Roy, that the Doric order consisted of three periods. This misapprehension had led to the erroneous conclusion that the temples represented the beginnings of architecture. Even if these were the oldest buildings, Paoli asked, how could we tell that the Dorics really built them? – an unanswerable question, which he followed up by exposing Le Roy's faulty historical interpretation of early architectural forms arising from an over-hasty analysis of his examples.

Paoli's polemic is remarkable. His new interpretation of the temples at Paestum completely undermined current ideas on the origins of architecture:

because [the temples] post-date the time when the doric order was already fixed to the height of six diameters, we cannot apply to them the primitive and very ancient method of building that we had supposed; on the contrary, we must view them as capricious constructions, in an antique style, if you like, but [one that was] poorly understood;

142 Paolo Antonio Paoli, comparison of the 'Tempio di Pesto' (Temple of Neptune) with an example (taken from Vitruvius) of an Etruscan temple, in *Paesti . . . rudera: Rovine della città di Pesto* (1784), plate XXIII.

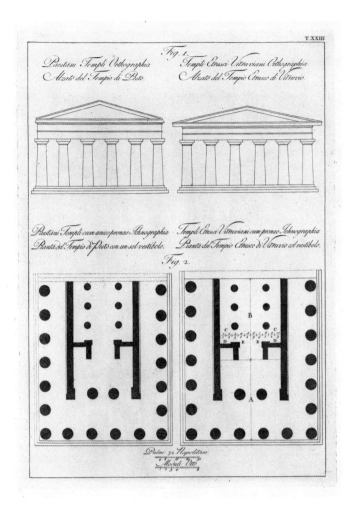

whether someone wanted to make use of the stones that were to hand, or whether there were some other circumstances would be hard to guess, and even useless to try to find out.[119]

In this significant passage Paoli disconnected 'primitive' in the sense of 'very ancient' from the application of particular forms in architecture that look primitive, claiming (in opposition to Winckelmann, Le Roy and other writers on ancient Greek architecture) that the architectural forms of the temples at Paestum do not necessarily indicate an ancient way of building. The temples might be ancient, but they should be seen as fanciful constructions, examples of a badly understood or oddly interpreted antique style – an idea that resonates with Piranesi's. Asking himself why these architectural forms were different from ancient classical architecture, Paoli concluded that it was because the builders had used the building material that happened to be available: thus primitive forms might result from an artistic or a practical choice, and have nothing to do with origins. This disconnection of primitive in the sense of early and original from primitive forms in the sense of rough and uncouth as a conscious choice is further explained in another passage:

We do not have to consider a work of art as ancient, or as evidence of one of the first attempts at this very art, for the simple reason that it is rough, misshapen, without proportions as a whole, and without decoration; because in modern times we have seen works appear that were badly conceived and executed without the least method.[120]

Here we can discern a new variety of primitivism: after primitivism as a cultural theory and primitivism as an aetiology, now we have aesthetic primitivism. Primitive, simple architectural forms do not automatically signify a beginning or the origins of architecture: they may indicate an artistic choice, made freely for any of a number of reasons at any time in history – late or early. In Paoli's view, this aesthetic primitive was appropriated as part of a repertory of artistic possibilities by the ancestors of the Italians, the Etruscans. It was independent of history. Because primitive was a choice that could be made at any moment in time, according to aesthetic preference and local circumstances, it had nothing to do with the beginnings of architecture.

Paoli presented his letter to Fea as a sort of summary of his publication on Paestum, referring to his volume in many of the notes. He explained how he had looked for evidence at the site – in the building materials, the architectural forms, and the degradation of the stone by erosion and decay. This physical evidence had convinced him that the temples were of Etruscan origin (Fig. 142): 'these monuments are of short proportions, and . . . are formed by large masses of stone; but I did not view that as sufficent evidence to identify the character of the works of these people [the Greeks], or the work of a period before the origin of the three Greek orders'.[121]

In the letter, Paoli conceded that the temples at Paestum were very similar to Greek temples – at least in their squat columns – but maintained that this was no reason to think that any of them was Greek. In truth, Paoli turned and twisted rather tortuously in order to make the point not so much that all three temples were Etruscan but rather that history had taken a different course from the one set out in books by Le Roy, Winckelmann and others, and that what they presented as proper to Greek architecture was in fact much older. This view contradicts what Paoli had said earlier, which in itself is of interest in the quest for a connection between Paestum and the origins of architecture. He aimed to prove that before the Greeks started to build, there existed enormous complexes constructed by the Etruscans. The Greeks, he claimed, were not the inventors of architecture: their only contribution was to have embellished buildings by introducing elegance of style and exquisite ornamentation.[122] In fact, Paoli located the very origins of this type of architecture in the Temple of Solomon in Jerusalem: 'Here, then, is the origin of that heavy, massive, solid architecture, which came to birth in the Orient . . . and which the Greeks adopted afterwards.'[123]

Paoli explicitly set aside the assumption that architecture was created out of trees, claiming never to have seen a tree that resembled a column with a base and a capital.[124] And instead of huts, he regarded natural grottos as the first shelters and as the models for the first dwellings.[125] Using stone as his material, man had made the first building, and thus it was not only the origin of architecture that was connected to stone, but its evolution as well.[126]

When Paoli came to deal with columns, he made the remarkable claim that Paestum proved that the origins of columns lay with the Egyptians. To him, the direct predecessors of Paestum's architecture were pyramids and more particularly obelisks:

So then, we have only to lop off the corners of an obelisk, and truncate it to a given height, and we shall have an antique column, broad at its base and narrowing in the form of a pyramid, like the oriental columns used to be, and those of the two temples [Neptune and Ceres] at Paestum still are.[127]

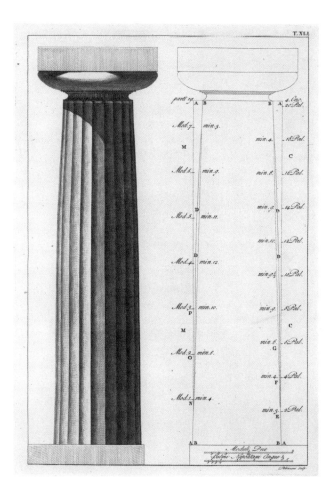

If one extended the lines of the columns of the Neptune temple, he went on, the resulting form would have the same proportions as an obelisk, and the same procedure applied to the columns of the Ceres Temple would produce the same proportions as the obelisk in St Peter's square in Rome.[128] What is so peculiar about this argument is that Paoli took no account at all of the structural aspects of architecture: architects who wrote about Paestum tried to work out how the ancients had constructed buildings, but Paoli completely ignored this question. Identifying 'the same taste and character' in obelisks as in columns, and having observed that they have the same proportions, he tried to clarify how an entasis (Fig. 143), which to him was an Etruscan invention, could be derived from an obelisk. In his view, this relationship explained the marked narrowing in the shafts of Etruscan columns 'and why the most ancient of this order had a pyramidal form'. To reduce the 'abruptness of the pyramidal outline', without compromising the solidity of the column, the Etruscans had introduced an entasis.[129] According to Paoli, even the fluting originated in the obelisk: by shaving off the corners of the obelisk to give it eight, sixteen or thirty-two faces (or – at Paestum – starting from a three-sided obelisk, to create six, then twelve, then twenty-four faces), and by making small hollows or channels in these faces to give them more elegance, 'one will obtain a round and fluted column'.[130] Both the entasis and the fluting indicated the antiquity of the columns and could never have originated in wood.[131] It is clear from this that Paoli viewed columns as ornament more than as con-

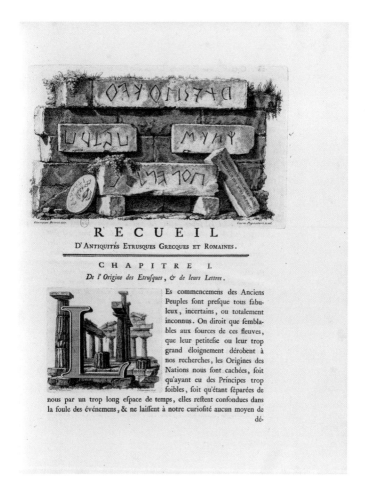

structional elements – perhaps because, as he said, he analysed his subject as a historian and not as an architect.[132]

The assumption that the temples were built by the Etruscans did not originate with Paoli.[133] As we saw in Chapter 1, in 1766 Pierre-François Hugues, known as Baron d'Hancarville (1719–1805), visited Paestum with William Hamilton, envoy-extraordinary to the court at Naples.[134] In his *Antiquités étrusques, grecques et romaines* (1766–7) d'Hancarville wrote as follows about the temples: 'In the midst of [these] ruins stand three Edifices of a sort of Architecture whose Members are Dorick, altho' its proportions are not so'.[135] While other authors, such as the Comte de Caylus, believed the Greeks to have been the successors of the Egyptians in architecture, d'Hancarville proposed the Etruscans as the architectural forefathers of the Greeks, and adduced Paestum to prove his theory. An image of the interior of the Neptune temple appears as a vignette to the first chapter of the *Antiquités*, on the origins of the Etruscans (Fig. 144), and at Paestum he found many traces of Etruscan presence, supporting his thesis that the buildings had been influenced by the Etruscans. D'Hancarville, a French art dealer, pseudo-aristocrat, and intimate friend of Winckelmann, was obviously not motivated by nationalist loyalties, as Paoli might have been, and in fact his argument is different: namely, because the buildings were on a site where there had earlier been an Etruscan settlement, the architecture had been influenced by these local conditions and showed Etruscan characteristics. So, he claimed, the Greek colonisers of Poseidonia inherited the old Tuscan order from their Etruscan forerunners and developed it into the Doric.[136] The Egyptian influence that Paoli would detect in the columns of the Paestum temples was also, in d'Hancarville's interpretation, transferred through the Etruscans.[137] D'Hancarville's ideas on the Etruscan heritage pre-date Paoli's by some seventeen years and also foreshadow theories that were to be developed in the nineteenth century: these related to the disposition and architectural forms of the buildings, which were attributed to function and 'decorum', and to the stylistic language created in the mind of the artist.

We have now surveyed three definitions of primitivism – as cultural theory, aetiology or history, and aesthetics – and have seen how, as these interpretations slowly diverge, the definitions become clearer. We have also encountered again the conflict between theory and experience: Paoli, Winckelmann and d'Hancarville all demonstrate that when travellers visited Paestum the primitivist theories they had developed at their desks did not hold water. Confronted with the architecture itself, Winckelmann was unable to integrate Paestum with his system of series and similarities. Paoli's archaeological quest led to the conclusion that the primitive forms of the temples were an artistic or practical choice, but he ignored the structural factors that affected the architecture. And d'Hancarville, in the attempt to rewrite history, tried to identify Etruscan and Egyptian elements in Paestum's architecture. A further question regarding primitivism emerges from this discussion of the roots of architecture: is there still room for artistic invention or creativity when the original is the norm? What are the 'motors of change' that explain why we now build differently from how we built at the time of the first dwellings? To clarify these questions we shall turn next to the theories of Quatremère de Quincy, who combined Winckelmann's reading of history in series with ideas about how change comes about.

Towards a Universal Architecture with Quatremère de Quincy

Antoine-Chrysostôme Quatremère de Quincy (1755–1849), man of letters, politician and art collector, published widely on his great interests – architecture and sculpture – and often discussed the topic of origins.[138] His library contained many publications on Egyptian architecture, various editions of Vitruvius, all the famous architectural treatises from Alberti to Serlio, and also works on the sublime and on primitivism.[139] He was trained as a sculptor in the atelier of Guillaume Coustou and at the Académie Royale de Peinture et de Sculpture in Paris, but his ambitions to become a sculptor were unfulfilled, and after a sojourn in Italy he decided to give up his dream of ever becoming an artist.[140] Although his Italian tour did not have the practical outcome he hoped for, it was important for the formation of his ideas on the arts. In 1776, when he was 21, he established himself in Rome among the European artists and the French *pensionnaires*, with whom he gained a reputation as an 'espèce de missionnaire de l'antiquité'.[141] Quatremère travelled for four years in Italy, visiting Rome, Naples, Paestum and Sicily, and collecting material for a publication on architecture as he went. In Rome he met Piranesi, and in 1779 he was in Naples with Jacques-Louis David, who painted his portrait showing Quatremère sitting at his desk holding a plan of a classical temple.[142] By 1780 he was back in Paris, but in 1783 and 1784 he returned to Italy, meeting William Hamilton and Antonio Canova there. He also travelled to Sicily again, with a letter of recommendation written by Vivant Denon, who was secretary at the French embassy in Naples at the time.

In his *De l'architecture égyptienne* (1803) Quatremère pursued ideas he had formulated earlier on the importance of the hut, the tent and the cave for the development of architecture. Although he expressed his debt to Laugier by citing him many times, Quatremère's idea of architectural origins and imitation differed fundamentally from Laugier's. First of all, Quatremère did not consider the hut as a means of returning to the natural simplicity of the original building type. The hut was not, in his view, a natural model nor was it directly reproducible: it was simply a work of art.[143] Unlike Laugier, he believed that the architect had to distance himself from the hut before he could make the transition from wood to stone; by his account, the Greeks had transformed the wooden skeleton of the hut into stone architecture. In his book on polychromy, *Le Jupiter Olympien* (1814), Quatremère drew out an interesting association with the primitive. He argued that the colouration of Greek architecture and sculpture linked them to ancient Middle Eastern art, and that they were manifestations of idolatry, which he considered a primitive and universal human instinct. Polychromy was, to him, an expression of the need of primitive humankind to connect colour and form.

Bearing in mind these ideas on primitive culture, what role did Paestum play in Quatremère's theories? Unfortunately, we cannot reconstruct his thoughts on Paestum at the time of his visit in 1779 since he left no account of his travels in Italy. But he wrote about the site in his publications, notably his reference work *Encyclopédie méthodique*, which was based on the *Encyclopédie, ou Dictionnaire raisonné des sciences, des arts et des métiers* by Diderot and d'Alembert, and was meant to complete and improve it. The 210 volumes of the *Encyclopédie méthodique* were published between 1782 and 1832 (157 volumes of texts, and fifty-three of images); three volumes, each in two parts, were devoted to architecture,[144] and here Quatremère set down his ideas on the origins of architecture. The entries 'Architecture' and 'Bois' (1788), 'Cabane' (1790), 'Dorique' (1801), 'Paestum' (1825) and 'Temple' (1828) offer particular insights. The 'Paestum' entry contains a very short description of the site, the situation, the city walls, the two Doric temples and the Basilica; it also mentions that the site includes other ruins, and refers to Delagardette's *Les Ruines de Paestum* ([1799]) for more information on the building materials and for ideas on the construction methods; the entry ends with mention of the type of stone used in all the buildings, the cement, and the stucco, on which traces of colour could still be seen.[145] The entry on Paestum does not contribute much on the topic of primitivism, but 'Dorique' and 'Temple' do. Here Quatremère analysed the Paestum temples in the context of the origins of architecture and of the baseless Doric order. And both 'Cabane' and 'Dorique' contain significant remarks on how he viewed the concept of the primitive hut. In these texts Quatremère drew on Winckelmann's construction of series and Laugier's ideas of the primitive hut, and on Vitruvius.

Quatremère had his own views on Paestum, but he also summarised other eighteenth-century ideas about the site. For example, in 'Dorique' the Basilica is not considered a temple, and it does not feature in the section on the different proportions of the Doric order, where a comparison is made between the proportions of the temples at Paestum and others in Sicily and Athens. In 'Temple', Quatremère described the origins of Greek temples, the progress of temple architecture and its different forms and developments, and cross-referred to the entries 'Architecture' and 'Cabane', where he explained the evolution from the primitive hut to the temple.[146] Paestum's Neptune and Ceres temples are mentioned simply as examples of a type of temple building, with a reference to Vitruvius,[147] but in 'Dorique' Quatremère's remarks are of more interest. Referring to the Doric as an order that expresses 'force' and 'solidity', he distinguished between the original Greek Doric order and false modifications of it in modern architecture – the result of architects' forgetting the ancient form; there follows a list, with short descriptions, of buildings (including Paestum) in which the baseless Doric had been used in Greece, Sicily and Italy, the aim of which was to show the similarities and differences between the original and modern forms of Doric. He stressed that 'all these Doric works [were,] without a single exception[,] in character, style, form and proportions unknown to the moderns before the recent discoveries that have increased the number of original monuments of Greek art.'[148] Like Winckelmann, we see Quatremère here concentrating on series and similarities, and focusing on the common characteristics of the temples rather than their idiosyncrasies. Because of a lack of knowledge of Greek architecture, he claimed, travellers were unable to appreciate the original Greek Doric when they encountered it at Paestum, and assumed that Paestum represented architecture in its infancy. They saw the order as exceptional because they were used to the modern Doric in their own cities, whereas, in fact, it must be the case that the temples represented the rule:[149]

> because of the contrast between the Greek Doric and the modern, & struck by the heaviness, the short proportion, the masculine and massive forms of the ancient Doric, they viewed it as a precursor of this order, & from the lack of a base, concluded that such a taste must go back to the infancy of art. This judgement was . . . false; the simplest reflection demonstrates it.[150]

Although Quatremère tried to prove that the monuments were simply part of Greek architecture, he admitted that it was difficult to combine the 'coarse' and 'barbaric' in the architecture of Magna Graecia with the luxury and culture of Greek civilisation and the perfection found in the other arts. So he asked how it was possible to reconcile this idea of infancy in architecture with the contemporary perfection in all the other arts of the Greeks. He explained this conundrum as follows: because weight and mass are used in the temples of the greatest gods and for the most important buildings in Greece, this characteristic expresses the grandeur and the dignity of the architecture of the Greeks. According to this reasoning the heavy style could be universal, a model rather than a first attempt or an early phase.[151] Here again we find Quatremère interpreting Paestum as a norm of Greek architecture, part of the general rule. While he connected the baseless Doric with the origins of architecture,[152] his main aim was to show the general aspects of the order, and not to distinguish specific variations.

Locating Paestum in the mainstream of Greek architecture allowed Quatremère to argue that it was ignorance that had resulted in the assumption on the part of Paoli and others that Paestum was, in fact, Etruscan. Betraying more than a hint of anxiety, Quatremère stated that if the Etruscans had, indeed, invented the Tuscan order, the history of the origins of architecture would be overturned. According to him, therefore, Paoli had been motivated by 'national self-esteem & the desire to give Italy a native architecture', and he pointed out that Paoli had even argued that the Etruscans looked for their models in Egypt, leaving the Greek contribution entirely out of count.[153] If Paoli had seen other Greek monuments, Quatremère stated, he would have argued differently.[154] What seems to have troubled Quatremère most is that Paoli based a whole historical system of architecture on his theory,[15] whereas, for us, Paoli's ideas prove, rather, that he saw Paestum as unique. In fact it was Quatremère himself, rather than Paoli, whose aim was to trace the similarities and emphasise the parallels between Paestum and other Greek monuments. He refused to acknowledge that Paestum was unique, which was why the idea of a Paestum order agitated him so much. To strengthen his argument that the baseless Doric order was simply part of general Greek Doric architecture, Quatremère compared the proportions of different temples, and indicated some specific features, variations or nuances in some of them.[156] He reaffirmed that Paestum was essential to an understanding of the origins of the Doric and thus of its revitalisation. The site now enjoyed 'a celebrity that it had lost many centuries ago . . . [its] closeness to Naples induced many artists to undertake this journey, & there are no antiquuities better known today than these'. Quatremère reminded his readers of the change in thinking at the end of the eighteenth century that had led to an understanding of the strange architecture of the temples:

> the discovery of the ruins of Paestum having preceded all others by a very long time, the Doric of these temples was the subject of controversy & of rather bizarre speculations until more numerous discoveries of the same kind put the greatest number of artists in the way of making parallels and generalising their ideas.[157]

By standardising its architecture, Quatremère turned Paestum into a norm, and a model for a contemporary version of it – a modern Doric. The two were, to him, separate orders, which should be used to express different characters. He criticised the eighteenth-century fashion for the pure Greek Doric order, demanding a return to simplicity and more caution in its use: 'The Doric order is too serious, too solemn to be employed other than seriously and with solemnity.'[158] He proposed the preservation of a pure form of the original baseless Doric, and a version, with base, for contemporary use, a mixture of Doric and Ionic orders.[159]

These ideas on the Doric order show Quatremère giving the origins of architecture an important role. If we now return to his thoughts about the primitive hut, we can pinpoint a further crucial element in his reasoning: the significance of cultural factors. Like Laugier, he regarded the primitive hut as an invention of nature: 'No man, no architect, could have had the honour of that invention.'[160] But he differed from Laugier in maintaining that the development from wooden hut to stone architecture was a process that needed time and experience: it could not have been 'the sudden result of only one attempt'. Before the hut could transmute into the Doric order, it had first to be perfected by a civilised people,[161] a process that Quatremère believed had been very lengthy.[162] Only the perfected wooden structure could serve as the predecessor of the first building in stone – the first true architecture. Whereas John Soane, in his lecture drawings, closely associated the primitive dwelling with Paestum, Quatremère placed the primitive hut at a remote distance from architecture in stone; to him, it was impossible to attribute this development to one city, country or architect.[163] What connected the two was a system of rules that derived from the transformation by the Greeks of the hut into the Doric order. This, Quatremère reasoned, introduced the spirit of nature into architecture, without which architecture would have been overtaken by caprice.[164]

Although Laugier's influence is traceable here, and Quatremère considered the primitive hut the only original type, he parted company with Laugier in allowing the existence of other types as well: the trio of cave, tent and hut as the first shelters. Quatremère connected these types of primitive dwelling with different cultures, believing that each had led to a different architecture: the cave – shelter of the hunter and fisherman – was the basis of the religious architecture of the Egyptians; the tent of the herdsman had influenced the wooden structures of the Chinese; and the hut of the farmer and cultivator had been the predecessor of stone Greek architecture. It is important to note Quatremère's focus on different regions and cultures in stressing that the primitive dwellings were culturally determined; this is in line with Montesquieu's ideas, in *De l'esprit des lois* (1748), about the influence of climate on material conditions, but more especially on humankind and society. We shall see in the next section how Labrouste interpreted these local differences.

Quatremère stated that character in architecture was the result of place and climate: architecture reflected the geography and climatic conditions of its surroundings and took its form from the people who had conceived it. The order, harmony, balance, nuance and delicacy of Greek architecture had been shaped by the soil, the climate and the temperature of its location (an argument that Winckelmann also used). It followed that to transplant architecture was difficult, and led to a loss of its essential nature. Just such a loss was exactly what resulted when architects tried to turn Paestum into a design model: the defining characteristics were no longer there. If an architect referred to Paestum in a design, as Soane did with his barn, all that was transferred to the new building was an idealisation or an abstraction of the architecture of the temples. As we have seen, despite declaring that the character of architecture was inextricably connected with its native soil, in his encyclopedia article 'Dorique' Quatremère endorsed the use of the simple baseless Doric as a model for contemporary architecture in Western Europe. Labrouste, as we shall shortly find, had no faith in this displacement.

Quatremère's theory on types of primitive dwelling was based less on historical or archaeological factors than on cultural specificity; instead of explaining the exceptional qualities of Greek architecture by reference to the primitive hut, he underlined the importance of Greek culture. According to his account, the origins of architecture were secular rather than sacred, as other authors had suggested, though his ideas about polychromy (see above) connected the primitive to idolatry and thus divinity. While he leant towards the influence of culture rather than history, Quatremère still drew a connection between the primitive hut and Greek Doric temples, though he maintained that the progress from wood to stone was long drawn out. In this respect we can trace a closer link with the ideas of Vitruvius than with those of Laugier.

In associating the geographical conditions of Greece with the magnificence of Greek architecture, Quatremère contrived to use location to define universal characteristics, and paid minimal attention to local or specific differences. This is amply clear from the example of Paestum, where the local and individual characteristics did not interest him: his focus was the temples' significance for Greek architecture as a whole. Labrouste saw things quite differently, and would clash directly with Quatremère on this very subject.

The Genius of the Place According to Labrouste

The work of the French architect Henri Labrouste (1801–1875) on Paestum illustrates how history increasingly replaced the central role of theory in architectural thought in the nineteenth century, a factor that is crucial to an understanding of the shifting relations between ideas on the origins of architecture, the primitive and the history of Greek architecture. In 1824 Labrouste won the Grand Prix de Rome and in January 1825 left for Italy to study for five years as a *pensionnaire* at the Académie de France in Rome.[165] For his fourth-year *envoi* ('submission'), which, by the rules of the Académie, must comprise a *restauration* ('restoration') of an ancient monument, he chose the temples at Paestum.[166] This project – the most important and prestigious for the students – usually consisted of precisely measured drawings of a Roman monument, accompanied by a historical description. Labrouste was the first *pensionnaire* to present a fourth-year *envoi* with *restauration* and *mémoire* on a Greek site.[167] The students' work was exhibited in Rome, at the Villa Médici,

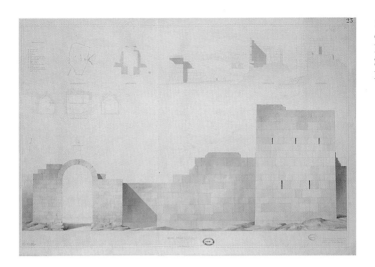

where the Académie de France was located, in the spring, and then in Paris in the autumn. The purpose of the *restaurations* was, together, to present a canon of classical architecture, to serve as a model for future architects; there was no requirement to carry out scientific archaeological research. However, Labrouste was not in search of a model for contemporary architecture; instead he aimed to reconstruct a historical development. Paestum was an excellent choice for this: it had three monuments, similar but clearly built at different times.

In addition to making drawings of the site in its present state (Fig. 145), Labrouste wrote a *mémoire* on the temples, with further drawings showing his own interpretation of their reconstruction. In this part of the project, he tried to establish the building chronology of the remains and situate them in history, an enterprise that involved a painstaking examination of the ruins. In pursuing these concerns, Labrouste offered a new perspective on Paestum, which in modern studies is often considered from the viewpoint of later nineteenth-century developments;[168] but a different insight emerges if we analyse them in the light of the eighteenth-century theories we have been discussing in this chapter.

Labrouste completed his *mémoire* in 1829. Although it remained unpublished until 1877,[169] it became known long before its publication, and was the catalyst for a fierce debate on the Paestum temples, and on Greek architecture and its significance and applicability for contemporary architecture. David van Zanten presents Labrouste's *envoi* as 'the first clear proclamation of the architectural revolution and . . . , at the time, the target of the Académie's bitterest criticisms'.[170] Labrouste and his fellow students Léon Vaudoyer (1803–1872), Félix Duban (1798–1870) and Louis Duc (1802–1879), were dubbed the 'Romantics', and the Paestum *mémoire* was Labrouste's revolutionary manifesto. The story is well known: in place of the doctrine of academic classicism, the four students proposed an eclectic and hybrid approach, using a combination of historical forms, and sometimes even a historical narrative of architectural experience.[171] In the earlier chapters of this book, however, it has already been shown that the eighteenth-century views against which these young architects reacted were not so clear cut: we cannot say simply that academicism ruled in the period, and that Labrouste and his group broke with this radically. What Labrouste launched in the 1820s was foreshadowed in the decades before.

Scholars still disagree on the exact nature of the debate between Labrouste and the Académie. Some see the controversy mostly as a personal battle between the Académie's

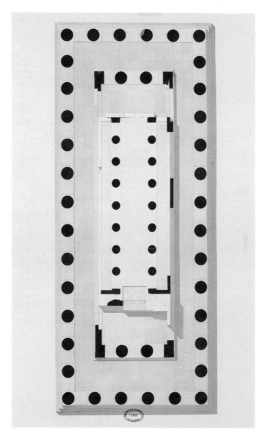
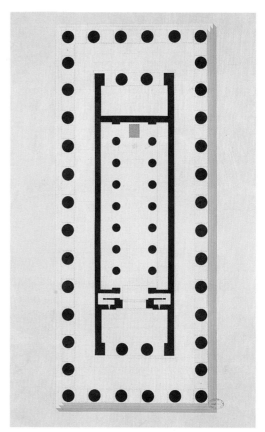

principals in Paris (Quatremère de Quincy, Secrétaire Perpétuel) and Rome (Horace Vernet, Director), and maintain that there was no dispute with Labrouste at all.[172] However, Quatremère de Quincy was certainly one of Labrouste's critics, and in letters between Léon Vaudoyer and his father Antoine-Laurent-Thomas, written at the very time that Labrouste delivered his *mémoire*,[173] there is talk of an 'affaire'.[174]

Labrouste's *mémoire* presented his ideas in nine sections: five on the history of the site, three on the individual temples and one on the other remains. The version published in 1877 has only six sections: one on the history of the site, three on the individual temples, one on other fragments and one on the city walls; here the text is mostly devoted to commentary on the twenty-one plates, of which eleven show the Neptune temple, three

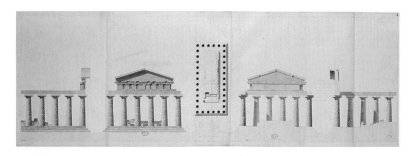

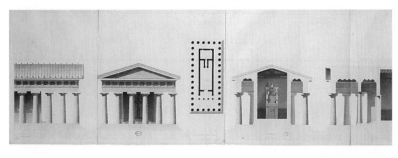

147a and b Henri Labrouste, elevations, plans and cross-sections of the Temple of Ceres, current and restored states, 1828. Paris, École Nationale Supérieure des Beaux-Arts, Env. 22.

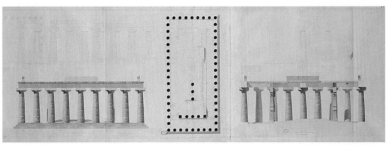

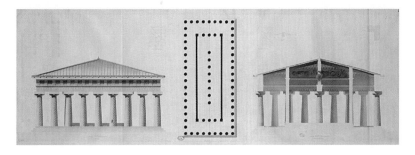

148a and b Henri Labrouste, elevations, plans and cross-sections of the Basilica, current and restored states, 1828. Paris, École Nationale Supérieure des Beaux-Arts, Env. 22.

the Ceres temple, five the Basilica, one other fragments and one the city walls. Labrouste presented himself as the first to have examined the monuments thoroughly,[175] a claim that the Academicians dismissed, suggesting that he would have done better to trust existing authoritive accounts.[176] In his introduction Labrouste lost no time in criticising the architects whose reports had helped to form the general opinion that the temples at Paestum showed art in its infancy.[177] He adopted a much more rigorous historical approach, and proceeded to describe the temples and explain their significance on the basis of the history and culture of Magna Graecia. In 1826 and 1828, when he had visited Paestum, he had also travelled to Sicily to examine the Greek temples there,[178] and compared his findings, often referring to the Sicilian temples to highlight the historical importance of Paestum.[179]

149 Henri Labrouste, detail of two superposed columns in the Temple of Neptune, 1828. Paris, École Nationale Supérieure des Beaux-Arts, Env. 22, fol. 4, PC 77823-7-192.

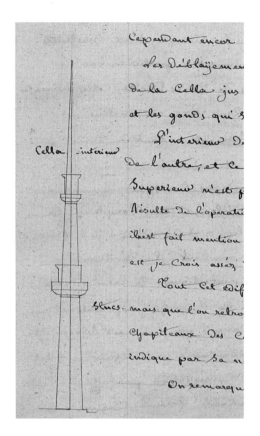

Following the rules of the Académie, Labrouste drew several reconstructions of the ruins (Figs 146–8), avoiding the kind of 'picturesque' perspectives that he disliked so much in other publications. Here, too, he drew on evidence from the Sicilian temples.[180]

Delagardette's monograph on Paestum ([1799]) had come to be acknowledged at the Académie in Paris as the seminal publication on the subject. But Labrouste contradicted Delagardette's opinions on many aspects of the three temples, often directly attacking the architect, and criticising him on almost every page of his *mémoire*; he also often challenged Paoli. This naturally alienated the Académie members, but their disapproval was more deeply rooted. Although Labrouste made some new and interesting remarks (which would later be reproduced by other travellers to the site), the Academicians mainly objected to his historical reconstruction, as opposed to Delagardette's precise analysis of the architecture.[181] They could not come to terms with Labrouste's new method of interpreting the temples by examining the buildings in the context of other monuments and comparing their function, style, period, and ethnic and cultural circumstances, while failing to offer a model for contemporary design.

It is interesting to compare Labrouste's publication with eighteenth-century ideas – Quatremère's and those of other Paestum theorists, such as Paoli. In his description of the Neptune temple, Labrouste presented a drawing of the superposed orders of columns (Fig. 149). We recognise the image and the description from Paoli's monograph and his letter to Fea on Winckelmann's *Geschichte*, where he compared the proportions of the columns with those of an Egyptian obelisk. By contrast, Labrouste's explanation of the form is – as so often – functional, and he found the double order in the Temple of Neptune admirably rational (Fig. 150):[182]

Rediscovering Architecture

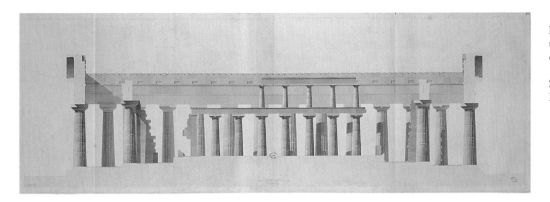

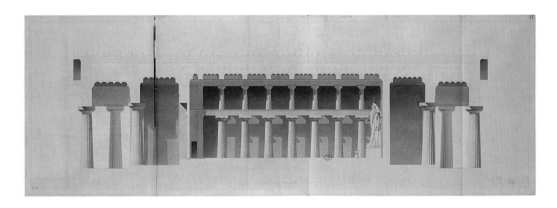

150a and b   Henri Labrouste,
longitudinal cross-section of
the Temple of Neptune,
current and restored states,
1828. Paris, École Nationale
Supérieure des Beaux-Arts,
Env. 22.

The interior of the cella is adorned with two orders placed one on top of the other; and what is very remarkable about this arrangement is that the upper order is, so to say, nothing more than the continuation of the lower order[.] (This fact results from the process carried through in a most rigorous way.) This feature, which no publication on the ruins of Poseidonia mentions, is I believe rather interesting for the study of architecture.[183]

In my view, Labrouste's unique contribution to the historiography of Paestum was his specific interpretation of the temples and his use of earlier accounts to support his historical approach to the question of architectural origins. Paoli and d'Hancarville had argued that the temples were Etruscan, and appropriated them to the Italian tradition. Delagardette was not sure who had built them: the Neptune temple clearly conformed with the Greek canon but he believed the other two to have been restored by the Romans, who had conquered Poseidonia. The columns of the oldest temples had been cut thinner by the Romans, he said, which explained their silhouette in relation to their squat proportions; he proposed that at the time of the Greeks they had no entasis, and that their current outline was the work of Roman architects whose purpose had been to reduce their barbaric primitiveness.

Thus Delagardette argued in favour of a continuous classical tradition, whereas Labrouste did not refer to Roman monuments at all: throughout his *mémoire* he presented Greek architecture in isolation and explained its forms by reference to function, and not as an ideal. He picked up on the eighteenth-century debate about universal continuity versus local specificity, present in the theories of Winckelmann and Quatremère de Quincy, and

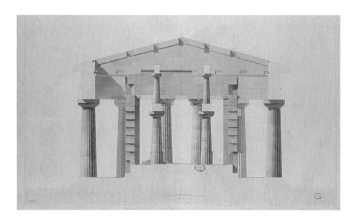

151a and b Henri Labrouste,
cross-section of the Temple of
Neptune, current and restored
states, 1828. Paris, École
Nationale Supérieure des
Beaux-Arts, Env. 22.

the identification of local characteristics at Paestum by Piranesi and Paoli, but he gave these ideas a new twist.

As becomes clear early in the *mémoire*, Labrouste's aim was to prove that the temples at Paestum represented the exact opposite of art in its infancy – in fact that they were 'art that had arrived at perfection'.[184] He used certain finds he had made at the site as evidence to support his claim that the Temple of Neptune was built just after the colonisation of Poseidonia. For example, he stated that the statue of Neptune (Fig. 151) had been carved in local stone, for the sculptors, just like the builders of the temples, had been obliged to use the materials they found at the site.[185] He believed that the stucco he had discovered in the Neptune temple, on the capitals and in the pronaos of the cella, had been added later.[186] He defended the idea that the Temple of Neptune was constructed first, and the Temple of Ceres and the Basilica (which he called 'le Portique' or Portico) only later. The Poseidonians would have raised a temple to their greatest god, the patron of the city, early on, but might not have honoured other divinities for many years. And it was only after the colony had established itself through military superiority and had acquired 'a certain degree of stability and power' that the Poseidonians would have built places of assembly 'where they could discuss matters of common interest. We should thus consider the Portico and the Temple of Ceres as later than the temple of Neptune.'[187] Thus Labrouste regarded the Temple of Neptune, which came closest to the classical architecture of Greece, as set apart from the other two monuments.

Labrouste accounted for his chronology of the temples by historical reasoning, but he also considered the evidence of the buildings themselves. Of the Ceres temple and the Basilica he wrote:

> indeed we see in these two monuments a very different Architecture from that of the Temple of Neptune. These two monuments are constructed in the same manner; the use of different materials, the mixture of hard and soft stones, is a sign if not of an advance, at least of a better knowledge of the materials provided by the locality; and the mixture of stones of different kind and colour made the Use of stucco necessary from the start. The Architecture of these two monuments is the same in respect of their forms, but these forms no longer have the primitive purity that we see in the Temple of Neptune.[188]

Labrouste here stated that the new architecture of the colonists represented progress, and identified the use of local building material as one of the motors of change. In the Ceres temple he detected that hard and soft stones were used according to particular functions in the building (Fig. 152):

> The construction of this monument offers a great deal of interest and yet none of the publications on the antiquities of Posidonia pay it any attention. We should note that in the construction of this Temple stones of two different kinds have been used: the columns, the architraves, the frieze and the pediment are constructed in a hard stone and the soft stone seems to have been reserved for the parts decorated with mouldings, such as the capitals, the mouldings of the architrave, the triglyphs and the cornice of the entablature.[189]

Like Piranesi and others, Labrouste considered the Basilica to have been a public building rather than a temple.[190] He reasoned that, in constructing the Neptune temple, the founders of Poseidonia had built according to the architectural rules of their homeland, but their descendants had chosen a different architecture for their other monuments:

> These observations lead one to consider the Temple of Neptune as Greek Architecture and constructed in a period when the . . . founders of Posidonia had not yet forgotten the principles of architecture that they had brought with them from Greece; and to consider the Portico and the Temple of Ceres as later than the Temple of Neptune and constructed in a Period when the Posidonians, having become more powerful, wanted to create a new architecture.[191]

Labrouste thus associated the urge to create a new architecture with the firm establishment of the colony and its independence from Greece. His argument challenged eighteenth-century thinking even more strongly when he claimed that this new architecture belonged exclusively to Poseidonia and not to any other country or people – that it expressed local characteristics: 'These two monuments alone offer the Type of the Architecture of Posidonia.'[192] Although, as we have seen, Quatremère de Quincy stressed the importance of local conditions for architecture, he aimed to draw connections between local variations and the norms of Greek architecture, so as to claim that there was a single unified style. Labrouste, while drawing on the ideas of Winckelmann and Quatremère, deconstructed this line of reasoning. In his view the specificity of buildings was decisive and, precisely because architecture depends on local circumstances, there could never be one general norm of Greek

152 (*below left*) Henri Labrouste, details of the Temple of Ceres, restored state, 1828. Paris, École Nationale Supérieure des Beaux-Arts, Env. 22.

153 (*below right*) Henri Labrouste, details of the Basilica, restored state, 1828. Paris, École Nationale Supérieure des Beaux-Arts, Env. 22.

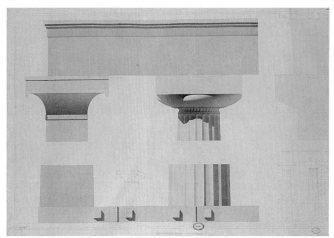

architecture: Paestum made clear that the concept of a unified Greek architecture (to be copied by nineteenth-century architects) was untenable. This is the crux of the 'Paestum affair' and justifies the view of it as a battle between Quatremère and Labrouste.

Labrouste's analysis attempted to trace the origins of architectural invention and the factors that drove architectural change. Unlike his predecessors, he did not assign precise dates to the temples, but he did place them in chronological order – a chronology that was very different from the one generally given in the monographs on Paestum. The established view was (and still is) that the Basilica temple was the oldest, followed by the Temple of Ceres, and that the Temple of Neptune, being closest to the Greek canon, was the youngest.[193] Authors often took the echinus of the capitals as indicative of date: the flat, bulky shape (Fig. 153) was considered the oldest, those that were less compressed were seen as more recent. Labrouste stated that because the 'pure' Neptune temple was closest to the Greek tradition it must be the oldest and would have been built soon after the Greeks settled in Poseidonia. The Basilica temple was the youngest because it was the furthest away from this tradition and showed the adaptation of architecture to local circumstances. He adduced further support for his thesis in his findings of two different types of stone in the Basilica and Ceres temples, but only one in the Neptune temple,[194] a sign that the later builders had better knowledge of local building materials and made more intelligent use of them. These younger temples, he argued, were more authentically 'of Posidonia' than the older one.[195]

To Neil Levine, Labrouste's theories about the authentic Paestum style implied that he believed the transfer of these building forms to France would require radical adaptation.[196] I would go further than that: in my view Labrouste was suggesting that the utilisation of Greek architecture in contemporary buildings was impossible. Another scholar, Martin Bressani, has attributed to Labrouste the idea that what he believed to be the youngest temples were a product of cultural contacts and exchanges between the Greeks and the Etruscans, living close to each other, which resulted in an Etruscan influence on Greek architecture.[197] However, no such statement is made explicitly in the *mémoire*, and Bressani's claim appears to be based mainly on assumption.[198] Labrouste said several times, unequivocally, that in his opinion all the temples were Greek, and even referred to Quatremère de Quincy's *Encyclopédie* to support this.[199] He appears never to have questioned the Greek origin of the monuments,[200] though, as a result of his examination of the temples, he did point to a mixture of Doric and Ionic columns in the Temple of Ceres – a claim that would not have pleased the Académie, since any corruption of the Doric meant that there was no longer a pure Greek model.[201] (The official line at the Académie was that Paestum represented the essence of Greek architecture. The Neptune temple was not in question, but any suggestion that the other two temples were a mixture of Greek and foreign influences – whether Labrouste's quite moderate claim or the more radical one that they displayed Greek, Roman and Etruscan characteristics – was unwelcome. It is noteworthy, however, that the Académie endorsed Delagardette's publication, even though he postulated Roman modifications to the Basilica and Ceres temples.)[202]

In my opinion these were not the most controversial points for the Académie: much more significant was the idea of progression represented in Labrouste's new chronology – that is, progression towards the primitive as an artistic choice. Instead of the accepted idea that architecture gradually improved towards perfection, Labrouste claimed that architecture seemed to adapt itself to local conditions, and thus to drift away from its original perfect state, which had pertained when the Basilica and Ceres temples were built. He explained their forms in terms of the building materials available at the site: locality had given rise to the architecture. Labrouste held that the perfect Greek temple – Neptune – was the result of the first building campaign by the original Greek colonists in Poseidonia, while the builders of the Basilica and Ceres temples, after living in the city for a time and getting to know the local conditions, deployed the local stone more carefully for different elements of the building and thus created a local and specific style that no longer looked like classical Greek architecture. To Labrouste this was a positive move: architectural forms had departed from the perfect example and developed into an architecture that was specific to its locale.

But how could a Greek architecture of such a kind provide a good model for contemporary design practice? Not only did Labrouste turn the image of Greek architecture upside down, he also proved that a building could not be transferred as a model from one time and place to another. For Levine, Labrouste demonstrated that a building can have meaning without conforming with Greek ideals.[203] In my opinion Labrouste thought it might have more meaning precisely when it fails to conform with these ideals, because then it is specific to its time and place and not an abstract model or a historically founded type.

Labrouste's *envoi* was a peculiarly acute critique of the Académie's view of the progress from Greek to Roman architecture because it came from inside the organisation, but similar ideas were already abroad outside the Académie's walls. While scholars have focused on Labrouste's revolutionary break with the Académie's rules, architectural theorists – Laugier, Winckelmann, Paoli and, remarkably, the Academician Quatremère – had been expressing their thoughts on the subject for as long as Greek architecture had been central to the Académie's curriculum, with Le Roy and then Léon Dufourny as professors. Delagardette had written his Paestum project for the Académie, presenting the temples as the canon – as perfection. Piranesi had identified the use of local resources at Paestum and reasoned from this that the temples had, as it were, grown out of nature. His version of the architect's invention prefigured Labrouste's notion that the newer temples were evidence of architectural innovation.[204] All these eighteenth-century forerunners of Labrouste had already broken with Vitruvius. That the Académie did not move at the same pace does not mean that Labrouste's vision was entirely new.

In focusing only on his conflict with the Académie, scholars have failed to see that Labrouste was an exponent of ideas that had been developing during the eighteenth century. He has always been seen as the beginning of something new, whereas in fact he stands at the end of a tradition – a tradition of revolutionary thought generated largely through reflections about Paestum.[205] This does not mean that Labrouste was simply a child of the eighteenth century. When considered in the context of the various versions of primitivism distinguished in this chapter, the novelty of his work becomes clearer: he not only presented a new chronology of a progression towards the primitive, he also definitively broke with the idea that the primitive as a model could be a solution for design practice. In putting the emphasis on historical development, connected to a sense of local circumstances, rather than searching for a (theoretical) model, Labrouste showed that the primitivist normative debates of the eighteenth century could not have value for contemporary architecture. According to his understanding, the primitive at Paestum grew out of the builders' concentrating on and gaining knowledge of the particular site, and may have had no connection with the origins of architecture.

In stating that the builders of Paestum aimed to 'create a new architecture' with the two 'younger' temples, Labrouste presented himself as viewing the temples with an architect's as well as a historian's eye. He referred, for example, to the functional decisions the builders had made, reconstructing their quest for construction solutions specific to the site and situation. He also adopted the perspective of an architect in imagining how these old structures could serve as an inspiration for contemporary architects – not by way of direct importation or model, but by suggesting an approach to design that depended on examining the site and using the natural resources and materials it offered. This solution was not self-evident to eighteenth-century architects: although we have seen similar ideas from Piranesi and Quatremère de Quincy, they were less well developed than Labrouste's. In the next chapter we shall see how some eighteenth-century architects tried in practical terms to make Paestum a norm of Greek architecture and to take it as a model. Now that we have examined Labrouste's solution, their attempts may seem ineffectual, but they will underline the importance of the site and clarify what essentials remained when its elements started to be exported.

While Labrouste's account of Paestum is the last of a long line of such works, and brings together many ideas on the subject, at the same time it reacts strongly against much of what went before. Labrouste saw the relationship between the origins of architecture and primitivism differently from most of his eighteenth-century predecessors. Only between Piranesi and Labrouste can we draw a clear connection, with Piranesi as Labrouste's intellectual forefather. What had begun with Piranesi's *Parere*, in which Roman, Greek and Etruscan architecture were discerned by means of research on the spot, and the importance of local conditions was brought out, culminated in Labrouste's research on site at Paestum. In doing comparative ethnographical research, Labrouste asked himself why architecture develops, and proposed the motors of change. He pursued Winckelmann's ideas on the development of history, but elaborated on them. And the ideas of Quatremère de Quincy on cultural typology echo in his theories as well; yet he deconstructed Quatremère's principle of universal progress, claiming that progress was a local phenomenon, dependent on local characteristics and conditions. Like Paoli, Labrouste did not equate primitive forms with the beginnings of architecture, but defined the primitive as an artistic choice.

Primitivism, Origins and History

The complicated relationship between archaeological quests and primitivism as a cultural theory became intensely uncomfortable when ideas on the primitive that originated in theoretical discourse coincided with exposure to very ancient architecture, as happened at Paestum. When visitors viewed Paestum from a primitivist perspective they certainly found ancient architecture, but they did not find a useful design model. If they went there to investigate its archaeology, they had to concede that the beginnings of architecture did not conform with a primitivist vision. There were no unequivocal answers to the many questions Paestum posed, but it was very clear from the evidence of the site that primitivism as a cultural normative theory was problematic. First of all, the hut was the first architectural model in primitive theories, but at Paestum the oldest building was a temple. Worse was that, although Paestum exemplified the origins of architecture (or was thought to), it did not offer a workable model.

But, in fact, the problem is more complex still: it has two aspects, relating to history and invention, and emerged from the various quests for the primitive that we have explored in this chapter. The primitive figures as the beginning of architectural history in the theories of Vitruvius, Chambers, Delagardette, Winckelmann and Quatremère de Quincy; Delagardette, Soane and Piranesi were all in search of design solutions, though only Delagardette saw the primitive as a possible model. Soane was inspired by the primitive hut in his designs and also presented it in his lectures as a historical antecedent of Paestum. Piranesi was interested in the origins of architecture from a historical viewpoint, but also looked at Paestum with the eyes of a designer. Then Winckelmann, Paoli, d'Hancarville, Quatremère de Quincy and Labrouste, all in their own ways, tried to write architectural history in relation to Paestum. In Paoli's and Labrouste's theories the line of history is not synonymous with progress: they disconnected ancient and primitive – origin and primitive – and therefore dissociated primitive models from design solutions, and presented the primitive as an artistic choice.

The sources show a slow shift towards a more historical approach that increasingly discounted Paestum as a design solution. Whereas Laugier undertook an ahistorical thought experiment that offered no stylistic evolution, Winckelmann adopted a historical approach, and Labrouste developed an archaeologically grounded chronology as a result of exploring the subject himself (he had other ideas on how to treat history). As Paestum was absorbed into the historical discourse, its possible role as a design model became more and more problematic; growing knowledge of the origins of architecture increasingly discredited the idea of the temples as a possible type for modern building. The more information architects had about Paestum, the less useful the temples were to their architecture – or rather, they became differently useful. To Labrouste they were valuable in proving how locality determines architectural forms, while to Piranesi they showed that a creative force had been at work in architecture from the beginning, which inspired him to invent new forms himself. In fact, Piranesi's vision of the origins of architecture was more radical than any other eighteenth-century theorist's, and his rejection of Vitruvius and classical architecture as a design model more thoroughgoing, leading to the ultimate conclusion that primitivism as a normative theory was both ahistorical and paradoxical.

This primitivism was paradoxical because, on the one hand, it confirmed the importance of history, and aimed to identify the oldest source of architecture. On the other hand, it rejected the relevance of history as a sequence of developments from the first beginnings of architecture until the present, precisely because it sought a return to the first origins. This was Piranesi's point in his *Parere*, where he dismissed all elements of classical architecture because, according to Vitruvius and his adherents, there is no clear origin. It is interesting to view these ideas in the light of the writings of Giambattista Vico, who in his *Principi di un scienza nuova* (1725; rev. and enlarged 1744) attempted to develop a history of civilisations. His work is of interest for its emphasis on the peculiarity of ancient Roman civilisation and its barbarian character, which led to the loss of its authority as an ideal society. Vico demonstrated that the brand of primitivism propagated by many later eighteenth-century theorists, such as Rousseau and Laugier – namely, that the earliest origins of a human practice are relevant to contemporary action – was twofold. This primitivism purveyed two definitions of history: history in the sense of the most distant past (the origins of human culture) and history in the sense of developments through time, from the origins to the present. Primitivism, in Vico's view, was not useful but history was. This illuminates the role Paestum played in primitivism in the eighteenth century. As we have seen, because Paestum was, at one and the same time, classical but uncanonical, it compromised classical architecture as a design model.

So much for history: invention was the second stumbling block in the way of a reconciliation between primitivism and the reality of Paestum. How to unite invention and the primitive in a single norm? If origins are the norm, is there still room for artistic change? The normative primitivists stressed a return to origins in a far-distant past, but eventually their project led to the dismissal either of history or of invention. In Piranesi, history and invention are present. He presented this very clearly, in his exaggeration of Laugier's idea of an architecture reduced to three elements, when he made his representative, Didascalo, speak of an architecture 'with no walls, no columns, no pilasters, no friezes, no cornices, no vaults, nor roofs. A clean sweep.'[206] Either history is dismissed, or primitivism has to be replaced by archaeological research. Piranesi attacked Laugier in the *Parere* with historical arguments: an architecture without ornament was impossible (thus he dismissed Laugier's model at a stroke), and ornament was the product of the architect's invention, drawing on forms from the beginnings of architecture onwards and from different cultures, and combining them in new designs. In writing about Paestum, having examined the temples with the eye of an architect, he underscored the importance of invention. As Piranesi and Paoli argued, an architect must apply his inventive talent to create a new, contemporary architecture, but this architecture could use primitive forms. Quatremère de Quincy and Labrouste asked themselves what drove or inspired people, at a certain time, to build differently from those who had constructed the first dwellings. The paradox of primitivism as a normative theory becomes even clearer when we realise that it leaves no room for motors of change. Labrouste went beyond Quatremère de Quincy and Piranesi in demonstrating that the causes of change can work with the primitive as an artistic choice, but rule out the cultural theory of the primitive as a design model. Thus Paestum's key role in the eighteenth-century intellectual debate is proven: it embodies the problem of adopting primitivism as a norm and justifies Labrouste's entirely different interpretation of the primitive.

Slowly, from Winckelmann via Quatremère de Quincy to Labrouste, theories and preoccupations formulated earlier were replaced by what the architect's eye discerned. Winckelmann focused on his claim to be the first German visitor to Paestum and on art-historical themes relating to the proportions of buildings and sculptures. Quatremère tried to fit Paestum into a historiographical model based on Winckelmann, which still relied on a cyclical interpretation of the development of human culture. Only Labrouste tried to collect as much data as possible, and to reason from the evidence. It was no wonder that he made the Académie nervous: in his work their theoretical and normative vision was replaced by empirical research.

Piranesi and Labrouste presented a vision of Paestum in which there was room for architectural invention and development. Labrouste's *mémoire* on Paestum did nothing less than to change thoughts about history. In showing how the most primitive temple – the Basilica – must be the youngest because it differs most markedly from classical Greek architecture, Labrouste proved that the passage of time does not necessarily mean ever-increasing refinement, as Winckelmann had claimed. Singlehandedly, Labrouste upset the primitivist paradigm by demonstrating that history is not the same as progress; at Paestum, exploitation of local conditions as time went on had led to a rougher and more primitive character in the architecture.

As it happens, Labrouste was wrong about the chronology of the temples: the Basilica temple is, in fact, the oldest. But that does not matter. What is important is that he focused on the place, the surroundings and the natural conditions of the architecture. In his view, Greek architecture could not be imported to France, or England or Germany: architecture had to evolve out of its locality. Primitivism as a cultural theory assumes that the beginnings of architecture – the original design – represent a perfect model: after that there can be nothing but decay; it leaves no room for development or evolution. Piranesi and Labrouste showed convincingly that one can look at the same object differently, in the light of development. Piranesi concentrated on the invention of new forms, starting from the primitive, by the exercise of the architect's creative talent. Labrouste saw primitive, rough and uncouth forms as an adjustment of architecture to its surroundings, an assertion of local and not universal progress.

Labrouste's positive reading of the primitive nature of Paestum had nothing to do with the origins of architecture and undermined eighteenth-century thinking about how architecture had come about: when primitive form is no longer regarded as the oldest, the idea of the earliest beginnings loses its value. If primitivism and origins are independent of history, further development is irrelevant, but according to Labrouste this is impossible, because an architectural form without historical evolution is unthinkable. This sheds light not only on the importance of history in nineteenth-century architectural thought, but also on primitivism. Primitive architecture need not be connected to origins: it can owe its existence to nature, to local conditions, to the genius of the place.

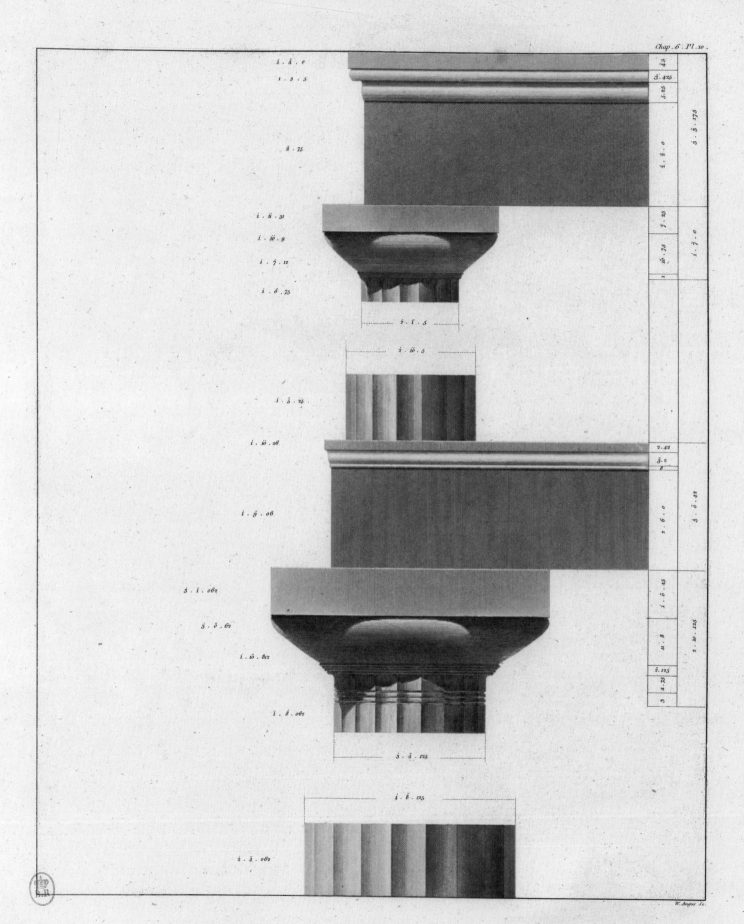

Published as the Act directs, June 1, 1806, by Longman, Hurst, Rees & Orme, Paternoster Row.

W. Angus Sc.

CHAPTER 6

The Eye of the Architect:
Paestum Exported

As soon as Paestum was rediscovered, it was evident that it was important for the history of architecture; but the question of its application to contemporary design was much more problematic. In 1781 the architect Pierre-Adrien Pâris on the one hand asserted the antiquity of the buildings:

> They are without a doubt of a very remote antiquity and the productions of the first Greeks who populated these regions; their style may perhaps prove that the migration of these people to Italy was of earlier date than we think and that it occurred very soon after the invention of the Doric order. This beautiful order is employed [at Paestum] in its first austerity . . . and though almost everything there breathes wildness, there reigns a connection between all the parts that gives a great deal of pleasure to the trained eye and makes the beauty of the relative proportions felt.

but on the other hand addressed the difficulty of their use in architecture:

> These monuments are not only precious for the history of architecture, there are still opportunities to use this style successfully; these occasions are truly very rare, and one has to avoid most carefully what many architects do at present[: namely,] to introduce this order into buildings that need only offer what is simultaneously simple and pleasurable, because they are meant for habitation: the abuse of the character is a fundamental flaw in architecture.[1]

The French architect Louis Combes (1754–1818), noted the same limits to the utility of Greek architecture in contemporary building:

> The Greek Doric order we see in the surviving temples in Sicily, and those of the ancient city of Paestum in Italy present without question a male and vigorous style . . . This order is only six diameters high, lacks a base and has a very heavy capital . . . an appearance of rustic character that seems to me to be suited only to buildings where this style has to be used, such as prisons, arsenals, or in buildings in a simple rural style.[2]

154 (*facing page*) Detail of Fig. 168a.

These two texts prove that, even while they were actually visiting Paestum, architects were already asking themselves whether the temples were relevant to contemporary architecture, and concluding that any such relevance was not evident. Pâris made an interesting observation on the importance of Paestum for the history of architecture, but was adamant that the Paestum order should not be applied in a building of a different character from the temples. Louis Combes made a similar remark, but was more specific. He referred to the 'male and vigorous style' of the architecture, and to its rusticity, which lends itself only to buildings of particular functions and characters. We can see his ideas expressed in his design for a prison (Fig. 155), in which the baseless Doric order he used has extremely heavy proportions and carries the vaults of a gloomy, cavernous, crypt-like space. It somewhat recalls the theatre designs by Pâris that featured crypts with baseless Doric columns and vaults (see Fig. 85). As we saw in Chapter 4, this baseless order was not a direct imitation of the temples at Paestum, but rather an abstracted combination of many columns Pâris had seen in Paestum and in publications on Greek architecture; it resulted from the historical and comparative analyses of ancient architecture made in the eighteenth century with the aim of developing design models. Elements of Paestum's baseless Doric were incorporated into this order, but to be of any use in contemporary architecture Paestum had to forfeit many of its key characteristics.

Pâris's remarks make explicit a divergence between the historical value of Paestum and its value as a design model. The same ambivalence is found in many other texts. When it was a matter of historical value, various authors placed Paestum alongside other examples of Greek architecture to provide the context or construct chronological or typological

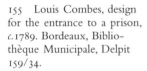

155   Louis Combes, design for the entrance to a prison, c.1789. Bordeaux, Bibliothèque Municipale, Delpit 159/34.

Rediscovering Architecture

series that located Paestum historically. When architects sought to establish its potential as a model for contemporary design, they reduced the architecture to an agglomeration of individual elements – for example, by isolating a particular order, proportions, or tectonic aspects. So we can discern two tendencies – historical contextualisation and formal and structural abstraction – and these are the subject of this chapter.

While in earlier chapters we have seen that the specificity of Paestum was important, and was either celebrated or dismissed, now we shall examine what happened when an experience of the site led to the desire to explain Paestum in a historical context and to disseminate it for application in contemporary architecture. How did the abstraction of Paestum take place, and which elements were selected and preserved for contemporary architecture? How was Paestum contextualised? What were the consequences of the historicising and disseminating tendencies and how do they relate? What is left of Paestum in these processes, and do architects still attach any importance to the experience of the site?

The advance of historical knowledge of the origins of architecture in the late eighteenth century shifted the focus from the uniqueness of Paestum to the similarities between Paestum and other classical temples, which involved aligning it with a general concept of Greek Doric temple architecture. Paestum took its place as just one of many in a historical series. At the same time, different attributes of the temples were isolated for their possible utility in contemporary architecture: for example, the order was identified as aesthetically pleasing, and the simplicity of the construction was the focus of interest because of its technical characteristics.

In order to analyse the normalisation of Paestum through these processes of contextualisation and abstraction, we shall first examine the ideas of an architect in whose thinking these two tendencies came together: namely, Pâris. Then we shall turn to Claude-Mathieu Delagardette, and his attempts to conceive a Paestum order. Next we shall examine the historical contextualisation of Paestum in two treatises on Greek architecture, by Julien-David Le Roy and William Wilkins, and through the presentation of Paestum in museum collections. Finally, we shall consider the theories of Jean Rondelet, who concentrated on construction, and those of Jean-Nicolas-Louis Durand, who situated an abstracted version of Paestum in a typological context. Slowly the importance accorded to Paestum as a unique entity will recede, as the temples fade into the general corpus of classical architecture.

Revising Treatises: Pâris on Desgodetz and Delagardette on Vignola

That Pierre-Adrien Pâris (1745–1819) thought Paestum was historically important enough to be considered part of the main corpus of ancient architecture is shown by his projected integration of Paestum into a new edition of a well-known treatise on classical architecture, *Les édifices antiques de Rome, dessinés et mesurés très exactement* (1682) by Antoine Desgodetz (1653–1728). To understand why, we need to go back to Pâris's writings about Paestum after his visit to the site in 1774.

Pâris's travel notes about his visit in fact concentrated mostly on the city in general.[3] His diary contains copious comments on the town plan, and he was one of the first to note that Greek and Etruscan cities were conceived on an orthogonal scheme. He concluded from this that the Etruscans and other Italian people might have learned from the Greeks how to lay out their cities and to surround them with walls.[4] When he turned to

156 Pierre-Adrien Pâris,
plan, elevation, cross-section
and details of the Temple of
Neptune, engraved by Pierre-
André Barabé, in Jean-Claude
Richard de Saint-Non, *Voyage
pittoresque, ou Description des
royaumes de Naples et de Sicile*,
vol. III (Paris, 1783), plate 87.

Plan et Elevation Géométrale, avec les Details en grand, du Temple Hipetre de Pestum.

the temples, he described them, to begin with, rather generally. His first reactions were mixed – he found the temples 'terrible' and 'distinctive'[5] – but altogether they seem to have made a positive impression, despite their awkward and unusual architectural forms, for Pâris paid them a high compliment in comparing them favourably with the Roman Pantheon (which he called 'la rotonde'):

> These precious monuments surely merit the difficult journey one makes to see them. None of the most beautiful pieces of antiquity, not even the [Panthéon], produce such an impressive effect. A harmony reigns there, above all in the largest temple, . . . so that even though the proportions are not the ones our eyes are used to, we are not revolted or shocked by the thickness of the columns, by the height of the entablature etc. Everything pleases, at least that is the effect I have experienced there.[6]

Pâris solved the problem of coming to terms with the temples by taking careful measurements, such as those of the columns of the Temple of Neptune, which he detailed in his travel notes.[7] In terms of images, what remain of his observations and researches at the site are a few drawings founded on precise measurements – plans, elevations and details, presented in a way that could be used in design. Some were published as engravings in Abbé Jean-Claude Richard de Saint-Non's *Voyage pittoresque, ou Description des royaumes de Naples et de Sicile* (1781–6), which contained other engravings from drawings by Hubert Robert; these tell us much more about the site than Pâris's details (see Chapter 3).[8] The preparatory drawings Pâris made for this publication some time after 1774 are lost; there are only two drawings of Paestum by him in the book (plates 87 and 88 in volume III). The first of these (Fig. 156) pictures a plan, elevation, cross-section and details of the Neptune temple; the second (Fig. 157) shows plans, elevations and details of the Basilica and the Ceres temple.[9] Another drawing that Pâris made of the Neptune temple is in his manuscript work 'Études d'architecture' (Fig. 158): it depicts a plan, two elevations, a cross-

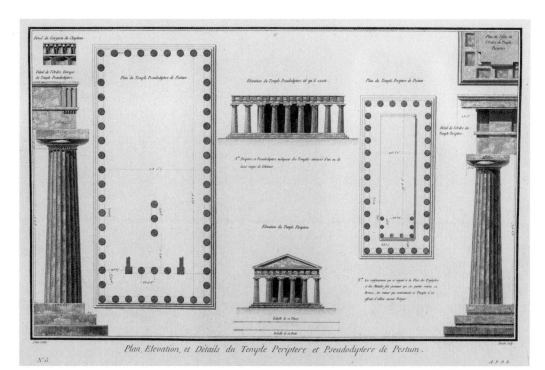

Plan, Elevation, et Détails du Temple Periptere et Pseudodiptere de Pestum.

157 Pierre-Adrien Pâris, plans, elevations and details of the Basilica and the Temple of Ceres, engraved by Pierre-André Barabé, in Jean-Claude Richard de Saint-Non, *Voyage pittoresque, ou Description des royaumes de Naples et de Sicile*, vol. III (Paris, 1783), plate 88.

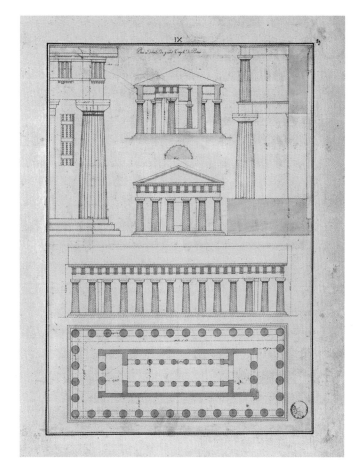

158 Pierre-Adrien Pâris, plan, elevations, cross-section and details of the Temple of Neptune, 1771. Besançon, Bibliothèque Municipale, Bibliothèque d'Étude et de Conservation, Collection Pierre-Adrien Pâris, vol. 476, no. 29.

section, and elevations of the exterior column, with details including the superposed columns in the interior.[10] All these drawings are geometrical 'translations' of his measurements, and express nothing of his experience of Paestum or his thoughts on the antiquity of the temples.[11]

His interest in the Paestum order and the geometry of the temples re-emerged a year after his visit to the site. Having returned from his journey, on 12 June 1775 Pâris gave a lecture to the Académie d'Architecture on the classical monuments he had examined in Italy, mentioning Paestum. As he reported later, Jacques-Germain Soufflot, the first foreign architect to have 'rediscovered' Paestum and thus an acknowledged authority, attacked him on the subject. Their dispute related specifically to the outline – curved or straight – of the columns of the Neptune temple. Soufflot thought the columns had no entasis, while Pâris claimed that they had, and that he had actually observed it himself. Pâris then sent three French architects to the site to check this feature, and they confirmed his opinion. In the same vein he dismissed an English publication (probably Thomas Major's *Ruins of Paestum*) for falsely depicting the pediment.[12] The debate about the curvature of the columns occurred at a time when the idea of using the Paestum order in new buildings was current: besides motives of prestige, resting on the question of which of the disputants had 'read' the temples correctly on the spot, Pâris and Soufflot participated in this discussion of a possible application in contemporary architecture.

Pâris's ideas on the use of Paestum's order were far from unequivocal: indeed, he found it rather problematic, as his reaction to a change made to one of his designs shows. He only once used a baseless Doric order – in the peristyle of the city hall at Neuchâtel (1783–4; Fig. 159).[13] There he chose to use columns with proportions inspired by the Temple of Hercules at Cori, but without his permission his building contractor decided to introduce flattened vaults, which shortened the columns and gave them the proportions of those at Paestum. Pâris called this 'barbaric', and declared that 'a large number of beautiful columns, already completed, have been mutilated in order to create deformed and shocking things, in a completely unprincipled way and against all the rules'.[14] The change turned the peristyle into a sort of 'cave' or crypt, instead of a light, clear space.[15] His reaction demonstrates the particularity that was ascribed to the Paestum order: as Louis Combes had stated, it was seen as appropriate for crypts or prisons, and was not to be carelessly or generally applied.

159a and b Pierre-Adrien Pâris, design for the city hall at Neuchâtel, transverse cross-section (*below left*) and longitudinal cross-section (*below right*), 1783–4. Besançon, Bibliothèque Municipale, Bibliothèque d'Étude et de Conservation, Collection Pierre-Adrien Pâris, vol. 484, nos 41, 42.

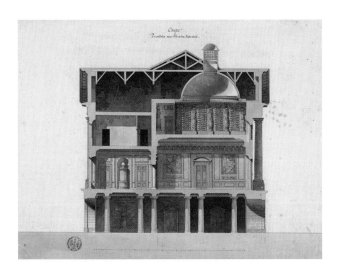

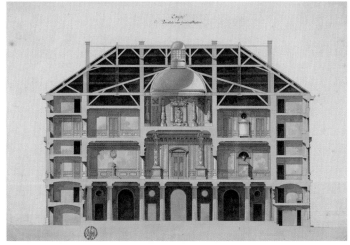

A second indication of Pâris's ideas about the use of the order is seen in his reaction to a student's design at the Académie d'Architecture. Among young architects, the application of the 'Paestum column' appears to have been in fashion in the 1780s, but the older generation was not enthusiastic. In the late 1780s a student named J.-A. Ch. Moreau submitted to the Académie d'Architecture a design for a building 'intended to unite everything to do with natural history'. Making its judgment in 1788, the jury, consisting of Étienne-Louis Boullée, Nicolas-Henri Jardin, Pierre-Louis Moreau-Desproux and Pâris, mentioned the problematic use of Paestum as a design model. The columns in the student's design were too small for their mass, and the jury seized the occasion to address 'the abuse young people make of the Paestum columns: often they use them in buildings that would be more suitably adorned with the regular orders, which have fixed, well-defined and more elegant proportions'. According to the jury, there were very few contexts where this type of architecture, 'which excludes every sort of richness', was appropriate. If its particular proportions were not rigorously observed, young architects would produce only 'an incoherent pile without interest or taste'.[16] Instead of elegance and richness, the order expressed poverty and simplicity to the jury, something that the students had not understood. In this particular project, it must be said, the so-called Paestum columns lack fluting and do not appear closely to resemble those of the temples, but the jury's judgment seems to indicate that it was the squat proportions of the columns, akin to those at Paestum, that they objected to, and the fact that there was as yet no such fixed or standardised order. Above all the jury highlighted the often inappropriate use of the columns, which were unsuited to most buildings.

Although Pâris admired the temples, he did not regard them as a model for contemporary architecture, but he did acknowledge their value as documents of architectural history, and placed them among the most important examples of classical architecture. This becomes fully evident when we consider that, some seven years after his visit to Paestum, Pâris began to plan a new edition of Desgodetz's widely read work on Roman architecture, *Les édifices de Rome* (1682),[17] in which he intended to include the temples. We find here a divergence between his appreciation of Paestum as a major example of classical architecture and a very cautious attitude to the possibility of using it as a design model – a dissociation between the cultural and historical value of Paestum and its value in contemporary architecture.

Desgodetz had been sent to Rome by Jean-Baptiste Colbert in 1674, under the auspices of Louis XIV, because, in order to inform modern architectural practice, the Académie in Paris was in urgent need of precise information on the system used by the Romans. Because Vitruvius did not provide any clear technical details, Desgodetz was asked to take measurements of the main Roman monuments *in situ*. He returned to Paris in 1677 with the results, which served to prove that there was no one common dimensional system, and that the data published by Serlio and Palladio were inaccurate. His *Édifices* was intended to be a handbook for architects and artists, which, the Académie believed, would offer an objective basis for beauty in architecture. It was to replace the works by Andrea Palladio (*L'antichità di Roma* (1554)) and Sebastiano Serlio (*Il terzo libro* (1540)) on Rome, because it gave better measurements, provided drawings of the buildings as they then survived alongside reconstructions, and presented other sorts of information, such as different types of plan and sectional views. It contained 137 plates of thirty-two antique monuments in Rome, the Temple of Vesta in Tivoli and the amphitheatre in Verona, accompanied by explanatory texts. Although the book presented detailed engravings of these antique buildings and was meant to determine the proportional systems that the

Romans had used, Desgodetz was unable to prove that there had been any consistent approach among the Roman architects, and moreover uncovered many conflicts between the proportional systems described in architectural treatises such as Palladio's.

Desgodetz's measurements of the Roman monuments soon met with criticism. Shortly after the publication of *Les édifices*, Claude Perrault pointed out, in his *Ordonnance des cinq espèces de colonnes selon la méthode des anciens* (1683), that the idea of setting architectural norms based on antique buildings was doomed to fail because, among other things, Desgodetz had proved that their dimensions differed greatly.[18] Towards the middle of the eighteenth century, though it was generally admired, Desgodetz's work was also criticised for 'its inconsistent modes of representation, the inaccuracy of its measurements, and its almost exclusive concentration on the religious and civic architecture of Rome itself'.[19] The criticisms became more strident when architects started to examine the Roman buildings with their own eyes, sometimes with Desgodetz's book in their hands.[20] A number of them, including Robert and James Adam, compiled albums in which they reacted to Desgodetz's findings. The Frenchmen Charles-Louis Clérisseau, Marie-Joseph Peyre, Charles de Wailly and Pierre-Louis Moreau-Desproux began work on a supplement to Desgodetz, and to improve their understanding of the remains undertook minor excavations in Rome. In 1779 the Académie d'Architecture acquired the manuscript of Desgodetz's work,[21] and in the same year the publisher Claude-Antoine Jombert obtained the copper plates from which the first edition had been printed. At the instigation of Marie-Joseph Peyre, one of the group of French architects who had been working on Desgodetz's text, Jombert decided to reissue the *Édifices*, but, despite all the criticisms that had been levelled at it and Peyre's urging that it be revised, the project to amend the treatise came to nothing: the book was simply reprinted from the original plates and published in Paris in 1779.[22]

As an admirer of Desgodetz, Pâris had made notes on the *Édifices* and conceived supplementary plates for the work when he was a *pensionnaire* at Rome in the years 1772–4. After Jombert's edition of 1779 appeared, he returned to the text, and in 1781 presented his 'Observations' on Desgodetz's work (1779–81) to the Académie.[23] Although Pâris would never publish his findings in a new Desgodetz edition, his 'Observations' are of interest. He first commented on the Roman buildings presented by Desgodetz, then proposed the addition of other classical monuments in the environs of Rome and the Kingdom of Naples – for example, at Herculaneum, Capua, Benevento and Paestum – stressing that they were important and singular for the history of architecture.[24] For each one, Pâris drafted a description, referring to his personal experience, and provided drawings.

After Pâris's proposals, further projects to revise Desgodetz were launched. The several eighteenth-century architects who conceived such plans included Jacques-Guillaume Legrand (1753–1808) and Jacques Molinos (1743–1831), who will feature later in this chapter.[25] In 1785 Legrand and Molinos took measurements in Rome, which contradicted those made by Desgodetz.[26] Like most other revisers, except for Pâris, they did not suggest adding Greek monuments: their concern was mainly with correcting Desgodetz's data, not with supplementing the treatise. Pâris's proposal was extraordinary not only because he aimed to include Greek monuments in a publication that concentrated on canonical Roman architecture, but also because his purpose seems to have been to write architectural history rather than to provide concrete models for architects; as he thought the application of Paestum in contemporary architecture was problematic, his intention to add Paestum to Desgodetz must have had to do with establishing its pre-eminent importance as an example of classical architecture (in line with other attempts to locate the temples in a historical context, which we saw in Chapter 5).

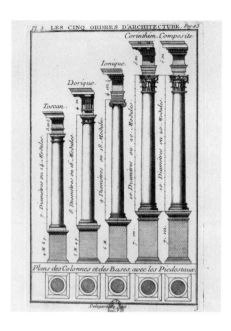

160a–c Claude-Mathieu Delagardette, *Règles des cinq ordres d'architecture de Vignole* (1786), title page (*above left*), frontispiece (*above centre*), and the five orders of architecture, plate 5 (*above right*).

Pâris's plans were never realised, but another such venture was more successful. The treatise in question was a book of orders, *Regola delli cinque ordini d'architettura* (1562) by Giacomo Barozzi da Vignola (1507–1573), and the revision that introduced Paestum was by Claude-Mathieu Delagardette (1762–1805). However, the motives for this addition were entirely different. While Pâris integrated Paestum into the history of architecture, Delagardette would try to embody Paestum in an order and add it to the classical repertory available to architects. What Pâris thought impossible, Delagardette set out to do in his *Règles des cinq ordres d'architecture de Vignole* (1786; Fig. 160).[27] At the time he added Paestum to Vignola's famous treatise, Delagardette had never even visited the site, but he was apparently so enchanted by the drawings of the temples made by other architects that he was persuaded to incorporate it in the principal orders of architecture. His aim was to make the 'beautiful Doric Order of Pœstum' widely available to students; Delagardette insisted that his precise measurements and calculations would help students to compare it with other orders and would make it easy for them to apply it in their designs.[28]

The lack of first-hand experience of the site did not, apparently, prevent Delagardette from considering the order of value, or from representing it correctly. It was not important to him to have seen the monuments himself: he could reproduce the dimensions of the columns from measurements taken by others, and in fact he based his order on measurements made by Soufflot and Dumont, the first French visitors to the site.[29] (Major had done the same, though he had also used measurements by others, as the preparatory drawings for his publication, eventually bought by Soane, testify.) Throughout the eighteenth century architects had repeatedly disagreed about the measurements, thus demonstrating that there were risks involved in using those of only one architect, even if he was 'architecte du Roi', as Soufflot was. Eventually Delagardette decided that he should visit the site himself, so he went to Paestum in 1793, and afterwards (1797) republished his Vignola edition, with new drawings and different dimensions. Nevertheless, this later edition still did not refer in any way to Delagardette's experience at the site, but gave a purely technical account of the monuments. The book became a success and was widely used as a manual by architects. It goes a long way towards clarifying how Paestum was imported into architectural practice.

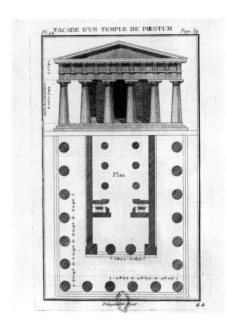

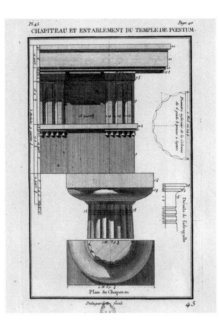

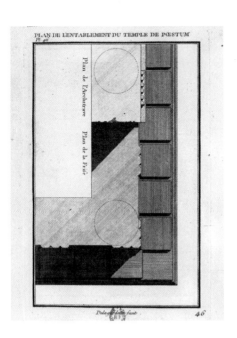

161a–c Claude-Mathieu
Delagardette, the Temple of
Neptune, elevation and plan
(*above left*), details of the order
and entablature (*above centre*)
and plan of the entablature
(*above right*), in *Règles des cinq
ordres d'architecture de Vignole*
(1786), plates 44, 45, 46.

While Pâris's drawings in the *Voyage pittoresque* and in his projected revision of Desgodetz were restricted to two-dimensional plans, elevations and details of the three temples, Delagardette went further. In both editions of *Règles des cinq ordres* Paestum's reduction to an order was, in fact, its reduction to the order of only one of the temples – the Temple of Neptune – which, like other architects before him, Delagardette chose for its majesty.[30] In the 1786 edition of his book he published three engravings of the Paestum order: an elevation of Neptune's front façade, details of the order and entablature and a plan of the entablature (Fig. 161).[31] In the 1797 edition he emphasised that he had meticulously measured the temples himself, to guarantee the exactitude of the details he gave.[32] His motives for adding the Paestum order were now slightly differently formulated, and he complained that, though the order was often and successfully employed, it was described only in rare and expensive publications, and he wished to make it available to a wider public. He now explained that he had chosen to present the exterior order of the Neptune temple, which was not only the most majestic of the three, but also the one whose details were 'the purest and the most ingeniously opposed'.[33] The distillation of the complexity of Paestum that was needed to achieve the end product disseminated in Delagardette's book was substantial: by choosing the Temple of Neptune for its majesty, purity and ingenuity, he discounted the city as a whole and the other two temples; then he reduced the scope still further by examining only the exterior columns of the Neptune temple. In the end, his Paestum order is based on just one type of column from one of the temples.

The second edition contained four engravings of the temple: 'Façade d'un temple de Pœstum', 'Entablement de Pœstum', 'Plan de l'entablement de Pœstum', and 'Proportions et détails des colonnes de Pœstum' (Fig. 162).[34] Apart from some changes to the measurements and, of course, the added factor of Delagardette's having seen Paestum with his own eyes, his account in the second edition is little different from the first. He had gone to Paestum with the well-defined aim of capturing the order for future architects. It was the only order he added to the five in Vignola's original publication; he claimed to have chosen it for its popularity among architects, but he probably also favoured it because it was novel and very different.

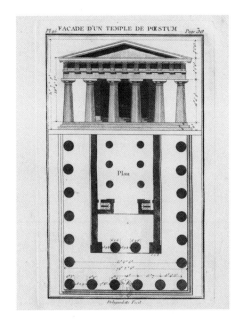

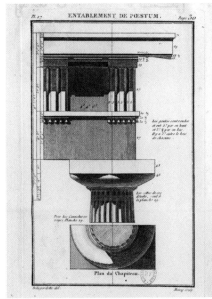

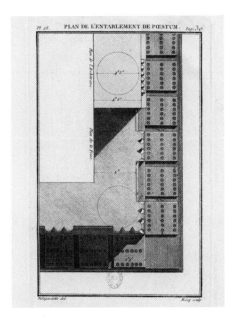

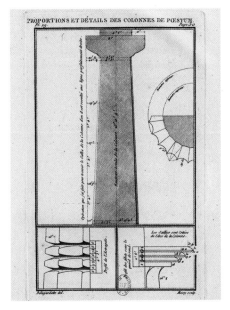

162a–d   Claude-Mathieu Delagardette, the Temple of Neptune, elevation and plan (*far left, top*), details of the order and entablature (*left, top*), plan of the entablature (*far left, bottom*), proportions and details of the columns (*left, bottom*), in *Regles des cinq ordres d'architecture, de Vignole,* 2nd edn (1797), plates 26, 27, 28, 29.

Delagardette's interest in Paestum did not stop with the definition of the order. He also pictured and described the temples in a monograph entitled *Les Ruines de Paestum*, which he published in 1799. In this work he made some remarkable statements on the earlier, widely used measurements of Soufflot and Dumont, as well as on other accounts of Paestum: 'Neither Soufflot nor Dumont ever saw, measured or drew the details of the cornice, the guttae of the architrave, the mouldings and the astragals of the capitals of the great temple at Paestum.'[35] By dismissing his predecessors for their failure to attend to the architectural details, Delagardette presented himself as the only authority on Paestum and the only one who had thoroughly examined and measured the temples. In a survey of previous publications, only Piranesi's engravings met with his unreserved approval, for their accuracy and completeness; this was probably because Piranesi had not published any measured drawings, but only perspective views, and for that reason was in no way a rival. As a matter of fact, Delagardette's claim to be the first to study the temples thoroughly on site was largely true: he made a lengthy stay at Paestum to carry out his work, while other authors had mostly relied on quickly executed drawings and measurements, or had depended on others to supply them with dimensions.

In his Vignola publication Delagardette provided no historical context for his decision to include Paestum. He focused on the primitive aspects of the temples but did not treat them in a chronological sequence. In Chapter 5 we discussed authors who took a diachronic approach to situating Paestum in its historical context; in this chapter the method is synchronic. By placing Paestum amid other examples of Greek architecture or Doric temples, writers constructed series in images and texts: such series might be chronological or achronological,[36] and were created for different purposes. The contextualisation of Paestum thus depended on the agenda of the architect, and also on the reading public for whom the books were intended.

As we saw in discussing the jury's reaction to Henri Labrouste's *mémoire* (Chapter 5), the Académie de l'Architecture considered Delagardette's monograph on Paestum a seminal publication. Many architects owned a copy, or even subscribed to the book before its publication.[37] One of these, himself the author of a work on Greek architecture, was Julien-David Le Roy (1724–1803). Delagardette often mentioned Le Roy's *Les ruines* to demonstrate the similarity of Paestum's temples to other Greek temples, and to reinforce his dating.[38] But where Delagardette offered only an order, Le Roy provided a much broader view of Greek architecture. We shall now turn to his work to see at close range how Paestum could be integrated into an overview of Greek classical architecture.

The Development of Greek Architecture According to Le Roy and Wilkins

Le Roy's *Les ruines des plus beaux monuments de la Grece* (1758), a combination of treatise, archaeological account and travelogue, published just after the rediscovery of Paestum, was the first systematic analysis of Greek architecture to appear in the eighteenth century.[39] Based on personal inspection and archaeological research in Greece, carried out during his tour of 1755, Le Roy's thorough historical and theoretical analysis resulted in a new way of viewing ruins. Although his work fuelled ideas on the Greek ideal in the eighteenth century, Le Roy did not, in fact, present a clear model or canon of Greek architecture; he 'was concerned rather to penetrate to the essential spirit that had conferred upon the architecture of ancient Greece its supreme distinction, the better to understand not only that architecture but also the very nature of all architecture that mattered.'[40] His book was an important step in the process of historical contextualisation, showing examples of Greek buildings as part of a historical series in which Greek architecture was presented as superior to Roman, and his initial aim was to locate Paestum within this series. In the prospectus for *Les ruines*, issued in 1756, he described his intention to present geometric plans, façades and profiles of buildings, with all their measurements:

> To make this part more interesting, we shall include the profiles of ancient Doric columns from the church of San Pietro in Vincoli in Rome, the columns and the entablature of the Theatre of Marcellus in the same city, & some parts of the temples of

Paestum in the Kingdom of Naples. These curious monuments compared with the Greek orders, will prove perceptibly and decisively what History teaches us only generally about the passage of Greek architecture into Italy.[41]

In the event, Le Roy did not publish images of Paestum in his book, but this passage from the prospectus clarifies his idea of situating Paestum within a chronology of Doric architecture, something that other writers picked up only later in the eighteenth century. Although he had no first-hand knowledge of Paestum, the prospectus shows that Le Roy's purpose in including its temples in his survey was to state something significant about how Greek architecture had been disseminated in Italy:[42] a comparison of the temples with other buildings would clarify the history of the Doric order. The fact that Le Roy used the temples – these 'curious monuments' – to advertise his book also indicates that Paestum already figured in architectural discourse and that his public was interested in the subject, even though, at the time, no publication about the site existed. Had Le Roy published images of Paestum so soon after its rediscovery, they would have been the first; as it was, his text on the temples pre-dated the first monograph about them (which did not appear until 1764), and established the historical approach that afterwards became the basis for publications about Paestum.[43]

The second edition of Le Roy's *Les ruines* (1770) did not appear until after five monographs on Paestum had been published. Again, he included no images of Paestum, but he mentioned it several times, referring to the antiquity of the Basilica and to works that had come out since 1758. In discussing the way in which the columns were originally arranged in Greek temples, he drew on 'two temples of the remotest antiquity':

The one in Italy at [Pesto, or] Paestum, an ancient city of Magna Graecia, some 22 leagues from Naples, has a range of columns down the middle of the interior, just as we suppose the first columns were placed in buildings . . . The public may form its own opinion as to the merits of this conjecture, partly deduced from the temples at Paestum. It has been to some extent confirmed in two books recently published on the ruins of that city: one by Mr. . . . Major, the other by Monsieur . . . Dumont. The chronology of the discovery of the temples by a Neapolitan painter, of the survey of them taken by Monsieur . . . Soufflot, and of the various works published on them is given [in the publication of] Dumont.[44]

That Le Roy already considered the Basilica to be a temple and not a public building is remarkable at a time when the function of this building was still debated. It is important to realise, however, that in this second edition of his book, Le Roy was not examining Paestum for its own sake, but simply to demonstrate his ideas about Greek architecture in general. He wrote, for example, about the Temple of Minerva in Athens (the Parthenon), noting the remarkable proportions of its two principal dimensions: with its eight by seventeen columns, the temple was more than twice as long as it was wide. He regarded this as a feature of Greek architecture, and named as examples the Temple of Theseus in Athens, the Temple of Jupiter at Olympia and the 'temples of great antiquity that stand to this day in the ruins of Paestum'.[45] By 1770, then, Le Roy was clearly labelling Paestum as Greek architecture, whereas in the prospectus of 1756 he had referred to its 'curious monuments' and proposed to compare its Doric order with the Greek orders so as to prove a historical development from Greek architecture to buildings in Italy.

Le Roy's only other reference to the temples again relates to their acclaimed antiquity and occurs in a passage on the ruins of a temple at Corinth:

To determine the approximate date of the ruins of a temple, I consider it necessary to examine not only the general proportions of its columns but also the taper of the shaft, the form of the capital, and the details of the profiles and entablature. Even columns less than six diameters high may well be so elaborate in their detailing that they cannot possibly antedate the time when – according to Vitruvius . . . the Greek colonies founded in Asia Minor by Ion . . . first had the idea of making their Doric columns six diameters high. And so, more cautious than those who, in a work published in Italy, have sought to assign to the temples of Paestum a date earlier than given by Vitruvius for the invention of the Doric, we shall say only that the temple at Corinth is of great antiquity and that it was probably built before the age of Pericles.[46]

To Le Roy, Paestum was simply an example of very ancient architecture – a moment in the history of architecture – and was of interest only in relation to other Greek temples. It would be nearly half a century before a history of Greek architecture and the definition of a design model, with Paestum in a central role, would be combined.

The work in question was *The Antiquities of Magna Graecia* (1807) by the English architect William Wilkins (1778–1839). Although Wilkins in some senses followed Le Roy's lead, his aim in *The Antiquities* was more specific: to identify a new general standard in Greek temple architecture.[47] At the turn of the century Wilkins was compiling the material from which he would later draw his design inspiration (Fig. 163); in the summer of 1803, having returned to England after a tour of Italy and Sicily, he made plans to publish his findings, and immediately began to work on his book.[48] Although its title is *The Antiquities*, the work in fact treats only temple architecture, as the very opening statement indicates: mentioning Vitruvius, Wilkins referred to the principles 'by which the construction of Grecian Temples appears to have been generally regulated'.[49] Vitruvius's analysis of Roman architecture was, he said, entirely inapplicable to Greek temples, as he claimed to have proved by his own examination of the remains.[50] His aim was to establish a new set of principles to account for the architecture of the temples in Greece and in the Grecian colonies.

According to Wilkins, the number of columns on the long sides of Grecian hexastyle–peripteral temples appeared to have been regulated not by the number on the front or short sides but by entirely different considerations. Challenging James Stuart's *The antiquities of Athens*, he argued that the number of columns on the short side was not always doubled and then exceeded by one to determine the number on the long side, as in the Temple of Theseus at Athens and at Agrigento: 'the temples of Aegina, Paestum, Argos, Syracuse, Aegesta, and Selinus, are examples in which [this] application fails. In all these, with the exception of the first, the number of columns in the flanks exceeds double the number in the fronts, by two or more.'[51] In naming Paestum as one of the examples that proved Stuart's rule to be false, Wilkins obviously did not address all three temples, since their proportions and the number of their columns vary: the Basilica has nine by eighteen columns; the Ceres temple has six by thirteen (the only one that conforms with Stuart's rule); only the Neptune temple, having six by fourteen columns, matches Wilkins's assertion. This point is noteworthy because, as we shall see, Wilkins more than once treated the Neptune temple as though it were synonymous with Paestum, just as Delagardette and others did. Wilkins's reason was that he believed it to be the only true example of ancient Greek architecture at the site: the two other temples were, in his opinion, Roman – or had perhaps been tampered with by the Romans. (He referred to Delagardette's earlier observation that the columns of the three temples had been produced by 'Grecian workmen', but the superstructures of the Basilica and the Ceres temple had been restored 'by the

163   William Wilkins, design for Grange Park, 1809. London, Royal Institute of British Architects, Drawings and Archives Collections, SC36/43 (1–2).

Romans'.)[52] It was, at all events, clear to Wilkins that the two smaller temples had a different building history from the Neptune temple and were of a different age.[53]

In his quest to establish a norm of Greek temple architecture, Wilkins focused on similarities in his analysis of the temples in the Greek colonies of Magna Graecia. It follows that he took account only of the features that Paestum shared with other temples and ignored those that were unique. Standardisation was the result, but only one temple at Paestum matched the type – the Temple of Neptune. Applied to Wilkins's text, the term 'standardisation' means selection and exclusion: he saw no room for exceptions or variations. His argument for this method is clear: without standardisation Greek architecture could not serve as a model. As the Basilica and Ceres temples did not fit his newly established norm, they were simply left out, dismissed as bad examples or accidents. Contemporary architects should concentrate on the one magnificent example at Paestum that confirmed the supremacy of the Greeks as temple builders. In the following passage it is abundantly clear that the standardisation of Paestum related to this one temple only:

> Of all these [ruins], perhaps, the only one which has claims to Grecian origin is the Great temple, supposed to have been dedicated to Neptune. This indeed possesses all the grand characteristics of that pre-eminent style of architecture. Solidity, combined with simplicity and grace, distinguish it from the other buildings, which, erected in subsequent ages, when the arts had been long on the decline, in a great degree want that chastity of design for which the early Grecian is so deservedly celebrated.[54]

To Wilkins, as to other architects, only the Temple of Neptune was ancient, and only the Temple of Neptune could be regarded as an example of Greek superiority.

In his urge to incorporate Paestum into a chronological series of Greek temples, Wilkins paid almost no attention to the evidence that experience of the site offered. Instead, he took one temple and tried to trace back its characteristics to the earliest example of temple architecture: Solomon's temple at Jerusalem.[55] By associating the Temple of Neptune with that of Solomon, on which he wrote at length in the introduction to *The Antiquities of*

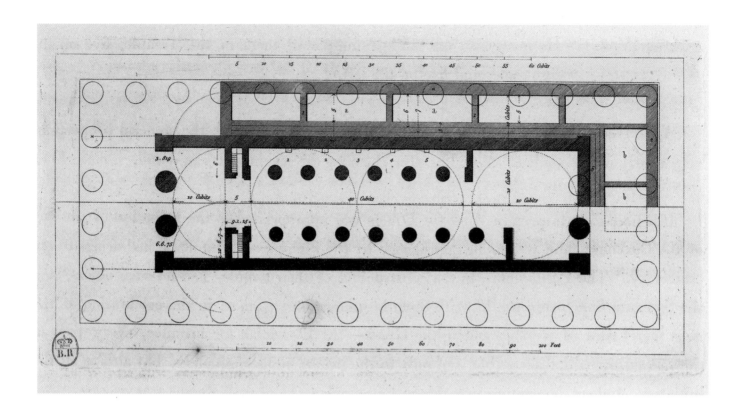

Magna Graecia, Wilkins attempted to shed some light on the history of architecture and
to explain the origins of the general principles and common features of the Greek temples:

> Let us then compare the plan and proportions of this celebrated structure with those
> of some of the earliest Grecian temples, such as at Paestum and Aegina. So great a
> resemblance will be found, upon investigation, to subsist between them, as to afford a
> presumptive proof that the architects both of Syria and Greece were guided by the same
> general principles in the distribution and proportion of the more essential parts of their
> buildings.[56]

Wilkins turned thus to what he supposed to be the origins of architecture in order to
show where the principles of Greek architecture had come from. Remarkably, he made a
direct connection with Paestum, and even illustrated this in engravings. He presented a
plan of Paestum, 'reduced from real admeasurements', integrated with a plan of the temple
at Jerusalem (Fig. 164), and in the vignette to his introduction he represented 'sections
through the Pronaos and Cella of the Temple of Solomon. The proportions are taken from
the Temple at Paestum' (Fig. 165).[57] Thus, in a curious reversal, the Temple of Neptune
was used to determine the proportions of the Temple of Solomon, which was presented
as embodying the beginnings of architecture. But, apart from observing that both temples
were very ancient,[58] and that the Temple of Solomon was the model for Greek architecture,
Wilkins did not elaborate further on the historical relationship between the two buildings.

Wilkins claimed to have been influenced by Isaac Newton's *Chronology* (1728) in making
this connection.[59] However, the idea that the Jerusalem temple was an ancestor of classical architecture was well established:[60] for example, as we saw in Chapter 5, the same connection featured in Paoli's letter published in Carlo Fea's edition of Winckelmann. While

Rediscovering Architecture

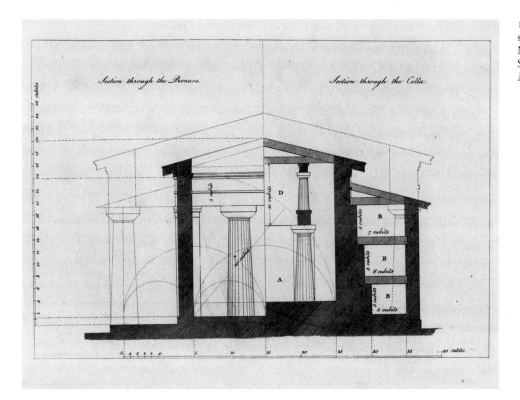

there are significant links between Wilkins's work and other theories of the origins of architecture, Wilkins had a specific purpose in tracing the roots of temple architecture: namely, to identify those common features that defined the 'norm' in Greek architecture. His intention was not to rewrite history or to present a new set of great examples of ancient architecture, but to inspire architects. Although he did not explain in literal terms how his drawings and descriptions could feed into a new contemporary architecture, his book was clearly aimed principally at the professional milieu, though he intended it to be of interest also to a public of connoisseurs. In the years after the publication of *The Antiquities*, which established him as a scholar, Wilkins became famous as an architect, designing public buildings and monuments in Greek Revival style in Cambridge; his designs referred mostly to Athenian architecture and Paestum seems to have played no particular role in his own work.

In the first fifteen pages of the introduction to *The Antiquities* Wilkins repeatedly compared the Temple of Neptune with Solomon's temple, basing his knowledge of the latter on Juan Bautista Villalpando's descriptions in *Ezechielem explanationes* (1596–1604) and on Newton. The ingenious drawing in which he combined cross-sections through the pronaos and the cella of the Temple of Neptune with a cross-section through Solomon's temple (see Fig. 165) sought to show that the proportions were the same, and he also identified other similarities between the two: 'the Temple at Paestum, as well as other Grecian temples of the same era, were actually designed after the model of the Temple at Jerusalem'.[61] He repeatedly underscored this:

> there existed a connection between the plans of ancient Grecian temples, particularly that of Paestum, and the Temple of Solomon. The proportions of the latter may therefore be assumed as the standard, by which the early Greeks were directed in the

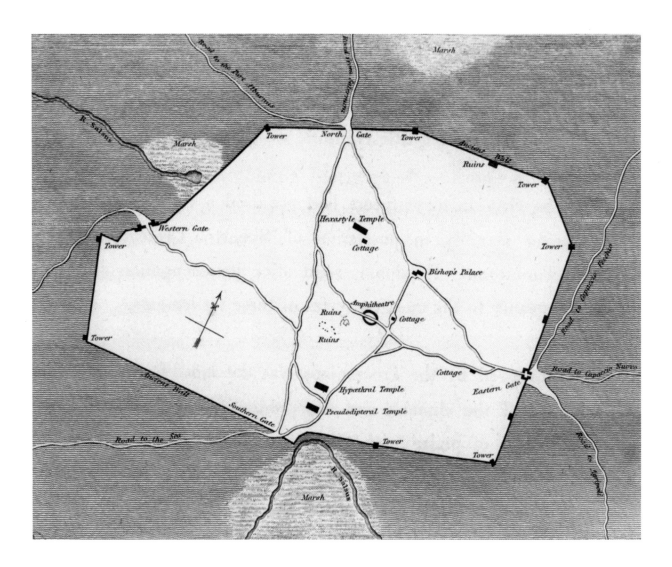

166　William Wilkins, plan of
Paestum, in *The Antiquities of
Magna Graecia* (1807).

construction of their temples; and which was followed, with little variation, by the
Greeks of later times.[62]

According to Wilkins, the influence from the Middle East entered Greece – and Italy –
through the 'channel' of Minos. In giving measurements of the 'Paestum temple' that corresponded more or less to those of the temple at Jerusalem, Wilkins even found a norm in the
exceptions to the general rule. Small differences in proportion, he claimed, became a common
feature of Greek architecture and part of the standard: 'We ought not . . . to be surprised that
the proportion of the height to the diameter of the columns does not more exactly correspond: among the early Greeks, it does not appear that there existed any rule for determin-
ing the height of columns from the diameter.'[63] This directly contradicts the idea, which we
encountered in earlier chapters, that Paestum was exceptional, and certainly not representative of a standard. In the process of regularisation Wilkins thus did everything possible to
emphasise that Paestum was not unique but just another example alongside many others.

Another passage from the introduction, expanding on the matter of small variations
between examples of Greek temple architecture, makes an interesting point about the
origins of the Paestum order:

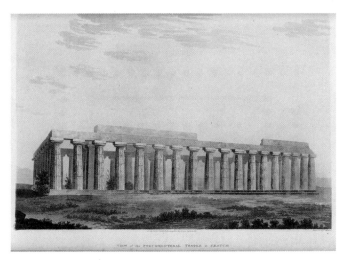

Since the proportions of the columns of this temple did not vary very considerably from those of the columns in several Grecian temples which are well known to us, it is fair to conclude that they were of that order which was subsequently called the Doric; and that the *bowls*, mentioned in the Book of Kings, were the circular parts of the capitals, which in the columns at Paestum have a great resemblance to antique bowls or cups, called by the Italians *Tazze*. The French style this member, in the capitals of Doric columns, the *Vase du chapiteau*.[64]

Here Wilkins contrived a historical explanation for the bizarre capitals that Lord North described as resembling 'props, on which our peasants in England sometimes put their corn, to prevent its being eaten by vermin' (see Chapter 1).[65] He presented this feature, too, as partaking of the general characteristics of the Doric and, again, related it to the same ancient topos of classical architectural history – the temple at Jerusalem.

After the introduction, *The Antiquities* has separate chapters on Sicily, Syracuse, Agrigento, Selinunte, Segesta and Paestum, all with plates. In the chapter on Paestum, after introducing the city, its history and inhabitants, Wilkins described the site (Fig. 166), evoking some elements of the sublime and the primitive:

167a–d William Wilkins, general view of Paestum (*top left*), perspective view of the Temple of Neptune (*top right*), perspective view of the Basilica (*bottom left*), perspective view of the Temple of Ceres (*bottom right*), in *The Antiquities of Magna Graecia* (1807), plates I, II, XII, XVII.

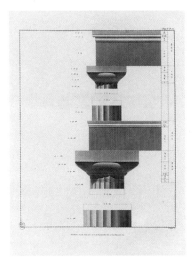

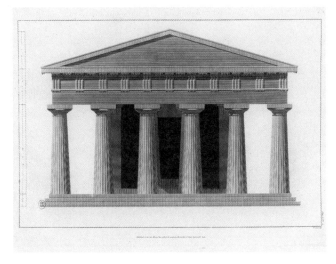

168a–d William Wilkins, the Temple of Neptune, detail of the order (*right*), elevation, restored state (*far right*), cross-section in front of the pronaos, restored state (*below left*), cross-section, restored state (*below right*), in *The Antiquities of Magna Graecia* (1807), plates X, IV, V, VI.

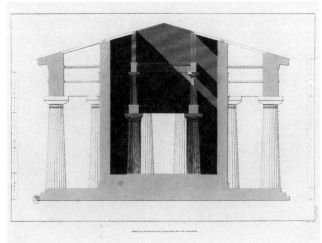

The air of desolation which reigns in the environs of this once populous city, heightened by the deserted aspect of the ruins, is in no degree relieved by the appearance of a few wretched hovels, which serve as temporary habitations to the keepers of the numerous herds of buffaloes. The uncouth wild appearance of these animals impresses more strongly the idea, that we are here far removed from the abode of civilized man.[66]

This brief evocation of the experience of being in a world far from civilisation is quickly overtaken by Wilkins's attempts to represent Paestum as part of the development of Greek temple architecture and the Neptune temple as a model for contemporary design. The book as a whole may be seen as a sequence of steps in the reduction of the site from its individual reality to the status of an exemplar: first the site is set aside, then the temples as an ensemble, until only one temple is left. This process is visible in the engravings that Wilkins included, which clearly show that his interest was at no point archaeological. Unlike other writers on Paestum, he published only a few drawings of the ruins in their present state. Instead, throughout the book he depicted the temples of Paestum and the

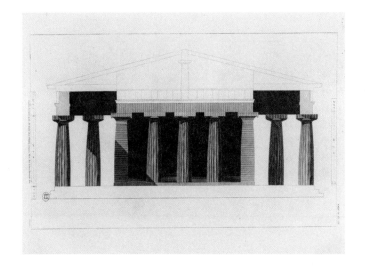
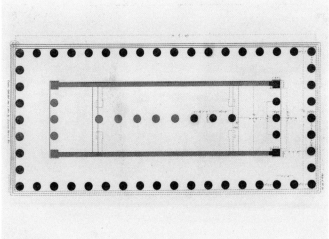
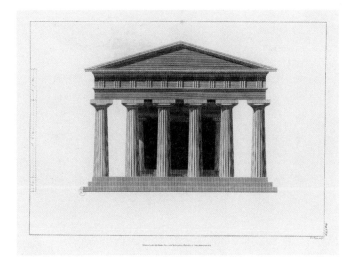
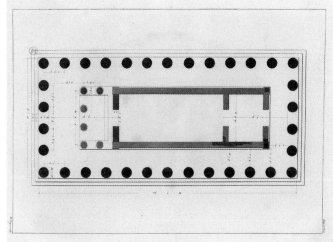

other Greek colonies in reconstructed versions, showing them in a perfect state. This helped readers to imagine what they had looked like in ancient times, and made the application of the Neptune temple to contemporary architecture more plausible. Wilkins included twenty-two engravings of the temples at Paestum: one general plan, one showing a view of the three temples, eleven of the Neptune temple, five of the Basilica, and four of the Temple of Ceres. Only the perspective views of the monuments in their surroundings depict the actual eighteenth-century situation (Fig. 167). Apart from these, the plan of the site and one interior perspective, all the other views, sixteen in total, are reconstructed plans, façades, cross-sections or details of the orders (Figs 168–9). In his ambition to present a general type of Greek architecture to inspire contemporary architects, Wilkins treated the Paestum temples as part of a general historical framework of Doric temple architecture; at the same time he singled out one temple – the Neptune – as an exemplar, 'cleaning up' its ruins and reconstructing the temple to make it available as a model for architecture in his own day. And to achieve that, he had to strip Paestum of its site, situation and specificity, and locate it on a historical continuum of Greek classical architecture.

169a–d William Wilkins, cross-section of the Basilica, restored state (*top, left*), plan of the Basilica, restored state (*top, right*), elevation of the Temple of Ceres, restored state (*bottom, left*), plan of the Temple of Ceres, restored state (*bottom, right*), in *The Antiquities of Magna Graecia* (1807), plates XIV, XIII, XIX, XVIII.

170 (*right, top*) Scale model of the Basilica, before 1822, cork (L 1845 × W 920 × H 400 mm, approximately 1:33). Naples, Museo Archeologico Nazionale.

171 (*far right*) Scale model of the Temple of Ceres, before 1822, cork (L 1760 × W 800 × H 430 mm, approximately 1:33). Naples, Museo Archeologico Nazionale.

172 (*right, bottom*) Scale model of the Temple of Neptune, before 1822, cork (L 1900 × W 910 × H 520 mm, approximately 1:33). Naples, Museo Archeologico Nazionale.

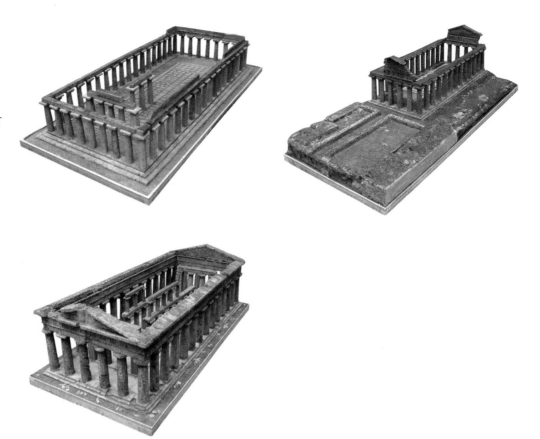

Paestum Abroad in Collections

While the projects and publications of Pâris, Delagardette, Le Roy and Wilkins were mainly aimed at a professional public of architects and artists, they were also disseminated among connoisseurs, and it was this larger public that another initiative sought to engage – the exhibition of collections of model buildings. These three-dimensional representations were often executed in cork, and they became a fashion in eighteenth-century Europe; created to scale, they were owned by private collectors or academic institutions and were on view in museums and academies, and in the homes of collectors.[67] To understand the reduction and contextualisation of Paestum, it is essential to survey the cork models of the temples (Figs 170–75); their circulation and public availability offered a three-dimensional, spatial and, to a certain degree, tactile appreciation of the temples, though in fact the known examples are almost all reproductions of the Neptune temple.[68]

The new industry of model building developed at the end of the eighteenth century,[69] and its invention is generally attributed to the architect Augusto Rosa (1738–1784).[70] In 1777 Rosa accompanied Giovanni Battista Piranesi and his son Francesco to Paestum, where the three of them took measurements – the Piranesis for their engravings, Rosa for his models. This process of measuring the buildings, an indication of the seriousness of their enterprise, was an Italian phenomenon as far as model making was concerned,[71] and the Italians were respected for the scientific accuracy of their work.[72]

Large three-dimensional cork models had many advantages. Despite their size, they were light and could be transported with relative ease. They were more easily 'readable' than

engravings, especially for amateurs, who could at a glance gain a clear impression of the monument concerned. Models were ideal as teaching aids. And they were less likely than the perspective views in engravings to arouse false expectations in prospective visitors to a site, as the proportions of the monuments in the model versions were identical with those of the originals. In the case of Paestum, there was the added advantage that the cork of the models bore a striking resemblance to the type of porous stone of which the temples were built.

Professional architects bought these objects for their own use, but models were also intended for a wider market and were put on display for the delectation of amateurs and the interested public. For example, in the early nineteenth century the French painter and engraver Louis-François Cassas (1756–1827) installed a gallery at 8 rue de la Seine in Paris,[73] where he presented models and other objects, paintings and engravings. An engraving of 1806 (Fig. 176) shows Egyptian monuments on the right, and Greek monuments behind and on the left. Jacques-Guillaume Legrand published an exhibition guide to Cassas's collection in 1806. One of the aims of the exhibition, he stated, was to allow visitors to trace the 'history and progress of architecture of all ancient and modern people'. The collection of 'masterpieces of Architecture' was not only a powerful means of instruction but also made possible a comparison of the architecture of different peoples by making available 'the most beautiful, the most famous, the most characteristic monuments of Egyptian, Indian, Persian, Greek, Palmyrian, Etruscan, Mexican, Roman, Gothic, Moorish, Italian . . . architecture'.[74] The various forms of these different architectural traditions could be properly appreciated, Legrand declared, only through three-dimensional models, which

173 (top, left) Domenico Padiglione, scale model of the Basilica, cork (L 1335 × W 617 × H 240 mm), London, Sir John Soane's Museum, MR22.

174 (top, right) Domenico Padiglione, scale model of the Temple of Ceres, cork (L 1320 × W 334 × H 320 mm) London, Sir John Soane's Museum, MR12.

175 (bottom) Domenico Padiglione, scale model of the Temple of Neptune, after 1802, cork with terracotta capitals, on a mahogany base (L 1324 × W 630 × H 374 mm, approximately 1:43). London, Sir John Soane's Museum, MR25.

could be skilfully lit to create effects of daylight, dusk and nighttime. Even the best drawings and engravings could not match the realism of a model.[75]

The models were so impressive, Legrand declared, that they rendered a visit to the monuments themselves unnecessary: when one wandered through the collection, comparing
the monuments with one another, it was easy to imagine them in their true settings:

> we shall see the burning or freezing sky under which [the building] is located: the site,
> mountainous or pleasant or wild, that surrounds it; the character of the rocks, the trees,
> the local plants; the [mode of] dress of the people who own it or sometimes visit it;
> well, we shall be transported, as if by magic, to the foot of these famous monuments,
> without enduring the fatigue of a journey, and we shall have the infinite advantage of
> being able instantly to compare Asian monuments with European or African ones,
> merely by taking a few steps.[76]

In fact, visiting the collection at the rue de la Seine surpassed the experience of the sites
themselves, because visitors were able to compare monuments that they could never nor-
mally see together. These were now within easy reach, at an accessible scale, displayed in
a pleasant exhibition space in the centre of Paris; using their own powers of fantasy, visitors could imagine wandering from one monument to another – from Egypt to India,
from Greece to Persia – in a few minutes.

As part of the coverage of Greek architecture, Cassas chose the Neptune temple from
Paestum, showing it next to monuments that were mostly in Athens.[77] Legrand explained
this choice as follows:

> It is the largest of the three buildings of the same type that still survive in the gulf of
> Salerno, and that all the travellers hasten to visit when they are in Naples, to gain an
> idea of Greek architecture. There is, in fact, a very close connection between this order
> and the Doric order used in Athenian monuments. Although the Paestum temples are

of less elegant, less pure proportions, which makes one assume they are more ancient, they nevertheless convey a very grand character.

According to Legrand, the cork model perfectly imitated the ruined state of the temple, 'which today presents to artists' paintbrushes an infinite number of viewpoints and rich colour tones'. His guide to the exhibits first gave a general introduction to Paestum and all three temples, the ruins of which, he claimed, were, along with those at Tivoli, the best-known and most often drawn remains in Italy.[78] He emphasised the similarities between the three temples and also focused on resemblances between them and other Greek monuments, notwithstanding the differences in their proportions. Then he singled out the Neptune temple as the best example of the three and discussed it in more detail, with reference to the model on show. Thus, like Wilkins, Cassas and Legrand began by ignoring the site, and then set aside the two smaller temples, to leave one representative of Paestum, which they placed in the general context of Greek architecture.

In the same spirit of diffusing knowledge of classical architecture to a large public, in 1800 Legrand and his fellow architect Jacques Molinos (who had collaborated earlier on the project of a new edition of Desgodetz – see p. 236), opened their 'musée de l'ordre dorique' at 6 rue de Saint-Florentin in Paris (a building that they had designed as their residence in 1792–4). The redesigned façade of the building, which was intended to announce the function of the interior, consisted of ten Doric columns, and the courtyard featured baseless Doric pilasters;[79] inside, plaster casts and models of buildings were displayed for the education of architects. In a letter to the editors of the *Journal des Arts, des Sciences et de la Littérature* about their new venture, Legrand and Molinos wrote:

> To . . . complete the collection [showing] the Greek Doric order, under the vestibule will be found four columns, that give a faithful likeness of the order of the Propylaea at Athens, of that of the Temple of Theseus, [of that] of the arch of Augustus in the same city, and of that of the great temple of Paestum in Magna Graecia, an order that Artists grieve to see often mutilated by masons who believe they are making Architecture.[80]

Their collection was based on personal experience during their travels, and was intended, as they stated, to exemplify the true Doric, instead of the false concept of the order that had become fashionable. They had visited Paestum together and had remarked on the sturdy proportions of the temples and their masculine style, which reminded them of the athletic forms of sculpted depictions of Hercules.[81] The objective of their museum being so restricted, they presented only one aspect of the totality of Paestum, and stripped down the complex reality to nothing more than an order, featured in their overview of Greek Doric architecture.

Among other architects who created large collections of architectural models was Jean Rondelet (1743–1829),[82] for whom his models had a mainly pedagogical purpose since he used them in his lectures. Rondelet had a different interest again in creating his collection, which shows another angle on the reduction of Paestum: Rondelet was interested above all in construction. Trained as an architect – he had been a pupil of Jacques-Germain Soufflot and Jacques-François Blondel – Rondelet taught stereotomy at the École des Beaux-Arts and was the author of *Traité théorique et pratique de l'art de bâtir* (1802–17).[83] In 1808 he began to convert the illustrations in his book into models, which he exhibited between 1808 and 1813 in the Galérie d'Architecture at the Louvre.[84] Between 1812 and 1821 his brother finished this task, and eventually the collection consisted of a total of 410 models.[85]

Rondelet's *Traité* played an important role in the process of deriving a type for Greek architecture from Paestum's temples. On a tour of Italy, Sicily and Malta in 1784, he had visited Paestum, taken measurements of the temples and paid keen attention to their tectonic aspects.[86] A letter of February 1784 recounts his visit, and focuses on the large blocks of travertine that were set one on another without mortar. Especially in the Neptune temple, he admired the cutting and laying of these stones: they were of the same size and so perfectly cut that the joints were almost invisible. In Naples, Rondelet continued to concentrate on construction, and researched the technical methods of other architects and masons in search of new ideas that could inform Parisian architecture.[87]

From the start, Rondelet planned to publish his findings from the tour,[88] which eventually bore fruit two decades later in his *Traité . . . de l'art de bâtir*. In his treatise Rondelet quoted at length from Vitruvius and commented on the text, setting out his own experiences at Roman sites such as the Villa Adriana and the Baths of Caracalla and dilating on the ancient construction methods he had studied. The *Traité*, to which many architects and engineers subscribed, became a standard text for successive generations of architects, together with Jean-Nicolas-Louis Durand's *Précis des leçons d'architecture données à l'École Polytechnique* (1802–5). While Durand focused on formal geometry, Rondelet concentrated on construction: many architects regarded the two books as complementary, because together they formulated the main issues of eighteenth-century architectural practice, and paved the way for that of the nineteenth century. Rondelet presented architecture as a science, not as an imaginative art: in his view, good architecture followed from good construction.[89] And, unlike Quatremère de Quincy, he was not much interested in history, as both the entries he wrote for Quatremère's *Encyclopédie méthodique* and his own work prove. The *Traité* covered building materials, the techniques of building and methods of

177 Jean Rondelet, comparative plans of churches and temples, in *Traité théorique et pratique de l'art de bâtir*, vol. III (1805), plate LXXV: (*left to right*) San Paolo fuori le Mura, Rome; (*above*) Santa Sabina and San Pietro in Vincoli, Rome; San Filippo Neri, Naples; (*below*) Temple of Neptune, Paestum; Temple of Juno and Temple of Concordia, Agrigento.

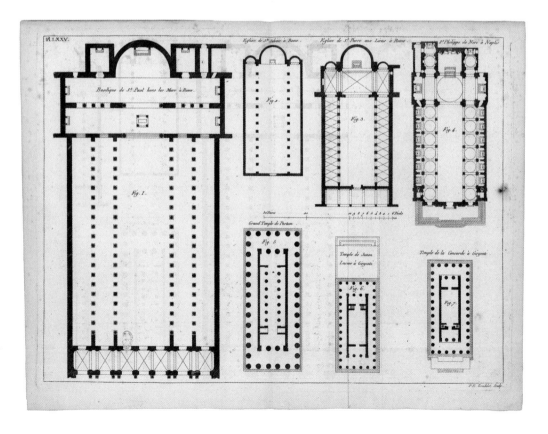

estimating building costs. Rondelet reflected lengthily on the use of iron, both in buildings and in bridges. He became well known for his work on the church of Sainte-
Geneviève in Paris (now the Panthéon), first as Soufflot's pupil but afterwards as the
technical expert in his own right; he planned and carried out the iron reinforcement of
parts of the church, including the dome, which was in danger of collapse.[90] Rondelet's
focus was thus always on building technology, and, together with Durand, he came to
stand for the separation, around 1800, of the professions of engineer and architect. Although
he considered Paestum technically interesting, he found objectionable the idea of its order
being used for ornamental reasons, like other fashionable styles – the Egyptian, Gothic and
Arab:[91] according to Rondelet, the constructional value of the Paestum order was much
more significant.

In the *Traité*, Rondelet presented the principal stones used for construction in Italy, and
analysed the stone types to be found from the north to the south of the country.[92] Of
Paestum's stone type he wrote, in volume I: 'The temples of Paestum are built of a hard
and calcareous stone, which is a sort of travertine full of holes, and less beautiful than the
one in Rome.'[93] In volume III he compared the structures of different buildings, among
which was the Neptune temple.[94] His purpose was to analyse the relation of the walls
and other load-bearing members to the dimensions of the buildings so as to establish how
mass and stability were connected. In pursuit of this end, Rondelet compared plans of the
Neptune temple, San Filippo Neri in Naples, and San Pietro in Vincoli, Santa Sabina and
San Paolo fuori le Mura in Rome, and presented his data in a table.[95] So, as far as Rondelet was concerned, Paestum was of interest in the context of engineering and building
materials: the series he devised were based on formal or constructional similarities and had
no chronological aim.

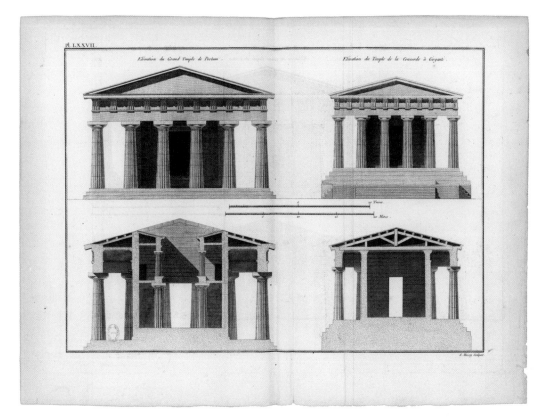

178 Jean Rondelet,
comparative elevations and
cross-sections of the Temple
of Neptune at Paestum (*left*)
and the Temple of Concordia
at Agrigento (*right*), in *Traité
théorique et pratique de l'art de
bâtir*, vol. III (1805), plate
LXXVII.

In volume III of Rondelet's treatise, Paestum features in two plates. One shows the plans of the four churches in Rome and Naples, and reconstructed plans, on the same scale, of two Sicilian temples (Concordia and Juno at Agrigento) and the Temple of Neptune at Paestum (Fig. 177).[96] The other depicts reconstructions, again at the same scale, of the 'Grand Temple de Pestum' and the 'Temple de la Concorde' (Concordia) in elevation and in cross-section (Fig. 178).[97] By means of these comparisons Rondelet aimed to show the similarities between the temples – the differences were mainly of size. One can see how much larger the Paestum temple is, and that its proportions are slightly different from those of the other temples, most markedly in the intercolumnium. In Fig. 178 the Temple of Neptune is shown elevated on three steps, whereas the Concordia Temple has four steps and a large base; in cross-section, the two storeys in the centre of the Neptune temple, with the two ranks of superposed columns, contrast with the single storey and one row of columns in the Concordia. Here Paestum – in the shape of the Neptune temple – is shown to be important for its structural features, selected as one of only three temples to demonstrate the type of Greek architecture. Other authors had proposed it as a historical and stylistic exemplar: now Rondelet identified it as a structural model for contemporary architects.

The Two-Dimensional Architecture of Durand

In *Recueil et parallèle des édifices de tout genre anciens et modernes remarquables par leur beauté* (1799–1800) Jean-Nicolas-Louis Durand (1760–1834), Étienne-Louis Boullée's favourite pupil and from 1795 onwards a professor of architecture at the École Polytechnique, went even further than Rondelet in the selective approach to Paestum, reducing the scope of his enquiry to specific architectural elements.[98] He offered a comparative method of presentation, derived from Le Roy (with whom he also studied), who, in *Histoire de la disposition et des formes différentes que les Chrétiens ont données à leur Temples* (1764), had presented the evolution of temple and church architecture on a single page of images; other publications that adopted the same approach were Le Roy's *Les ruines des plus beaux monuments de la Grèce* (1758), and Gabriel-Pierre-Martin Dumont's publications on theatres. Following their example, Durand provided comparative diagrams, in which he juxtaposed forms and not styles.[99] He grouped together different buildings on the same page, drawing them all at the same scale so that they could be compared as types; by this means he constructed typological series, ignoring the idiosyncrasies and stylistic characteristics of the individual buildings.

When it came to Paestum, Durand outdid even Delagardette in his dissection of architectural details. Delagardette, whose *Ruines de Paestum* was published almost simultaneously with Durand's *Recueil*, made comparisons between the different manifestations of the Doric order at Paestum and in other temples (Fig. 179),[100] with the purpose of dating the temples (see Chapter 5).[101] By centring his analysis on the Paestum order, Delagardette eliminated the distinctiveness of the temples, claiming to see an analogy between all these buildings, which were, he asserted, 'conceived according to the same principles'. He went on: 'we find the same type, the same genius, the same stage in the arrangement of harmonious details'.[102]

In similar fashion, Durand's *Recueil* sets out 'la pureté de l'Architecture Grecque', presenting in the engravings only details of the Paestum temples, such as a capital or an entablature, among many other examples of Greek architectural details (Fig. 180).[103] However,

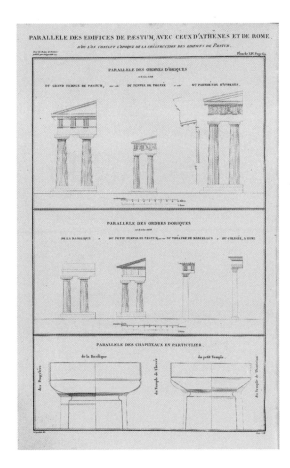

PARALLELE DES EDIFICES DE PÆSTUM, AVEC CEUX D'ATHENES ET DE ROME.
D'OU L'ON CONCLUT L'ÉPOQUE DE LA CONSTRUCTION DES EDIFICES DE PÆSTUM.

PARALLELE DES ORDRES D'ORIQUES

DU GRAND TEMPLE DE PÆSTUM, DU TEMPLE DE THESEE DU PARTHENON D'ATHENES.

PARALLELE DES ORDRES DORIQUES

DE LA BASILIQUE DU PETIT TEMPLE DE PÆSTUM, DU THEATRE DE MARCELLUS DU COLISÉE, A ROME.

PARALLELE DES CHAPITEAUX EN PARTICULIER.

de la Basilique   du petit Temple.

179 Claude-Mathieu Delagardette, comparative details of the Doric order of Paestum and of other buildings, in *Les Ruines de Paestum* ([1799]), plate XIV: (*left to right, above*) Temple of Neptune, Paestum; Temple of Theseus and the Parthenon, Athens; (*middle*) the Basilica and Temple of Ceres, Paestum; Theatre of Marcellus and the Coliseum, Rome; (*below*) the Basilica and Temple of Ceres, Paestum.

unlike Rondelet and others, Durand did not ignore the Basilica: even though he dubbed the Neptune temple simply the 'Temple de Pestum', he showed the capitals of both temples. In the text accompanying the plates, Durand explained how he had brought together the principal examples of the original Doric order used by the Greeks in Athens, Sicily and elsewhere, and had drawn them at the same scale so as to make it easier to see the variety of their proportions and 'compare their relative grandeur'.[104] The aim of this comparison was to expose the different characters of the columns, expressed as a result of their proportions. Durand claimed that his diagrams provided the reader with a tool for judging the relation between the thickness and the height of the columns, their features and stature. It was, he said, like examining a line of human beings of different ages, shapes and figures: 'we recognise the elegance and lightness of youth in some, and the vigour and force of mature age or the decline of old age in others'.[105]

Durand criticised his fellow architects for adopting a method of designing Doric columns by multiplying the diameter by eight to calculate the height and adding a base – a thing the Greeks had never done. Instead of such mechanical procedures, he made a plea for a thorough study and knowledge of the art of drawing, recommended the comparison of monuments by travelling to see them, and appealed to the architect to pursue 'the continuous observation of nature . . . [and] the numerous combinations she presents him with'. In explaining his ideas on the applicability of Greek architecture, he claimed that architecture must follow its surroundings. He suggested that architects had 'irritated' the Doric order, taken away its character and grandeur, 'its male solidity', by extending its

180 Jean-Nicolas-Louis
Durand, comparative details
of orders, in *Recueil et parallèle
des édifices de tout genre anciens
et modernes*, vol. II (1800),
plates 63, 65.

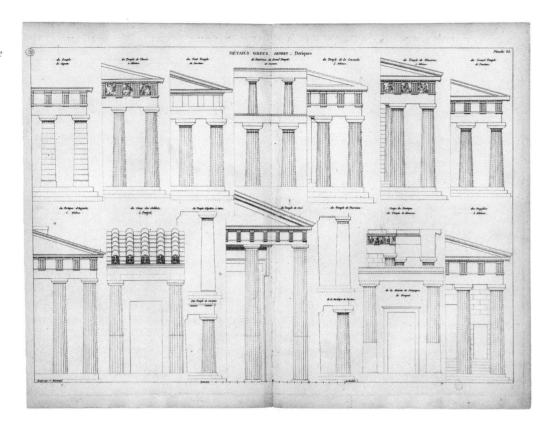

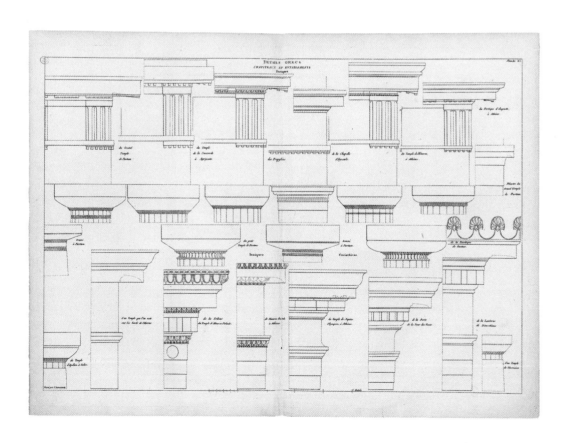

height to eight diameters, and robbed it of its originality 'by adding a base'. He referred to the monuments in Athens, Paestum and Sicily, where the substructure of the buildings was more solid and more appropriate. It was up to artists, he said, to 'examine, compare, choose, and apply' from among the examples he had drawn and assembled in a single plate, and he made a case for the 'pure, simple, gracious, noble and grand style of Greek architecture', which modern taste had despoiled by forcing it to take its place alongside the five orders of architecture.[106]

While Durand referred to nature and the setting of a building as having an influence on its design, he did not require the architect to integrate the building with its surroundings in the way that Labrouste would do some thirty years later. It was much more important to go back to the source, to the original architectural forms, and to reproduce the original order. This return to the pure beginnings of Doric architecture was prompted by aesthetic motives. Durand distilled one order out of the features of many Greek temples, a baseless Doric that was set up in opposition to the Ionic and Tuscan orders and could take its place between them.[107] But Durand's order is not derived from Paestum: it is a mixture of many baseless Doric columns from different buildings. In his *Recueil* he continually praised Greek architecture, which he described as proud and original, delicate, executed with genius and superiority; architects could achieve the same qualities in their own contemporary buildings, if they would only use his engravings as models and execute the forms they found there.

Durand never travelled to Paestum, and so had never seen the temples with his own eyes. But, in fact, that hardly mattered, for what he did in his *Recueil* was to distil Greek architecture down to a collection of elements that could be copied in contemporary design; for his engravings he simply took these elements from other publications and redrew them. Durand's presentation of Paestum did not, therefore, call on any experience at the site: on the contrary, it was probably better, from the point of view of ease and clarity, for his series not to have to translate from three-dimensional reality but to be able to rely on existing two-dimensional representations of the relevant features of the temples. In this enterprise, the actual geographical site of Paestum ceased to have any importance, and its specific character disappeared completely. Such an abstraction, reduction and standardisation of its architecture meant that Paestum itself was no longer in any way truly present in the outcome. In place of its unique and strange reality, it was pared down to a single example among many other examples, swallowed up in a sea of details of Greek temple architecture. The process of the abstraction of Paestum that we have analysed in this chapter reached its climax in Durand's work, where experience was superseded completely by synthetic scholarship.

Architecture without Experience

In contrast with the richness of experiences analysed in the other five chapters of this book, this chapter shows the poverty of selecting nothing but an order from the architecture of Paestum, and of the reductionist strategy generally. The site, as experienced by the protagonists of the earlier chapters, no longer had any significance, which is why Labrouste's stance (see Chapter 5), is so deeply interesting. Labrouste located Paestum in a new chronology of architectural history, but argued against transplanting the architecture of the temples to France, claiming that it was impossible to transfer architecture from one country to another. He opposed the architectural theorists who were of the opinion that there is a universal Greek architecture, and claimed that this was nonsense. In trying to treat Paestum as a design model and consequently mixing it with the dimensions and elements of other baseless Doric temples, architects did not re-create the original – indeed, what they created lacked the essence and the particularity of Paestum. Reproducing a column did not result in reproducing the interior and the space, much less the site as a whole or the landscape. All the approaches we have discussed in the course of this book – the sublime, the picturesque, physical experience, theatricality and primitivism – were lost when the Paestum order was isolated and used in eighteenth-century architecture. Architecture based solely on an order is no longer grounded in the experience associated with the order in its original context, and cannot reproduce that experience.

Whereas in earlier chapters we explored the different reactions of visitors to the site itself, in this chapter we have seen interest shift to mere features of Paestum that could be singled out and exported to the native countries of the architects. The complex reality of Paestum was steadily diminished: first the architecture was divested of its setting – its landscape and topography; next the site was reduced to the temples, then to one temple, to the proportions of Greek temple architecture, and to constructional characteristics, until all that was left was a single column. The stages in this process are echoed by the material manifestation of the theorists' work. We might say that Paestum's site is still present in the taking of measurements of the monuments on the spot – a process that involved intimate physical contact with the architecture; the cork models that were fabricated in Rome replicated the temples but eliminated the landscape and the rest of the city, and destroyed the ensemble by treating each one as a disembodied individual. In published works, Delagardette restricted Paestum to an order, Wilkins to proportions and Rondelet to engineering. Then each of them arranged his favoured feature in a series with equivalent features from other buildings, and Paestum became nothing more than a representative of the baseless Doric, or harmonious proportions, or Greek building methods.

The dissemination of knowledge was the objective of all these attempts at contextualisation and abstraction. Recording the site and making it known through publications, as opposed to the more explorative approaches of the authors of the first monographs, evolved towards Delagardette's architectural approach. It was Delagardette who identified the Neptune temple as the only example of pure Greek architecture, and then restricted his scope still further by homing in on the order, which he delineated in his Vignola edition. As the eyes of the architects focused ever more searchingly on the applicability of Paestum to contemporary architecture, their main concern became the need for accurate measurements, and the geometry – whether curved or straight – of the column. They looked for similarities between Greek buildings, and played down or denied differences and idiosyncrasies. Pâris noted the difficulty of using the Paestum order, and made clear that its definition in the context of eighteenth-century architecture was a vexed question: a stumpy, baseless Doric was, regardless of its other characteristics, automatically attributed to Paestum. As Quatremère de Quincy observed, this had more to do with Paestum's celebrated status and the fact that the temples were known to have a heavy baseless order, than with any actual likeness between this order and those of the temples.

Chapter 5 pursued the role of Paestum in the history and origins of architecture. As the historical significance of the temples became evident, the efforts of architects to position Paestum on the continuum of classical architecture gathered pace. At the same time, history also began to have an influence on design practice: to place Paestum within a historical development justified its use in design, which in turn conferred cultural value on the resulting architecture. We have traced the contextualisation of Paestum in a number of projects: Pâris added Paestum to Desgodetz's canon of classical architecture; Le Roy and Wilkins sought to draw out the similarities between different buildings in the Greek temple tradition; Cassas, Legrand and Molinos aimed to educate connoisseurs and professionals through comparative displays; and Rondelet devoted his attention to techniques of construction. Although practically all these exponents of Paestum had travelled to the site, Durand deployed the geometry of Paestum without feeling the need to go there, and Legrand recommended that examining a three-dimensional model of Paestum's temples in Paris was, if anything, better than the experience to be had on the spot in Italy. While Delagardette did feel the urge to see Paestum with his own eyes, his experience is totally absent from the account he afterwards gave: he referred to columns, capitals and entablatures, and gave information that could be largely obtained from any of the existing publications. In his estimation, clearly, it was no longer necessary to have the experience: it sufficed to study the books.

In all the works quoted in this chapter, Paestum was stripped of its experiential dimension. In exporting the order, the proportions or the constructional techniques, architects distanced themselves from the site. Paradoxically, while in one sense knowledge increased, in another genuine comprehension of Paestum and the experience of its complex reality disappeared in the process of abstraction, and the version disseminated to the public and professional realms was emasculated and generalised. This limited function contrasts strongly with the sublime responses that many travellers had experienced in the presence of Paestum's remains. In the course of the development described in this chapter, Paestum ceased to be strange and unique and vanished into the amorphous mass of Greek architecture.

Conclusion

Fifty years of experience at Paestum generated more than half a century of debate on architecture. Topics that were at the centre of eighteenth-century discourse were brought to the site and tested against it. At the same time, other themes originated at Paestum, often because preconceptions were overturned by the sight and in the presence of its unusual buildings. Thus it was that Paestum played a key role in eighteenth-century architectural thinking.

Paestum presented itself as a conundrum to visitors, but simultaneously never failed to fascinate, a fascination that was multi-layered and complex. The responses to the site seem to embody a network of paradoxes, which tell us something not only about Paestum, but also about eighteenth-century ideas of architecture. The six chapters of this book have explored these paradoxes, from the first impressions that baffled and overwhelmed travellers to the conscious and scholarly transformation of Paestum in architectural handbooks. They have shown the diverse interactions between the site and architectural thought: the confrontation between expectation and experience, theory and practice, assumptions and encounters.

First, we discovered that the sublime was invoked to express the awe-inspiring and contradictory experiences of a visit to Paestum. It was the sublime in all its facets, theorised by Longinus, Boileau, Burke and others, that provided visitors with a framework for their sensations and a vocabulary to articulate them in images and texts. The paradox of the sublime at Paestum was that it broke with the laws of beauty defined in classicism, even while they were applied to classical buildings. A second paradox emerged out of the experience of the picturesque at Paestum. In picturesque theories, the desired approach was to view a landscape and the buildings in it from a distance, framing them to produce a pleasing composition, as if they were the subject of a painting. But by observing the site from far off, the observer could no longer discern its specific features: within the picture frame, Paestum's temples were simply some unidentifiable ruins, incidents in a landscape, like follies in a garden. So Part I of this study functioned as a diptych: each chapter analysed a major aesthetic theory and its role at Paestum. The two concepts are strongly contrasted and have

181 *(facing page)* Detail of Fig. 96a.

very different outcomes: whereas the sublime exposed all the specificities of the site, ranging from the stages of the journey towards it to all the feelings evoked on the spot, the picturesque offered nothing more than a pleasant painting of what might be any ruin in beautiful scenery. The sublime was much better able to capture the particularities and contradictions of Paestum, yet the picturesque made a contribution of its own to the experience by drawing on movement as an important ingredient in perceiving architecture.

Movement became a major part of the process of examining the temples. Part II of this book demonstrated how moving towards, in and around the buildings was the means by which visitors were able to come to terms with the architecture. By entering the ruins and relating themselves physically to the buildings, exploring, and in various ways – both literal and imaginative – experiencing mass, load and support, space, openness and closedness, scale and situation, with multiple senses, visitors could comprehend the temples: spatiality, structure and texture could only be felt through the body. The different stages of exploring the site through movement were disseminated, and to some extent determined, by the many publications that appeared on Paestum, as Chapter 4 showed. In navigating and observing the site, visitors followed sequences of experiences that, in their diversity, can be likened to the concept of theatre. At this point the perspective begins to shift away from experience towards the gaining and propagation of knowledge.

In Part III we saw that increasing knowledge of Paestum, deployed in the search for origins, an account of historical progress and a model for contemporary architecture, also brought to light some paradoxes. It transpired that theories of the primitive did not correspond with the reality of ancient ruins on the ground; and while the primitive hut of cultural normative theory was presented as a model for contemporary architecture, the real remains at Paestum could not serve as such. The search for the origins of architecture suggested a return to the earliest source, but at the same time denied or ignored the developments that followed from these first beginnings, and was in that sense ahistorical. History needed to accommodate both the dawning of civilisation and the sequence of development from the origins up to the present. Another problem of primitivism was that, in its insistence on the original as the norm, it denied a place for invention. Only in Piranesi's ideas of origins as a creative force, and in Paoli's and Labrouste's primitive as an artistic choice was there room for ingenuity on the part of the architect.

Every increase in knowledge seemed to complicate the theoretical explanations and their application. The same was true of attempts to export Paestum by means of architectural handbooks, treatises and exhibits aimed at presenting it either as part of a historical development of classical architecture or as a model for contemporary design. These efforts resulted in reducing Paestum on the one hand to a single element – an order, architectural proportions or tectonics – and on the other to a single non-specific example of the corpus of classical architecture. Above all, nothing was left of the experience of the site, which was the source of all the ideas that had been formulated about Paestum. Architects went to the site with a certain agenda – to look for a model for their own work, or to locate the temples within architectural history – but when they were confronted with the real, and very strange remains, they had to adopt a non-intellectual strategy: to move about, wander inside and outside the ruins, observe and experience their reality in order to understand them. It is this process of observation, with all its implications, that is at the heart of this study, and the subject of the detailed analysis we have pursued from different theoretical viewpoints. For the first time, architectural experience is here examined systematically, on the basis of a single supremely important case, to illuminate eighteenth-century ideas and practice.

Rediscovering Architecture

In the middle of the eighteenth century, at the time that Paestum was rediscovered, the importance of experience in architecture, and its significance for design had become a focal point for many architects and architectural theorists. Works written by Julien-David Le Roy, Marc-Antoine Laugier, Nicolas Le Camus de Mézières, Thomas Whately, Richard Payne Knight and John Soane, to name only a few, are pervasive examples of this new interest. Architectural experience was used to analyse existing buildings, and this analysis provided the architect with tools to enable him to design with the experience of environment, space and changing perspectives already in mind. It is by exploring experience – the impact of a building on its beholder and user – that many of the developments in the thinking of the Enlightenment are revealed. That is why it has formed the backbone of this study of Paestum in the context of the long eighteenth century.

Interactions between experience and theory figure in all three parts of this book, informing the key themes of perception, representation and use, and running like a cross-section through the chapters. We have examined aesthetic, physical and contextual experiences, which we have discussed as depending, respectively, on observation and sensation, movement and contact, and scholarly study. As Le Roy argued, following the ideas of philosophers such as John Locke and Étienne Bonnot de Condillac, history and theory are irrelevant to sensory experience, which arises from the reactions of the mind and body to the stimuli received at a given time and place. The experience of Paestum clearly had no connection with Vitruvian analysis and categorisation of architecture through orders, plans and proportions, which were not what counted for the visitor on the spot; it was this recognition that led architects to break with the classicist way of thinking about buildings.

The sensory experience of Paestum went through different stages, starting with the journey and unfolding as the visitor came upon the temples and finally entered them. All the senses worked together: though sight was paramount, hearing, smell and touch were far from absent. The traveller was assailed by the sounds, smells, dangers and discomforts of a long and difficult trip from Naples, the delights or desolation of Paestum's setting, depending on the season of the year, the weather and the time of day, and the physical sensations of clambering about the ruins and touching their time-worn stone. Every aspect of experience was explored. This approach is entirely comprehensible in the context of Enlightenment empiricism: questions about how a building can be understood and how it affects the beholder could be answered only by an individual's confrontation with, and exploration of, the three-dimensional reality on the site.

But the Paestum experience went much further than pure empiricism. Paestum – the city and its setting – permitted the visitor to test the impressions a building could make in all their diversity. The vast extent of the site made it possible to take a view from a great distance and then, quite consciously, to stage different scenes as one approached the temples. The experience did not end with the sensations of the sublime evoked by the infinite landscape or the strange architecture of the temples. The next stage was to take in the buildings by walking around them and eventually inside them. The complexity of these enormous structures offered architects the opportunity to explore their spatial qualities, which changed at every turn. The fact that the temples were ruined but still remarkably intact meant that inside and outside were interlinked, the boundaries were sometimes unclear, and thus by wandering through them a myriad of different perspectives presented themselves to view. This was why Delagardette and Labrouste stayed for weeks at Paestum: not only did they measure the temples in detail, but more importantly they were able to capture the impact of different conditions of weather and light on the buildings, to get to know them intimately from diverse angles; as Piranesi's engravings show, every step the visitor took offered a new perspective.

Experience on the ground did not only prove to visitors that the buildings worked on the beholder by means of sensory perception, it also launched architectural theories and provided the means of developing, testing and sometimes overturning them. The subjects that were at the centre of architectural discourse in the eighteenth century – the sublime, the picturesque, the origins and history of architecture and the search for design models – all came together and were enlivened through the experience of architecture, with Paestum in a leading role.

The evolution of architectural thought from the second half of the eighteenth century into the nineteenth is visible in the themes analysed in this book, even though the structure of the account is not entirely chronological. Generally, two major developments may be distinguished: the importance of science and the importance of history. The evolution of the scientific approach was expressed, for example, in the ideas of John Locke and Isaac Newton on how knowledge could be acquired through sensory perception. The sensationalist attitude towards the world, in which emotional responses and knowledge were linked, is a constant theme in the eighteenth-century records of Paestum. But gradually we can discern a shift from motives connected with the connoisseurship of amateurs, who visited Paestum in the course of the Grand Tour, towards scientific reasons for exploring the site, including the beginnings of an interest in archaeological research. An increase in more scientifically orientated publications is detectable towards the end of the eighteenth century.

This period saw an ever widening public enthusiasm for architecture, fostered by the appearance of pamphlets, articles and books, the salon culture, the availability of museum exhibits, and the pursuit of architectural debates in periodical publications, in which non-architects often had an important say – as they did in disputes about Paestum. Here, too, the influence of science was felt in a new interest in classification, and the construction of series. Starting with the art-historical sequences devised by Winckelmann, architectural books from Le Roy's *Les ruines* to the treatises by Rondelet and Durand demonstrated the urge to codify knowledge. It was this desire for system that eventually negated the specificity of Paestum's temples: raided for the elements they had in common with other Greek temples, their uniqueness was eclipsed by a single composite image of Greek architecture.

The importance accorded to history in the eighteenth century – the second development in architectural thinking – is also documented in the treatment of Paestum in contemporary publications. It was included in various chronological series and was located in a historical context according to different interpretations. The search for architectural origins, partly motivated by critical questioning of the present state of architecture, had a direct result in the writing of the history of architecture from the first beginnings to the present. The prominence given to the historical past in theoretical works also guaranteed history a place in design practice. It was not only criticism of contemporary architecture that prompted the search for design exemplars in historical buildings. This was the period in which new and unprecedented building types, such as museums, public theatres and libraries, were first projected, and to answer the question of what they should look like inspiration was sought in the past; the explorations of ancient sites provided important examples.

When we analyse Paestum in the context of these developments we can discern how sensory experience, the dissemination to the public of knowledge about the site, and the development of the scientific approach gave way to an emphasis on history, which eventually supplanted theory. Through the meticulous study of Paestum's role in architectural thought we have seen how the history of architecture began: at Paestum we can see history in the making. The greater paradox of Paestum is also historical: the true Paestum could not be incorporated into contemporary architecture; it did not conform with the classical ideals; no prior knowledge was necessary to appreciate and comprehend its architecture (indeed, such knowledge was a positive hindrance); and the experience of the temples was, in fact, ahistorical. Nevertheless, it was eventually through the primacy of history that Paestum gained its place as a design model: when it was exported, as a disembodied representation of the origins of architecture, nothing was left of Paestum in all its strange and idiosyncratic reality. We might say that, at the same time, history both saved and demolished Paestum.

Notes

Introduction

1 'D. Ferdinando Sanfelice Patrizio Napolitano . . . avendo inteso che li son state presentate certe mostre di pietra bianca per fare gl'ornamenti del real Palazzo nella Villa di Capo di Monte, e considerando che per tagliare e trasportare tanta quantità di pietra, oltre della spesa vi vuole gran tempo . . . rapprenta alla M.V. che per avanzare il tempo e la spesa si portrebbe prendere le pietre che sono nell'antica città di Pesto, situato nel territorio di Capaccio, che fu antica colonia dei Romani, dove vi sono tante quantità d'edificij mezzi diruti, essendovi più di cento colonne di dismisurata grandezza con i loro capitelli, architravi, freggi e cornicioni di pezzi così grandi che fan conoscere la potenza degl'antichi Romani; questi si portrebbero trasportare con grandissima facoltà per mare, essendo la detta città fabbricata accosto la marina.' Ferdinando Sanfelice, letter to Carlo di Borbone, 10 July 1740, Naples, Archivio di Stato, Casa Reale Antica, fascio 1537, inc. 44 bis, fol. 3. Sanfelice's letter is quoted in Pietro Laveglia, *Paestum, dalla decadenza alla riscoperta fino al 1860* (Naples: Libreria Scientifica Editrice, 1971), 72–3. See also Raffaelle Ajello, 'Le origini della politica mercantilistica nel Regno di Napoli', in Franco Strazzullo, *Le manifatture d'arte di Carlo di Borbone* (Naples: Liguori Editore, 1979), 11–17.

2 On Sanfelice see Alastair Ward, *The Architecture of Ferdinando Sanfelice* (New York: Garland, 1988); Alfonso Gambardella (ed.), *Ferdinando Sanfelice: Napoli e l'Europa* (Naples: Edizioni Scientifiche Italiane, 2004).

3 According to Mario Gioffredo: 'Dovremmo qui porre un' idea della prima Architettura Etrusca e Dorica ne' tre tempj di *Pesti*, che servirebbe a giovani vaghi di vedere i primi prodotti dell'arte: ma lasciamo volentieri quella, come ogni altra cosa che ci ritarda, o ci allontana dallo scopo propostoci. Nel 1746, passando per Pesti, vidi quelle ruine, che in appresso si sono ammirate da' stranieri piucché da' nostri Letterati, come i più celebri monumenti dell'antichità. Le manifestai a molti amici,

e tra gli altri al Conte GAZOLA, a Mons. SUFFLOT, ed al Signor NATALI Pittore d'Architettura, con cui nel 1750, e nel 1752, summo a misurare e disegnare i tre templi con tuttociò ch'esiste in quella città.' Mario Gioffredo, *Dell'architettura di Mario Gioffredo architetto Napoletano, Parte prima. Nella quale si tratta degli ordini dell'archittetura de' Greci, e degl'Italiani, e si danno le regole più spedite per disegnarli* (Naples: s.n., 1768), 7, n. 3, cited in Benedetto Gravagnuolo (ed.), *Mario Gioffredo* (Naples: Guida, 2002). Contrary to Gioffredo's statement, Soufflot was already back in Lyon in 1752, but he had visited the temples of Paestum in 1750.

4 'En me plaignant de ce qu'on jouissoit si peu des decouvertes d'Herculanée a un homme plein de goust en place et fort curieux que j'avois l'honneur de voir souvent a Naples, il me parla d'une ville qui en etoit eloignée d'environ 30 lieux par mer, il ne l'avoit point vue mais un peintre habile qu'il aimoit et estimoit avec raison y avoit fait un voyage pour y voir de grands temples d'architecture grecque.' Jacques-Germain Soufflot, in a lecture on his journey to Vesuvius, Herculaneum and Paestum, 'Diverses remarques sur l'Italie. Etat du Mont Vesuve dans le mois de juin 1750 et dans le mois de novembre de la même année', read to the Académie de Lyon on 12 April 1752. Lyon, Bibliothèque de l'Académie des Sciences, Belles-Lettres et Arts, Recueil 136, fols 2–12 (no. 810). The lecture is published in *L'Œuvre de Soufflot à Lyon: Études et documents* (Lyon: Presses Universitaires de Lyon, 1982), for Paestum see 213–14. Here and throughout I reproduce the texts as they were written (that is, eighteenth-century spelling and authors' errors remain unchanged).

5 Gabriel-Pierre-Martin Dumont, *Suitte [Suite] de plans, coupes, profils, élévations géométrales et perspectives de trois temples antiques, tels qu'ils existaient en 1750 dans la bourgade de Poesto, qui est la ville Poestum de Pline . . .* (Paris: Dumont, 1764), was followed by: Filippo Morghen, untitled [*Sei vedute delle rovine di Pesto*] (Naples: s.n., n.d. [1765]); [John Longfield] (published anony-

mously), *The Ruins of Poestum or Posidonia, containing a description and views of the remaining antiquities, with the ancient and modern history, inscriptions, etc.* (London: s.n., 1767); Thomas Major, *The ruins of Paestum, otherwise Posidonia, in Magna Græcia* (London: s.n., 1768) / *Les ruines de Paestum* (London: T. Major, 1768); Gabriel-Pierre-Martin Dumont, *Les ruines de Paestum, autrement Posidonia, ville de l'ancienne grande Grèce, au Royaume de Naples: ouvrage contenant l'histoire ancienne & moderne de cette ville, la description & les vues de ses antiquités, ses inscriptions, &c.: avec des observations sur l'ancien Ordre Dorique,* partly based on [John Longfield], *The ruins of Poestum,* trans. Jacques Varenne de Béost (London / Paris: C.-A. Jombert, 1769); Giovanni Battista Piranesi, *Différentes vues de quelques restes de trois grands édifices qui subsistent encore dans le milieu de l'ancienne ville de Pesto, autrement Possidonia qui est située dans la Lucanie* (Rome: s.n., 1778); Paolo Antonio Paoli, *Paesti, quod Posidoniam etiam dixere, rudera: Rovine della città di Pesto, detta ancora Posidonia* (Rome: [in typographio Paleariniano], 1784); Claude-Mathieu Delagardette, *Les Ruines de Paestum, ou Posidona, ancienne ville de la Grande-Grèce* (Paris: l'auteur / H. Barbou, an VII [1799]).

6 'il me parla surtout d'une Temple de Pestum que Vanvitelli vouloit exécuter dans le jardin anglois de Caserta'. Léon Dufourny, 'Journal . . . à Palerme, 8 juillet 1789 – 29 septembre 1793', Paris, Bibliothèque Nationale, Cabinet des Estampes, Ub 236, 40, vol. II, fol. 156 (entry for 16 July 1790); It. trans. in Léon Dufourny, *Diario di un Giacobino a Palermo, 1789–1793,* introduction by Geneviève Bresc-Bautier, trans. Raimondo A. Cannizzo (Palermo: Fondazione Lauro Chiazzese della Sicilcassa, 1991), 187.

7 Magna Graecia is the name given to the coastal areas of southern Italy (including Sicily) that were colonised by the Greeks from about the eighth century BC.

8 For an art-historical description of Paestum in Greek and Roman times see John Griffiths Pedley, *Paestum: Greeks and Romans in Southern Italy* (London: Thames and Hudson, 1990). Other studies on Paestum were published by some of the main archaeologists of the site. In the 1930s excavations were conducted by Vittorio Spinazzola, Antonio Marzullo, Amedeo Maiuri and Friedrich Krauss; their studies include Friedrich Krauss, *Paestum: Die griechischen Tempel,* 3rd, enlarged, edn (Berlin: Mann, 1976) [first published 1941]. Pellegrino Sestieri excavated in the 1950s, and Mario Napoli in the 1960s. Napoli, who discovered the Tomba del Tuffatore, or Tomb of the Diver, the Greek painted tomb of the early fifth century BC, published: *Paestum* (Novara: Istituto Geografico de Agostini, 1970); *La Tomba del Tuffatore: La scoperta della grande pittura greca* (Bari: De Donato, 1970). More recently Emanuele Greco and Dinu Theodorescu have done archaeological work; their publications include *Poseidonia – Paestum,* 4 vols (Rome: École Française de Rome, 1980–99). Restorations of the temples were conducted by Dieter Mertens (*Der Tempel von Segesta und die dorische Tempelbaukunst des griechischen Westens in klassischer Zeit* (Mainz: P. von Zabern, 1984); *Der alte Heratempel in Paestum und die archaische Baukunst in Unteritalien* (Mainz: P. von Zabern, 1993)), and of the city walls by Mertens and the German Archaeological Institute.

9 Cella: the sanctuary of the temple, usually containing the cult statue.

10 Pedley, *Paestum,* 44.

11 Entasis: swelling of the columns, which visibly affects their profile. Echinus: a quarter-round, cushion-like, convex projection or moulding, supporting the abacus (flat slab), which forms the top of a capital.

12 Comparisons may be made with Doric temples in other Greek colonies of Magna Graecia. At Syracuse: the Temple of Apollo (sixth century BC six columns by seventeen); and the Temple of Athena (now the Duomo, *c.*480 BC, six columns by fourteen). At Agrigento (Acragas): the Temple of Juno Lacinia (*c.*450 BC, six columns by thirteen); the Temple of Concordia (*c.*440–430 BC, six columns by thirteen); the Temple of Zeus Olympios (*c.*480 BC, seven columns by fourteen); and the Temple of Herakles (sixth century BC, six columns by fifteen). At Selinunte (Selinus): seven temples, including Temple C (*c.*550 BC, six columns by seventeen); Temple E or the Temple of Hera (*c.*470–460 BC, six columns by fifteen); and Temple G (*c.*520 BC, eight columns by seventeen). And at Segesta: the Temple of Athena (*c.*430–420 BC, six columns by fourteen, unfluted). In the eighteenth century none of these was in so complete a state as the Paestum temples; in the twentieth century some of them have been reconstructed (for example, at Agrigento and Selinunte), even though by then, in a number of cases, no column remained standing. On the Greek mainland, major Doric temples were: at Athens, the Temple of Athena and Hephaestus (*c.*449 BC, six columns by thirteen), and the Parthenon (447–432 BC, eight columns by seventeen); at Corinth, the Temple of Apollo (*c.*540 BC, six columns by fifteen); at Delphi, the Temple of Apollo (*c.*525 BC, six columns by fifteen); at Olympia, the Temple of Zeus (*c.*470 BC, six columns by thirteen); and at Aegina, the Temple of Aphaea (*c.*500 BC, six columns by twelve). The last named had, like the Temple of Neptune at Paestum, two superposed rows of columns in the interior, supporting the roof and dividing the cella into nave and aisles. See A. W. [Arnold Walter] Lawrence, *Greek Architecture,* 5th edn, rev. R. A. Tomlinson (New Haven (Conn.) / London: Yale University Press, 1996) [first published 1957]; Luca Cerchiai, Lorena Jannelli and Fausto Longo, *Greek Cities of Magna Graecia and Sicily* (San Giovanni Lupatoto: Arsenale Editrice, 2007) [first published 2004].

13 Emanuele Greco and Fausto Longo (eds), *Paestum: Scavi, studi, ricerche. Bilancio di un decennio (1988–1998)* (Paestum (Salerno): Pandemos / Fondazione Paestum, 2000).

14 For eighteenth-century architectural theory see Anthony Vidler, *The Writing of the Walls: Architectural Theory in the Late Enlightenment* (Princeton (NJ): Princeton Architectural Press, 1987); Chantal Grell, *Le Dix-huitième Siècle et l'antiquité en France, 1680–1789,* 2 vols (Oxford: Voltaire Foundation, 1995); David Watkin (ed.), *Sir John Soane: Enlightenment Thought and the Royal Academy Lectures* (Cambridge: Cambridge University Press, 1996). For a broader perspective see Peter Collins, *Changing Ideals in Modern Architecture, 1750–1950* (London: Faber & Faber, 1965); Caroline van Eck, *Organicism in Nineteenth-Century Architecture: An Inquiry into its Theoretical and*

Philosophical Background (Amsterdam: Architectura & Natura, 1994); Hanno-Walter Kruft, *A History of Architectural Theory: From Vitruvius to the Present*, trans. Ronald Taylor, Elsie Callander and Antony Wood (London / New York: Zwemmer / Princeton Architectural Press, 1994) [first published in German 1985].

15 For aesthetic theory in France see Baldine Saint Girons, *Esthétiques du XVIIIe siècle: Le Modèle français* (Paris: P. Sers, 1990); Annie Becq, *Genèse de l'esthétique française moderne: De la raison classique à l'imagination créatrice, 1680–1814* (Paris: Albin Michel, 1994) [first published 1984].

16 Joseph Rykwert, *On Adam's House in Paradise: The Idea of the Primitive Hut in Architectural History*, 2nd edn (Cambridge (Mass.) / London: MIT Press, 1981) [first published 1972]; Chantal Grell and Christian Michel (eds), *Primitivisme et mythes des origines dans la France des Lumières, 1680–1820* (Paris: Presses de l'Université de Paris-Sorbonne, 1989).

17 See, for example, Werner Szambien, *Symétrie, goût, caractère: Théorie et terminologie de l'architecture à l'âge classique, 1550–1800* (Paris: Picard, 1986); Caroline van Eck, *Classical Rhetoric and the Visual Arts in Early Modern Europe* (Cambridge: Cambridge University Press, 2007).

18 For France see Dora Wiebenson and Claire Baines, *French Books: Sixteenth through Nineteenth Centuries* (Washington (DC) / New York: National Gallery of Art / G. Braziller, 1993). For England see Eileen Harris and Nicholas Savage, *British Architectural Books and Writers, 1556–1785* (Cambridge: Cambridge University Press, 1990); Robin Middleton, Gerald Beasley, Nicholas Savage et al., *British Books: Seventeenth through Nineteenth Centuries* (Washington (DC) / New York: National Gallery of Art / G. Braziller, 1998); for the earlier period, Caroline van Eck (ed.), *British Architectural Theory, 1540–1750: An Anthology of Texts* (Aldershot (Surrey): Ashgate, 2003). Useful general anthologies include Adolf K. Placzek and Angela Giral (eds), *Avery's Choice: Five Centuries of Great Architectural Books, One Hundred Years of an Architectural Library, 1890–1990* (New York / London: G. K. Hall / Prentice Hall International, 1997); Harry Francis Mallgrave (ed.), *Architectural Theory*, vol. I: *An Anthology from Vitruvius to 1870* (Malden (Mass.): Blackwell, 2006). For a general history of architecture in the eighteenth century, the following are useful: Robin Middleton and David Watkin, *Neo-Classical and 19th Century Architecture* (New York: Harry N. Abrams, 1980); Antoine Picon, *Architectes et ingénieurs au siècle des Lumières* (Marseille: Parenthèses, 1988); Harry Francis Mallgrave, *Modern Architectural Theory: A Historical Survey, 1673–1968* (Cambridge: Cambridge University Press, 2005).

19 General studies that treat the Greek Revival in architecture are Dora Wiebenson, *Sources of Greek Revival Architecture* (London: A. Zwemmer, 1969); Michael McCarthy, 'Documents on the Greek Revival in Architecture', *Burlington Magazine*, 114 (November 1972), 760–69; J. Mordaunt Crook, *The Greek Revival: Neo-Classical Attitudes in British Architecture, 1760–1870* (London: John Murray, 1995) [first published 1972]; Robin Middleton and David Watkin, *Architecture of the Nineteenth Century* (Milan: Electa, 2003) [first published 1980].

20 Susan Lang, 'The Early Publications of the Temples at Paestum', *Journal of the Warburg and Courtauld Institutes*, 13 (1950), 48–64, gives an introduction to a selection of the eight monographs on Paestum. Domenico Mustilli, 'Prime memorie delle rovine di Paestum', in *Studi in onore di Riccardo Filangieri*, vol. III (Naples: L'Arte Tipografica, 1959), 105–21, discusses the first texts. Laveglia, *Paestum dalla decadenza alla riscoperta fino* gives an overview of the written sources to 1860. Joselita Raspi Serra (ed.), *La fortuna di Paestum e la memoria moderna del dorico, 1750–1830*, 2 vols (Florence: Centro Di, 1986), an exhibition catalogue, provides a good survey of written and visual material on the site, but focuses on the impact of Paestum on buildings and lacks a larger cultural context; a selection of the essays from the catalogue in English translation appear in Joselita Raspi Serra (ed.), *Paestum and the Doric Revival, 1750–1830* (Florence: Centro Di, 1986). Mario Mello, 'Visitare Paestum: Aspetti e problemi dall riscoperta ad oggi', in Italo Gallo (ed.), *Momenti si storia salernitana nell'antichità. Atti del Covegno Nazionale AICC di Salerno-Fisciano, 12–13 nov. 1988* (Naples: Arte Tipografica, 1989), 91–123, presents eye-witness accounts of the temples. Joselita Raspi Serra (ed.), *Paestum: Idea e immagine. Antologia di testi critici e di immagini di Paestum, 1750–1836* (Modena: Franco Cosimo Panini, 1990) is an anthology of texts. Thomas Lutz, 'Die Wiederentdeckung der Tempel von Paestum: Ihre Wirkung auf die Architektur und Architekturtheorie besonders in Deutschland', unpublished PhD thesis, Albert-Ludwigs-Universität Freiburg, 1987, offers the German perspective. Élisabeth Chevallier, 'Les Voyageurs et la découverte de Paestum', in Élisabeth Chevallier and Raymond Chevallier, *Iter Italicum: Les Voyageurs français à la découverte de l'Italie ancienne* (Paris: Les Belles Lettres, 1984), 61–71, concentrates on French travellers. The exhibition catalogue by Bernard Andreae, Michael Philipp, Nina Simone Schepkowski and Ortrud Westheider, *Malerei für die Ewigkeit: Die Gräber von Paestum* (Munich: Hirmer, 2007), covers responses to Paestum in paintings and drawings (notably, Nina Simone Schepkowski, 'Die Tempel von Paestum: Künstlerische Rezeption, 1750 bis 1850, und Katalog der Gemälde und Zeichnungen', 154–215). On Soane and Piranesi see John Wilton-Ely, *Piranesi, Paestum & Soane* (London: Azimuth, 2002; rev. and enlarged edn, Munich / London / New York: Prestel, 2013); in the revised edition, Wilton-Ely gives an incorrect date (1974) for my PhD thesis, 'Rediscovering Architecture: Paestum in Eighteenth-Century Architectural Experience and Theory', unpublished, Leiden University, 2010.

21 Giovanna Ceserani, *Italy's Lost Greece: Magna Graecia and the Making of Modern Archaeology* (Oxford / New York: Oxford University Press, 2012).

22 For the earlier results of my research see Sigrid de Jong, 'Staging Ruins: Paestum and Theatricality', *Art History*, 33 / 2 (April 2010) [special issue], 334–51, and in Caroline van Eck and Stijn Bussels (eds), *Theatricality in Early Modern Art and Architecture* (Chichester: Wiley-Blackwell, 2011), 134–51; Sigrid de Jong, 'Paradoxical Encounters: Eighteenth-Century Architectural Experiences and the Sublime', in Caroline van

Eck, Stijn Bussels, Maarten Delbeke and Jürgen Pieters (eds), *Translations of the Sublime: The Early Modern Reception and Dissemination of Longinus' Peri hupsous in Rhetoric, the Visual Arts, Architecture and the Theatre* (Leiden: Brill, 2012), 247–67.

23 Chantal Grell, *Herculanum et Pompéi dans les récits des voyageurs français du XVIIIe siècle* (Naples: Centre Jean Bérard, 1982); William L. MacDonald and John A. Pinto, *Hadrian's Villa and its Legacy* (New Haven (Conn.) / London: Yale University Press, 1995). For Sicily see Arnaldo Momigliano, 'The Rediscovery of Greek History in the Eighteenth Century: The Case of Sicily', *Studies in Eighteenth Century Culture*, 9 (1979), 167–87; see also Hélène Tuzet, *La Sicile au XVIIIe siècle vue par les voyageurs étrangers* (Strasbourg: P. H. Heitz, 1955).

24 The most important studies of the Grand Tour are Jeremy Black, *The British and the Grand Tour* (London: Croom Helm, 1985); Andrew Wilton and Ilaria Bignamini, *Grand Tour: The Lure of Italy in the Eighteenth Century* (London: Tate Gallery, 1996); Jeremy Black, *The British Abroad: The Grand Tour in the Eighteenth Century* (London: Sandpiper Books, 1999) [first published 1992]; Cesare De Seta, *Vedutisti e viaggiatori in Italia tra Settecento e Ottocento* (Turin: Bollati Boringhieri, 1999); Cesare De Seta, *L'Italia del Grand Tour: Da Montaigne a Goethe* (Naples: Electa Napoli, 2001) [first published 1992]. See also Ludwig Schudt, *Italienreisen im 17. und 18. Jahrhundert* (Vienna: Schroll-Verlag, 1959). A relevant study that focuses on architects' sojourns in Rome and covers some of the architects treated in this book is Janine Barrier, *Les Architectes européens à Rome, 1740–1765* (Paris: Monum / Éditions du Patrimoine, 2005). On travel publications see Charles L. Batten, *Pleasurable Instruction: Form and Convention in Eighteenth-Century Travel Literature* (Berkeley, Los Angeles and London: University of California Press, 1978). On Naples and archaeology from the eighteenth century see Carol C. Mattusch (ed.), *Rediscovering the Ancient World on the Bay of Naples, 1710–1890* (New Haven (Conn.): Yale University Press, 2012).

25 For example, in Frank Salmon, *Building on Ruins: The Rediscovery of Rome and English Architecture* (Aldershot (Surrey): Ashgate, 2000); Jean-Philippe Garric, *Recueils d'Italie: Les Modèles italiens dans les livres d'architecture français* (Sprimont (Liège): Pierre Mardaga, 2004).

26 Steen Eiler Rasmussen, *Experiencing Architecture*, trans. Eve Wendt (Cambridge (Mass.): MIT Press, 1995) [first published in Danish 1957]; Juhani Pallasmaa, *The Eyes of the Skin: Architecture and the Senses* (Chichester: John Wiley & Sons, 2005) [first published 1996]. See also Steven Holl, Juhani Pallasmaa and Alberto Pérez-Gómez, *Questions of Perception: Phenomenology of Architecture* (Tokyo: a + u publishers, 1994); Peter MacKeith (ed.), *Archipelago: Essays on Architecture, for Juhani Pallasmaa* (Helsinki: Rakennustieto, 2006). All of these deal with modern architecture and design and draw on Maurice Merleau-Ponty, *Le Visible et l'invisible* (Paris: Gallimard, 1964) and *Phénoménologie de la perception* (Paris: Gallimard, 1945), or Gaston Bachelard, *La Poétique de l'espace* (Paris: Presses Universitaires de France, 1957). See for a history of the concept of experience in philosophy, politics, or history (but not in architecture): Martin Jay, *Songs of Experience: Modern American and European Variations on a Universal Theme* (Berkeley / Los Angeles: University of California Press, 2005); Harry Francis Mallgrave, *The Architect's Brain: Neuroscience, Creativity and Architecture* (Chichester: Wiley-Blackwell, 2010) is more on perception than on experience.

27 On architectural experience in the eighteenth century related to the ideas of Julien-David Le Roy see Robin Middleton, Introduction to Julien-David Le Roy, *The Ruins of the Most Beautiful Monuments of Greece*, 2nd edn [1770], trans. David Britt (Los Angeles: Getty Research Institute, 2004), and his Soane Annual Lecture published as *Julien-David Leroy: In Search of Architecture* (London: Sir John Soane's Museum, 2003); Christopher Drew Armstrong, *Julien-David Leroy and the Making of Architectural History* (London / New York: Routledge, 2012). On architectural experience as related to the ideas of Le Camus de Mézières see Robin Middleton, Introduction to Nicolas Le Camus de Mézières, *The Genius of Architecture, or The Analogy of that Art with our Sensations* [1780], trans. David Britt (Santa Monica (Call.): Getty Center for the History of Art and the Humanities, 1992), and (mainly on Le Camus de Mézières) Louise Pelletier, *Architecture in Words: Theatre, Language and the Sensuous Space of Architecture* (London: Routledge, 2006). Richard Wittman, *Architecture, Print Culture, and the Public Sphere in Eighteenth-Century France* (London / New York: Routledge, 2007) is interesting for its focus on the experience of public space and the city of Paris. See also my article on architectural experience in the eighteenth century: 'Experiencing Architectural Space', in Caroline van Eck and Sigrid de Jong (eds), *Companion to Eighteenth-Century Architecture* (Chichester: Wiley-Blackwell, forthcoming, 2015).

Chapter 1

1 'Ce sont de grands quarrés longs formés par des rangs de colonnes cannelées sans bases et avec des chapiteaux qui ont à peu près la forme d'un vase ou plutôt d'une tasse'. Jean-Claude Richard de Saint-Non, *Panopticon italiano: Un diario di viaggio ritrovato, 1759–1761*, ed. Pierre Rosenberg (Rome: Ed. dell'Elefante, 2000), 124. Jean-Claude Richard de Saint-Non was at Paestum in 1760. On Saint-Non see also Petra Lamers, *Il viaggio nel sud dell'Abbé de Saint-Non: Il 'Voyage pittoresque à Naples et en Sicile': La genesi, i disegni preparatori, le incisioni* (Naples: Electa, 1995); Jean-Claude Richard de Saint-Non, *Da Napoli a Malta: Voyage pittoresque, ou Description des royaumes de Naples et de Sicile di Jean Claude Richard Abbé de Saint-Non, 1781–1786*, ed. Silverio Salamon and Elisabetta Rollier (Turin: L'Arte Antica, S. Salamon, 2001).

2 See Sigrid de Jong, 'Paradoxical Encounters: Eighteenth-Century Architectural Experiences and the Sublime', in Caroline van Eck, Stijn Bussels, Maarten Delbeke and Jürgen Pieters (eds), *Translations of the Sublime: The Early Modern Reception and Dissemination of Longinus' Peri hupsous in Rhetoric, the Visual Arts, Architecture and the Theatre* (Leiden: Brill, 2012), 247–67.

3 Susan Pearce and Frank Salmon, 'Charles Heathcote Tatham in Italy, 1794–96: Letters, Drawings and Fragments, and Part of an Autobiography', *Walpole Society*, 67 (2005), 86.

4   James Adam, letter to Janet Adam, 21 November 1761, quoted in John Fleming, 'James Adam in Naples', in Edward Chaney and Neil Ritchie (eds), *Oxford, China and Italy: Writings in Honour of Sir Harold Acton on his Eightieth Birthday* (London: Thames and Hudson, 1984), 175. Adam added: 'Here there is not to be had nor milk to one's tea nor butter to one's bread, nor bread but what strangers bring. We send for water at 4 miles distance and in short there is a plenty of nothing but of fleas which exist here in a quantity not to be imagin'd. What, however is amazing is that by a letter of recommendation we have got very tolerable beds, that is free of bugs, which I assure you, in this blessed country is the height of luxury.' In his travel diary Adam wrote: 'There are here the remains of two Basilica, and one temple of the Doric order; it is an early, inelegant, and unenriched Doric, without bases and without proportion.' James Adam, 'Journal of a Tour in Italy', *Library of the Fine Arts*, 2/8 (September 1831), 236. For Adam see also John Fleming, *Robert Adam and his Circle in Edinburgh & Rome* (London: John Murray, 1962), on Paestum pp. 292–4; Thomas J. McCormick, 'An Unknown Collection of Drawings by Charles-Louis Clérisseau', *Journal of the Society of Architectural Historians*, 22 (1963), 119–26, on Paestum p. 126; Joseph and Anne Rykwert, *The Brothers Adam: The Men and the Style* (London: Collins, 1985), on his Grand Tour pp. 55–9. On Clérisseau the seminal study is Thomas J. McCormick, *Charles-Louis Clérisseau and the Genesis of Neo-Classism* (Cambridge (Mass.): MIT Press, 1990), on Paestum pp. 71–2. For the large collection of Clérisseau's drawings see Valery Chevtchenko, Sabine Cotté, Madeleine Pinault-Sørensen et al., *Charles-Louis Clérisseau, 1721–1820: Dessins du Musée de l'Ermitage, Saint-Petersbourg* (Paris: Réunion des Musées Nationaux, 1995). For Johann Joachim Winckelmann and Clérisseau see Francesca Lui, *L'antichità tra scienza e invenzione: Studi su Winckelmann e Clérisseau* (Bologna: Minerva, 2006).

5   See Fleming, *Robert Adam and his Circle*, 293, and John Ingamells, *A Dictionary of British and Irish Travellers in Italy, 1701–1800* (New Haven (Conn.) / London: Published for the Paul Mellon Centre for Studies in British Art by Yale University Press, 1997), 4–5.

6   Gabriel-Pierre-Martin Dumont, *Suitte [Suite] de plans, coupes, profils, élévations géométrales et perspectives de trois temples antiques, tels qu'ils existaient en 1750 dans la bourgade de Poesto* (Paris: Dumont, 1764); [John Longfield], *The ruins of Poestum or Posidonia, containing a description and views of the remaining antiquities, with the ancient and modern history, inscriptions, etc.* (London: s.n., 1767). Adam could have talked with other British architects who had travelled to Paestum – for instance, Stephen Riou (1753) and Robert Mylne (1756). Their drawings became part of the collection of Thomas Major, who based his engravings in *The ruins of Paestum, otherwise Posidonia, in Magna Graecia* (London: s.n., 1768) on these and on drawings by Jacques-Germain Soufflot, Julien-David Le Roy and Gaetano Magri. This collection of Paestum drawings and a copy of the English edition of Major's book are now in London, Sir John Soane's Museum, Drawings Collection, Drawer 60, Set 1. Other early British travellers to Paestum were Lascelles Raymond Iremonger (1752), Frederick, Lord North, and William Legge, 2nd Earl of Dartmouth (1753), John Brudenell and Henry Lyte (1756); Brudenell's draftsman was Antonio Joli, whose paintings and drawings of Paestum became the basis of many engravings in publications of the site (see Chapter 4).

7   'La vue de cette ville nous frappa d'étonnement et de pitié considérant son étendue, la magnificence des bâtiments dont on voit encore des restes et la ruine entière de la plus grande partie des édifices dont elle était ornée et dont la place est labourée ou couverte de monceaux de pierre'. Pierre-Louis Moreau, 'Notes sur mon voyage', Paris, Institut National d'Histoire de l'Art, Collection Jacques Doucet, MS 98, fol. 16r, published in *Le Voyage d'Italie de Pierre-Louis Moreau: Journal intime d'un architecte des Lumières (1754–1757)*, ed. Sophie Descat (Pessac: Presses Universitaires de Bordeaux, 2004), 126.

8   Lascelles Raymond Iremonger, letter to Sir Roger Newdigate, Naples, 22 July 1752, Warwick County Record Office, published in Michael McCarthy, 'Documents on the Greek Revival in Architecture', *Burlington Magazine*, 114 (November 1972), 761. In this letter Iremonger referred to the temples as being 'all marble': in fact they are built entirely of limestone.

9   Lord North, letter to Charles Dampier, Lyon, 1 September 1753 – Bern, 9 September 1753, Warwick County Record Office, published in McCarthy, 'Documents on the Greek Revival', 761–5.

10 'Du milieu de ses ruines, s'élevent trois Edifices d'une sorte d'Architecture, dont les membres sont Doriques bien que les proportions ne le soient pas . . . dans un quatrieme voyage que nous fimes il y a quelques mois à Pesti, nous nous y arrêtames plusieurs jours pour examiner à loisir ces ruines magnifiques, qui étonnent & imposent d'avantage à mesure qu'elles sont examinées avec plus de soin & revues plus souvent.' Pierre-François Hugues d'Hancarville, *Antiquités étrusques, grecques et romaines, tirées du cabinet de M. Hamilton / Collection of Etruscan, Greek and Roman Antiquities from the Cabinet of the Hon. William Hamilton*, 4 vols (Naples: s.n., 1766–7), vol. 1, 96–7.

11 'On voit dans les ruines de Pestum ou Posidonia, trois temples dont un surtout est assés bien conservé. Je ne connois rien d'aussi terrible, d'aussi imposant, ni d'aussi caracterisé que ces temples.' Pierre-Adrien Pâris, 'Notes et lavis de Pierre-Adrien Pâris, intercalés par lui, avec différentes estampes', in Antoine Desgodets [Desgodetz], *Les édifices antiques de Rome, dessinés et mesurés très exactement* [1682], new edn (Paris: Claude-Antoine Jombert fils aîné, Libraire du Roi, 1779), Paris, Institut de France, MS 1906, fol. 329.

12 'Nun sind unsere Augen und durch sie unser ganzes inneres Wesen an schlankere Baukunst hinangetrieben und entschieden bestimmt, so daßuns diese stumpfen, kegelförmigen, enggedrängten Säulenmassen lästig, ja furchtbar erscheinen.' Johann Wolfgang von Goethe, *Italienische Reise [1786–8]* [1829] (Munich: Wilhelm Goldmann Verlag, 1988), 205; Eng. trans. in Johann Wolfgang von Goethe, *Italian Journey [1786–8]* [1829], trans. W. H. Auden and Elizabeth Mayer (London: Penguin, 1970) [first published 1962], 218.

13 On the history of the sublime see Baldine Saint Girons, *Fiat lux: Une philosophie du sublime* (Paris: Quai Voltaire, 1993); Andrew Ashfield and Peter de Bolla, *The Sublime: A Reader in British Eighteenth-Century Aesthetic Theory* (Cambridge: Cambridge University Press, 1996); Baldine Saint Girons, *Le Sublime de l'antiquité à nos jours* (Paris: Desjonquères, 2005). Earlier, fundamental studies are Walter John Hipple, *The Beautiful, the Sublime & the Picturesque in Eighteenth-Century British Aesthetic Theory* (Carbondale: Southern Illinois University Press, 1957); Samuel Holt Monk, *The Sublime: A Study of Critical Theories in XVIII-Century England* (Ann Arbor: University of Michigan Press, 1960) [first published 1935]; Marjorie Hope Nicolson, *Mountain Gloom and Mountain Glory: The Development of the Aesthetics of the Infinite* (Seattle / London: University of Washington Press, 1997) [first published 1959].

14 Evidence of the ownership of relevant works is known in the case of Pierre-Adrien Pâris, Giovanni Battista Piranesi, Quatremère de Quincy and Jean Rondelet. On Pâris see Charles Weiss, *Catalogue de la bibliothèque de M. Paris, architecte et dessinateur de la Chambre du Roi . . . suivi de la description de son cabinet* (Besançon: Librairie de Deis, 1821). On Piranesi see Didier Laroque, *Le Discours de Piranèse: L'Ornement sublime et le suspens de l'architecture; suivi d'un tableau de l'œuvre écrit de Piranèse et d'une nouvelle traduction de 'Ragionamento apologetico in difesa dell'architettura Egizia e Toscana', 1769* (Paris: Les Éditions de la Passion, 1999), 8. On Quatremère de Quincy see *Bibliothèque de M. Quatremère de Quincy . . . Collection d'ouvrages relatifs aux beaux-arts et à l'archéologie . . . Vente le 27 mai 1850 et jours suivants, rue de Condé, no 14. Préface de R. Merlin* (Paris: Imprimerie d'Adrien Le Clere et Cie, 1850). On Rondelet's library and those of other eighteenth-century architects see Robin Middleton, 'Rondelet's Library', in Robin Middleton and Marie-Noëlle Baudouin-Matuszek, *Jean Rondelet: The Architect as Technician* (New Haven (Conn.) / London: Yale University Press, 2007), 271–88. See also Annie-Charon Parent, 'Enquête à travers les catalogues de vente de bibliothèques d'architectes du XVIIIe siècle: La Bibliothèque de Jacques-Germain Soufflot', in Jean-Michel Leniaud and Béatrice Bouvier (eds), *Le Livre d'architecture XVe–XXe siècle: Édition, réprésentations et bibliothèques* (Paris: École des Chartes, 2002), 187–98.

15 The Greek text, in a manuscript from the tenth century, formed the basis of all the later versions. The title says 'by Dionysios Longinus' but the first page says 'Dionysios or Longinus'. Bernard Weinberg, 'Translations and Commentaries of Longinus' On the Sublime to 1600: A Bibliography', *Modern Philology*, 47 (1950), 145–51; Marc Fumaroli, 'Rhétorique d'école et rhétorique adulte: Remarques sur la réception européenne du traité *Du sublime* au XVIe et au XVIIe siècle', *Revue d'Histoire Littéraire de la France*, 86 (1986), 35–6, 39–40. See also Pseudo-Longin, *De la sublimité du discours*, ed. Emma Gilby (Chambéry: L'Act Mem, 2007), 28–9.

16 Pseudo-Longin, *De la sublimité*, ed. Gilby, 49–50. See Craig Kallendorf, Carsten Zelle and Christine Pries, 'Erhabene, das', in Gert Ueding (ed.), *Historisches Wörterbuch der Rhetorik*, vol. II (Tübingen: M. Niemeyer, 1994), cols 1357–89.

17 But see van Eck, Bussels, Delbeke and Pieters (eds), *Translations of the Sublime.*

18 Longinus, *On the Sublime*, ed. and trans. W. Hamilton Fyfe and W. Rhys Roberts, rev. Donald Russell, in Aristotle, *Poetics . . . Longinus, On the Sublime . . . Demetrius, On Style*, Loeb Classical Library, 199, 2nd edn (Cambridge (Mass.) / London: Harvard University Press, 1995), I. 125.

19 For example, the writings by Cicero, who is like 'a flash of lightning or a thunder-bolt', ibid., XII. 165.

20 Ibid., VIII. 141.

21 Ibid., VII. 139.

22 Ibid., XI. 163.

23 Ibid., XXXV. 227.

24 Ibid., XXI. 193, on inversion as a method.

25 Ibid., XXXVI. 229.

26 Ibid., XVII. 187.

27 Ibid., XXVIII. 205–7.

28 Ibid., XXX. 209. For analogies between words and music see XXXIX. 234–5; XLI. 241.

29 Ibid., X. 160–61.

30 The solemnity and awfulness in the church architecture of Hawksmoor and Vanbrugh can thus be explained. See Caroline van Eck, 'Longinus' Essay on the Sublime and the "most solemn and awfull appearance" of Hawksmoor's Churches', *Georgian Group Journal*, 15 (2006), 1–7; Sophie Ploeg, 'Staged Experiences: Architecture and Rhetoric in the Work of Sir Henry Wotton, Nicholas Hawksmoor and Sir John Vanbrugh', unpublished PhD thesis, Rijksuniversiteit Groningen, 2006. On sublime architecture see Caroline van Eck, *Classical Rhetoric and the Visual Arts in Early Modern Europe* (Cambridge: Cambridge University Press, 2007), 110–22.

31 See Introduction to Nicolas Boileau-Despréaux (trans.), *Longin, Traité du sublime* [1674], ed. Francis Goyet (Paris: Librairie Générale Française, 1995).

32 Ibid., 6.

33 'cet extraordinaire et ce merveilleux qui frappe dans le discours, et qui fait qu'un ouvrage enlève, ravit, transporte'. Boileau-Despréaux, Preface, *Longin, Traité du sublime*, ed. Goyet, 70.

34 'Le Sublime est une certaine force de discours, propre à élever et à ravir l'âme, et qui provient ou de la grandeur de la pensée et de la noblesse du sentiment, ou de la magnificence des paroles ou du tour harmonieux, vif et animé de l'expression; c'est-à-dire d'une de ces choses regardées séparément, ou ce qui fait le parfait Sublime, de ces trois choses jointes ensemble.' Ibid., 155. Boileau defined the sublime in four lines: 'la grandeur de la pensée, la noblesse du sentiment, la magnificence des paroles, et l'harmonie de l'expression'. Ibid., 156. *Réflexions* was written in 1694–1710.

35 'Il faut donc savoir que par Sublime, Longin n'entend pas ce que les orateurs appellent le style sublime: mais cet extraordinaire et ce merveilleux qui frappe dans le discours, et qui fait qu'un ouvrage enlève, ravit, transporte. Le style sublime veut toujours de grands mots; mais le Sublime se peut trouver dans une seule pensée, dans une seule figure, dans un seul tour de paroles.' Boileau-Despréaux, Preface, *Longin, Traité du sublime*, ed. Goyet, 70.

36 'Longtemps plaire et jamais ne lasser', Nicolas Boileau-Despréaux, *L'art poétique* (1674), III. v. 256, in *Œuvres complètes*, ed. Françoise Escal (Paris: Gallimard, 1966), 174, as quoted in Saint Girons, *Le Sublime*, 63.

37 'le bas et le précieux, le burlesque et le grandiose, le rationnel et le "je ne sais quoi" . . . l'invraisemblable et le vrai'. Quoted in Saint Girons, *Le Sublime*, 63.

38 James I. Porter, 'Lucretius and the Sublime', in Stuart Gillespie and Philip Hardie (eds), *The Cambridge Companion to Lucretius* (Cambridge: Cambridge University Press, 2007), 167–84. On Burke see also Eric Baker, 'Lucretius in the European Enlightenment', in Gillespie and Hardie (eds), *The Cambridge Companion to Lucretius*, 284–5.

39 Editions of Burke's *Philosophical Enquiry* were published in 1757, 1759, 1761, 1766, 1764, 1767, 1770, 1772, 1773, 1776, 1782, 1787, 1793 and 1796; a French edition was published in 1765 as *Recherches philosophiques sur l'origine des idées que nous avons du beau et du sublime*; a German edition was published in 1773 as *Philosophische Untersuchungen über den Ursprung unsrer Begriffe vom Erhabnen und Schönen*. The *Enquiry* was reviewed positively in French as early as 1757, in the *Journal Encyclopédique* (July 1757), 17: 'L'Auteur de cet Ouvrage nous paroît homme de génie; ses idées sont neuves et hardies; son style est mâle et concis.' Biographical studies on Burke deal mainly with his politics or his writings on the French Revolution, as, for example, Christopher Reid, *Edmund Burke and the Practice of Political Writing* (Dublin / New York: Gill and Macmillan / St. Martin's Press, 1986); Peter James Stanlis, *Edmund Burke: The Enlightenment and Revolution* (New Brunswick (NJ) / London: Transaction, 1991). Some more general studies are Francis Canavan, *Edmund Burke: Prescription and Providence* (Durham (NC): Carolina Academic Press, 1987); Stanley Ayling, *Edmund Burke: His Life and Opinions* (London: Murray, 1988); Conor Cruise O'Brien, *The Great Melody: A Thematic Biography and Commented Anthology of Edmund Burke* (London: Sinclair-Stevenson, 1992); Stephen K. White, *Edmund Burke: Modernity, Politics and Aesthetics* (Thousand Oaks (Cal.) / London: Sage Publications, 1994); Frederick P. Lock, *Edmund Burke*, vol. 1 (Oxford: Clarendon Press, 1998).

40 Edmund Burke, *A Philosophical Enquiry into the Origin of our Ideas of the Sublime and Beautiful* [1757], ed. James T. Boulton (London / New York: Routledge, 2008), 123.

41 Ibid., 77.

42 The influence of the sublime on Revolutionary architecture has been discussed in, for example, Emil Kaufmann, *Three Revolutionary Architects: Boullée, Ledoux, and Lequeu* (Philadelphia: American Philosophical Society, 1952) and Saint-Girons, *Fiat lux*, but the influence of the sublime on the experience of architecture has received little attention. Didier Laroque, 'Boullée et le sublime', in Elisabetta Matelli (ed.), *Il sublime: Fortuna di un testo e di un'idea* (Milan: Vita e Pensiero, 2007), 263–72, discusses mainly Boullée.

43 Burke, *A Philosophical Enquiry*, ed. Boulton, 62.

44 'en parlant du sublime, [Longin] est lui-même très sublime'. Boileau-Despréaux, Preface, *Longin, Traité du sublime*, ed. Goyet, 65.

45 'Esprit sublime! Génie vaste et profond! Etre divin! Newton, daigne agréer l'hommage de mes faibles talents! Ah! si j'ose le rendre public, c'est à cause de la persuasion que j'ai de m'être surpassé dans l'ouvrage dont je vais parler. O Newton! Si par l'étendue de tes lumières et la sublimité de ton génie, tu as déterminé la figure de la terre, moi j'ai conçu le projet de t'envelopper de ta découverte. C'est en quelque façon t'avoir enveloppé de toi-même . . . En me servant, Newton, de ton divin système pour former la lampe sépulcrale qui éclaire ta tombe, je me suis rendu, ce me semble, sublime.' Étienne-Louis Boullée, *Architecture: Essai sur l'art*, ed. Jean-Marie Pérouse de Montclos (Paris: Hermann, 1968), 137–8 (from Paris, Bibliothèque Nationale de France, MS 9153, c.1794); Eng. trans. as 'Architecture, Essay on Art', in Helen Rosenau, *Boullée and Visionary Architecture* (London / New York: Academy Editions / Harmony Books, 1976), 107. See the publications cited for more background on Boullée's ideas. See also Étienne-Louis Boullée, *Architecture: Essai sur l'art*, ed. Helen Rosenau as *Boullée's Treatise on Architecture: A Complete Presentation of the 'Architecture, essai sur l'art' which Forms Part of the Boullée Papers (Ms. 9153) in the Bibliothèque Nationale, Paris* (London: Tiranti, 1953); Philippe Madec, *Boullée* (Paris: F. Hazan, 1986); Jean-Marie Pérouse de Montclos, *Etienne-Louis Boullée* (Paris: Flammarion, 1994); Daniel Rabreau and Dominique Massounie (eds), *Claude Nicolas Ledoux et le livre d'architecture en français: Étienne Louis Boullée, l'utopie et la poésie d'art* (Paris: Monum / Éditions du Patrimoine, 2006).

46 Sophie Hache has identified the sublime in French discourse in the seventeenth century before Boileau in *La Langue du ciel: Le Sublime en France au XVIIe siècle* (Paris: H. Champion, 2000). For painting and the sublime see Clélia Nau, *Le Temps du sublime: Longin et le paysage poussinien* (Rennes: Presses Universitaires de Rennes, 2005). For the sublime before Burke see also Théodore A. Litman, *Le Sublime en France, 1660–1714* (Paris: A. G. Nizet, 1971); Theodore Edmundson Brown Wood, *The Word 'Sublime' and its Context, 1650–1760* (The Hague / Paris: Mouton, 1972); Nicolson, *Mountain Gloom*.

47 An English translation of Longinus by John Hall appeared in 1652, and after that four others, all based on Boileau, in 1680, 1698, 1712 and 1739: John Hall, *Peri hupsous, or, Dionysius Longinus on the Height of Eloquence. Rendered out of the original by J. H.* (London, 1652); John Pulteney, *A treatise of the loftiness or elegancy of speech* (London, 1680); the anonymous *Essay upon sublime, translated from the Greek of Dionysius Longinus Cassius the rhetorician: compar'd with the French of the Sieur Despreaux Boileau* (Oxford: printed by Leon. Lichfield, 1698); Leonard Welsted, *Dionysius Longinus' Treatise on the Sublime. Translated from the Greek* (London: printed for Sam. Briscoe, 1712); William Smith, *Dionysius Longinus On the Sublime: Translated . . . with notes and observations, and some account of the life and writings and character of the author* (London: J. Watts / W. Innys and R. Manby, 1739). The translation of Longinus by William Smith reached its fifth edition in 1800.

48 Van Eck, 'Longinus' Essay on the Sublime'; Ploeg, 'Staged Experiences', PhD thesis; Sophie Ploeg, 'Staged Experiences:

The Church Designs of Nicholas Hawksmoor', in Caroline van Eck and Edward Winters (eds), *Dealing with the Visual: Art History, Aesthetics and Visual Culture* (Aldershot (Surrey): Ashgate, 2005), 167–90.

49 Van Eck, 'Longinus' Essay on the Sublime'; Ploeg, 'Staged Experiences', PhD thesis.

50 Joseph Addison, 'The Pleasures of the Imagination' [1712], in Richard Steele and Joseph Addison, *Selections from the Tatler and The Spectator*, ed. with an introduction and notes by Angus Ross (London: Penguin Books, 1982), 364–406.

51 Ploeg, 'Staged Experiences', PhD thesis, 263.

52 For the concept of the infinite in the sublime see Nicolson, *Mountain Gloom*, which focuses on descriptions of nature in seventeenth- to nineteenth-century literature (architecture plays a very small role); the chapter on the aesthetics of the infinite is of particular interest.

53 Joseph Addison, 'A Letter from Italy, to the Right Honourable Charles Lord Halifax, in the Year MDCCI', in *Remarks on several parts of Italy, &c., in the Years 1701, 1702, 1703*, 2nd edn (London: J. Tonson, 1718), p. v.

54 *A Letter from Italy to the Right Honourable Charles Lord Hallifax, by Mr Joseph Addison, MDCCI* (London: s.n., 1703), in *The Miscellaneous Works of Joseph Addison*, ed. A. C. Guthkelch, vol. 1 (London: G. Bell and Sons, 1914), 55 (ll. 69–74). The equivalent passage in the manuscript version (Oxford, Bodleian Library) reads: 'How dos the mighty Scene my soul amaze / When on proud Rome's Immortal seats I Gaze, / Where piles of Ruine scatter'd all around, / Magnificently strow the pompous ground! / An Amphitheater's transcendant height / Here fills my Eye with terrour and delight', in *The Miscellaneous Works*, ed. Guthkelch, 54 (ll. 85–90).

55 Joseph Addison, 'Paper V: On the Pleasures of the Imagination', *The Spectator*, no. 415 (26 June 1712); repr. in *The Spectator, in Eight Volumes* (London: Sharpe and Hailes, 1811), 501.

56 Ibid., 500–01.

57 Porter, 'Lucretius and the Sublime', 167–84.

58 Burke, *A Philosophical Enquiry*, ed. Boulton, 60. The reference is to *Paradise Lost*, Book 2, lines 666–73, though Burke misquotes Milton's original.

59 Burke, *A Philosophical Enquiry*, ed. Boulton, 61–2.

60 Ibid., 72.

61 'the eye not being able to perceive the bounds of many things, they seem to be infinite, and they produce the same effects as if they were really so.' Ibid., 73.

62 Ibid., 76.

63 Ibid., 81.

64 Ibid., 82.

65 The only biography of Blondel published to date is: Auguste Prost, *J.-F. Blondel et son œuvre* (Metz: Rousseau-Pallez, 1860). On his teaching and theory see Robin Middleton, 'Jacques-François Blondel and the *Cours d'architecture*', *Journal of the Society of Architectural Historians*, 18 (December 1959), 140–48; Antoine Picon, 'Vers une architecture classique: Jacques-François Blondel et le *Cours d'architecture*', *Cahiers de la Recherche Architecturale*, 18 (1985), 28–37; Werner Szambien, *Symétrie, goût, caractère: Théorie et terminologie de l'architecture à*

l'âge classique, 1550–1800 (Paris: Picard, 1986). On his influence on foreign architects see Freek H. Schmidt, 'Expose Ignorance and Revive the *Bon Goût*: Foreign Architects at Jacques-François Blondel's École des Arts', *Journal of the Society of Architectural Historians*, 61 (2002), 4–29.

66 'un style sublime, noble, élevé'; 'un caractère naïf, simple, vrai'. Jacques-François Blondel, *Cours d'architecture, ou Traité de la décoration, distribution et construction des bâtiments: contenant les leçons données en 1750 et les années suivantes*, 6 vols (Paris: Desaint, 1771–7), vol. I, 373.

67 'cette poésie muette, ce coloris suave, intéressant, ferme ou vigoureux; en un mot, cette mélodie tendre, touchante, forte ou terrible qu'on peut emprunter de la Poésie, de la Peinture ou de la Musique, & qu'on peut rapporter aux diverses compositions qui émanent de l'Architecture'. Ibid., 376.

68 'Pour définir le sublime dont nous voulons parles, il faudroit soi-même être sublime (et nous sommes bien éloignés de cette perfection).' Ibid., 377.

69 'Un colosse sans proportion & composé, pour ainsi dire, de pieces rapportées, ne peut obtenir les suffrages des hommes de goût, ni des hommes raisonnables, quelque grande qu'en ait pu être l'idée.' Ibid.

70 'il faudroit réunir . . . le savoir, le génie, la beauté, la régularité, la convenance, la solidité & la commodité; mais cependant il faut songer que l'esprit méthodique, la méditation, le flegme, peuvent produire un bon Architecte, & que le génie, l'ame, l'enthousiasme, élevent seuls l'Artiste au sublime: que l'esprit définit, que le sentiment peint, & que celui-ci donne la vie à toutes les productions. En un mot, il seroit à desirer qu'un édifice puisse, à son aspect, entraîner, émouvoir, & pour ainsi dire, élever l'ame du spectateur, en le portant à une admiration contemplative, dont il ne pourroit lui-même se rendre compte au premier coup d'œil, quoique suffisamment instruit des connaissances profondes de l'Art.' Ibid., 377–8.

71 'elle éleve l'esprit de l'eximinateur, le saisit, l'étonne: les vrais Connoisseurs la reconnoissent par une régularité qui n'a rien de monotone, par des accompagnements assortis; en un mot, par un accord général, qui se fait admirer & approuver dans tous les temps.' Ibid., 380.

72 Ibid.

73 Ibid. See further: 'il faut donc que la beauté de l'ordonnance des dehors d'un bâtiment, la commodité des dedans & la solidité de sa construction, ne se démentent jamais, & que ces trois objets y semblent réunis de manière à ne laisser rien à desirer absolument.' Ibid., 383.

74 Ibid., 426–7.

75 Ibid.

76 'Le genre terrible est l'effet de la grandeur combinée avec la force. On peut comparer la terreur qu'inspire une scène de la nature à celle qui naît d'une scène dramatique; l'ame est fortement ébranlée, mais ses sensations ne sont agréables que lorsqu'elles tiennent à la terreur sans avoir rien de choquant. On peut employer les ressources de l'Art pour rendre ces sensations plus vives; il s'agit de développer les objets dont la grandeur est le caractere, & de donner plus de vigueur à ceux qui se distinguent par la force; on marquera avec soin ceux qui impriment la terreur, en jettant çà & là

quelques teintes obscures & propres à inspirer de la tristesse.' Nicolas Le Camus de Mézières, *Le Génie de l'architecture, ou L'Analogie de cet art avec nos sensations* (Paris: l'auteur, 1780), 59. For Le Camus de Mézières see Nicolas Le Camus de Mézières, *The Genius of Architecture, or The Analogy of that Art with our Sensations* [1780], introduction by Robin Middleton, trans. David Britt (Santa Monica (Cal.): Getty Center for the History of Art and the Humanities, 1992) ; Louise Pelletier, *Architecture in Words: Theatre, Language and the Sensuous Space of Architecture* (London: Routledge, 2006).

77 'Les avant-corps saillans sont un des moyens dont on peut se servir; quelques percés qui se terminent sur un endroit sombre & obscur, où la vue puisse à peine pénétrer à travers les ténèbres, seront une vraie ressource: d'un autre côté on laissera appercevoir, si l'occasion le permet, de ces lointains vagues & non déterminés, où il ne se présente aucun objet sur lequel la vue puisse se reposer. Rien de plus terrible, l'ame est étonnée, elle frémit. Les masses fieres & hardies, sur lesquelles les yeux ont été fixés d'abord, l'ont préparée à cette sensation.' Le Camus de Mézières, *Le Génie de l'architecture*, 60; Eng. trans. in Le Camus de Mézières, *The Genius of Architecture*, trans. Britt, 94.

78 'L'Océan lui-même, par sa majesté, nous dédommage à peine de son immensité. En effet, pour qu'il forme une perspective agréable, il faut qu'on puisse appercevoir à une distance médiocre un rivage, un cap, une isle: ces objets variés donnent au tout la figure & la vie . . . La grandeur est essentielle au genre terrible, ainsi que les masses fieres & marquées sont l'apanage du majestueux.' Ibid., 60–61.

79 'Sommes-nous placés sur le bord d'une riviere, la simple agitation de l'eau engourdit nos sens, nous endort; plus de rapidité est portée à l'excès, elle jette l'alarme dans nos sens; c'est un torrent dont le fracas, la force & l'impétuosité inspirent la terreur, sensation étroitement liée avec la sublimité, soit qu'on la regarde comme cause ou comme effet.' Ibid., 59–61.

80 There are interesting studies that use the sublime as the key concept in the analysis of artworks: for example, the paintings of Poussin, in which the depiction of different weather effects has destabilising results (Nau, *Le Temps du sublime*) or the abstract works of ett Newman (Renée van de Vall, *Een subliem gevoel van plaats: Een filosofische interpretatie van het werk van Barnett Newman* (Groningen: Historische Uitgeverij, 1994)). The few studies on (specific aspects of) the sublime in seventeenth-century architecture are: Ploeg, 'Staged Experiences', in *Dealing with the Visual*, 167–90; Ploeg, 'Staged Experiences', PhD thesis; van Eck, 'Longinus' Essay on the Sublime'. Caroline van Eck, *Inigo Jones on Stonehenge: Architectural Representation, Memory and Narrative* (Amsterdam: Architectura & Natura, 2009) briefly discusses the topic. For the eighteenth century, focusing mainly on Piranesi, see Laroque, *Le Discours de Piranèse*. For landscape and the sublime see Baldine Saint Girons, 'Le Paysage et la question du sublime', in Chrystèle Burgard, Baldine Saint Girons, Marie-Ceciello-Bachy et al., *Le Paysage et la question du sublime* (Paris / Lyon: Réunion des Musées Nationaux / ARAC, 1997), 75–118.

81 Dance visited Naples in June 1764, but apparently did not go to Paestum. Ingamells, *A Dictionary of British and Irish Travellers in Italy*, 273–4.

82 Dance thought the *Philosophical Enquiry* 'a very excellent work. – That part on taste the best He has ever seen on the subject'. *The Diary of Joseph Farington*, ed. Kenneth Garlick and Angus Macintyre, vol. III (s.l.: Yale University Press, 1979), 784 (entry for 3 March 1797), quoted in David Watkin (ed.), *Sir John Soane: Enlightenment Thought and the Royal Academy Lectures* (Cambridge: Cambridge University Press, 1996), 59.

83 Barry Bergdoll, *European Architecture, 1750–1890* (Oxford / New York: Oxford University Press, 2000), 145, 128.

84 On the history and influence of this street see Werner Szambien, *De la rue des Colonnes à la rue de Rivoli* (Paris: Délégation à l'Action Artistique de la Ville de Paris, 1992).

85 William Chambers, notes for Royal Academy lectures, London, Royal Institute for British Architects (RIBA), Drawings and Archives Collection, CHA 1/8. ii.

86 'To give therefore an historical account of architecture from the beginning to the present time will not I trust be deemed foreign to our purpose since it will bring before us the immense works of the Assyrians and Egyptians, Persians, Greeks, Jews, Roman and other famous people of antiquity as well as of some modern peoples justly celebrated for the magnificence of their structures.' Chambers, notes, RIBA, Drawings and Archives Collection, CHA 2/3.

87 William Chambers, notes, RIBA, Drawings and Archives Collection, CHA 2/26, cited in Watkin (ed.), *Sir John Soane*, 34.

88 Bergdoll, *European Architecture*, 67.

89 Edward K. A. Wendt, 'The Burkean Sublime in British Architecture', unpublished PhD thesis, Columbia University, New York, 2002, 53–60.

90 Soane owned the 1810 edition of Nicolas Boileau-Despréaux, *Œuvres complètes . . . contenant . . . sa traduction de Longin*, 3 vols. (Paris: Mame, 1810), two other editions of Boileau's Longinus in French, and an English translation, *The works of Monsieur Boileau. Made English from the last Paris edition, by several hands* (London: E. Sanger, and E. Curll, 1712); see Watkin (ed.), *Sir John Soane*, 190.

91 Watkin (ed.), *Sir John Soane*, 329.

92 Dora Wiebenson suggests 1768 as a date when the lectures were written, adducing as evidence that in the 1791 edition of his *Treatise on the decorative part of civil architecture* Chambers wrote that his criticism of Greek architecture had been meant for the second edition (1768) of the treatise. Dora Wiebenson, *Sources of Greek Revival Architecture* (London: A. Zwemmer, 1969), 26.

93 Eileen Harris, 'Burke and Chambers on the Sublime and the Beautiful', in Douglas Fraser, Howard Hibbard and Milton J. Lewine (eds), *Essays in the History of Architecture Presented to Rudolf Wittkower* (London: Phaidon Press, 1967), 207–13.

94 Chambers, notes, RIBA, Drawings and Archives Collection, CHA 1/3, fol. 42.

95 'The French and Italians have a method of rendering the most trifling Compositions Considerable which Vanbrugh

alone amongst the English has ventured to Imitate. They raise their buildings considerably above the Surface of the Ground then surround them with terrasses proportioned to the buildings the Angles of which are Marked by Groups of figures . . . Statues or Vases and the centers of each Side with flights of Steps the Whole so Contrived as to Connect with and Seem a Part of the design by Which means the most Pleasing forms are produced and an air of Importance is imparted to the Composition which without such artifice twice the expence would not produce Versailles Marli Triganon Frescati Tivoli & Several of the Villas about Rome furnish many Examples of this practice very deserving of Imitation'. William Chambers, notes, RIBA, Drawings and Archives Collection, CHA 1/6.

96 Chambers, notes, RIBA, Drawings and Archives Collection, CHA 1/8 iii.

97 'Gloom is alwais productive of Grandeur.' Chambers, notes, RIBA, Drawings and Archives Collection, CHA 1/8 iv.

98 Chambers, notes, RIBA, Drawings and Archives Collection, CHA 1/4, fol. 39. On the close contacts between Chambers and Julien-David Le Roy see Janine Barrier, *William Chambers: Une architecture empreinte de culture française. Suivi de correspondance avec la France* (Paris: PUPS, Université Paris-Sorbonne, 2010).

99 On Willey Reveley see Obituary of Willey Reveley, *Gentleman's Magazine*, 59/2 (1799), 627; Terry Friedman, 'Willey Reveley's All Saints', Southampton', *Georgian Group Journal*, 12 (2002), 74–95; Howard M. Colvin, *A Biographical Dictionary of British Architects, 1600–1840*, 4th edn (New Haven (Conn.) / London: Yale University Press, 2008) [first published 1954], 856–7; Frank Salmon, 'The Forgotten "Athenian": Drawings by Willey Reveley', in Christopher White, Elizabeth Einberg, Martin Postle et al., *Windows on that World: Essays on British Art Presented to Brian Allen* (London: Paul Mellon Centre for Studies in British Art, 2012), 143–82. On Reveley in Italy see Ingamells, *A Dictionary of British and Irish Travellers in Italy*, 807–8. On his introduction to Stuart see 'Review of New Publications: The Antiquities of Athens, measured and delineated by James Stuart, F.R.S. and F.S.A. and Nicholas Revett, Painters and Architects. Volume the Third', *Gentleman's Magazine*, 65 (February 1795), 137; *Gentleman's Magazine*, 71 (May 1801), 419–20.

100 Obituary of Willey Reveley, *Gentleman's Magazine*, 627.

101 Willey Reveley, travel journal, RIBA, Drawings and Archives Collection, ReW/1.

102 Chambers, who denigrated Greek architecture in his *Treatise*, wrote in his lecture notes for the Royal Academy: 'At first Sight it appears extraordinary that a People so renowned for Poetry, Rhetoric, & every sort of Polite Literature and who carried Sculpture farther than any of the ancient nations should be so deficient in Architecture.' Chambers, notes, RIBA, Drawings and Archives Collection, CHA 1/4, fol. 27.

103 'Went by Sea to Pœstum, crost the Gulf of Salerno, set out upon good wind. but was afterwards becalmed – Arrived there ab. Midday – Three Temples all in the same Stile Doric – Middle one the largest & best Preserved – Pediments very low, but have a good Effect, Entab: remarkably high –

Columns very low.' Thomas Hardwick, journal, RIBA, Drawings and Archives Collection, SKB103/3, fol. 17v; Hardwick, sketchbook, RIBA, Drawings and Archives Collection, SKB105/1.

104 Thomas Hardwick, *A Memoir of the Life of Sir William Chambers* (London: s.n., 1825), 3–4.

105 Wiebenson, *Sources of Greek Revival Architecture*, 60.

106 Ibid., 61. In '"L'Architecture terrible" and the "jardin anglo-chinois"', *Journal of the Society of Architectural Historians*, 27 (May 1968), 136–9, Wiebenson sees a connection with the ideas of Boullée and Chambers on the sublime.

107 James Stuart and Nicholas Revett, *The antiquities of Athens measured and delineated by James Stuart F.R.S. and F.S.A. and Nicholas Revett painters and architects*, 4 vols, vol. III, ed. Willey Reveley (London: John Nichols, 1794), p. xiv.

108 Reveley, notes and sketches for a proposed dictionary of architecture, RIBA, Drawings and Archives Collection, ReW/1, fol. 12r.

109 Ibid., fol. 12v.

110 Ibid., fol. 13r. Reveley gives as examples of design that is too ornamented and confused the Horse Guards building at Whitehall, the façade of Saint Peter's in Rome and that of San Moisè in Venice. The first example 'does not fill the mind, but leaves a great vacancy: & the latter because it is too complicated for the mind to comprehend at a glance, & the time necessary to consider it takes of the effect of the first impression', fol. 12v.

111 'On verra un monument dans le lequel le spectateur se trouverait, comme par echantement, transporté dans les airs et porté sur des vapeurs de nuages dans l'immensité de l'espace.' Boullée, *Architecture*, ed. Pérouse de Montclos, 138.

112 Burke, *A Philosophical Enquiry*, ed. Boulton, 79–81.

113 Boullée never travelled to Italy and did not appreciate Greek architecture: to him the temples all looked alike and had no character. 'Leurs temples ont une similitude frappante; il ont tous à peu près la même forme. Comment les hommes de génie comme les Grecs ont-ils pu négliger de manifester la poésie de l'architecture dans des monuments qui en étaient aussi susceptibles par les attributions diverses qu'ils reconnaissent dans le pouvoir de leurs divinités?' Boullée, *Architecture*, ed. Pérouse de Montclos, 161.

114 Barry Bergdoll, *Léon Vaudoyer: Historicism in the Age of Industry* (New York / Cambridge (Mass.) / London: Architectural History Foundation / MIT Press, 1994), 19–20.

115 'de développer à nos yeux la plus grande surface, ce qui le rend majestueux; d'avoir la forme la plus simple, beauté qui provient de ce que sa surface est sans interruption aucune; et de joindre à toutes ces qualités celle de la grâce, car le contour qui dessine ce corps est aussi doux, aussi coulant qu'il soit possible.' Boullée, *Architecture*, ed. Pérouse de Montclos, 64; Eng. trans. in Rosenau, *Boullée and Visionary Architecture*, 86.

116 'Le premier sentiment que nous éprouvons alors vient évidemment de la manière dont l'objet nous affecte. Et j'appelle caractère l'effet qui résulte de cet objet et cause en nous une impression quelconque.' Boullée, *Architecture*, Eng. trans. in Rosenau, *Boullée and Visionary Architecture*, 89. More specif-

ically, in relation to architecture: 'Mettre du caractère dans un ouvrage, c'est employer avec justesse tous les moyens propres à ne nous faire éprouver d'autres sensations que celles qui doivent résulter du sujet.' This 'character' is best explained by appealing to the sensations that nature produces in the mind of the spectator. In describing these feelings, Boullée used expressions of the sublime: 'les transports de notre admiration sont sans bornes ... Quel bonheur pur ce spectacle répand au fond de nos cœurs! Quel ravissement il cause en nous! Non, il n'est pas possible de l'exprimer.' Boullée, *Architecture*, ed. Pérouse de Montclos, 73.

117 'astonishment is that state of the soul, in which all its motions are suspended, with some degree of horror. In this case the mind is so entirely filled with its object, that it cannot entertain any other, nor by consequence reason on that object which employs it'. Burke, *A Philosophical Enquiry*, ed. Boulton, 57.

118 Ibid., 134.

119 Ibid., 57.

120 Ibid., 58.

121 Ibid., 157–8.

122 'un si horrible désert', Charles-Marguerite-Jean-Baptiste Mercier Dupaty, *Lettres sur l'Italie en 1785*, 2 vols (Paris: De Senne, 1788), vol. II, 195. On Dupaty see *Studies on Voltaire and the Eighteenth Century*, vol. CCXXX (Oxford / Paris: Voltaire Foundation / J. Touzot, 1985); Jean-Louis Prouteau, *Charles Dupaty: Un magistrat-philosophe du siècle des Lumières* (La Rochelle: J.-L. Prouteau, 1989).

123 'Comment donc des Sybarites on-ils imaginé et mis debout des colonnes d'un nombre si prodigieux, d'une matière si vile, d'un travail si brut, d'une masse si lourde et d'une forme si monotone?'. Dupaty, *Lettres sur l'Italie*, vol. II, 196; Eng. trans. in *Travels through Italy, in a series of letters; written in the year 1785, by President Dupaty. Translated from the French by an English Gentleman* (London: G. G. J. and J. Robinson, 1788), 324.

124 'Cependant il faut convenir que, malgré leur rusticité, ces temples offrent des beautés: ils offrent du moins la simplicité, l'unité, l'ensemble, qui sont les premières des beautés: l'imagination peut supléer presque toutes les autres, elle ne peut supléer celles-ci.' Dupaty, *Lettres sur l'Italie*, vol. II, 197; Eng. trans. in *Travels through Italy*, 324–5.

125 'Quel dommage qu'il faille si-tôt quitter ces lieux ... Mais la chaleur est extrême; il n'y a d'abri nulle part. Je voudrois pourtant bien recueillir et remporter dans mon cœur toutes les sensations que je viens d'éprouver. – Qu'on me laisse puiser encore, dans cette solitude, dans ce désert, dans ces ruines, je ne sais quelle horreur, qui me charme.' Dupaty, *Lettres sur l'Italie*, vol. II, 199; Eng. trans. in *Travels through Italy*, 326.

126 'le génie ... est indépendant du hasard et de la fortune, c'est un don du ciel, où la terre n'a point de part; c'est je ne sais quoi de divin'. Quoted in Litman, *Le Sublime en France*, note 115, 24; Eng. trans. in Robin Middleton, Introduction to Julien-David Le Roy, *The Ruins of the Most Beautiful Monuments of Greece*, 2nd edn [1770], trans. David Britt (Los Angeles: Getty Research Institute, 2004), 52.

127 'un plan bien plus vaste et de plus nobles manières que Virgile, qu'il a une plus grande étendue de caractère, qu'il a un air plus grand et je ne sais quoi de sublime, qu'il peint beaucoup mieux les choses; que ses images mêmes sont plus achevées'. Quoted in Litman, *Le Sublime en France*, n. 115, 32; Eng. trans. in Middleton, Introduction to Le Roy, *The Ruins*, 52.

128 Burke mentioned the inexplicable in another context – namely, Part III of the *Enquiry*, on beauty. Here he compared gracefulness to beauty: 'In this ease, this roundness, this delicacy of attitude and emotion, it is that all the magic of grace consists, and what is called its *je ne sais quoi*.' Burke, *A Philosophical Enquiry*, ed. Boulton, 119.

129 'After a residence of three weeks during which I once only went to the Theatre of San Carlo the finest in the world, I engaged a Vetturino for Paestum with the Master of the Hotel for my Compagnon de Voyage who turned out an excellent English hearted fellow. We passed the first night in a wretched Inn & laid down in our cloathes & pistols by our sides. There was an uncouth set of people within the walls who did not inspire me with much confidence. We remained safely, & slept at intervals amidst noise & confusion, & started early in the morning in quest of the Temples.' Pearce and Salmon, 'Charles Heathcote Tatham', 86. Other studies on Tatham include David Udy, 'The Neo-Classicism of Charles Heathcote Tatham', *The Connoisseur*, 177 (1971), 269–76; Frank Salmon, 'Charles Heathcote Tatham and the Accademia di S. Luca, Rome, *Burlington Magazine*, 140 (February 1998), 85–92.

130 In addition to the drawings in the Victoria and Albert Museum in London (Prints and Drawings Collection, 93.G.8), Sir John Soane's Museum in London holds another scale drawing of the Neptune temple by Tatham, in Charles Heathcote Tatham, Italian drawings, Vol. 109.

131 Pearce and Salmon, 'Charles Heathcote Tatham', 86.

132 Burke, *A Philosophical Enquiry*, ed. Boulton, 140 (Part IV Section xiii).

133 Ibid., 139.

134 Henry Swinburne, *Travels in the Two Sicilies ... in the years 1777, 1778, 1779, and 1780*, 2 vols (London: P. Elmsly, 1783–5), vol. II, 136–7; see also the section 'Journey to Paestum', ibid., 131–9.

135 John Flaxman, letter to George Romney, Rome, 25 May 1788, in John Romney, *Memoirs of the Life and the Works of George Romney, Including Various Letters, and Testimonies to his Genius &c.; also Some Particulars of the Life of Peter Romney, his Brother* (London: Baldwin and Cradock, 1830), 204–7.

136 John Flaxman, letter to William Hayley, Rome, 17 July 1788, London, British Library, Add. MS 39780, fol. 44r.

137 Brydone presents Paestum, falsely, as not having been visible before its discovery: 'the discovery of Pestum, a Grecian city, that had not been heard of for many ages; till of late some of its lofty temples were seen, peeping over the tops of the woods; upbraiding mankind for their shameful neglect; and calling upon them to bring it once more to light. According curiosity, and the hopes of gain, a still more powerfull motive, soon opened a passage, and exposed to view these valuable

and respectable relics.' Patrick Brydone, *A tour through Sicily and Malta, in a series of letters to William Beckford*, 3rd edn, 2 vols (London: W. Strahan & T. Cadell, 1775), vol. 1, 46–7. Longinus, *On the Sublime: Translated . . . By William Smith.*

138 Uvedale Price, 'On Architecture and Buildings', in *Sir Uvedale Price on the Picturesque: With an Essay on the Origin of Taste, and Much Original Matter, by Sir Thomas Dick Lauder, Bart., and Sixty Illustrations, Designed and Drawn on the Wood by Montagu Stanley, R. S. A.* (Edinburgh / London: Caldwell, Lloyd and Co. / Wm. S. Orr and Co., 1842), 341. In his notes Price wrote: 'those which from their size and character are of acknowledged grandeur – such as the vast and massy structures of Pœstum and Selinus . . .'. Ibid., 579. See also Uvedale Price, *Essays on the Picturesque, as Compared with the Sublime and the Beautiful; and, on the Use of Studying Pictures, for the Purpose of Improving Real Landscape*, 3 vols (London: J. Mawman, 1810), vol. II, 203–4.

139 For more on Price and the picturesque see Chapter 2.

140 Lauder in Price, *Sir Uvedale Price on the Picturesque*, 82–3.

141 Price, 'On Architecture and Buildings', in *Sir Uvedale Price on the Picturesque*, 360, 396.

142 Ibid., 338–9. Further: 'If, again, we consider modern building, no mansion of regular, finished, ornamental architecture that I have yet seen, has, from such a number of different points, so grand an appearance as Blenheim; and never was the reproach of heaviness so unceasingly applied to any building. It would hardly be supposed that the *heaviness* of Blenheim would ever have been mentioned as a compliment to the noble owner; yet I remember an instance of it. The conversation happened to turn upon the immense weight that an egg would support if pressed exactly in a perpendicular direction; – no weight, they said, would break it. A person who was sitting at some distance from the Duke of Marlborough, called out to him, "My Lord Duke! if they were to put Blenheim upon it . . . I believe it would crush the egg." How far the heaviness of the ancient temples or of the modern palace might be diminished, without diminution of their grandeur, may be a question; but I believe it is very clear, that after a certain point, as they gained more in lightness, they would become less majestic, and, beyond that again, less beautiful.' Ibid., 341.

143 Price gives the example of an avenue of lofty trees: 'Mr. Burke observes, that the sublime in building requires solidity, and even massiness; and, in my idea, no single cause acts so powerfully, and can so little be dispensed with as massiness; but as massiness is so nearly allied to heaviness, it is – in this age especially – by no means a popular quality; for in whatever regards the mind itself, or the works that proceed from it, the reproach of heaviness is, of all others, the least patiently endured. It is a reproach, however, that has been made to some of the most striking buildings, both ancient and modern.' Ibid., 340.

144 *Le Voyage d'Italie de . . . Moreau*, ed. Descat (see note 7); see also Sophie Descat, 'Deux architectes-urbanistes dans l'Europe des Lumières: Pierre-Louis Moreau et George Dance à Paris et à Londres (1763–1815)', unpublished PhD thesis, Université de Paris 1 Panthéon-Sorbonne, 2000.

145 'La grandeur de cette malheureuse ville était considérable'; 'la plaine d'un grandeur fort considérable'. Moreau, 'Notes sur mon voyage' (see note 7), fol. 46r; *Le Voyage d'Italie de . . . Moreau*, ed. Descat, 126.

146 'l'ordre dorique est employé à tous les trois [temples] dans toute la sévérité et la grandeur de style qu'eux seuls ont pratiquées'. Moreau, 'Notes sur mon voyage', fol. 46v; *Le Voyage d'Italie de . . . Moreau*, ed. Descat, 127. In his contribution to an anonymous publication on Paestum, Gabriel-Pierre-Martin Dumont spoke about: 'l'empêche de s'élever à ce point de sublime & de grandeur qui caractérisa la maniere de faire des anciens architectes'. Gabriel-Pierre-Martin Dumont, *Les ruines de Paestum, autrement Posidonia, ville de l'ancienne grande Grèce, au Royaume de Naples: ouvrage contenant l'histoire ancienne & moderne de cette ville, la description & les vues de ses antiquités, ses inscriptions, &c.: avec des observations sur l'ancien Ordre Dorique*, partly based on [John Longfield], *The ruins of Poestum*, trans. Jacques Varenne de Béost (London / Paris: C.-A. Jombert, 1769), 11.

147 'C'est un des spectacles les plus agréables que j'aie vu de ma vie. Les peintres en font leur délice et véritablement il n'y a rien de si pittoresque que les effets singuliers de cette cascade . . . Les rochers et le paysage qui couvrent toute cette côte sont des objets capables de former les meilleurs peintres de ce genre.'; 'Rien n'est plus étonnant que la chute presque entière du fleuve dans la grande cascade et surtout la vue des effects qu'il produit au-dessous du pont. Le risque que j'y courus augmente peut-être l'étonnement que me donna ce spectacle.' Moreau, *Le Voyage d'Italie de . . . Moreau*, ed. Descat, 76.

148 'La vue de cette ville nous frappa d'étonnement et de pitié considérant son étendue, la magnificence des bâtiments dont on voit encore des restes et la ruine entière de la plus grande partie des édifices dont elle était ornée et dont la place est labourée ou couverte de monceaux de pierre'. Moreau, 'Notes sur mon voyage', fol. 46r; *Le Voyage d'Italie de . . . Moreau*, ed. Descat, 26.

149 'Les seuls habitants qu'on y voit sont des pasteurs et quelques gens vêtus de peaux d'animaux qui ressemblent à des sauvages comme le lieu ressemble à un désert.' Moreau, 'Notes sur mon voyage', fol. 46r; *Le Voyage d'Italie de . . . Moreau*, ed. Descat, 26.

150 On the reception of Hadrian's Villa at Tivoli see William L. MacDonald and John A. Pinto, *Hadrian's Villa and its Legacy* (New Haven (Conn.) / London: Yale University Press, 1995).

151 Studies on Vaudoyer include Bergdoll's seminal *Léon Vaudoyer*; also César Daly, 'Notices nécrologiques: MM. Vaudoyer et Baltard', *Revue de l'Architecture et des Travaux Publics*, 6 (1845–6), 547–52; *Dessins d'architectes XVIIIe et XIXe siècles: Antoine, Léon et Alfred Vaudoyer. Vente à Paris, Hôtel Drouot, 11 avril 1986* (s.l.: s.n., 1986); Barry Bergdoll (ed.), *Les Vaudoyer: Une dynastie d'architectes* (Paris: Réunion des Musées Nationaux, 1991). In connection with the possible sources of Vaudoyer's knowledge of Paestum, Daly makes the pertinent comment: 'M. Vaudoyer avait une belle bibliothèque d'architecture où se rencontraient des hommes illustres de tous les temps et de pays très divers; il en prêtait les volumes précieux à

ses élèves avec une généreuse bienveillance.' Daly, 'Notices nécrologiques', 550.

152 The works concerned were: Dumont, *Suitte* [*Suite*] *de plans* (see note 6); Filippo Morghen, untitled [*Sei vedute delle rovine di Pesto*] (Naples: s.n., n.d. [1765]); repr. in *Le antichità di Pozzuoli, Baja e Cuma, incise in rame* (Naples: s.n., 1769); [Longfield], *The ruins of Poestum or Posidonia* (see note 6); Thomas Major, *The ruins of Paestum, otherwise Posidonia* (see note 6) and *Les ruines de Paestum* (London: T. Major, 1768); Dumont, *Les ruines de Paestum, autrement Posidonia* (see note 146); Giovanni Battista Piranesi, *Différentes vues de quelques restes de trois grands édifices qui subsistent encore dans le milieu de l'ancienne ville de Pesto, autrement Possidonia qui est située dans la Lucanie* (Rome: s.n., 1778). The next work, after Paolo Antonio Paoli, *Paesti, quod Posidoniam etiam dixere, rudera: Rovine della città di Pesto, detta ancora Posidonia* (Rome: [in typographio Paleariniano], 1784), was Claude-Mathieu Delagardette, *Les Ruines de Paestum, ou Posidona, ancienne ville de la Grande-Grèce* (Paris: l'auteur / H. Barbou, an VII [1799]).

153 'a Roma gunio 1786 Vaudoyer architetto', annotation in Paoli, *Paesti . . . rudera: Rovine della città di Pesto*, in the library collection of the Institut National d'Histoire de l'Art, Paris.

154 During the time that Vaudoyer was at the Académie de France, the following architects and travellers visited the city: L. A. Trouard (in Italy 1781–5, in Rome 1783), Louis Combes (in Italy 1782–6, in Rome 1785) and Pierre Bernard (in Italy 1783–7, in Rome 1785). British architects who were in Italy during the same period and must have visited Rome were Willey Reveley (1784–8), Thomas Johnson (1785–6), John Thomas Groves (1786) and Thomas O'Brien (1786–98); see Frank Salmon, *Building on Ruins: The Rediscovery of Rome and English Architecture* (Aldershot (Surrey): Ashgate, 2000), 231.

155 'Le caractère et les proportions de cet ordre portent la tristesse, mais en même temps la fermeté, allusion à celle qu'on doit avoir dans les malheurs.' Antoine-Laurent-Thomas Vaudoyer, letter to Hippolyte Lebas, Rome, 10 August 1785, in Antoine-Laurent-Thomas Vaudoyer, 'Voyage pittoresque en diverses parties de l'Italie: Extraits de lettres adressées à Paris à M. Lebas père, par A. L. T. Vaudoyer, architecte, pensionnaire du Roi à l'Académie de France à Rome, années 1786, 1787, 1788', Paris, private collection, letter no. 49. Bergdoll quoted the letter in *Léon Vaudoyer*, 32, but with an incorrect date.

156 On *caractère* see Szambien, *Symétrie, goût, caractère*.

157 See note 115.

158 'Mettre du caractère dans un ouvrage, c'est employer avec justesse tous les moyens propres à ne nous faire éprouver d'autres sensations que celles qui doivent résulter du sujet.' Boullée, *Architecture*, ed. Pérouse de Montclos, 73; Eng. trans. in Rosenau, *Boullée and Visionary Architecture*, 89. See also Alice T. Friedman, 'Academic Theory and A.L.T. Vaudoyer's Dissertation sur l'architecture', *Art Bulletin*, 67 (March 1985), 118.

159 'Toute cette architecture est, en général, d'un caractère très lourd et très pesant; les colonnes sont courtes, très serrées, de gros chapiteaux, pas de base; le pied pose sur trois gros gradins; l'Entablement est très fort et très saillant'. Antoine-

Laurent-Thomas Vaudoyer, 'Voyage de Rome à Poestum et tout le Royaume de Naples', 1787, Paris, private collection, fol. 123.

160 'cet effet; son aspect Mâle et imposant m'a fait beaucoup de plaisir et j'y ai trouvé, si l'on peut dire, ainsi, la forme, les grâces et finesses de l'hercule.' Vaudoyer, 'Voyage de Rome à Poestum', Paris, private collection, fol. 123.

161 'Son effet est toujours imposant, cela vient de son extreme simplicité, dela multitude des colonnes, du caractère fier et Male de son architecture, et dela belle couleur des pierres'. Hubert Rohault de Fleury, 'Voyage de l'architecte Rohault de Fleury en Italie, 1804–1805', 4 vols, Paris, Bibliothèque Nationale de France, Département des Manuscrits, NAF 23696, vol. II, 155. For Rohault de Fleury see Jean-Pierre Willesme, 'Hubert Rohault de Fleury (1777–1846): Un grand commis de l'architecture. Biographie et catalogue des dessins des albums conservés au Musée Carnavalet (Paris)', unpublished PhD thesis, École Pratique des Hautes Études, Paris, 2007.

162 Vitruvius, *De architectura libri decem*, I. ii. 5, in *Vitruvius on Architecture*, ed. Thomas Gordon Smith (New York: Monacelli Press, 2003), 68.

163 'à droite, très près du Grand Temple, on trouve une Colonnade de grande face, qui ressemble assez à un portique ou promenoir'. Vaudoyer, 'Voyage de Rome à Poestum', Paris, private collection, fol 123.

164 'l'architecture du petit temple ne le vaut pas et encore moins celle du portique'. Ibid., fol. 123.

165 'Nun sind unsere Augen und durch sie unser ganzes inneres Wesen an schlankere Baukunst hinangetrieben und entschieden bestimmt, so daßuns diese stumpfen, kegelförmigen, enggedrängten Säulenmassen lästig, ja furchtbar erscheinen.' Goethe, *Italienische Reise*, 205; Eng. trans. in Goethe, *Italian Journey*, trans. Auden and Mayer, 218. Goethe's account will be treated more thoroughly in Chapter 3.

166 'Beim frühsten Morgen fuhren wir auf ungebahnten, oft morastigen Wegen einem Paar schön geformten Bergen zu, wir kamen durch Bach und Gewässer, wo wir den nilpferdischen Büffeln in die blutroten wilden Augen sahen. Das Land ward immer flacher und wüster, wenige Gebäude deuteten auf kärgliche Landwirtschaft. Endlich, ungewiss, ob wir durch Felsen oder Trümmer führen, konnten wir einige grösse länglich-viereckige Massen, die wir in der Ferne schon bemerkt hatten, als überbliebene Tempel und Denkmale einer ehemals so prächtigen Stadt unterscheiden.' Goethe, *Italienische Reise*, 205; Eng. trans. in Goethe, *Italian Journey*, trans. Auden and Mayer, 218.

167 Reveley, notes and sketches, RIBA, Drawings and Archives Collection,, ReW/1, fol. 171v.

168 '28th of Feb we set out with these priests, one of whom seemed fitter for a brothel than a church, their oddities were the only amusement as they were all very ignorant, the old woman had an ingenious way of leaning out of the caless, & watering the road without detaining us by getting out as any other person would have done, it was the only proof of her ingenuity that I saw.' Ibid., fol. 172v. Further: 'the ancient & modern poets have sung the praises of the Pœstan Roses,

whose blossoms were renewed twice a year with the richest fragrance But in the course of time the water insensibly stagnated & putrified the teritory became Marshy, & at present the air is extreemly noxius, during the hot months & this once favoured spot is now almost a desert, these being on the scite of the ancient city only the Cathedral & Bishops palace adjoining to it, one osteria consisting of one room above for the residence of the family & a stable under it, & about 6 or 8 cottages of the most mean & miserable description'. Ibid., first of two unnumbered sheets before fol. 244.

169 Reveley, Introduction to Stuart and Revett, *The antiquities of Athens*, vol. III, p. xiii.

170 Ibid., p. xv. On Stuart and *The antiquities of Athens* see David Watkin, *Athenian Stuart: Pioneer of the Greek Revival* (London / Boston: George Allen and Unwin, 1982); Susan Weber Soros (ed.), *James 'Athenian' Stuart, 1713–1788: The Rediscovery of Antiquity* (New Haven (Conn.) / London: Yale University Press for the Bard Graduate Center for Studies in the Decorative Arts, Design, and Culture, New York, 2006).

171 'On voit dans les ruines de Pestum ou Posidonia, trois temples dont un surtout est assés bien conservé. Je ne connois rien d'aussi terrible, d'aussi imposant, ni d'aussi caracterisé que ces temples.' Pierre-Adrien Pâris, 'Notes et lavis', in Desgodets [Desgodetz], *Les édifices antiques de Rome*, Paris, Institut de France, MS 1906, fol. 329.

172 'Ce qu'on doit entendre par une Architecture terrible', Blondel, *Cours d'architecture*, vol. I, 426–7.

173 'De la difference qu'il y a entre le caractere mâle, ferme ou viril dans l'Architecture.' Blondel, *Cours d'architecture*, vol. I, 411–13.

174 'mâle: sans être pesante, conserve dans son ordonnance un caractere de fermeté assorti à la grandeur des lieux & au genre de l'édifice; celle qui est simple dans sa composition générale, sage dans ses formes, & peu chargée de détails dans ses ornements; celle qui s'annonce par des plans rectilignes, par des angles droits, par des corps avancés qui portent de grandes ombres; celle qui, destinée aux marchés publics, aux Foires, aux Hôpitaux & sur-tout aux Edifices Militaires, doit être composée de belles masses, dans lesquelles on prend soin d'éviter les petites parties, le chétif & le grand ne pouvant aller ensemble. Souvent on croit faire une Architecture mâle, on la fait lourde, massive, matérielle; on prend le mot pour la chose. On croit faire du neuf, & l'on ne ramene sur la scène que la charge des belles productions des Michel-Ange, des le Brun, des le Pautre, sans se douter que les Debrosses, les Hardouin Mansard, les François Blondel, nous ont laissé des exemples immortels en ce genre, dans la composition, la grandeur & la solidité du Palais du Luxembourg, des Ecuries & de l'Orangerie de Versailles, dans la porte triomphale de S. Denis; productions admirables qui, incontestablement, doivent servir d'autorités pour l'ordonnance des divers édifices qui exigent le caractere mâle dont nous voulons parler.' Ibid., vol. I, 411–12. See also Caroline van Eck, ' "Par le style on atteint au sublime": The Meaning of the Term "Style" in French Architectural Theory of the Late Eighteenth Century', in Caroline van Eck, James McAllister and Renée van de Vall (eds), *The Question of Style in Philosophy and the*

Arts (Cambridge: Cambridge University Press, 1995), 89–107.

175 'Une Architecture ferme differe d'une Architecture mâle par les masses: l'Architecture ferme annonce moins de pesanteur, mais néanmoins dans ses parties, dans sa division, elle présente des formes décidées dont les surfaces & les angles sont droits; partout elle montre une certitude, une articulation, qui impose, qui frappe, & qui satisfait les yeux intelligents. Les ouvrages de François Mansard, de le Veau, de le Mercier, portent assez généralement ce caractere de fermeté, dans les Châteaux de Misons, de Vincennes & de Richelieu: productions qui moins mâles que les précédentes, ont aussi quelque chose de plus intéressant, & sont plus du ressort des bâtiments d'habitation.' Blondel, *Cours d'architecture*, vol. I, 412.

176 'mais lorsqu'une fois cet ordre est présent dans la décoration des façades, il faut s'attendre qu'il ne tolere aucun détail, aucun accessoire qui ne soit puisé dans sa virilité: lorsqu'il préside dans l'ordonnance de l'édifice, il ne veut souffrir aucune espece de mêlange, il est même jaloux de communiquer son caractere aux autres ordres qu'on lui associe souvent dans les différents étages du bâtiment . . . Quoiqu'il paroisse qu'une Architecture virile differe peu des deux précédentes, il est cependant vrai qu'on peut donner ce nom à celle dans l'ordonnance de laquelle préside l'ordre Dorique. Une Architecture mâle considérée séparément, une Architecture ferme, proprement dite, n'exigent souvent que l'expression rustique ou solide, & non la présence de l'ordre dont nous parlons'. Ibid., vol. I, 412–13.

177 See *The Letters of Percy Bysshe Shelley*, ed. Frederick L. Jones, 2 vols (Oxford: Oxford University Press, 1964), vol. II: *Shelley in Italy*; Angela Leighton, *Shelley and the Sublime: An Interpretation of the Major Poems* (Cambridge: Cambridge University Press, 1984); Cian Duffy, *Shelley and the Revolutionary Sublime* (Cambridge: Cambridge University Press, 2005).

178 Mary Wollstonecraft Shelley (1797–1851), Journal 116 (entry for Wednesday 24 February 1819), published in *The Journals of Mary Shelley, 1814–1844*, ed. Paula R. Feldman and Diana Scott-Kilvert, 2 vols (Oxford: Clarendon Press, 1987).

179 Percy Bysshe Shelley, letter to Thomas Love Peacock, Naples, 25 February 1819, in Shelley, *The Letters*, vol. II, 77–82.

180 Ibid., 79.

181 Ibid.

182 Ibid., 80.

183 Marguerite, Countess of Blessington, *Lady Blessington at Naples*, ed. Edith Clay, introduction by Harold Acton (London: Hamish Hamilton, 1979), 88–9.

184 Ibid., 89.

185 On Turner's Italian tour see Cecilia Powell, *Turner in the South: Rome, Naples, Florence* (New Haven (Conn.) / London: Yale University Press for the Paul Mellon Centre for Studies in British Art, 1987); James Hamilton, *Turner & Italy* (Edinburgh: National Galleries of Scotland, 2009). When Turner left Paestum and returned to Naples by boat he made some small sketches of the coastal landscape.

186 Hakewill travelled in Italy in 1816–17, and on his return published *A Picturesque Tour of Italy from Drawings made in 1816–*

17 by J. H. (London: s.n., 1820). Turner made the watercolours on the basis of Hakewill's travel sketches.

187 Turner's sketches of Paestum are in the collection of Tate Britain in London.

188 Powell, *Turner in the South*, 85.

189 Maurice Davies, *Turner as Professor: The Artist and Linear Perspective* (London: Tate Gallery Publications, 1992), 23. Turner's lecture notes are in London, British Library, Add. MS 46151 A–BB. See also D. S. MacColl, 'Notes on English Artists, II: Turner's Lectures at the Academy', *Burlington Magazine*, 12 (1908), 343–6; Alexander Joseph Finberg, *A Complete Inventory of the Drawings of the Turner Bequest: with which are Included the Twenty-Three Drawings Bequeathed by Mr. Henry Vaughan*, 2 vols (London: Stationery Office, 1909); W. T. Whitley, 'Turner as a Lecturer', *Burlington Magazine*, 22 (February 1913), 202–8, 255–9.

190 In Helen Dorey, *John Soane & J M W Turner: Illuminating a Friendship* (London: Sir John Soane's Museum, 2007), 24, it is suggested that Turner used the original preparatory drawings by Piranesi that were in the Soane collection; but it is also a possibility that he used the engraving in the publication.

191 Samuel Rogers, *Italy: A Poem* (London: T. Cadell, 1830). Rogers had visited Paestum in 1815, a visit recorded in his diary: 'Country open and level; did not see the Paestum Temples till we approached them. The temples in a plain, on three sides shut in by the mountains, on the fourth open to the sea, and the sea itself half shut in by them, by the promontory of Sorrentum, within which are the isles of the sirens. A magnificent theatre, worthy of such objects; the columns almost bare, broken, and of an iron-brown, like iron rust; the floor green with moss and herbage; the columns and cornices of the richest tints and climbed by the green lizards that fly into a thousand chinks and crevices at your approach; the snail adheres to them, the butterfly flutters among them, and the kite is sailing over them; fluted fragments of columns and moulded cornices among briars strew the middle space between the temple and the basilica.' *The Italian Journal of Samuel Rogers*, ed. J. R. Hale (London: Faber and Faber, 1956). His 'Lines Written at Paestum March 4, 1815' was originally published as a section of *Human Life: A Poem (Lines Written at Paestum – The Boy of Egremond)* (London: John Murray, 1819), 83–94; it was later re-used in *Italy: A Poem*. Turner's illustration stands at the head of the poem, which begins with an evocation of the sublime in its description of the temples: 'They stand between the mountains and the sea; / Awful memorials, but of whom we know not!'

192 Powell, *Turner in the South*, 85.

193 'The neolithic circle of Stonehenge has always been recognised as an object specially evocative of the sublime'. Louis Hawes, *Constable's Stonehenge* (London: Victoria and Albert Museum, 1975), 163. In 1740 William Stukeley wrote: 'When you enter the building, whether on foot or horseback and cast your eyes around, upon the yawning ruins, you are struck into an exstatic reverie, which none can describe, and they only can be sensible of, that feel it.' William Stukeley, *Stonehenge: A temple restor'd to the British druids* (London: W.

Innys and R. Manby, 1740), 12. Subsequent poets and tourists also found inspiration in its antiquity, mystery, and desolate situation: see William Gilpin, *Observations on the western parts of England, relative chiefly to picturesque beauty* (London: T. Cadell jun. and W. Davies, 1798), 77; Linda Marie Zimmerman, 'Representations of Stonehenge in British Art (1300–1900): Antiquity, Ideology, and Nationalism', unpublished PhD thesis, Stanford University, 1997.

194 Andrew Wilton, *Turner and the Sublime* (London: British Museum Publications for the Art Gallery of Ontario, the Yale Center for British Art, the Trustees of the British Museum, 1980), 159. Wilton quotes *The Works of John Ruskin*, ed. E. T. Cook and Alexander Wedderburn, 39 vols (London: George Allen, 1903–12), vol. XXI, 223.

195 The connection between Paestum and Stonehenge is not only in the sublime, but also in primitivism. We shall return to this in Chapter 5.

196 Wilton, *Turner and the Sublime*, 166.

197 Ibid., 66.

198 Ibid., 115.

Chapter 2

1 'On fait des descriptions si étranges, et on prend des idées si monstrueuses d'après ce qu'on lit, et ce qu'on entend raconter, que je croyais trouver Paestum dans un désert marécageux, ses temples perdus ou enfouis dans les joncs ou les broussailles, son air infect et exhalé de la fange; au lieu de cela, je trouvai une belle situation, un golfe, une belle plaine entourée de belles montagnes, un pays cultivé en vignes et en blé.' [Dominique] Vivant Denon, *Voyage au Royaume de Naples* [1778], ed. Mathieu Couty (Paris: Perrin 1997), 288.

2 After completing his Italian tour, Denon stayed in Italy and became secretary at the French embassy in Naples. He lived in Italy from 1778 to 1785, returning to Paris in 1786. On Denon see Pierre Lelièvre, *Vivant Denon: Homme des Lumières, 'ministre des arts' de Napoléon* (Paris: Picard, 1993), on his Italian period pp. 27–38; Marie-Anne Dupuy-Vachey, *Les Itinéraires de Vivant-Denon, dessinateur et illustrateur*, Collection Musée Denon (Manosque: Le Bec en l'Air, 2007); Marie-Anne Dupuy-Vachey (ed.), *Vivant Denon et le 'Voyage pittoresque': Un manuscrit inconnu* (Paris: Fondation Custodia, 2009); Pierre Rosenberg (ed.), *Naples et Pompéi: Les Itinéraires de Vivant-Denon* (Chalon-sur-Saône / Manosque: Musée Denon / Le Bec en l'Air, 2009).

3 Gabriel-Pierre-Martin Dumont, *Suitte [Suite] de plans, coupes, profils, élévations géométrales et perspectives de trois temples antiques, tels qu'ils existaient en 1750 dans la bourgade de Poesto* (Paris: Dumont, 1764); Filippo Morghen, untitled [*Sei vedute delle rovine di Pesto*] (Naples: s.n., n.d. [1765]); repr. in *Le antichità di Pozzuoli, Baja e Cuma, incise in rame* (Naples: s.n., 1769); [John Longfield] (published anonymously), *The ruins of Poestum or Posidonia, containing a description and views of the remaining antiquities, with the ancient and modern history, inscriptions, etc.* (London: s.n., 1767); Thomas Major, *The ruins of Paestum, otherwise Posidonia, in Magna Graecia* (London: s.n.,

1768) and *Les ruines de Paestum* (London: T. Major, 1768); Gabriel-Pierre-Martin Dumont, *Les ruines de Paestum, autrement Posidonia, ville de l'ancienne grande Grèce, au Royaume de Naples: ouvrage contenant l'histoire ancienne & moderne de cette ville, la description & les vues de ses antiquités, ses inscriptions, &c.: avec des observations sur l'ancien Ordre Dorique*, partly based on [John Longfield], *The ruins of Poestum*, trans. Jacques Varenne de Béost (London / Paris: C.-A. Jombert, 1769); Giovanni Battista Piranesi, *Différentes vues de quelques restes de trois grands édifices qui subsistent encore dans le milieu de l'ancienne ville de Pesto, autrement Possidonia qui est située dans la Lucanie* (Rome: s.n., 1778). Piranesi's work, though published in Rome, was written in French and aimed at the French market; Denon could also have seen the Piranesi engravings in Rome.

4 On Jean-Claude Richard de Saint-Non, a French engraver and draughtsman, and his group of artists and architects see Petra Lamers, *Il viaggio nel sud dell'Abbé de Saint-Non: Il 'Voyage pittoresque à Naples et en Sicile': La genesi, i disegni preparatori, le incisioni* (Naples: Electa, 1995); Jean-Claude Richard de Saint-Non, *Da Napoli a Malta: Voyage pittoresque, ou Description des royaumes de Naples et de Sicile di Jean Claude Richard Abbé de Saint-Non, 1781–1786*, ed. Silverio Salamon and Elisabetta Rollier (Turin: L'Arte Antica, S. Salamon, 2001). On Saint-Non's first voyage to Italy, with the painters Jean-Honoré Fragonard and Hubert Robert, see Jean-Claude Richard de Saint-Non, *Panopticon italiano: Un diario di viaggio ritrovato, 1759–1761*, ed. Pierre Rosenberg (Rome: Ed. dell'Elefante, 2000); the travellers were in Paestum in 1760.

5 Jean-Claude Richard de Saint-Non, *Voyage pittoresque, ou Description des royaumes de Naples et de Sicile*, 5 parts in 4 vols (Paris: Clousier, 1781–6), with 542 engravings; for Denon's text see vol. III, 153–61. The following plates of Paestum were included: 'Vue générale des temples de Pæstum, prise en arrivant du côté du couchant'; 'Vue générale et plus détaillée des trois temples de Pæstum, prise du côté du Levant'; 'Vue du petit temple exastile périptere de Paestum'; Vue intérieures et extérieures du grand temple périptere de Paestum'; 'Coupes, plans & détails des temples de Paestum': vol. III, 153, 156, 157, 158, 160, plates 82–8.

6 On this topic see John Whale, 'Romantics, Explorers and Picturesque Travellers', in Stephen Copley and Peter Garside (eds), *The Politics of the Picturesque: Literature, Landscape and Aesthetics since 1770* (Cambridge: Cambridge University Press, 1994), 175–95. For tourism and the picturesque in Britain see Malcolm Andrews, *The Search for the Picturesque: Landscape Aesthetics and Tourism in Britain, 1760–1800* (Stanford (Cal.): Stanford University Press, 1989).

7 Nikolaus Pevsner, 'Richard Payne Knight', *Art Bulletin*, 31 (December 1949), 300–01; Christopher Hussey, *The Picturesque: Studies in a Point of View*, rev. edn, with a new preface by the author (Hamden (Conn.): Archon Books, 1967) [first published 1927].

8 As early as 1748, in *A dialogue upon the gardens of the Right Honourable the Lord Viscount Cobham, at Stowe in Buckinghamshire* (London: B. Seeley, 1748), William Gilpin wrote about the picturesque as 'that which is suited to pictorial representation'.

9 See, for example, Lord Kames [Henry Home], *Introduction to the Art of Thinking* (Edinburgh: A. Kincaid and J. Bell 1761); Thomas Whately, *Observations on modern gardening* (London: T. Payne, 1770); William Chambers, *A dissertation on oriental gardening* (London: W. Griffin, 1772). In France, Roger de Piles introduced the term *pittoresque* in his *Cours de peinture par principes* (Paris: J. Estienne, 1708); Claude-Henri Watelet wrote the first French treatise on the picturesque garden, *Essai sur les jardins* (Paris: Impr. de Prault, 1774).

10 See also William Gilpin, *Three essays: on picturesque beauty; on picturesque travel; and on sketching landscape: to which is added a poem, on landscape painting* (London: R. Blamire, 1792); Uvedale Price, *A Dialogue on the Distinct Characters of the Picturesque and the Beautiful. In Answer to the Objections of Mr. Knight* (Hereford: s.n., 1801).

11 Gilpin, *Three essays*, 47–8.

12 John Dixon Hunt, *Gardens and the Picturesque: Studies in the History of Landscape Architecture* (Cambridge (Mass.) / London: MIT Press, 1992), 178–9.

13 Hussey, *The Picturesque*, 4–5.

14 Walter John Hipple, *The Beautiful, the Sublime & the Picturesque in Eighteenth-Century British Aesthetic Theory* (Carbondale: Southern Illinois University Press, 1957).

15 John Dixon Hunt and Peter Willis (eds), *The Genius of the Place: The English Landscape Garden, 1620–1820* (London: Paul Elek, 1975); John Dixon Hunt, *The Figure in the Landscape: Poetry, Painting, and Gardening during the Eighteenth Century* (Baltimore: Johns Hopkins University Press, 1976). Sidney K. Robinson's *Inquiry into the Picturesque* (Chicago: University of Chicago Press, 1991) deals mainly with Britain in the eighteenth century and the role of the picturesque in music, poetry, landscape design, painting and politics, with Price and Knight as the main protagonists. A more cultural–historical approach is found in the essays in Copley and Garside (eds), *The Politics of the Picturesque*, focusing on the late eighteenth and nineteenth century. John Dixon Hunt, *The Afterlife of Gardens* (London: Reaktion Books, 2004) is especially interesting for its treatment of experience and movement in gardens.

16 Hunt, *Gardens and the Picturesque*, 243–84; John Dixon Hunt, *The Picturesque Garden in Europe* (London: Thames and Hudson, 2002), 104–39; Dora Wiebenson, *The Picturesque Garden in France* (Princeton (NJ): Princeton University Press, 1978); Caroline van Eck, Jeroen van den Eynde, Wilfred van Leeuwen (eds), *Het schilderachtige: Studies over het schilderachtige in de Nederlandse kunsttheorie en architectuur, 1650–1900* (Amsterdam: Architectura & Natura, 1994).

17 Hunt, 'Beyond Anglomania', in *The Picturesque Garden in Europe*, 140–93.

18 Nikolaus Pevsner, 'The Picturesque in Architecture', *RIBA Journal*, 55 (1947), 55–61; Emil Kaufmann, *Architecture in the Age of Reason: Baroque and Post-Baroque in England, Italy, and France* (Cambridge (Mass.): Harvard University Press, 1955).

19 For a different approach to the picturesque in architecture see Caroline van Eck, *Organicism in Nineteenth-Century Architecture: An Inquiry into its Theoretical and Philosophical Background* (Amsterdam: Architectura & Natura, 1994), 74–83;

Caroline van Eck, *Classical Rhetoric and the Visual Arts in Early Modern Europe* (Cambridge: Cambridge University Press, 2007), 123–6; John Macarthur, *The Picturesque: Architecture, Disgust and other Irregularities* (London / New York: Routledge, 2007).

20 On Price see Andrew Ballantyne, *Architecture, Landscape and Liberty: Richard Payne Knight and the Picturesque* (Cambridge: Cambridge University Press, 1997).

21 Hussey, *The Picturesque*; John Mordaunt Crook, 'The Consequences of the Picturesque', in *The Dilemma of Style: Architectural Ideas from the Picturesque to the Post-Modern* (London: John Murray, 1989) [first published 1987], 13–41.

22 Hussey, *The Picturesque*, 217.

23 Caroll L. V. Meeks, 'Picturesque Eclecticism', *Art Bulletin*, 32 (September 1950), 226–35; Reyner Banham, 'Revenge of the Picturesque: English Architectural Polemics, 1945–1965', in John Summerson (ed.), *Concerning Architecture: Essays on Architectural Writers and Writing Presented to Nikolaus Pevsner* (London: Allen Lane, 1968), 265–73.

24 Meeks argued that these five elements are all in opposition to classicism. Meeks, 'Picturesque Eclecticism', 227–8.

25 Uvedale Price, *Essays on the Picturesque, as Compared with the Sublime and the Beautiful; and, on the Use of Studying Pictures, for the Purpose of Improving Real Landscape*, 3 vols (London: J. Mawman, 1810), vol. I, 37.

26 Ibid., 76. 'I felt that there were numberless objects which give great delight to the eye, and yet differ as widely from the beautiful as from the sublime. The reflections I have since been led to make have convinced me that these objects form a distinct class, and belong to what may properly be called the picturesque.' Ibid., 41. For the difference between the picturesque, the beautiful and the sublime see also ibid., 76, 80–81ff.

27 Uvedale Price, *An essay on the picturesque as compared with the sublime and the beautiful: and on the use of studying pictures, for the purpose of improving real landscape* (London: J. Robson, 1794), 108–9.

28 Ibid., 44–5.

29 Ibid., 111.

30 Price, *Essays on the Picturesque* (1810), vol. I, 51–2.

31 Price, *An essay on the picturesque* (1794), 46.

32 Ibid., 50.

33 William Gilpin, *Observations, relative chiefly to picturesque beauty, made in the year 1772, on several parts of England; particularly the mountains, and lakes of Cumberland, and Westmoreland*, 2 vols (London: R. Blamire, 1786), vol. II, 188.

34 Richard Payne Knight, *An Analytical Inquiry into the Principles of Taste* (London: printed by Luke Hansard for T. Payne and J. White, 1805), 70.

35 Ibid.

36 Ibid., 57.

37 'It may not be amiss for the Architect to take advantage *sometimes* of that to which I am sure the Painter ought always to have his eyes open, I mean the use of accidents: to follow when they lead, and to improve them, rather than always to trust to a regular plan. It often happens that additions have been made to houses, at various times, for use or pleasure. As such buildings depart from regularity, they now and then acquire something of scenery by this accident, which I should think might not unsuccessfully be adopted by an Architect, in an original plan, if it does not too much interfere with convenience.' Joshua Reynolds, Discourse XIII, 1786, in *Discourses* [1797], ed. with an introduction and notes by Pat Rogers (Harmondsworth: Penguin, 1992), 297–8.

38 Pevsner, 'Richard Payne Knight', 293–320; Ballantyne, *Architecture, Landscape and Liberty*, 260–68. We shall come back to this later in the chapter (see pp. 99–102).

39 Charles Barry, travel diary of Rome, London, Royal Institute of British Architects, Drawings and Archives Collection, SKB401/2.

40 Price in 'An Essay on Architecture and Buildings', in *Essays on the Picturesque* (1810), vol. II, 268.

41 Ibid., 186–230.

42 Ibid., vol. I, 349.

43 Reynolds, Discourse XIII, 1786, in *Discourses*, ed. Rogers, 298.

44 Ibid.

45 Price, *Essays on the Picturesque* (1810), vol. II, 212–13.

46 Hunt, *The Afterlife of Gardens*, has a chapter on the role of movement, 145–72. See also van Eck, *Classical Rhetoric*, 233–61; Macarthur, *The Picturesque*.

47 Hussey, *The Picturesque*, 188, 189, 202. On Vanbrugh see Vaughan Hart, *Sir John Vanbrugh: Storyteller in Stone* (New Haven (Conn.): Published for the Paul Mellon Centre for Studies in British Art by Yale University Press, 2008).

48 John Soane, Royal Academy Lecture V, in David Watkin (ed.), *Sir John Soane: Enlightenment Thought and the Royal Academy Lectures* (Cambridge: Cambridge University Press, 1996), 563. Blenheim Palace (1705–24), designed by John Vanbrugh and Nicholas Hawksmoor, is in Oxfordshire.

49 Robert Adam and James Adam, *The Works in Architecture of Robert and James Adam, Esquires* [1778], ed. with an introduction by Robert Oreskó (London: Academy Editions, 1975), 46.

50 Adam and Adam, *The Works in Architecture*, ed. Oreskó, 45–6. According to Mallgrave, 'it is only in the footnotes that we find an articulation of their ideas'. Harry Francis Mallgrave (ed.), *Architectural Theory*, vol. I: *An Anthology from Vitruvius to 1870* (Malden (Mass.): Blackwell, 2006), 287.

51 Price, *Essays on the Picturesque* (1810), vol. I, 331.

52 James Adam, unfinished draft of an essay on architectural theory, written in Rome, November 1762, Edinburgh, H.M. Register House, Clerk of Penicuik collection, quoted in John Fleming, *Robert Adam and his Circle in Edinburgh & Rome* (London: John Murray, 1962), 315–19.

53 'I have seen buildings which without anything to recommend them but merely a considerable degree of this sort of movement, have by that alone been rendered agreeable and even interesting, such is Blenheim and Heriot's Hospital at Edinburgh.' James Adam, unfinished draft of an essay on architectural theory, 1762, quoted in Fleming, *Robert Adam and his Circle*, 316.

54 '[Les tribunes – open arcades overlooking the nave] de Notre Dame a Paris, sont d'une etendue considerable et produisent

un effet surprenant en offrant à la vuë, pour ainsi dire, une seconde eglise, dont la clarté contrastante avec l'espece d'obscurité qui regne dans les dessous, la fait paroître et plus vague et plus elevée, et fait distinguer aux spectateurs comme dans un lointain mille objets qui, tantost perdus, tantost retrouvés, leurs donnent a mesure qu'ils s'en eloignent ou s'en aprochent des spectacles qui les ravissent a eux mêmes.' Jacques-Germain Soufflot, 'Mémoire sur l'architecture gothique', read before the Académie in Lyon, 12 April 1741, in *L'Œuvre de Soufflot à Lyon: Études et documents* (Lyon: Presses Universitaires de Lyon, 1982), 191. On Soufflot see Jean Mondain-Monval, *Soufflot: Sa vie, son œuvre, son esthétique (1713–1780)* (Paris: A. Lemerre, 1918); *Soufflot et son temps: 1780–1980* (Paris: Caisse Nationale des Monuments Historiques et des Sites, 1980); Monique Mosser and Daniel Rabreau (eds), *Soufflot et l'architecture des Lumières* (Paris: École Nationale Supérieure des Beaux-Arts, 1986); Jean-Marie Pérouse de Montclos, *Jacques-Germain Soufflot* (Paris: Monum/Éditions du Patrimoine, 2004). See also Sigrid de Jong, 'Experiencing Architectural Space', in Caroline van Eck and Sigrid de Jong (eds), *Companion to Eighteenth-Century Architecture* (Chichester: Wiley-Blackwell, forthcoming, 2015).

55 'cette partie métaphysique de l'architecture'. Le Roy quoted in Richard Etlin, 'Grandeur et décadence d'un modèle: L'Église Sainte-Geneviève et les changements de valeur esthétique au XVIIIe siècle', in Mosser and Rabreau (eds), *Soufflot et l'architecture des Lumières*, 30; Etlin gives as a reference for the quotation Le Roy's *Lettres choisies* (1792), 64.

56 Robin Middleton, Introduction to Julien-David Le Roy, *The Ruins of the Most Beautiful Monuments of Greece*, 2nd edn [1770], trans. David Britt (Los Angeles: Getty Research Institute, 2004), 141.

57 Lord Kames [Henry Home], 'Gardening and Architecture', in *Elements of Criticism*, 3 vols (Edinburgh: s.n., 1762), vol. III, 313.

58 'Si vous vous promenez dans un jardin, à quelque distance & le long d'une rangée d'arbres plantés réguliérement, dont tous les troncs touchent un mur percé d'arcades ; la situation respective des arbres avec ces arcades, ne vous paroîtra changer que d'une maniere très-insensible, & votre ame n'éprouvera aucune sensation nouvelle, quoique vous ayez parcouru assez vite un espace considérable. Mais si cette rangée d'arbres est éloignée du mur ; en vous promenant de même, vous jouïrez d'un spectacle nouveau, par les différents espaces du mur que les arbres paroîtront, à chaque pas que vous serez, couvrir successivement ... Ainsi, quoique nous ayons supposé le mur décoré réguliérement, & les arbres également éloignés, la premiere des décorations semblera immobile, pendant que l'autre au contraire s'animent en quelque sorte par le mouvement du spectateur, lui présentera une succession de vues très-variées, qui résulteront de la combinaison infinie des objets simples qu'il apperçoit.' Julien-David Le Roy, *Les ruines des plus beaux monuments de la Grèce, considérées du côté de l'histoire et du côté de l'architecture*, 2nd edn, 2 vols (Paris: Louis-François Delatour, 1770), vol. II, p. vii. Eng. trans. in Le Roy, *The Ruins*, trans. Britt, 371.

59 '[une voûte] couronne la colonnade de la manière la plus majestueuse; en ce que les colonnes n'étant pas surchargées par les masses supérieures des voûtes, conservent leur dignité et la grâce qui leur est propre; enfin, en ce que le spectateur éprouveroit à chaque pas, l'effet le plus piquant de l'architecture, ce piquant effet qui naît de ce que nos regards ne sauroient parcourir des objets isolés dont la disposition les présente en divers sens, et d'une manière symétrique, sans que ces objets ne nous semblent se mettre en mouvement avec nous et que nous paroissions leur donner la vie.' Étienne-Louis Boullée, *Architecture: Essai sur l'art*, ed. Jean-Marie Pérouse de Montclos (Paris: Hermann, 1968), 93; Eng. trans. Étienne-Louis Boullée, 'Architecture, Essay on Art', in Helen Rosenau, *Boullée and Visionary Architecture* (London/New York: Academy Editions/Harmony Books, 1976), 93. For more on this topic see de Jong, 'Experiencing Architectural Space'.

60 Arthur Young, *A six months' tour through the North of England, containing an account of the present state of agriculture, manufactures and population in several Counties of this Kingdom*, 2nd edn, 4 vols (London: W. Strahan, 1771), vol. II, 302. For Young see John G. Gazley, *The Life of Arthur Young, 1741–1820* (Philadelphia: American Philosophical Society, 1973).

61 Knight, *An Analytical Inquiry*, 156.

62 'On arrive à Pæstum par un chemin où les amis de la nature en retrouvent toutes les beautés. Rien de plus frais, de plus varié, de plus pittoresque, que les aspects qu'il présente ... comme aussi rien de plus aride, rien de plus triste que Pæstum lui-même.' Auguste Creuzé de Lesser, *Voyage en Italie et en Sicile, fait en 1801 et 1802* (Paris: P. Didot l'aîné, 1806), 195–6.

63 'les peintres peuvent y trouver des études à faire. Nous y avons rencontré des Bufles, animaux horribles et méchans dans un très beau site ils s'étoient plongés tous dans l'eau, ce qui animoit le paysage.' Rohault de Fleury, 'Voyage de l'architecte Rohault de Fleury en Italie, 1804–1805', 4 vols, Paris, Bibliothèque Nationale de France, Département des Manuscrits, NAF 23696, vol. II, 153.

64 'Les Peintres y trouveront également differents points de vüe fort interessants, soit par ses differentes ouvertures, soit par la varieté des plantes champetres, qui l'environnent de toutes parts; ou bien par celle de plusieurs troupeaux de diverses couleurs, que les Bergers y conduisent.' Giovanni Battista Piranesi, *Différentes vues de ... Pesto*, text on plate X.

65 'quelques-uns même de ces Auteurs, semblent n'être allés à Pæstum que par simple curiosité, ou dans le dessein d'y faire un dîné pittoresque'. Claude-Mathieu Delagardette, *Les Ruines de Paestum, ou Posidonia, ancienne ville de la grande Grèce ... levées, mesurées et dessinées ... en l'an II* (Paris: l'auteur, an VI [1798]) [prospectus for forthcoming publication], 2.

66 Mariana Starke, *Letters from Italy, between the Years 1792 and 1798* (London: R. Philips, 1800), 140. Starke was an English author who wrote poetry, plays and travelogues. Besides *Letters from Italy*, her other travel books include *Travels on the Continent* (1820); *Information and Directions for Travellers on the Continent* (1824); *Travels in Europe for the Use of Travellers on the Continent and Likewise in the Island of Sicily, to which is Added an Account of the Remains of Ancient Italy* (1832).

67 Marguerite, Countess of Blessington, *Lady Blessington at Naples*, ed. Edith Clay, introduction by Harold Acton (London: Hamish Hamilton, 1979), 90. George Howard recited the poem, which was 'so admirable, and so spirited, as to convey an impression, that it must have been written on the spot, and under the inspiration of the actual scene'. The idea that Paestum – the site and the temples – functioned as a stage will be discussed in Chapter 4.

68 'Ces ruines ont un attrait peut-être dangereux pour les architectes: leur forme pittoresque, le caractère d'abandon et même de désolation que porte le pays qui les environne, frappent, au premier abord, trop puissamment les regards; souvent on ne résiste pas au désir de dessiner les vues pittoresques, et ces vues, faites à la hâte et inexactement, dans lesquelles le caractère de fermeté de l'architecture, étant outré, devient lourd et vicieux, perpétuent des erreurs, malheureusement accréditées dans les écoles.' Henri Labrouste, *Les Temples de Paestum: Restauration exécutée en 1829 par Henri Labrouste*, Restaurations des Monuments Antiques par les Architectes Pensionnaires de l'Académie de France à Rome, vol. III (Paris: Firmin-Didot, 1877), 3. See Chapter 5 for Labrouste, and Chapters 5 and 6 for Delagardette.

69 Publications by Knight include: *An Account of the Remains of the Worship of Priapus* (London: T. Spilsbury, 1786); *An analytical essay on the Greek alphabet* (London: P. Elmsly, 1791); the poems *The Landscape: A didactic poem, in three books. Addressed to Uvedale Price* (London: W. Bulmer and Co., 1794), and *The progress of civil society: A didactic poem* (London: G. Nicol, 1796); *An Analytical Inquiry* (1805); *Carmina Homerica, Ilias et Odyssea* (London: G. Bulmer, 1808); *An Inquiry into the Symbolical Language of Ancient Art and Mythology* (London: privately printed, 1818).

70 On Knight see Ballantyne, *Architecture, Landscape and Liberty*. For essays on his theories and different aspects of his life and work see Michael Clarke and Nicolas Penny (eds), *The Arrogant Connoisseur: Richard Payne Knight, 1751–1824* (Manchester: Manchester University Press, 1982). Pevsner, 'Richard Payne Knight', 293–320, drew attention for the first time to Knight's journal and published the text (in his own English translation of Goethe's German translation). See also Jean-Jacques Mayoux, *Richard Payne Knight et le pittoresque: Essai sur une phase esthétique* (Paris: Presses Modernes, 1932); Susan Lang, 'Richard Payne Knight and the Idea of Modernity', in Summerson (ed.), *Concerning Architecture*, 85–97; Frank J. Messmann, *Richard Payne Knight: The Twilight of Virtuosity* (The Hague / Paris: Mouton, 1974), on Downton and the Grand Tour pp. 13–36.

71 Ballantyne, *Architecture, Landscape and Liberty*; Bruce Redford, *Dilettanti: The Antic and the Antique in Eighteenth-Century England* (Los Angeles: J. Paul Getty Museum / Getty Research Institute, 2008), contains a chapter on Knight's journey.

72 Richard Payne Knight, *Expedition into Sicily*, ed. Claudia Stumpf (London: British Museum Publications, 1986).

73 Knight had inherited a large part of the family fortune through his uncle Richard Knight, which financed his Grand Tour to France and Italy in 1772–3. A third visit to Italy would follow in 1785.

74 Cozens's Swiss sketches are in the collection of the British Museum. On Cozens see C. F. Bell and T. Girtin, *The Drawings and Sketches of John Robert Cozens*, Walpole Society, vol. XXIII (Oxford: printed for the Walpole Society by John Johnson at the University Press, 1935); A. P. Oppé, *Alexander and John Robert Cozens* (London: A. & C. Black, 1952); Francis W. Hawcroft, *Watercolours by John Robert Cozens* (Wilmslow (Cheshire): Richmond Press, 1971); Francis W. Hawcroft, 'Grand Tour Sketchbooks of John Robert Cozens, 1782–1783', *Gazette des Beaux-Arts*, 91 (March 1978), 99–106; Andrew Wilton, *The Art of Alexander and John Robert Cozens* (New Haven (Conn.): Yale Center for British Art, 1980).

75 Knight and Hackert might have met in 1772 on Knight's first trip to Naples. Hackert worked from 1770 for the Neapolitan court and was appointed court painter in 1786. They travelled at a time when royal permission was needed to draw the sites on Sicilian territory; Knight wrote of their being arrested for drawing a watchtower, and of Hackert's saving them from detention by showing letters of recommendation from the royal court. Hackert's watercolours of Sicily survive in the bequest of Knight in the British Museum, and there are views in German collections. Prince August von Sachsen-Gotha-Altenburg admired the finished watercolours of the Sicilian voyage when he saw them in Hackert's studio on 6 December 1777; see Stumpf, Introduction to Knight, *Expedition into Sicily*, 30 n. 59, 113. Only one of Hackert's drawings of Paestum has been preserved (in a private collection).

76 Bell and Girtin, and Oppé suggested that Knight and Cozens had quarrelled: Bell and Girtin, *The Drawings and Sketches*, 11; Oppé, *Alexander and John Robert Cozens*, 112. Messmann, *Richard Payne Knight*, 29 n. 75, suggested that Cozens stayed in Rome for financial reasons.

77 They left Naples on 12 April; on the 13th they were in Paestum. From there Knight listed the places on their itinerary as follows: 'Porto Palinuro – Stromboli – Lipari – Milazzo – Tindaro – Aquadolce – Cefalu – Termini – Himera – La Bagaria – Palermo – Montreale – Aegesta [Segesta] – Selinus – Sciacca – Girgenti [Agrigento] – Alicata – Biscari – Syracuse – Catania – Aetna – Aci Reale – Taormina – Messina – Naples'.

78 Charles Gore's sketches of the tour are in the Department of Prints and Drawings of the British Museum, London; watercolour drawings show the temples and ruins in Agrigento, Selinunte, Segesta and Syracuse, and also the islands of Stromboli and Procida and Mount Etna (LB 1–20). On Gore's record of the tour see Alexander Rosenbaum, 'Charles Gores Reisealbum *Voyage de Sicile 1777*', *Zeitschrift für Kunstgeschichte*, 69 (2006), 17–36. Knight's diary is preserved in the Goethe–Schiller Archiv in Weimar (see note 82 below), along with 112 sketches and watercolours by Gore (Th. Scr. 2.2³ ff.).

79 The drawings collection in the Victoria and Albert Museum in London holds a drawing of Paestum by Cozens, but this is from a trip he made in 1782 and not from Knight's visit. Knight probably wrote up the final version of his diary after his return to England, and in 1782 he gave Hackert's and Gore's watercolours to Thomas Hearne to make definitive

illustrations. Gore possibly took with him a copy of Knight's diary as a souvenir of their trip when he moved to Weimar in 1792.

80 John Dryden, *A voyage to Sicily and Malta . . . in the years 1700 and 1701* (London: J. Brew, 1776); Jacques Philippe d'Orville, *Jacobi Philippi d'Orville Sicula, quibus Siciliae veteris rudera . . . illustrantur*, 2 vols (Amsterdam: G. Tielenburg, 1764); Patrick Brydone, *A tour through Sicily and Malta, in a series of letters to William Beckford*, 2 vols (London: W. Strahan and T. Cadell, 1773); J. H. von Riedesel, *Reise durch Sicilien und Grossgriechenland* (Zurich: Orell, Gessner, Füesslin & Co., 1771).

81 Arnaldo Momigliano, 'The Rediscovery of Greek History in the Eighteenth Century: The Case of Sicily', *Studies in Eighteenth-Century Culture*, 9 (1979), 167–187. See also Arnaldo Momigliano, 'Ancient History and the Antiquarian', *Journal of the Warburg and Courtauld Institutes*, 13 (1950), 285–315; Hélène Tuzet, *La Sicile au XVIIIe siècle vue par les voyageurs étrangers* (Strasbourg: P. H. Heitz, 1955).

82 A handwritten copy of Knight's diary, 120 pages long and entitled 'Expedition into Sicily', is in the Goethe–Schiller Archiv in Weimar. Unfortunately it is not clear who wrote the manuscript: the handwriting is not Knight's, and the copy is not dated. As Claudia Stumpf has shown, a letter by Goethe (Weimar, 15 January 1810, Goethe–Schiller Archiv, xlix, 3.6) is in the same hand, and she suggests it is that of Goethe's secretary; see Claudia Stumpf, 'The "Expedition into Sicily"', in Clarke and Penny (eds), *The Arrogant Connoisseur*, 112 n. 8. Goethe translated parts of Knight's diary into German and published them in 1810 in a biography of his friend Hackert; ibid., 19–31. Knight himself, who wrote many books and often moved from one subject to another, was already preoccupied with another topic a few years after the trip. The second part of the diary, a sociological reflection on the people of Sicily, represents a clear break with the more archaeological content of the first part, and may have been written up several years after the expedition took place. In his long exposé Knight stated how, after the degeneration of Latin as a language, taste was destroyed, and he wrote about the purity of antiquity. See Knight, *Expedition into Sicily*, ed. Stumpf, 30–31. Goethe left the general passage on the Sicilian people out of his translation (Stumpf, 'The "Expedition into Sicily"', 113 n. 65). In 1949 Pevsner translated into English the parts of the journal that Goethe published; Pevsner, 'Richard Payne Knight', 311–20. Hussey refers to the diary (*The Picturesque*, 124 n. 1), referring to the disappearance of the original English version. Thomas Weidner argues that Stumpf's 'Entdeckerfreude' is exaggerated, because others had written about the diary before; see Weidner, *Jakob Philipp Hackert: Landschaftsmaler im 18. Jahrhundert* (Berlin: Deutscher Verlag für Kunstwissenschaft, 1998), 201 n. 28.

83 Knight bequeathed his collection of antiquities and drawings to the British Museum in London (Department of Prints and Drawings, O.0.4-(2–41); it included 39 drawings from the Sicilian expedition, some by Gore and Hackert, others copied from their originals by Cozens and Hearne. Knight returned to England in 1778 and may have had the Sicilian

watercolours with him, or Gore may have kept them and taken them back to England in 1779. Gore's Sicilian views, 112 watercolours and sketches with annotations, are in the Goethe-Nationalmuseum in Weimar, Th. Scr. 2.2.3. See Rosenbaum, 'Charles Gores Reisealbum', 17–36.

84 Unless otherwise indicated, all quotations from Knight's account of his Sicilian expedition are from pp. 26–66 of the handwritten copy of his travel diary in the Goethe–Schiller Archiv in Weimar. The voyage from Naples, the journey to Paestum, and Knight's experiences at the site are described on pp. 26–9.

85 Knight owned an edition of the *Georgics* of 1746. See *Catalogue of a Select Portion of the Valuable Library of John Crosse . . . and a Portion of the Library of the Late Richard Payne Knight* (London: s.n., 1829), lot 743: 'Virgili Opera, Burmanni 1746'.

86 'Round the groves of Silarus and the green holm oaks of Alburnus swarms a fly, whose Roman name is *asilus*, but the Greeks have called it in their speech *oestrus* [the gadfly]. Fierce it is, and sharp of note; before it whole herds scatter in terror through the woods: with their bellowings the air is stunned and maddened, the groves, too, and the banks of parched Tanager.' Virgil, *Georgics*, III. 146–51, in Virgil, *Eclogues, Georgics, Aeneid i–vi*, trans. H. Rushton Fairclough, rev. G. P. Goold (Cambridge (Mass.) / London: Harvard University Press 1999), 186–7.

87 Knight, *Expedition into Sicily*, ed. Stumpf, 29. 'Besides the three Temples, there are the foundations of a small Amphitheatre, and considerable remains of the City Walls, within which the ground is all overspread with broken Columns and other fragments of ruined Edifices, which show the former magnificence of this ancient City. Among these one may trace the Ruins of a small Temple of a very singular kind. It stood between the great Temple or (as others suppose) the Basilica, and the Amphitheatre and appears to have been of the usual Doric form. The Columns are fluted in the Corinthian manner, with interstices between the flutes, and the Capitals are of the same order, but very rude and simple. The entablature is Doric, but more charged with Members than that of the other buildings of Paestum. Between the Trigliffs are basso rilievos, the design of which appears to have been pure and elegant, but they are so corroded and mutilated in the small fragments which remain, that one cannot judge of the execution. Whether this Temple was built before the perfection of the Corinthian order, or after its decline, is uncertain. I am inclined to think the former for many reasons. The Corinthian order does not appear from any monuments extant, to have been perfected before the time of Augustus, nor to have declined till that of the Antonines. As for the Story of its having been invented by an Architect of Corinth, from seeing an Acanthus, growing round a basket of flowers, it deserves little attention.' Ibid., 28–9.

88 'The City of Paestum must have been in a state of decay long before the corruption, or even perfection of the Corinthian order, as Strabo mentions its being deserted and unhealthy in his time, and it is never spoken of as a place of any importance by the Historians of the Roman Wars in Italy.' Ibid., 29. Of the existing publications Dumont, Major,

Longfield and Grosley, for example, refer to Strabo: Dumont, *Suitte* [*Suite*] *de Plans*; [Longfield,] *The ruins of Poestum or Posidonia*; Dumont, *Les ruines de Paestum, autrement Posidonia*; Pierre-Jean Grosley, *Observations sur l'Italie et sur les italiens, données en 1764, sous le nom de 'Deux gentilshommes suédois'* (London: s.n., 1770). The original passage in Strabo reads as follows: 'the Poseidonian Gulf . . . is now called the Paestan Gulf; and the city of Poseidonia, which is situated in the centre of the gulf, is now called Paestus. The Sybaritae, it is true, had erected fortifications on the sea, but the settlers removed them farther inland; later on, however, the Leucani took the city away from the Sybaritae, and, in turn, the Romans took it away from the Leucani. But the city is rendered unhealthy by a river that spreads out into the marshes in the neighbourhood.' Strabo, *Geography*, 5.4.13, in *The Geography of Strabo*, trans. Horace Leonard Jones (Cambridge (Mass.) / London: Harvard University Press, 1988), vol. II, 469.

89 For Major's references to Strabo, see *The ruins of Paestum, otherwise Posidonia*, 13. '. . . were I not . . . about to furl my sails . . . I might sing . . . of Paestum whose rose beds bloom twice yearly', Virgil, *Georgics*, IV. 119, in Virgil, *Eclogues, Georgics, Aeneid i–vi*, trans. Fairclough, rev. Goold. 'I have seen rose-beds of fragrant Paestum that promised enduring bloom lying withered by the scirocco's morning blast', Propertius IV. 5. 59, in Propertius, *Elegies*, ed. and trans. G. P. Goold (Cambridge (Mass) / London: Harvard University Press, 1990). 'Let his forehead be low and his nostrils not too large and slightly aquiline, let his red lips vie with the roses of Paestum', Martial IV. 42. 9. '. . . whose breath was fragrant as a Paestan rose bed or new honey', Martial, V. 37. 9. '. . . the charm of fragrant Flora, so splendid the glory of the Paestan countryside', Martial, VI. 80. 6. 'Whether you were born in Paestum's fields', Martial, IX. 60. 1. Martial, *Epigrams*, ed. and trans. D. R. Shackleton Bailey, 2 vols (Cambridge (Mass.) / London: Harvard University Press, 1993).

90 'The Buildings of the lower ages of Rome, when Architecture was corrupted, are also in a different Stile from that above mention'd. The Romans being Masters of the World, and having the rich quarries of Africa, Greece and Sicily, at their command, never imployed so much work upon so coarse a Material; But the Greek Republics being confined to a small place, were obliged to use whatever Material their own territory produced.' Knight, *Expedition into Sicily*, ed. Stumpf, 29. Knight's view is similar to Piranesi's, as we shall see in Chapter 5.

91 'The exact time of the rise or fall of Paestum is not known, tho' both were probably very early. Its remains owe their preservation to the pestiferous quality of the Air, for had the place been habitable, they would have shared the fate of most of the works of the Greeks and Romans, and have been pulled in pieces, in order to imploy the materials in modern edifices . . . This poisonous air is produced by a salt stream, which flows from the mountains and stagnates under the Walls, where it petrifies and forms the kind of Stone of which the City was built. The petrification is extremely rapid, and some have supposed, that the Columns were cast in molds, as they consist of reeds, rushes etc. petrified

by this Water; but I am inclined to think this opinion ill-founded.' Ibid.

92 'The city was quadrangular, as appears by the Walls, which seem formerly to have been washed by the Sea, though now (owing to the petrifying stream) they are upwards of 500. yards distant from it. The new ground is very distinguishable from the old, being all nude petrification of Saltmarsh, whereas the old soil, within the Walls, and between them and the Mountains, is dry and fertile, worthy of the rosaria Paesti, so celebrated by the Roman Poets.' Ibid. Virgil's text reads: 'In fact, were I not, with my task well-nigh done, about to furl my sails and making haste to turn my prow to land, perchance I might sing what careful tendance clothes rich gardens in flower, and might sing of Paestum whose rose beds bloom twice yearly, how the endive rejoices in drinking streams, the verdant banks in celery; how the cucumber, coiling through the grass, swells into a paunch. Nor should I have passed in silence the late-flowering narcissus, the twining tendril of the acanthus, pale ivy sprays, or the shore-loving myrtle.' Virgil, *Georgics*, IV. 116–24, in Virgil, *Eclogues, Georgics, Aeneid i–vi*, trans. Fairclough, rev. Goold, 226–7.

93 Knight, *Expedition into Sicily*, ed. Stumpf, 31.
94 Ibid., 43.
95 Ibid., 59–60.
96 'I could not measure, not being able to procure a Ladder.' Ibid., 39.
97 Ibid., 38.
98 Ibid., 40.
99 Soon after his arrival in Rome, Knight was already preoccupied with the need to verify his thinking by reference to his library at home: 'you will excuse inaccuracies and remember, that I write as a traveller without books and memorandums', he wrote to the painter George Romney on 24 November 1776; John Romney, *Memoirs of the Life and Works of George Romney, Including Various Letters, and Testimonies to his Genius, &c.* (London: Baldwin and Cradock, 1830), 332. The suggestion by Stumpf (Knight, *Expedition into Sicily*, ed. Stumpf, 15) that these plans to publish an illustrated volume about the journey were abandoned a few years later because Knight was deterred by the appearance in the 1780s of a number of grand folios, has never been proved. Abbé Jean-Claude Richard de Saint-Non's five-part *Voyage pittoresque, ou Description des royaumes de Naples et de la Sicile* appeared in Paris from 1781 to 1786; Ignazio Paternò Castello, Prince of Biscari, a scholar and collector, published a travel guide to the antiquities of Sicily in 1781; and Jean-Pierre-Louis-Laurent Houël's *Voyage pittoresque des Isles de Sicile, de Malte et de Lipari* appeared in Paris in 1782–7 in four volumes. For more on Knight's abandoning his project to publish his travel diary, see Stumpf's introduction to Knight, *Expedition into Sicily*, 30–31.

100 Two of Cozens's Grand Tour sketchbooks, 1782–3, are now in the Whitworth Art Gallery in Manchester; see Clarke and Penny (eds), *The Arrogant Connoisseur*, 162–3. During that tour he worked as a draughtsman for William Beckford (1759–1844), author and patron; see Oppé, *Alexander and John Robert Cozens*; Kim Sloan, *Alexander and John Robert Cozens:*

The Poetry of Landscape (New Haven (Conn.) / London: Yale University Press, 1986); John Ingamells, *A Dictionary of British and Irish Travellers in Italy, 1701–1800* (New Haven (Conn.) / London: Published for the Paul Mellon Centre for Studies in British Art by Yale University Press, 1997), 249. There are six watercolours of Paestum by Cozens in the Whitworth Art Gallery in Manchester, of which three are reproduced here (Figs 57, 58, 60): *The Ferry between Eboli and Paestum*, 7 November 1782; *The Three Temples at Paestum*, 7 November 1782; *The Temple of Neptune and the Basilica at Paestum*, 7 November 1782; *View of the Temple of Neptune and the Basilica at Paestum*, 1782; *The Small Temple at Paestum*, 1782; *The Small Temple at Paestum*. Another is in the Victoria and Albert Museum, London (Fig. 59), and two more are in the Gallery Oldham (see Figs 61, 62).

101 On light in Cozens's paintings see Isabelle von Marschall, *Zwischen Skizze und Gemälde: John Robert Cozens (1752–1797) und das englische Landschaftsaquarell* (Munich: Scaneg, 2005).

102 Knight, *Expedition into Sicily*, ed. Stumpf, 29.

103 Cozens was in Paestum on 7 November 1782. Three drawings, of the small temple (Ceres), of the 'two great temples' and of the three temples, were part of the Beckford collection and are listed (without images) in *Catalogue of a Collection of Drawings by John Robert Cozens with some Decorative Furniture and other Objects of Art* (London: Burlington Fine Arts Club, n.d. [1923]), 22–23. The catalogue describes the last drawing as showing: 'Dark stormy sky with heavy cumulus clouds.' See also note 100.

104 Richard Payne Knight, *The Landscape: A didactic poem, in three books*, 2nd edn (1795), 19.

105 David Hume, 'Of the Standard of Taste', in *Four Dissertations* (1757), quoted in Mallgrave (ed.), *Architectural Theory*, vol. I, 271.

106 For example, Gilpin, *Observations, relative chiefly to picturesque beauty*.

107 '. . . the recollection or conception of *other* objects which are associated in our imaginations with those before us'. [Francis Jeffrey] (published anonymously), 'Essay on Beauty', review of Archibald Alison, *Essays on the nature and principles of taste*, in *Edinburgh Review*, 18 (May 1811), 3.

108 See van Eck, *Organicism in Nineteenth-Century Architecture*, 74–83, which also deals with the role of rhetoric; Caroline van Eck, '"The splendid effects of architecture, and its power to affect the mind": The Workings of Picturesque Association', in Jan Birksted (ed.), *Landscapes of Memory and Experience* (London: Spon Press, 2000), 245–58.

109 For example, Knight attacked Burke for his ideas on the sublime in these terms: 'But, to say nothing of [the] assumed connection between the causes of pain and the ideas of the sublime, the slightest knowledge of optics would have informed him that the sheet of paper, upon which he was writing, seen thus close to the eye, reflected a greater, and more forcible mass of light; and, consequently, produced more irritation and tension, than the Peak of Teneriffe or Mount St. Elias would, if seen at the distance of a few miles: – yet, surely he would not say that the sheet of paper excited more grand and perfect ideas of the sublime.' Knight, *An Analytical Inquiry*, 60. In another passage, he remarked that

Burke was a 'respectable' man, with a 'sublime character', without anyone being in 'awe' of him: 'If . . . he had suddenly appeared among the mangers in Westminsterhall without his wig and coat; or had walked up St. James's street without his breeches, it would have occasioned great and universal *astonishment*; and if he had, at the same time, carried a loaded blunderbuss in his hand, the astonishment would have been mixed with no small portion of *terror*: but I do not believe that the united effects of these powerful passions would have produced any sentiment or sensation approaching to sublime, even in the breasts of those, who had the strongest sense of self-preservation, and the quickest sensibility of danger.' Ibid., 380–81.

110 'Of the Sublime and the Pathetic', ibid., 315–409.

111 Ibid., 371.

112 Ibid., 377. Knight also wrote about the sublime in his letter to the painter George Romney, published in Romney, *Memoirs of the Life*, 321–32.

113 Knight, *An Analytical Inquiry*, 54.

114 Ibid., 145–6.

115 Ibid., 146.

116 Ibid.

117 Ibid.

118 Ibid., 68. In a footnote Knight wrote: 'According to Mr. Price, however, beauty, even in architecture, implies the freshness of youth; or, at least, a state of high and perfect preservation; and buildings are mouldered out of beauty into *picturesqueness.*' Ibid.

119 Ibid., 151.

120 Ibid., 152.

121 Ibid., 195.

122 Knight, *The Landscape* (1794), 64–5, ll. 257–60.

123 Ibid., 14–15, ll. 233–6.

124 Ibid., 35, ll. 242–7.

125 Ibid., 12, ll. 193–6.

126 '. . . a Doric fireplace, its columns modelled specifically on those at Paestum, but without their ruggedness, a much higher degree of finish being appropriate to their tamed domestic setting'. Ballantyne, *Architecture, Landscape and Liberty*, 32–3, also 259. For an image of this chimney piece see Michael Clarke, Nicholas Penny (ed.), *The Arrogant Connoisseur*, 37 (plate 19) and see my 'Rediscovering Architecture: Paestum in Eighteenth-Century Architectural Experience and Theory', unpublished PhD thesis, Leiden University, 2010, 185, fig. 2.25.

127 Knight, *An Analytical Inquiry*, 220–21.

128 Humphry Repton, *Fragments on the Theory and Practice of Landscape Gardening, Including some Remarks on Grecian and Gothic Architecture* (London: s.n., 1816), 157. On Repton see André Rogger, *Landscapes of Taste: The Art of Humphry Repton's Red Books* (London / New York: Routledge, 2007).

129 Knight, *The Landscape*, 36–37, ll. 268–87.

130 Soane, Royal Academy Lecture X, in Watkin (ed.), *Sir John Soane*, 169. Soane further stated: 'In our parks and gardens, on the contrary, they [reproductions of Greek and Roman temples] stand wholly unconnected with all that surround them – mere unmeaning excrescences; or, what is worse, manifestly meant for ornament, and therefore having no

accessory character, but that of ostentatious vanity: so that, instead of exciting any interest, they vitiate and destroy that, which the naturalized objects of the country connected with them would otherwise excite. Even if the landscape scenery should be rendered really beautiful by such ornaments, its beauty will be that of a vain and affected coquette; which, though it may allure the sense, offends the understanding; and, on the whole, excites more disgust than pleasure.' Ibid., 170.

131 Knight, *An Analytical Inquiry*, 169.

132 Ibid., 221.

133 Ibid., 160.

134 Ballantyne, *Architecture, Landscape and Liberty*, 288.

135 Knight, *An Analytical Inquiry*, 221.

136 For example, James Wyatt's Fonthill Abbey (1795–1807) for William Beckford, or John Nash's East Cowes Castle (1789), his own house.

137 On Strawberry Hill see Michael Snodin, *Horace Walpole's Strawberry Hill* (New Haven (Conn.) / London: Yale University Press, 2009).

138 See Lang, 'Richard Payne Knight and the Idea of Modernity'; Lang also writes about Knight's ideas on style.

Chapter 3

1 'Denn im architektonischen Aufriß erscheinen sie eleganter, in perspektivischer Darstellung plumper, als sie sind, nur wenn man sich um sie her, durch sie durch bewegt, teilt man ihnen das eigentliche Leben mit; man fühlt es wieder aus ihnen heraus, welches der Baumeister beabsichtigte, ja hineinschuf. Und so verbrachte ich den ganzen Tag, indessen Kniep nicht säumte, uns die genausten Umrisse zuzueignen.' Johann Wolfgang von Goethe, *Italienische Reise [1786–8]* [1829] (Munich: Wilhelm Goldmann Verlag, 1988), 206; Eng. trans. in Johann Wolfgang von Goethe, *Italian Journey [1786–8]*, trans. W. H. Auden and Elizabeth Mayer (London: Penguin, 1970) [first published 1962], 218.

2 John Soane, Royal Academy Lecture V, in David Watkin (ed.), *Sir John Soane: Enlightenment Thought and the Royal Academy Lectures* (Cambridge: Cambridge University Press, 1996), 557. Christopher Woodward gives a Romantic twist to this situation: 'Tired of wandering through the columns which lie scattered in the dust like giant, chopped celery, the tall, skinny youth stretched out inside a flute to rest. For the next fifty years his life was a heroic struggle to measure himself against the grandeur of antiquity.' Christopher Woodward, *In Ruins* (London: Chatto & Windus, 2001), 176.

3 'Les colonnes etoient si grosses qu'un homme pouvoit se cacher dans une des cannelures au raport de Diodore de Sicile.' Jean Rondelet, letter to the Comte d'Angiviller, Rome, 25 February 1784, published in Robin Middleton and Marie-Noëlle Baudouin-Matuszek, *Jean Rondelet: The Architect as Technician* (New Haven (Conn.) / London: Yale University Press, 2007), 313.

4 Thomas Whately, *Observations on modern gardening* (London: T. Payne, 1770), 131–2, 155.

5 Constantin-François de Volney, *Les ruines, ou Méditations sur les révolutions des empires* [1791], in *Observations générales sur les Indiens, Les ruines . . .* [1791] (Paris: Coda, 2009). On ruins in eighteenth-century thought see Roland Mortier, *La Poétique des ruines en France: Ses origines, ses variations de la Renaissance à Victor Hugo* (Geneva: Droz, 1974), esp. chapters 'Diderot: Créateur et théoricien d'une "poétique des ruines"', 88–106, and 'Les Ruines de Volney: Une philosophie rationaliste de l'histoire', 136–41; Nina L. Dubin, *Futures & Ruins: Eighteenth-Century Paris and the Art of Hubert Robert* (Los Angeles: Getty Research Institute, 2010); John A. Pinto, *Speaking Ruins: Piranesi, Architects, and Antiquity in Eighteenth-Century Rome* (Ann Arbor: University of Michigan Press, 2012). For the aesthetics of ruins and the ideas of Volney see Sophie Lacroix, *Ce que nous disent les ruines: La Fonction critique des ruines* (Paris: L'Harmattan, 2007). For a more philosophical approach see Sophie Lacroix, *Ruine* (Paris: Éditions de la Villette, 2008). See also Rose Macaulay, *Pleasure of Ruins* (London: Thames and Hudson, 1984) [first published 1953]. For the appeal of ruins for artists see Brian Dillon, *Ruin Lust: Artists' Fascination with Ruins from Turner to the Present Day* (London: Tate Publishing, 2014).

6 Lacroix, *Ce que nous disent les ruines*, 200–02.

7 'Souvent je rencontrais d'antiques monuments, des débris de temples, de palais et de forteresses; des colonnes, des aqueducs, des tombeaux - et ce spectacle tourna mon esprit vers la méditation des temps passés, et suscita dans mon coeur des pensées graves et profondes.' Volney, *Les ruines*, 51; Eng. trans. in *Volney's Ruins, or Meditation on the Revolutions of Empires. Translated, under the Immediate Inspection of the Author, from the Latest Paris Edition* (New York: G. Vale, 1853).

8 Edward Gibbon, *Miscellaneous works . . . With Memoirs of his life and writings . . . illustrated from his letters*, 2 vols (London: A. Strahan and T. Cadell jun., 1796), vol. I, 129. Gibbon was referring to his *History of the Decline and Fall of the Roman Empire*, 6 vols (London: s.n., 1776–88). On Gibbon see Harold Bond, *The Literary Art of Edward Gibbon* (Oxford: Clarendon Press, 1960).

9 'Les idées que les ruines réveillent en moi sont grandes. Tout s'anéantit, tout périt, tout passe. Il n'y a que le monde qui reste. Il n'y a que le temps qui dure. Qu'il est vieux ce monde! Je marche entre deux éternités'. [Denis] Diderot, *Salons III: Ruines et paysages: Salons de 1767*, ed. Else Marie Bukdahl, Michel Delon and Annette Lorenceau (Paris: Hermann, 1995), 338. For a biography of Diderot see Arthur McCandless Wilson, *Diderot: Sa vie et son œuvre* (Paris: Laffont, 1985). For Diderot and ruins see Jean Seznec, *Essais sur Diderot et l'antiquité* (Oxford: Clarendon Press, 1957).

10 Diderot wrote about the Salons of 1759, 1761, 1763, 1765, 1767, 1769, 1771, 1775 and 1781. On the Salons see Else Marie Bukdahl, *Diderot, critique d'art*, 2 vols (Copenhagen: Rosenkilde and Bagger, 1980); Philippe Dean, *Diderot devant l'image* (Paris / Montreal: L'Harmattan, 2000); Jean-Christophe Abramovici, Pierre Frantz, Jean Goulemot and Frédéric Calas, *Diderot: Salons* (Neuilly: Atlande, 2007); Denis Diderot, *Écrits sur l'art et les artistes*, ed. Jean Seznec, new edn with introductory texts by Jean Starobinski, Michel Delon and Arthur Cohen (Paris: Hermann, 2007) [first published 1967]; Stéphane Lojkine, *L'Œil révolté: Les 'Salons' de Diderot* (Paris

/ Arles: J. Chambon / Actes Sud, 2007); Pierre Frantz and Élisabeth Lavezzi (eds), *Les 'Salons' de Diderot: Théorie et écriture* (Paris: PUPS, Université Paris-Sorbonne, 2008).

11 On Robert see Dubin, *Futures & Ruins*. On his designs and depictions of gardens see Jean de Cayeux, *Hubert Robert et les jardins* (Paris: Éditions Herscher, 1987). On his reactions to the French Revolution see Catherine Boulot, *Hubert Robert et la Révolution* (Valence: Musée de Valence, 1989).

12 'L'obscurité seule, la majesté de l'édifice, la grandeur de la fabrique, l'étendue, la tranquillité, le retentissement sourd de l'espace m'aurait fait frémir. Je n'aurais jamais pu me défendre d'aller rêver sous cette voûte, de m'asseoir entre ces colonnes, d'entrer dans votre tableau.' Diderot, *Salons III: Ruines et paysages*, ed. Bukdahl, Delon and Lorenceau, 338.

13 'Si le lieu d'une ruine est périlleux, je frémis. Si je m'y promets le secret et la sécurité, je suis plus libre, plus seul, plus à moi, plus près de moi.' Ibid., 339.

14 'Dans cet asile désert, solitaire et vaste, je n'entends rien ; j'ai rompu avec tous les embarras de la vie. Personne ne me presse et ne m'écoute. Je puis me parler tout haut, m'affliger, verser des larmes sans contrainte.' Ibid., 339.

15 Richard Sennett, *The Fall of Public Man* (London: Penguin Books, 2002) [first published 1974], 98.

16 'L'effet de ces compositions, bonnes ou mauvaises, c'est de vous laisser dans une douce mélancolie. Nous attachons nos regards sur les débris d'un arc de triomphe, d'un portique, d'une pyramide, d'un temple, d'un palais; et nous revenons sur nous-mêmes; nous anticipons sur les ravages du temps; et notre imagination disperse sur la terre les édifices mêmes que nous habitons. A l'instant la solitude et le silence règnent autour de nous. Nous restons seuls de toute une nation qui n'est plus. Et voilà la première ligne de la poétique des ruines.' Diderot, *Salons III: Ruines et paysages*, ed. Bukdahl, Delon and Lorenceau, 335.

17 'Il faut ruiner un palais pour en faire un objet d'interêt.' Ibid., 348.

18 The *Vue imaginaire* is only one of a number of such paintings that Robert produced: see Marie-Catherine Sahut, *Le Louvre d'Hubert Robert* (Paris: Éditions de la Réunion des Musées Nationaux, 1979), and Stéphanie Thuilliez, 'La Poétique de la variété: Les Ruines et la terre', *Bulletin de l'Association des Historiens de l'Art Italien*, 2 (1996), 26–33.

19 Jean-Claude Richard de Saint-Non, *Panopticon italiano: Un diario di viaggio ritrovato, 1759–1761*, ed. Pierre Rosenberg (Rome: Ed. dell'Elefante, 2000).

20 Robert's Paestum drawings were sold in Paris on 22 June 1933, without having been being photographed. The Musée des Beaux-Arts in Rouen and the Archives de Besançon each hold a single drawing of Paestum by Robert, as does the Pierpont Morgan Library in New York; ibid., 284 n. 218. For Saint-Non's diary notes on Paestum, see ibid., 12–14. See also Pinto, *Speaking Ruins*. For Joli see Chapter 4.

21 These drawings, of which three are reproduced here (Figs 74–6), are published in Petra Lamers, *Il viaggio nel sud dell'Abbé de Saint-Non: Il 'Voyage pittoresque à Naples et en Sicile': La genesi, i disegni preparatori, le incisioni* (Naples: Electa, 1995), 356–9.

22 Saint-Non's *Voyage pittoresque* also contained engravings after drawings by other architects and artists; see Chapter 2, pp. 68–9. See also Lamers, *Il viaggio*.

23 On Gandy see Brian Lukacher and Desmond Hill, *Joseph Michael Gandy, 1771–1843* (London: Architectural Association, 1982); Brian Lukacher, 'Joseph Michael Gandy: The Poetical Representation and Mythography of Architecture', unpublished PhD thesis, University of Delaware, 1987; Brian Lukacher, 'Joseph Gandy and the Mythography of Architecture', *Journal of the Society of Architectural Historians*, 53 (1994), 280–99; Brian Lukacher, *Joseph Gandy: An Architectural Visionary in Georgian England* (London: Thames and Hudson, 2006).

24 John Summerson named the Bank of England Soane's key project, and praised it as showing 'the most original architectural language in Europe at that moment'. John Summerson, *Architecture in Britain, 1530–1830* (New Haven (Conn.) / London: Yale University Press, 1993) [first published 1953], 435.

25 For a discussion of Soane's possible motives in commissioning an image of his project in a ruined state see *Visions of Ruin: Architectural Fantasies & Designs for Garden Follies, with Crude Hints towards a History of my House by John Soane* (London: Sir John Soane's Museum, 1999), 28–9.

26 John Soane, letter to John Horsley Palmer, Governor of the Bank of England, 8 April 1833, London, Sir John Soane's Museum, Personal Correspondence, XIV/J/1.2; quoted in Margaret Richardson and MaryAnne Stevens (eds), *John Soane, Architect: Master of Space and Light* (London: Royal Academy of Arts, 1999), 210.

27 The Four and Five Per Cent Office was designed and built in 1793–7, the Rotunda in 1794–5.

28 *The Times* (1 May 1925), published in Christopher Woodward, *In Ruins* (London: Chatto & Windus, 2001), 163.

29 On constructed ruins see David Watkin, 'Built Ruins: The Hermitage as a Retreat', and Christopher Woodward, 'Scenes from the Future', in *Visions of Ruin*, 5–14, 15–17.

30 John Soane, account of the 'ruins' at Pitshanger Manor, headed 'Ealing / June 1802', London, Sir John Soane's Museum, SM AL Soane Case 31.

31 John Soane, manuscript on Pitshanger Manor, London, Sir John Soane's Museum, Library, Soane Case 170, fols 134–5, quoted in Watkin (ed.), *Sir John Soane*, 187–8.

32 Soane owned two copies of the French translation of *Hypnerotomachia Poliphili* (1546), and a copy of the reprint of the first edition (1545). In seventeenth-century France the work was very influential; see Anthony Blunt, 'The Hypnerotomachia Poliphili in 17th-century France', *Journal of the Warburg Institute*, 1 (1937–8), 117–37. For Soane's own translation of part of the work and his marginal notes in one of his copies, see Watkin (ed.), *Sir John Soane*, 246–8. See also John Dixon Hunt, *The Afterlife of Gardens* (London: Reaktion Books, 2004), 57–76.

33 'Crude Hints towards an History of my House in L[incoln's] I[nn] Fields', 1812, London, Sir John Soane's Museum, SM AL Soane Case 31; ed. as *Crude Hints towards a History of my House*, in *Visions of Ruin*', 61–74. The words 'crude hints'

appear often in the early drafts of Soane's Royal Academy lectures, where they mean 'rough draft'.

34 Soane, *Crude Hints*, 64.

35 Ibid., 69.

36 Ibid., 72.

37 Ibid.

38 Ibid., 73.

39 In yet another version of the ending, Soane writes '. . . from my almost paralysed hand'. Ibid., 74.

40 'Ce matin à 5 heures nous partons pour Paestum; pays triste, désert, marais, air lourd; à 10 heures nous arrivons à Paestum. Les trois temples de Cérès; celui de Neptune, et la basilique; heureuse proportion du temple de Cérès; celui de Neptune est un peu lourd; colonnes trop recherchées dans la basilique; je dessine le temple de Neptune; air pesant, soleil, je ne suis pas à mon aise.' Eugène-Emmanuel Viollet-le-Duc, *Lettres d'Italie, 1836–1837, adressées à sa famille*, ed. Geneviève Viollet le Duc (Paris: Léonce Laget, 1971), 372. Viollet-le-Duc visited Paestum on 24 July 1836.

41 'Le temple de Neptune est supérieurement construit, tous trois sont d'une pierre remplie de cavités et fort dure; quelques portions stuquées existent encore.' Ibid.

42 'Les colonnes grecques n'avoient pas coutume d'écraser le sol; elles montoient avec légéreté dans les airs; elles s'élançoient: celles-ci, au contraire, s'affaissent avec pesanteur sur la terre; elles tombent. Les colonnes grecques avoient une taille élégant et svelte, autour de laquelle le regard fuyoit toujours; celles-ci ont une taille évasée et pesante, autour de laquelle les yeux ne sauroient tourner: nos crayons et nos burins, qui flattent tous les monumens, ont cherché vainement à l'amincir.' Charles-Marguerite-Jean-Baptiste Mercier Dupaty, *Lettres sur l'Italie en 1785*, 2 vols (Paris: De Senne, 1788), 196–7; Eng. trans. in Charles-Marguerite-Jean-Baptiste Mercier Dupaty, *Travels through Italy, in a series of letters; written in the year 1785, by President Dupaty. Translated from the French by an English Gentleman* (London: G. G. J. and J. Robinson, 1788), 324.

43 'Denn im architektonischen Aufriß erscheinen sie eleganter, in perspektivischer Darstellung plumper, als sie sind, nur wenn man sich um sie her, durch sie durch bewegt, teilt man ihnen das eigentliche Leben mit; man fühlt es wieder aus ihnen heraus, welches der Baumeister beabsichtigte, ja hineinschuf.' Goethe, *Italienische Reise*, 206; Eng. trans. in Goethe, *Italian Journey*, trans. Auden and Mayer, 218.

44 'Nun sind unsere Augen und durch sie unser ganzes inneres Wesen an schlankere Baukunst hinangetrieben und entschieden bestimmt, so daß uns diese stumpfen, kegelförmigen, enggedrängten Säulenmassen lästig, ja furchtbar erscheinen.' Goethe, *Italienische Reise*, 205; Eng. trans. in Goethe, *Italian Journey*, trans. Auden and Mayer, 218.

45 Harry Francis Mallgrave and Eleftherios Ikonomou (eds), *Empathy, Form, and Space: Problems in German Aesthetics, 1873–1893* (Santa Monica (Cal.): Getty Center for the History of Art and the Humanities, 1994), 91–2.

46 'Doch nahm ich mich bald zusammen, erinnerte mich der Kunstgeschichte, gedachte der Zeit, deren Geist solche Bauart gemäß fand, vergegenwärtigte mir den strengen Stil der Plastik, und in weniger als einer Stunde fühlte ich mich befreundet, ja ich pries den Genius, daß er mich diese so wohl erhaltenen Reste mit Augen sehen ließ, da sich von ihnen durch Abbildung kein Begriff geben läßt.' Goethe, *Italienische Reise*, 205–6; Eng. trans. in Goethe, *Italian Journey*, trans. Auden and Mayer, 218.

47 'Here we left the carriage, and waded to a lone cottage-inn, where thieves and thief-catchers often meet to negotiate. Some of the latter, being fortunately there, lent us their mules and escorted us to Pæstum. On arriving at the Sele, we found more mules waiting for the ferry-boat. These when embarked, grew so furious that some of the passengers caught hold of ropes and stood ready to plunge into the river. The rage of those wicked brutes seemed contagious, as if excited by the gad-fly, which ever since Virgil's time has infested these banks.' Joseph Forsyth, *Remarks on Antiquities, Arts, and Letters, during an Excursion in Italy in the Years 1802 and 1803* (London: T. Cadell and W. Davies, 1813), 339. On Forsyth see the Introduction to Joseph Forsyth, *Remarks on Antiquities, Arts, and Letters during an Excursion in Italy, in the Years 1802 and 1803*, ed. Keith Crook (Newark: University of Delaware Press, 2001), pp. xi–lxiii.

48 Forsyth, *Remarks on Antiquities*, 339.

49 Baldine Saint Girons, *Fiat lux: Une philosophie du sublime* (Paris: Quai Voltaire, 1993), 42–9.

50 Forsyth, *Remarks on Antiquities*, 343.

51 Ibid., 341.

52 Forsyth, *Remarks on Antiquities*, 4th edn (London: John Murray, 1835), n. 319.

53 Forsyth, *Remarks on Antiquities* (1813), 341–2. Forsyth calls the third 'structure', 'still more singular' and the stone 'probably formed at Paestum itself, by the brackish water of the Salso acting on vegetable earth, roots and plants; for you can distinguish their petrified tubes in very column.'

54 Shelley's letters from Italy were published after his death by Mary Shelley in *Essays, Letters from Abroad: Translations and Fragments*, 2 vols (London: E. Moxon, 1840). They have received little attention from scholars, but see Alan M. Weinberg, *Shelley's Italian Experience* (London: Macmillan, 1991); Benjamin Colbert, *Shelley's Eye: Travel Writing and Aesthetic Vision* (Aldershot (Surrey): Ashgate, 2005).

55 Eustace died of malaria in Naples in 1815, never having completed his tour. Sir Richard Colt Hoare later wrote *A Classical Tour through Italy and Sicily, Tending to Illustrate some Districts, which have not been Described by Mr Eustace, in his Classical Tour* (London: s.n., 1819).

56 John Chetwode Eustace, *A Tour through Italy, Exhibiting a View of its Scenery, its Antiquities, and its Monuments, Particularly as they are Objects of Classical Interest and Elucidation*, 2 vols (London: J. Mawman, 1813), vol. II, 27.

57 Ibid., vol. II, 17. He wrote: 'Of all the objects that lie within the compass of an excursion from Naples, *Pæstum*, though the most distant, is perhaps the most curious and most interesting. In scenery, without doubt, it yields, not only to *Baia* and *Puteoli*, but to every town in the vicinity of the *Crater*; but in noble and well preserved monuments of antiquity it surpasses every city in Italy, her immortal capital Rome alone

excepted' (vol. II, 9). He further reflected on the rediscovery of Paestum: 'That it was not much visited, we know, but this was owing rather to the indifference than to the ignorance of the learned, and perhaps a little to the state of the country, ever lawless and unsafe while under the domination of absent sovereigns. We are too apt to conclude, that nobody had seen what we did not see, and that what travellers have not recorded, was not known to exist; without reflecting that the ignorance of the latter is often the consequence of the little acquaintance which many of them have with the language and natives of the countries they undertake to describe' (vol. II, 10).

58 Ibid., vol. II, 24. Eustace also referred to measurements taken by William Wilkins, and to the columns being covered by stucco (vol. II, 26). We shall return to Wilkins in Chapter 6.

59 Ibid., vol. II, 24. He continued: 'It was now dusk, and on our entrance into the bishop's villa we found a plentiful repast, and excellent wines waiting our arrival. Our beds and rooms were all good, and every thing calculated to make our visit to *Pæstum* as agreeable in its accompaniments as it was interesting in its object.'

60 Ibid., vol. ii, 18.

61 Ibid., vol. II, 16–17.

62 Ibid., vol. II, 19–20.

63 Ibid., vol. II, 21–2.

64 Percy Bysshe Shelley, *The Letters of Percy Bysshe Shelley*, ed. Frederick L. Jones, 2 vols (Oxford: Clarendon Press, 1964), vol. II, 59.

65 Colbert, *Shelley's Eye*, 179–82. In his description of the Coliseum in *Prometheus Unbound* (1819) Shelley emphasised the fact that the 'marble wilderness' of the Coliseum is 'sublime' and 'impressive' precisely because it is a ruin; see Shelley, *The Letters*, ed. Jones, vol. II, 59. In his poem *Childe Harold's Pilgrimage*, Byron described the Coliseum as 'This long-explored but still exhaustless mine / Of contemplation', Canto IV, 128, ll. 1162–3. See Carolyn Springer, *The Marble Wilderness: Ruins and Representation in Italian Romanticism, 1775–1850* (Cambridge: Cambridge University Press, 1987).

66 Shelley, *The Letters*, ed. Jones, vol. II, 87–8.

67 Ibid., vol. II, 85. Written upon the 'mountainous ruins' of Caracalla, Shelley's verse drama *Prometheus Unbound* (1819) mingled his impressions of Rome and Naples; see, for example, Act III, Scene iv, ll. 111–21, in *The Poems of Shelley*, ed. Kelvin Everest and Geoffrey Matthews, vol. II (1817–1819) (Harlow: Longman, 2000), 604–5.

68 Shelley, *The Letters*, ed. Jones, vol. II, 74–5. According to Jones, Shelley invented the word 'upaithric', from the Greek adjective *hupaithrios* ('open to the air', 'having no roof').

69 Ibid., vol. II, 73.

70 'I employed my mornings . . . in translating the Symposium, which I accomplished in ten days.' Shelley, letter to Thomas Love Peacock, 25 July 1818, in ibid., vol. II, 26; Colbert, *Shelley's Eye*, 133.

71 Colbert, *Shelley's Eye*, 191.

72 Preface to *Hellas* (1821), in *Shelley's Poetry and Prose: Authoritative Texts, Criticism*, selected and ed. Donald H. Reiman and Neil Fraistat (New York / London: W. W. Norton & Company,

2002), 431. 'I have been reading scarcely anything but Greek, and a little Italian poetry with Mary.' Shelley, letter to Thomas Love Peacock, 25 July 1818, in *The Letters*, ed. Jones, vol. II, 26.

73 *Shelley's Poetry and Prose*, ed. Reiman and Fraistat, 520; see also Colbert, *Shelley's Eye*, 145.

74 Shelley, letter to Thomas Love Peacock, Naples, 25 February 1819, in *The Letters*, ed. Jones, vol. II, 79.

75 Ibid.

76 Ibid.

77 Cammy Brothers, *Michelangelo: Drawing and the Invention of Architecture* (New Haven (Conn.): Yale University Press, 2008), 189–91; Brothers did not rely on contemporary (sixteenth-century) experiences but analysed the building from the perspective of bodily experience, referring to Wölfflin's *Prolegomena* (at p. 190 n. 52)

78 Brothers, *Michelangelo*, 190.

79 'Körperliche Formen können charakteristisch sein nur dadurch, daß wir selbst einen Körper besitzen . . . Als Menschen aber mit einem Leibe, der uns kennen lehrt, was Schwere, Kontraktion, Kraft usw. ist, sammeln wir an uns die Erfahrungen, die uns erst die Zustände fremder Gestalten mitzuempfinden befähigen . . . Wir haben Lasten getragen und erfahren, was Druck und Gegendruck ist . . . und darum wissen wir das stolze Glück einer Säule zu schätzen und begreifen den Drang allen Stoffes, am Boden formlos sich auszubreiten.' Heinrich Wölfflin, *Prolegomena zu einer Psychologie der Architektur* (Berlin: Mann, 1999) [first published 1886], 9; Eng. trans. in Mallgrave and Ikonomou (eds), *Empathy, Form, and Space*, 151.

80 Joseph Rykwert, *The Dancing Column: On Order in Architecture* (Cambridge (Mass.) / London: MIT Press, 1996).

81 'Sie können uns nur das mitteilen, was wir selbst mit ihren Eigenschaften ausdrücken.' Wölfflin, *Prolegomena*, 10; Eng. trans. in Mallgrave and Ikonomou (eds), *Empathy, Form, and Space*, 152.

82 '. . . mit unserer körperlichen Organisation mitmachen . . . Mit der bestimmten Erstreckung und Bewegung unseres Körpers ist ein Wohl- und Wehegefühl verbunden, das wir als eigentümlichen Genuß jener Naturgestalten selber auffassen.' Wölfflin, *Prolegomena*, 11; Eng. trans in Mallgrave and Ikonomou (eds), *Empathy, Form, and Space*, 153.

83 '"Zählen des Auges" zu sein, wesentlich in einem unmittelbaren körperlichen Gefühl beruhe.' Wölfflin, *Prolegomena*, 12–13; Eng. trans in Mallgrave and Ikonomou (eds), *Empathy, Form, and Space*, 155.

84 'Just as the human mind is sufficiently active to be reminded of something by seeing something similar, it is also sufficiently occupied with, directed toward, and conscious of itself to find everywhere resemblances between external things and its own mental states, experiences, sensations [*Empfindungen*], moods, emotions, and passions. It finds in everything a counterpart to itself and a symbol of its humanity.' ('Wie der menschliche Geist lebendig genug ist, um durch Aehnliches an Aehnliches erinnert zu wrden, so ist er auch stark genug mit sich selber beschäftigt, auf sich selber gerichtet, sein selber sich bewusst, um namentlich Aehn-

lichkeiten äusserer Dinge mit seinen eigenen Zuständen, Erlebnissen, Empfindungen, Stimmungen, Affekten, Leidenschaften überall wahrzunehmen, in Allem sich ein Gegenbild von sich, ein Symbol des Menschlichen wiederzufinden.') Robert Vischer, *Über das optische Formgefühl: Ein Beitrag zur Aesthetik* (Leipzig: Hermann Credner, 1873), p. vi; Eng. trans. in Mallgrave and Ikonomou (eds), *Empathy, Form, and Space*, 91–2. From Karl Albert Scherner's book *Das Leben des Traum* (1861) Vischer derived the idea that the body 'consciously projects its own bodily form – and with this also the soul – into the form of the object. From this I derived the notion that I call [*Einfühlung*].' ('Es ist also ein unbewusstes Versetzen der eigenen Leibform und hiermit auch der Seele in die Objektsform. Hieraus ergab sich mir der Begriff, den ich Einfühlung nenne.') Vischer, *Über das optische Formgefühl*, p. vii; Eng. trans. in Mallgrave and Ikonomou (eds), *Empathy, Form, and Space*, 91–2.

85 'das stolze Glück eine Säule . . . den Drang alles Stoffes, am Boden formlos sich auszubreiten'. Wölfflin, *Prolegomena*, 9; Eng. trans. in Mallgrave and Ikonomou (eds), *Empathy, Form, and Space*, 151.

Chapter 4

1 David Watkin (ed.), *Sir John Soane: Enlightenment Thought and the Royal Academy Lectures* (Cambridge: Cambridge University Press, 1996), 188 (Lecture V).

2 Most publications on theatre and architecture concentrate on buildings. For example, *Victor Louis et le théâtre: Scénographie, mise en scène et architecture théâtrale aux XVIIIe et XIXe siècles* (Paris: Éditions du Centre National de la Recherche Scientifique, 1982); Daniel Rabreau, 'The Theatre-Monument: A Century of "French" Typology, 1750–1850', *Zodiac*, 2 (September 1989), 44–69; Briant Hamor Lee, *European Post-Baroque Neoclassical Theatre Architecture* (Lewiston (NY): E. Mellen, 1996); Daniel Rabreau, *Le Théâtre de l'Odéon: Du monument de la nation au Théâtre de l'Europe: Naissance du monument de loisir urbain au XVIIIe siècle* (Paris: Belin, 2007); Daniel Rabreau, *Apollon dans la ville: Essai sur le théâtre et l'urbanisme à l'époque des Lumières* (Paris: Éditions du Patrimoine / Centre des Monuments Nationaux, 2008). The interesting exception is Louise Pelletier, *Architecture in Words: Theatre, Language and the Sensuous Space of Architecture* (London: Routledge, 2006).

3 See Sigrid de Jong, 'Staging Ruins: Paestum and Theatricality', *Art History*, 33/2 (April 2010) [special issue], 334–51; Sigrid de Jong, 'Staging Ruins: Paestum and Theatricality', in Caroline van Eck and Stijn Bussels (eds), *Theatricality in Early Modern Art and Architecture* (Chichester: Wiley-Blackwell, 2011), 134–151. See that volume for more on the role of theatricality in the arts.

4 The interior of the Neptune temple (see Fig. 99e) was the backdrop for 'Sçene Vme. du IIme Acte de la Tragédie de Philotecte'; the caption of the image of the Basilica (see Fig. 104d) reads: 'Vestiges de l'intérieur d'un Temple ou Basilique de l'ancienne ville de Pœstum tels qu'ils existoient en 1750. Pirrhus seul dans la Sçene premiere de l'Acte V. de la Tragédie de Philotecte.' *Catalogue de l'Œuvre des gravures d'architecture de*

Dumont, architecte à Paris (Paris, 1775), unnumbered plates [24, 25]. The Académie Royale added an endorsement to this publication, congratulating Dumont for bringing the temples of Paestum to public notice: 'M. Dumont a mis au jour des Plans et Elévations des Temples de Pœstum ou Possidonia . . . qui sont d'autant plus importants pour l'Architecture qu'ils donnent connoissance de l'ordre Dorique dans des tems plus rapprochés de son origine.'

5 On the decors or temporary structures Pâris designed for royal feasts see Alain-Charles Gruber, *Les Grandes Fêtes et leurs décors à l'époque de Louis XVI* (Geneva: Droz, 1972); on his designs for the court in general see Alain-Charles Gruber, *L'Œuvre de Pierre-Adrien Pâris à la cour de France, 1779–1791* (Paris: F. De Nobele, 1974). On Pâris and antiquity see Pierre Pinon, *Pierre-Adrien Pâris (1745–1819), architecte, et les monuments antiques de Rome et de la Campanie* (Rome: École Française de Rome, 2007).

6 Marc-Henri Jordan, 'L'Érudition et l'imagination: Les Décors de scène', in *Le Cabinet de Pierre-Adrien Pâris: Architecte, dessinateur des menus-plaisirs* (Besançon / Paris: Musée des Beaux-Arts et d'Archéologie de Besançon / Hazan, 2008), 68–81.

7 Jordan also named Paestum as an inspiration for the stage set of *Iphigénie en Tauride*, ibid.,72.

8 For *Oedipe à Colone* by Antonio Sacchini (premiere 1786), Pâris designed a 'temple rustique' and a 'temple antique des Euménides', both rather primitivist. We shall address some of the issues regarding the role of nature in ideas on the origins of architecture and on primitivism in Chapter 5.

9 Roland Barthes, 'Diderot, Brecht, Eisenstein', in *Image, Music, Text*, essays selected and trans. Stephen Heath (London: Fontana Press, 1977), 69: 'The theatre is precisely that practice which calculates the place of things *as they are observed*: if I set the spectacle here, the spectator will see this; if I put it elsewhere, he will not, and I can avail myself of this masking effect and play on the illusion it provides. The stage is the line which stands across the path of the optic pencil, tracing at once the point at which it is brought to a stop and, as it were, the threshold of its ramification. Thus is founded – against music (against the text) – *representation*.'

10 For Joli see Ralph Toledano, *Antonio Joli: Modena, 1700–1777, Napoli* (Turin: Artema, 2006); the entire series of paintings of Paestum is reproduced on pp. 390–401. See also Mario Manzelli, *Antonio Joli: Opera pittorica* (Venice: Studio LT2, 2000); Roberto Middione, *Antonio Joli* (Soncino (Cremona): Edizioni dei Soncino, 1995).

11 A *veduta* is a realistic, detailed picture of a town scene with buildings of interest; the genre is represented by eighteenth-century Italian artists such as Canaletto, Guardi and Piranesi (*Oxford English Dictionary*).

12 The painting is in oil on canvas (76 × 102 cm), Caserta, Palazzo Reale, inv. 314 [1905]. As for many of Joli's stage-set designs, it is not known for which opera this design was created, but Manzelli believed it could be a design for a lyric opera (*Antonio Joli*, 134); Toledano dated the painting between 1762 and 1777, but denied that it was for a stage set (*Antonio Joli*, 102). See also Middione, *Antonio Joli*, 39–42. Riccardo Lattuada, however, believed it to be a stage design,

dated it *c.*1760–70, and entitled it 'Un'esedra dorica in rovina, aperta su navate a volta' (in *Antonio Joli tra Napoli, Roma e Madrid: Le vedute, le rovine, i capricci, le scenografie teatrali* (Naples: Edizioni Scientifiche Italiane, 2012)).

13 A capriccio is a drawing, or painted or engraved composition, combining features of imaginary and real architecture, ruined or intact, in a picturesque setting. In its fantastic character it is the opposite of the *veduta* (see *Grove Art Online*).

14 See Giuseppe Galli Bibiena, *Architectural and Perspective Designs* [1740] (New York: Dover Publications, 1964).

15 Filippo Morghen, untitled [*Sei vedute delle rovine di Pesto*] (Naples: s.n., n.d. [1765]); repr. in *Le antichità di Pozzuoli, Baja e Cuma, incise in rame* (Naples: s.n., 1769); [John Longfield] (published anonymously), *The ruins of Poestum or Posidonia, containing a description and views of the remaining antiquities, with the ancient and modern history, inscriptions, etc.* (London: s.n., 1767); Thomas Major, *The ruins of Paestum, otherwise Posidonia, in Magna Graecia* (London: s.n., 1768); Gabriel-Pierre-Martin Dumont, *Les ruines de Paestum, autrement Posidonia, ville de l'ancienne grande Grèce, au Royaume de Naples: ouvrage contenant l'histoire ancienne & moderne de cette ville, la description & les vues de ses antiquités, ses inscriptions, &c.: avec des observations sur l'ancien Ordre Dorique*, partly based on [John Longfield], *The ruins of Poestum*, trans. Jacques Varenne de Béost (London / Paris: C.-A. Jombert, 1769). Joli's paintings were used for other travelogues as well: for example, Jérôme de La Lande, *Voyage d'un françois en Italie, fait dans les années 1765 et 1766, contenant l'histoire & les anecdotes les plus singulieres de l'Italie, & sa description, les mœurs, les usages, le gouvernement, le commerce, la littérature, les arts, l'histoire naturelle, & les antiquités*, 8 vols and atlas (Paris: Chez Desaint, 1769); Jean Barbault, *Recueil de divers monumens anciens répandus en plusieurs endroits de l'Italie* (Rome: Bouchard et Gravier, 1770).

16 Giovanni Battista Piranesi, *Différentes vues de quelques restes de trois grands édifices qui subsistent encore dans le milieu de l'ancienne ville de Pesto, autrement Possidonia qui est située dans la Lucanie* (Rome: s.n., 1778); Paolo Antonio Paoli, *Paesti, quod Posidoniam etiam dixere, rudera: Rovine della città di Pesto, detta ancora Posidonia* (Rome: [in typographio Paleariniano], 1784); Claude-Mathieu Delagardette, *Les Ruines de Paestum, ou Posidona, ancienne ville de la Grande-Grèce* (Paris: l'auteur / H. Barbou, an VII [1799])

17 The eleven pictures by Joli (see Toledano, *Antonio Joli*, 390–401) are: (1) Perspective view of the three temples from the south-east (three variants), possibly commissioned by Lord Brudenell, now in the collection of the Duke of Buccleuch and Queensberry, Bowhill, Selkirk, Scotland, and private collection (ibid., 390–93) (Figs 93a–c); (2) Bird's-eye perspective view of the three temples from the west (two variants), Norton Simon Art Foundation, Pasadena, California, and private collection (ibid., 394–5) (Figs 91a, b); (3) Perspective view of the façades seen from the south, private collection, formerly in the collection of Sir James Gray and then that of his brother Major-General George Gray (ibid., 396) (Fig. 94a); (4) Perspective view through the gate from the east (two variants), private collection, one formerly in the collection of Sir James Gray (ibid., 398–9) (Figs 92a, b); (5)

Perspective view of the Temple of Ceres from the west, private collection (ibid., 401) (Fig. 106a); (6) Interior perspective of the Temple of Neptune from the south-west, Palazzo Reale, Caserta (ibid., 400) (Fig. 98a); (7) Interior perspective of the Temple of Neptune from the east, private collection (ibid., 397) (Fig. 100a). Morghen ([1765] 1769) published nos 2, 3, 5 and 6 (engravings dated 1765); Longfield (1767) nos 2, 3 and 5; Major (1768) nos 2, 3 and 4; Dumont (1769) no. 2; La Lande (1769) no. 2; Barbault (1770) nos 2, 3, 5 and 7.

18 Another cultural agent in Naples was Count Felice Gazzola, officer at the Neapolitan court, who was one of the first visitors to Paestum after its rediscovery in 1740. The drawings made on his request at the time by Gian Battista Natali and Gaetano Magri were shown to Jacques-Germain Soufflot before his visit to Paestum in 1750, and were used in Major's and Paoli's publications; see Paoli, *Paesti . . . rudera: Rovine della città di Pesto*, 4–7. Susan Lang, 'The Early Publications of the Temples at Paestum', *Journal of the Warburg and Courtauld Institutes*, 13 (1950), 48–64; Michael McCarthy, 'New Light on Thomas Major's "Paestum" and Later English Drawings of Paestum', in Joselita Raspi Serra (ed.), *Paestum and the Doric Revival, 1750–1830* (Florence: Centro Di, 1986), 47–50.

19 'This view was taken in Presence of his Excellency Sir James Gray, and engraved from a fine Painting in the Collection of Major General Gray.' Major, *The ruins of Paestum, otherwise Posidonia*, 43 (referring to plates II and III); see Toledano, *Antonio Joli*, 396, 398. For Sir James Gray see John Ingamells, *A Dictionary of British and Irish Travellers in Italy, 1701–1800* (New Haven (Conn.) / London: Published for the Paul Mellon Centre for Studies in British Art by Yale University Press, 1997), 424.

20 The Yale Center for British Art at New Haven (Conn.) holds Bruce's collection of Paestum drawings (C27 Sh2 B1944.14.8493–8512), of which five are reproduced in this chapter (Figs 97b, 99c, 102b, 104c, 105b), and his travel diary (C27 Sh3).

21 See, for example, Janine Barrier, *Les Architectes européens à Rome, 1740–1765: La Naissance du goût à la grecque* (Paris: Monum / Éditions du Patrimoine, 2005).

22 Quoted in Watkin (ed.), *Sir John Soane*, 372–3.

23 Nicholas Savage, 'Shadow, Shading and Outline in Architectural Engraving from Fréart to Letarouilly', in Caroline van Eck and Edward Winters (eds), *Dealing with the Visual: Art History, Aesthetics and Visual Culture* (Aldershot (Surrey): Ashgate, 2005), 248.

24 James Stuart and Nicholas Revett, *The antiquities of Athens measured and delineated by James Stuart F.R.S. and F.S.A. and Nicholas Revett painters and architects*, 4 vols (vol. II ed. W. Newton, vol. III ed. W. Reveley, vol. IV ed. J. Woods) (London: John Nichols, 1762–1816); Robert Wood, *The ruins of Palmyra, otherwise Tedmor, in the desart* (London: s.n., 1753); Robert Wood, *The ruins of Balbec, otherwise Heliopolis, in Coelosyria* (London: s.n., 1757); Julien-David Le Roy, *Les ruines des plus beaux monuments de la Grèce* (Paris: H. L. Guérin et L. F. Delatour, 1758; 2nd edn 1770); Robert Adam, *Ruins of the Palace*

of the Emperor Diocletian at Spalatro, London: printed for the author, 1764).

25 Robin Middleton, Introduction to Julien-David Le Roy, *The Ruins of the Most Beautiful Monuments of Greece*, 2nd edn [1770], trans. David Britt (Los Angeles: Getty Research Institute, 2004), 103–4.

26 'parcourons des yeux toute l'étendue du péristyle du Louvre, en marchant le long des maisons qui lui font face; éloignons-nous-en pour en saisir l'ensemble; approchons-nous-en d'assez près pour découvrir la richesse de son plafond, de ses niches, de ses médaillons: saisissons le moment où le soleil y produit encore les effets les plus piquants, en faisant briller quelques parties du plus grand éclat, tandis que d'autres couvertes d'ombres les font ressortir: combien la magnificene du fond de ce péristyle, combinée de mille façons différentes, avec le contour agréable des colonnes qui sont devant, & avec la maniere dont il est éclairé, ne nous offriront-ils pas de tableaux enchanteurs!' Julien-David Le Roy, *Les ruines des plus beaux monuments de la Grèce, considérées du côté de l'histoire et du côté de l'architecture*, 2nd edn, 2 vols (Paris: Louis-François Delatour, 1770), vol. II, p. viii; Eng. trans. in Le Roy, *The Ruins*, trans. Britt, 372.

27 '. . . the plot, by which I mean the ordering of the particular actions'. Aristotle, *Poetics*, 1450a–1451a; Eng. trans. in D. A. Russell and M. Winterbottom (eds), *Ancient Literary Criticism: The Principal Texts in New Translations* (s.l. [London]: Clarendon Press, 1972), 97–101.

28 Aristotle, *Poetics*, 1411b; Eng. trans. in Russell and Winterbottom (eds), *Ancient Literary Criticism*, 24ff.

29 On the parallels between looking at a building and watching a play see van Eck, *Classical Rhetoric and the Visual Arts in Early Modern Europe* (Cambridge: Cambridge University Press, 2007), 127–34.

30 'Lorsque nous nous en approchons, un spectacle different nous affecte; l'ensemble de la masse nous échappe, mais la proximité où nous sommes des colonnes nous en dédommage; et les changements de lieu, sont plus frappans, plus rapides et plus varies. Mais si le spectateur entre sous le peristyle même, un spectacle tout nouveau s'offre à ses regards, à chaque pas qu'il fait, la situation des colonnes avec les objets qu'il découvre en dehors du peristyle varie, soit que ce qu'il découvre soit un paisage, ou la disposition pitoresque des maisons d'une ville, ou la magnificence d'un intérieur.' Le Roy, *Les ruines* (1770), vol. II, p. viii; Eng. trans. in Le Roy, *The Ruins*, trans. Britt, 372.

31 'Chaque piece doit avoir son caractere particulier. L'analogie, le rapport des proportions decident nos sensations; une piece fait désirer l'autre, cette agitation occupe & tient en suspens les esprits, c'est un genre de jouissance qui satisfait.' Nicolas Le Camus de Mézières, *Le Génie de l'architecture, ou L'Analogie de cet art avec nos sensations* (Paris: l'auteur, 1780), 45; Eng. trans. in Nicolas Le Camus de Mézières, *The Genius of Architecture, or The Analogy of that Art with our Sensations* [1780], introduction by Robin Middleton, trans. David Britt (Santa Monica (Cal.): Getty Center for the History of Art and the Humanities, 1992), 88. See also Pelletier, *Architecture in Words*.

32 'C'est par le grand ensemble qu'on attire & que l'on fixe l'attention; c'est lui seul qui peut intéresser tout à la fois & l'ame & les yeux. Le premier coup d'œil doit nous frapper, il enchaîne nos sens; les détails, les masses de la décoration, les profils, les jours conduisent à ce but. Les grandes parties, la pureté des profils, des jours ni trop vifs ni trop sombres, de beaux percés, les masses bien cadencées, beaucoup d'harmonie annoncent la grandeur & la magnificence.' Le Camus de Mézières, *Le Génie de l'architecture*, 64; Eng. trans. in Le Camus de Mézières, *The Genius of Architecture*, trans. Britt, 96.

33 Richard Payne Knight, *Expedition into Sicily*, ed. Claudia Stumpf (London: British Museum Publications, 1986), 28.

34 'Cette ville est située à un demi mille du bord de la mer, et adossée à une chaîne de belles montagnes. Ce qui fait un très bel aspect quand on se recule assez pour jouir d'un coup d'œil des trois monuments, rien n'est tel que de monter au haut de la tour sur le bord de la mer, en face le grand Temple.' Antoine-Laurent-Thomas Vaudoyer, 'Voyage de Rome à Poestum et tout le Royaume de Naples', 1787, 123, Paris, private collection.

35 Major's collection of drawings is now in Sir John Soane's Museum in London, together with his publication. Soane obtained the whole set in 1800. Thomas Major, 'The Original Drawings for a Work Intituled the Ruins of Paestum or Posidonia Engraved by T. Major 1768', London, Sir John Soane's Museum, Drawings Collection, Vol. 27; Thomas Major, *The ruins of Paestum, otherwise Posidonia, in Magna Graecia* (London: T. Major, 1768), London, Sir John Soane's Museum, Drawings Collection, Vol. 28.

36 La Lande, *Voyage d'un françois en Italie*, 8 vols and atlas; in the atlas La Lande published mainly city plans of towns in Italy, some views of Rome, and one of Paestum. The first edition of 1769 contained twenty-three plates relating to the different volumes; the second edition of 1786 had thirty-six.

37 'M. le Comte de Gazola, Grand-Maître de l'Artillerie, en fit tirer les plans & dessiner les élévations; plusieurs Peintres ont été sur les lieux pour les peindre sous différens aspects. J'en ai vu chez Don Antoine Jolli, Peintre & Décorateur du théâtre de S. *Carlo*, différens tableaux fort intéressans, parmi d'autres vues de Naples, de Venise, de Malte, de Madrid, &c. & M. Morghan, en 1767, les a fait graver en six feuilles, d'après les desseins de M. Jolli.' La Lande, *Voyage d'un françois en Italie*, vol. VII, 216.

38 'J'ai place à la fin de cet ouvrage un extrait de ces gravures en une seule planche. La premiere des six feuilles présente la vue extérieure & intérieure de la porte septentrionale, la seule des quatre portes qui soit encore sur pied . . . La seconde planche est une vue générale de l'emplacement de Pæstum, prise du côté du midi . . . La troisieme représente les trois Temples, vus de plus près, par un observateur situé à la partie orientale . . . La quatrieme & la cinquieme sont les vues intérieures du Temple qui est dans le milieu . . . La sixieme planche . . . est la vue du Temple exastilepérytere [Ceres temple] assez éloigné des deux autres.' Ibid., 216–18.

39 'colonnes Doriques cannelées, sans bases, ainsi qu'on le pratiquoit dans les temps les plus reculés'; '[Les temples] peuvent servir de modele aux Artistes qui connoissent & qui aiment les beautés de l'architecture Grecque'. Ibid., 218, 219.

40 La Lande was referring to [Longfield], *The ruins of Poestum or Posidonia*, see note 15.

41 Richard Norris, travel journal, 'No. 4', fol. 16r (entry for Saturday 5 January 1771), London, British Library, Add. MS 52497B.

42 Ibid., fols 24r–25r (entry for Friday 11 January 1771).

43 Before arriving at Paestum, the party slept at Salerno: 'Thursday Jany 10th 1771 Sett off at Eight oClock in Cartaches to go to Pestum. Slept at Salerno abt. 30 Miles. Went through several Towns which are very populous – but very nasty – the Roads pretty good, but dirty – some very romantic. Prospects towards Salerno and the Roads very good at about two Miles before you arrive at Salerno you see to the Right a Town upon the declivity of a Moun.n with which you have a fine View of the Sea – and sols to Salerno which is on the Sea Side – Slept at the Inn.' Ibid., fol. 23v (entry for Thursday 10 January 1771).

44 'Nous entrâmes par [la porte], et aperçûmes les trois grands temples rangés en flanc, qui partagent un peu obliquement toute la largeur de la ville.' [Dominique] Vivant Denon, *Voyage au Royaume de Naples* [1778], ed. Mathieu Couty (Paris: Perrin, 1997), 288–9.

45 Morghen, [*Sei vedute delle rovine di Pesto*], plate III; [Longfield], *The ruins of Poestum or Posidonia*, plate IV; Major, *The ruins of Paestum, otherwise Posidonia*, plate II; Barbault, *Recueil de divers monumens anciens*, plate 7.

46 'J'avance à travers des campagnes désertes, dans un chemin affreux, loin de toutes traces humaines, au pied de montagnes décharnées, sur des rivages où la mer est seule; et tout-à-coup, voilà un temple, en voilà deux, en voilà trois: j'approche à travers les herbes, je monte sur le socle d'une colonne ou sur les débris d'un fronton.' Charles-Marguerite-Jean-Baptiste Mercier Dupaty, *Lettres sur l'Italie en 1785*, 2 vols (Paris: De Senne, 1788), vol. II, 198; Eng. trans. in Charles-Marguerite-Jean-Baptiste Mercier Dupaty, *Travels through Italy in a series of letters; written in the year 1785, by President Dupaty. Translated from the French by an English Gentleman* (London: G. G. J. and J. Robinson, 1788), 325.

47 'une nuée de corbeaux prend son vol: des vaches mugissent dans le fond d'un sanctuaire: la couleuvre, entre les colonnes et les ronces, siffle et s'échappe: cependant, un jeune pâtre, appuyé nonchalamment sur une corniche, remplit, des sons d'un chalumeau, le vaste silence de ce désert'. Dupaty, *Lettres sur l'Italie*, vol. II, 198; Eng. trans. in Dupaty, *Travels through Italy*, 325.

48 'Et à la vérité quelle scène imposante pour un Artiste observateur, que celle de voir sur les rivages de la mer, un espace immense et aride, entouré de murailles, couvert de colonnes et de monuments majestueux, où sous un beau ciel qu'aucun nuage n'obscurcit, regne le silence le plus absolu: n'ayant d'autres habitans autour de lui que ces compagnons de voyage, que quelques rustres occupés à faire paître des buffles, que des pierres et des serpents.' Delagardette, *Les Ruines de Paestum*, 3.

49 'Vivement ému, j'étais dans une sorte de délire, à l'aspect du tableau extraordinaire qui se déroulait devant moi. Mais portant mes regards sur chacun des monuments en particulier, je crus appercevoir [*sic*] ce génie sublime qui avait présidé à l'invention de ces chef-d'œuvres, et le savoir profond qui avait conduit leur exécution.' Ibid., 3–4.

50 Brenna's drawings are in the drawings collection of the Victoria and Albert Museum, London. For those of Paestum see 8478.12;VI 1–31, 8478 13–17. For Brenna see Gerard Vaughan, '"Vincenzo Brenna Romanus, architectus et pictor": Drawing from the Antique in Late Eighteenth-Century Rome', *Apollo*, 144 (October 1996), 37–41.

51 Giovanni Battista Piranesi, study drawings for *Différentes vues de . . . Pesto*, London, Sir John Soane's Museum, Drawings Collection: plates II (F20 (71)), III (F9 (51)), IV (F78 (146)), V (F24 (76)), VI (F23 (75)), VII (F10 (54)), VIII (F70 (133)), IX (F64 (125)), X (F21 (72)), XI (F19 (70)), XII (F18 (69)), XIII (F22 (74)), XIV (F25 (77)), XVI (F76 (139)), XVII (F77 (140)). Two others ended up in the collection of the Bibliothèque Nationale de France in Paris and the Rijksmuseum in Amsterdam. All were published as engravings in Piranesi, *Différentes vues de . . . Pesto*. Piranesi died during the engraving process and his son finished the work.

52 The publications on Greek architecture by Stuart and Revett (*The antiquities of Athens*) and Le Roy (*Les ruines des plus beaux monuments de la Grèce*) offered a mixture of archaeological account, architectural theory and travelogue of Greece; design instructions based on Greek architecture were not yet an independent category.

53 'La représentation en avait été si vraie, qu'oubliant en plusieurs endroits que j'étais spectateur, et spectateur ignoré, j'avais été sur le point de sortir de ma place, et d'ajouter un personnage réel à la scène.' Denis Diderot, *Œuvres esthétiques*, ed. Paul Vernière (Paris: Garnier, 1994), 78.

54 'Je n'aurais jamais pu me défendre d'aller rêver sous cette voûte, de m'asseoir entre ces colonnes, d'entrer dans votre tableau.' [Denis] Diderot, *Salons III: Ruines et paysages: Salons de 1767*, ed. Else Marie Bukdahl, Michel Delon and Annette Lorenceau (Paris: Hermann, 1995), 338.

55 'plus je retois a Pæstum, plus je trouvois ce temple beau, je l'ai éxaminé sous toutes les faces, toujours un spectacle nouveau, au soleil couchant le matin, avant et après le lever du soleil. c'est le caractere de la simplicité de ne pas autant séduire au premier coup d'oeil, et de gagner à l'examen'. Hubert Rohault de Fleury, 'Voyage de l'architecte Rohault de Fleury en Italie, 1804–1805', 4 vols, Paris, Bibliothèque Nationale, Département des Manuscrits, NAF 23696, vol. II, fol. 156.

Chapter 5

1 'à en juger par le pesant et le massif de ses proportions, il est indubitable que ces Monumens ont été construits par les Grecs dans l'origine de l'Architecture, et qu'ils sont de la première antiquité, étant très certain que tout ce qui reste en Italie de Temples et de Monumens construits par les Romains est d'une architecture bien plus légère, et de proportion et de forme toute différente'. Jean-Claude Richard de Saint-Non, *Panopticon italiano: Un diario di viaggio ritrovato, 1759–1761*, ed. Pierre Rosenberg (Rome: Ed. dell'Elefante, 2000), 124.

2 'il est clair que la date de leur construction remante à l'origine de l'architecture.' [Donatien Alphonse François de] Marquis de Sade, *Voyage à Naples*, ed. Chantal Thomas (Paris: Payot and Rivages, 2008), 294.

3 Arthur O. Lovejoy and George Boas, *Primitivism and Related Ideas in Antiquity* (Baltimore: Johns Hopkins Press, 1935). See also George Boas, 'Primitivism', in Philip P. Wiener (ed.), *Dictionary of the History of Ideas*, vol. III (New York: Charles Scribner's Sons, 1968), 578–98.

4 Michel de Montaigne, 'Des cannibales', in *Essais de Messire Michel, Seigneur de Montaigne . . . Livre premier et second* (Bordeaux: S. Millanges, 1580), Book I, 31.

5 On ideas on the peasant in eighteenth-century France see Amy S. Wyngaard, *From Savage to Citizen: The Invention of the Peasant in the French Enlightenment* (Newark: University of Delaware Press, 2004).

6 A. Owen Aldridge, 'Primitivism in the Eighteenth Century', in Wiener (ed.), *Dictionary of the History of Ideas'*, 598–605. See also Paul Hazard, *La Pensée européenne au XVIIIe siècle, de Montesquieu à Lessing: Notes et références* (Paris: Boivin, 1946). Eighteenth-century publications include Antoine Court de Gébelin, *Le monde primitif analysé et comparé avec le monde moderne*, 9 vols (Paris: s.n., 1775–84); Delisle de Sales, *Histoire philosophique du monde primitif*, 4th edn, 7 vols (Paris: Chez Gay et Gide, 1793–5).

7 Anthony Ashley Cooper, 3rd Earl of Shaftesbury, *Characteristicks* (s.l.: s.n. [London: J. Darby], 1711), vol. III, 255.

8 'Tout est bien sortant des mains de l'Auteur des choses, tout dégénère entre les mains de l'homme.' It has been argued that Rousseau was not a pure primitivist: see Arthur O. Lovejoy, 'The Supposed Primitivism of Rousseau's Discourse on Inequality', in *Essays in the History of Ideas* (Baltimore: Johns Hopkins Press, 1948), 14–37. Cf. 'So long as men remained content with their rustic huts . . . they lived free, healthy, honest and happy lives'. Jean-Jacques Rousseau, *Confessions*, vol. VII of *Collection complète des œuvres de J. J. Rousseau* (Geneva: s.n., 1782), 47–8.

9 For a more cultural–historical approach to the terms 'primitive' and 'savage' see Marianna Torgovnick, *Gone Primitive: Savage Intellects, Modern Lives* (Chicago: University of Chicago Press, 1990). See also Lois Whitney, *Primitivism and the Idea of Progress in English Popular Literature of the Eighteenth Century* (Baltimore: Johns Hopkins Press, 1934).

10 'La vie sauvage est si simple, et nos sociétés sont des machines si compliquées! L'Otaïtien touche à l'origine du monde, et l'Européen touche à sa vieillesse.' [Denis] Diderot, *Supplément au voyage de Bougainville* [written in 1772, first published in 1796], ed. Paul-Édouard Levayer (Paris: Librairie Générale Française, 1995), 37.

11 'Before, in the time of Homer, the peoples, who were almost all body and almost no reflection, must have been all vivid sensation in perceiving particulars, strong imagination in apprehending and enlarging them . . . and robust memory in retaining them.' Giambattista Vico, *The New Science of Giambattista Vico* [1744], trans. Thomas Goddard Bergin and Max Harold Fisch (Ithaca (NY): Cornell University Press, 1984), 116. 'Since barbarians lack reflection, which, when ill-used, is the mother of falsehood, the first heroic . . . poets sang true histories . . . And in virtue of this same nature of barbarism, which for lack of reflection does not know how to feign (whence it is naturally truthful, open, faithful, generous, and magnanimous).' Ibid., 312.

12 Ibid., 75, 77.

13 'For it has been shown that it was deficiency of human reasoning power that gave rise to poetry so sublime that the philosophers which came afterward, the arts of poetry and of criticism, have produced none equal or better, and have even prevented its production.' Ibid., 120.

14 For a new light on the Perrault–Blondel debate see Anthony Gerbino, *François Blondel: Architecture, Erudition, and the Scientific Revolution* (London / New York: Routledge, 2010), 148–65.

15 For example, Lovejoy and Boas, *Primitivism and Related Ideas in Antiquity*; Christian Marouby, *Utopie et primitivisme: Essai sur l'imaginaire anthropologique à l'âge classique* (Paris: Seuil, 1990); Pascal Griener, 'Théorie de l'art et théorie pessimiste de l'histoire: un paradoxe', in Christian Michel and Carl Magnusson (eds), *Penser l'art dans la seconde moitié du XVIIIe siècle: Théorie, critique, philosophie, histoire* (Paris: Somogy, 2013), 699–711.

16 Christian Michel, 'L'Argument des origines dans les théories des arts en France à l'époque des Lumières', in Chantal Grell and Christian Michel (eds), *Primitivisme et mythes des origines dans la France des Lumières, 1680–1820* (Paris: Presses de l'Université Paris-Sorbonne, 1989), 35–45.

17 For example, Robert Goldwater, *Primitivism in Modern Painting* (New York / London: Harper & Bros., 1938) and William Rubin (ed.), *'Primitivism' in Twentieth-Century Art: Affinity of the Tribal and the Modern*, 2 vols (New York: Museum of Modern Art, 1984). For the nineteenth century see Melinda Curtis (ed.), *The Search for Innocence: Primitive and Primitivistic Art of the Nineteenth Century* (College Park: University of Maryland Art Gallery, 1975); Susan Hiller (ed.), *The Myth of Primitivism: Perspectives on Art* (London / New York: Routledge, 1991). On the primitivist aesthetic see Barbara Maria Stafford, *Symbol and Myth: Humbert de Superville's Essay on Absolute Signs in Art* (Cranbury (NJ) / London: Associated University Press, 1979). On primitivism as opposed to classicism in art see E. Foundoukidis (ed.), *Primitivisme et classicisme: Les Deux Faces de l'histoire de l'art* (Paris: Centre International des Instituts de Recherche, Art, Archéologie, Ethnologie, 1946).

18 Frances S. Connelly, *The Sleep of Reason: Primitivism in Modern European Art and Aesthetics, 1725–1907* (University Park: Pennsylvania State University Press, 1995). Three publications are forthcoming from the NWO-VIDI project 'The Quest for the Legitimacy of Architecture 1750–1850' at Leiden University, by Maarten Delbeke, Linda Bleijenberg and Sigrid de Jong on primitivism and the origins of architecture in architectural thought. One of the papers that will appear in advance: Sigrid de Jong, 'Origins of Architecture', in Caroline van Eck and Sigrid de Jong (eds), *Companion to Eighteenth-Century Architecture* (Chichester: Wiley-Blackwell, forthcoming, 2015).

19 For example, Wolfgang Herrmann, *Laugier and Eighteenth Century French Theory* (London: A. Zwemmer, 1962); Sylvia

Lavin, *Quatremère de Quincy and the Invention of a Modern Language of Architecture* (Cambridge (Mass.) / London: MIT Press, 1992); Adolf Max Vogt, *Le Corbusier, der edle Wilde: Zur Archäologie der Moderne* (Braunschweig: Vieweg, 1996); Pierre de La Ruffinière Du Prey, *Hawksmoor's London Churches: Architecture and Theology* (Chicago: University of Chicago Press, 2000). Other publications on primitivism in architecture, in which the subject is mostly treated in relation to modernism, include Anthony Vidler, 'Rebuilding the Primitive Hut', in *The Writing of the Walls: Architectural Theory in the Late Enlightenment* (Princeton (NJ): Princeton Architectural Press, 1987); Jo Odgers, Flora Samuel and Adam Sharr (eds), *Primitive: Original Matters in Architecture* (London: Routledge, 2006); 'The Primitive in Modern Architecture and Urbanism', *Journal of Architecture*, 13/4 (August 2008) [special issue], 355–64.

20 Ernst Hans Gombrich, 'Dream Houses' [review of Joseph Rykwert, *On Adam's House in Paradise: The Idea of the Primitive Hut in Architectural History* (1972)], *New York Review of Books*, 20 (29 November 1973), 35–7. See also Ernst Hans Gombrich, 'The Debate on Primitivism in Ancient Rhetoric', *Journal of the Warburg and Courtauld Institutes*, 29 (1966), 24–38; Ernst Hans Gombrich, *The Preference for the Primitive: Episodes in the History of Western Taste and Art* (London: Phaidon, 2002). Gombrich's book concentrates on art and only briefly evokes Gothic architecture. He connected primitivism first and foremost to the question of growth and decay in the arts, showing the 'longue durée' of the preference for the primitive, beginning with Plato, Aristotle and Cicero; he traced a revival of primitivism in the eighteenth century, and again in the twentieth century.

21 Grell and Michel (eds.), *Primitivisme et mythes des origines*; Odgers, Samuel, and Sharr (eds.), *Primitive: Original Matters in Architecture*.

22 Vitruvius, *De architectura libri decum / Ten Books on Architecture*, trans. Ingrid D. Rowland, commentary and illustrations by Thomas N. Howe (Cambridge: Cambridge University Press, 1999), 34, on 'The Invention of the Arts and of Building'. The passage continues: 'Because people are by nature imitative and easily taught, they daily showed one another the success of their constructions, taking pride in creation, so that by daily exercising their ingenuity in competition they achieved greater insight with the passage of time. First they erected forked uprights, and weaving twigs in between they covered the whole with mud. Others, letting clods of mud go dry, began to construct walls of them, joining them together with wood, and to avoid rains and heat they covered them over with reeds and leafy branches. Later, when these coverings proved unable to endure through the storms of winter, they made eaves with moulded clay, and set in rainspouts on inclined roofs.' Ibid. Vitruvius's account is probably based on Lucretius, whose publications he is said to have read with admiration (ibid., commentary, 173).

23 Cicero, *De Oratore*, [Book III]: *De fato, Paradoxa stoicorum, De partitione oratoria*, trans. H. Rackham (Cambridge (Mass.) / London: Harvard University Press / William Heinemann, 1982), 143 (xlv.179–xlvi.180). Next, Cicero makes a comparison

with speech, demonstrating the necessity for perfect speech as shown by the example of architecture. Gombrich quoted this as a crucial passage on primitivism and architecture ('Dream Houses', 35–7); he discussed Cicero again in *The Preference for the Primitive*, 22–9. For further context on Vitruvius and other sources see Lovejoy and Boas, *Primitivism and Related Ideas in Antiquity*.

24 [Marc-Antoine Laugier], *Essai sur l'architecture* (Paris: Chez Duchesne, 1753). Laugier's book was controversial and was the target of adverse criticism soon after publication – for instance, in Étienne La Font de Saint-Yenne, *Examen d'un essai sur l'architecture* (Paris: Michel Lambert, 1753); repr. in Duperron, *Discours sur le peinture et sur l'architecture* [1758] (Geneva: Minkoff Reprint, 1973), and in an article in the *Mercure de France* by Amédée-François Frézier (1682–1773); Laugier reacted to some of the objections in the second edition of the *Essai*. The critics were outspoken: for example, 'Je serai fort trompé si l'autorité de ce maître moderne [Laugier] a assés de poids pour faire changer de pratique à nos Architectes, & les engage d'imiter les arbres dans leurs colonnes.' La Font de Saint-Yenne, *Examen d'un essai sur l'architecture*, 12–13. In the same volume, however, we find a positive reaction to Laugier: 'Si l'on veut avoir un détail plus circonstancié de l'origine de l'Architecture, on peut ouvrir le nouvel Essai qui a fait tant de bruit. Cet Ouvrage est écrit avec grace, l'Auteur par la parure & par les charmes d'un style délicat; a sçu rendre intéressant un Art que les François regardoient avec trop d'indifférence.' Duperron, *Discours sur la peinture et sur l'architecture* (Paris: Prault, 1758), 1. On Laugier see Herrmann, *Laugier and Eighteenth Century French Theory*.

25 Marc-Antoine Laugier, *Essai sur l'architecture, nouvelle édition . . . avec un dictionnaire des termes, et des planches qui en facilitent l'explication* (Paris: Chez Duchesne, 1755); for contemporary reviews of the *Essai* see Herrmann, *Laugier and Eighteenth Century French Theory*, 256.

26 The first chapter is entitled 'Des principes généraux de l'Architecture'; the next five chapters are on the architectural orders, the art of building (solidity, commodity and propriety), building churches, and embellishing cities and gardens.

27 'mon principal dessein est de former le goût des Architectes'. Laugier, *Essai . . . nouvelle édition*, p. xliii. To this second edition Laugier added a glossary and some plates by way of clarification: 'Moyennant ces nouveaux soins j'espere que cette édition sera moins indigne que la précédente de l'approbation du public.' Ibid., p. xxxii.

28 'Il en est de l'Architecture comme de tous les autres Arts: ses principes sont fondés sur la simple nature, & dans les procédés de celle-ci se trouvent clairement marquées les règles de celle-là. Considérons l'homme dans sa premiere origine sans autre secours; sans autre guide que l'instinct naturel de ses besoins. Il lui faut un lieu de repos. Au bord d'un tranquile ruisseau, il apperçoit un gason; sa verdure naissante plaît à ses yeux, son tendre duvet l'invite; il vient, & mollement étendu sur ce tapis émaillé, il ne songe qu'à jouir en paix des dons de la nature: rien ne lui manque, il ne désire rien. Mais bientôt l'ardeur du Soleil qui le brule, l'oblige à chercher un abri. Il apperçoit une forêt qui lui offre la

fraîcheur de ses ombres; il court se cacher dans son épaisseur, & le voilà content. Cependant mille vapeurs élevées au hasard se rencontrent & se rassemblent, d'épais nuages couvrent les airs, une pluie effroyable se précipite comme un torrent sur cette forêt délicieuse. L'homme mal couvert à l'abri de ses feuilles, ne sçait plus comment se défendre d'une humidité incommode qui le pénétre de toute part. Une caverne se présente, il s'y glisse, & se trouvant à sec, il s'applaudit de sa découverte. Mais de nouveaux désagremens le dégoutent encore de ce séjour. Il s'y voit dans les ténébres, il y respire un air mal sain, il en sort résolu de suppléer, par son industrie, aux inattentions & aux négligences de la nature. L'homme veut se faire un logement qui le couvre sans l'ensevelir.' Ibid., 8–9.

29 'Quelques branches abbatues dans la forêt sont les matériaux propres à son dessein. Il en choisit quatre des plus fortes qu'il éleve perpendiculairement, & qu'il dispose en quarré. Au-dessus il en met quatre autres en travers; & sur celle-ci il en éleve qui s'inclinent, & qui se réunissent en pointe de deux côtés. Cette espece de toit est couvert de feuilles assez serrées pour que ni le soleil, ni la pluie ne puissent y pénétrer; & voilà l'homme logé.' Ibid., 9. Contemporary architects should build in the same way: 'Tous les jours nous voyons des Artistes ignorans produire des choses excellentes, sans autre secours que l'heureux instinct qu'ils ont reçu de la nature, guide beaucoup meilleur que tous les principes scientifiques.' Ibid., 261 (annotated 'Réponse aux remarques de M. Frezier, inserées dans le Mercure de juillet 1754').

30 J.-L. de Cordemoy, in his *Nouveau traité de toute l'architecture, ou L'art de bastir, utile aux entrepreneurs at aux ouvriers* [1706], 2nd edn (Paris: J.-B. Coignard, 1714). Cordemoy argued for an architecture without ornament, and urged the truth and simplicity of the structural principles found in both Greek and Gothic architecture. John Soane, who owned two copies of Cordemoy, approved of his argument that the frieze and the cornice of interior entablatures should be restrained, not only to prevent them obstructing the light but also because indoors they did not fulfil their true function of protecting the columns from rainfall. Soane annotated this point in one of his copies: 'as in one of the temples at Paestum [the Temple of Neptune]'. David Watkin (ed.), *Sir John Soane: Enlightenment Thought and the Royal Academy Lectures* (Cambridge: Cambridge University Press, 1996), 140–41.

31 'En considérant avec attention nos plus grands & nos plus beaux Edifices, mon ame a toujours éprouvé diverses impressions. Quelquefois le charme étoit si fort, qu'il produisoit en moi un plaisir mêlé de transport & d'enthousiasme. D'autres fois, sans être si vivement entraîné, je me sentois occupé d'une maniere satisfaisante; c'étoit un plaisir moindre, mais pourtant un vrai plaisir. Souvent je demeurois tout à fait insensible; souvent aussi j'étois dégoûté, choqué, revolté. J'ai réfléchi longtems sur tous ces différens effets.' Laugier, *Essai . . . nouvelle édition*, pp. xxxviii–xxxix; Eng. trans. in Marc-Antoine Laugier, *An essay on the study and practice of architecture* (London: Stanley Crowder and Henry Woodgate, 1756), pp. x–xi. A little further on Laugier added: 'La vûe d'un édifice construit dans toute la perfection de l'art, cause un plaisir & un enchantement dont on n'est pas maître de se défendre. Ce spectacle réveille dans l'ame des idées nobles & touchantes. Il nous fait éprouver cette douce émotion, & cet agréable transport qu'excitent les ouvrages qui portent l'empreinte d'une vraie supériorité d'esprit. Un bel édifice parle éloquemment pour son Architecte. M. Perrault dans ses écrits n'est tout au plus qu'un Sçavant : la colonade du Louvre le décide grand Homme.' Laugier, *Essai . . . nouvelle édition*, 2–3.

32 '1°. qu'il y avoit dans l'Architecture des beautés essentielles, indépendantes de l'habitude des sens, ou de la convention des hommes. 2°. Que la composition d'un morceau d'Architecture étoit comme tous les ouvrages d'esprit, susceptible de froideur & de vivacité, de justesse & de désordre. 3°. Qu'il devoit y avoir pour cet Art comme pour tous les autres, un talent qui ne s'acquiert point, une mesure de génie que la nature donne; & que ce talent, ce génie avoient besoin cependant d'être assujettis & captivés par des loix.' Ibid., p. xl.

33 'Tout à coup il s'est fait à mes yeux un grand jour.' Ibid., p. xli.

34 'Telle est la marche de la simple nature: c'est à l'imitation de ses procédés que l'art doit sa naissance. La petite cabane rustique que je viens de décrire, est le modele sur lequel on a imaginé toutes les magnificences de l'Architecture. C'est en se raprochant dans l'exécution de la simplicité de ce premier modele, que l'on évite les défauts essentiels, que l'on saisit les perfections véritables.' Ibid., 9–10; Eng. trans. in Laugier, *An essay*, 11.

35 'Les pieces de bois élevées perpendiculairement nous ont donné l'idée des colonnes. Les pieces horisontales qui les surmontent, nous ont donné l'idée des entablemens. Enfin les pieces inclinés qui forment le toit, nous ont donné l'idée des frontons: voilà ce que tous les Maîtres de l'Art ont reconnu.' Laugier, *Essai . . . nouvelle édition*, 10; Eng. trans. in Laugier, *An essay on the study and practice of architecture*, 12.

36 'Ne perdons point de vûe notre petite cabane rustique. Je n'y vois que des colonnes, un plancher ou entablement, un toit pointu dont les deux extrêmités forment chacune ce que nous nommons un fronton. Jusqu'ici point de voûte, encore moins d'arcade, point de piédestaux, point d'attique, point de porte même, point de fenêtre. Je conclus donc, & je dis: Dans tout ordre d'Architecture, il n'y a que la colonne, l'entablement & le fronton qui puissent entrer essentiellement dans sa composition. Si chacune de ces trois parties se trouve placée dans la situation & avec la forme qui lui convient, il n'y aura rien à ajouter pour que l'ouvrage soit parfait.' Laugier, *Essai . . . nouvelle édition*, 10–11; Eng. trans. in Laugier, *An essay on the study and practice of architecture*, 13.

37 'une innovation bisarre, qui n'étant fondée en nature d'aucune façon, & n'étant autorisée par aucun besoin, n'a pu être adoptée que par ignorance, & n'est encore tolérée que par habitude.' Laugier, *Essai . . . nouvelle édition*, 17.

38 'la nature fait rien de quarré'. Ibid., p. xii (reacting to Saint-Yenne, *Examen d'un essai sur l'architecture* (1753)).

39 'des colonnes isolées qui portent leur entablement en platebande, ne laisseront jamais de doute sur la vérité du specta-

cle d'Architecture qu'elles présentent; parce qu'on sent bien qu'on ne pourroit toucher à aucune de ces parties, sans endommager & ruiner l'édifice'. Laugier, *Essai . . . nouvelle édition*, p. xviii.

40 'For every body consists entirely of parts that are fixed and individual; if these are removed, enlarged, reduced, or transferred somewhere inappropriate, the very composition will be spoiled that gives the body its seemly appearance.' Leon Battista Alberti, *De re aedificatoria*, 1443–1452, Book 9, in Leon Battista Alberti, *De re aedificatoria / On the Art of Building in Ten Books*, trans. Joseph Rykwert, Neil Leach and Robert Tavernor (Cambridge (Mass.): MIT Press, 1988), 302.

41 'Je ne crois pas que la nature ait jamais rien produit qui puisse autoriser ce renflement.' Laugier, *Essai . . . nouvelle édition*, 21.

42 Although the first publication about Paestum did not appear until 1764, from the early 1750s travellers returned from Italy with drawings in their portfolios: Soufflot and Dumont, who were there in 1750, Mylne and Le Roy all brought their drawings back to Paris.

43 Otherwise, to Laugier, the Greeks were superior to the Romans: 'L'Architecture doit ce qu'elle a de plus parfait aux Grecs, Nation privilégiée, à qui il étoit réservé de ne rien ignorer dans les Sciences, & de tout inventer dans les Arts. Les Romains dignes d'admirer, capables de copier les modeles excellens que la Grece leur fournissoit, voulurent y ajouter du leur, & ne firent qu'apprendre à tout l'Univers, que quand le dégré de perfection est atteint, il n'y a plus qu'à imiter ou à déchoir.' After that there was only the 'barbarie des siècles postérieures.' Laugier, *Essai . . . nouvelle édition*, 3. In his *Observations sur l'architecture* (The Hague: Saillant, 1765), Laugier wrote about a copy of a copy: 'Cette premiere imitation imparfaite, fut répétée & altérée tant de fois, que les derniers ouvrages ne conserverent avec le premier modéle d'autre rapport que celui qu'on apperçoit entre les espéces qui ont le plus dégénéré, & l'espéce originale & primitive.' Laugier, *Observations*, 79.

44 'tout y est selon les vrai principes de l'Architecture. Un quarré long où trente colonnes supportent un entablement & un toit terminé aux deux extrêmités par un fronton; voilà tout ce dont il s'agit. Cet assemblage a une simplicité & une noblesse qui frappe tous les yeux.' Laugier, *Essai . . . nouvelle édition*, 11; Eng. trans. in Laugier, *An essay on the study and practice of architecture*, 14.

45 'Leur beauté frappe tout le monde, parce qu'elle est naturelle, parce qu'elle est vraie. Il est étonnant qu'avec de tels modeles sous les yeux, nos Architectes en reviennent toujours à leurs misérables arcades.' Laugier, *Essai . . . nouvelle édition*, 31.

46 'tout ce qui est contre nature, peut être singulier; mais il ne sera jamais beau; Dans un édifice il faut que tout porte dès les fondemens: Voilà une regle dont il n'est jamais permis de s'écarter'. Ibid., 48.

47 'On m'objectera peut-être encore que je réduis l'Architecture presqu'à rien; puisqu'à la réserve des colonnes, des entablements, des frontons, des portes & des fenêtres, je retranche à peu près tout le reste.' Ibid., 56–7.

48 The importance of historical progress becomes clear in Vitruvius's treatment of *decor* ('decorum' or correctness). He expanded on this definition, rendering it: 'things as they are and as they have been handed down through the course of history'. To Vitruvius, history was 'a critical process of discovery' that accumulates across many generations. Things become accepted by 'proven means' (*probatis rebus*) – that is, by being tested – and by 'achieving a certain general acceptance'; and 'the mutual attention to the activities and accomplishments of others is a positive force in the growth of culture'. To Vitruvius *decor* was a function laid down by tradition, and tradition is commonly accepted through general use. So correctness meant: first, formal cultural rules; second, that which is tacitly accepted in a culture; and third, that which is clearly described by nature. See Vitruvius, *De architectura*, 1.2.5, trans. Rowland, commentary, 150–51.

49 Herrmann drew attention to this (*Laugier and Eighteenth Century French Theory*, 49). On Laugier's hut see also Caroline van Eck, *Organicism in Nineteenth-Century Architecture: An Inquiry into its Theoretical and Philosophical Background* (Amsterdam: Architectura & Natura, 1994), 89–98.

50 In 1755 two rival translations were made, of which only one (by an unknown translator) was published: *An essay on architecture in which its true principles are explained and invariable rules proposed . . . Adorned with a frontispiece, designed by Mr. Wale* (London: T. Osborne & Shipton, 1755). See Eileen Harris and Nicholas Savage, *British Architectural Books and Writers, 1556–1785* (Cambridge: Cambridge University Press, 1990), 281–2. No mention was made of Laugier or of the French original. The book was not a success in England, though many English architects read it.

51 In his study on Laugier, the historian Wolfgang Herrmann made a short inventory of images of the primitive hut, and others are discussed in Joachim Gaus, 'Die Urhütte: Über ein Modell in der Baukunst und ein Motiv in der bildenden Kunst', *Wallraf-Richartz-Jahrbuch*, 33 (1971), 7–70; Joseph Rykwert, *On Adam's House in Paradise: The Idea of the Primitive Hut in Architectural History*, 2nd edn (Cambridge (Mass.)/London: MIT Press, 1981) [first published 1972]. As Herrmann stated, the frontispiece of the second edition of the *Essai* is the first image of the primitive hut as a 'product of nature' (*Laugier and Eighteenth Century French Theory*, 215). A similar image appeared later as the frontispiece of Francesco Milizia's *Le vite de' più celebri architetti d'ogni nazione e d'ogni tempo* (Rome, 1768). Representations of men creating a hut had already been published in the fifteenth century: for instance, in Antonio Averlino Filarete, *Trattato d'architettura* (1470), II.I.140; and in two editions of Vitruvius (Como, 1521), fol. 32; (Paris, 1547), fol. 16. See Erwin Panofsky, 'The Early History of Man in Two Cycles of Paintings by Piero di Cosimo', in *Studies in Iconology: Humanistic Themes in the Art of the Renaissance* (New York: Oxford University Press, 1939), 33, plates XI and XII.

52 The primitive hut is treated in many other eighteenth-century publications, such as Pietro Marquez, *Delle case di città degli antichi Romani seconda la dottrina di Vitruvio* (Rome, 1795), which deals with the origins of architecture and the

role of the primitive hut. Soane made lengthy notes on this book, which is no longer in his library; see Watkin (ed.), *Sir John Soane*, 116. Other publications include William Wrighte, *Grotesque architecture, or Rural amusement; consisting of plans, elevations, and sections, for huts, retreats, summer and winter hermitages, terminaries . . . The whole containing twenty-eight new designs . . . To which is added, an explanation, with the method of executing them* (London, 1767), plate 1 (façade and plan of the primitive hut). The transformation of wooden into stone architecture is often illustrated: see Abraham Bosse, *Traité des manières de dessiner les ordres de l'architecture antique* (Paris, 1664), plate XI; Claude Perrault, *Dix livres d'architecture de Vitruve corrigés et traduits nouvellement en français* (Paris: Chez Jean Baptiste Coignard, 1673), plates VIII, XXXII, XXXIII; William Chambers, *A treatise on civil architecture, in which the principles of that art are laid down, and illustrated by a great number of plates* (London: printed for the author, 1759), plate 1; Giovanni Battista Piranesi, *Della magnificenza ed architettura de' Romani* (Rome, 1761), plates XXXIII–XXIX, XXXII; Jacques-François Blondel, *Cours d'architecture, ou Traité de la décoration, distribution et construction des bâtiments*, 6 vols (Paris: Desaint, 1771–7), vol. I, plate I. A number of authors examined the topic of origins in relation to architecture, such as John Wood, *The Origin of Building*, 5 vols (London, 1741), who connected origins with religious factors, which is not an issue in relation to Paestum.

53 Chambers, *A treatise on civil architecture*. A second edition was published in London in 1768, and a third in 1791. A French translation based on the second edition appeared in Paris in the 1770s. The third edition, *A treatise on the decorative part of civil architecture, illustrated by fifty original, and three additional plates* (London: printed by Joseph Smeeton, 1791), was considerably revised and extended and is considered the most complete representation of his thinking. See Harris and Savage, *British Architectural Books*, 155–64.

54 See Janine Barrier, *Les Architectes européens à Rome, 1740–1765: La Naissance du goût à la grecque* (Paris: Monum/Éditions du Patrimoine, 2005), 8–9.

55 Chambers, *A treatise on the decorative part of civil architecture*, 16. In the first edition: 'Antiently, says Vitruvius, Men lived in woods, and inhabited caves; but in time, taking perhaps example from birds, who with great industry build their nests, they made themselves huts. At first they made these huts, very probably, of a Conic Figure; because that is a form of the simplest structure; and, like the birds, whom they imitated, composed them of branches of trees, spreading them wide at the bottom, and joining them in a point at the top; covering the whole with reeds, leaves, and clay, to screen them from tempests and rain.' Chambers, *A treatise on civil architecture*, 10. As Robin Middleton has pointed out, the huts Chambers proposed in his *Treatise* are based on Vitruvius's Phrygian and Chalkian huts; Robin Middleton, 'Chambers, W., "A Treatise on Civil Architecture", London 1759', in John Harris and Michael Snodin (eds), *Sir William Chambers: Architect to George III* (New Haven (Conn.)/London: Yale University Press, 1996), 70.

56 Chambers, *A treatise on the decorative part of civil architecture*, 16. In the first edition: 'But finding the Conic Figure inconvenient, on account of its inclined sides, they changed both the form and construction of their huts, giving them a Cubical figure.' Chambers, *A treatise on civil architecture*, 10.

57 Middleton, 'Chambers, W., "A Treatise"', 68–76, suggests that he was possibly influenced by Joseph-François Lafitau's *Moeurs des sauvages ameriquains, comparées aux moeurs des premiers temps* (1724).

58 Johann Joachim Winckelmann, letter to Heinrich von Bünau, Naples, 26 April 1758, in *Johann Joachim Winckelmann, Briefe*, ed. Walther Rehm and Hans Diepolder, 4 vols (Berlin: Walter de Gruyter, 1952–7), vol. I, 350.

59 'C'est dans ces ruines où l'on trouve l'Ordre Dorique exécuté dans toute sa pureté primitive; c'est dans ces ruines où l'Architecture porte ce caractère à la fois simple et sublime que les Doriens imprimoient à tous leurs ouvrages, et qui les fit distinguer des autres peuples de la Grèce.' Claude-Mathieu Delagardette, *Les Ruines de Paestum, ou Posidonia, ancienne ville de la grande Grèce* (Paris: l'auteur, an VI [1798]) [prospectus for forthcoming publication], 5.

60 Delagardette's edition of Vignola was published by Chéreau in Paris, and was reissued in new editions in 1797 (repr. 1823), 1840 and 1851. Delagardette's other works for young architects were: *Leçons élémentaires des ombres dans l'architecture, faisant suite aux règles des cinq ordres de Vignole* (Paris: Chéreau, 1786) and *Nouvelles règles pour la pratique du dessin et du lavis de l'architecture civile et militaire* (Paris: Barrois, an XI [1803]). In a few editions the *Vignole* and the *Dessin* are bound together in one volume.

61 'La nécessité de se garantir des injures, des saisons & des insultes des bêtes féroces, enseigna, sans doute, aux hommes la manière de se construire des habitations. Ils commencèrent, nous dit Vitruve, à se loger dans des cavités faites en terre; mais les familles devenant plus nombreuses & plus industrieuses, on inventa de nouvelles habitations; on les fit d'abord avec des perches plantées en terre, que l'on entrelassa de branchages & qu'on revêtit de boue extérieurement, en leur donnant la forme de cônes pour faciliter l'écoulement des eaux. De semblables logemens étoient peu commodes, & pouvoient aisément être renversés par les vents ou par les inondations. A mesure que la société se forma, on perfectionna les habitations, & à la place des huttes, on construisit des cabanes'. Claude-Mathieu Delagardette, *Les Ruines de Paestum, ou Posidona, ancienne ville de la Grande-Grèce'* (Paris: l'auteur/H. Barbou, an VII [1799]), 16.

62 'Stimulé moi-même, par le désir de fixer l'attention des nos jeunes Eleves, sur la pureté primitive de l'Architecture de ces peuples, j'ai inséré de confiance, dans la première édition de mon traité des cinq Ordres, publié en 1787, les détails d'un ordre dorique de Pæstum, qui me furent donnés par l'Auteur d'un de ces ouvrages. Mais alors je n'avois pas vû l'original.' Delagardette, *Les Ruines* ([1798]) [prospectus], 6.

63 John Soane, 'Italian Sketches/J: Soane/1779', London, Sir John Soane's Museum, Drawings Collection, sketchbook, Vol. 39, 32–4 (entry for 26 January).

64 John Wilton-Ely, *Piranesi, Paestum & Soane* (London: Azimuth, 2002), 52–6, takes the contrary view to mine, holding that the use of baseless Doric columns is Paestum's legacy in Soane's work. A revised version of this book appeared in 2013: John Wilton-Ely, *Piranesi, Paestum & Soane*, rev. and enlarged edn (Munich / London / New York: Prestel, 2013). For a photograph of the barn see Margaret Richardson and MaryAnne Stevens (eds), *John Soane, Architect: Master of Space and Light* (London: Royal Academy of Arts, 1999), 116.

65 'An English architect by name Soane who is an ingenious young man now studying at Rome accompanied us thither & measured the buildings.' Philip Yorke, letter of 31 January 1779, London, British Library, Add. MS 35378, fols 302r–305v. See John Ingamells, *A Dictionary of British and Irish Travellers in Italy, 1701–1800* (New Haven (Conn.) / London: Published for the Paul Mellon Centre for Studies in British Art by Yale University Press, 1997), 1035–6. Yorke kept a journal of his Grand Tour, 'Travels thro Holland, Germany, Italy & Switzerland &c. in the years 1777, 1778 and 1779', London, British Library, Add. MSS 36258–36260; an anonymous travel journal, New Haven (Conn.), Yale University, Beinecke Library, Osborne MSS, c. 332, is probably also by him.

66 Pierre de La Ruffinière Du Prey, 'John Soane, Philip Yorke, and their Quest for Primitive Architecture', in Gervase Jackson-Stops (ed.), *National Trust Studies, 1979* (London: Philip Wilson Publishers for Sotheby Parke Bernet Publications, 1978), 28–38. Soane designed several buildings at Yorke's estate in Hertfordshire, and also redesigned Wimpole Hall, Cambridgeshire, for him. The dairy was Yorke's wedding present to his wife. See also Pierre de La Ruffinière du Prey, *John Soane: The Making of an Architect* (Chicago / London: Academy Editions, 1982), 248. Gillian Darley, *John Soane: An Accidental Romantic* (New Haven (Conn.) / London: Yale University Press, 1999), 64–5.

67 Watkin's assertion that the 'timber columns recalled the supposedly primitivist Greek Doric columns of the temples at Paestum' is not Soane's. Watkin (ed.), *Sir John Soane*, 116.

68 See the entry on Hamels Park in Richardson and Stevens (eds), *John Soane, Architect: Master of Space and Light*, 118. The building consisted of two rooms: a dairy and a parlour for eating strawberries and cream. It was demolished in the nineteenth century.

69 The same lecture was repeated four more times: on 8 January 1810 at the start of the main series of lectures, 12 February 1813 (altered), 20 February 1817 (altered) and 18 February 1819 (altered). This last version was delivered three times more by the Academician Henry Howard: on 16 February 1832, 9 January 1834, 7 January 1836. See Watkin (ed.), *Sir John Soane*, 731–2.

70 London, Sir John Soane's Museum, Drawings Collection, Royal Academy lecture drawing, undated, Drawer 27, Set 2, no. 4.

71 Besides the drawings, it seems likely that Soane illustrated his ideas at this lecture by showing models of a primitive hut. Several such models exist in his collection, including: model of a primitive hut, mahogany, 278 × 345 × 531 mm, London, Sir John Soane's Museum, M1298; model of a primitive hut (more advanced state), mahogany, 231 × 260 × 430 mm, London, Sir John Soane's Museum, SC1; these were among the few models used during the lectures, see Richardson and Stevens (eds), *John Soane, Architect*, 119. In his inventory Soane wrote of the first model: 'Small model explanatory of the principle of Construction supposed to have been adopted in the Primitive Huts, and the origin of the several members of the Orders of Architecture.'

72 These are among the Royal Academy lecture drawings in London, Sir John Soane's Museum, Drawer 27, Set 2; the descriptions are those assigned by the museum. The first and last drawings are undated, the second (flat roof) is dated 20 May 1807 and the third (pedimented roof) is dated 1807. This set contains ten drawings of different types of primitive huts; Drawer 86, Set 1, contains two perspectives of huts (nos 1 and 2).

73 Watkin (ed.), *Sir John Soane*, Lecture I, 497. Soane also referred to an Egyptian temple, of which he showed an image, but which is not further identified.

74 Watkin (ed.), *Sir John Soane*, Lecture I, 498.

75 Other drawings of Paestum were shown in Lecture III (a section and a perspective of the Temple of Neptune), and Lecture V (an interior view of the Temple of Neptune, and a perspective view of the three temples, from Thomas Major, *The ruins of Paestum, otherwise Posidonia* (1768)): London, Sir John Soane's Museum, Royal Academy lecture drawings, Drawer 19, Set 5, nos 1–5; Drawer 23, Set 3, no. 8. In Lecture II Soane compared the columns of the Paestum temple with those of the temple of Corinth, of the temples of Theseus, Minerva and Augustus in Athens, but only in respect of their dimensions, the diameter of their columns and the proportion of the entablature to the height of the columns (see the drawing in Drawer 25, Set 1, no. 1). Watkin (ed.), *Sir John Soane*, Lecture II, 504.

76 Ibid., 503.

77 Ibid., 507n.

78 The three works were published in a single volume as *Osservazioni di Gio. Battista Piranesi sopra la lettre de M. Mariette aux auteurs de la Gazette Littéraire de l'Europe, inserita nel supplemento, dell'istessa Gazzetta stampata dimanche 4. novembre, MDCCLIV: & parere su l'architettura, con una prefazione ad un nuovo tratatto della introduzione e del progresso delle belle arti in Europa ne' tempi antichi* (Rome: s.n. [Generoso Salomoni e G. B. Piranesi], 1765); Eng. trans. in Giovanni Battista Piranesi, *Observations on the Letter of Monsieur Mariette, with Opinions on Architecture, and a Preface to a New Treatise on the Introduction and Progress of the Fine Arts in Europe in Ancient Times* [1765], introduction by John Wilton-Ely, trans. Caroline Beamish and David Britt (Los Angeles: Getty Research Institute, 2002).

79 'vil métier où l'on ne feroit que copier'. Giovanni Battista Piranesi, *Parere su l'architettura: Dialogo* (Rome, 1765), 14; Eng. trans in Piranesi, *Observations*, trans. Beamish and Britt, 111. Piranesi is quoting Le Roy.

80 'Osserviamo le pareti d'un edifizio sì di dentro, che di fuori. Queste in cima terminano con gli architravi, e col resto, che vi va sopra; e sotto questi architravi per lo più vi si dispongono delle colonne semidiametrali, o de' pilastri. Or domando,

che cosa regge il tetto dell'edifizio? Se la parete, questa non ha bisogno d'architravi; se le colonne, o i pilastri, la parete che vi fa ella? Via scegliete, Signor Protopiro, che cosa volete abbattere? le pareti, o i pilastri? Non rispondete? E io distruggerò tutto. Mettete da parte, *Edifizi senza pareti, senza colonne, senza pilastri, senza fregi, senza cornici, senza volte, senza tetti; piazza, piazza, campagna rasa.*' Piranesi, *Parere su l'architettura*, 11; Eng. trans. in Piranesi, *Observations*, trans. Beamish and Britt, 106.

81 'Non v'ho io detto, che a fare un edifizio secondo que' principi che vi siete posti in capo, cioè di far tutto con ragione e verità, ci vorreste ridurre a stare in tante capanne?' Piranesi, *Parere su l'architettura*, 11; Eng. trans. in Piranesi, *Observations*, trans. Beamish and Britt, 106.

82 'Biasimate l'esperienza di quella moltitudine di professori che, da quando fu inventato un tal genere d'Architettura, finchè non restò sepolto fra le rovine, fece sempre così'. Piranesi, *Parere su l'architettura*, 12; Eng. trans. in Piranesi, *Observations*, trans. Beamish and Britt, 108.

83 'Quel tale visita le antichità, e riporta le misure d'una colonna, d'un ftegio [*sic*], d'una cornice, con l'intenzione di dare all'Architettura proporzione differenti da quelle alle quali finora abbiamo assuefatto la vista.' Piranesi, *Parere su l'architettura*, 12; Eng. trans. in Piranesi, *Observations*, trans. Beamish and Britt, 108.

84 For example, in Robin Middleton, 'The Abbé de Cordemoy and the Graeco-Gothic Ideal: A Prelude to Romantic Classicism', *Journal of the Warburg and Courtauld Institutes*, 25 (1962), 278–320; 26 (1963), 90–123; Roberto Pane, *Paestum nelle acqueforti di Piranesi* (Milan: Edizioni di Comunità, 1980); Norbert Miller, *Archäologie des Traums: Versuch über Giovanni Battista Piranesi* (Munich: Deutscher Taschenbuch Verlag, 1994) [first published 1978].

85 'Cet Ouvrage montre bien que l'Architecte étoit maitre de son art qu'il n'étoit point retenu par des Systemes imaginés capricieusement, ou même dependants de l'imitation des ouvrages en bois.' Giovanni Battista Piranesi, *Différentes vues de quelques restes de trois grands édifices qui subsistent encore dans le milieu de l'ancienne ville de Pesto, autrement Possidonia qui est située dans la Lucanie* (Rome: s.n., 1778), plate XII.

86 'L'on voit cependant ici des traits d'une invention, à la quelle on ne s'attendoit pas, et qui malgré leur hardiesse obligent d'avoüer, que l'on ne pouvoit pas mieux se conduire en pareil cas.' Ibid., plate VI.

87 'le frise, qui est d'une médiocre grandeur, est propre à orner toute cette façade, comme l'a bien senti l'Artiste en donnant à cette entrée un aspect grave et majesteux, ce qui forme le second point de vuë de ceux qui entroient.' Ibid., plate XII.

88 'Ce Temple là ne presente aucune bisarerie dans ses ornements.' Ibid., plate X.

89 'Les Grecs mêmes voulant adoucir l'ordre Dorique, le chargerent de quelques ornements, ce qui fur imité par les Romains au point qu'ils rencherirent encore sur leurs models; car ceux qui n'ont pas la vraie théorie de l'art preférent toujours une architecture chargée de guirlandes, de fleurs et d'autres ornements à celle qui n'a qu'une simple pureté.' Ibid. 'En cela l'on a voulu faire voir, que ces sortes

de monuments étant construits d'une matiere dure, il étoit dans les vrais principes de l'art de n'en point trop alterer la nature, et qu'un édifice tout de pierre devoit conserver un grand air de force, et de solidité.' Ibid.

90 'Pour ce qui est de ce temple, soit que ce fut la coûtume de la nation, qui tendoit au grave, et au simple, soit que ce fut sagesse dans l'Architecte, il est clair que cette entreprise fut conduite, et terminée avec dignité par la supression de la plus grande partie des ornements, pour le rendre solide, et grave.' Ibid.

91 'que ces sortes de monuments étant construits d'une matiere dure, il étoit dans les vrais principes de l'art de n'en trop alterer la nature, et qu'un édifice tout de pierre devoit conserver un grand air de force, et de solidité.' Ibid.

92 'il faillot . . . remonter à la Théorie primitive, c'est-à-dire, à la Nature même'. Ribart de Chamoust, *L'Ordre françois trouvé dans la nature, présenté au Roi, le 21 septembre 1776, par M. Ribart de Chamoust. Orné de planches gravées d'après les dessins de l'auteur* (Paris: Nyon l'aîné, 1783), p. ii.

93 'Le principe d'origine prime la vérité archéologique.' Élisabeth Décultot, *Johann Joachim Winckelmann: Enquête sur la genèse de l'histoire de l'art* (Paris: Presses Universitaires de France, 2000), 124.

94 'Der eintzige Weg für uns groß, ja wenn es möglich ist, unnachahmlich zu werden, ist die Nachahmung der Alten.' Johann Joachim Winckelmann, *Gedanken über die Nachahmung der griechischen Werke in der Malerei und Bildhauerkunst* (Dresden / Leipzig, 1765), 14. Décultot has shown that there is a contradiction in Winckelmann's theories between going back to origins and being original: *Johann Joachim Winckelmann*, 106–12.

95 Décultot refers to Greece as Winckelmann's 'non-lieu': ibid., 149; for Winckelmann's diminishing eagerness to visit Greece see ibid., 147.

96 Ibid., 123–4. On Winckelmann's ideas of history as a system see Alex Potts, *Flesh and the Ideal: Winckelmann and the Origins of Art History* (New Haven (Conn.) / London: Yale University Press, 2000) [first published 1994], 33–46.

97 On chronology as a science: Chantal Grell, *Le Dix-huitième Siècle et l'antiquité en France, 1680–1789*, 2 vols (Oxford: Voltaire Foundation, 1995), vol. II, 791–881.

98 Mylne was preparing a publication entitled *Antiquities of Sicily*, but this was never finished or published. He referred to it in several letters, now in the archives of the Royal Institute of British Architects, London.

99 'Heureux! si je pourrois parcourir toute la Magna Graecia. Les trois temples à Pesto 50 milles de Naples d'une Architecture plus ancienne peût-être que celle du tems de Pericles dont on n'a parlé que depuis deux ans, bienqu'ils sont presque entiers, ayant été de tout tems à decouvert, cette negligence me fait croire qu'il y pourroit y avoir une infinité de belles choses dispersées et negligées surtout à Tarente et aux environs. Je serois determiné d'y aller meme à pieds.' Winckelmann, letter to Giovanni Lodovico Bianconi, Rome, 29 August 1756, in *Johann Joachim Winckelmann, Briefe*, ed. Rehm and Diepolder, vol. I, 243.

100 'Ich habe verschiedene Reisen weit ins Land hinein gethan, um alles zu sehen: unter anderen bin ich nach Pesto am

Salernitanischen Meerbusen gegangen, um 3 alte dorische Tempel oder Portici, welche fast ganz erhalten sind, zu sehen; dieses ist das ältesten was wir in der Baukunst in der Welt außer Egypten haben. Die Mauren der Stadt sind noch an 2 Mann hoch und 32 Neapelsche Palmen dick . . . Ich würde über die Grenzen eines Briefes gehen, wenn ich von diesen erstaunenden Ueberbleibseln einigen Begriff geben wollte; ich werde aber sowohl von diesen als von dem entdeckten Foro und Tempel zu Pozzuolo einige Nachricht in Druck gehen lassen. Die Gebäude zu Pesto sind allezeit so wie sie itzo sind, zu sehen gewesen, aber man hat allererst vor 6 Jahren davon angefangen zu reden. Itzo werden sie in Kupfer gestochen. Das Land bis Salerno ist eine Gegend, die sich niemand schöner bilden kann'. Winckelmann, letter to Heinrich von Bünau, Naples, 26 April 1758, in ibid., vol. I, 350. Winckelmann was in Paestum in 1758 with the Danish sculptor Johannes Wiedewelt (1731–1803) and Peter Dietrich Volkmann (1735–1792), ibid., vol. IV, 15.

101 Winckelmann, letter to Michelangelo Bianconi, Rome, 13 May 1758, in ibid., vol. I, 355–6.

102 'Vielleicht bin ich . . . der erste Deutsche der da gewesen.' Winckelmann to his intimate friend the lawyer Hieronymus Dietrich Berendis, Rome, 15 May 1758, in ibid., vol. I, 366.

103 Winckelmann, letter to Adam Friedrich Oeser, Rome, 15 May 1758, in ibid., vol. I, 362; Winckelmann, letter to Muzel Stosch, Rome, 20 May 1758, ibid., vol. I, 371.

104 Winckelmann, letters to Johann Caspar Füssli, Rome, 27 July 1758, ibid., vol. I, 400; his patron Heinrich Wilhelm von Muzell-Stosch, Rome, 5 August 175, ibid., vol. I, 403, and 11 August 1758, ibid., vol. I, 404; Giovanni Bianconi, Rome, 24 June 1759, ibid., vol. II, 9; the archaeologist Abbé Jean-Jacques Barthélemy, Rome, 13 September 1760, ibid., vol. II, 101; Johann Jacob Volkmann, Rome, 27 March 1761, ibid., vol. II, 129; the poet Christian Felix Weisse, Rome, 15 August 1761, ibid., vol. II, 173; Giovanni Bianconi, Rome, 10 January 1762, ibid., vol. II, 201; Johannes Wiedewelt, Rome, 3 March 1762, ibid., vol. II, 209; J. J. Volkmann, Rome, 3 March 1762, ibid., vol. II, 211. In his letter to Salomon Gessner, Rome 17 January 1761, ibid., vol. II, 113, Winckelmann referred to the site when he wrote about Peter Dietrich Volkmann, with whom he travelled to Paestum.

105 Winckelmann, letters to the librarian Johann Michael Francke, Rome, 28 January 1764, ibid., vol. III, 14, on his plan to go in February to Naples and to Paestum (though in the event he did not go to Paestum, see ibid., vol. III, 425); the librarian and collector Paolo Maria Paciaudi, Rome, 8 November 1765, ibid., vol. III, 136; the librarian and professor Christian Gottlob Heyne, Rome, 28 December 1765, ibid., vol. III, 146.

106 'L'Architettura non s'è formata sull'imitazione di qualche cosa nella natura rassomigliava a una casa, ma il Scultore aveva il suo archetipo nella natura perfetto e determinato. Le regole della proporzione bisogna convenire che sieno prese dal corpo umano, dunque stabilite da' Scultori.' Winckelmann added a reference to the stability of the columns at Paestum, which he attributed to their entasis: 'questa forma conica le rende stabili e se non saranno distratte con viva forza, rester-

anno in piedi sin'alla fine del mondo.' Winckelmann, letter to Giovanni Lodovico Bianconi, Rome, mid-July 1758, ibid., vol. I, 384–5.

107 Potts, Flesh and the Ideal, 39–40. The philosopher Johann Gottfried Herder argued that Winckelmann 'offered a system of doctrines rather than a history', and gave 'categories by which to group and judge the monuments of antiquity', according to Gombrich, The Preference for the Primitive, 71.

108 'Das Stück Säule ist von dem einen Tempel zu Pesto genommen, von welchen Gebäuden ich in der Vorrede zu den Anmerkungen über die Baukunst der Alten die erste Nachricht gegeben habe. Diese Tempel sind vermutlich nicht lange nach der zwei und siebenzigsten Olympias gebauet, und allem Ansehen nach älter, als alles, was in Griechenland selbst von Gebäuden übrig ist. Die Säule sollte kegelmässiger gehen, welches der Zeichner nicht beobachtet hat.' Johann Joachim Winckelmann, Geschichte der Kunst des Alterthums (Dresden: Walther, 1764), pp. XLIX–L; Eng. trans. in Johann Joachim Winckelmann, History of the Art of Antiquity [1764], introduction by Alex Potts, trans. Harry Francis Mallgrave (Los Angeles: Getty Research Institute, 2006), 82.

109 'Dieses sind ohne Zweifel die ältesten Griechischen Gebäude, und nebst dem Tempel zu Girgenti in Sizilien, und dem Pantheon zu Rom, ist kein anderes Werk der Baukunst, welches sich so völlig erhalten hat'. Johann Joachim Winckelmann, 'Vorbericht', in Anmerkungen über die Baukunst der Alten, entworfen von Johann Winkelmann (Leipzig: Johann Gottfried Dyck, 1762), 4.

110 'Die Verzierungen an dem Tempel zu Girgenti und an denen zu Pesto sind, wie überhaupt in den ältesten Zeiten, groß und einfältig. Die Alten sucheten das Große, worinn die wahre Pracht bestehet: daher springen die Glieder an diesen Tempeln mächtig hervor, und viel stärker, als zu Vitruvius Zeiten, oder wie er selbst lehret.' Johann Joachim Winckelmann, 'Anmerkungen über die Baukunst der alten Tempel zu Girgenti in Sicilien', in Johann Joachim Winckelmann, Kleine Schriften, ed. Walther Rehm (Berlin: Walter de Gruyter, 1968), 179.

111 Paolo Antonio Paoli, 'Lettre sur l'origine et l'antiquité de l'architecture', in Johann Joachim Winckelmann, Histoire de l'art chez les anciens, par Winckelmann; traduit de l'allemand avec des notes historiques et critiques de différens auteurs, vol. II (Paris: Gide, an XI [1803]), 1–55. I have used this edition for th e quotes.

112 The 1779 translation was by Carlo Amoretti, with annotations by Angelo Fumagalli; it was published in Milan.

113 For more background on Fea's publication see Ronald T. Ridley, The Pope's Archaeologist: The Life and Times of Carlo Fea (Rome: Quasar, 2000), 32–46. Immediately after he arrived in Rome, Goethe bought a copy of Fea's edition: 'Winckelmanns Kunstgeschichte, übersetzt von Fea, die neue Ausgabe, is ein sehr brauchbares Werk, das ich gleich angeschafft habe und hier am Orte in guter, auslegender und belehrender Gesellschaft sehr nützlich finde.' Johann Wolfgang Goethe, Italienische Reise [1829] (Munich: Wilhelm Goldmann Verlag, 1988), 139; Eng. trans. in Johann Wolfgang Goethe, Italian Journey [1786–8], trans. W. H. Auden and Elizabeth Mayer (London: Penguin, 1970) [first published 1962], 148.

114 A review by Onofrio Boni, in *Memorie per le Belli Arti* (March–June 1786) criticised Fea for unthinkingly publishing Paoli's letter asserting that the Paestum temples were Etruscan, when Winckelmann had rightly shown that they were Doric. (Boni had already reviewed Paoli's monograph on Paestum in *Memorie per le Belle Arti* (August–December 1785).) Fea replied lengthily to Boni's criticism, in *Memorie delle Belle Arti* (July–December 1786).

115 'sur-tout lorsqu'elles [les ouvrages] sont exécutées par un esprit ardent, dont le travail rapide ne s'accorde pas toujours avec de lentes et utiles réflexions'. Paoli, 'Lettre', in Winckelmann, *Histoire*, vol. II, 2.

116 'aussi dois-je attribuer à votre véritable attachement pour moi, ou plutôt à votre modestie et à votre défiance de vousmême, de m'avoir communiqué vos savantes observations, et de m'avoir forcé à vous exposer mon sentiment sur quelques remarques de Winckelmann sur l'architecture des anciens, et spécialement sur les ruines de Pestum, dont il parle en différens endroits de son ouvrage'. Ibid., 3.

117 'les dimensions données dans les planches de mon ouvrage, sont non-seulement les plus exactes qui aient paru jusqu'ici; mais elles correspondent aussi parfaitement aux monumens sur lequels elles ont été prises'. Ibid., 4.

118 Paolo Antonio Paoli, 'Osservazioni sull'architettura degli antichi', in Johann Joachim Winckelmann, *Storia delle arti del disegno presso gli antichi di Giovanni Winkelmann, tradotta dal tedesco e corretta e aumentata dall'abate Carlo Fea* (1783–4), 3 vols (Rome: Pagliarini, 1783–4), vol. III, 1–106.

119 'car ils sont postérieurs au temps auquel l'ordre dorique étoit déjà fixé à la hauteur de six diamètres, il est impossible de leur appliquer cette méthode primitive et très-ancienne de bâtir qu'on a supposée: on devroit, au contraire, les regarder comme des constructions fantasques, d'un style, si l'on veut, antique, mais mal entendu; soit qu'on ait voulu se servir des pierres qu'on avoit sous la main, soit par l'effet de quelques autres circonstances, qu'il seroit difficile de deviner, et inutile même de vouloir chercher à connoître'. Paoli, 'Lettre', in Winckelmann, *Histoire*, vol. II, 8.

120 'On ne doit pas considérer un ouvrage de l'art comme antique, ou comme attestant un des premiers essais de ce même art, par la raison seulement qu'il est grossier, difforme, sans proportions dans son ensemble, et privé d'ornemens; puisque, dans des temps modernes, on a vu paroître des ouvrages mal conçus et executés sans la moindre méthode.' Ibid.

121 'leur origine étrusque, de ce que ces monumens sont de courte proportion, et qu'ils sont formés de grandes masses de pierre; mais je ne regardai pas cela comme des preuves suffisantes pour y reconnoître le caractère des travaux de ces peuples, et comme l'ouvrage d'un temps antérieur à l'origine des trois ordres grecs'. Ibid., 9. Here he referred to Le Roy's idea, formulated in his *Les ruines des plus beaux monumens de la Grèce* (1758; 2nd edn 1770), that there had existed a 'primitive' Doric before the Doric order that was known – a shorter and 'deformed' version of the order. According to Paoli, this theory was unconvincing: 'Le Roi auroit . . . dû produire quelques preuves de l'antiquité des deux monu-

ments dont il s'agit [temples at Corinth and Athens], s'il eût voulu nous convaincre qu'ils sont du temps plus reculé que celui de l'ordre dorique qui nous est connu.' Paoli, 'Lettre', in Winckelmann, *Histoire*, vol. II, 8. In another passage, Paoli took again as a starting point Le Roy's description of these two temples, one near Corinth and the Theseus temple in Athens, and argued against Le Roy's claim that these were not Greek: 'plus le Roi fera d'efforts pour nous représenter ces monumens comme lourds et sans grâce, moins il parviendra à prouver qu'ils ont été construits par les Grecs'. Ibid., 13. The idea still persisted that Greek architecture was simple and graceful, and that buildings that did not correspond to this idea were of a puzzling derivation, as they were to Winckelmann.

122 'Il eût même suffi de ce que j'ai dit, dans mon ouvrage, sur Pestum [*Paesti . . . rudera: Rovine della città di Pesto* (1784), 7ff.], pour répondre à le Roi, et pour le convaincre qu'on ne doit pas attribuer aux Grecs l'invention de l'architecture; mais seulement son élégance et ses ornemens les plus recherchés. Et véritablement, je me flatte d'avoir prouvé que quand les premiers Grecs vinrent de la Phocide en Italie, non-seulement les Tyrréniens étoient déjà avancés dans l'architecture, mais que même ceux de Pestum étoient en état d'enseigner aux nouveaux habitans l'art de bâtir une ville.' Paoli, 'Lettre', in Winckelmann, *Histoire*, vol. II, 16. Further: 'La science des Grecs par rapport à l'architecture s'est principalement manifestée dans l'élégance des colonnes, dans la variété de leurs bases, et dans la beauté de leurs chapiteaux.' Ibid., 34.

123 '[Le] temple de Salomon, nous indique les proportions . . . Voici donc l'origine de cette architecture lourde, massive et solide, qui prit naissance en Orient, qui, dans les contrées méridionales, fut adoptée par les Tyrréniens, et que les Grecs adoptèrent ensuite.' Ibid., 20.

124 'Quant à moi, je n'ai jamais vu d'arbres dont la partie inférieure ressemblât à un socle, et qui fussent terminés à leur cîme par un chapiteau.' Ibid., 22.

125 'Je me conforme volontiers à l'opinion de ceux qui, en admettant les cabanes, regardent cependant les grottes et les antres, comme les premières et les plus anciennes retraites de l'homme . . . cabanes qu'en second lieu.' Ibid., 25.

126 'Ainsi, la méthode d'élever des murs en liant les pierres avec de la boue, et de durcir la terre humide par le moyen d'un élément plus actif que la seule chaleur du soleil, en les cuisant au feu, ne me semblent pas chose de difficile invention. C'est cependant à quoi l'on doit l'origine et les progrès de l'architecture.' Ibid., 31.

127 'En effet, que l'on abatte les angles d'une aiguille, qu'on la tronque à une hauteur donnée, et on aura une colonne antique, large à sa base et se retrécissant en forme de pyramide, comme l'étoient les colonnes orientales, et comme le sont encore celles de deux temples de Pestum.' Ibid., 36.

128 'Cela posé, la colonne du grand temple de Pestum est retrécie d'environ une quatrième partie de sa base, à la hauteur d'environ quatre diamètres; si l'on prolonge ses lignes jusqu'au point du retrécissement d'une troisième partie, elle formera une colonne haute de cinq diamètres et deux tiers . . . Si l'on considère ensuite la colonne du petit temple de Pestum, qui

est moins ancien que l'autre, et dont par conséquent le rétré-cissement est moins considérable, on verra qu'elle répond en quelque manière aux proportions de l'obélisque de la place Saint-Pierre.' Ibid., 37.

129 'Voilà donc la raison du grand retrécissement des colonnes étrusques, et pourquoi les plus anciennes de cet ordre avoient une forme pyramidale. Il se pourroit aussi que cela eût fourni l'idée de l'*entasis* ou renflement des colonnes, dont les Etrusques furent également les inventeurs, et qui se voit au troisième et le moins ancien monument de Pestum. Lorsque, dans la suite, ces anciens habiles architectes sentirent la néces-sité de renfler leurs colonnes vers le milieu, pour leur ôter la sécheresse de cette ligne pyramidale, et conserver, en même temps, leur solidité, ils imaginèrent cette sage et ingénieuse proportion dont j'ai longuement parlé dans mon ouvrage, et à laquelle les Grecs ont donné le nom d'*entasis* . . . le même gout et le même caractère.' Ibid., 37–8.

130 'on obtiendra une colonne ronde et cannelée . . . et ce sont-là précisément les colonnes de Pestum'. Ibid., 38–9.

131 '[if we consider that columns and flutings] ne doivent pas leurs origine aux pyramides ou aux obélisques; je voudrois bien savoir comment la vue d'un arbre a pu en donner l'idée? car assurément l'arbre ne porte avec lui ni renflement vers le milieu, ni cannelures dans son fût. Cependant l'in-vention de la colonne et de ses cannelures remont à la plus haute antiquité; et le renflement d'une agréable proportion, qu'on nomme entasis, est également fort ancien.' Ibid., 43.

132 'je vais continuer à vous exposer ce que je pense sur l'orig-ine et les progrès de cet art admirable: pour cet effet, je con-tinuerai à traiter cette matière purement en historien, et non en architecte ni en professeur d'aucune partie pratique de l'art, dans lequel j'avoue n'avoir des connoissances suffisantes'. Ibid., 22.

133 Mario Guarnacci, *Origini italiche, o siano Memorie istorico-etrusche sopra l'antichissimo regno d'Italia e sopra i di lei primi abitatori nei secoli più remoti* (Lucca: L. Venturini, 1767), presented the temples as Etruscan, as did Baron d'Hancarville (see next note).

134 'Dans un quatrieme voyage que nous fimes il y a quelques mois à Pœsti, nous nous y arrêtames plusieurs jours pour examiner à loisir ces ruines magnifiques, qui étonnent & imposent d'avantage à mesure qu'elles sont examinées avec plus de soin, & revues plus souvent. En recherchant, avec Mr. Hamilton, tout ce qui pouvoit nous instruire du plan et de la grandeur de cette Ville, dont nous fimes plusieurs fois le tour.' Pierre-François Hugues d'Hancarville, *Antiqui-tés étrusques, grecques et romaines, tirées du cabinet de M. Hamil-ton / Collection of Etruscan, Greek and Roman Antiquities from the Cabinet of the Hon. William Hamilton*, 4 vols (Naples: s.n., 1766–7), vol. 1, 53.

135 'Du milieu de ses ruines, s'élèvent trois Edifices d'une sorte d'Architecture, dont les membres sont Doriques bien que les proportions ne le soient pas'. Ibid., vol. 1, 96–7. The publica-tion was meant to illustrate Hamilton's rich collection of vases. The section where Paestum is covered is called 'De l'o-rigine des Etrusques et de leurs Lettres'. On d'Hancarville see Francis Haskell, 'The Baron d'Hancarville: An Adventurer and

Art Historian in Eighteenth-Century Europe', in Edward Chaney and Neil Ritchie (eds), *Oxford, China and Italy: Writings in Honour of Sir Harold Acton on his Eightieth Birthday* (London: Thames and Hudson, 1984), 177–91; Noah Hering-man, *Sciences of Antiquity: Romantic Antiquarianism, Natural History, and Knowledge Work* (Oxford: Oxford University Press, 2013), 125–54. D'Hancarville also published *Recherches sur l'o-rigine, l'esprit et les progrès des arts de la Grèce, sur leurs connec-tions avec les arts et la religion des plus anciens peuples connus, sur les monuments antiques de l'Inde, de la Perse, du reste de l'Asie, de l'Europe et de l'Égypte*, 3 vols (London: P. Appleyard, 1785).

136 'Nevertheless those [buildings] of Pesti neither keeping to that rule [of Vitruvius], nor to the symmetry assign'd to the Spaces between the Pillars of the Order, they must have been built at a time preceeding the rule, that is before the Epoch of the establishment of the Greeks in Ionia . . . its grandeur and solidity; these two articles composed the Character which the Etruscans endeavoured to give to their Architec-ture, and we find both the one and the other in the Temples of Pesti. It is then credible that the Temples of Pesti erected before the discovery of the rules, in a Country where the Dorians had certainly Etruscan edifices before their Eyes, fol-lowed the Symmetry of the antient Tuscan Order, as differ-ent from that of which Vitruvius gives the proportions, as the Dorick of Pesti is to that of the Ionians . . . After having pointed out the Age to which may be attributed the con-struction of the Temples of Pesti; after having shewn the Etruscan edifices which may have been their models, we have proved that the Grecians borrowed sometimes a part of the system of the Etruscans in Architecture, and we have ended with shewing that this system is employed at Pesti.' D'Hancarville, *Antiquités étrusques, grecques et romaines / Col-lection of Etruscan, Greek and Roman Antiquities*, vol. 1, 96–7.

137 'The pyramidal form of the Pillars at Pesti, has made some think that the Grecians had borrowed that form from the Egyptians, although at the time they were raised, there was no communication between these two people; on the con-trary it is known that the taste of the Etruscans, though assuredly Original, resembled in many things that of the Egyptians'. Ibid., 108, 110.

138 For example, in *Considérations sur les arts du dessin en France, suivies d'un plan d'Académie ou d'École publique et d'un système d'encouragement* (Paris, 1791); *De l'architecture égyptienne consid-érée dans son origine, ses principes et son goût, et comparée sous les mêmes rapports à l'architecture grecque* (Paris, 1803); *Le Jupiter Olympien, ou L'Art de la sculpture antique* (Paris, 1814); *Essai sur la nature, le but et les moyens de l'imitation dans les beaux-arts* (Paris, 1823).

139 *Bibliothèque de M. Quatremère de Quincy . . . Collection d'ou-vrages relatifs aux beaux-arts et à l'archéologie . . . Vente le 27 mai 1850 et jours suivants, rue de Condé, no 14. Préface de R. Merlin* (Paris: Imprimerie d'Adrien Le Clere et Cie, 1850).

140 Not much has been published on Quatremère de Quincy. A recent study, focusing mainly on architecture and language, is Lavin, *Quatremère de Quincy*. The only biographical study is René Schneider, *Quatremère de Quincy et son intervention dans les arts (1788–1830)* (Paris: Hachette, 1910). For his theo-

ries see René Schneider, *L'esthétique classique chez Quatremère de Quincy (1805–1823)* (Paris: Hachette, 1910).

141 An inheritance enabled him to spend this period in Italy: see Joseph Daniel Guigniaut, *Institut impérial de France: Notice historique sur la vie et les travaux de M. Quatremère de Quincy, lue dans la séance publique . . . le 5 août 1864* (Paris: Firmin Didot frères, 1866), 6. 'A Pæstum, il eut la première apparition de l'architecture hellénique, dans la simplicité sévère du style dorien, qui lui révéla toute l'histoire de ce grand art chez les Grecs . . . Dans l'année 1779, il était en Sicile, où il en évoquait les images parmi les ruines des édifices doriques de cette île. Il y vit, entre autres, celles du temple de Jupiter à Agrigente, restitué par lui dans ses proportions colossales, d'après la description rectifiée de Diodore de Sicile: ce fut le sujet du premier Mémoire qu'il lut devant vous et comme l'un de vous, à vingt-cinq ans de là.' Ibid., 8.

142 Now in a private collection, this is the earliest known portrait of Quatremère; it is reproduced in Lavin, *Quatremère de Quincy*, 4.

143 'Ce modèle, réel ou fictif, quel qu'il fût, étoit déjà lui-même un ouvrage de l'art', Antoine C. Quatremère de Quincy, *Encyclopédie méthodique: Architecture, dédiée et présentée à Monseigneur de Lamoignon, garde des sceaux de France, &c.*, 3 vols (Paris: Chez Panckoucke, 1788–1825), vol. 1 (1790), 454.

144 The architecture volumes were written with the collaboration of Jean Rondelet until 1801, followed by Nicolas Huyot and Antoine-Laurent Castellan. Volume III is almost entirely by Quatremère de Quincy. The volumes were published as follows: volume I in 1788 (1–320) and 1790 (321–730); volume II in 1801 (1–358) and 1820 (361–744); volume III in 1825 (1–344) and 1828 (345–664). See Laurent Baridon, 'Le Dictionnaire d'architecture de Quatremère de Quincy: Codifier le néoclassicisme', in Claude Blanckaert and Michel Porret (eds), *L'Encyclopédie méthodique (1782–1832): Des Lumières au positivisme* (Geneva: Droz, 2006), 691–718.

145 'Plusieurs parties de cet enduit ont conservé des restes de couleurs.' Quatremère de Quincy, 'Paestum', in *Encyclopédie méthodique*, vol. III, 57.

146 'Temple', ibid., 448–57.

147 Ibid., 454.

148 'tous ces ouvrages doriques sont sans aucune exception dans le caractère, le style, la forme & les proportions inconnues aux modernes avant les récentes découvertes qui ont reproduit les monumens originaux de l'art des Grecs'. 'Dorique', ibid., vol. II, 234.

149 'c'est en Grèce exclusivement qu'on doit aller puiser les modèles de cet ordre. Ainsi ceux qui, sur la première vue de monumens doriques grecs retrouvés & dessinés pour la première fois vers le milieu de ce siècle à Pæstum, avoient jugé que cette ordonnance dorique n'étoit qu'un style local & d'exception, manquoient des données nécessaires au jugement qu'ils portoient. Leurs idées n'avoient pu se généraliser assez pour embrasser la question dans toute son étendue. On prenoit le dorique moderne pour règle; l'autre devoit être exception. Le tableau qu'on vient de donner fait assez voir de quel côté doit être la règle.' Ibid., 235.

150 'par l'effet du contraste du dorique grec avec le moderne, & frappés de la pesanteur, de la courte proportion, des formes mâles & massives de l'ancien dorique, le regardèrent comme une ébauche de cet ordre, & de la privation de base, conclurent qu'un tel goût remontoit à l'enfance de l'art. Ce jugement étoit tout aussi erroné; la plus simple réflexion le démontre.' Ibid.

151 Ibid., 235–6.

152 'Parler de l'ordre dorique, c'est parler de l'architecture grecque; ainsi parler de l'origine de cet ordre, ce seroit remonter à la naissance de l'architecture.' Ibid., 237.

153 'amour-propre national & le désir de donner à l'Italie une architecture indigène . . . plutôt parce qu'il lui importoit dans son système de donner à son toscan une origine étrangère à la Grèce.' Ibid., 239.

154 'la différence qui existe entre l'architecture de Pæstum & le dorique, tels que les modernes l'ont pratiqué, ne pourroit laisser de doute sur cette question qu'autant que les monumens de Pæstum seroient seuls de leur espèce; & c'est dans cette hypothèse qu'a raisonné le père Paoli, & c'est dans cette seule hypothèse que sa théorie devient tolérable . . . si ceux de Pæstum sont toscans, ceux d'Athènes sont aussi toscans.' Ibid., 238. This discussion of the strangeness of Paestum, Quatremère's defence of its being Doric, and his cautious endorsememt of its constituting a canon or norm disappeared from the second edition of the *Encyclopédie* (1835), because by that time these points were no longer an object of debate.

155 'Si le père Paoli eut eu connoissance de ce nombre prodigieux de monumens grecs, tous semblables à ceux de Pæstum, il est probable qu'il n'eût pas aussi légèrement bâti sur un point isolé le système général dont on vient de parler; mais ce système même joint au silence qu'il garde sur tous les autres monumens du même genre, prouve qu'il n'a connu que Pæstum; dès lors il est tout-à-fait caduc, & je n'en parlé aussi longuement que parce que la grande érudition de l'auteur, & la célébrité de l'ouvrage ne permettoient pas de laisser l'un & l'autre sans réfutation.' Quatremère de Quincy, 'Dorique', in *Encyclopédie méthodique*, vol. II, 239.

156 Here Quatremère referred to his own examination of the bases of the columns in the pronaos of the Ceres temple at Paestum: ibid., 247. In this part of 'Dorique' he also referred to Delagardette's publication, reverting to it again on p. 250.

157 'une célébrité qu'elle avoit perdue depuis bien des siècles. Enfin la proximité de Naples détermina beaucoup d'artistes à entreprendre ce voyage, & il n'y a pas d'antiquités mieux connues aujourd'hui que celles-là . . . Cependant la découverte des ruines de Pæstum ayant précédé de fort long-temps toutes les autres, le dorique de ses temples a été un sujet de controverse & de conjectures assez bizarres, jusqu'à ce que de plus nombreuses découvertes dans le même genre, eussent mis le plus grand nombre des artistes à portée de faire des parallèles & de généraliser les idées . . . Nous avons déjà parlé du système erroné du Père Paoli, précédé par M. d'Hancarville dans l'opinion que les temples de Pæstum étoient d'ordre toscan. Cela vint du défaut de notions générales sur cette matière. Il est résulté de même beaucoup d'erreurs de

goût, de préjugés & d'opinions hasardées sur le dorique de Pæstum – Toutes furent l'effet de cette découverte isolée & partielle, mais elles n'en ont pas moins contribué à jeter quelque défaveur sur la rénovation du véritable dorique.' Ibid., 252.

158 'L'ordre dorique est trop sérieux, trop grave pour être employé autrement que sérieusement & avec gravité.' Ibid., 255.

159 'Il faut que le dorique grec, le seul véritable dorique, ramène constamment l'architecture à son origine, & en reproduisant toujours ces premières pratiques de la construction en bois qui lui donnèrent l'être, apprenne aux artistes que c'est dans la simplicité des premières inventions que le génie doit aller puiser les motifs toujours nouveaux d'un art qui, comme un fleuve grossi par des torrens, n'est jamais pur qu'à sa source.' Ibid., 256.

160 'Nul homme, nul architecte n'a pu avoir l'honneur de cette invention.' Ibid., 240.

161 '. . . le fruit subit d'un seul essai . . . La cabane, sans perdre de la simplicité de sa forme première, aura vu ses supports, ses combles, ses porches, ses plafonds, ses proportions, se combiner, se modifier, s'embellir successivement, & se disposer avec plus de recherche & d'élégance.' Ibid.

162 'L'art ne transforma pas tout de suite & du premier coup les arbres en colonnes; . . . C'est en remplissant cet intervalle par les essais successifs d'une industrie toujours croissante, qu'on peut se rendre compte de la formation d'une architecture & de l'invention d'un ordre.' Ibid.

163 'c'est en vain qu'on chercheroit à attribuer l'honneur de son invention à telle ville, à tel pays, à tel architecte, à tel prince . . . l'ordre dorique est le perfectionnement de la construction chez les Grecs; c'est le complément d'un système fondé sur la nature de leur construction primitive.' Ibid., 241.

164 'L'architecture n'ayant aucun modèle positif dans la nature, eut été livrée à tous les caprices & à toutes les incertitudes de l'esprit de l'homme, si quelque forme simple, fondée en raison & déterminée par le besoin, n'eût pu servir de règle comme de terme aux efforts de l'imagination.' Ibid., 241–2.

165 For Labrouste see Neil Levine, 'The Romantic Idea of Architectural Legibility: Henri Labrouste and the Néo-Grec', in Arthur Drexler (ed.), *The Architecture of the École des Beaux-Arts* (New York/Cambridge (Mass.): Museum of Modern Art/MIT Press, 1977), 325–416; Pierre Saddy, *Henri Labrouste architecte, 1801–1875* (Paris: Caisse Nationale des Monuments Historiques et des Sites, 1977); Renzo Dubbini (ed.), *Henri Labrouste, 1801–1875* (Milan: Electa, 2002); Corinne Bélier, Barry Bergdoll and Marc Le Cœur (eds), *Henri Labrouste: Structure Brought to Light* (New York: Museum of Modern Art, 2013).

166 'J'ai fait plusieurs voyages à Pesto, à plusieurs années d'intervalle, et toujours frappé de la Beauté et de l'interêt de ces monuments, je me suis décidé a en présenter à l'académie l'Etat actuel et la restauration comme travail de ma quatrième année.' Henri Labrouste, 'Antiquités de Pestum Posidonia, Labrouste jeune 1829', *mémoire*, Paris, École Nationale Supérieure des Beaux-Arts, PC 77832–7, fol. 1; published in Henri Labrouste, *Les Temples de Paestum: Restauration exécutée en 1829 par Henri Labrouste*, Restaurations des Monuments

Antiques par les Architectes Pensionnaires de l'Académie de France à Rome, vol. III (Paris: Firmin–Didot, 1877), 4.

167 Marie-Christine Hellmann, Philippe Fraisse and Annie Jacques, *Paris–Rome–Athènes: Le Voyage en Grèce des architectes français aux XIXe et XXe siècles* (Paris: École Nationale Superieure des Beaux-Arts, 1982), 132–45. Other students to work on Paestum for submissions to the Académie were: Delagardette (*envoi*, 1793); Louis-Nicolas-Marie Destouches (second year, 1818, not delivered); S.-Cl. Constant-Duffeux (first year, 1831, two drawings); P. Morey (second year, 1834, three drawings); Félix Thomas (*restauration* and *mémoire*, fourth year, 1849; ibid., 146–51); P. Bigot (second year, 1903); Ch-H. Nicod (first year, one drawing); and René Mirland (third year, 1915, five drawings; ibid., 152–5), dealing with the Temple of Neptune only. See also Pierre Pinon and François-Xavier Amprimoz, *Les Envois de Rome (1778–1968): Architecture et archéologie* (Rome: École Française de Rome, 1988), 408–9.

168 See, for example, Levine, 'The Romantic Idea', 325–416; and Dubbini (ed.), *Henri Labrouste*.

169 Labrouste, *Les Temples de Paestum* (see note 166).

170 David van Zanten, *Designing Paris: The Architecture of Duban, Labrouste, Duc, and Vaudoyer* (Cambridge (Mass.): MIT Press, 1987), 11.

171 Ibid. See also Richard Wittman, 'Félix Duban's Didactic Restoration of the Château de Blois: A History of France in Stone', *Journal of the Society of Architectural Historians*, 55 (1996), 412–34.

172 Henry Lapauze, *Histoire de l'Académie de France à Rome*, 2 vols (Paris: Plon, Nourrit et Cie, 1924), vol. II, 190–200, cited the long correspondence between Quatremère and Vernet. Pinon and Amprimoz, *Les Envois de Rome*, 248–9, 322–4, use the original documents to prove that there was no *affaire* over the Académie's doctrines or polychromy, but that it was all a personal battle ('Il n'y a jamais eu de révolte de H. Labrouste contre l'Académie, mais un conflit Vernet–Quatremère de Quincy'), arguing that scholars have simply copied the opinions of Labrouste's advocates. See J. Musy, 'La Grèce et l'École des Beaux-Arts: L'Envoi d'Henri Labrouste', *Archéologia*, 167 (1982), 15–17; Marie-Françoise Billot: 'Recherches au XVIIIe et XIXe siècles sur la polychromie de l'architecture grecque', in Hellmann, Fraisse and Jacques, *Paris–Rome–Athènes*, 61–125; and Levine, 'The Romantic Idea', who, according to Pinon and Amprimoz, fails to take account of the original sources. Pinon and Amprimoz regard the debate as having been about architectural details, and not a conflict of academicism. For the correspondence between Quatremère de Quincy and Vernet, May–June 1829, see 'Rapport sur les voyages des architectes pensionnaires', 6 June 1829, and 'Pièces annexes des proces-verbaux de l'Académie des Beaux-Arts', Paris, Institut de France, Archives de l'Académie des Beaux-Arts, 1829 5 E 19; published in Lapauze, *Histoire de l'Académie*, and Schneider, *Quatremère*, 301–5.

173 Labrouste's project was received in Paris on 5 August 1829 and the exhibition of work was from 24 August to 3 October. Quatremère criticised Labrouste's *envoi*, while Vernet defended him and set up a commission to check Labrouste's findings at Paestum itself.

174 Apparently, Léon Vaudoyer also thought about choosing Paestum as his *envoi* subject, but his father discouraged him because he thought travelling to the site was dangerous. Vaudoyer wrote to his father about Labrouste trying to find ladders in Naples: 'Henry avait à retourner à Pestum pour terminer son travail en faisant porter des échelles de Naples; il y eut allé avec son frère et moi avec Duc. L'aspect de cette belle antiquité m'a ravi, c'est une des choses qui m'ait fait le plus d'effet.' Léon Vaudoyer, letter to Antoine-Laurent-Thomas Vaudoyer, received 6 December 1828 (letter XXXII). 'N'ayant point l'intention de faire un travail à Pestum, travail très important qui demande beaucoup de temps, et qui d'ailleurs, va être très bien fait par Henry. Je suis parti seulement pour bien voir et raisonner sur les lieux avec Henry, Duc et Labrouste. Nous avons couché à Salerne deux fois en allant et en revenant. Nous sommes restés 4 heures à Pestum où il n'y a pas de quoi manger, mais nous avions apporté des provisions, puis nous sommes revenus le soir à Salerne.' Rome, 29 January 1829 (letter XXXIV). Antoine-Laurent-Thomas Vaudoyer et Léon Vaudoyer, 'Correspondance échangée pendant le séjour à Rome de Léon Vaudoyer, 1826–1832', Voyage d'Italie d'A.-L.-T. Vaudoyer, 1786–1787', Paris, Institut Nationale d'Histoire de l'Art, MS 747 (1–2).

175 'Ces ruines qui appartiennent evidemment à des monumens d'Architecture grecque, présentent un très grand interêt pour l'architecte tant par la singularité de leur disposition et le caractère de leurs détails, que par leur etat de conservation. malheureusement les Architectes qui se rendent à Pesto, sont obligés de se contenter d'un court Examen, l'état d'abandon dans le quel se trouvent ces ruines, leur situation dans un payis inhabité, malsain, éloigné des grandes villes du Royaume de Naples, ne permettent de trouver aucun des moyens Necessaires pour y sejourner, et les mesurer et etudier convenablement; ces raisons qui privent les Architectes des etudes que pouraient leur presenter les ruines de Possidonia, peuvent, je crois, donner un interet de plus a celles que je presente. C'est a ces mêmes raisons qu'on doit attribuer l'origine d'une opinion, malheureusement trop connue, qui fait regarder l'architecture de ces monuments comme appartenant à l'Enfance de l'art, et qui l'a condamné comme impure et grossiere.' Labrouste, 'Antiquités de Pestum Posidonia', fol. 1.

176 'Mr henri Labrouste, qui a fait plusieurs voyages à Pœstum et qui y a séjourné longtems pour observer avec soin tous les details des restes d'antiquités que renferme cette ville, n'ayant pas dû mettre dans son travail la précipitation qu'il reproche aux architectes qui les ont visitées avant lui, aurait pu par ces recherches ajouter à son travail un intérêt de plus qu'à celui de ses prédécesseurs auxquels nous croyons qu'il ne rend pas tout à fait assez de justice sur certains points.' Horace Vernet, 'Rapport de la Section d'Architecture Sur la Restauration des monumens de Pestum par Mr Labrouste henri (jeune)', Paris, École Nationale Supérieure des Beaux-Arts, PC 77832–7, fol. 2.

177 'qui fait regarder l'architecture de ces monuments comme appartenant à l'Enfance de l'art'.

178 'la précipitation que mettent ordinairement les Architectes qui vont a Pesto, leur fait negliger les monumens connus sous les noms de Basilique et de Temple de Cerès; mon premier voyage en 1826 et les deux voyages que j'y ai fait en 1828 m'ont permis de mesurer toutes les Antiquités de Posidonia et d'y dessiner des fragmens que je crois inconnus et d'un grand interet; dans l'interval de ces deux voyages, j'ai parcouru la Sicile dont j'ai rapporté les materiaux qui me manquaient pour la Restauration.' Labrouste, 'Antiquités de Pestum Posidonia', fol. 1.

179 Labrouste made comparisons with the temples at Segesta, and the temples of Concord and Olympian Jupiter at Agrigento. Ibid., fols 3, 4, 7, 8, 12, 14.

180 'Ces divers fragmens trouvés en Sicile et qui m'ont servi d'autorité pour la restauration de la couverture du temple de Neptune, me paraissent interessants et neufs, j'ai cru convenable de les dessiner et d'en donner la dimension sur la feuille n° 12.' Ibid., fol. 8.

181 Path-breaking aspects of Labrouste's study relate to the proportions of the superposed orders in the Neptune temple ('Le diamètre inférieur du second ordre est donné par le prolongement de l'ordre inférieur', ibid., fol. 4) – a phenomenon that Viollet-le-Duc later noted; a reconstruction of the pediment of the Ceres temple; and observations on the polychromy of Greek architecture.

182 Compare, for example, his argument, based on functionality, about the Basilica's having only one line of columns, which was 'inspirée par le Besoin de couvrir un grand Espace à peu de frais. Car une Certaine economie etait nécessaire dans l'Eréction de ces Portiques, monumens d'utilité.' Ibid., fol. 11.

183 'L'intérieur de la cella est Decoré de deux ordres places l'un au dessus de l'autre; et ce qui est très remarquable dans cette disposition c'est que l'ordre superieur n'est pour ainsi dire que le prolongement de l'ordre inferieur (Ce fait résulte de l'opération faite de la maniere la plus rigoureuse). Cette particularité dont il est fait mention dans aucun des ouvrages publiés sur les ruines de Possidonia est je crois assez intéressante pour l'Etude de l'architecture.' Ibid., fol. 4. 'Ce temple est je crois le seul Exemple que l'on connaisse de deux ordres de colonnes placés l'un au dessus de l'autre dans l'interieur de la cella.' Ibid., fol. 5.

184 Labrouste made this point in talking about 'l'appareil des Triglyphes et des métopes de la frise est digne de remarque surtout à l'angle du monument': 'il ne décide en rien l'enfance de l'art, mais bien l'art arrivé à sa perfection.' Ibid., fol. 3. In speaking of the Temple of Neptune, he emphasised its 'caractère d'unité et de solidité qui regne dans toutes les parties de ce monument'. Ibid., fol. 6. In his *restauraton*, Labrouste chose to close the roof instead of leaving it open, as did Vitruvius and others – hence the description 'hypaethral' (having no roof). His text on the Neptune temple discredits Vitruvius as a source; his interpretation of the two superposed ranks of columns as indicating a preoccupation with structure is also a claim of the superiority of Greek over Roman architecture, and thus a taunt directed at the Académie, whose dogma was that Roman architecture represented perfection.

185 'il est à présumer que la nécessité obligea dabord à se servir des materiaux trouvés sur les lieux, surtout dans les premiers Edifices qu'on voulait construire; et les Posidoniens durent mettre leurs premiers soins à construire le Temple de Neptune, leur protecteur.' Ibid., fol. 9.

186 'Ce stuc indique par sa nature une epoque posterieure à celle de la fondation du Temple. On remarque souvent sur les monumens anciens des stucs ajoutés après coup'; Labrouste attributed the later addition of stucco to 'l'usage de renouveller la décoration', as in Rome, where they often decide to 'repeindre la façade des Eglises'. Ibid., fols 4–5.

187 'on ne peut pas supposer avec autant de vraisemblance que les nouveau colons mirent le même Emprèssement à Elever des Temples aux autres Divinités et à construire des monumens déstinés aux assemblées des magistrats. Ce ne fut qu'après plusieurs années de posterité que les nouveaux Colons durent penser à Elever un Temple à Cérès en reconnaissance de la fertilité de leurs campagnes [. . .] Ce ne fut aussi qu'après plusieurs succès dus à leurs armes, et lorsque la colonie eut acqui un certain dégré de Stabilité et de puissance que les possidoniens durent penser à construire des Portiques destinés aux assemblées ou l'on discutait des interets communs. On doit donc considerer le Portique et le Temple de Cérès comme posterieurs au temple de Neptune.' Ibid., fol. 10.

188 'en effet on remarque dans ces deux monumens une Architecture bien differente de celle du Temple de Neptune. Ces deux monumens sont construits de le même maniere; l'emploi des materiaux differans, le melange de pierres dures et de pierre tendres annonce si non un perfectionnement, du moins une plus ample connaissance des materiaux fournis par le pays; et ce mélange de pierres differantes de nature et même de couleur, a nécessité l'Emploi d'un stuc des l'origine. l'Architecture de ces deux monumens est la même quant aux formes, mais ces formes n'ont plus la pureté primitive qu'on remarque dans le Temple de Neptune.' Ibid., fols 10–11.

189 'La construction de ce monument offre beaucoup d'interet et cependant on n'en a rendu compte dans aucun ouvrage publiés sur les antiquités de Posidonia. Il est à remarquer qu'on a employé dans la construction de ce Temple des pierres de deux natures differentes: les colonnes, les architraves, le frise et le fronton sont construits en pierre dure et la pierre tendre semble avoir été réservée pour les parties ornées de moulures telles que les chapiteaux, les moulures de l'architrave, les trigliphes et la corniche de l'entablement.' Ibid., fol. 14.

190 Labrouste claimed that this building had been a 'portique' rather than a basilica because of the uneven number of columns on the front and rear façades and the row of columns down the central axis: 'Cette disposition m'a déterminé à le considerer comme un de les portiques ou les anciens se réunisaient pour discuter les affaires publiques. Ces portiques etaient d'une grande utilité chez les grecs, car toutes les villes en contenaient un ou plusieurs.' Ibid., fol. 10. In his *restauration* drawing of the Basilica, he showed shields and other weapons decorating the interior of the building,

as if these had been put up 'shortly after a ceremony' (see Barry Bergdoll, 'Labrouste and Italy', in Bélier, Bergdoll and Le Cœur (eds), *Henri Labrouste*, 69).

191 'Ces observations conduisent à considerer le Temple de Neptune comme etant d'Architecture grecque et construit à l'epoque ou les Trisieneux originaires du Péleponèze et fondateurs de Posidonia n'avaient pas encor oublié les Principes de l'architecture qu'ils avaient apportés de la grèce; et à considerer le Portique et le Temple de Cérès comme posterieures au Temple de Neptune et construits à une Epoque ou les Posidoniens devenus plus puissants voulurent se créer une Architecture nouvelle'. Labrouste, 'Antiquités de Pestum Posidonia', fol. 11.

192 'Ces deux monumens seuls offrent le Type de l'Architecture de Posidonia.' Ibid.

193 See the Introduction, pp. 4–6.

194 'Tout ce temple [de Neptune] est construit en pierre, elle est dans toutes les parties de cet Edifice de même nature et de même qualité.' Labrouste, 'Antiquités de Pestum Posidonia', fol. 3.

195 Labrouste, *Les Temples de Paestum*, 13.

196 Neil Levine, 'Architectural Reasoning in the Age of Positivism: The Neo-Grec Idea of Henri Labrouste's Bibliothèque Sainte-Geneviève', unpublished PhD thesis, Yale University, 1975, 792, quoted in Martin Bressani, 'The Hybrid: Labrouste's Paestum', *Chora*, 5 (2007), 124.

197 Labrouste, *Les Temples de Paestum*, 5. In his interesting article on Labrouste's *restauration*, 'The Hybrid', Bressani claims that it was a combination of Greek and Etruscan architecture and then explores the nineteenth-century context of the Etruscan debate. He remarks that Labrouste's account must be interpreted 'as a more engrossing story of an architecture returning to the primitive: Greek architecture travelling back in time toward its own origin'. But, of course, as we have seen, Labrouste did not see Paestum as the origins of Greek architecture. See also Martin Bressani, 'The Paestum Controversy', in Bélier, Bergdoll and Le Cœur (eds), *Henri Labrouste*, 88–93.

198 See Bressani, 'The Hybrid', 82–126, and Levine, 'The Romantic Idea', 325–416.

199 'on ne peut non plus admettre l'opinion du pere Paoli qui attribue aux Etrusques les monumens de Posidonia. on retrouve dans [ces] monumens la même architecture et le même art de construire que dans ceux de la Sicile, qui sont a n'en pas douter construits par des colonies grecques. Cette opinion d'ailleurs est suffisamment réfutée dans l'Encyclopédie methodique (dictionnaire d'Arch. au mot Dorique) pour qu'il soit, je crois nécessaire de la combattre d'avantage.' Labrouste, 'Antiquités de Pestum Posidonia', fol. 2. He also referred to Quatremère's *Le Jupiter Olympien, ou L'Art de la sculpture antique* for the statues (fol. 14).

200 'J'ai cru devoir presenter ici plusieurs Exemples pris dans les monumens de la Sicile: ce rapprochement pourrait prouver, si l'on en doutait encore, que les habitans de Posidonia ainsi que les peuples de la Sicile etaient originaires du même pays, puisque ces divers peuples se servaient non seulement des mêmes formes d'architecture, mais qu'ils Employaient aussi

les mêmes moyens dans la construction des monumens.' Labrouste, 'Antiquités de Pestum Posidonia', fol. 12.

201 Labrouste wrote of the pronaos of the Ceres temple: 'Les Bases le nombre des cannelures et la proportion élevée de ces colonnes, à en juger par leur diamètre inferieur, m'ont fait supposer que cet ordre etait Jonique, et j'ai imité dans la réstauration, l'ordre jonique du Tombeau de Theron à Agrigente en Sicile.' Ibid., fol. 13. The reaction of the Académie was: 'La base encore existante à l'entrée du Pronaos n'est pas, selon nous, une preuve suffisante de l'existence d'un ordre Ionique puisque l'on voit des Doriques avec base comme par exemple au temple de Cora, et qu'assez généralement dans les temples du caractère de ceux de Pœstum on trouve des Doriques de différentes proportions.' Ibid., fol. 7.

202 The commentary on Labrouste's *envoi* referred often to Delagardette and to William Wilkins (see Chapter 6) for an authoritative account of Paestum. In that sense, the Labrouste affair sheds light on eighteenth-century thinking because Delagardette was seen as an authority. A more positive reaction to Labrouste's work was: 'Ces beaux dessins qui nous font connaitre les profils et details tant intérieurs qu'extérieurs du temple de Neptune, nous ont paru rendus avec cette simplicité et cette exactitude qui conviennent à des bonnes études d'architecture.' The commentary also stated that the work was 'fait avec intelligence et fort intéressant'. Horace Vernet, 'Rapport . . . Sur la Restauration . . . de Paestum', fols 1–7.

203 Levine, 'The Romantic Idea', 389.

204 While the thought of creating a new architecture is seen by Levine as an idea of the Romantics in the 1820s to the 1840s, we have seen it already with Piranesi.

205 Neil Levine, for example, restricted his attention to Delagardette's work, the most canonised representation of Paestum, while ignoring other eighteenth-century debates on Paestum. He used mainly later writers who mythified Labrouste, such as Eugène Emmanuel Viollet-le-Duc, who said that Labrouste's *envoi* was 'purely and simply a revolution on a few sheets of double elephant paper'. Viollet-le-Duc, 'Lettres extra-parlementaires', 5 March 1877, quoted in Levine, 'The Romantic Idea', 365.

206 Piranesi, *Parere su l'architettura*, 11; Eng. trans. in Piranesi, *Observations*, trans. Beamish and Britt, 106.

Chapter 6

1 'Ils sont sans doute d'une antiquité très reculée et les productions des premiers Grecs qui ont peuplé ces côtés; leur stile prouveroit peut-être que la migration de ces peuples en Italie est d'une époque plus ancienne qu'on ne le croit et qu'elle a suivi de très près l'invention de l'ordre Dorique. Ce bel ordre est employé là dans sa première austérité: presque tout y en quarré dans les profils, et quoique tous y respire l'air sauvage, il y règne un rapport entre toutes les parties qui fait beaucoup de plaisir aux yeux exercés et fait pour sentir la beauté des proportions relatives.' 'Ces monuments sont non seulement précieux pour l'histoire de l'architecture,

mais encore il est des occasions ou ce stile peut être employé avec succès; ces occasions sont à la vérité fort rares, et il faut éviter avec le plus grand soin ce que beaucoup d'architectes font actuellement; de faire entrer cet ordre dans des édifices qui ne doivent rien présenter que de simple et agréable en même tems, puisqu'ils sont destinés à l'habitation: l'abus du caractère étant un défaut essentiel en architecture.' Pierre-Adrien Pâris, 'Notes et lavis de Pierre-Adrien Pâris, intercalés par lui, avec différentes estampes', in Antoine Desgodets [Desgodetz], *Les édifices antiques de Rome, dessinés et mesurés très exactement* [1682], new edn (Paris: Claude-Antoine Jombert fils aîné, Libraire du Roi, 1779), Paris, Institut de France, MS 1906, fol. 329.

2 'L'ordre Dorique des Grecs tel qu'on le voit dans les restes des temples de la Sicile, et dans ceux de l'ancienne ville de Pestum en Italie presente sans doute un style mâle et vigoureux: mais il n'a pas celui de la Beauté et de la Majesté qui semble plus convenable a la deviation des temples. Cet ordre porte seulement a six diamètres de hauteur sans baze avec un chapiteau très lourd, . . . un aspect de rusticité qui me semble convenir que dans les edifices ou ce style doit être employé, tel que les prisons, les arsenaux ou dans des batimens d'un style simple et agreste.' Louis Combes, 'Des Progrès & de la Décadence de l'Architecture Grècque en France Depuis les Romains jusqu'à nos jours', Bordeaux, Archives Municipales, Fonds Delpit, 66 S 272 (MS 48), fol. 6v. On Combes see François-Georges Pariset, 'Les Théories artistiques d'un architecte du néoclassicisme, Louis Combes, de Bordeaux', *Annales du Midi*, 76 (1964) 68–9, 543–54; François-Georges Pariset, 'Louis Combes', *Revue Historique de Bordeaux et du Département de la Gironde*, 22 (1973), 1–40; François-Georges Pariset, *L'Architecte Combes* (Bordeaux: Biscaye Frères, 1974).

3 'Cette ville doit son origine aux Grecs comme toutes celles de cette côte. L'enceinte de ses murs qui subsistent encore en partie formoit un quarré ou tout au moins un rectangle. La construction des murs ainsi que la forme d'une porte de la ville qui existe encore ressemble parfaitement aux murs et à la Porte de l'ancienne ville Falerie.' Pierre-Adrien Pâris, 'Route de Rome à Naples', Besançon, Bibliothèque Municipale, Fonds Pâris, MS 12, fol. 115r.

4 'les anciens donnoient la forme quarrée à leur ville comme étant la plus simple et la plus facile à tracer sur le terrain: on pourroit peut-être en conclure encore que c'est des Grecs que les Etrusques et autres peuples d'Italie ont appris à former des villes et à les entourer de murailles'. Quoted in Pierre Pinon, *Pierre-Adrien Pâris (1745–1819), architecte, et les monuments antiques de Rome et de la Campanie* (Rome: École Française de Rome, 2007), 320.

5 'On voit dans les ruines de Pestum ou Posidonia, trois temples dont un surtout est assés bien conservé. Je ne connois rien d'aussi terrible, d'aussi imposant, d'aussi caractérisé que ces temples. Ils sont sans doute d'une antiquité très reculée, et les productions des premiers Grecs qui ont peuplé ces côtés . . . Les plans, élévations, et autres détails que je joins ici, me dispensent de faire la description de ces temples. J'observerai seulement que les gouttes du plafond

sont creusées ici au lieu d'être saillantes, comme elles sont partout ailleurs: cette singularité n'a été observée ni dans l'ouvrage anglois de Major, ni dans ce que Dumont a publié sur ces monumens d'après Mr Soufflot.' Pâris, 'Notes et lavis', fols 329, 332. Pâris travelled to Italy again in 1783 and 1807, but he did not pay a second visit to Paestum, which according to Pinon (*Pierre-Adrien Pâris*, 321) suggests that he did not find the site very interesting. I disagree, given his reactions to Paestum and his plan to include it in Desgodetz. Pâris was in Paestum in July or August 1774. In his library he had three publications on Paestum: Gabriel-Pierre-Martin Dumont, *Les ruines de Paestum, autrement Posidonia, ville de l'ancienne grande Grèce, au Royaume de Naples: ouvrage contenant l'histoire ancienne & moderne de cette ville, la description & les vues de ses antiquités, ses inscriptions, &c.: avec des observations sur l'ancien Ordre Doriqu*e, partly based on [John Longfield], *The ruins of Poestum*, trans. Jacques Varenne de Béost (London / Paris: C.-A. Jombert,1769); Paolo Antonio Paoli, *Paesti, quod Posidoniam etiam dixere, rudera: Rovine della città di Pesto, detta ancora Posidonia* (Rome: [in typographio Paleariniano], 1784); Claude-Mathieu Delagardette, *Les Ruines de Paestum, ou Posidona, ancienne ville de la Grande-Grèce* (Paris: l'auteur / H. Barbou, an VII [1799]). For his library see Charles Weiss, *Catalogue de la bibliothèque de M. Paris, architecte et dessinateur de la Chambre du Roi . . . suivi de la description de son cabinet* (Besançon: Librairie de Deis, 1821).

6   'Ces précieux monumens méritent bien le pénible voyage qu'on fait pour les voir. Aucun des plus beaux morceaux de l'antiquité, la rotonde même ne produisent un effet aussi imposant. Il y règne, surtout dans le plus grand, une harmonie dans le parti qu'on y a pris qui fait que quoique les proportions soient de celles auxquelles nos yeux ne sont pas accoutumés on y est point révolté ou choqué de la grosseur des colonnes, de la hauteur de l'entablement &c. Le tout plaît, du moins c'est l'effet que j'y ai éprouvé.' Pâris, 'Route de Rome à Naples', fols 118–19. From Naples, Pâris also visited Pompeii, Herculaneum, Pozzuoli and Baia; Pinon, *Pierre-Adrien Pâris*, 7.

7   'ce qui intéresse ceux qui font ce voyage sont trois temples dont celui du milieu est presque dans son entier. L'aspect de ces temples est ce que j'ai vu de plus imposant. Ils sont d'ordre dorique. Les colonnes qui sont sans base n'ont guerre que 4 diamètres de hauteur ayant 6ᴾ 3° [6 feet 3 inches] de diamètre et 26ᴾ [26 feet] de hauteur. Le chapiteau des colonnes est composé d'un talloir très saillant, d'une moulure ensuite qui tient lieu de notre quart de rond mais qui ne lui ressemble pas étant très applatie. Il y a ensuite quatre petites baguettes après lesquelles naissent les canelures qui continuent jusqu'en bas au nombre de 24.' Pâris, 'Route de Rome', fol. 115r.

8   For Saint-Non, Pâris drew in total sixty-three plates, of which two were of Paestum, for volume III of the *Voyage pittoresque*. See Petra Lamers, *Il viaggio nel sud dell'Abbé de Saint-Non: Il 'Voyage pittoresque à Naples et en Sicile': La genesi, i disegni preparatori, le incisioni* (Naples: Electa, 1995), 73–6, and 310–32.

9   Plate 87 'Plan et élévation géométrale avec les détails en grand du Temple Hipètre de Pestum', plate 88 'Plan, éléva-tion et détails du Temple Périptère et pseudodiptère de Pestum'.

10 Pierre-Adrien Pâris, 'Études d'Architecture faites en Italie pendant les années 1771, 1772, 1773 et 1774. Premier volume contenant les antiquités', Besançon, Bibliothèque Municipale, Fonds Pâris, MS 476, vol. I, plate IX recto, 'Plan et détails du grand Temple de Pestum', plate IX verso 'Charpente et toiture du "petit Temple de Pestum"'. In the 'Observations', added to Antoine Desgodets [Desgodetz], *Les édifices antiques de Rome, dessinés et mesurés très exactement* [1682], new edn (Paris: Claude-Antoine Jombert fils aîné, Librairie du Roi, 1779), Besançon, Bibliothèque Municipale, Fonds Pâris, inv. 12.421, Pâris added (following p. 140) notes on the 'Temples de Paestum' and a plate engraved after one of his drawings for Saint-Non's *Voyage pittoresque*.

11 In respect of the age of the temples, and referring to the temple of Sibyl in Tivoli, Pâris wrote: 'Tout concourt à me faire penser que ce temple, celui de la Fortune Prenestine, ainsi que ceux d'Hercule et de Castor de Cori, sont non seulement du même tems, mais encore qu'ils sont peut-être des plus anciens que l'architecture grecque ait produit en Italie. J'en excepte ceux de Pestum qui portent décidément le caractère de la plus haute antiquité.' Pâris, 'Notes et lavis', fol. 80r. Pâris's writings have never been published, but they were circulated: his notes in a copy of Desgodetz (now in the Institut de France) went from the library of the Académie d'Architecture to Léon Dufourny, who may have used them in his own writings. Pinon, *Pierre-Adrien Pâris*, 375.

12 'J'ajouterai que les colonnes m'ayant paru avoir une courbe pour le contour vertical de leur fust, je le traçai ainsi sur les dessins que j'ai fait de ces temples. Mr. Soufflot m'en fit un procès lorsque je présentai en 1775 mes Études à l'Académie: quelque peu intéressant que cela fut, je me piquai, et je chargeai Mrs. Renard, Huvé et Desprès architectes qui ont fait ce voyage, d'examiner le fait; le résultat est qu'en effet je ne me suis pas trompé; que le contour de ces colonnes est une courbe au lieu d'une ligne droite qui selon Mr. Soufflot prend du sol et va jusque sous le chapiteau, sentiment qui est faux en tous points. L'ouvrage anglois contient aussi une erreur notable en ce qu'il donne une cimaise au fronton du grand temple tandis qu'il n'y en a pas, ce qui est facile à voir, ce fronton étant presque entier.' Pâris, 'Notes et lavis', fol. 329; by 'l'ouvrage anglois' he probably meant Thomas Major's *The ruins of Paestum* (1768). Pâris also raised the issue in his (undated) 'Études d'Architecture': 'La forme des colonnes est bien telle qu'on la voit dans le détail en grand. Lorsque je fis voir les Études à l'Académie, Mr Soufflot prétendit que je m'étois trompé et que ces colonnes étoient coniques; son autorité me donna de la défiance sur la manière dont je les avois vues; j'engageai plusieurs personnes qui sont allées depuis moi à Pestum, et particulièrement Mrs Huvé et Bélisard, à examiner la chose avec attention; ils m'ont assuré que je ne m'étois pas trompé, et que le trait des colonnes, au lieu d'être en ligne droite comme le disoit Mr Soufflot, est une courbe, ainsi que je l'ai fait.' Pâris, 'Études d'Architecture', vol. I, plate IX.

13 Besançon, Bibliothèque Municipale, Fonds Pâris, vol. 484, nos 36–43; the two sections (Fig. 159) are nos 41–2.

14 '. . . [une] chose barbare', Pierre-Adrien Pâris, letter to J.-Fr. de Montmollin, 4 April 1785, Archives de la Ville de Neuchâtel, 'Correspondence relative à la succession de Mr. le baron de Pury de Lisbonne'; 'on a mutilé une grande quantité de belles colonnes toutes faites pour faire sans aucuns principes et contre toutes règles des choses difformes et choquantes', Pâris, letter to 'Quatre Ministraux de l'État à Neuchâtel', 29 May 1786, Archives de la Ville de Neuchâtel, 'Correspondance avec Pâris'; quoted in Pinon, *Pierre-Adrien Pâris*, 34.

15 Pierre-Adrien Pâris, letter to 'Quatre Ministraux', 14 May 1785 (minute), Besançon, Bibliothèque Municipale, Fonds Pâris, MS 1, fol. 30v; quoted in Pinon, *Pierre-Adrien Pâris*, 34.

16 Moreau's design was described as a building 'destiné à réunir tout ce qui concerne l'histoire naturelle'. The jury's report read: 'La partie de l'élévation qui occupe le premier plan présente une grande façade percée de trois arcades portées par des colonnes de l'espèce de celles des temples de Pestum, mais sans cannelures; ces colonnes qui forment un portique dans toute la largeur de l'édifice sont beaucoup trop petites pour la masse . . . C'est peut-être ici le lieu d'observer les inconveniens de l'abus que les jeunes gens font des colonnes de Pestum; souvent ils les employent à des édifices qui seroient décorés d'une manière plus convenable par des ordres réguliers qui ont des proportions fixes, déterminées et plus élégantes. Il est très peu d'occasions où ce genre d'architecture qui exclut toute espèce de richesse puisse convenir, et si les rapports qui lui sont propres ne sont pas rigoureusement observés, on n'y voit plus qu'un amas incohérent sans intérêt, comme sans goût.' Extrait des registres de l'Académie d'Architecture, séance du 14 janvier 1788, Paris, Archives Nationales, O¹ 1931; quoted in Pinon, *Pierre-Adrien Pâris*, 32.

17 On Desgodetz see Antoine Desgodets, *Les édifices antiques de Rome* [1682]; repr. with introduction by Hélène Rousteau-Chambon (Paris: Picard, 2008), 13–30. See also Wolfgang Herrmann, 'Antoine Desgodets and the Académie Royale d'Architecture', *Art Bulletin*, 40 (March 1958), 23–53; Antoine Picon, *Architectes et ingénieurs au siècle des Lumières* (Marseille: Parenthèses, 1988); Eng. trans. as *French Architects and Engineers in the Age of Enlightenment* (Cambridge / New York: Cambridge University Press, 1992); Hilary Ballon, *Louis Le Vau Mazarin's Collège: Colbert's Revenge* (Princeton (NJ): Princeton University Press, 1999).

18 Wolfgang Herrmann, *The Theory of Claude Perrault* (London: A. Zwemmer, 1973), 79–81; Antoine Picon, *Claude Perrault, 1613–1688, ou, La Curiosité d'un classique* (Paris: Picard / Caisse Nationale des Monuments Historiques et des Sites / Délégation à l'Action Artistique de la Ville de Paris, 1988), 141–4, 150.

19 Frank Salmon, *Building on Ruins: The Rediscovery of Rome and English Architecture* (Aldershot (Surrey): Ashgate, 2000), 35.

20 Ibid., 35–41.

21 Antoine Desgodetz, 'Recœuil des études d'architectures que j'ay fait à Rome pendant l'espace de seize mois que j'y ay demeuré dans les années 1676 et 1677', Paris, Bibliothèque de l'Institut de France, MS 2718.

22 The following reference to Peyre's role appears below the table of contents: 'Messieurs Peyre l'aîné, Guillaumot, Peyre le jeune, qui avoient été nommés pour examiner un Ouvrage de M. Desgodetz, *sur les Edifices antiques de Rome*, en ayant fait leur rapport, l'Académie a jugé que cet Ouvrage, déja connu & favorablement accueilli du Public, méritoit d'être réimprimé, avec l'Approbation & sous le Privilège de l'Académie; en soi de quoi j'ai signé le présent Certificat. A Paris, ce 8 Août 1779. J. M. Sedaine'. Antoine Desgodets [Desgodetz], *Les édifices antiques de Rome*, p. xii. See also Alan Braham, *The Architecture of the French Enlightenment* (London: Thames and Hudson, 1980), 90; Eileen Harris and Nicholas Savage, *British Architectural Books and Writers, 1556–1785* (Cambridge: Cambridge University Press, 1990), 73, 89 note 19; Rousteau-Chambon, introduction to Desgodets, *Les édifices antiques de Rome*, 29–30. On Clérisseau and Adam see Thomas J. McCormick, *Charles-Louis Clérisseau and the Genesis of Neo-Classicism* (Cambridge (Mass.): MIT Press, 1990), 34–5.

23 Pierre-Adrien Pâris, 'Notes et lavis de Pierre-Adrien Pâris, intercalés par lui, avec différentes estampes', 1779–81, in Desgodetz, *Les édifices*, new edn (1779), Paris, Institut de France, MS 1906; this is Pâris's own copy, presented to the Académie d'Architecture in 1781, of his 'Observations', 1779–81, Besançon, Bibliothèque Municipale, inv. 12.421. On the re-edition and Pâris's 'Observations' see Pinon, *Pierre-Adrien Pâris*, 12–13, 56–70. See also Joselita Raspi Serra, 'Les Édifices antiques de Rome mesurés et dessinés exactement par Antoine, testo annotato da Adrien Pâris. Un metodo d'intervento: Misura e verifica dei monumenti romani', in Antonio Cadei, Marina Righetti Tosti-Croce, Anna Segagni Malacart and Alessandro Tomei (eds), *Arte d'occidente: Temi e metodi. Studi in onore di Angiola Maria Romanini*, vol. III (Rome: Edizioni Sintesi, 1999), 1215–20.

24 'J'y ai ajouté quelques plans qu'il avoit négligé et même des vues qui rappellent ces lieux toujours si intéressans pour ceux qui les ont vu. J'ai cru devoir y joindre la colonne Trajane; les plus beaux obélisques; le cirque de Caracalla, monument unique aujourd'huy . . . Enfin j'y ai ajouté encore nombre de monumens antiques répandus soit aux environs de Rome, soit dans le royaume de Naples parce qu'il m'a paru qu'ils présentoient quelques singularités intéressantes pour l'histoire de l'architecture: tels sont le temple d'Hercule à Cori, celui de la Fortune de Préneste, l'édifice qui sert aujourd'huy d'église de Nocera de Pagani, le théâtre d'Herculanum, l'amphithéâtre de Capoue, l'arc de Trajan à Bénévent et les temples grecs de Pestum.' Quoted in Pinon, *Pierre-Adrien Pâris*, 57.

25 Ibid., 68–9; see also Salmon, *Building on Ruins*, 35–9. Robert Adam noted the popularity of the book to his brother: 'Desgodetz's book is almost entirely out of print. Neither in England, France or Italy can one get a copy of it under double price.' Quoted in John Fleming, *Robert Adam and his Circle in Edinburgh & Rome* (London: John Murray, 1962), 170.

26 'J'ai fait un examen attentif et scrupuleux de cet Auteur, en comparant chaque planche de son Ouvrage au pied des monumens antiques, lors de mon voyage à Rome en 1785,

avec M. Molinos, mon collègue et mon ami. Cette curieuse étude nous a mis à même de reconnaître une multitude de fautes dans la seule configuration des Monumens. Nous avons en conséquence rectifié ces erreurs par des notes et des figures, tracées sur le lieu même, en marge du livre; et nous avons en outre fait mouler plusieurs détails des ornemens, pour démontrer les différences qui existent dans la forme et dans le caractère de ceux qu'il a représentés, et pour prouver aux plus incrédules l'absolue nécessité de ces vérifications.' Jacques-Guillaume Legrand, *Essai sur l'histoire générale de l'architecture . . . pour servir de texte explicatif au Recueil et Parallèle des édifices de tout genre . . . nouvelle édition . . .* (Paris: s.n. [L. Ch. Soyer], 1809) [written 1799, first published 1803], 45; quoted in Werner Szambien, *Le Musée d'architecture* (Paris: Picard, 1988), 23.

27 Claude-Mathieu Delagardette, *Règles des cinq ordres d'architecture de Vignole, avec un détail d'un ordre dorique de Poestum* (Paris: Chéreau, 1786). On Delagardette's gravestone in 1805 was written: 'A la mémoire de Ch. M. Delagardette, architecte, né a Paris en 1762. Il fut le Vignole de son temps. Lui seul fit bien connaitre les ruines de Pæstum et mourut pauvre a l'age de 45 ans. Simple et pur dans ses moeurs comme dans ses compositions, il fut l'ami et le père de ses élèves.' H. Herluison and Paul Leroy, *L'Architecte Delagardette* (Orléans: Herluison, 1896), 15. As this indicates, Delagardette was considered the Vignola of his day, and the principal expert on the topic of Paestum.

28 'J'ai cru devoir ajouter aux Ordres de Vignole les détails d'un bel Ordre Dorique de Pæstum qui ne se trouvent que dans peu d'ouvrages assez rares & d'un prix considérable. On emploie actuellement cet Ordre avec succès & assez fréquemment pour qu'il soit intéressant de la faire connoître aux personnes qui étudient l'Architecture & qui ne peuvent facilement se procurer les ouvrages où il est traité . . . J'ai mis tout le soin & toute l'exactitude dont je suis capable dans les calculs qu'il fallu faire pour parvenir à réduire en modules les subdivisions de la toise & du pied, & j'ai cru cela nécessaire pour que les étudians fissent plus facilement la comparaison de cet Ordre avec les autres, & aussi parce que le module est la mesure ordinaire dont ils se servent.' Delagardette, 'Ordre de Pœstum', in *Règles des cinq ordres*, 39.

29 'M. Dumont, Professeur d'Architecture, connu par ses divers ouvrages & par son zèle pour les progrès des Eleves, a bien voulu me confier les dessins originaux que feu M. Soufflot, son Ami, Architecte du Roi, avoit faits à Pœstum & sur lesquels il avoit marqué toutes les mesures avec la plus grande exactitude. Ce sont ces mêmes dessins qui ont été gravés dans l'ouvrage de M. Dumont sur les ruines de Pœstum, & dans celui qui a été publié à Londres par Thomas Major.' Ibid.

30 'J'ai choisi dans les trois Temples de Pœstum celui qui m'a paru le plus majestueux, c'est celui qu'on nomme Amphyprostyle, Hexastyle; *Amphyprostyle* signifie qui a deux faces semblables une à chaque extrémité: *Hexastyle* dont les faces ont six colonnes de front. Ce Temple étoit aussi *Hyptère*, c'est-à-dire qu'il étoit découvert. Je n'en donne que la façade,

les détails & la moitié du plan; ce qui m'a paru suffisant dans un livre élémentaire.' Ibid., 39–40.

31 Plates XLIV–XLVI, ibid., 40 (description of the plates).

32 'mais, sur-tout, je me suis fait un devoir de donner les détails d'un Ordre dorique de Pœstum; & le voyage que j'ai fait sur les lieux mêmes, m'a mis à portée d'en garantir l'exactitude.' Claude-Mathieu Delagardette, *Regles des cinq ordres d'architecture, de Vignole*, new edn (Paris: Joubert, 1797), 5.

33 'J'ai promis de donner les détails d'un ordre dorique de Poestum, tel que je l'ai mesuré moi-même sur les lieux; je remplis ma promesse d'autant plus volontiers, qu'on emploie cet ordre fréquemment & avec succès aujourd'hui, & qu'il n'est décrit que dans les ouvrages rares & chers . . . J'ai choisi dans les trois temples que l'on voit à Poestum, l'ordre extérieur de celui qu'on dit avoir été dédié à Neptune, & qui m'a paru le plus majestueux; c'est aussi celui dont les détails sont les plus purs & les plus ingénieusement opposés.' Ibid., 29.

34 Plates XXVI–XXIX, ibid., 29–30 (description of the plates).

35 'Ni Soufflot ni Dumont n'ont jamais vu, mésuré et dessiné à Pæstum, les détails de la corniche, les gouttes de l'architrave, la moulure et les astragales des chapiteaux du grand temple qu'ils nous ont donnés.' Delagardette, *Les Ruines de Paestum* ([1799]), 4. This passage is followed by a critical review of all the other monographs on Paestum: 'Ces erreurs, ces contradictions dans la représentation d'un même objet, font penser naturellement que tous ces ouvrages sont plutôt des productions d'amateurs curieux et peu versés dans l'étude, que le résultat d'un travail approfondi d'Artistes observateurs.' Ibid. Of all the earlier publications, Delagardette favoured Paoli, *Paesti . . . rudera: Rovine della città di Pesto*, but pride of place went to Piranesi: 'La collection la plus complette et la plus fidelle des vûes de Pæstum, est celle donnée à Rome par Piranese: on y voit réellement les Ruines de Pæstum.' Delagardette, *Les Ruines de Paestum* ([1799]), 4.

36 See, later in this chapter, the discussion of the works of Le Roy and Wilkins, who devised chronological series to show a development, and the plates of Rondelet and Durand, which are not arranged according to a chronology.

37 Among the subscribers were Julien-David Le Roy, Jacques-Guillaume Legrand, Jacques Molinos, Louis-François Cassas, Léon Dufourny and Jacques-Nicolas-Louis Durand, for all of whom, see below. Others were: Charles Percier and Pierre-François-Léonard Fontaine, Jean-Augustin Renard, Jacques-François Blondel, Charles-François Viel de Saint-Maux, Pierre-Charles-Joseph Normand and Jacques-Denis Antoine. See 'Liste des souscripteurs', in Delagardette, *Les Ruines de Paestum* ([1799]), p. v.

38 Ibid., 72; see 25, 32, 41, 53, 71 for other references to Le Roy.

39 Julien-David Le Roy, *Les ruines des plus beaux monuments de la Grece* (Paris: H. L. Guérin et L. F. Delatour, 1758). On Julien-David Le Roy see Robin Middleton, *Julien-David Leroy: In Search of Architecture* (London: Sir John Soane's Museum, 2003); Robin Middleton, introduction to Julien-David Le Roy, *The Ruins of the Most Beautiful Monuments of Greece*, 2nd edn [1770], trans. David Britt (Los Angeles:

Getty Research Institute, 2004), 1–199; Christopher Drew Armstrong, *Julien-David Leroy and the Making of Architectural History* (London / New York: Routledge, 2012).

40 Middleton, introduction to Le Roy, *The Ruins*, trans. Britt, 83.

41 'Afin de rendre cette partie plus intéressante, on y joindra les profils des Colonnes doriques antiques de l'Eglise de S. Pierre au liens à Rome, ceux des Colonnes & de l'entablement du Théatre de Marcellus dans la même Ville, & quelques parties des Temples de Pæstum au Royaume de Naples. Ces monumens curieux comparés avec les ordres Grecs, prouveront d'une manière sensible & décisive ce que l'Histoire ne nous apprend qu'en général sur le passage de l'Architecture grecque en Italie.' Julien-David Le Roy, *Les Ruines des plus beaux monumens de la Grèce* (Paris: H. L. Guérin and L. F. Delatour, 1756) [prospectus for forthcoming publication], 3.

42 It is not known why there were no images of Paestum in *Les ruines*. Le Roy could have obtained drawings from Dumont and Soufflot, who brought a number back to France in 1751; perhaps, wishing to publish these themselves, they refused to allow them to be used by other authors. That Le Roy had copied their drawings is shown by the large collection of drawings of Paestum owned by Thomas Major, which formed the basis for his engravings in *The ruins of Paestum* (1768); Soane obtained the whole set in 1800, London, Sir John Soane's Museum, Drawings Collection, Vol. 27. See also Michael McCarthy, 'New Light on Thomas Major's "Paestum" and Later English Drawings of Paestum', in Joselita Raspi Serra (ed.), *Paestum and the Doric Revival, 1750–1830* (Florence: Centro Di, 1986), 47–50.

43 Major and Delagardette both referred to Le Roy in their monographs; see Armstrong, *Julien-David Leroy*, 127.

44 'J'ai formé cette conjecture sur la maniere dont les colonnes ont été placées d'abord dans les Temples Grecs, d'après la construction de deux Temples de la plus haute Antiquité: l'un que l'on voit en Italie à Pæstum, ville ancienne de la Grande Grece, située à 22 lieues de Naples, a une file de colonnes rangées dans le milieu de l'intérieur, précisément, comme nous supposons qu'ont été d'abord placées les premieres colonnes dans les Edifices . . . Le Public est en état de juger à présent du cas qu'il doit faire de cette conjecture, que j'ai formée en partie d'après les Temples de Pæstum. On l'a en quelque sorte confirmée dans deux Livres publiés depuis peu sur les ruines de cette ville. L'un est de M. Major, l'autre de M. Dumont. On peut voir sur ce qui concerne le temps où ces Temples ont été decouverts par un Peintre Napolitain, & mesurés par M. Souflot, & sur l'époque des différents ouvrages qu'on a publié sur ces Edifices . . . dans l'ouvrage de M. Dumont.' Julien-David Le Roy, *Les ruines des plus beaux monuments de la Grèce, considérées du côté de l'histoire et du côté de l'architecture*, 2nd edn, 2 vols (Paris: Louis-François Delatour, 1770), vol. I, pp. xiii–xiv; Eng. trans. in Le Roy, *The Ruins*, trans. Britt, 232.

45 '. . . des Temples d'une antiquité très-reculée, qu'on trouve encore dans les débris de Pestum'. Le Roy, *Les ruines* (1770), vol. I, pt 2, 42; Eng. trans. in Le Roy, *The Ruins*, trans. Britt, 322.

46 'Pour fixer à peu-près le temps dans lequel un Temple dont on voit les ruines, a été construit, nous croyons qu'on ne doit pas se borner à examiner seulement la proportion générale de ses colonnes, nous pensons que leur diminution, la forme de leur chapiteau, les particularités de leurs profils, & celles de l'entablement de l'Edifice, doivent entrer dans cet examen; & ces détails pourroient être tels, ils pourroient montrer, par exemple, dans des colonnes qui n'auroient pas six diametres de hauteur, une telle recherche qu'on ne sauroit avec vraisemblance supposer qu'elles fussent élevées avant le temps où les colonies Grecques qui passerent dans l'Asie Mineure, sous la conduite d'Ion, fils de Xuthus, imaginerent, selon Vitruve [*De architectura libri decem*, Book 4, chapter 1, 5–6], de donner six diametres de hauteur aux colonnes Doriques. Ainsi plus circonspect qu'on ne l'a été, dans un ouvrage publié en Italie, où l'on s'est efforcé de faire remonter la construction des Temples de Pœstum avant le temps que Vitruve marque pour l'invention de l'Ordre Dorique, nous nous contenterons de dire que le Temple de Corinthe est d'une haute antiquité, & qu'il a été construit vraisemblablement avant le siecle de Périclès.' Le Roy, *Les ruines* (1770), vol. II, pt 2, 44–5; Eng. trans. in Le Roy, *The Ruins*, trans. Britt, 475, 477. This is the passage to which Paoli reacted in his letter to Carlo Fea (Chapter 5, pp. 205–7).

47 William Wilkins, *The Antiquities of Magna Graecia* (London: Longman, Hurst, Orme and Rees, 1807). For Wilkins see R. W. Liscombe, *William Wilkins, 1778–1839* (Cambridge: Cambridge University Press, 1980); see also David Watkin, *Thomas Hope, 1769–1831, and the Neo-Classical Idea* (London: John Murray, 1968), 57–74; David Watkin, *The Triumph of the Classical: Cambridge Architecture, 1804–1834* (Cambridge / New York: Cambridge University Press for the Fitzwilliam Museum, 1977); Cinzia Maria Sicca, *Committed to Classicism: The Buildings of Downing College, Cambridge* (Cambridge: Downing College, 1987); J. Mordaunt Crook, *The Greek Revival: Neo-Classical Attitudes in British Architecture, 1760–1870* (London: John Murray, 1995) [first published 1972]; Howard M. Colvin, *A Biographical Dictionary of British Architects, 1600–1840*, 4th edn (New Haven (Conn.) / London: Yale University Press, 2008) [first published 1954], 893–6.

48 William Wilkins probably visited Paestum in 1802, en route between Naples and Selinunte, whence he continued to Segesta, Athens, Sounion, Rhamnus, Eleusis, Olympia and Aegina. In his *Antiquities*, he cited the works of Delagardette, Denon, Paoli, Piranesi and Winckelmann (in the Fea edition); Liscombe, *William Wilkins*, 33. The British Library holds a letter of 27 October 1805, in which Wilkins mentioned Paestum (BL, Add. MS 43229.CXCI.99). His other publications on Greek architecture include: *Atheniensia, or Remarks on the Topography and Buildings of Athens* (London: s.n., 1816); *The Unedited Antiquities of Attica, Comprising the Architectural Remains of Eleusis, Rhamnus, Sunium and Thoricus* (London: Longman, Hurst, Rees, Orme and Brown, 1817).

49 Wilkins, *The Antiquities of Magna Graecia*, p. i.

50 For instance: 'The general principles, which are given by Vitruvius in the fourth chapter of the fourth book, for the division of the aedes, or temple within the peristyle, of the

Romans, will be found, upon investigation, to fail entirely in their application to the temples of the Greeks.' Ibid., p. vi.

51 Willey Reveley demonstrated Stuart's error in claiming that the Temple of Jupiter Olympius had twenty-one columns in the flanks: there were actually twenty, as Reveley noticed when he visited Greece himself. Willey Reveley, introduction to James Stuart and Nicholas Revett, *The antiquities of Athens measured and delineated by James Stuart F.R.S. and F.S.A. and Nicholas Revett painters and architects*, vol. III, ed. W. Reveley (London: John Nichols, 1794).

52 'le grand Temple, le petit Temple, et la Basilique, ont été construits par les Grecs; mais . . . les deux derniers ont été restaurés par les Romains à des époques que nous croyons pouvoir déterminer par le caractère même des édifices, et par celui des details des restaurations.' Delagardette, *Les Ruines de Paestum* ([1799]), 71.

53 About the Basilica temple, Wilkins wrote: 'The form of the temple may be considered as a variety of that which admitted of interior columns; and the deviation from the rule generally observed of placing an even number of columns in the fronts to have arisen from the determination to adopt a single instead of a double range of columns within the Cella for the support of the roof. Such a striking deviation from the simple style of ancient architecture can only be attributed to the vitiated taste of the age in which this temple was designed. This observation leads to the consideration of the probable period of its construction. From the great similarity of the capitals of this and the lesser temple, and the general character of the mouldings, we may adopt the opinion so generally prevalent, that they were coëval.' Wilkins, *The Antiquities of Magna Græcia*, 62–3. '[The Basilica] differs from the pseudo-dipteral of Vitruvius in the number of the columns in the fronts and flanks. The antae of the Pronaos, contrary to the uniform practice of the Greeks, diminish in the same manner as the columns, and are crowned with a projecting capital of a singular form.' Ibid., 64. On the 'lesser temple' (Temple of Ceres), Wilkins stated that its having six by thirteen columns 'agrees with the received idea of a Grecian hexastyle temple' (ibid., 65), but shortly afterwards: 'The cornice has no resemblance whatsoever to the Grecian Doric; it is without mutules: instead of these, pannels are sunk in the soffite of the principal member.' Ibid., 66.

54 The text continues: 'There can exist little doubt, in the minds of those who are accustomed to contemplate the features of ancient architecture, that this building was coëval with the very earliest period of the Grecian migration to the south of Italy. The Grecian character is too strongly marked to admit of any argument, whether its origin was prior or subsequent to the possession of Posidonia by that people. Low columns with a great diminution of the shaft, bold projecting capitals, a massive entablature, and triglyphs placed at the angle of the zophorus, are strong presumptive proofs of its great antiquity. The shafts of the columns diminish in a straight line from the base to the top, although at first sight they have the appearance of swelling in the middle. This deception is caused by the decay of the stone in the lower part of the shafts, which there has taken place in a greater degree than elsewhere. The sharp angles of the flutes are within the reach of every hand, and as they offer little or no resistance to the attacks of wanton or incidental dilapidation, they have not failed to experience the evils to which they were exposed by their delicacy and situation.' Ibid., 59. Wilkins added a note citing Paoli, who suggested that the temples were Etruscan, built before the arrival of the Greeks in Italy – according to Wilkins, because his 'ideas of Grecian proportions are founded upon the authority of Vitruvius'. Ibid.

55 'The Temple at Jerusalem is the earliest of which we have any written documents. Upon its claims to attention, as it is connected with our holy religion, it were surely needless to expatiate. But, independently of the interest excited by its antiquity and sanctity, we shall find that an enquiry into the arrangement and dimensions of its component parts will be amply repaid by the light which it tends to diffuse upon the history of Architecture in general.' Ibid., p. vi.

56 Ibid.

57 Ibid., p. vii.

58 'Having thus shown the great precision which obtained in the proportions of these interesting monuments of ancient taste, I proceed to add a few observations to confirm the assertions advanced in the course of the preceding inquiry, and to strengthen the proposition that the Temple at Paestum, as well as other Grecian temples of the same area, were actually designed after the model of the Temple at Jerusalem.' Ibid., p. xiv.

59 He named Newton twice in a note, referring to the *Chronology*; Wilkins, *The Antiquities of Magna Graecia*, pp. vii, xv, see also p. xvii. He also referred to Juan Bautista Villalpando (1552–1608), the Spanish Jesuit scholar, mathematician and architect, whose *Ezechielem explanationes* (1596–1604), in which he described and illustrated Solomon's temple, was widely influential on architects' ideas about the temple; Wilkins, *The Antiquities of Magna Graecia*, pp. ix, x, xii.

60 For studies of the temple at Jerusalem see Wolfgang Herrmann, 'Unknown Designs for the "Temple of Jerusalem" by Claude Perrault', in Douglas Fraser, Howard Hibbard and Milton J. Lewine (eds), *Essays in the History of Architecture Presented to Rudolf Wittkower* (London: Phaidon Press, 1967), 143–58; Helen Rosenau, *Visions of the Temple: The Image of the Temple of Jerusalem in Judaism and Christianity* (London: Oresko Books, 1979). On Villalpando see René Taylor, 'El Padre Villalpando (1552–1608) y sus ideas estéticas', in *Academia: Anales y Boletín de la Real Academia de Bellas Artes de San Fernando*, 3rd ser., I (1951), 409–73; and on his influence René Taylor, 'Hermetism and Mystical Architecture in the Society of Jesus', in Rudolf Wittkower and Irma B. Jaffe (eds), *Baroque Art: The Jesuit Contribution* (New York: Fordham University Press, 1972), 63–97. See also Sergey R. Kravtsov, 'Juan Bautista Villalpando and Sacred Architecture in the Seventeenth Century', *Journal of the Society of Architectural Historians*, 64 (2005), 312–39.

61 Wilkins, *The Antiquities of Magna Graecia*, p. xiv.

62 Ibid., p. xv.

63 Ibid., p. ix. In a note Wilkins added: 'The proportions of the columns of the Jewish Temple do not differ much from those of the Temple of Juno at Agrigentum. The following scale shews the height of columns in various Grecian temples of the Doric order of architecture, the diameter being supposed unity.'

64 Ibid., pp. x–xi (original italics).

65 Lord North, letter to Charles Dampier, Lyon, 1 September 1753 – Bern, 9 September 1753, Warwick County Record Office, published in McCarthy, 'Documents on the Greek Revival', 761–5.

66 Wilkins, *The Antiquities of Magna Graecia*, 58–9.

67 Richard Dubourg opened a cork model museum in London, which was destroyed in 1785 in a fire caused by an ill-fated demonstration of Vesuvius erupting; by 1798 he had opened a new display. Salmon, *Building on Ruins*, 47.

68 The thirty-six architectural models in the collection of the antiquarian Marie-Gabriel-Florent-Auguste de Choiseul-Gouffier, the author of *Voyage pittoresque de la Grèce* (1795), included one model of Paestum. There were two out of a total of fourteen (mostly by Chichi, see note 70) in the collection of the Comte d'Orsay of 1793, and one in the Galerie of the École Nationale des Ponts et Chaussées in 1787. Cassas made a Paestum temple part of his 1806 exhibition (see below), and there was one in the collection of Léon Dufourny in 1804. The purpose of all these collections was to educate the public about ancient architecture, and the architecture of the temples of Paestum was an essential part of this. John Soane owned a model of the Neptune temple (Fig. 175), and two others of the Ceres temple (London, Sir John Soane Museum, SM MR12: L 1320 × W 334 × H 320 mm) and the Basilica (SM MR22: L 1335 × W 617 × H 240 mm) (Figs 173–4). Other models are in the Museo Archeologico Nazionale in Naples, and in the Rijksmuseum van Oudheden in Leiden. For inventories of the French collections see Szambien, *Le Musée*, 122–35. See also Bernard Andreae, 'Die Tempel von Paestum: Korkmodelle aus der Zeit des Klassizismus', in Bernard Andreae et al., *Malerei für die Ewigkeit: Die Gräber von Paestum* (Munich: Hirmer, 2007), 216–19.

69 On models, see Szambien, *Le Musée*, 13–16; Peter Gercke and Nina Zimmermann-Elseify (eds), *Antike Bauten: Korkmodelle von Antonio Chichi, 1777–1782* (Kassel: Staatliche Museen, 2001). See also Martin S. Briggs, 'Architectural Models', *Burlington Magazine*, 54 (April–May 1929), 174–83, 245–52; John Wilton-Ely, 'The Architectural Models of Sir John Soane: A Catalogue', *Architectural History*, 12 (1969), 5–101; Monique Mosser, 'Französische Architekturmodelle im Zeitalter der Aufklärung', *Daidalos*, 2 (1981), 85–95; Jannic Durand, 'Une collection oubliée: Les Maquettes du Musée des Antiquités Nationales', *Antiquités Nationales*, 14–15 (1982–3), 118–35.

70 Other successful model makers were Antonio Chichi (1743–1816), who had a large clientele in Rome, among whom were many Germans, and Giovanni Altieri and Carlo Lochangeli, who exported several models to England and France.

71 Others relied on engravings for their dimensions. Szambien, *Le Musée*, 14.

72 The École Nationale Supérieure des Beaux-Arts in Paris owns a model of the Neptune temple signed by Rosa (dated 1777), possibly from the collection of the Comte d'Orsay, Saint-Germain-en-Laye, Musée des Antiquités Nationales, inv. 49.795; see 'Les Maquettes d'architecture', *Revue de l'Art*, 58–9 (1982–3), 123–41, catalogue ('Répertoire des maquettes d'architecture, modèles et plan-reliefs'), 128–41.

73 Szambien, *Le Musée*, 62, 102. On Cassas see Annie Gilet and Uwe Westfehling, *Louis-François Cassas, 1756–1827: Dessinateur-voyageur* (Mainz: P. von Zabern, 1994); Mechthild Haas, *Orient auf Papier: Von Louis-François Cassas bis Eugen Bracht* (Darmstadt: Graphische Sammlung, Hessisches Landesmuseum Darmstadt, 2002).

74 '. . . histoire et progrès de l'architecture chez tous les peuples anciens et modernes . . . La collection des chefs-d'œuvre de l'Architecture, exécutée en modèles dans leur justes proportions, et rapprochée sur des échelles convenables, offre seule un puissant moyen d'instruction en ce genre; et c'est un spectacle digne de tous les esprits cultivés que la comparaison à faire sur ces modèles du caractère particulier des différens peuples. L'artiste qui la met aujourd'hui sous les yeux des amateurs, par une exposition publique, rend à l'art un service essentiel, en facilitant ainsi son étude par le choix raisonné qu'il a fait des monumens les plus beaux, les plus célèbres, les plus caractéristiques de l'architecture égyptienne, indienne, persanne, grecque, palmyrénienne, étrusque, mexicaine, romaine, gotique, mauresque, italienne, etc.' Jacques-Guillaume Legrand, *Collection des chefs-d'oeuvre de l'architecture des différens peuples, exécutés en modèles, sous la direction de L.-F. Cassas, auteur des voyages d'Istrie, Dalmatie, Syrie, Phœnicie, Palestine, Bass-Égypte, etc.* (Paris: Leblanc, 1806), p. x.

75 'La variété des formes adoptées par chacun de ces peuples ne pouvait être bien sentie que par des modèles en reliefs, susceptibles d'être éclairés à tous les effets du jour, ou de recevoir la nuit au moyen de lumières adroitement ménagées; un clair-obscur pittoresque et souvent magique, dont les peintres d'histoire et de décorations peuvent tirer le parti le plus avantageux, pour mettre dans leurs tableaux le style convenable au sujet qu'ils traitent et la vérité la plus parfaite. Les dessins les mieux faits, les gravures les plus soignées, ne pouvaient remplacer pour cet objet l'avantage incomparable des modèles, qui font ainsi contraster toutes les formes, et les gravent dans la mémoire en traits ineffaçables, sans obliger à cet effort d'attention qu'exige la comparaison de plans, de coupes, d'élévations difficiles à concevoir pour l'artiste même, difficultés que ne résout pas entièrement le dessin en perspective le plus exact et le mieux présenté.' Ibid., pp. xi–xii.

76 'on verra le ciel brûlant ou glacé sous lequel il est placé; le site montagneux, ou riant, ou sauvage, qui l'environne; la nature des rochers, des arbres, des plantes du pays; le costume des peuples qui le possèdent ou qui vont quelquefois le visiter; enfin, on sera transporté, comme par enchantement, au pied de ces monumens célèbres, sans éprouver la fatigue du voyage, et l'on aura l'avantage infini de pouvoir comparer au même instant les monumens de l'Asie avec ceux de l'Eu-

rope ou de l'Afrique, en faisant quelques pas seulement.' Ibid., p. xviii.

77 Cassas's model of the Neptune temple was possibly by Chichi, at a scale of approximately 1:50. Among the Athenian monuments represented in the collection were the Temple of Minerva, the Propylaea, the Temple of Minerva Polias, the Erechtheion, the Tower of the Winds, the monument to Thrasyllus, and some tombs and sarcophagi. Ibid., 89–111 (nos 14–30).

78 'C'est le plus grand des trois édifices du même genre qui subsistent encore dans le golfe de Salerne, et que tous les voyageurs s'empressent d'aller visiter lorsqu'ils sont à Naples, pour avoir une idée de l'architecture grecque. Il y a, en effet, un très-grand rapport entre cet ordre et l'ordre dorique employé dans les monumens d'Athènes. Quoique les temples de Pæstum soient d'une proportion moins élégante et moins pure, ce qui les fait supposer plus anciens; ils n'en portent pas moins un très-grand caractère. On croit qu'une colonie de Sybarites s'est emparée de Posidonia, et peut y avoir érigé ces grand monumens; dans cette supposition, on s'attendrait à y trouver plus de délicatesse et l'emploi des ordres dorique ou corynthien. L'exécution de ce modèle en liège, imite parfaitement l'état de ruine et de vétuste où se trouve cet édifice, qui présente aujourd'hui une infinité de points de vue et de riches tons de couleurs aux pinceaux des artistes. Aussi ces ruines et celles de Tivoli sont-elles les plus connues et les plus souvent dessinées de toute l'Italie.' Ibid., 106 (no. 24, 'Le grand Temple de Pæstum ou Posidonia dans la grande Grèce, à vingt-deux lieues de Naples').

79 Szambien, Le Musée, 52; on the 'musée dorique', 49–53.

80 'Pour compléter aussi la collection de l'Ordre Dorique des Grecs, on trouvera sous le vestibule quatre colonnes qui donneront le portrait fidèle de l'ordre des Propylées d'Athènes, de celui du Temple de Thésée, du portique d'Auguste dans la même ville, et de celui du grand temple de Paestum dans la grande Grèce, ordre que les Artistes ont la douleur de voir si souvent estropier par les maçons qui croient faire de l'Architecture.' Jacques-Guillaume Legrand and Jacques Molinos, 'Lettre aux rédacteurs', Journal des Arts, des Sciences et de la Littérature, 46 (10 March 1800), 1–2, quoted in Szambien, Le Musée, 137. On the Doric order as the most solid see Werner Szambien, Symétrie, goût, caractère: Théorie et terminologie de l'architecture à l'âge classique, 1550–1800 (Paris: Picard, 1986), 131–40.

81 'Ils quittèrent Rome et portèrent leurs pas sur les temples de Pæstum, pour y recueillir des observations utiles sur l'architecture grecque, dans l'ordre dorique. Ils virent que ses proportions robustes et son style mâle rappelaient à l'esprit les formes athlétiques d'Hercule auquel il fut toujours consacré, tandis que les modernes en ont souvent fait un faux emploi, pour suivre la mode bien plus que la raison.' Jean-Jacques-François Le Barbier, 'Notice nécrologique sur M. Legrand, architecte, membre de l'Académie Celtique', Mémoires de l'Académie Celtique, vol. II (Paris: L.-P. Dubray, 1808), 300–01. Legrand was a student of Jacques-François Blondel and of Charles-Louis Clérisseau.

82 Szambien, Le Musée, 73.

83 Jean Rondelet, Traité théorique et pratique de l'art de bâtir, 5 parts in 7 vols (Paris: l'auteur, 1802–17). Rondelet also wrote 176 entries on construction for Quatremère de Quincy's Encyclopédie méthodique (1782–1832). On Rondelet see Robin Middleton and Marie-Noëlle Baudouin-Matuszek, Jean Rondelet: The Architect as Technician (New Haven (Conn.) / London: Yale University Press, 2007), esp. 'Rondelet's Italian Journey, April 1783 to December 1784', 79–88, and, on the Encyclopédie, 199–207. Rondelet's large library contained 891 titles (2018 volumes). In comparison Boullée owned 100 titles, Durand 533, Pâris 777, Soufflot 726, Legrand 1231, and Quatremère de Quincy 1485; architect Maximilien-Joseph Hurtault, a collaborator of Rondelet, owned 3450 volumes. On Rondelet's library and those of other eighteenth-century architects see Robin Middleton, 'Rondelet's library', in Middleton and Baudouin-Matuszek, Jean Rondelet, 271–88. See also Annie-Charon Parent, 'Enquête à travers les catalogues de vente de bibliothèques d'architectes du XVIIIe siècle: La Bibliothèque de Jacques-Germain Soufflot', in Jean-Michel Leniaud and Béatrice Bouvier (eds), Le Livre d'architecture, XVe–XXe siècle: Édition, réprésentations et bibliothèques (Paris: École des Chartes, 2002), 187–98.

84 For an inventory see Paris, Archives Nationales, AJ 52 446. The formation of the collection could have been an assignment from the École des Beaux-Arts. Szambien, Le Musée, 73.

85 Ibid.

86 'De Pompeïa j'ai été a Pestum ou l'on voit trois temples antiques semblables a ceux qui sont decrit dans Vitruve qu'il apele periptere. Ils sont environnés de colonnes Doriques sans bases. Ils sont bâtis en grandes pierres de taille semblables au travertin de Rome. Toutes ces pierres sont posées sans mortier. Le temple du milieu est le mieux conservé. On y voit une partie du mur du Pronaos ou vestibule qui est si bien appareillé qu'a peine on voit les joins, toutes les pierres sont de même grandeur et les assises de même hauteur. Nous avons levé le plan de ces trois temples pour avoir occasion de les mieux examiner et j'ai fait des nottes sur ce qu'il y avoit de particulier dans leur construction. De retour a Naples je me suis occupé des constructions modernes, apres avoir visité tous les édifices remarquables et levé quelques plans qui m'ont paru interessans tant pour la disposition que pour la construction.' Jean Rondelet, letter to the Comte d'Angiviller, Rome, 25 February 1784, Los Angeles, Getty Research Institute, Research Library, 850122, published in Middleton and Baudouin-Matuszek, Jean Rondelet, 312. Rondelet's other Italian letters to the Comte d'Angiviller are in Paris, Archives Nationales, O¹ 1916 and O¹ 1917 (letters 1–5, 7–9, 11) and Traité théorique et pratique de l'art de bâtir, 6th edn (1830), vol. IV, 354–5 (letter 6); published in Middleton and Baudouin-Matuszek, Jean Rondelet, 307–13.

87 'J'ai été voir les bâtiments que l'on construit. J'ai fait connaissance avec les architectes et les maîtres maçons. Je les ai questionné et j'ai examiné avec attention tous les procedes dont ils se servent et les matteriaux qu'ils employent. On a fait exprès devant moi differens ouvrages pour me faire mieux comprendre leur procedés, comme par exemple la

maniere de preparer le *lastrico* pour le pavé des appartemens et les couvertures des maisons qui sont presque toutes en terrasse. J'ai tenu notte de tout. J'ai cherché a connoitre les differentes espèces de Pouzzolane et la maniere de les mêler pour les ouvrages dans l'eau et hors de l'eau. J'en ai même emporté plusieurs echantillons dans des boites pour les confronter avec celle de Rome et des autres pays ou j'en pourai trouver en retournant en France et même pour en faire quel qu'essaie avec la chaux de Paris.' Jean Rondelet, letter to the Comte d'Angiviller, 25 February 1784 (see note 86).

88 'J'espere de toutes ces observations former un ouvrage raisoné qui pourra etre utile aux constructeurs et aux architectes, vous en pourres juger d'après ce que j'ai fait et que j'aurai l'honneur de vous presenter a mon arrivée à Paris . . . Lorsque je suis parti pour Naples je croyois avoir fini tout ce qui concernoit les constructions antiques. Cependant j'ai trouvé a Pompeja a Pestum et en Sicile beaucoup de choses interessantes a ajouter d'autres a Corriger parce que je n'avois pu les voir qu'en très mauvais etat dans les ruines de Rome.' Jean Rondelet, letter to the Comte d'Angiviller, received / reply sent 19 September 1784, Paris, Archives Nationales, O¹ 1917 323, published in Middleton and Baudouin-Matuszek, *Jean Rondelet*, 313.

89 Ibid., 213.

90 Ibid., 89–138, 179–98.

91 '. . . tous les projets chimériques, ruineux et souvent inexécutables qui résultent des concours, où l'on voit que l'objet principal est toujours sacrifié à de vains accessoires; où l'on ne fait aucune attention à l'usage auquel un édifice est destiné; où l'on voit que c'est le genre de décoration à la mode qui décide la plus grand nombre des concurrents. Tantôt c'est l'ordre de Pestum ou l'Egyptien, tantôt le Gotique ou l'Arabesque qu'ils adoptent sans discernement.' Rondelet, *Traité théorique* (1802–17), vol. 1, 8–9.

92 The stone type of Paestum is no. 327, ibid., 196.

93 'Les temples de Pestum sont construits avec une pierre dure et calcaire, qui est une espèce de travertin rempli de trous, et moins beau que celui de Rome.' Ibid., 205.

94 'Le plan représenté par la figure 5 est celui du grand temple de Pestum: sa superficie, à compter du nu extérieur des colonnes par le bas, est de 1426 mètres 9/10 ou 375 toises 1/2, dont 64 toises 3/4 ou points d'appui c'est-à-dire plus du sixième ou 4/23 la superficie totale, et 4/19 de la superficie libre ou plus du cinquième . . . Ces trois exemples prouvent que dans les temples grecs qui n'étaient couverts que par un toit en charpente et des plafonds en bois ou en pierre de taille, les murs et points d'appui sont doubles de ceux des églises en basilique, dont il vient d'être question.' Ibid., vol. III, 210–11. Rondelet then moved on to the temples at Agrigento.

95 'Table qui indique le rapport des murs et points d'appui de plusieurs édifices, avec la superficie totale qu'ils occupent', ibid., 232. The table shows, for example, buildings in Paris, Rome, Florence, Ravenna and Naples, the Neptune temple at Paestum and the temples at Agrigento, the Panthéon in Paris and in Rome, and Egyptian temples.

96 Ibid., plate LXXV.

97 Ibid., plate LXXVII.

98 Jean-Nicolas-Louis Durand, *Recueil et parallèle des édifices de tout genre anciens et modernes remarquables par leur beauté*, 2 vols (Paris: Gillé fils, an VIII – an IX [1799–1800]). For studies of Durand see Werner Szambien, *Jean-Nicolas-Louis Durand, 1760–1834: De l'imitation à la norme* (Paris: Picard, 1984); Sergio Villari, *J. N. L. Durand (1760–1834): Art and Science of Architecture*, trans. Eli Gottlieb (New York: Rizzoli International, 1990) [first published in Italian].

99 Other publications with comparative diagrams were Jacques Tarade, *Desseins de toutes les parties de l'église de Saint Pierre de Rome* (Paris, n.d. [1700–10]); Juste-Aurèle Meissonnier, *Traité sur l'architecture universelle*, of which only the plates were published (c.1745–50); Gabriel-Pierre-Martin Dumont's *Détails des plus intéressantes parties d'architecture de la basilique de St. Pierre de Rome* (Paris, 1763). See Middleton, introduction to Le Roy, *The Ruins*, trans. Britt, 90–101. For further nineteenth-century context see Mari Hvattum, 'The Comparative Method', in *Gottfried Semper and the Problem of Historicism* (Cambridge / New York: Cambridge University Press, 2004), 114–36.

100 Delagardette, *Les Ruines de Paestum* ([1799]). His chapters present: (1) the history of the city; (2) a topographical description; (3) a description of the Neptune temple; (4) an essay on the reconstruction of the Neptune temple; (5) an essay on the covering of the Neptune temple; (6) a description of the Temple of Ceres; (7) a description of the Basilica; (8) a description of the other monuments at Paestum; (9) a description of the building materials; (10) a comparison with Doric orders in temples at Rome and Athens; (11) a description of the medals found at Paestum; (12) and a table showing the linear system of measurements in France.

101 'Parallele des edifices de Pæstum, avec ceux d'Athènes et de Rome, d'ou l'on conclut l'époque de la construction des edifices de Pæstum.' Delagardette, *Les Ruines de Paestum* ([1799]), 69, plate XIV.

102 'ont . . . été conçus dans les mêmes principes', ibid. 68; 'on y retrouvera le même type, le même génie, la même marche dans la distribution des détails harmoniques', ibid., 69.

103 Durand, *Recueil et parallèle des édifices de tout genre*, vol. I, 8; engravings, vol. II, 63–5.

104 'Tous ces ordres sont dessinés sur un même diamètre, afin de faire mieux apercevoir la variété de leurs proportions, et parce que leurs grandeurs relatives peuvent se comparer.' Ibid., vol. I, 48.

105 'Il n'est ici question que de juger du rapport de la grosseur de la colonne avec sa hauteur, et de saisir la physionomie et en quelque sorte la stature de ces ordres, comme on ferait en examinant une file d'hommes de différens ages et de proportions variées, où nous reconnaissons dans les uns l'élégance et la légéreté de la jeunesse, la vigueur et la force de l'âge mûr, ou la décadence de la vieillesse.' Ibid.

106 'N'a-t-on pas énervé l'ordre Dorique; ne lui a-t-on pas enlevé son caractère et sa grandeur, sa mâle solidité, en l'allongeant jusqu'à huit diamètres? N'a-t-on pas perdu son originalité, en y ajoutant cette base qui semble destinée à soutenir des fûts plus délicats; et les trois gradins élevés que les Grecs lui ont

substitué dans les monumens d'Athènes, dans les Temples de Pestum et dans quelques autres de la Sicile, ne lui forment-ils pas un soubassement plus ferme et plus convenable? C'est aux Artistes à examiner, à comparer, à choisir et appliquer, suivant les cas. Je ne me permettrai point de rien prescrire à cet égard; je doute que ceux que seront bien pénétrés de ce style pur, simple, gracieux, et si noble; et si grand, de l'Architecture Grecque, dont les principaux ordres Doriques sont rapportés dans cette planche, puissent contempler avec le même plaisir, cette colonne que le goût des modernes amollit, énerva, pour l'enchainer entre le lourd Toscan et l'Ionique dépouillé de sa grace naive, et lui faire prendre son rang parmi les cinq ordres d'Architecture.' Ibid., 49.

107 Delagardette had proposed a similar disposition of the base-less Doric on a continuum between the Tuscan and Ionic. *Règles des cinq ordres* (1786).

Bibliography

PRIMARY SOURCES

Manuscripts

FRANCE

Besançon, Bibliothèque Municipale
Pâris, Pierre-Adrien, 'Études d'Architecture faites en Italie pendant les années 1771, 1772, 1773 et 1774. Premier volume contenant les antiquités', Fonds Pâris, MS 476
———— 'Observations', notes and drawings, added to Antoine Desgodets [Desgodetz], *Les édifices antiques de Rome, dessinés et mesurés très exactement* [1682], new edn (Paris: Claude-Antoine Jombert fils aîné, Libraire du Roi, 1779), inv. 12.421
———— 'Route de Rome à Naples', Fonds Pâris, MS 12

Bordeaux, Archives Municipales
Combes, Louis, 'Des Progrès & de la Décadence de l'Architecture Grècque en France Depuis les Romains jusqu'à nos jours', Fonds Delpit, 66 S 272 (MS 48)
———— 'Reflections sur les temples antiques et modernes de Rome', Fonds Delpit, 66 S 273 (MS 49)

Champs-sur-Marne, École Nationale des Ponts et Chaussées
Dumont, Gabriel-Pierre-Martin, drawings, Fonds ancien, MS, fol. 208

Paris, Archives Nationales
Académie Royale d'Architecture, Archives, O¹ 1931–1934
Léon Dufourny Papers, 138 AP 212

Paris, Bibliothèque Nationale de France
Dufourny, Léon, 'Journal . . . à Palerme, 8 juillet 1789 – 29 septembre 1793', Cabinet des Estampes, Ub 236, 40

———— 'Notes rapportées d'un voyage en Sicile', Cabinet des Estampes, Ub 236, 40
Dupaty, Charles-Marguerite-Jean-Baptiste Mercier, 'Lettres sur l'Italie en 1785', Département des Manuscrits, MS 6762
Rohault de Fleury, Hubert, 'Voyage de l'architecte Rohault de Fleury en Italie, 1804–1805', 4 vols, Département des Manuscrits, NAF 23696
Piranesi, Giovanni Battista, study drawing for *Différentes vues de . . . Pesto* (Rome: s.n., 1778), plate 1, Département des Estampes et de la Photographie, Reserve B-11-FT 4 Piranèse

Paris, École Nationale Supérieure des Beaux-Arts
Léon Dufourny Papers, MS 805, A–D; MS 807, W–Z
Labrouste, Henri, 'Antiquités de Pestum Posidonia, Labrouste jeune 1829', *mémoire*, PC 77832–7

Paris, Fondation Custodia
Taurel, Jacques-François, 'Paysage avec les temples de Paestum', drawing , Album va, 1993-T.8

Paris, Institut de France
Delannoy, François-Jacques, 'Voyage de Naples et de Pestum. Avril et mai 1781', MS 1920
Pâris, Pierre-Adrien, 'Notes et lavis de Pierre-Adrien Pâris, intercalés par lui, avec différentes estampes', in Antoine Desgodets [Desgodetz], *Les édifices antiques de Rome, dessinés et mesurés très exactement* [1682], new edn (Paris: Claude-Antoine Jombert fils aîné, Libraire du Roi, 1779), MS 1906

Paris, Institut National d'Histoire de l'Art
Moreau-Desproux, Pierre-Louis, 'Notes sur mon voyage', Collection Jacques Doucet, MS 98
Vaudoyer, Antoine-Laurent-Thomas, and Léon Vaudoyer, 'Correspondance échangée pendant le séjour à Rome de Léon

Vaudoyer, 1826–1832', 'Voyage d'Italie d'A.-L.-T. Vaudoyer, 1786–1787', MS 747 (1–2)

Paris, Private collection
Vaudoyer, Antoine-Laurent-Thomas, 'Voyage de Rome à Poestum et tout le Royaume de Naples', 1787
———— 'Voyage pittoresque en diverses parties de l'Italie: Extraits de lettres adressées à Paris à M. Lebas père, par A. L. T. Vaudoyer, architecte, pensionnaire du Roi à l'Académie de France à Rome, années 1786, 1787, 1788'

ITALY

Naples, Archivio di Stato
Casa Reale Antica, fascio 1537

NETHERLANDS

Amsterdam, Rijksmuseum, Rijksprentenkabinet
Piranesi, Giovanni Battista, study drawing for *Différentes vues de . . . Pesto* (Rome: s.n., 1778), plate XIX, RP-T-1960-205

UNITED KINGDOM

London, British Library, Department of Manuscripts
Flaxman, John, correspondence, Add. MS 39780
Norris, Richard, travel journal, 'No. 4', Naples and Rome, 31 December 1770 – 29 June 1771, Add. MS 52497 B
Turner, Joseph Mallord William, Royal Academy lectures, 1806–27, Add. MS 46151 A–BB
Yorke, Philip, correspondence, 1777–1779, Add. MS 35378
———— 'Travels thro Holland, Germany, Italy & Switzerland &c. in the years 1777, 1778 and 1779', Add. MSS 36258–36260

London, British Museum, Archive
Brenna, Vincenzo, letters to Charles Townley, BM Townley Papers, TY 7/1030–43
Townley, Charles, travel diary, Naples to Paestum, BM Townley Papers, TY 1/3

London, British Museum, Department of Prints and Drawings
Barry, Charles, drawing of Paestum, L.B. 1, 1875-8-14-1159
Châtelet, Claude-Louis, drawing of Paestum, Lucas Collection, BM 1918-5-9-1
Crouch, W., drawing of Paestum, L.B. 1, 1890-0512-39
Gore, Charles, drawings of expedition into Sicily, LB 1–20
Hackert, Jakob Philipp, drawings made on an expedition into Sicily, O.o.4-7, 27, 28
Tresham, Henry, drawing of Paestum, 1955-11-17-5
Turner, Joseph Mallord William, drawings of Paestum, 1919-6-14-3, 1940-6-1-30

London, Paul Mellon Centre, Library and Archive
Sir Brinsley Ford Archive

London, Royal Institute of British Architects, Drawings and Archives Collections
Barry, Charles, travel diary of Rome, SKB401/2
Chambers, William, notes for Royal Academy lectures, CHA 1/3, 1/4, 1/6, 1/8, 2/3, 2/26
Hardwick, Thomas, notebooks, sketchbooks, journal and album from an Italian journey, 1777–9, SKB103, SKB104/3, SKB105/1, SKB105/4
Mylne, Robert, letters from Italy, 1754–9, MSS Add. Mylne 4/8/1–4, 6; MSS Add. Mylne 4/17/2–15, 4/18/1
Reveley, Willey, notes and sketches for a proposed dictionary of architecture, travel journal, ReW/1

London, Sir John Soane's Museum, Drawings Collection
Major, Thomas, 'The Original Drawings for a Work Intituled the Ruins of Paestum or Posidonia Engraved by T. Major 1768', Vol. 27
———— *The ruins of Paestum, otherwise Posidonia, in Magna Graecia* (London: T. Major, 1768), Vol. 28
'Major's Paestum proof etchings & additional engravings & 12 drawings', Drawer 60, Set 1
Piranesi, Giovanni Battista, study drawings for *Différentes vues de . . . Pesto* (Rome: s.n., 1778), plates II–XIV, XVI–XVII, F9 (51)–F10 (54); F18 (69)–F25 (77); F64 (125); F70 (133); F76 (139)–F 78 (146)
Reveley, Willey, volume of tracings and sketches of Greek and Roman ornament and miscellaneous subjects, Vol. 31
Soane, John, 'Italian Sketches / J: Soane / 1779', sketchbook, Vol. 39
———— Royal Academy lecture drawings of buildings at Paestum, Drawer 19, Set 5
———— Royal Academy lecture drawings of Greek Doric temples and the Doric order, Drawer 23, Set 3
———— Royal Academy lecture drawings to illustrate Greek Doric orders, Drawer 25, Set 1
———— Royal Academy lecture drawings to illustrate primitive huts, Drawer 27, Set 2
———— Royal Academy lecture drawings to illustrate primitive huts and the growth of trees, Drawer 86, Set 1
———— 'Sir John Soane / Notes Italy & Italian Language', Vol. 162
Tatham, Charles Heathcote, Italian drawings, Vol. 109

London, Victoria and Albert Museum, Prints and Drawings Collection
Brenna, Vinzenco, drawings of Paestum, 8478.12; map VI 1–31, 8478 13–17
Cozens, John, drawing of Paestum, P.2-1973
Morghen, Filippo, engravings of Paestum, 92.D.23
Reveley, Willey, drawings of Paestum and Greece, D.140-1888, D.446-1887
Tatham, Charles Heathcote, letters and sketches, 99.A.3, nos 2, 3
———— album, 93.G.8

UNITED STATES

New Haven (Conn.), Yale University, Beinecke Rare Book and Manuscript Library, Osborn Manuscript Files
Paoli, Paolo Antonio, letters, 1781–7, 11351–11359

New Haven (Conn.), Yale University, Yale Center for British Art, Paul Mellon Collection
Bruce, James (and Luigi Balugani), drawings of Paestum, C27 Sh2 B1944.14.8493–8512
Bruce, James, travel diary, C27 Sh3
Reveley, Willey, 'Views in the Levant', incl. drawings of Paestum, B1977.14.19434, 19454
Riou, Stephen, letters, travel journal 'Part of a tour in Greece, & other papers by SR', 1750–78, DG424.R56 P37 1750

Published sources

Adam, James, 'Journal of a Tour in Italy', *Library of the Fine Arts*, 2/8 (September 1831)
Adam, Robert, *Ruins of the Palace of the Emperor Diocletian at Spalatro* (London: printed for the author, 1764)
Adam, Robert, and James Adam, *The Works in Architecture of Robert and James Adam, Esquires* [1778], ed. with an introduction by Robert Oresko (London: Academy Editions, 1975)
Addison, Joseph, 'Paper V: On the Pleasures of the Imagination', *The Spectator*, no. 415 (26 June 1712); repr. in *The Spectator, in Eight Volumes* (London: Sharpe and Hailes, 1811)
——— 'The Pleasures of the Imagination' [1712], in Richard Steele and Joseph Addison, *Selections from the Tatler and The Spectator*, ed. with an introduction and notes by Angus Ross (London: Penguin Books, 1982), 364–406
——— *Remarks on several parts of Italy, &c., in the Years 1701, 1702, 1703* [1705], 2nd edn (London: J. Tonson, 1718)
——— *The Miscellaneous Works of Joseph Addison*, ed. A. C. Guthkelch, vol. 1 (London: G. Bell and Sons, 1914)
Alberti, Leon Battista, *De re aedificatoria / On the Art of Building in Ten Books*, trans. Joseph Rykwert, Neil Leach and Robert Tavernor (Cambridge (Mass.): MIT Press, 1988)
Alison, Archibald, *Essays on the nature and principles of taste* (Dublin: P. Byrne, 1790)
Aloë, Stanislas d', *Naples: Ses monuments et ses curiosités, avec une description de Pompei, Herculanum, Stabies, Paestum, Pouzzoles, Cumes, Capoue* (Naples: Imprimerie Virgile, 1847)
Aristotle, *Poetics*, in D. [Donald] A. Russell and M. [Michael] Winterbottom (eds), *Ancient Literary Criticism: The Principal Texts in New Translations* (s.l. [London]: Clarendon Press, 1972)
Barbault, Jean, *Recueil de divers monumens anciens répandus en plusieurs endroits de l'Italie, dessinés par feu M. Barbault peintre pensionnaire du Roy à Rome, et gravés en 166 planches avec leur explication historique pour servir de suite aux 'Monumens de Rome ancienne'* (Rome: Bouchard et Gravier, 1770)

Beulé, Charles Ernest, 'L'Architecture au siècle de Pisistrate, Chapitre VIII: Les Temples de Paestum', *Revue Générale de l'Architecture et des Travaux Publics*, 16 (1858), 8–25
Bibliothèque de M. Quatremère de Quincy . . . Collection d'ouvrages relatifs aux beaux-arts et à l'archéologie . . . Vente le 27 mai 1850 et jours suivants, rue de Condé, no. 14. Préface de R. Merlin (Paris: Imprimerie d'Adrien Le Clere et Cie, 1850)
Blessington, Marguerite, Countess of, *Lady Blessington at Naples*, ed. Edith Clay, introduction by Harold Acton (London: Hamish Hamilton, 1979)
Blondel, Jacques-François, *Cours d'architecture, ou Traité de la décoration, distribution et construction des bâtiments: contenant les leçons données en 1750 et les années suivantes*, 6 vols (Paris: Desaint, 1771–7)
Boffrand, Germain, *Book of Architecture, Containing the General Principles of the Art and the Plans, Elevations and Sections of Some of the Edifices Built in France and in Foreign Countries* [1745], ed. and introduced by Caroline van Eck, trans. David Britt (Aldershot (Surrey): Ashgate 2002)
Boileau-Despréaux, Nicolas (trans.), *Longin, Traité du sublime* [1674], ed. Francis Goyet (Paris: Librairie Générale Française, 1995)
Boullée, Étienne-Louis, *Architecture: Essai sur l'art*, ed. Helen Rosenau as *Boullée's Treatise on Architecture: A Complete Presentation of the 'Architecture, essai sur l'art' which Forms Part of the Boullée Papers (Ms. 9153) in the Bibliothèque Nationale, Paris* (London: Tiranti, 1953)
——— *Architecture: Essai sur l'art*, ed. Jean-Marie Pérouse de Montclos (Paris: Hermann, 1968)
——— 'Architecture, Essay on Art', in Helen Rosenau, *Boullée and Visionary Architecture* (London / New York: Academy Editions / Harmony Books, 1976)
Brydone, Patrick, *A tour through Sicily and Malta, in a series of letters to William Beckford*, 2 vols (London: W. Strahan and T. Cadell, 1773)
——— *A tour through Sicily and Malta, in a series of letters to William Beckford*, 3rd edn, 2 vols (London: W. Strahan and T. Cadell, 1775)
Burke, Edmund, *A Philosophical Enquiry into the Origin of our Ideas of the Sublime and Beautiful* [1757], ed. James T. Boulton (London / New York: Routledge, 2008)
——— *Recherche philosophique sur l'origine de nos idées du sublime et du beau*, trans. E. Lagentie de Lavaisse, foreword by Baldine Saint-Girons (Paris: J. Vrin, 1973)
Catalogue de l'Œuvre des gravures d'architecture de Dumont, architecte à Paris (Paris: s.n., 1775)
Catalogue of a Select Portion of the Valuable Library of John Crosse . . . and a Portion of the Library of the Late Richard Payne Knight (London: s.n., 1829)
Caylus, Comte de, *Recueil d'antiquités égyptiennes, étrusques, grecques et romaines*, 7 vols (Paris: Desaint et Saillant, 1752–67)
Chambers, William, *A treatise on civil architecture, in which the*

principles of that art are laid down, and illustrated by a great number of plates . . . designed, and . . . engraved by the best hands (London: printed for the author, 1759)

————— A dissertation on oriental gardening (London: W. Griffin, 1772)

————— A treatise on the decorative part of civil architecture, illustrated by fifty original, and three additional plates, engraved by Old Rooker, Old Foudrinier, Charles Grignion, and other eminent hands (London: printed by Joseph Smeeton, 1791) [3rd, rev. and enlarged, edn of A treatise on civil architecture (1759)]

Cicero, De oratore, [Book III]: De fato, Paradoxa stoicorum, De partitione oratoria, trans. H. Rackham (Cambridge (Mass.) / London: Harvard University Press / William Heinemann, 1982)

Condillac, Étienne Bonnot de, Essai sur l'origine des connoissances humaines (Amsterdam: Pierre Mortier, 1746)

————— Traité des sensations (London / Paris: Debure, 1754)

Cordemoy, J.-L. de, Nouveau traité de toute l'architecture, ou L'art de bastir, utile aux entrepreneurs et aux ouvriers [1706], 2nd edn (Paris: J.-B. Coignard, 1714)

Creuzé de Lesser, Auguste, Voyage en Italie et en Sicile, fait en 1801 et 1802 (Paris: P. Didot l'aîné, 1806)

Daly, César, 'Notices nécrologiques: MM. Vaudoyer et Baltard', Revue de l'Architecture et des Travaux Publics, 6 (1845–6), 547–52

Delagardette, Claude-Mathieu, Règles des cinq ordres d'architecture de Vignole, avec un détail d'un ordre dorique de Poestum, suivies d'une seconde partie, contenant les Leçons élémentaires des ombres dans l'architecture, démontrées par principes pris dans la nature (Paris: Chéreau, 1786)

————— Regles des cinq ordres d'architecture, de Vignole. Ouvrage dans lequel on donne: Une idée de la Géométrie; les définitions des figures géométriques nécessaires à l'étude de l'Architecture; la formation des Ordres, rigoureusement démontrée, dans l'origine de l'architecture; leur division générale; les proportions particulières à chacun d'eux; les différences qui les caractérisent; une méthode facile pour les dessiner; les détails d'un Ordre-dorique de Poestum, mésurés par l'Auteur, sur les lieux mêmes; enfin, les notions nécessaires sur les Ordres appelés accessoires, new edn (Paris: Joubert, 1797)

————— Les Ruines de Paestum, ou Posidonia, ancienne ville de la grande Grèce . . . levées, mesurées et dessinées . . . en l'an II (Paris: l'auteur, an VI [1798]) [prospectus for forthcoming publication]

————— Les Ruines de Paestum, ou Posidona, ancienne ville de la Grande-Grèce, a vingt-deux lieues de Naples, dans le golfe de Salerne: Levées, mesurées et dessinées sur les lieux, en l'an ii (Paris: l'auteur / H. Barbou, an VII [1799])

Delannoy, François-Jacques, Souvenirs de la vie et des ouvrages de F.-J. Delannoy, architecte (Paris: A. Éverat et Cie, 1839)

Denon, [Dominique] Vivant, Voyage au Royaume de Naples [1778], ed. Mathieu Couty (Paris: Perrin, 1997)

Denon, Dominique Vivant, Voyage en Sicile [1788], introduced by Patrick Mauriès (Paris: Gallimard, 1993)

————— Vivant Denon et le 'Voyage pittoresque': Un manuscrit inconnu, ed. Marie-Anne Dupuy-Vachey (Paris: Fondation Custodia, 2009)

Desgodets [Desgodetz], Antoine, Les édifices antiques de Rome, dessinés et mesurés tres exactement par feu M. Desgodetz, Architecte du Roi [1682], new edn (Paris: Claude-Antoine Jombert fils aîné, Libraire du Roi, 1779)

————— Les édifices antiques de Rome [1682]; repr. with introduction by Hélène Rousteau-Chambon (Paris: Picard, 2008)

Diderot, [Denis], Supplément au voyage de Bougainville [1796], ed. Paul-Édouard Levayer (Paris: Librairie Générale Française, 1995) [written in 1772]

Diderot, Denis, Écrits sur l'art et les artistes, ed. Jean Seznec, new edn with introductory texts by Jean Starobinski, Michel Delon and Arthur Cohen (Paris: Hermann, 2007) [first published 1967]

————— Œuvres esthétiques, ed. Paul Vernière (Paris: Garnier, 1994)

Diderot, [Denis], Salons III: Ruines et paysages: Salons de 1767, ed. Else Marie Bukdahl, Michel Delon and Annette Lorenceau (Paris: Hermann, 1995)

————— Salons, ed. Michel Delon (Paris: Gallimard, 2008)

Dryden, John, A voyage to Sicily and Malta, written by Mr. John Dryden, Junior, when he accompanied Mr Cecill in that expedition, in the years 1700 and 1701 (London: J. Brew, 1776)

Dubois, L. J. J., Catalogue d'antiquités égyptiennes, grecques et romaines; sculptures modernes, émaux et terres émaillées; vitraux peints, etc., etc., qui composent l'une des collections d'objets d'arts, formées par feu M. Léon Dufourny (Paris: s.n., 1819)

Dufourny, Léon, Diario di un Giacobino a Palermo, 1789–1793, introduction by Geneviève Bresc-Bautier, trans. Raimondo A. Cannizzo (Palermo: Fondazione Culturale Lauro Chiazzese della Sicilcassa, 1991)

Dumont, Gabriel-Pierre-Martin, Suitte [Suite] de plans, coupes, profils, élévations géométrales et perspectives de trois temples antiques, tels qu'ils existaient en 1750 dans la bourgade de Poesto, qui est la ville Poestum de Pline . . . Ils ont été mesurés et dessinés par J.-G. Soufflot, . . . en 1750, et mis au jour par les soins de G.-M. Dumont en 1764 (Paris: Dumont, 1764)

————— Parallèle de plans des plus belles salles de spectacles d'Italie et de France, avec des détails de machines théâtrales (Paris: s.n., n.d. [c.1765])

————— Les ruines de Paestum, autrement Posidonia, ville de l'ancienne grande Grèce, au Royaume de Naples: ouvrage contenant l'histoire ancienne & moderne de cette ville, la description & les vues de ses antiquités, ses inscriptions, &c.: avec des observations sur l'ancien Ordre Dorique, partly based on [John Longfield], The ruins of Poestum, trans. Jacques Varenne de Béost (London / Paris: C.-A. Jombert, 1769)

Dupaty, Charles-Marguerite-Jean-Baptiste Mercier, Lettres sur l'Italie en 1785, 2 vols (Paris: De Senne, 1788)

————— Travels through Italy, in a series of letters; written in the year 1785, by President Dupaty. Translated from the French by an

English Gentleman (London: G. G. J. and J. Robinson, 1788)

————— *Sentimental letters on Italy; written in French by President Dupaty, in 1785. Published at Rome in 1788, and translated the same year by J. Povoleri, at Paris* (London: J. Crowder, 1789)

Duperron, *Discours sur la peinture et sur l'architecture* (Paris: Prault, 1758); repr. with Étienne La Font de Saint-Yenne, *Examen d'un essai sur l'architecture* [1753] (Geneva: Minkoff Reprint, 1973)

Durand, Jean-Nicolas-Louis, *Recueil et parallèle des édifices de tout genre anciens et modernes remarquables par leur beauté*, 2 vols (Paris: Gillé fils, an VIII – an IX [1799–1800])

Eustace, John Chetwode, *A Tour through Italy, Exhibiting a View of its Scenery, its Antiquities, and its Monuments, Particularly as they are Objects of Classical Interest and Elucidation: With an Account of the Present State of its Cities and Towns, and Occasional Observations on the Recent Spoliations of the French*, 2 vols (London: J. Mawman, 1813)

Flaxman, John, letter to George Romney, Rome, 25 May 1788, in John Romney, *Memoirs of the Life and Works of George Romney, Including Various Letters, and Testimonies to his Genius &c.; also Some Particulars of the Life of Peter Romney, his Brother* (London: Baldwin and Cradock, 1830), 204–7

Flloyd, Thomas, *An Essay on Architecture* (London: T. Osborne and Shipton, 1755) [trans. of Marc-Antoine Laugier's *Essai sur l'architecture* (1753)]

Forsyth, Joseph, *Remarks on Antiquities, Arts, and Letters, during an Excursion in Italy in the Years 1802 and 1803* (London: T. Cadell and W. Davies, 1813)

————— *Remarks on Antiquities, Arts, and Letters, during an Excursion in Italy in the Years 1802 and 1803*, 4th edn (London: John Murray, 1835)

————— *Remarks on Antiquities, Arts, and Letters during an Excursion in Italy, in the Years 1802 and 1803*, ed. Keith Crook (Newark: University of Delaware Press, 2001)

Frézier, Amédée-François, 'Remarques sur quelques livres nouveaux concernant la beauté & le bon goût de l'architecture', *Mercure de France* (July 1754), 7–59

————— 'Résultat de la dispute entre le P. Laugier et M. Frézier, concernant le goût de l'architecture', *Mercure de France* (May 1755), 143–74

Galli Bibiena, Giuseppe, *Architectural and Perspective Designs* [1740] (New York: Dover Publications, 1964)

Gibbon, Edward, *The History of the Decline and Fall of the Roman Empire*, 6 vols (London: s.n., 1776–88)

————— *Miscellaneous works . . . With Memoirs of his life and writings . . . illustrated from his letters*, 2 vols (London: A. Strahan and T. Cadell jun., 1796)

Gilpin, William, *A dialogue upon the gardens of the Right Honourable the Lord Viscount Cobham, at Stowe in Buckinghamshire* (London: B. Seeley, 1748)

————— *An essay upon prints; containing remarks upon the principles of picturesque beauty, etc.* (London: J. Robson, 1768)

————— *Observations, relative chiefly to picturesque beauty, made in the year 1772, on several parts of England; particularly the mountains, and lakes of Cumberland, and Westmoreland*, 2 vols (London: R. Blamire, 1786)

————— *Three essays: on picturesque beauty; on picturesque travel; and on sketching landscape: to which is added a poem, on landscape painting* (London: R. Blamire, 1792)

————— *Observations on the western parts of England, relative chiefly to picturesque beauty. To which are added, a few remarks on the picturesque beauties of the Isle of Wight* (London: T. Cadell jun. and W. Davies, 1798)

Gioffredo, Mario, *Dell'architettura di Mario Gioffredo, architetto Napoletano, Parte prima. Nella quale si tratta degli ordini dell'archittetura de' Greci, e degl'Italiani, e si danno le regole più spedite per disegnarli* (Naples: s.n., 1768)

Goethe, Johann Wolfgang von, *Philipp Hackert: Biographische Skizze, meist nach dessen eigenen Aufsätzen entworfen von Goethe* (Tübingen: In der J. G. Cottaischen Buchhandlung, 1811)

————— *Italienische Reise [1786–8]* [1829] (Munich: Wilhelm Goldmann Verlag, 1988)

————— *Italian Journey [1786–8]* [1829], trans. W. H. Auden and Elizabeth Mayer (London: Penguin, 1970) [first published 1962]

Grosley, Pierre-Jean, *Observations sur l'Italie et sur les italiens, données en 1764, sous le nom de 'Deux gentilshommes suédois'* (London: s.n., 1770)

Guarnacci, Mario, *Origini italiche, o siano Memorie istorico-etrusche sopra l'antichissimo regno d'Italia e sopra i di lei primi abitatori nei secoli più remoti* (Lucca: L. Venturini, 1767)

Hakewill, James, *A Picturesque Tour of Italy from Drawings made in 1816–17 by J. H.* (London: s.n., 1820)

Hancarville, Pierre-François Hugues d', *Antiquités étrusques, grecques et romaines, tirées du cabinet de M. Hamilton / Collection of Etruscan, Greek and Roman Antiquities from the Cabinet of the Hon. William Hamilton*, 4 vols (Naples: s.n., 1766–7)

————— *Recherches sur l'origine, l'esprit et les progrès des arts de la Grèce, sur leurs connections avec les arts et la religion des plus anciens peuples connus, sur les monumens antiques de l'Inde, de la Perse, du reste de l'Asie, de l'Europe et de l'Égypte*, 3 vols (London: P. Appleyard, 1785)

Hardwick, Thomas, *A Memoir of the Life of Sir William Chambers* (London: s.n., 1825)

Hoare, Richard Colt, *A Classical Tour through Italy and Sicily, Tending to Illustrate some Districts, which have not been Described by Mr Eustace, in his Classical Tour* (London: s.n., 1819)

[Jeffrey, Francis] (published anonymously), 'Essay on Beauty', review of Archibald Alison, *Essay on the Nature and Principles of Taste*, *Edinburgh Review*, 18 (May 1811), 1–45

Kames, Lord [Henry Home], *Introduction to the Art of Thinking* (Edinburgh: A. Kincaid and J. Bell, 1761)

————— *Elements of Criticism*, 3 vols (Edinburgh: s.n., 1762)

Knight, Richard Payne, *The Landscape: A didactic poem, in three* books. *Addressed to Uvedale Price* (London: W. Bulmer and Co. 1794; 2nd edn 1795)

——— *An Analytical Inquiry into the Principles of Taste* (London: printed by Luke Hansard for T. Payne and J. White, 1805)

——— *Expedition into Sicily*, ed. Claudia Stumpf (London: British Museum Publications, 1986)

Labrouste, Henri, *Les Temples de Paestum: Restauration exécutée en 1829 par Henri Labrouste*, Restaurations des Monuments Antiques par les Architectes Pensionnaires de l'Académie de France à Rome, vol. III (Paris: Firmin–Didot, 1877)

La Font de Saint-Yenne, Étienne, *Examen d'un essai sur l'architecture* (Paris: Michel Lambert, 1753); repr. in Duperron, *Discours sur le peinture et sur l'architecture* [1758] (Geneva: Minkoff Reprint, 1973)

La Lande, Jérôme de, *Voyage d'un françois en Italie, fait dans les années 1765 et 1766, contenant l'histoire & les anecdotes les plus singulieres de l'Italie, & sa description, les mœurs, les usages, le gouvernement, le commerce, la littérature, les arts, l'histoire naturelle, & les antiquités; avec des jugements sur les ouvrages de peinture, sculpture & architecture, & les plans de toutes les grandes villes d'Italie*, 8 vols and atlas (Paris: Chez Desaint, 1769)

——— *Voyage en Italie, contenant l'histoire & les anecdotes les plus singulieres de l'Italie, & sa description, les usages, le gouvernement, le commerce, la littérature, les arts, l'histoire naturelle, & les antiquités*, 2nd edn, 8 vols and atlas (Paris: Chez la Veuve Desaint, 1786)

La Querelle des anciens et des modernes, XVIIe–XVIIIe siècles, ed. Anne-Marie Lecoq (Paris: Gallimard, 2001)

La Rive, Pierre-Louis de, *Lettres du peintre Pierre-Louis de La Rive pendant son séjour en Italie (1784–1786)*, ed. Georges de Morsier (Geneva: s.n., 1972)

[Laugier, Marc-Antoine], *Essai sur l'architecture* (Paris: Chez Duchesne, 1753)

Laugier, Marc-Antoine, *Essai sur l'architecture, nouvelle édition . . . avec un dictionnaire des termes, et des planches qui en facilitent l'explication* (Paris: Chez Duchesne, 1755)

——— *An essay on architecture in which its true principles are explained and invariable rules proposed . . . Adorned with a frontispiece, designed by Mr. Wale* (London: T. Osborne & Shipton, 1755) [Eng. trans. of Laugier, *Essai sur l'architecture* (1753)]; repr. as *An essay on the study and practice of architecture: Explaining the true principles of the science* (London: Stanley Crowder and Henry Woodgate, 1756)

——— *Observations sur l'architecture* (The Hague: Saillant, 1765)

Le Barbier, Jean-Jacques-François, 'Notice nécrologique sur M. Legrand, architecte, membre de l'Académie Celtique', *Mémoires de l'Académie Celtique*, vol. II (Paris: L.-P. Dubray, 1808)

Le Camus de Mézières, Nicolas, *Le Génie de l'architecture, ou L'Analogie de cet art avec nos sensations* (Paris: l'auteur, 1780)

——— *The Genius of Architecture, or The Analogy of that Art with our Sensations* [1780], introduction by Robin Middleton, trans.

David Britt (Santa Monica (Cal.): Getty Center for the History of Art and the Humanities, 1992)

Legrand, Jacques-Guillaume, *Essai sur l'histoire générale de l'architecture . . . pour servir de texte explicatif au Recueil et Parallèle des édifices de tout genre, anciens et modernes, remarquables par leur beauté, leur grandeur, ou leur singularité, et dessinés sur une même échelle; Par J. N. L. Durand . . . nouvelle édition corrigée et augmentée d'une notice historique sur J. G. L.* [1803] (Paris : s.n. [L. Ch. Soyer], 1809)

——— *Collection des chefs-d'œuvre de l'architecture des différens peuples, exécutés en modèles, sous la direction de L.-F. Cassas, auteur des voyages d'Istrie, Dalmatie, Syrie, Phœnicie, Palestine, Bass-Égypte, etc.; décrite et analysée par J.-G. Legrand* (Paris: Leblanc, 1806)

Le Roy, Julien-David, *Les Ruines des plus beaux monumens de la Grèce, ou Recueil de desseins et de vues de ces monumens; avec leur histoire, et des reflexions sur les progres de l'Architecture, par M. Le Roy* (Paris: H. L. Guérin and L. F. Delatour, 1756) [prospectus for forthcoming publication]

——— *Les ruines des plus beaux monuments de la Grece: ouvrage divisé en deux parties, où l'on considere, dans la premiere, ces monuments du côté de l'histoire; et, dans la seconde, du côté de l'architecture* (Paris: H. L. Guérin et L. F. Delatour, 1758)

——— *Histoire de la disposition et des formes différentes que les Chrétiens ont données à leurs Temples, depuis le règne de Constantin le Grand, jusqu'à nous* (Paris: Chez Desaint & Saillant, 1764)

——— *Les ruines des plus beaux monuments de la Grèce, considérées du côté de l'histoire et du côté de l'architecture*, 2nd edn, 2 vols (Paris: Louis-François Delatour, 1770)

——— *The Ruins of the Most Beautiful Monuments of Greece*, 2nd edn [1770], introduction by Robin Middleton, trans. David Britt (Los Angeles: Getty Research Institute, 2004)

Locke, John, *An Essay Concerning Human Understanding* [1689], ed. Roger Woolhouse (London: Penguin, 1997)

[Longfield, John] (published anonymously), *The ruins of Poestum or Posidonia, containing a description and views of the remaining antiquities, with the ancient and modern history, inscriptions, etc.* (London: s.n., 1767)

Longinus, *Dionysius Longinus On the Sublime: Translated . . . with notes and observations, and some account of the life and writings and character of the author. By William Smith* (London: J. Watts / W. Innys and R. Manby, 1739)

——— *On the Sublime*, ed. and trans. W. Hamilton Fyfe and W. Rhys Roberts, rev. Donald Russell, in Aristotle, *Poetics . . . Longinus, On the Sublime . . . Demetrius, On Style*, Loeb Classical Library, 199, 2nd edn (Cambridge (Mass.) / London: Harvard University Press, 1995)

Major, Thomas, *The ruins of Paestum, otherwise Posidonia, in Magna Graecia* (London: s.n., 1768)

——— *Les ruines de Paestum* (London: T. Major, 1768)

Martial, *Epigrams*, ed. and trans. D. R. Shackleton Bailey, 2 vols

(Cambridge (Mass.) / London: Harvard University Press, 1993)

Montaigne, Michel de, *Essais de Messire Michel, Seigneur de Montaigne . . . Livre premier et second* (Bordeaux: S. Millanges, 1580)

Moreau-Desproux, Pierre-Louis, *Le Voyage d'Italie de Pierre-Louis Moreau: Journal intime d'un architecte des Lumières (1754–1757)*, ed. Sophie Descat (Pessac: Presses Universitaires de Bordeaux, 2004)

Morghen, Filippo, untitled [*Sei vedute delle rovine di Pesto*] (Naples: s.n., n.d. [1765]); repr. in *Le antichità di Pozzuoli, Baja e Cuma, incise in rame* (Naples: s.n., 1769)

Obituary of Willey Reveley, *Gentleman's Magazine*, 59/2 (1799), 627

Orville, Jacques Philippe d', *Jacobi Philippi d'Orville Sicula, quibus Siciliae veteris rudera . . . illustrantur*, 2 vols (Amsterdam: G. Tielenburg, 1764)

Paoli, Paolo Antonio, 'Lettera sull'origine ed antichità dell'architettura al Signor Abate Fea', in Johann Joachim Winckelmann, *Storia delle arti del disegno presso gli antichi di Giovanni Winkelmann, tradotta dal tedesco e corretta e aumentata dall'abate Carlo Fea*, 3 vols (Rome: Pagliarini, 1783–4), vol. III, 127–86

——— *Paesti, quod Posidoniam etiam dixere, rudera: Rovine della città di Pesto, detta ancora Posidonia* (Rome: [in typographio Paleariniano], 1784)

——— 'Lettre sur l'origine et l'antiquité de l'architecture', in Johann Joachim Winckelmann, *Histoire de l'art chez les anciens, par Winckelmann; traduit de l'allemand avec des notes historiques et critiques de différens auteurs*, vol. II (Paris: Gide, an XI [1803]), 1–55

Piles, Roger de, *Cours de peinture par principes* (Paris: J. Estienne, 1708)

Piranesi, Giovanni Battista, *Osservazioni di Gio. Battista Piranesi sopra la lettre de M. Mariette aux auteurs de la Gazette Littéraire de l'Europe, inserita nel supplemento, dell'istessa Gazzetta stampata dimanche 4. novembre, MDCCLIV: & parere su l'architettura, con una prefazione ad un nuovo tratatto della introduzione e del progresso delle belle arti in Europa ne' tempi antichi* (Rome: s.n. [Generoso Salomoni e G. B. Piranesi], 1765)

——— *Parere su l'architettura: Dialogo* (Rome, 1765)

——— *Observations on the Letter of Monsieur Mariette, with Opinions on Architecture, and a Preface to a New Treatise on the Introduction and Progress of the Fine Arts in Europe in Ancient Times* [1765], introduction by John Wilton-Ely, trans. Caroline Beamish and David Britt (Los Angeles: Getty Research Institute, 2002)

——— *Différentes vues de quelques restes de trois grands édifices qui subsistent encore dans le milieu de l'ancienne ville de Pesto, autrement Possidonia qui est située dans la Lucanie* (Rome: s.n., 1778)

Price, Uvedale, *An essay on the picturesque as compared with the sublime and the beautiful: and on the use of studying pictures, for the purpose of improving real landscape* (London: J. Robson, 1794; rev. 2nd edn, 2 vols, 1796–8) [revisions in 2nd edn include the addition of 'An Essay on Architecture and Buildings as Connected with Scenery']

——— *A Dialogue on the Distinct Characters of the Picturesque and the Beautiful. In Answer to the Objections of Mr. Knight* (Hereford: s.n., 1801)

——— *Essays on the Picturesque, as Compared with the Sublime and the Beautiful; and, on the Use of Studying Pictures, for the Purpose of Improving Real Landscape*, 3 vols (London: J. Mawman, 1810) [3rd edn of *An essay on the picturesque as compared with the sublime and the beautiful* (1794)]

——— *Sir Uvedale Price on the Picturesque: With an Essay on the Origin of Taste, and Much Original Matter, by Sir Thomas Dick Lauder, Bart., and Sixty Illustrations, Designed and Drawn on the Wood by Montagu Stanley, R. S. A.* (Edinburgh / London: Caldwell, Lloyd and Co. / Wm. S. Orr and Co., 1842)

Propertius, Sextus, *Elegies*, ed. and trans. G. P. Goold (Cambridge (Mass.) / London: Harvard University Press, 1990)

Pseudo-Longin, *De la sublimité du discours*, ed. Emma Gilby (Chambéry: L'Act Mem, 2007)

Quatremère de Quincy, Antoine C., *Encyclopédie méthodique: Architecture, dédiée et présentée à Monseigneur de Lamoignon, garde des sceaux de France, &c.*, 3 vols (Paris: Chez Panckoucke, 1788–1825)

——— *De l'architecture égyptienne: Considérée dans son origine, ses principes et son goût et comparée sous les mêmes rapports à l'architecture grecque* (Paris: Chez Barrois l'aîné et fils, 1803)

Repton, Humphry, *Sketches and hints on landscape gardening: Collected from designs and observations now in the possession of the different noblemen and gentlemen, for whose use they were originally made. The Whole Tending to Establish Fixed Principles in the Art of Laying out Ground* (London: W. Bulmer and Co., Shakespeare Printing-Office, n.d. [1795])

——— *Fragments on the Theory and Practice of Landscape Gardening, Including some Remarks on Grecian and Gothic Architecture* (London: s.n., 1816)

Reynolds, Joshua, *Discourses* [1797], ed. with an introduction and notes by Pat Rogers (Harmondsworth: Penguin, 1992)

Ribart de Chamoust, *L'Ordre françois trouvé dans la nature, présenté au Roi, le 21 septembre 1776, par M. Ribart de Chamoust. Orné de planches gravées d'après les dessins de l'auteur* (Paris: Nyon l'aîné, 1783)

Riedesel, J. H. [Johann Hermann] von, *Reise durch Sicilien und Grossgriechenland* (Zurich: Orell, Gessner, Füesslin & Co., 1771)

——— *Voyage en Sicile et dans la grande Grèce, adressé par l'auteur à son ami M. Winckelmann; traduit de l'allemand, accompagné de notes du traducteur et d'autres additions intéressantes* (Lausanne: F. Grasset, 1773)

——— *Travels through Sicily and that part of Italy formerly called Magna Graecia: And a tour through Egypt, with an accurate description of its cities. . . . Translated from the German, by J.-R. Forster* (London: E. and C. Dilly, 1773)

Rive, P.-L. de la, *Notice biographique de M. P.-L. de la Rive, peintre* de paysage, membre de la société des arts, écrite par lui-même (Geneva: A. L. Vignier, 1832)

Rogers, Samuel, *Human Life: A Poem (Lines Written at Paestum — The Boy of Egremond)* (London: John Murray, 1819)

———— *Italy: A Poem* (London: T. Cadell, 1830)

———— *The Italian Journal of Samuel Rogers*, ed. J. R. Hale (London: Faber and Faber, 1956)

Romanelli, Domenico, *Viaggio a Pompei, a Pesto, e di ritorno ad Ercolano, colla illustrazione di tutti monumenti finora scoverti . . . dall'Ab. Domenico Romanelli* (Naples: Perger, 1811)

Romney, John, *Memoirs of the Life and Works of George Romney, Including Various Letters, and Testimonies to his Genius, &c.; also Some Particulars of the Life of Peter Romney, his Brother* (London: Baldwin and Cradock, 1830)

Rondelet, Jean, *Traité théorique et pratique de l'art de bâtir*, 5 parts in 7 vols (Paris: l'auteur, 1802–17; 6th edn, 1830)

Rousseau, Jean-Jacques, *Confessions*, vol. VII of *Collection complète des œuvres de J. J. Rousseau* (Geneva: s.n., 1782)

Sade, [Donatien Alphonse François de], Marquis de, *Voyage à Naples*, ed. Chantal Thomas (Paris: Payot and Rivages, 2008)

Saint-Non, Jean-Claude Richard de, *Voyage pittoresque, ou Description des royaumes de Naples et de Sicile*, 5 parts in 4 vols (Paris: Clousier, 1781–6)

———— *Panopticon italiano: Un diario di viaggio ritrovato, 1759–1761*, ed. Pierre Rosenberg (Rome: Ed. dell'Elefante, 2000)

———— *Da Napoli a Malta: Voyage pittoresque, ou Description des royaumes de Naples et de Sicile di Jean Claude Richard Abbé de Saint-Non, 1781–1786*, ed. Silverio Salamon and Elisabetta Rollier (Turin: L'Arte Antica, S. Salamon, 2001)

Shelley, Mary Wollstonecraft, *Mary Shelley's Journal*, ed. Frederick L. Jones (Norman: University of Oklahoma Press, 1947)

———— *The Journals of Mary Shelley, 1814–1844*, ed. Paula R. Feldman and Diana Scott-Kilvert, 2 vols (Oxford: Clarendon Press, 1987)

Shelley, Percy Bysshe, *Essays, Letters from Abroad: Translations and Fragments*, ed. Mary Shelley, 2 vols (London: E. Moxon, 1840)

———— *The Letters of Percy Bysshe Shelley*, ed. Frederick L. Jones, 2 vols (Oxford: Clarendon Press, 1964)

———— *The Poems of Shelley*, ed. Kelvin Everest and Geoffrey Matthews, vol. II (1817–1819) (Harlow: Longman, 2000)

———— *Shelley's Poetry and Prose: Authoritative Texts, Criticism*, selected and ed. Donald H. Reiman and Neil Fraistat (New York / London: W. W. Norton & Company, 2002)

Soane, John, 'The Royal Academy Lectures', in David Watkin (ed.), *Enlightenment Thought and the Royal Academy Lectures* (Cambridge: Cambridge University Press, 1996)

———— *The Royal Academy Lectures*, ed. David Watkin (Cambridge: Cambridge University Press, 2000)

Starke, Mariana, *Letters from Italy, between the Years 1792 and 1798, Containing a View of the Revolution in that Country, from the Capture of Nice by the French Republic to the Expulsion of Pius VI from the Ecclesiastical State* (London: R. Philips, 1800)

Strabo, *The Geography of Strabo*, trans. Horace Leonard Jones, vol. II, (Cambridge (Mass.) / London: Harvard University Press, 1988)

Stuart, James, and Nicholas Revett, *The antiquities of Athens measured and delineated by James Stuart F.R.S. and F.S.A. and Nicholas Revett painters and architects*, 4 vols (vol. II ed. W. Newton, vol. III ed. W. Reveley, vol. IV ed. J. Woods) (London: John Nichols, 1762–1816)

Stukeley, William, *Stonehenge: A temple restor'd to the British druids* (London: W. Innys and R. Manby, 1740)

Swinburne, Henry, *Travels in the two Sicilies . . . in the years 1777, 1778, 1779, and 1780*, 2 vols (London: P. Elmsly, 1783–5)

Vico, Giambattista, *The New Science of Giambattista Vico* [1744], trans. Thomas Goddard Bergin and Max Harold Fisch (Ithaca (NY): Cornell University Press, 1984)

———— *New Science* [1744], trans. David Marsh with an introduction by Anthony Grafton (London: Penguin Books, 1999)

Vigée Le Brun, Élisabeth, *'Les Femmes régnaient alors, la Révolution les a détrônées': Souvenirs, 1755–1842*, ed. Didier Masseau (Paris: Tallandier, 2009)

Viollet-le-Duc, Eugène-Emmanuel, *Lettres d'Italie, 1836–1837, adressées à sa famille*, ed. Geneviève Viollet le Duc (Paris: Léonce Laget, 1971)

Virgil, *Eclogues, Georgics, Aeneid i–vi*, trans. H. Rushton Fairclough, rev. G. P. Goold (Cambridge (Mass.) / London: Harvard University Press, 1999)

Vitruvius, *De architectura libri decem / Ten Books on Architecture*, trans. Ingrid D. Rowland, commentary and illustrations by Thomas N. Howe (Cambridge: Cambridge University Press, 1999)

———— *Vitruvius on Architecture*, ed. Thomas Gordon Smith (New York: Monacelli Press, 2003)

Volney, Constantin-François de, *Observations générales sur les Indiens ou sauvages d'Amérique du Nord, Les ruines . . .* [1791], *La loi naturelle* (Paris: Coda, 2009)

———— *Volney's Ruins, or Meditation on the Revolutions of Empires. Translated, under the Immediate Inspection of the Author, from the Latest Paris Edition* (New York: G. Vale, 1853)

Watelet, Claude-Henri, *Essai sur les jardins* (Paris: Impr. de Prault, 1774)

Weiss, Charles, *Catalogue de la bibliothèque de M. Paris, architecte et dessinateur de la Chambre du Roi . . . suivi de la description de son cabinet* (Besançon: Librairie de Deis, 1821)

Whately, Thomas, *Observations on modern gardening, illustrated by descriptions* (London: T. Payne, 1770)

Wilkins, William, *The Antiquities of Magna Graecia* (London: Longman, Hurst, Orme and Rees, 1807)

———— *Atheniensia, or Remarks on the Topography and Buildings of Athens* (London: s.n., 1816)

———— *The Unedited Antiquities of Attica, Comprising the Architectural Remains of Eleusis, Rhamnus, Sunium and Thoricus* (London: Longman, Hurst, Rees, Orme and Brown, 1817)

Winckelmann, Johann Joachim, *Anmerkungen über die Baukunst der Alten, entworfen von Johann Winkelmann* (Leipzig: Johann Gottfried Dyck, 1762)

———— *Geschichte der Kunst des Alterthums* (Dresden: Walther, 1764)

———— *History of the Art of Antiquity* [1764], introduction by Alex Potts, trans. Harry Francis Mallgrave (Los Angeles: Getty Research Institute, 2006)

———— *Gedanken über die Nachahmung der griechischen Werke in der Malerei und Bildhauerkunst* (Dresden / Leipzig, 1765)

———— *Lettres familières de M. Winckelmann* (Amsterdam / Paris: Couturier fils, 1781)

———— *Histoire de l'art chez les anciens, par Winckelmann; traduit de l'allemand avec des notes historiques et critiques de différens auteurs*, vol. II (Paris: Gide, an XI [1803])

———— *Johann Joachim Winckelmann, Briefe*, ed. Walther Rehm and Hans Diepolder, 4 vols (Berlin: Walter de Gruyter, 1952–7)

———— *Kleine Schriften*, ed. Walther Rehm (Berlin: Walter de Gruyter, 1968)

———— *Een portret in brieven*, ed. Hein L. van Dolen and Eric M. Moormann (Baarn: Ambo, 1993)

———— *Johann Joachim Winckelmann, Schriften und Nachlass*, ed. Stephanie-Gerrit Bruer and Max Kunze (Mainz: P. von Zabern, 1996)

———— *Anmerkungen über die Baukunst der alten Tempel zu Girgenti in Sicilien, Anmerkungen über die Baukunst der Alten, Fragment einer neuen Bearbeitung der Anmerkungen über die Baukunst der Alten, sowie zeitgenössische Rezensionen*, ed. Marianne Gross, Adolf H. Borbein and Max Kunze (Mainz: P. von Zabern, 2001)

Wood, Robert, *The ruins of Palmyra, otherwise Tedmor, in the desart* (London: s.n., 1753)

———— *The ruins of Balbec, otherwise Heliopolis, in Coelosyria* (London: s.n., 1757)

Young, Arthur, *A six months tour through the North of England, containing an account of the present state of agriculture, manufactures and population, in several Counties of this Kingdom . . . Interspersed with Descriptions of the Seats of the Nobility and Gentry* [1769], 2nd edn, 4 vols (London: W. Strahan, 1771)

SECONDARY LITERATURE

Abramovici, Jean-Christophe, Pierre Frantz, Jean Goulemot and Frédéric Calas, *Diderot: Salons* (Neuilly: Atlande, 2007)

Agassiz, D., *A. L. Du Cros, peintre graveur (1748–1810): Étude biographique* (Lausanne: Imprimerie de la Société Suisse de Publicité, 1927)

Ajello, Raffaele, 'Le origini della politica mercantilistica nel Regno di Napoli', in Franco Strazzullo, *Le manifatture d'arte di Carlo di Borbone* (Naples: Liguori Editore, 1979), 11–17

Aldridge, A. Owen, 'Primitivism in the Eighteenth Century', in Philip P. Wiener (ed.), *Dictionary of the History of Ideas*, vol. III (New York: Charles Scribner's Sons, 1968), 598–605

Andreae, Bernard, Michael Philipp, Nina Simone Schepkowski and Ortrud Westheider, *Malerei für die Ewigkeit: Die Gräber von Paestum* (Munich: Hirmer, 2007)

Andrews, Malcolm, *The Search for the Picturesque: Landscape Aesthetics and Tourism in Britain, 1760–1800* (Stanford (Cal.): Stanford University Press, 1989)

Ankersmit, Frank, *De sublieme historische ervaring* (Groningen: Historische Uitgeverij, 2007)

Antonio Joli tra Napoli, Roma e Madrid: Le vedute, le rovine, i capricci, le scenografie teatrali (Naples: Edizioni Scientifiche Italiane, 2012)

Aquarelles de Abraham-Louis-Rodolphe Du Cros (1748–1810) (Lausanne: Musée Cantonal des Beaux-Arts de Lausanne, 1953)

Armstrong, Christop her Drew, *Julien-David Leroy and the Making of Architectural History* (London / New York: Routledge, 2012)

Arnold, Dana, and Andrew Ballantyne (eds), *Architecture as Experience: Radical Change in Spatial Practice* (London: Routledge, 2004)

Arnold, Dana, and Stephen Bending (eds), *Tracing Architecture: The Aesthetics of Antiquarianism* (Oxford: Blackwell, 2003)

Ashfield, Andrew, and Peter de Bolla, *The Sublime: A Reader in British Eighteenth-Century Aesthetic Theory* (Cambridge: Cambridge University Press, 1996)

Bachelard, Gaston, *La Poétique de l'espace* (Paris: Presses Universitaires de France, 1957)

Baker, Eric, 'Lucretius in the European Enlightenment', in Stuart Gillespie and Philip Hardie (eds), *The Cambridge Companion to Lucretius* (Cambridge: Cambridge University Press, 2007), 274–88

Ballantyne, Andrew, *Architecture, Landscape and Liberty: Richard Payne Knight and the Picturesque* (Cambridge: Cambridge University Press, 1997)

Ballon, Hilary, *Louis Le Vau Mazarin's Collège: Colbert's Revenge* (Princeton (NJ): Princeton University Press, 1999)

Banham, Reyner, 'Revenge of the Picturesque: English Architectural Polemics, 1945–1965', in John Summerson (ed.), *Concerning Architecture: Essays on Architectural Writers and Writing Presented to Nikolaus Pevsner* (London: Allen Lane, 1968), 265–73

Baridon, Laurent, 'Le Dictionnaire d'architecture de Quatremère de Quincy: Codifier le néoclassicisme', in Claude Blanckaert and Michel Porret (eds), *L'Encyclopédie méthodique (1782–1832): Des Lumières au positivisme* (Geneva: Droz, 2006), 691–718

Baridon, Laurent, and Martial Guédron, *Corps et arts: Physionomies et physiologies dans les arts visuels* (Paris / Montreal: L'Harmattan, 1999)

Barkan, Leonard, *Unearthing the Past: Archaeology and Aesthetics in the Making of Renaissance Culture* (New Haven (Conn.) / London: Yale University Press, 1999)

Barrier, Janine, *Les Architectes européens à Rome, 1740–1765: La Naissance du goût à la grecque* (Paris: Monum / Éditions du Patrimoine, 2005)

———— *William Chambers: Une architecture empreinte de culture française. Suivi de correspondance avec la France* (Paris: PUPS, Université Paris-Sorbonne, 2010)

Barthes, Roland, 'Diderot, Brecht, Eisenstein', in *Image, Music, Text*, essays selected and trans. Stephen Heath (London: Fontana Press, 1977), 69–78

Batten, Charles L., *Pleasurable Instruction: Form and Convention in Eighteenth-Century Travel Literature* (Berkeley, Los Angeles and London: University of California Press, 1978)

Bayer, Thora Ilin, and Donald Phillip Verene (eds), *Giambattista Vico: Keys to the New Science. Translations, Commentaries, and Essays* (Ithaca (NY) / London: Cornell University Press, 2009)

Becq, Annie, *Genèse de l'esthétique française moderne: De la raison classique à l'imagination créatrice, 1680–1814* (Paris: Albin Michel, 1994) [first published 1984]

Bélier, Corinne, Barry Bergdoll and Marc Le Cœur (eds), *Henri Labrouste: Structure Brought to Light* (New York: Museum of Modern Art, 2013)

Bell, C. F. [Charles Francis], and T. [Thomas] Girtin, *The Drawings and Sketches of John Robert Cozens*, Walpole Society, vol. XXIII (Oxford: printed for the Walpole Society by John Johnson at the University Press, 1935)

Bellenger, Sylvain, and Françoise Hamon, *Félix Duban, 1798–1870: Les Couleurs de l'architecte* (Paris: Gallimard / Electa, 1996)

Bellier de La Chavignerie, Émile, *Les Artistes français du XVIII siècle oubliés ou dédaignés* (Paris: Renouard, 1865)

Benhamou, Reed, 'Continuing Education and other Innovations: An Eighteenth-Century Case Study', *Studies in Eighteenth-Century Culture*, 15 (1986), 67–76

Bergdoll, Barry, 'Competing in the Academy and the Marketplace: European Architectural Competitions, 1401–1927', in Hélène Lipstadt (ed.), *The Experimental Tradition: Essays on Competitions in Architecture* (New York: Princeton Architectural Press, 1989), 21–52

———— (ed.), *Les Vaudoyer: Une dynastie d'architectes* (Paris: Réunion des Musées Nationaux, 1991)

———— *Léon Vaudoyer: Historicism in the Age of Industry* (New York / Cambridge (Mass.) / London: Architectural History Foundation / MIT Press, 1994)

———— *European Architecture, 1750–1890* (Oxford / New York: Oxford University Press, 2000)

Bevilacqua, Mario, Mario Gori Sassoli and Fabio Barry (eds), *The Rome of Piranesi: The Eighteenth-Century City in the Great Vedute* (Rome: Artemide, 2006)

Black, Jeremy, *The British and the Grand Tour* (London: Croom Helm, 1985)

———— *The British Abroad: The Grand Tour in the Eighteenth Century* (London: Sandpiper Books, 1999) [first published 1992]

Blunt, Anthony, 'The Hypnerotomachia Poliphili in 17th-Century France', *Journal of the Warburg Institute*, 1 (1937–8), 117–37

Boas, George, 'Primitivism', in Philip P. Wiener (ed.), *Dictionary of the History of Ideas*, vol. III (New York: Charles Scribner's Sons, 1968), 578–98

Bois, Yve-Alain, 'A Picturesque Stroll around *Clara-Clara*', *October*, 29 (Summer, 1984), 32–62

Bond, Harold, *The Literary Art of Edward Gibbon* (Oxford: Clarendon Press, 1960)

Boulot, Catherine, *Hubert Robert et la Révolution* (Valence: Musée de Valence, 1989)

Braham, Allan, *The Architecture of the French Enlightenment* (London: Thames and Hudson, 1980)

Bressani, Martin, 'Étienne-Louis Boullée: Empiricism and the Cenotaph for Newton', *Architectura*, 23/1 (1993), 37–58

———— 'The Hybrid: Labrouste's Paestum', *Chora*, 5 (2007), 81–126

———— 'The Paestum Controversy', in Corinne Bélier, Barry Bergdoll and Marc Le Cœur (eds), *Henri Labrouste: Structure Brought to Light* (New York: Museum of Modern Art, 2013), 88–93

Briggs, Martin S., 'Architectural Models', *Burlington Magazine*, 54 (April–May 1929), 174–83, 245–52

Broglio, Ron, *Technologies of the Picturesque: British Art, Poetry, and Instruments, 1750–1830* (Lewisburg (Penn.): Bucknell University Press, 2008)

Brothers, Cammy, *Michelangelo: Drawing and the Invention of Architecture* (New Haven (Conn.): Yale University Press, 2008)

Brunel, Georges (ed.), *Piranèse et les Français* (Rome: Edizioni dell'Elefante, 1978)

Bukdahl, Else Marie, *Diderot, critique d'art*, 2 vols (Copenhagen: Rosenkilde and Bagger, 1980)

Burda, Hubert, *Die Ruine in den Bildern Hubert Roberts* (Munich: Wilhelm Fink, 1969)

Carter, George, *Humphrey Repton Landscape Gardener, 1752–1818* (Norwich: Sainsbury Centre for Visual Arts, 1982)

Castiglione Minischetti, Vito, Giovanni Dotoli and Roger Musnik, *Le Voyage français en Italie des origines au XVIIIe siècle: Bibliographie analytique* (Fasano / Paris: Schena / Lanore, 2006)

Catalogue of a Collection of Drawings by John Robert Cozens with some Decorative Furniture and other Objects of Art, with an introduction signed C. F. B. [Charles Francis Bell] (London: Burlington Fine Arts Club, n.d. [1923])

Cayeux, Jean de, *Hubert Robert et les jardins* (Paris: Éditions Herscher, 1987)

Cerchiai, Luca, Lorena Jannelli and Fausto Longo, *Greek Cities of Magna Graecia and Sicily* (San Giovanni Lupatoto: Arsenale Editrice, 2007) [first published 2004]

Ceserani, Giovanna, *Italy's Lost Greece: Magna Graecia and the Making of Modern Archaeology* (Oxford / New York: Oxford University Press, 2012)

Chessex, Pierre, *Quelques documents sur un aquarelliste et marchand vaudois à Rome à la fin du XVIIIe siècle: A. L. R. Ducros* (Chavannes: SVHA-Archives Cantonales Vaudoises, 1982) [first published in *Revue Historique Vaudoise*, 90 (1982), 35–71]

———— *A. L. R. Ducros (1748–1810): Paysages d'Italie à l'époque de Goethe* (Geneva: Éditions du Tricorne, 1986)

Chevallier, Élisabeth, 'Les Voyageurs et la découverte de Paestum', in Élisabeth Chevallier and Raymond Chevallier, *Iter Italicum: Les Voyageurs français à la découverte de l'Italie ancienne* (Paris: Les Belles Lettres, 1984), 61–71

Chevtchenko, Valery, Sabine Cotté, Madeleine Pinault-Sørensen et al., *Charles-Louis Clérisseau, 1721–1820: Dessins du Musée de l'Ermitage, Saint-Petersbourg* (Paris: Réunion des Musées Nationaux, 1995)

Cirillo, Ornella, *Carlo Vanvitelli: Architettura e città nella seconda metà del Settecento* (Florence: Alinea Editrice, 2008)

Clarke, Michael, and Nicholas Penny (eds), *The Arrogant Connoisseur: Richard Payne Knight, 1751–1824* (Manchester: Manchester University Press, 1982)

Colbert, Benjamin, *Shelley's Eye: Travel Writing and Aesthetic Vision* (Aldershot (Surrey): Ashgate, 2005)

Coleman, Francis X. J., *The Aesthetic Thought of the French Enlightenment* (Pittsburgh: University of Pittsburgh Press, 1971)

Collins, Peter, *Changing Ideals in Modern Architecture, 1750–1950* (London: Faber & Faber, 1965)

Colvin, Howard M., *A Biographical Dictionary of British Architects, 1600–1840*, 4th edn (New Haven (Conn.) / London: Yale University Press, 2008) [first published 1954]

Connelly, Frances S., *The Sleep of Reason: Primitivism in Modern European Art and Aesthetics, 1725–1907* (University Park: Pennsylvania State University Press, 1995)

Copley, Stephen, and Peter Garside (eds), *The Politics of the Picturesque: Literature, Landscape and Aesthetics since 1770* (Cambridge: Cambridge University Press, 1994)

Coulton, J. J., *Ancient Greek Architects at Work: Problems of Structure and Design* (Oxford: Oxbow Books, 1995) [first published 1977]

Crook, J. Mordaunt, *Haileybury and the Greek Revival: The Architecture of William Wilkins, R.A.* (Leicester: The Author, 1964)

———— *The Dilemma of Style: Architectural Ideas from the Picturesque to the Post-Modern* (London: John Murray, 1989) [first published 1987]

———— *The Greek Revival: Neo-Classical Attitudes in British Architecture, 1760–1870* (London: John Murray, 1995) [first published 1972]

Crow, Thomas, *Painters and Public Life in Eighteenth-Century Paris* (New Haven (Conn.) / London: Yale University Press, 1985)

Curl, James Stevens, *The Egyptian Revival: Ancient Egypt as the Inspiration for Design Motives in the West* (London / New York: Routledge, 2005)

Curtis, Melinda (ed.), *The Search for Innocence: Primitive and Primitivistic Art of the Nineteenth Century* (College Park: University of Maryland Art Gallery, 1975)

Curtis, William J. R., *Modern Architecture, Mythical Landscapes & Ancient Ruins* (London: Sir John Soane's Museum, 1997)

Darley, Gillian, *John Soane: An Accidental Romantic* (New Haven (Conn.) / London: Yale University Press, 1999)

Davies, Maurice, *Turner as Professor: The Artist and Linear Perspective* (London: Tate Gallery Publications, 1992)

Dean, Philippe, *Diderot devant l'image* (Paris / Montreal: L'Harmattan, 2000)

Décultot, Élisabeth, *Johann Joachim Winckelmann: Enquête sur la genèse de l'histoire de l'art* (Paris: Presses Universitaires de France, 2000)

Delbeke, Maarten, Dirk De Meyer, Bas Rogiers and Bart Verschaffel (eds), *Piranesi: De prentencollectie van de Universiteit Gent* (Ghent: A&S Books, 2008)

Descat, Sophie, 'Deux architectes-urbanistes dans l'Europe des Lumières: Pierre-Louis Moreau et George Dance à Paris et à Londres (1763–1815)', unpublished PhD thesis, Université de Paris 1 Panthéon-Sorbonne, 2000

De Seta, Cesare, *Vedutisti e viaggiatori in Italia tra Settecento e Ottocento* (Turin: Bollati Boringhieri, 1999)

———— *L'Italia del Grand Tour: Da Montaigne a Goethe* (Naples: Electa Napoli, 2001) [first published 1992]

Dessins d'architectes XVIIIe et XIXe siècles: Antoine, Léon et Alfred Vaudoyer. Vente à Paris, Hôtel Drouot, 11 avril 1986 (s.l.: s.n., 1986)

Dillon, Brian, *Ruin Lust: Artists' Fascination with Ruins from Turner to the Present Day* (London: Tate Publishing, 2014)

Dodds, George, and Robert Tavernor (eds), *Body and Building: Essays on the Changing Relation of Body and Architecture* (Cambridge (Mass.) / London: MIT Press, 2002)

Dorey, Helen, *John Soane & J M W Turner: Illuminating a Friendship* (London: Sir John Soane's Museum, 2007)

Drexler, Arthur (ed.), *The Architecture of the École des Beaux-Arts* (New York / Cambridge (Mass.): Museum of Modern Art / MIT Press, 1977)

Dripps, R. D., *The First House: Myth, Paradigm, and the Task of Architecture* (Cambridge (Mass.) / London: MIT Press, 1997)

Dubbini, Renzo (ed.), *Henri Labrouste, 1801–1875* (Milan: Electa, 2002)

Dubin, Nina L., *Futures & Ruins: Eighteenth-Century Paris and the Art of Hubert Robert* (Los Angeles: Getty Research Institute, 2010)

Duffy, Cian, *Shelley and the Revolutionary Sublime* (Cambridge: Cambridge University Press, 2005)

Du Prey, Pierre de La Ruffinière, 'John Soane, Philip Yorke, and their Quest for Primitive Architecture', in Gervase Jackson-Stops (ed.), *National Trust Studies, 1979* (London: Philip Wilson Publishers for Sotheby Parke Bernet Publications, 1978), 28–38

——— *John Soane: The Making of an Architect* (Chicago / London: Academy Editions, 1982)

——— *Hawksmoor's London Churches: Architecture and Theology* (Chicago: University of Chicago Press, 2000)

Dupuy-Vachey, Marie-Anne, *Les Itinéraires de Vivant-Denon, dessinateur et illustrateur*, collection Musée Denon (Manosque: Le Bec en l'Air, 2007)

——— *Vivant Denon et le 'Voyage pittoresque': Un manuscrit inconnu* (Paris: Fondation Custodia, 2009)

Durand, Jannic, 'Une collection oubliée: Les Maquettes du Musée des Antiquités Nationales', *Antiquités Nationales*, 14–15 (1982–3), 118–135

Du sublime, introduction by Jean-Luc Nancy (Paris: Belin, 2009) [first published 1988]

Eck, Caroline van, *Organicism in Nineteenth-Century Architecture: An Inquiry into its Theoretical and Philosophical Background* (Amsterdam: Architectura & Natura, 1994)

——— '"Par le style on atteint au sublime": The Meaning of the Term "Style" in French Architectural Theory of the Late Eighteenth Century', in Caroline van Eck, James W. McAllister and Renée van de Vall (eds), *The Question of Style in Philosophy and the Arts* (Cambridge: Cambridge University Press, 1995), 89–107

——— '"The splendid effects of architecture, and its power to affect the mind": The Workings of Picturesque Association', in Jan Birksted (ed.), *Landscapes of Memory and Experience* (London: Spon Press, 2000), 245–58

——— (ed.), *British Architectural Theory, 1540–1750: An Anthology of Texts* (Aldershot (Surrey): Ashgate, 2003)

——— 'Longinus' Essay on the Sublime and the "most solemn and awfull appearance" of Hawksmoor's Churches', *Georgian Group Journal*, 15 (2006), 1–7

——— *Classical Rhetoric and the Visual Arts in Early Modern Europe* (Cambridge: Cambridge University Press, 2007)

——— *Inigo Jones on Stonehenge: Architectural Representation, Memory and Narrative* (Amsterdam: Architectura & Natura, 2009)

Eck, Caroline van, and Stijn Bussels, 'The Visual Arts and the Theatre in Early Modern Europe', *Art History*, 33/2 (April 2010) [special issue], 208–23

Eck, Caroline van, Stijn Bussels, Maarten Delbeke and Jürgen Pieters (eds), *Translations of the Sublime: The Early Modern Reception and Dissemination of Longinus' Peri hupsous in Rhetoric, the Visual Arts, Architecture and the Theatre* (Leiden: Brill, 2012)

Eck, Caroline van, Jeroen van den Eynde and Wilfred van Leeuwen (eds), *Het schilderachtige: Studies over het schilderachtige in de Nederlandse kunsttheorie en architectuur, 1650–1900* (Amsterdam: Architectura & Natura, 1994)

Eck, Caroline van, and Edward Winters (eds), *Dealing with the Visual: Art History, Aesthetics and Visual Culture* (Aldershot (Surrey): Ashgate, 2005)

Egbert, Donald Drew, *The Beaux-Arts Tradition in French Architecture: Illustrated by the Grands Prix de Rome*, ed. David van Zanten (Princeton (NJ): Princeton University Press, 1980)

Eriksen, Svend, *Early Neo-Classicism in France: The Creation of the Louis Seize Style in Architectural Decoration, Furniture and Ormolu, Gold and Silver, and Sèvres Porcelain in the Mid-Eighteenth Century*, trans. from the Danish and ed. Peter Thornton (London: Faber, 1974)

Etlin, Richard A., *Symbolic Space, French Enlightenment Architecture and its Legacy* (Chicago / London: University of Chicago Press, 1994)

Ferris, David S., *Silent Urns: Romanticism, Hellenism, Modernity* (Stanford (Cal.): Stanford University Press, 2000)

Finberg, Alexander Joseph, *A Complete Inventory of the Drawings of the Turner Bequest: with which are Included the Twenty-Three Drawings Bequeathed by Mr. Henry Vaughan*, 2 vols (London: Stationery Office, 1909)

Fleming, John, *Robert Adam and his Circle in Edinburgh & Rome* (London: John Murray, 1962)

——— 'James Adam in Naples', in Edward Chaney and Neil Ritchie (eds), *Oxford, China and Italy: Writings in Honour of Sir Harold Acton on his Eightieth Birthday* (London: Thames and Hudson, 1984), 169–76

Focillon, Henri, *Giovanni Battista Piranesi* (Gollion (Switzerland): InFolio, 2001) [first published 1918]

Fothergill, Brian, *Sir William Hamilton: Envoy Extraordinary* (Stroud (Gloucestershire): Nonsuch, 2005) [first published 1969]

Foundoukidis, E. (ed.), *Primitivisme et classicisme: Les Deux Faces de l'histoire de l'art* (Paris: Centre International des Instituts de Recherche, Art, Archéologie, Ethnologie, 1946)

Franchi dell'Orto, Luisa, and Antonio Varone (eds), *Rediscovering Pompeii* (Rome: 'L'Erma' di Bretschneider, 1992)

Frantz, Pierre, and Élisabeth Lavezzi (eds), *Les 'Salons' de Diderot: Théorie et écriture* (Paris: PUPS, Université Paris-Sorbonne, 2008)

Fried, Michael, *Absorption and Theatricality: Painting and Beholder in the Age of Diderot* (Berkeley / Los Angeles / London: University of California Press, 1980)

Friedman, Alice T., 'Academic Theory and A. L. T. Vaudoyer's Dissertation sur l'architecture', *Art Bulletin*, 67 (March 1985), 110–23

Friedman, Terry, 'Willey Reveley's All Saints', Southampton', *Georgian Group Journal*, 12 (2002), 74–95

Fritzsche, Peter, *Stranded in the Present: Modern Time and the Melancholy of History* (Cambridge (Mass.): Harvard University Press, 2004)

Fumaroli, Marc, 'Rhétorique d'école et rhétorique adulte: Remarques sur la réception européenne du traité *Du sublime* au XVIe et au XVIIe siècle', *Revue d'Histoire Littéraire de la France*, 86 (1986), 33–51

Gallo, Italo (ed.), *Momenti di storia salernitana nell'antichità* (Naples: Arte Tipografica, 1989)

Gambardella, Alfonso (ed.), *Ferdinando Sanfelice: Napoli e l'Europa* (Naples: Edizioni Scientifiche Italiane, 2004)

Garric, Jean-Philippe, *Recueils d'Italie: Les Modèles italiens dans les livres d'architecture français* (Sprimont (Liège): Pierre Mardaga, 2004)

Gaus, Joachim, 'Die Urhütte: Über ein Modell in der Baukunst und ein Motiv in der bildenden Kunst', *Wallraf-Richartz-Jahrbuch*, 33 (1971), 7–70

Gazley, John G., *The Life of Arthur Young, 1741–1820* (Philadelphia: American Philosophical Society, 1973)

Gerbino, Anthony, *François Blondel: Architecture, Erudition, and the Scientific Revolution* (London / New York: Routledge, 2010)

Gercke, Peter (ed.), *Antike Bauten in Modell und Zeichnung um 1800* (Kassel: Staatliche Kunstsammlungen, 1986)

Gercke, Peter, and Nina Zimmermann-Elseify (eds), *Antike Bauten: Korkmodelle von Antonio Chichi, 1777–1782* (Kassel: Staatliche Museen, 2001)

Germann, Georg, *Einführung in die Geschichte der Architekturtheorie* (Darmstadt: Wissenschaftliche Buchgesellschaft, 1987) [first published 1980]

Gilet, Annie, and Uwe Westfehling, *Louis-François Cassas, 1756–1827: Dessinateur-voyageur* (Mainz: P. von Zabern, 1994)

Glacken, Clarence J., *Traces on the Rhodian Shore: Nature and Culture in Western Thought from Ancient Times to the End of the Eighteenth Century* (Berkeley / Los Angeles / London: University of California Press, 1967)

Goldwater, Robert, *Primitivism in Modern Painting* (New York / London: Harper & Bros., 1938)

Gombrich, Ernst Hans, 'The Debate on Primitivism in Ancient Rhetoric', *Journal of the Warburg and Courtauld Institutes*, 29 (1966), 24–38

———— 'Dream Houses' [review of Joseph Rykwert, *On Adam's House in Paradise: The Idea of the Primitive Hut in Architectural History* (1972)], *New York Review of Books*, 20 (29 November 1973), 35–7

———— *The Preference for the Primitive: Episodes in the History of Western Taste and Art* (London: Phaidon, 2002)

Goodman, Dena, *The Republic of Letters: A Cultural History of the French Enlightenment* (Ithaca (NY) / London: Cornell University Press, 1994)

Gordon, Alden R., 'Jérôme-Charles Bellicard's Italian Notebook of 1750–51: The Discoveries at Herculaneum and Observations on Ancient and Modern Architecture', *Metropolitan Museum Journal*, 25 (1990), 49–142

———— *The Houses and Collections of the Marquis de Marigny* (Los Angeles: Getty Trust Publications, 2003)

Gravagnuolo, Benedetto (ed.), *Mario Gioffredo* (Naples: Guida, 2002)

Greco, Emanuele, and Fausto Longo (eds), *Paestum: Scavi, studi, ricerche. Bilancio di un decennio (1988–1998)* (Paestum (Salerno): Pandemos / Fondazione Paestum, 2000)

Greco, Emanuele, and Dinu Theodorescu, *Poseidonia–Paestum*, 4 vols (Rome: École Française de Rome, 1980–99)

Grell, Chantal, *Herculanum et Pompéi dans les récits des voyageurs français du XVIIIe siècle* (Naples: Centre Jean Bérard, 1982)

———— *Le Dix-huitième Siècle et l'antiquité en France, 1680–1789*, 2 vols (Oxford: Voltaire Foundation, 1995)

Grell, Chantal, and Christian Michel (eds), *Primitivisme et mythes des origines dans la France des Lumières, 1680–1820* (Paris: Presses de l'Université de Paris-Sorbonne, 1989)

Griener, Pascal, 'Ottaviano di Guasco, intermédiaire entre la philosophie française et les antiquités de Rome', in Letizia Norci Cagiano (ed.), *Roma triumphans? L'attualità dell'antico nella Francia del Settecento* (Rome: Edizioni di Storia Letteratura, 2007), 25–51

———— 'Théorie de l'art et théorie pessimiste de l'histoire: un paradoxe', in Christian Michel and Carl Magnusson (eds), *Penser l'art dans la seconde moitié du XVIIIe siècle: Théorie, critique, philosophie, histoire* (Paris: Somogy, 2013)

Gruber, Alain-Charles, *Les Grandes Fêtes et leurs décors à l'époque de Louis XVI* (Geneva: Droz, 1972)

———— *L'Œuvre de Pierre-Adrien Pâris à la cour de France, 1779–1791* (Paris: F. De Nobele, 1974)

Guerretta, Patrick-André, *Pierre-Louis de La Rive ou la belle nature: Vie et œuvre peint (1753–1817)* (Chêne-Bourg (Geneva) / Paris: Georg Éditeur, 2002)

Guigniaut, Joseph Daniel, *Institut impérial de France: Notice historique sur la vie et les travaux de M. Quatremère de Quincy, lue dans la séance publique . . . le 5 août 1864* (Paris: Firmin Didot frères, 1866)

Guillaume, Jean (ed.), *Les Traités d'architecture de la Renaissance: Actes du colloque tenu à Tours du 1er au 11 juillet 1981* (Paris: Picard, 1988)

Haas, Mechthild, *Orient auf Papier: Von Louis-François Cassas bis Eugen Bracht* (Darmstadt: Graphische Sammlung, Hessisches Landesmuseum Darmstadt, 2002)

Hache, Sophie, *La Langue du ciel: Le Sublime en France au XVIIe siècle* (Paris: H. Champion, 2000)

Hamilton, James, *Turner & Italy* (Edinburgh: National Galleries of Scotland, 2009)

Harrington, Kevin, *Changing Ideas of Architecture in the 'Encyclopédie', 1750–1776* (Ann Arbor (Mich.): UMI Research Press, 1985)

Harris, Eileen, 'Burke and Chambers on the Sublime and the Beautiful', in Douglas Fraser, Howard Hibbard and Milton J. Lewine (eds), *Essays in the History of Architecture Presented to Rudolf Wittkower* (London: Phaidon Press, 1967), 207–13

Harris, Eileen, and Nicholas Savage, *British Architectural Books and Writers, 1556–1785* (Cambridge: Cambridge University Press, 1990)

Harris, John, and Michael Snodin (eds), *Sir William Chambers, Architect to George III* (New Haven (Conn.) / London: Yale University Press, 1996)

Hart, Vaughan, *Sir John Vanbrugh: Storyteller in Stone* (New Haven (Conn.): Published for the Paul Mellon Centre for Studies in British Art by Yale University Press, 2008)

Haskell, Francis, 'The Baron d'Hancarville: An Adventurer and Art Historian in Eighteenth-Century Europe', in Edward Chaney and Neil Ritchie (eds), *Oxford, China and Italy: Writings in Honour of Sir Harold Acton on his Eightieth Birthday* (London: Thames and Hudson, 1984), 177–91

Haskell, Francis, and Nicholas Penny, *Taste and the Antique* (New Haven (Conn.) / London: Yale University Press, 1981)

Hautecœur, Louis, *Histoire de l'architecture classique en France.* vol. IV: *Seconde moitié du XVIIIe siècle: Le Style Louis XVI, 1750–1792* (Paris: Picard, 1952)

Hawcroft, Francis W., *Watercolours by John Robert Cozens* (Wilmslow (Cheshire): Richmond Press, 1971)

—————— 'Grand Tour Sketchbooks of John Robert Cozens, 1782–1783', *Gazette des Beaux-Arts*, 91 (March 1978), 99–106

Hawes, Louis, *Constable's Stonehenge* (London: Victoria and Albert Museum, 1975)

Hazard, Paul, *La Pensée européenne au XVIIIe siècle, de Montesquieu à Lessing: Notes et références* (Paris: Boivin, 1946)

Hellmann, Marie-Christine, Philippe Fraisse and Annie Jacques, *Paris–Rome–Athènes: Le Voyage en Grèce des architectes français aux XIXe et XXe siècles* (Paris: École Nationale Supérieure des Beaux-Arts, 1982)

Heringman, Noah, *Sciences of Antiquity: Romantic Antiquarianism, Natural History, and Knowledge Work* (Oxford: Oxford University Press, 2013)

Herluison, H., and Paul Leroy, *L'Architecte Delagardette* (Orléans: Herluison, 1896)

Hermans, Lex, *'Alles wat zuilen heeft is klassiek': Classicistische ideeën over bouwkunst in Nederland, 1765–1850* (Rotterdam: Uitgeverij 010, 2005)

Herrmann, Wolfgang, 'Antoine Desgodets and the Académie Royale d'Architecture', *Art Bulletin*, 40 (March 1958), 23–53

—————— *Laugier and Eighteenth Century French Theory* (London: A. Zwemmer, 1962)

—————— 'Unknown Designs for the "Temple of Jerusalem" by Claude Perrault', in Douglas Fraser, Howard Hibbard and Milton J. Lewine (eds), *Essays in the History of Architecture Presented to Rudolf Wittkower* (London: Phaidon Press, 1967), 143–58

—————— *The Theory of Claude Perrault* (London: A. Zwemmer, 1973)

Hersey, George, *The Lost Meaning of Classical Architecture* (Cambridge (Mass.) / London: MIT Press, 1988)

Hiller, Susan (ed.), *The Myth of Primitivism: Perspectives on Art* (London / New York: Routledge, 1991)

Hipple, Walter John, *The Beautiful, the Sublime & the Picturesque in Eighteenth-Century British Aesthetic Theory* (Carbondale: Southern Illinois University Press, 1957)

Hobsbawm, Eric, *Nations and Nationalism since 1780: Programme, Myth, Reality* (Cambridge: Cambridge University Press, 1990)

Hobsbawm, Eric, and Terence Ranger (eds), *The Invention of Tradition* (Cambridge: Cambridge University Press, 1983)

Holl, Steven, Juhani Pallasmaa and Alberto Pérez-Gómez, *Questions of Perception: Phenomenology of Architecture* (Tokyo: a + u publishers, 1994)

Honour, Hugh, *Neo-Classicism* (London: Penguin, 1991) [first published 1968]

Hunt, John Dixon, *The Figure in the Landscape: Poetry, Painting, and Gardening during the Eighteenth Century* (Baltimore: Johns Hopkins University Press, 1976)

—————— 'Wondrous Deep and Dark: Turner and the Sublime', *Georgia Review*, 30 (1976), 139–64

—————— *Gardens and the Picturesque: Studies in the History of Landscape Architecture* (Cambridge (Mass.) / London: MIT Press, 1992)

—————— *The Picturesque Garden in Europe* (London: Thames and Hudson, 2002)

—————— *The Afterlife of Gardens* (London: Reaktion Books, 2004)

Hunt, John Dixon, and Peter Willis (eds), *The Genius of the Place: The English Landscape Garden, 1620–1820* (London: Paul Elek, 1975)

Hussey, Christopher, *English Gardens and Landscapes, 1700–1750* (London / New York: Country Life / Funk & Wagnalls, 1967)

—————— *The Picturesque: Studies in a Point of View*, rev. edn, with a new preface by the author (Hamden (Conn.): Archon Books, 1967) [first published 1927]

Hvattum, Mari, *Gottfried Semper and the Problem of Historicism* (Cambridge / New York: Cambridge University Press, 2004)

Il teatro di corte di Caserta: Storia e restauro (Naples: Electa Napoli, 1995)

Imbruglia, Girolamo, *Naples in the Eighteenth Century: The Birth and Death of a Nation State* (Cambridge: Cambridge University Press, 2000)

Ingamells, John, *A Dictionary of British and Irish Travellers in Italy, 1701–1800* (New Haven (Conn.) / London: Published for the Paul Mellon Centre for Studies in British Art by Yale University Press, 1997)

Jacques, Annie, and Jean-Pierre Mouilleseaux, *Les Architectes de la liberté* (Paris: Gallimard, 1988)

Jay, Martin, *Songs of Experience: Modern American and European Variations on a Universal Theme* (Berkeley / Los Angeles: University of California Press, 2005)

Jong, Sigrid de, 'Rediscovering Architecture: Paestum in Eighteenth-Century Architectural Experience and Theory', unpublished PhD thesis, Leiden University, 2010

—————— 'Staging Ruins: Paestum and Theatricality', *Art History*, 33/2 (April 2010) [special issue], 334–51

—————— 'Staging Ruins: Paestum and Theatricality', in Caroline van Eck and Stijn Bussels (eds), *Theatricality in Early Modern Art and Architecture* (Chichester: Wiley-Blackwell, 2011), 134–51

—————— 'Paradoxical Encounters: Eighteenth-Century Architectural Experiences and the Sublime', in Caroline van Eck, Stijn Bussels, Maarten Delbeke and Jürgen Pieters (eds), *Translations of the Sublime: The Early Modern Reception and Dissemination of Longinus' Peri hupsous in Rhetoric, the*

Visual Arts, Architecture and the Theatre (Leiden: Brill, 2012), 247–67

———— 'Origins of Architecture', in Caroline van Eck and Sigrid de Jong (eds), *Companion to Eighteenth-Century Architecture* (Chichester: Wiley-Blackwell, forthcoming 2015)

———— 'Experiencing Architectural Space', in Caroline van Eck and Sigrid de Jong (eds), *Companion to Eighteenth-Century Architecture* (Chichester: Wiley-Blackwell, forthcoming 2015)

Kallendorf, Craig, Carsten Zelle and Christine Pries, 'Erhabene, das', in Gert Ueding (ed.), *Historisches Wörterbuch der Rhetorik*, vol. II (Tübingen: M. Niemeyer, 1994), cols 1357–89

Kalnein, Wend von, *Architecture in France in the Eighteenth Century*, trans. from the German by David Britt (New Haven (Conn.): Yale University Press, 1995)

Kantor-Kazovsky, Lola, *Piranesi as Interpreter of Roman Architecture and the Origins of his Intellectual World* (Florence: Leo S. Olschki Editore, 2006)

Kaufmann, Emil, *Von Ledoux bis Le Corbusier: Ursprung und Entwicklung der autonomen Architektur* (Vienna / Leipzig: Rolf Passer, 1933)

———— *Three Revolutionary Architects: Boullée, Ledoux, and Lequeu* (Philadelphia: American Philosophical Society, 1952)

———— *Architecture in the Age of Reason: Baroque and Post-Baroque in England, Italy, and France* (Cambridge (Mass.): Harvard University Press, 1955)

Knight, Carlo, *Il Giardino Inglese di Caserta: Un'avventura settecentesca* (Napoli: Peerson, 1986)

———— *Hamilton a Napoli: Cultura, svaghi, civiltà di una grande capitale europea* (Naples: Electa, 2003) [first published 1990]

Krauss, Friedrich, *Paestum: Die griechischen Tempel*, 3rd, enlarged, edn (Berlin: Mann, 1976) [first published 1941]

Kravtsov, Sergey R., 'Juan Bautista Villalpando and Sacred Architecture in the Seventeenth Century', *Journal of the Society of Architectural Historians*, 64 (2005), 312–39

Kruft, Hanno-Walter, *A History of Architectural Theory: From Vitruvius to the Present*, trans. Ronald Taylor, Elsie Callander and Antony Wood (London / New York: Zwemmer / Princeton Architectural Press, 1994) [first published in German 1985]

Lacroix, Sophie, *Ce que nous disent les ruines: La Fonction critique des ruines* (Paris: L'Harmattan, 2007)

———— *Ruine* (Paris: Éditions de la Villette, 2008)

Lamers, Petra, *Il viaggio nel sud dell'Abbé de Saint-Non: Il 'Voyage pittoresque à Naples et en Sicile': La genesi, i disegni preparatori, le incisioni* (Naples: Electa, 1995)

Lang, Susan, 'The Early Publications of the Temples at Paestum', *Journal of the Warburg and Courtauld Institutes*, 13 (1950), 48–64

Lang, S. [Susan], 'Richard Payne Knight and the Idea of Modernity', in John Summerson (ed.), *Concerning Architecture: Essays on Architectural Writers and Writing Presented to Nikolaus Pevsner* (London: Allen Lane, 1968), 85–97

Lapauze, Henry, *Histoire de l'Académie de France à Rome*, 2 vols (Paris: Plon, Nourrit et Cie, 1924)

Laroque, Didier, *Le Discours de Piranèse: L'Ornement sublime et le suspens de l'architecture; suivi d'un tableau de l'œuvre écrit de Piranèse et d'une nouvelle traduction de 'Ragionamento apologetico in difesa dell'architettura Egizia e Toscana', 1769* (Paris: Les Éditions de la Passion, 1999)

———— 'Boullée et le sublime', in Elisabetta Matelli (ed.), *Il sublime: Fortuna di un testo e di un'idea* (Milan: Vita e Pensiero, 2007), 263–72

Laveglia, Pietro, *Paestum, dalla decadenza alla riscoperta fino al 1860* (Naples: Libreria Scientifica Editrice, 1971)

Lavin, Sylvia, *Quatremère de Quincy and the Invention of a Modern Language of Architecture* (Cambridge (Mass.) / London: MIT Press, 1992)

Lawrence, A. W. [Arnold Walter], *Greek Architecture*, 5th edn, rev. R. A. Tomlinson (New Haven (Conn.) / London: Yale University Press, 1996) [first published 1957]

Le Cabinet de Pierre-Adrien Pâris: Architecte, dessinateur des menus-plaisirs (Besançon / Paris: Musée des Beaux-Arts et d'Archéologie de Besançon / Hazan, 2008)

Lee, Briant Hamor, *European Post-Baroque Neoclassical Theatre Architecture* (Lewiston (NY): E. Mellen, 1996)

Leighton, Angela, *Shelley and the Sublime: An Interpretation of the Major Poems* (Cambridge: Cambridge University Press, 1984)

Lelièvre, Pierre, *Vivant Denon: Homme des Lumières, 'ministre des arts' de Napoléon* (Paris: Picard, 1993)

Le Panthéon: Symbole des révolutions: De l'église de la nation au temple des grands hommes (Montreal / Paris: Centre Canadien d'Architecture / Caisse National des Monuments Historiques et des Sites / Picard, 1989)

Levine, Neil, 'The Romantic Idea of Architectural Legibility: Henri Labrouste and the Néo-Grec', in Arthur Drexler (ed.), *The Architecture of the École des Beaux-Arts*, New York / Cambridge (Mass.): Museum of Modern Art / MIT Press, 1977), 325–416

Liscombe, R. W., *William Wilkins, 1778–1839* (Cambridge: Cambridge University Press, 1980)

Litman, Théodore A., *Le Sublime en France, 1660–1714* (Paris: A. G. Nizet, 1971)

L'Œuvre de Soufflot à Lyon: Études et documents (Lyon: Presses Universitaires de Lyon, 1982)

Lohse, Bruno, *Jakob Philipp Hackert: Leben und Anfänge seiner Kunst* (Emsdetten (North Rhine-Westphalia): Lechte, 1936)

Lojkine, Stéphane, *L'Œil révolté: Les 'Salons' de Diderot* (Paris / Arles: J. Chambon / Actes Sud, 2007)

Lovejoy, Arthur O., *Essays in the History of Ideas* (Baltimore: Johns Hopkins Press, 1948)

Lovejoy, Arthur O., and George Boas, *Primitivism and Related Ideas in Antiquity* (Baltimore: Johns Hopkins Press, 1935)

Lui, Francesca, *L'antichità tra scienza e invenzione: Studi su Winckelmann e Clérisseau* (Bologna: Minerva, 2006)

Lukacher, Brian, 'Joseph Michael Gandy: The Poetical Representation and Mythography of Architecture', unpublished PhD thesis, University of Delaware, 1987

————— 'Joseph Gandy and the Mythography of Architecture', *Journal of the Society of Architectural Historians*, 53 (1994), 280–99

————— *Joseph Gandy: An Architectural Visionary in Georgian England* (London: Thames and Hudson, 2006)

Lukacher, Brian, and Desmond Hill, *Joseph Michael Gandy, 1771–1843* (London: Architectural Association, 1982)

Lutz, Thomas, 'Die Wiederentdeckung der Tempel von Paestum: Ihre Wirkung auf die Architektur und Architekturtheorie besonders in Deutschland', unpublished PhD thesis, Albert-Ludwigs-Universität Freiburg, 1987

Macarthur, John, *The Picturesque: Architecture, Disgust and other Irregularities* (London / New York: Routledge, 2007)

McCarthy, Michael, 'Documents on the Greek Revival in Architecture', *Burlington Magazine*, 114 (November 1972), 760–69

————— 'Sir Roger Newdigate: Some Piranesian Drawings', *The Burlington Magazine*, 120 (October 1978), 671–4

————— 'New Light on Thomas Major's "Paestum" and Later English Drawings of Paestum', in Joselita Raspi Serra (ed.), *Paestum and the Doric Revival, 1750–1830* (Florence: Centro Di, 1986), 47–50

Macaulay, Rose, *Pleasure of Ruins* (London: Thames and Hudson, 1984) [first published 1953)

McClellan, Andrew, *Inventing the Louvre: Art, Politics, and the Origins of the Modern Museum in Eighteenth-Century Paris* (Cambridge: Cambridge University Press, 1994)

MacColl, D. S., 'Notes on English Artists, II: Turner's Lectures at the Academy', *Burlington Magazine*, 12 (1908), 343–6

McCormick, Thomas J., 'An Unknown Collection of Drawings by Charles-Louis Clérisseau', *Journal of the Society of Architectural Historians*, 22 (October 1963), 119–26

————— *Charles-Louis Clérisseau and the Genesis of Neo-Classicism* (Cambridge (Mass.): MIT Press, 1990)

MacDonald, William L., and John A. Pinto, *Hadrian's Villa and its Legacy* (New Haven (Conn.) / London: Yale University Press, 1995)

McGowan, Margaret M., *The Vision of Rome in Late Renaissance France* (New Haven (Conn.) / London: Yale University Press, 2000)

MacKeith, Peter (ed.), *Archipelago: Essays on Architecture, for Juhani Pallasmaa* (Helsinki: Rakennustieto, 2006)

McMordie, Colin, 'Louis-François Cassas: The Formation of a Neo-Classical Landscapist', *Apollo*, 103 (1976), 228–30

Madec, Philippe, *Boullée* (Paris: F. Hazan, 1986)

Mallgrave, Harry Francis, *Modern Architectural Theory: A Historical Survey, 1673–1968* (Cambridge: Cambridge University Press, 2005)

————— (ed.), *Architectural Theory*, vol. I: *An Anthology from Vitruvius to 1870* (Malden (Mass.): Blackwell, 2006)

————— *The Architect's Brain: Neuroscience, Creativity and Architecture* (Chichester: Wiley-Blackwell, 2010)

Mallgrave, Harry Francis, and Christina Contandriopoulos (eds), *Architectural Theory*, vol. II: *An Anthology from 1871 to 2005* (Malden (Mass.): Blackwell, 2008)

Mallgrave, Harry Francis, and Eleftherios Ikonomou (eds), *Empathy, Form, and Space: Problems in German Aesthetics, 1873–1893* (Santa Monica (Cal.): Getty Center for the History of Art and the Humanities, 1994)

Manzelli, Mario, *Antonio Joli: Opera pittorica* (Venice: Studio LT2, 2000)

Marouby, Christian, *Utopie et primitivisme: Essai sur l'imaginaire anthropologique à l'âge classique* (Paris: Seuil, 1990)

Marschall, Isabelle von, *Zwischen Skizze und Gemälde: John Robert Cozens (1752–1797) und das englische Landschaftsaquarell* (Munich: Scaneg, 2005)

Martin, Raymond, and John Barresi, *The Rise and Fall of Soul and Self: An Intellectual History of Personal Identity* (New York: Columbia University Press, 2006)

Marzullo, A., *Paestum* (Rome: Enit, 1933)

Mattusch, Carol C. (ed.), *Rediscovering the Ancient World on the Bay of Naples, 1710–1890* (New Haven (Conn.): Yale University Press, 2012)

Mayoux, Jean-Jacques, *Richard Payne Knight et le pittoresque: Essai sur une phase esthétique* (Paris: Presses Modernes, 1932)

Meeks, Caroll L. V., 'Picturesque Eclecticism', *Art Bulletin*, 32 (September 1950), 226–35

Mello, Mario, 'Visitare Paestum: Aspetti e problemi dall riscoperta ad oggi', in Italo Gallo (ed.), *Momenti di storia salernitana nell'antichità. Atti del Covegno Nazionale AICC di Salerno-Fisciano, 12–13 nov. 1988* (Naples: Arte Tipografica, 1989), 91–123

Merleau-Ponty, Maurice, *Phénoménologie de la perception* (Paris: Gallimard, 1945)

————— *Le Visible et l'invisible* (Paris: Gallimard, 1964)

Mertens, Dieter, *Der Tempel von Segesta und die dorische Tempelbaukunst des griechischen Westens in klassischer Zeit* (Mainz: P. von Zabern, 1984)

————— *Der alte Heratempel in Paestum und die archaische Baukunst in Unteritalien* (Mainz: P. von Zabern, 1993)

Messmann, Frank J., *Richard Payne Knight: The Twilight of Virtuosity* (The Hague / Paris: Mouton, 1974)

Michel, Christian, 'L'Argument des origines dans les théories des arts en France à l'époque des Lumières', in Chantal Grell and Christian Michel (eds), *Primitivisme et mythes des origines dans la France des Lumières, 1680–1820* (Paris: Presses de l'Université Paris-Sorbonne, 1989), 35–45

Middione, Roberto, *Antonio Joli* (Soncino (Cremona): Edizioni dei Soncino, 1995)

Middleton, Robin, 'Jacques-François Blondel and the *Cours d'architecture*', *Journal of the Society of Architectural Historians*, 18 (December 1959), 140–48

————— 'The Abbé de Cordemoy and the Graeco-Gothic Ideal: A Prelude to Romantic Classicism', *Journal of the Warburg and Courtauld Institutes*, 25 (1962), 278–320; 26 (1963), 90–123

———— (ed.), *The Beaux-Arts and Nineteenth-Century French Architecture* (London: Thames and Hudson, 1982)

———— 'Boullée and the Exotic', *AA Files*, 19 (1990), 35–49

———— 'Chambers, W., "A Treatise on Civil Architecture", London 1759', in John Harris and Michael Snodin (eds), *Sir William Chambers: Architect to George III* (New Haven (Conn.) / London: Yale University Press, 1996), 68–76

———— *Julien-David Leroy: In Search of Architecture* (London: Sir John Soane's Museum, 2003)

Middleton, Robin, and Marie-Noëlle Baudouin-Matuszek, *Jean Rondelet: The Architect as Technician* (New Haven (Conn.) / London: Yale University Press, 2007)

Middleton, Robin, Gerald Beasley, Nicholas Savage et al., *British Books: Seventeenth through Nineteenth Centuries* (Washington (DC) / New York: National Gallery of Art / G. Braziller, 1998)

Middleton, Robin, and David Watkin, *Neo-Classical and 19th Century Architecture* (New York: Harry N. Abrams, 1980)

———— and ———— *Architecture of the Nineteenth Century* (Milan: Electa, 2003) [first published 1980]

Miller, Norbert, *Archäologie des Traums: Versuch über Giovanni Battista Piranesi* (Munich: Deutscher Taschenbuch Verlag, 1994) [first published 1978]

Mitias, Michael H. (ed.), *Architecture and Civilization* (Amsterdam / Atlanta (Ga.): Rodopi, 1999)

Momigliano, Arnaldo, 'Ancient History and the Antiquarian', *Journal of the Warburg and Courtauld Institutes*, 13 (1950), 285–315

———— *Essays in Ancient and Modern Historiography* (Oxford: Basil Blackwell, 1977)

———— 'The Rediscovery of Greek History in the Eighteenth Century: The Case of Sicily', *Studies in Eighteenth-Century Culture*, 9 (1979), 167–87

Mondain-Monval, Jean, *Soufflot: Sa vie, son œuvre, son esthétique (1713–1780)* (Paris: A. Lemerre, 1918)

Monk, Samuel Holt, *The Sublime: A Study of Critical Theories in XVIII-Century England* (Ann Arbor: University of Michigan Press, 1960) [first published 1935]

Mortier, Roland, *La Poétique des ruines en France: Ses origines, ses variations de la Renaissance à Victor Hugo* (Geneva: Droz, 1974)

Mosser, Monique, 'Französische Architekturmodelle im Zeitalter der Aufklärung', *Daidalos*, 2 (1981), 85–95

Mosser, Monique, and Daniel Rabreau (eds), *Soufflot et l'architecture des Lumières* (Paris: École Nationale Supérieure des Beaux-Arts, 1986)

Mustilli, Domenico, 'Prime memorie delle rovine di Paestum', in *Studi in onore di Riccardo Filangieri*, vol. III (Naples: L'Arte Tipografica, 1959), 105–21

Musy, J., 'La Grèce et l'École des Beaux-Arts: L'Envoi d'Henri Labrouste', *Archéologia*, 167 (1982), 15–17

Napoli, Mario, *La Tomba del Tuffatore: La scoperta della grande pittura greca* (Bari: De Donato, 1970)

———— *Paestum* (Novara: Istituto Geografico de Agostini, 1970)

Nau, Clélia, *Le Temps du sublime: Longin et le paysage poussinien* (Rennes: Presses Universitaires de Rennes, 2005)

Nicolson, Marjorie Hope, *Mountain Gloom and Mountain Glory: The Development of the Aesthetics of the Infinite* (Seattle / London: University of Washington Press, 1997) [first published 1959]

Nyberg, Dorothea, 'La Sainte Antiquité: Focus of an Eighteenth-Century Architectural Debate', in Douglas Fraser, Howard Hibbard and Milton J. Lewine (eds), *Essays in the History of Architecture Presented to Rudolf Wittkower* (London: Phaidon Press, 1967), 159–69

Odgers, Jo, Flora Samuel and Adam Sharr (eds), *Primitive: Original Matters in Architecture* (London: Routledge, 2006)

O'Neal, John C., *The Authority of Experience: Sensationist Theory in the French Enlightenment* (University Park: Pennsylvania State University Press, 1996)

Oppé, A. P. [Adolf Paul], *Alexander and John Robert Cozens* (London: A. & C. Black, 1952)

Pallasmaa, Juhani, *The Eyes of the Skin: Architecture and the Senses* (Chichester: John Wiley & Sons, 2005) [first published 1996]

Palmaerts, Geert, *Eclecticisme: Over moderne architectuur in de negentiende eeuw* (Rotterdam: 010 Publishers, 2005)

Pane, Roberto, *Paestum nelle acqueforti di Piranesi* (Milan: Edizioni di Comunità, 1980)

Panofsky, Erwin, *Studies in Iconology: Humanistic Themes in the Art of the Renaissance* (New York: Oxford University Press, 1939)

Parent, Annie-Charon, 'Enquête à travers les catalogues de vente de bibliothèques d'architectes du XVIIIe siècle: La Bibliothèque de Jacques-Germain Soufflot', in Jean-Michel Leniaud and Béatrice Bouvier (eds), *Le Livre d'architecture, XVe–XXe siècle: Édition, réprésentations et bibliothèques* (Paris: École des Chartes, 2002), 187–98

Pariset, François-Georges, 'Les Théories artistiques d'un architecte du néoclassicisme, Louis Combes, de Bordeaux', *Annales du Midi*, 76 (1964), 68–9, 543–54

———— 'Louis Combes', *Revue Historique de Bordeaux et du Département de la Gironde*, 22 (1973), 1–40

———— *L'Architecte Combes* (Bordeaux: Biscaye Frères, 1974)

Parslow, Christopher Charles, *Rediscovering Antiquity: Karl Weber and the Excavation of Herculaneum, Pompeii, and Stabiae* (Cambridge: Cambridge University Press, 1995)

Pearce, Susan, and Frank Salmon, 'Charles Heathcote Tatham in Italy, 1794–96: Letters, Drawings and Fragments, and Part of an Autobiography', *Walpole Society*, 67 (2005), 1–92

Pedley, John Griffiths, *Paestum: Greeks and Romans in Southern Italy* (London: Thames and Hudson, 1990)

Pelletier, Louise, *Architecture in Words: Theatre, Language and the Sensuous Space of Architecture* (London: Routledge, 2006)

Perkins, Jean A., *The Concept of the Self in the French Enlightenment* (Geneva: Droz, 1969)

Perlove, Shelley Karen, 'Piranesi's *Tomb of the Scipios* of *Le antichità romane* and Marc-Antoine Laugier's Primitive Hut', *Gazette des Beaux-Arts*, 112 (March 1989), 115–20

Pérouse de Montclos, Jean-Marie, *Etienne-Louis Boullée (1728–1799), de l'architecture classique à l'architecture révolutionnaire* (Paris: Arts et Métiers, 1969)

———— *Histoire de l'architecture française*, vol. II (Paris: CNMHS, 1989)

———— *Étienne-Louis Boullée* (Paris: Flammarion, 1994)

———— *Jacques-Germain Soufflot* (Paris: Monum / Éditions du Patrimoine, 2004)

Petzet, Michael, *Soufflots Sainte Geneviève und der französische Kirchenbau des 18. Jahrhunderts* (Berlin: W. de Gruyter, 1961)

Pevsner, Nikolaus, 'The Picturesque in Architecture', *RIBA Journal*, 55 (1947), 55–61

———— 'Richard Payne Knight', *Art Bulletin*, 31 (December 1949), 293–320

———— *Studies in Art, Architecture and Design*, 2 vols (London: Thames and Hudson, 1968)

———— *Some Architectural Writers of the Nineteenth Century* (Oxford: Clarendon Press, 1972)

———— (ed.), *The Picturesque Garden and its Influence Outside the British Isles* (Washington (DC): Dumbarton Oaks Trustees for Harvard University, 1974)

Picon, Antoine, 'Vers une architecture classique: Jacques-François Blondel et le *Cours d'architecture*', *Cahiers de la Recherche Architecturale*, 18 (1985), 28–37

———— *Architectes et ingénieurs au siècle des Lumières* (Marseille: Parenthèses, 1988); Eng. trans. as *French Architects and Engineers in the Age of Enlightenment* (Cambridge / New York: Cambridge University Press, 1992)

———— *Claude Perrault, 1613–1688, ou, La Curiosité d'un classique* (Paris: Picard / Caisse Nationale des Monuments Historiques et des Sites / Délégation à l'Action Artistique de la Ville de Paris, 1988)

Pinon, Pierre, *Pierre-Adrien Pâris (1745–1819), architecte, et les monuments antiques de Rome et de la Campanie* (Rome: École Française de Rome, 2007)

Pinon, Pierre, and François-Xavier Amprimoz, *Les Envois de Rome (1778–1968): Architecture et archéologie* (Rome: École Française de Rome, 1988)

Pinto, John A., *Speaking Ruins: Piranesi, Architects, and Antiquity in Eighteenth-Century Rome* (Ann Arbor: University of Michigan Press, 2012)

Placzek, Adolf K., and Angela Giral (eds), *Avery's Choice: Five Centuries of Great Architectural Books, One Hundred Years of an Architectural Library, 1890–1990* (New York / London: G. K. Hall / Prentice Hall International, 1997)

Ploeg, Sophie, 'Staged Experiences: The Church Designs of Nicholas Hawksmoor', in Caroline van Eck and Edward Winters (eds), *Dealing with the Visual: Art History, Aesthetics and Visual Culture* (Aldershot (Surrey): Ashgate, 2005), 167–90

———— 'Staged Experiences: Architecture and Rhetoric in the Work of Sir Henry Wotton, Nicholas Hawksmoor and Sir John Vanbrugh', unpublished PhD thesis, Rijksuniversiteit Groningen, 2006

Ponte, Alessandra, *Le Paysage des origines: Le Voyage en Sicile (1777) de Richard Payne Knight* (Besançon: Les Éditions de l'Imprimeur, 2000)

Porter, James I., 'Lucretius and the Sublime', in Stuart Gillespie and Philip Hardie (eds), *The Cambridge Companion to Lucretius* (Cambridge: Cambridge University Press, 2007), 167–84

Potts, Alex, *Flesh and the Ideal: Winckelmann and the Origins of Art History* (New Haven (Conn.) / London: Yale University Press, 2000) [first published 1994]

Pousin, Frédéric, *L'Architecture mise en scène: Essai sur la représentation du modèle grec au XVIIe siècle* (Paris: Éditions Arguments, 1995)

Powell, Cecilia, *Turner in the South: Rome, Naples, Florence* (New Haven (Conn.) / London: Yale University Press for the Paul Mellon Centre for Studies in British Art, 1987)

Prost, Auguste, *J.-F. Blondel et son œuvre* (Metz: Rousseau-Pallez, 1860)

Prouteau, Jean-Louis, *Charles Dupaty: Un magistrat-philosophe du siècle des Lumières* (La Rochelle: J.-L. Prouteau, 1989)

Rabreau, Daniel, 'La Basilique Sainte-Geneviève de Soufflot', in *Le Panthéon: Symbole des révolutions: De l'église de la nation au temple des grands hommes* (Montreal / Paris: Centre Canadien d'Architecture / Caisse National des Monuments Historiques et des Sites / Picard, 1989), 37–96

———— 'The Theatre-Monument: A Century of "French" Typology, 1750–1850', *Zodiac*, 2 (September 1989), 44–69

———— *Le Théâtre de l'Odéon: Du monument de la nation au Théâtre de l'Europe: Naissance du monument de loisir urbain au XVIIIe siècle* (Paris: Belin, 2007)

———— *Apollon dans la ville: Essai sur le théâtre et l'urbanisme à l'époque des Lumières* (Paris: Éditions du Patrimoine / Centre des Monuments Nationaux, 2008)

Rabreau, Daniel, and Dominique Massounie (eds), *Claude Nicolas Ledoux et le livre d'architecture en français: Étienne Louis Boullée, l'utopie et la poésie d'art* (Paris: Monum / Éditions du Patrimoine, 2006)

Rasmussen, Steen Eiler, *Experiencing Architecture*, trans. Eve Wendt (Cambridge (Mass.): MIT Press, 1995) [first published in Danish 1957]

Raspi Serra, Joselita (ed.), *La fortuna di Paestum e la memoria moderna del dorico, 1750–1830*, 2 vols (Florence: Centro Di, 1986)

———— (ed.), *Paestum and the Doric Revival, 1750–1830* (Florence: Centro Di, 1986)

———— (ed.), *Paestum: Idea e immagine. Antologia di testi critici e di immagini di Paestum, 1750–1836* (Modena: Franco Cosimo Panini, 1990)

———— 'Les Édifices antiques de Rome mesurés et dessinés exactement par Antoine, testo annotato da Adrien Pâris.

Un metodo d'intervento: Misura e verifica dei monumenti romani', in Antonio Cadei, Marina Righetti Tosti-Croce, Anna Segagni Malacart and Alessandro Tomei (eds), *Arte d'occidente: Temi e metodi. Studi in onore di Angiola Maria Romanini*, vol. III (Rome: Edizioni Sintesi, 1999), 1215–20

Redford, Bruce, *Dilettanti: The Antic and the Antique in Eighteenth-Century England* (Los Angeles: J. Paul Getty Museum / Getty Research Institute, 2008)

Reid, Christopher, *Edmund Burke and the Practice of Political Writing* (Dublin / New York: Gill and Macmillan / St. Martin's Press, 1986)

Richardson, Margaret, and MaryAnne Stevens (eds), *John Soane, Architect: Master of Space and Light* (London: Royal Academy of Arts, 1999)

Ridley, Ronald T., *The Pope's Archaeologist: The Life and Times of Carlo Fea* (Rome: Quasar, 2000)

Robinson, Sidney K., *Inquiry into the Picturesque* (Chicago: University of Chicago Press, 1991)

Rogger, André, *Landscapes of Taste: The Art of Humphrey Repton's Red Books* (London / New York: Routledge, 2007)

Rosenau, Helen, *Visions of the Temple: The Image of the Temple of Jerusalem in Judaism and Christianity* (London: Oresko Books, 1979)

Rosenbaum, Alexander, 'Charles Gores Reisealbum *Voyage de Sicile 1777*', *Zeitschrift für Kunstgeschichte*, 69 (2006), 17–36

Rosenberg, Pierre (ed.), *Naples et Pompéi: Les Itinéraires de Vivant-Denon* (Chalon-sur-Saône / Manosque: Musée Denon / Le Bec en l'Air, 2009)

Roujon, Henry, *Le Voyage en Italie de M. de Vandières et de sa compagnie (1749–1751). Lu dans la séance publique annuelle des Cinq Académies du mercredi 25 octobre 1899* (Paris: s.n., 1909)

Rubin, William (ed.), *'Primitivism' in Twentieth-Century Art: Affinity of the Tribal and the Modern*, 2 vols (New York: Museum of Modern Art, 1984)

Rykwert, Joseph, *The First Moderns: The Architects of the Eighteenth Century* (Cambridge (Mass.) / London: MIT Press, 1980)

——— *On Adam's House in Paradise: The Idea of the Primitive Hut in Architectural History*, 2nd edn (Cambridge (Mass.) / London: MIT Press, 1981) [first published 1972]

——— *The Dancing Column: On Order in Architecture* (Cambridge (Mass.) / London: MIT Press, 1996)

Rykwert, Joseph, and Anne Rykwert, *The Brothers Adam: The Men and the Style* (London: Collins, 1985)

Saddy, Pierre, *Henri Labrouste architecte, 1801–1875* (Paris: Caisse Nationale des Monuments Historiques et des Sites, 1977)

Sahut, Marie-Catherine, *Le Louvre d'Hubert Robert* (Paris: Éditions de la Réunion des Musées Nationaux, 1979)

Saint Girons, Baldine, *Esthétiques du XVIIIe siècle: Le Modèle français* (Paris: P. Sers, 1990)

——— *Fiat Lux: Une philosophie du sublime* (Paris: Quai Voltaire, 1993)

——— 'Le Paysage et la question du sublime', in Chrystèle Burgard, Baldine Saint Girons, Marie-Ceciello-Bachy et al., *Le Paysage et la question du sublime* (Paris / Lyon: Réunion des Musées Nationaux / ARAC, 1997), 75–118

——— (ed.), *Art et science à l'âge classique* (Nanterre: Université Paris X, 2000)

——— *Le Sublime de l'antiquité à nos jours* (Paris: Desjonquères, 2005)

Salmon, Frank, 'Charles Heathcote Tatham and the Accademia di S. Luca, Rome', *Burlington Magazine*, 140 (February 1998), 85–92

——— *Building on Ruins: The Rediscovery of Rome and English Architecture* (Aldershot (Surrey): Ashgate, 2000)

——— (ed.), *The Persistence of the Classical: Essays on Architecture presented to David Watkin* (London: Philipp Wilson, 2008)

——— 'The Forgotten "Athenian": Drawings by Willey Reveley', in Christopher White, Elizabeth Einberg, Martin Postle et al., *Windows on that World: Essays on British Art Presented to Brian Allen* (London: Paul Mellon Centre for Studies in British Art, 2012), 143–82

Savage, Nicholas, 'Shadow, Shading and Outline in Architectural Engraving from Fréart to Letarouilly', in Caroline van Eck and Edward Winters (eds), *Dealing with the Visual: Art History, Aesthetics and Visual Culture* (Aldershot (Surrey): Ashgate, 2005), 242–83

Schirmer, Wulf, and Barry Bergdoll (eds), *Friedrich Weinbrenner, 1766–1826* (London: Architectural Association, 1982)

Schmidt, Freek H., 'Expose Ignorance and Revive the *Bon Goût*: Foreign Architects at Jacques-François Blondel's École des Arts', *Journal of the Society of Architectural Historians*, 61 (2002), 4–29

Schnapp, Alain, *The Discovery of the Past*, trans. Ian Kinnes and Gillian Varndell (London: British Museum Press, 1996) [first published in French 1993]

Schneider, René, *L'Esthétique classique chez Quatremère de Quincy (1805–1823)* (Paris: Hachette, 1910)

——— *Quatremère de Quincy et son intervention dans les arts (1788–1830)* (Paris: Hachette, 1910)

Schöller, Wolfgang, *Die Académie Royale d'Architecture, 1671–1793: Anatomie einer Institution* (Cologne / Weimar / Vienna: Böhlau, 1993)

Schudt, Ludwig, *Italienreisen im 17. und 18. Jahrhundert* (Vienna: Schroll-Verlag, 1959)

Schumann-Bacia, Eva, *John Soane and the Bank of England* (London / New York: Longman, 1991) [first published in German 1989]

Scott, Geoffrey, *The Architecture of Humanism: A Study in the History of Taste* (London: Constable, 1924) [first published 1914]

Scott, Ian Jonathan, *Piranesi* (London / New York: Academy Editions / St. Martin's Press, 1975)

Scully, Vincent, *The Earth, the Temple, and the Gods: Greek Sacred Architecture* (New Haven (Conn.): Yale University Press, 1962)

Seegmullser, Rainer Karl, 'Shelley and Architecture: Romanticism and the Semiotics of the Architectural Descriptions in Shelley's Letters from Italy', unpublished PhD thesis, University of Oxford, 1989

Sennett, Richard, *The Fall of Public Man* (London: Penguin Books, 2002) [first published 1974]

Seznec, Jean, *Essais sur Diderot et l'antiquité* (Oxford: Clarendon Press, 1957)

Shanks, Michael, *Classical Archaeology of Greece: Experiences of the Discipline* (London / New York: Routledge, 1996)

Sicca, Cinzia Maria, *Committed to Classicism: The Buildings of Downing College, Cambridge* (Cambridge: Downing College, 1987)

Sloan, Kim, *Alexander and John Robert Cozens: The Poetry of Landscape* (New Haven (Conn.) / London: Yale University Press, 1986)

Snodin, Michael, *Horace Walpole's Strawberry Hill* (New Haven (Conn.) / London: Yale University Press, 2009)

Soros, Susan Weber (ed.), *James 'Athenian' Stuart, 1713–1788: The Rediscovery of Antiquity* (New Haven (Conn.) / London: Yale University Press for the Bard Graduate Center for Studies in the Decorative Arts, Design, and Culture, New York, 2006)

Soufflot et son temps, 1780–1980 (Paris: Caisse Nationale des Monuments Historiques et des Sites, 1980)

Springer, Carolyn, *The Marble Wilderness: Ruins and Representation in Italian Romanticism, 1775–1850* (Cambridge: Cambridge University Press, 1987)

Stafford, Barbara Maria, 'Rude Sublime: The Taste for Nature's Colossi in the Late Eighteenth and Early Nineteenth Centuries', *Gazette des Beaux-Arts*, 118 (April 1976), 113–26

────── *Symbol and Myth: Humbert de Superville's Essay on Absolute Signs in Art* (Cranbury (NJ) / London: Associated University Press, 1979)

────── 'Beauty of the Invisible: Winckelmann and the Aesthetics of Imperceptibility', *Zeitschrift für Kunstgeschichte*, 43 (1980), 65–78

────── *Voyage into Substance: Art, Science, Nature and the Illustrated Travel Account, 1760–1840* (Cambridge (Mass.) / London: MIT Press, 1984)

Stanlis, Peter James, *Edmund Burke: The Enlightenment and Revolution* (New Brunswick (NJ) / London: Transaction, 1991)

Stern, Ralph, 'Winckelmann, Piranesi and the Graeco-Roman Controversies: A Late Exchange in the *Querelle des anciens et des modernes*', *Architectura*, 33 (2003), 62–94.

Stillman, Damie, *English Neo-Classical Architecture*, 2 vols (London: A. Zwemmer, 1988)

Stroud, Dorothy, *Humphry Repton* (London: Country Life, 1962)

────── *George Dance, Architect, 1741–1825* (London: Faber & Faber, 1971)

────── *Capability Brown*, introduction by Christopher Hussey (London / Boston: Faber & Faber, 1984) [first published 1975]

Studies on Voltaire and the Eighteenth Century, vol. CCXXX (Oxford / Paris: Voltaire Foundation / J. Touzot, 1985)

Stumpf, Claudia, 'The "Expedition into Sicily"', in Michael Clarke and Nicolas Penny (eds), *The Arrogant Connoisseur: Richard Payne Knight, 1751–1824* (Manchester: Manchester University Press, 1982), 19–31

Summerson, John, *Georgian London* (London: Barrie and Jenkins, 1978) [first published 1945]

────── *The Classical Language of Architecture* (London: Thames and Hudson, 1980) [first published 1963]

────── 'Soane: The Man and the Style', in *John Soane* (London / New York: Academy Editions / St. Martin's Press, 1983) [adapted from Summerson, *Sir John Soane, 1753–1837* (London: Art and Technics, 1952)]

────── *The Architecture of the Eighteenth Century* (London: Thames and Hudson, 1986)

────── *The Unromantic Castle and other Essays* (London: Thames and Hudson, 1990)

────── *Architecture in Britain, 1530–1830* (New Haven (Conn.) / London: Yale University Press, 1993) [first published 1953]

Szambien, Werner, *Jean-Nicolas-Louis Durand, 1760–1843: De l'imitation à la norme* (Paris: Picard, 1984)

────── *Symétrie, goût, caractère: Théorie et terminologie de l'architecture à l'âge classique, 1550–1800* (Paris: Picard, 1986)

────── *Le Musée d'architecture* (Paris: Picard, 1988)

────── *De la rue des Colonnes à la rue de Rivoli* (Paris: Délégation à l'Action Artistique de la Ville de Paris, 1992)

Taillard, Christian, *Bordeaux à l'âge classique* (Bordeaux: Mollat, 1997)

Taylor, René, 'El Padre Villalpando (1552–1608) y sus ideas estéticas', in *Academia: Anales y Boletín de la Real Academia de Bellas Artes de San Fernando*, 3rd ser., I (1951), 409–73

────── 'Hermetism and Mystical Architecture in the Society of Jesus', in Rudolf Wittkower and Irma B. Jaffe (eds), *Baroque Art: The Jesuit Contribution* (New York: Fordham University Press, 1972), 63–97

'The Primitive in Modern Architecture and Urbanism', *Journal of Architecture*, 13/4 (August 2008) [special issue], 355–64

Thuilliez, Stéphanie, 'La Poétique de la variété: Les Ruines et la terre', *Bulletin de l'Association des Historiens de l'Art Italien*, 2 (1996), 26–33

Toledano, Ralph, *Antonio Joli: Modena, 1700–1777, Napoli* (Turin: Artema, 2006)

Torgovnick, Marianna, *Gone Primitive: Savage Intellects, Modern Lives* (Chicago: University of Chicago Press, 1990)

Tuveson, Ernest Lee, 'Space, Deity, and the "Natural Sublime"', *Modern Language Quarterly*, 12 (1951), 20–38

Tuzet, Hélène, *La Sicile au XVIIIe siècle vue par les voyageurs étrangers* (Strasbourg: P. H. Heitz, 1955)

Udy, David, 'The Neo-Classicism of Charles Heathcote Tatham', *The Connoisseur*, 177 (1971), 269–76

Ustárroz, Alberto, *La lección de las ruinas: Presencia del pensamiento* griego y del pensamiento romano en la arquitectura (Barcelona: Fundación Caja de Arquitectos, 1997)

Vall, Renée van de, *Een subliem gevoel van plaats: Een filosofische interpretatie van het werk van Barnett Newman* (Groningen: Historische Uitgeverij, 1994)

Van Zanten, David, *The Architectural Polychromy of the 1830s* (New York: Garland, 1977)

——— *Designing Paris: The Architecture of Duban, Labrouste, Duc, and Vaudoyer* (Cambridge (Mass.): MIT Press, 1987)

Vaughan, Gerard, 'The Townley Zoffany: Reflections on *Charles Townley and his Friends*', *Apollo*, 144 (November 1996), 32–5

——— '"Vincenzo Brenna Romanus, architectus et pictor": Drawing from the Antique in Late Eighteenth-Century Rome', *Apollo*, 144 (October 1996), 37–41

Victor Louis et le théâtre: Scénographie, mise en scène et architecture théâtrale aux XVIIIe et XIXe siècles (Paris: Éditions du Centre National de la Recherche Scientifique, 1982)

Vidler, Anthony, *The Writing of the Walls: Architectural Theory in the Late Enlightenment* (Princeton (NJ): Princeton Architectural Press, 1987)

——— *Claude-Nicolas Ledoux: Architecture and Social Reform at the End of the Ancien Régime* (Cambridge (Mass.): MIT Press, 1990)

Villari, Sergio, *J. N. L. Durand (1760–1834): Art and Science of Architecture*, trans. Eli Gottlieb (New York: Rizzoli International, 1990) [first published in Italian]

Vischer, Robert, *Über das optische Formgefühl: Ein Beitrag zur Aesthetik* (Leipzig: Hermann Credner, 1873)

Visions of Ruin: Architectural Fantasies & Designs for Garden Follies, with Crude Hints towards a History of my House by John Soane (London: Sir John Soane's Museum, 1999)

Vogt, Adolf Max, *Boullées Newton-Denkmal: Sakralbau und Kugelidee* (Basel / Stuttgart: Birkhäuser, 1969)

——— *Le Corbusier, der edle Wilde: Zur Archäologie der Moderne* (Braunschweig: Vieweg, 1996)

Ward, Alastair, *The Architecture of Ferdinando Sanfelice* (New York: Garland, 1988)

Watkin, David, *Thomas Hope, 1769–1831, and the Neo-Classical Idea* (London: John Murray, 1968)

——— *The Triumph of the Classical: Cambridge Architecture, 1804–1834* (Cambridge / New York: Cambridge University Press for the Fitzwilliam Museum, 1977)

——— *Athenian Stuart: Pioneer of the Greek Revival* (London / Boston: George Allen and Unwin, 1982)

——— *The English Vision: The Picturesque in Architecture, Landscape, and Garden Design* (London: John Murray, 1982)

——— (ed.), *Sir John Soane: Enlightenment Thought and the Royal Academy Lectures* (Cambridge: Cambridge University Press, 1996)

Watkin, David, and Tilman Mellinghoff, *German Architecture and the Classical Ideal* (London: Thames and Hudson, 1987)

Weidner, Thomas, *Jakob Philipp Hackert: Landschaftsmaler im 18.*

Jahrhundert (Berlin: Deutscher Verlag für Kunstwissenschaft, 1998)

Weinberg, Alan M., *Shelley's Italian Experience* (London: Macmillan, 1991)

Weinberg, Bernard, 'Translations and Commentaries of Longinus' On the Sublime to 1600: A Bibliography', *Modern Philology*, 47 (1950), 145–51

Weiskel, Thomas, *The Romantic Sublime: Studies in the Structure and Psychology of Transcendence* (Baltimore: Johns Hopkins University Press, 1976)

Wendt, Edward K. A., 'The Burkean Sublime in British Architecture', unpublished PhD thesis, Columbia University, New York, 2002

Whale, John, 'Romantics, Explorers and Picturesque Travellers', in Stephen Copley and Peter Garside (eds), *The Politics of the Picturesque: Literature, Landscape and Aesthetics since 1770* (Cambridge: Cambridge University Press, 1994), 175–95

Whitley, W. T., 'Turner as a Lecturer', *Burlington Magazine*, 22 (February 1913), 202–8, 255–9

Whitney, Lois, *Primitivism and the Idea of Progress in English Popular Literature of the Eighteenth Century* (Baltimore: Johns Hopkins Press, 1934)

Wiebenson, Dora, '"L'Architecture terrible" and the "jardin anglo-chinois"', *Journal of the Society of Architectural Historians*, 27 (May 1968), 136–9

——— *Sources of Greek Revival Architecture* (London: A. Zwemmer, 1969)

——— *The Picturesque Garden in France* (Princeton (NJ): Princeton University Press, 1978)

Wiebenson, Dora, and Claire Baines, *French Books: Sixteenth through Nineteenth Centuries* (Washington (DC) / New York: National Gallery of Art / G. Braziller, 1993)

Willesme, Jean-Pierre, 'Hubert Rohault de Fleury (1777–1846): Un grand commis de l'architecture. Biographie et catalogue des dessins des albums conservés au Musée Carnavalet (Paris)', unpublished PhD thesis, École Pratique des Hautes Études, Paris, 2007

Wilson, Arthur McCandless, *Diderot: Sa vie et son œuvre* (Paris: Laffont, 1985)

Wilton, Andrew, *The Art of Alexander and John Robert Cozens* (New Haven (Conn.): Yale Center for British Art, 1980)

——— *Turner and the Sublime* (London: British Museum Publications for the Art Gallery of Ontario, the Yale Center for British Art, the Trustees of the British Museum, 1980)

Wilton, Andrew, and Ilaria Bignamini, *Grand Tour: The Lure of Italy in the Eighteenth Century* (London: Tate Gallery, 1996)

Wilton-Ely, John, 'The Architectural Models of Sir John Soane: A Catalogue', *Architectural History*, 12 (1969), 5–101

——— *The Mind and Art of Giovanni Battista Piranesi* (London: Thames and Hudson, 1978)

——— *Piranesi, Paestum & Soane* (London: Azimuth, 2002)

——— *Piranesi, Paestum & Soane*, rev. and enlarged edn (Munich

/ London / New York: Prestel, 2013)

Wittkower, Rudolf, 'Piranesi's "Parere su L'architettura"', *Journal of the Warburg Institute*, 2 (1938), 147–58

———— 'Piranesi's Architectural Creed', in *Studies in the Italian Baroque* (London: Thames and Hudson, 1975), 235–46

Wittman, Richard, 'Felix Duban's Didactic Restoration of the Château de Blois: A History of France in Stone', *Journal of the Society of Architectural Historians*, 55 (1996), 412–34

———— *Architecture, Print Culture, and the Public Sphere in Eighteenth-Century France* (London / New York: Routledge, 2007)

———— 'The Hut and the Altar: Architectural Origins and the Public Sphere in Eighteenth-Century France', *Studies in Eighteenth-Century Culture*, 36 (2007), 235–59

Wölfflin, Heinrich, *Prolegomena zu einer Psychologie der Architektur* (Berlin: Mann, 1999) [first published 1886]

Wood, Theodore Edmundson Brown, *The Word 'Sublime' and its Context, 1650–1760* (The Hague / Paris: Mouton, 1972)

Woodbridge, Kenneth, *Landscape and Antiquity: Aspects of English Culture at Stourhead, 1718 to 1838* (London: Clarendon Press, 1970)

Woodward, Christopher, *In Ruins* (London: Chatto & Windus, 2001)

Woud, Auke van der, *De Bataafse hut: Denken over het oudste Nederland (1750–1850)* (Amsterdam / Antwerp: Uitgeverij Contact, 1998)

———— *The Art of Building, from Classicism to Modernity: The Dutch Architectural Debate, 1840–1900* (Aldershot (Surrey): Ashgate, 2002)

Wyngaard, Amy S., *From Savage to Citizen: The Invention of the Peasant in the French Enlightenment* (Newark: University of Delaware Press, 2004)

Zimmerman, Linda Marie, 'Representations of Stonehenge in British Art (1300–1900): Antiquity, Ideology, and Nationalism', unpublished PhD thesis, Stanford University, 1997

Zucker, Paul, 'Ruins: An Aesthetic Hybrid', *Journal of Aesthetics and Art Criticism*, 20 (1961), 119–30

Zutter, Jörg (ed.), *Abraham-Louis-Rodolphe Ducros: Un peintre suisse en Italie* (Geneva / Lausanne: Skira / Musée des Beaux-Arts de Lausanne, 1998)

Photograph Credits

© Agnew's, London / Bridgeman Images: 96c; © Alinari Archives, Florence, Dist. RMN-Grand Palais / Fratelli Alinari: 1; Architekturmuseum der TU München: 95c, 97e; © The Art Institute of Chicago: 71; Author: 2–6; Beaux-Arts de Paris, Dist. RMN-Grand Palais / image Beaux-Arts de Paris: 120, 145–53; Beinecke Rare Book and Manuscript Library, Yale University, New Haven: 40, 41, 43–6, 91f–g, 108a, 110, 111–13, 126, 156–7, 179; © Bibliothèque Municipale de Besançon: 17, 76, 85–6, 158–9; Bibliothèque municipale de Bordeaux: 155; Crédit photographique Bibliothèque municipale de Lyon: 99h; Bibliothèque Nationale de France, Paris: 12, 19, 22, 91i, 93e, 94c, 94h, 104d, 118a, 123, 128, 140, 144, 154, 160–62, 164–9, 176–8, 180; © The Trustees of the British Museum, London: 38, 42, 47, 50, 52–6, 137; By kind permission of the Duke of Buccleuch & Queensberry KBE: 93a; Reproduced by kind permission of the Syndics of Cambridge University Library: 35; Collection Centre Canadien d'Architecture / Canadian Centre for Architecture, Montréal: 23, 48, 94i; Compton Verney, Warwickshire, UK / Bridgeman Images: 98c; © École nationale des ponts et chaussées: 104a; © Collection École polytechnique - Palaiseau, France: 18; Goethe-Museum / Anton-und-Katharina-Kippenberg-Stiftung, Düsseldorf: 25, 104g; Image courtesy of Robert B. Haas Family Arts Library, Yale University: 125; Heidelberg University Library: 91d (C 3673-4 Gross RES), 91h (C 3311 Gross RES), 91j (C 3611 RES); Herefordshire County Records Office: 64; Houghton Library, Harvard University (pfTyp 725.69580): 67, 91c, 94b, 98b, 100b, 106b; Klassik Stiftung Weimar: 11; KsDW, Bildarchiv, Heinz Fräßdorf: 7; Musée cantonal des Beaux-Arts de Lausanne. Collection Ducros. Acquisition, 1816: 94f, 99i; Musée de Picardie, Amiens (photo Marc Jeanneteau – Musée de Picardie): 69; © Musées de la Ville de Rouen, photo C. Lancien, C. Loisel: 68, 74; Naples, Soprintendenza per i Beni Archeologici di Napoli: 170–72; Norton Simon Art Foundation, Gift of Mr. Norton Simon: 84, 88, 91a; Oldham Gallery, Oldham: 8, 61–2; Palazzo Reale di Caserta / photo Antonio Gentile: 87, 98a; The Pierpont Morgan Library, New York. 1982.102, Purchased on the Sunny Crawford von Bülow Fund 1978: 75; Private Collection / Archives Charmet / Bridgeman Images: 20; RIBA British Architectural Library, RIBA Library Drawings Collection, London: *front endpapers*, 16, 94k, 163; Rijksmuseum, Amsterdam: 118q; Rijksmuseum van Oudheden, Leiden: 100d, 106c; © RMN-Grand Palais (musée du Louvre) / Jean-Gilles Berizzi: 73; © RMN-Grand Palais (musée d'Orsay) / Michèle Bellot: 83; Supplied by Royal Collection Trust / © HM Queen Elizabeth II 2012: 127; Royal Libary, The Hague: 13 (1367 F 30), 102c, 107b; Scottish National Gallery, Edinburgh: 49; By Courtesy of the Trustees of Sir John Soane's Museum, London: 14, 77–81, 95a, 97a, 99b, 101a, 102a, 104b, 105a, 107a, 118b–p, 129, 130–34, 136, 173–5 (photo Ardon Bar Hama: 14, 132, 136); Staatsbibliothek zu Berlin – Preußischer Kulturbesitz, Abteilung Historische Drucke: 99d; © The State Hermitage Museum, St Petersburg / photo by Vladimir Terebenin: 10, 70, 72; © Tate, London, 2014: *back endpapers*, 9, 30–32, 34, 36–7, 39; University of Amsterdam, Special Collections, UBM: NOG 03-63: 21; University Library, Ghent: 33, 82, 119, 121, 138–9; University Library Leiden, UB Plano 42 C 1: 91e, 92c, 94d, 95b, 97c, 99f, 101b, 103a, 104f, 105c, 135, 141; University Library Utrecht: 94e; Victoria and Albert Museum, London: 28–9, 59, 65, 99j, 114–17; Ville de Nîmes, Carré d'art bibliothèque, 33172/2: 124; Whitworth Art Gallery, Manchester: 60; Yale Center for British Art, New Haven: 15, 26–7, 63, 97b, 99c, 102b, 104c, 105b.

Index

and the picturesque 81, 82, 104

Règles des cinq ordres d'architecture de Vignole 187–8, 237–8, *237, 238, 239*, 240, 260

Les Ruines de Paestum 144, 145, 160–64, *160, 161*, 189, 193, 218, 239–40, 256, *257*

on spectator's role 168, 169

Delphi: Temple of Apollo 269n12

Denon, Dominique Vivant 42–3, 67, 71, 159, 210

Desgodetz, Antoine 231, 235–6

Desprez, Louis-Jean *31, 36*, 67, *69*

Desquauvilliers, François *68*

Diderot, Denis 111, 114, 134, 168, 175

Donaldson, Thomas Leverton 55

Doric order of architecture

beginnings of 259

Forsyth on 126

grandeur of 257

manifestations of 256

Paris: 'musée de l'ordre dorique' 253

Reveley on 52–3

Soane's use of 118

in theatre sets 139

Downton Castle (Herefordshire) 99, *99*, *101*, 102, *102*

Dryden, John 84, 175

Duban, Félix 215

Dubourg, Richard 318n67

Duc, Louis 215

Ducros, Abraham-Louis-Rodolphe *146, 149*

Dufourny, Léon 223

Dumont, Gabriel-Pierre-Martin 84, 138, *149, 152, 154*, 239, 241, 256, 301n42, 316n42

and measurement of Paestum 239

Les ruines de Paestum 144, 158, 279n146

Suitte de plans . . . de Pœsto 2

and theatre 138, 256

Duparc, Marc Alexandre *69, 70*

Dupaty, Charles-Marguerite-Jean-Baptiste Mercier 39–40, 124, 132, 159–60

Durand, Jean-Nicolas-Louis 254, 255, 256–9, *258*, 261, 319n83

Edinburgh Review 95

Einfühlung 125, 134

Eisen, Charles 178, *179*, 183

Elmes, Joseph *146*

empathy 125, 127

Etna, Mount 90, 91

Etruscan architecture 208, 209

Etruscans 4, 195, 212, 231

Eustace, John Chetwode 128, 132

Fabris, Pietro *148*

Fea, Carlo 205

Ferdinando di Borbone, King of the Two Sicilies 2, 141

Filarete, Antonio 301n51

Flaxman, John 41–2, *42*

Florence: Biblioteca Laurenziana 133

follies 2

Fonthill Abbey (Wiltshire) 29–30, 102

Forsyth, Joseph 125–7, 132

Fragonard, Jean-Honoré 71, 114

Fumagalli, Angelo 305n112

Füssli, Johann Caspar 203

Gainsborough, Thomas *73*

galleries *see under* Paris

Galli di Bibiena, Giuseppe 141, 142

Gandy, Joseph Michael 117, 118, *118, 119, 146*

gardens

and architecture 79

Caserta 2

Italian style 101

landscape 72, 94

ruins in 119

Syracuse 88

Gärtner, Friedrich von *148*

Gazette Littéraire de l'Europe 196

Gazzola, Felice, Count 1, 2, 143, 158

genius

of architects 24, 27–8, 180, 182, 199–200

Bouhours on 40

Knight on 87

Longinus on 19

of Newton 23

Paestum temples as 162, 256, 259

of place 214–24, 227

of Vanbrugh 78

Genoa: Madona del Cargnano church 32

Germain, Louis *69, 70*

German Archaeological Institute 269n8

Gessner, Salomon 203

Gibbon, Edward 111

Gilly, Friedrich *29*, 30

Gilpin, William 72, 75, 95, 97, 110

Gioffredo, Mario 1

Giorgione 97

Gluck, Christoph Willibald 141

Goethe, Johann Wolfgang von *18*, 19, 48–9, 109, 124–5, 132, 133, 287n82, 305n113

on architecture 133

on Paestum *18*, 19, 48–9, 124–5, 132

and Winckelmann's *Geschichte* 305n113

Gore, Charles 83, 90, 91

Gothic architecture 31, 75, 99, 100

Grand Tour 11, 82, 266

Knight, Richard Payne 82–8

grandeur 41, 43, 126

Gray, Sir James 143

Greece: Middle Eastern influence on 246

Greek architecture

despoliation of 259

diversity of 260

Durand's praise of 259

historical contextualisation of 240

as a model for contemporary design 222, 223

excavations at *174*
gates 3
landscape at 85
models of 250–53, *250, 251*
origins of 2, 4, 219
and origins of architecture 260
picturesque quality of 80–82, 97, 104, 263, 264
plans of *155*, 164–5, *246*
publications on 16, 43, 46, 67, 142, 203–4, 241, 260, 261
Roman remains at 86–7
Roman writers on 87
Romans in 4
roses of 87
sacred associations of 126
and Stonehenge compared 60, *61*, 62
stones for building 87, 255
streets 4
sublime nature of 17, 19, 48, 54, 64–5, 85, 94, 162, 263, 264
Temple of Athena (Ceres) 3, *4, 5*–6, 7, *51, 70, 91, 92,* 115–16, *117, 153, 154,* 217, 221, *233,* 289n103
　cella 5
　character 48
　columns 5, 115–16, 130, 242
　construction 222, 223
　decoration 6
　Doric order *257*
　elevations of *161, 163, 189, 249*
　plans of *4, 161, 163, 249*
　porch 5
　scale models of *250, 251*
　staircases 5
Temple of Hera I (Basilica) 4–5, 7, *47, 69,* 115, *150, 151,* 187, *189,* 193, 201, 211, *221,* 241
　ambulatory 5
　capitals 5, 257
　cella 5
　chronology 226
　columns 4–5, 48, *161,* 242
　construction of 220, 221, 222, 223
　cross-section *249*
　decoration 5
　Doric details *257*
　elevations *161, 163,* 217
　plans of *4, 163,* 217, *249*
　scale models of *250, 251*
Temple of Hera II (Neptune) 6–7, *47, 50, 51, 69,* 115, *116, 117,* 142, *147, 148, 161, 188,* 198–200, 201, 218–19, *233,* 243, *248,* 278n130
　archaic elements 7
　capitals 257
　character 47, 48, 52
　columns 6, 7, 33, 34, 52, 56, *208, 218,* 232, 234, 238, 242, 256
　compared with an Etruscan temple *204, 206*
　construction 220, 221, 222, 223
　cross-sections *162, 219, 220, 232, 233, 245, 245, 248*
　Doric order detail *257*
　elevations of *44, 162, 216, 232, 233, 248*
　entablature 7, 33, 34, 57

floors 6
'grandeur' of 41, 52
as a model for contemporary design 249
order and plan, details *162*
plans *4, 44, 216, 232, 233, 238, 239, 244, 244, 254, 256*
purity of 260
scale models of *250, 251,* 252–3
statue of Neptune 220, *220,* 262
as a structural model 256
structure of 255
stylobate 6
the sublime in 33, 34
use of travertine in 254
triglyphs 6
temples
　building materials 220–21, 222
　chronology of 220, 222, 226
　columns 124–5, 246–7
　construction of 223–4
　harmoniousness of 256
　masculinity of 52
　models of 250–53, *250, 251,* 260, 261
　origin of 165, 166, 173, 222
　and the picturesque 104–5
　replicas of 2
　restorations of 269n8
　and Solomon's temple compared 246–7
　theatricality of 138, 164–6
'Paestum affair' 221–2
painting
　architecture as 103–5
　Burke on 22, 26, 38
　landscape 72
　Longinus on 20
Palladio, Andrea 235
Palmyra 111
Panini, Giovanni Paolo 141
Paoli, Paolo Antonio 46, *145, 149, 151, 154, 155,* 164, *204,* 205–10, *208,* 212, 218, 223, 225, 226, *244,* 264
Paolini, Lorenzo *147, 262*
Paris
　8, rue de la Seine (gallery) 251
　Académie d'Architecture 31, 234, 235, 236, 240
　Académie des Beaux-Arts 111
　École des Beaux-Arts 37
　École Nationale des Ponts et Chaussées 37
　Louvre 28, 41, 115, 156–7, 182, 251, 252, *252,* 253
　'musée de l'ordre dorique' 253
　Notre Dame cathedral 79
　Porte Saint-Denis 28
　rue des Colonnes *29, 30, 30*
　Sainte-Geneviève (now the Panthéon) 79, 255
　Val-de-Grâce hospital 28
Pâris, Pierre-Adrien 18–19, 53, 71, *138, 139,* 229, 230–32, *232, 233, 234, 234,* 260
　Académie d'Architecture lecture 234
　and Desgodetz's *Les édifices de Rome* 235, 236–7, 261